HABAKKUK

VOLUME 25

THE ANCHOR BIBLE is a fresh approach to the world's greatest classic. Its object is to make the Bible accessible to the modern reader; its method is to arrive at the meaning of biblical literature through exact translation and extended exposition, and to reconstruct the ancient setting of the biblical story, as well as the circumstances of its transcription and the characteristics of its transcribers.

THE ANCHOR BIBLE is a project of international and interfaith scope: Protestant, Catholic, and Jewish scholars from many countries contribute individual volumes. The project is not sponsored by any ecclesiastical organization and is not intended to reflect any particular theological doctrine. Prepared under our joint supervision, THE ANCHOR BIBLE is an effort to make available all the significant historical and linguistic knowledge which bears on the interpretation of the biblical record.

THE ANCHOR BIBLE is aimed at the general reader with no special formal training in biblical studies; yet it is written with the most exacting standards of scholarship, reflecting the highest technical accomplishment.

This project marks the beginning of a new era of cooperation among scholars in biblical research, thus forming a common body of knowledge to be shared by all.

William Foxwell Albright
David Noel Freedman
GENERAL EDITORS

HABAKKUK

◆

A New Translation
with Introduction and Commentary

FRANCIS I. ANDERSEN

THE ANCHOR BIBLE
Doubleday
New York   London   Toronto   Sydney   Auckland

THE ANCHOR BIBLE
PUBLISHED BY DOUBLEDAY
a division of Random House, Inc.
1540 Broadway, New York, New York 10036

THE ANCHOR BIBLE DOUBLEDAY, and the portrayal
of an anchor with the letters A and B are trademarks of
Doubleday, a division of Random House, Inc.

LIBRARY OF CONGRESS CATALOGING-IN-PUBLICATION DATA

Bible. O.T. Habakkuk. English. Andersen. 2001.
  Habakkuk : a new translation with introduction and commentary /
  Francis I. Andersen — 1st ed.
    p.   cm. — (The Anchor Bible; v. 25)
  Includes bibliographical references and index.
  1. Bible, O.T. Habakkuk—Commentaries.   I. Andersen, Francis I., 1925–.
  II. Title.   III. Bible. English. Anchor Bible. 1964 ; v. 25.

BS.192.2A1 1964.G3 vol. 25.
[BS1635.3]
224′.95077 dc21   00-031673

ISBN 0-385-08396-3

10 9 8 7 6 5 4 3 2 1

To Lois (Garrett) Andersen

Devoted wife of Frank Andersen for fifty years
Mother of John, David, Martin, Nedra, Kathryn
Grandmother of Sean, Lalita,
Vivienne, Erin, Michael,
Tiria

Honoured as
a distinguished
physician in the Vera
Scantlebury Brown
award by the State of
Victoria for outstanding
service to child health, by the
Johns Hopkins Hospital
as Fellow in Pediatrics,
"pursuing excellence
in the care of
children."

Student
and teacher of
the Bible; Associate
Professor of Christian
Studies at New College,
Berkeley, California;
friend and spiritual guide
to many and many;
overcoming disability;
living deeply in the
mystery of the
love of God.

Creator
of beauty in
home and garden.

רַבּוֹת בָּנוֹת עָשׂוּ חָיִל
וְאַתְּ עָלִית עַל־כֻּלָּנָה:

CONTENTS

◆

PREFACE

◆

The Anchor Bible is intended for the general reader as well as the professional scholar. Writers on technical subjects sometimes give the impression that the mysteries of their research are trade secrets, guarded by the solemn obscurity of academic jargon. If any tidbits or crumbs from the table are dropped for the uninitiated, it is likely to be done with condescension and for that mythical "intelligent" layperson.

Instead of hoping that the reader will feel that "it must be profound because I don't understand it," we would like to explain things so that anyone who is interested in the Bible will be able to grasp what he or she reads. Such readers will not get their money's worth if we go soft on scientific seriousness for the sake of popular appeal.

Being simple and clear is only part of the job. It is not enough to supply customers with just the results of research, hoping that they will trust the expert. We want to show them where the results came from and how they were obtained. We prefer to have readers looking over our shoulder as we work with our tools on the bench. At the same time, we do not want to go overboard and waste space publishing our lab notes.

Talking about a book of the Bible (in this instance, the book of Habakkuk) requires many skills. Translating an ancient and sacred text uses knowledge of history, archaeology, social anthropology, and linguistics. We have to bring back to life the culture and values of an ancient society (in this instance, the people of Israel). We have to relive the experience of a man (the prophet Habakkuk) whose only testament is this little book. We have to understand what he was doing, what he was feeling, when he wrote it. We have to understand the literary forms available to him, which were familiar to his readers, but possibly strange to us. We need some knowledge of history in order to appreciate the situation that Habakkuk was in. We have to let Habakkuk be who he was and the people of Israel be who they were. We are here to listen, not to judge.

It is our intention to produce the relevant facts and to walk the readers through the arguments that lead to the NOTES and COMMENTS. It should not be necessary, however, to import masses of data that are readily available in standard reference works. When only representative data are deployed, we will give pointers to sources that list the evidence more completely. To save space, we will rarely quote biblical passages that are part of the discussion. To get the point, readers are encouraged, indeed urged, to look the references up in order to satisfy themselves that the point is valid.

The main aim of this study is to understand the prophecy of Habakkuk as a book, as an artistic creation. We are interested in its total structure and in its fine texture as a literary composition. Our hope is to combine a sense of the identity and integrity of the whole work—the big picture—with appreciation of the tight weaving of its thematic threads—the close-ups. There will be intensive analysis of the literary organization of the whole and of the linguistic connections of the parts in order to make decisions about textual readings and to choose among competing interpretations.

There are some common faults of biblical commentaries that we will try to avoid. The first is a vague appeal to "style" as a factor in making an exegetical judgment. This gets us nowhere unless the specific stylistic features that turn an argument are clearly identified and their contribution to solving a problem is fully discussed. The second is an equally fatuous claim that a certain result "fits the context" or "is required by the context." Interpretation out of context is worse, of course; but if context is to settle an issue, we have to be shown *how.* A text such as the book of Habakkuk, the whole or a part, has three kinds of context, and its connections with all of them must be analyzed in a systematic and disciplined way. First, there is the verbal and linguistic context of each word, phrase, and clause in the discourse of the book. This philological and literary dimension of the book has its setting in the language and the speech traditions of ancient Israel. Then there is the historical setting of Habakkuk and his book in the actual world, with its social, economic, religious, and political realities. Third, all of this belongs to the culture of ancient Israel, which has a larger background in the civilizations of the ancient Near East.

The identification of the "background" makes a big difference to the way the book is read. It can be very tricky, and at many points we are frustrated by the limitations of our knowledge. An exact fix may elude us. Then honesty requires suspended judgment and the discomfort of uncertainty.

The time has come to be candid about the many things we need to know, but do not know, when trying to solve the problems of the book of Habakkuk. With candor should go modesty and tolerance. But these virtues should not be perverted into license for ignorant and undisciplined readings as having just as much validity as the results (however tentative or inconclusive) of responsible investigation. It might put a dismal face on the enterprise to say that it is easier to show that a certain opinion or interpretation is unlikely, or even plain wrong, than to demonstrate beyond reasonable doubt that a particular result is correct. That cannot be helped.

Among the things about the book of Habakkuk that we do not know, but would like to know, are the date of its composition (and therefore its immediate historical setting) and the way it originated (whether the work of one author—it is sufficiently autobiographical to suggest the prophet himself—or the result of a complex development, over who knows how long, involving who knows how many contributors). Since the rise of modern critical biblical scholarship and the commitment to historical and literary interpretation, these questions—date, author, composition—have been at the top of the agenda. That enterprise seems to have exhausted its resources, and no consensus has emerged. We have to manage somehow without solutions to the problems that alert readers' notice sooner or later. It will be part of our task to receive the gains from past work, and we have a few improvements to offer. We see no need to labor the point, and we do not wish to disparage in any way the rich legacy of Habakkuk studies represented by the extensive bibliography included in this commentary. But we do not propose to write a commentary on the commentaries.

What we do have is the book of Habakkuk in the Hebrew Bible. If we do what can be done—study it for what it is, explore its design (or, rather, see how much design there might be in the final form), pay more attention to its poetic features than commentators usually do, and toil patiently at the linguistic side of the text in the light of our growing knowledge of the history of the Hebrew language—if we attempt that, there will be more than enough to do, and perhaps even some new insights to share.

The dedication to my wife, Lois, is designed after the Mesopotamian amulets that are discussed in the COMMENTARY on Habakkuk 3.

PRINCIPAL ABBREVIATIONS

◆

Abbreviations not listed are the same as those in *The Anchor Bible Dictionary*. The Dead Sea Scrolls and related manuscript sources are referred to using the now standard sigla, as listed in Emanuel Tov, "A List of the Texts from the Judaean Desert," in Peter W. Flint and James C. VanderKam, *The Dead Sea Scrolls After Fifty Years: A Comprehensive Assessment*, 2:669–717. (Leiden: Brill, 1999).

AB	The Anchor Bible (Commentary)
ABD	*Anchor Bible Dictionary*
ABR	*Australian Biblical Review*
AHw	W. von Soden, *Akkadisches Handwörterbuch*. 3 vols. Wiesbaden: Harrassowitz, 1965–81
AJBI	*Annual of the Japanese Biblical Institute*
AJSL	*American Journal of Semitic Languages and Literatures*
Akk	Akkadian (a language of ancient Mesopotamia)
AnBib	Analecta Biblica
ANET	*Ancient Near Eastern Texts Relating to the Old Testament*, ed. J. B. Pritchard. 3d ed. with suppl. Princeton: Princeton University Press, 1955, 1969
ANVAO	Avhandlinger utgitt av der Norske Videnskaps-Akademi i Olso
AOAT	Alter Orient und Altes Testament
ARAB	Luckenbill, D.D., *Ancient Records of Assyria and Babylon*. 2 vols. Chicago: The University of Chicago, 1928
ArOr	*Archiv orientální*
ASV	American Standard Version
ATD	Das Alte Testament Deutsch
BA	*Biblical Archaeologist*
BASOR	*Bulletin of the American Schools of Oriental Research*
BAT	Die Botschaft des Alten Testaments
BBB	Bonner biblische Beiträge
B.C.E.	Before the Common Era (= B.C.)
BDB	F. Brown, S. R. Driver, and C. A. Briggs, *Hebrew and English Lexicon of the Old Testament*. Oxford: Oxford University Press, 1907, 1955
BFCT	Beiträge zur Förderung christlicher Theologie
BH³	Biblia Hebraica, 3rd ed.
BHS	Biblia Hebraica Stuttgartensia
BHT	Beiträge zur historischen Theologie
Bib	*Biblica*

BibOr	Biblica et orientalia
BK	*Bibel und Kirche*
BJRL	*Bulletin of the John Rylands University Library of Manchester*
BN	*Biblische Notizen*
BRev	*Bible Review*
BSac	*Bibliotheca Sacra*
BSt	Biblische Studien
BWL	W. G. Lambert, *Babylonian Wisdom Literature*. Oxford: Clarendon Press (1960).
BZAW	Beihefte zur Zeitschrift für die alttestamentliche Wissenschaft
C	Cairo Codex of the Prophets
CAD	*The Assyrian Dictionary of the University of Chicago*, ed. L. Oppenheim et al. Chicago: University of Chicago Press, 1956–
CAT	Commentaire de l'Ancient Testament
CB	*Cultura biblica*
CBQ	*Catholic Biblical Quarterly*
CBQMS	Catholic Biblical Quarterly Monograph Series
C.E.	Common Era (= A.D.)
CH	Codex of Hammurapi
chap(s).	chapter(s)
col.	column
ConBot	Coniectnea biblica, Old Testament
CT	*Cuneiform Texts from Babylonian Tablets . . . in the British Museum*, London, 1896–
CTA	A. Herdner. *Corpus des tablettes en cunéiformes alphabétiques découvertes à Ras Shamra-Ugarit de 1929 à 1939*. Mission de Ras Shamra 10. Paris: Paul Geuther, 1963.
D^{62}	The Karasu-Bazar Codex of the Latter Prophets in the Library of the Oriental Institute of the Academy of Sciences, Saint Petersburg
DCH	*The Dictionary of Classical Hebrew*, ed. David J. A. Clines, Sheffield: Sheffield Academic Press, 1993–
DD	*Dor le Dor*
DJD	Discoveries in the Judaean Desert of Jordan
DNWSI	*Dictionary of the North-West Semitic Inscriptions*, ed. J. Hoftijzer and K. Jongeling, Leiden: Brill, 1995.
DSD	*Dead Sea Discoveries*
DSS	Dead Sea Scrolls
EAEHL	*Encyclopedia of Archaeological Excavations in the Holy Land*
EAJT	*East Asia Journal of Theology*
EB	Early Bronze (Age)
EBib	Études bibliques
EI	*Eretz Israel*
EncJud	*Encyclopedia Judaica*
EPRO	Études préliminaires aux religions orientales dans l'Empire romain

EstBib	*Estudios Bíblicos*
EstEcl	*Estudios Eclesiásticos*
EstTeo	*Estudios Teológicos*
'et	*Nota accusativi,* the sign of the definite object in Hebrew
ÉTR	*Études théologiques et religieuses*
ExB	Expositor's Bible
ExpT	*Expository Times*
EvQ	*Evangelical Quarterly*
GKC	*Gesenius' Hebrew Grammar* (2nd ed.), ed. E. Kautzsch, trans. A. E. Cowley. Oxford: Clarendon Press, 1910
HAL	L. Koehler and W. Baumgartner, *Hebräische und aramäische Lexicon zum alten Testament.* 3rd ed. Leiden: Brill, 1967–
HAR	*Hebrew Annual Review*
HAT	Handbuch zum Alten Testament
HSAT	Die Heilige Schrift des Alten Testaments
HSM	Harvard Semitic Monographs
HSS	Harvard Semitic Studies
HTR	*Harvard Theological Review*
HUCA	*Hebrew Union College Annual*
IBS	*Irish Biblical Studies*
ICC	International Critical Commentary
IEJ	*Israel Exploration Journal*
IM	Tablets in the collection of the Iraq Museum, Baghdad
ITC	International Theological Commentary
JAC	*Jahrbuch für Antike und Christentum*
JANES	*Journal of the Ancient Near Eastern Society*
JAOS	*Journal of the American Oriental Society*
JB	Jerusalem Bible
JBL	*Journal of Biblical Literature*
JJS	*Journal of Jewish Studies*
JNES	*Journal of Near Eastern Studies*
JNSL	*Journal of Northwest Semitic Languages*
JPOS	*Journal of the Palestine Oriental Society*
JQR	*Jewish Quarterly Review*
JSOT	*Journal for the Study of the Old Testament*
JSOTSup	Journal for the Study of the Old Testament Supplement Series
JSS	*Journal of Semitic Studies*
JTS	*Journal of Theological Studies*
KAT	Kommentar zum alten Testament
KEHAT	*Kurzgefasstes exegetisches Handbuch zum Alten Testament*
KHC	Kurzger Hand-Commentar zum Alten Testament
KJV	*The Holy Bible Containing the Old and New Testaments* or Authorized Version (= King James Version)
KTU	*The Cuneiform Alphabetic Texts from Ugarit, Ras Ibn Hani and Other Places (KTU: second, enlarged edition).* Manfred Diet-

	rich, Oswalt Lorctz, and Joaquín Sanmartin, eds. Münster: Ugarit-Verlag, 1995.
L	*Codex Leningradensis*
LAPO	Littératures anciennes du Proche-Orient
LB	*Linguistica Biblica*
LD	Lectio divina
LXX	Septuagint
MDP	Mémoires de la Délégation en Perse
MGWJ	*Monatsschrift für Geschichte und Wissenschaft des Judentums*
MT	Masoretic Text
MUN	Mémoires de l'Université de Neuchâtel
MVAG	Mitteilungen der vorder-asiatisch ägyptischen Gesellschaft
NAB	New American Bible
NASB	New American Standard Bible
NEB	New English Bible
NEBib	Neue Echter Bibel
NGTT	*Nederduits Gereformeerde Teologiese Tydscrif*
NIDOTTE	*New International Dictionary of Old Testament Theology and Exegesis.* Willem A. VanGemeren, ed. Grand Rapids: Zondervan, 1997.
NIB	*The New Interpreter's Bible.* Nashville: Abingdon, 1996
NIV	New International Version
NJB	New Jerusalem Bible
NJPS	The New Jewish Publication Society of America translations of the Holy Scriptures: *The Torah,* 2nd ed., Philadelphia, 1967; *The Prophets: Nevi'im,* Philadelphia, 1978; *The Writings: Kethubim,* Philadelphia, 1978
NKJV	New King James Version
NorTT	*Norsk Teologisk Tidsskrift*
NRSV	New Revised Standard Version
NT	New Testament
NTS	*New Testament Studies*
O	grammatical object
OBO	Orbis biblicus et orientalis
OLP	*Orientalia louvaniensia periodica*
OLZ	*Orientalische Literaturzeitung*
Or	*Orientalia*
OT	Old Testament
OTE	*Old Testament Essays*
OTL	Old Testament Library
OTMS	*The Old Testament and Modern Study. A Generation of Discovery and Research.* Essays by Members of the Society for Old Testament Study. Rowley, H. H., ed. Oxford: Clarendon Press, 1951.

OTP	*Old Testament Pseudepigrapha*, 2 vols., ed. J. Charlesworth, Garden City: Doubleday, NY, 1983–87.
OTS	*Oudtestamentische Studiën*
P	Priestly Source in the Pentateuch
PEQ	*Palestine Exploration Quarterly*
PL	J. Migne, *Patrologia latina*
PouT	De Prediking van het Oude Testament
PSB	*Princeton Seminary Bulletin*
1QH	*Hodayoth*
1QpHab	Qumran *pešer* of the book of Habakkuk
4QDibHam[a]	*Dibre hamme'orot* (4Q504)
RArch	*Revue archéologique*
RB	*Revue biblique*
REB	Revised English Bible
RGG	*Religion in Geschichte und Gegenwart*
RHPR	*Revue d'histoire et de philosophie réligieuses*
RelSRev	*Religious Studies Review*
RevQ	*Revue de Qumrân*
RSV	Revised Standard Version
S	grammatical subject
SAOC	Studies in Ancient Oriental Civilization
SBLDS	Society of Biblical Literature Dissertation Series
SBLMS	Society of Biblical Literature Monograph Series
ScrHier	*Scripta Hierosolymitana*
SEÅ	*Svensk Exegetisk Årsbok*
Sef	*Sefarad*
Sem	*Semitica*
SJOT	*Scandinavian Journal of the Old Testament*
SNVAO	*Skrifter utgitt av det Norske Videnscaps-Akademie i Olso*
SPB	Studia postbiblica
SS	Studi semitici
SSN	Studia Semitica Neerlandica
ST	*Studia theologica*
STDJ	Studies on the Texts of the Desert of Judah
StTh	*Studies in Theology*
TA	*Tel Aviv*
TBC	Torch Bible Commentary
TDOT	*Theological Dictionary of the Old Testament*, ed. G. J. Botterweck and H. Ringgren. Grand Rapids: Eerdmans, 1974–
Tg	Targum
ThViat	*Theologia Viatorum*
TSK	*Theologische Studien und Kritiken*
TynBul	*Tyndale Bulletin*
TZ	*Theologische Zeitschrift*

UF	*Ugarit-Forschungen*
UT	C. H. Gordon, *Ugaritic Textbook*. Rome, 1965; Supplement, 1967
V	Vulgate
v(v)	verse(s)
VT	*Vetus Testamentum*
VTSup	Vetus Testamentum Supplements
WBC	Word Biblical Commentary
WC	Westminster Commentary
WMANT	Wissenschaftliche Monographien zum Alten und Neuen Testaments
ZA	*Zeitschrift für Assyriologie*
ZAH	*Zeitschrift für Althebräistik*
ZAW	*Zeitschrift für die alttestamentliche Wissenschaft*
ZB	Zürcher Bibelkommentare
ZNW	*Zeitschrift für die nuetestamentliche Wissenschaft*
ZDMG	*Zeitschrift der deutschen morgenlandischen Gesellschaft*
ZDPV	*Zeitschrift des Palästina-Vereins*

HABAKKUK: A TRANSLATION

◆

I.   *Title* (1:1)
1   The burden that Habakkuk the prophet saw:

PART ONE.   ENCOUNTER BETWEEN HABAKKUK AND
                        YAHWEH (1:2–2:20)

Part One A.   DIALOGUE (1:2–2:5)

II. *Habakkuk's first prayer* (1:2–4)

2aA   How long (will it be), Yahweh?
                I have called out,
2aB   and thou* didst not listen?
2bA   I protested to thee "Lawlessness!"
2bB   and thou didst not rescue.
3aAα   Why didst thou make me see iniquity,
3aAβ   and look at wretchedness,
3aB   and the devastation and lawlessness that are before me?
3bA   And there was disputation,
3bB   and contention rose up.
4aA   That's why the Torah has become paralyzed,
4aB   and justice never came forth.
4bA   In fact the wicked restricted the righteous!
4bB   That's why justice came forth perverted.

III. *Yahweh's first response* (1:5–11)

5aA   Look among the nations and gaze!
5aB   And be astonished, be astounded!
5bA   For I am doing a deed in your days;
5bB   you won't believe when it is reported.
6aA   For behold I am raising up the Chaldeans,
6aB   the bitter and impetuous people,
6bA   that marches over the breadth of the earth,
6bB   to seize territories not its own.
7a   Dreadful and terrifying is he.
7b   His justice and status proceed from himself.
8aAα   And his horses are swifter than leopards,
8aAβ   and they are more savage than evening wolves.
8aB   And his cavalry dashes ahead,
8bA   and his cavalry gallops vast distances.

---

*We use the archaic English pronoun out of respect for the Hebrew language, which distinguishes singular from plural. We will not abolish gender distinctions; contrived inclusive language often obscures the authentic representation of Israelite culture in biblical texts. The richness of Hebrew should not be sacrificed to the poverty of English. Our choice of verb tenses likewise aims at keeping as close as possible to the time perspective of the Hebrew verb system.

3

8bB	They swoop on their prey like a swift eagle to devour.
9aA	All of them come for violence.
9aB	The *mgmt* of their faces is to the front.
9b	And he gathered prisoners like sand.
10aA	And he, he ridiculed kings,
10aB	and rulers were a laughingstock for him;
10bA	he, he laughed at every fortress.
10bB	And he heaped up earth and captured it.
11a	Then the spirit swept on and passed by;
11b	and he was guilty — he whose strength is his god.

IV. *Habakkuk's second prayer* (1:12–17)

12aA	Art thou not eternal, Yahweh,
12aB	my God, my Holy One, who never dies?
12bA	O Yahweh, for judgment thou didst appoint him;
12bB	and, O Rock, for accusation thou didst establish him.
13aA	Thine eyes are too pure to look on evil,
13aB	and to watch wrong thou art not able:
13bA	why then didst thou watch cheats,
13bB	and (why) wast thou silent when the wicked swallowed someone more righteous than himself?
14a	And thou didst make humankind like fishes of the sea,
14b	like reptiles, who have no ruler.
15aA	All of them with a hook he brought up;
15aB	and he dragged out each one with his net;
15aC	and he collected each one with his mesh.
15b	That's why he was happy and celebrated.
16aA	That's why he made a sacrifice to his net,
16aB	and burned incense to his mesh;
16bA	because with them his portion was fat,
16bB	and his food was plump.
17a	Will he therefore empty his net,
17b	and for ever slay nations without qualms? ס

V. *Habakkuk's response* (2:1)

1aA	Upon my lookout I will stand;
1aB	I will stand on guard on the tower:
1bA	and I will look out to see what he will say in me,
1bB	and what I will reply concerning my protest.

VI. *Yahweh's second response* (2:2–5)

2aA	And Yahweh answered me and said:
2aB	Write down the vision,
2aC	and explain it upon the tablets,
2b	so that he who reads it can run!

3aA   For the vision is still for the appointed time.
3aBα   And he is a witness to the end,
3aBβ   and he will not deceive.
3bA   If he delays, wait for him;
3bBα   for he will certainly come,
3bBβ   he won't be late.
4a   Behold, swollen, not straight, is his throat in him,
4b   and the righteous person by its trustworthiness will survive.
5aA   And yet indeed the wine is treacherous,
5aB   the man is presumptuous and he will not endure,
5bAα   who enlarged his throat like Sheol,
5bAβ   and he is like Death, and he will not be satisfied.
5bB   And he gathered to himself all the nations,
5bC   and he collected to himself all the peoples.

Part One B. THE FIVE WOE ORACLES (2:6–20)

VII.1. *Introduction to the woe oracles* (2:6a)

6aA Will not these — all of them — raise a proverb against him,
6aB   and derision, enigmas for him?
6bA   And he will say:

VII.2. *The first woe oracle* (2:6b–8)

6bB   Woe to him who accumulated what is not his!
6bC   —for how long?—
6bD   and got rich with unpaid debts!
7aA   Won't thy creditors suddenly rise up,
7aB   and (won't) those who agitate thee wake up?
7b   And thou shalt be loot for them.
8aA   Because thou, thou didst plunder many nations,
8aB   all the other peoples will plunder thee;
8bA   *from the blood of humankind,*
                and the lawlessness of the land,
8bB   *the city, and all who live in it.*   פ

VII.3. *The second woe oracle* (2:9–11)

9aA   Woe to him who became rich with fraudulent profits . . .† →
9aB   —Let evil come to his estate!—
9bA   to put his nest on the height,
9bB   and to make himself secure from the fist of evil . . .‡ →
10aA   Thou didst scheme!
10aB   —Let shame come to thine estate! —
10bA   → ‡ . . . to cut off many peoples.
10bB   → † . . . and thy soul is sinful.
11a   *For a stone from the wall will cry out,*
11b   *and a beam from the woodwork will echo it.*   פ

VII.4. *The third woe oracle* (2:12–14)

12a	Woe to him who built a town with blood,
12b	and established a city with iniquity!
13a	Isn't this—Behold!—from Yahweh Sebaoth?
13bA	And peoples labored only for fire,
13bB	and nations only for nothing exhausted themselves.
14a	*But the earth will be filled with the knowledge of the glory of Yahweh,*
14b	*as the waters cover the sea.* ס

VII.5. *The fourth woe oracle* (2:15–17)

15aA	Woe to him who made his neighbor drink,
15aBα	who poured out his anger,
15aBβ	and even made him drunk —
15b	so as to gaze on their nakedness!
16aA	Thou didst satiate thyself with shame instead of glory.
16aB	Drink, thou also! And expose thy nakedness!
16bA	The cup in Yahweh's right hand will circulate to thee,
16bB	and shameful vomit upon thy glory.
17aA	For the lawlessness of Lebanon will cover thee,
17aB	and the devastation of beasts will terrify thee —
17bA	*from the blood of humankind,*
	and the lawlessness of the land,
17bB	*the city, and all who live in it.* ס

VII.6. *The fifth woe oracle* (2.18–19)

18aA	How does an image benefit?
	For its craftsman has carved it;
18aB	a metal casting, and a teacher of lies.
18bA	For he who shapes his own shape has trusted in it,
18bB	to make dumb false gods. ס
19aA	Woe to him who says to a tree, "Wake up!"
19aB	"Get up!" to a dumb stone!
19bA	He gives instruction.
19bBα	Behold it is overlaid with gold and silver;
19bBβ	and there is no breath inside it.

VII.7. *Conclusion* (2:20)

20a	*But Yahweh is in his holy temple;*
20b	*be silent in his presence, all the earth!* פ

PART TWO. THE PSALM OF HABAKKUK (3:1–19)

VIII.1. *Title* (3:1)

1a	A prayer of Habakkuk the prophet
1b	(upon Shigyonoth).

VIII.2. *The prayer* (3:2–19)
VIII.2.i. *Invocation* (3:2)

2aAα	Yahweh! I heard the report about thee.
2aAβ	I was frightened, Yahweh, by thy deed.
2aAγ	In our midst, once more, by the life of Yahweh,
2aB	in our midst, once more, thou didst reveal,
2b	In (my) distress thou didst proclaim (thy name)—Compassionate.

VIII.2.ii. *The March in the South* (3:3–7)

3aA	Eloh came out from Teman,
3aB	even Qadosh from Mount Paran. [Selah]
3bA	His glory covered the sky,
3bB	and his praise filled the earth.
4aA	And his radiance was like the sun.
4aB	He had horns (coming) from his hand,
4b	and there he (un-)veiled his power.
5a	In front of him marched Plague;
5b	and Pestilence came out behind him.
6aAα	He stood and spanned the earth;
6aAβ	he looked and made the nations tremble.
6aB	And the primeval mountains were shattered,
6aC	the ancient peaks dissolved;
6b	the ancient highways were ruined.
7aA*	Under affliction I saw [it].
7aB	The tents of Kushan were agitated,
7b	the curtains of the land of Midian.

VIII. 2. iii. *The Victory over the Waters* (3:8–15)

8aA	Was thine anger against the rivers, Yahweh?
8aB	Was thy rage against the rivers?
8aC	Was thy fury against the sea?
8bA	When thou didst mount thy horses,
8bB	thy chariots of deliverance?
9aA	Thou didst strip the cover from thy bow,
9aB	Seven clubs thou didst bring to view. [Selah]
9b	Thou didst split open the streams of earth.
10aA	The mountains saw thee and writhed;
10aB	the cyclone passed over;
10bA	the abyss gave forth its voice.
10bB†	The exalted sun raised his hands,
11a	the princely moon stood still;

---

*This division does not match the Masoretic punctuation, which has *zaqef gadol* on "iniquity."
†The word "sun" has been attached to this colon from v 11.

11bA	thine arrows went streaming to the light,
11bB	thy flashing javelin to the bright one.
12a	In thine anger thou didst trample the earth;
12b	in thy rage thou didst thresh the nations.
13aA	Thou didst march out to deliver thy people,
13aB	to deliver thy messiah thou didst come.
13bA	Thou didst mash the head of the wicked,
13bB	Thou didst slash them from backside to neck. [Selah] פ
14aA	Thou didst smash their heads with thy two maces.
14aB	Their hair thou didst scatter to the wind.
14bA	Thou didst gloat over them. . .
14bB	like the oppressed feasting in the secret place.
15a	Thou didst trample the sea with thy horses,
15b	Thou didst churn up the many waters.

VIII.2.iv. *Habakkuk's Response* (3:16–19a)

16aAα	I heard, and my stomach churned
16aAβ	at the sound my lips trembled;
16aBα	rottenness entered my bones,
16aBβ	and my feet shook beneath me.
16bA	I waited for the day of disaster
16bB	to come up against the people who had invaded us.
17aAα	Although the fig-tree has not sprouted,
17aAβ	and there is no yield from the vines;
17aBα	although the olive crop has failed,
17aBβ	and the fields have made no food;
17bA	although the flocks are cut off from the fold,
17bB	and there are no cattle in the yards —
18a	Nevertheless I will rejoice in Yahweh,
18b	I will exult in the God of my deliverance;
19a	in Yahweh the Lord of my success.
19bA	And he made my legs like does,
19bB	and he made me trample on my high places.

VIII.3. *Dedication* (3:19c)

19c	For the conductor in my string ensemble.

INTRODUCTION

◆

The book of Habakkuk is an intensely personal testament. It arose from the agony of one man's struggle to live with God in this world. The way things are in this world does not match a God who is supposed to be good, strong, compassionate, wise, just. There is no way of experiencing human life in this world as it is and believing at the same time that this is the right way for everything to be, if this world is owned and managed by a Creator who is competent and fair.

The book of Habakkuk documents that experience. The two realities—God and the world—do not seem to fit. The task of making them fit is daunting. When the misery of existence becomes intolerable there are two ways out, both extreme, by denying one or the other of the two realities. God can be detached from the world; either he isn't interested, or he isn't even there. A person can detach from the world; the world can be rejected as meaningless, corrupt, or an illusion. In its most radical form, such disengagement can deny the reality of both God and the world, seeking relief in the nirvana of nothingness.

Biblical faith holds on tenaciously to both realities. The world is real; the God who made it all is also real. This is what Habakkuk believes. He manages somehow to survive by faith (2:4b).*

Habakkuk is caught in the existential predicament of all humans, trying to make sense of their experiences, grasping something beyond those experiences and refusing to let it go, refusing to accept things as they are, refusing to deny the reality of evil that seems endless and boundless, refusing to surrrender to inevitable fate but, rather, asserting human freedom, refusing to be silent, crying out, not just in angry protest, but in desperate prayers to the God who is reponsible for it all, daring to complain, to demand from God himself explanation and action. And, when things go on longer than anyone can endure, when the silence of God becomes insufferable and the actions of God become even more incomprehensible and more morally indefensible than his inaction, the prophet remained at attention on the watchtower, waiting for God to respond (2:1).

Habakkuk's spirituality, like the spirituality of all Israel's prophets, was shaped by his people's involvement in history. He found himself at a crisis point in that history, set in the larger perspective of the history of all humankind.

The questions that arose in Habakkuk's tormented soul were argued out with God, and the frame of reference was enlarged. The space frame was enlarged

---

*All references in this style are to chapter and verse of the book of Habakkuk.

11

from his immediate situation in the land of Judah to include the whole world, and the time frame was enlarged from the prophet's brief life to embrace all of time from beginning to end. The prophet's agitation was caused as much by perplexity about God as by moral outrage over wickedness in the world. His argument with God took the form of prayers, and God responded with oracular messages. Eventually, Habakkuk had a vision of God, set forth in a stupendous poem (Habakkuk 3). That vision experience brought him some kind of resolution, even reconciliation with the situation and peace with God.

The book of Habakkuk reports and records the prophet's vision of God. The vision was granted only after strenuous and dangerous prayers. In a response whose delay tested the prophet's faith even more, God showed him a vision and gave him a message. That response brought its own peculiar ecstasy and pain. This is how Habakkuk (3:16) describes the effect of God's self-disclosure on him:

> I heard, and my stomach churned,
>   at the sound my lips trembled;
> rottenness entered my bones,
>   and my feet shook beneath me.

Yet—somehow—in spite of (because of?) the added terror and mystery of the revelation, Habakkuk came to reconcilement with the world as it is and with the only God who is. The book of Habakkuk attests the terrible dangers that await people who try to grope their way to God, to tear aside the veil of secrecy with which God hides himself most of the time. The light is blinding, the flame, searing. This is how Habakkuk (3:3–7) tried to describe it:

> Eloh came out from Teman,
>   even Qadosh from Mount Paran.
> His glory covered the sky,
>   and his praise filled the earth.
> And his radiance was like the sun.
>   He had horns (coming) from his hand,
>   and there he (un-)veiled his power.
> In front of him marched Plague;
>   and Pestilence came out behind him.
> He stood and spanned the earth;
>   he looked and made the nations tremble.
> And the primeval mountains were shattered,
>   the ancient peaks dissolved;
>   the ancient highways were ruined.
> Under iniquity I saw [it].
> The tents of Kushan were agitated,
>   the curtains of the land of Midian.

Habakkuk's (3:2) response:

> LORD, I heard your report,
>> I was terrified, LORD, by your action.

It is not clear whether this prayer recites an ancient theophany or reports Habakkuk's own ecstatic vision; it is not clear whether the composition is liturgical or private. The vision is not the unreportable and unrepeatable experience of a solitary; it becomes a prophecy for wide distribution. In form, the revelation is traditional, part of Israel's national heritage. Those memories nurtured Habakkuk and re-created in him the realities of which they were memories. The stories of Yahweh's mighy achievements in primal creation and past salvivic interventions were ritually reenacted in the recitation of the story and reactualized in the perception of the prophet.

Habakkuk's experience is a classic instance of encounter with the energies of the living God. For heroic, authentic spirits like Habakkuk, to venture into this peril zone, to touch the ultimate holiness, was daunting, devastating.

It would be easier to hide, to give up.

In our fragile existence as humans, we confront many horrors, and by some we are deeply injured. Sooner or later, the perils of our uncertain, finite, vulnerable life wound us, perhaps badly, incurably. They always threaten us, and simply to anticipate possible disasters can be terrifying.

A psalmist once said to God, "Show me how frail I am!" (*meh-ḥādēl 'ānî* [Ps 39:4]). No need to pray that. We find out how little we can control what happens to us, how helpless we are against the forces that destroy our achievements and cancel our hopes.

In the life experiences that bring this home to us, it requires an extraordinarily robust faith to see the good hand of God in all such things, to find enjoyable the close presence of God in the most calamitous events, to uphold with intellectual integrity an uncompromising biblical, monotheistic belief, to recognize that the whole universe—every creature and every event—comes from the sovereign determination of the one and only actual God, who is to be identified as none other than Yahweh, the God of Israel and the Father of Jesus Christ. We see in the book of Habakkuk how one man grappled with this terrible threat to faith.

When writing a book or making a speech to be admired, it is easy to say that everything exists and happens only in the will of the one real God and to affirm the rightness of it all. But it is not easy to believe it, to believe that God does everything and that everything he does is right, to believe it with the full consent of the mind and the full endorsement of the conscience.

Everything is not right. God is the Creator. That is an article of the creed. Just think! Each and every individual in the vast human population of this planet was made by God. As Habakkuk tells Yahweh, "You made humankind (*'ādām*) like the fishes of the sea" (1:14); and, like all the little things that creep on the

ground and wriggle in the waters, humans are weak, helpless, with no ruler or
protector. Yet the pitiless extermination of vast swarms of defenseless humans
has continued from Habakkuk's time to our own, reaching a scale in the twentieth century many times greater than the slaughter and enslavement that
Habakkuk witnessed and dreaded.

We relive Habakkuk's agony. The recitation of Israel's story brought Habakkuk
to acquiescence and a measure of tranquillity, even joy, in the end. Is it possible that he still has a message for us in our time?

OUTLINE OF THE BOOK OF HABAKKUK

The revelation that Habakkuk the prophet saw consists of two portions:

- Part One. Interchange Between Habakkuk and Yahweh (Habakkuk 1 and 2)
- Part Two. The Prayer-Hymn of Habakkuk (Habakkuk 3)

The first part might be called a public message because it results in a set of "woe
oracles" suitable for proclamation. The second part is called a prayer, but
whether it should be understood as a private prayer, composed by the prophet
for his own use, or whether that title is a comment on his prophecy added by a
later editor is a critical question that will be discussed in the INTRODUCTION to
the second part.

Each part of the book has its own heading (1:1; 3:1). Each title contains the
name of the prophet. The first part is called "The Burden that Habakkuk the
Prophet Saw." The second is "A Prayer for (by?) Habakkuk the Prophet." It is
almost as though each part were an independent work. The boundaries of the
final hymn are well marked by a conventional heading (see the NOTES on Hab
3:1) and colophon (see the NOTES on Hab 3:19c). The "prayer of Habakkuk" is
just like a poem in the Psalter. In content and literary character it is strikingly
different from the rest of the book of Habakkuk. This contrast suggests that
Habakkuk 3 is a composition with its own literary history. Some scholars have
concluded from its hymnic character that the final poem has nothing to do with
Habakkuk's prophecy, except in the mind of a later editor. The final hymn is
certainly different from the other material, but in due time we shall review the
organization of the whole book and shall point out that Habakkuk 3 contains
themes and vocabulary that connect it back to Habakkuk 1 and 2.

The first part of the book, while clearly oracular, or at least containing pieces
of identifiable oracular discourse, is by no means uniform in character. One
readily identified block of material consists of a series of "woe oracles" (2:6b–20).
The remainder consists of speeches in which Habakkuk addresses Yahweh directly by name (1:2, 12), interspersed with other material in which Yahweh
replies to these prayers. Such a response is clearly identified in Hab 2:2, and
presumably another one begins at Hab 1:5, even though in that verse nothing
is said about who is speaking.

The distinctive character of the series of "woe oracles," in contrast with the features of the dialogue contained in Hab 1:2–2:6a, has suggested to many scholars that Hab 2:6b–20 is a separate prophetic composition complete in itself. Viewed in this way, the book of Habakkuk is an assemblage of three relatively independent pieces of different genre, which need not even have been written by the same person:

1. Dialogue between the prophet and God (1:1–2:6a)
2. Woe oracles (2:6b–20)
3. The Psalm of Habakkuk (3:1–19)

There are, however, arguments for regarding the "woe oracles" as integral to the dialogue, indeed as the culmination of the encounter between the prophet and Yahweh and as the "burden" (*hammaśśā'* [1:1]) secured in the vision (*ḥāzâ* [1:1]; *ḥāzôn* [2:2]). The dialogue is then the vehicle of this message of woe.

Interspersed through this material are brief remarks: two titles (1:1; 3:1a), two liturgical rubrics (3:1b; 3:19c), two meditative soliloquies (2:1; 3:17–19a), two narrative reports (2:2aA; 3:16), two exhortations (2:6a; 2:20).

We use an outline that shows six main components in all, mingled with these smaller, diverse pieces:

I.		Title (1:1)
II.		Habakkuk's first prayer (1:2–4)
III.		Yahweh's first response (1:5–11)
IV.		Habakkuk's second prayer (1:12–17)
V.	A soliloquy (2:1)	
	Narrative (2:2aA)	
VI.		Yahweh's second response (2:2aB–20), including
VII.1		Exhortation (2:6a), and
VII.2–7.		The "woe oracles" (2:6b–20)
VIII.	The Prayer of Habakkuk (Habakkuk 3)	
VIII.1	Title (3:1a)	
	Rubric (3:1b)	
VIII.2.i–iii.		The vision of Habakkuk (3:2–15)
VIII.2.iv	Narrative (3:16)	
	Soliloquy (3:17–19b)	
VIII.3.	Rubric (3:19c)	

If the complete book is accepted as a report of a visionary encounter with God, Habakkuk 3 (VIII) is part of the whole—indeed, the climax and resolution of the experience. The total design consists of five utterances alternating between the prophet (II, IV, VIII) and God (III, VI–VII).

In the first prayer (1:2–4 [II]), the prophet complains that God has been unresponsive to his cry for help against the "wicked." In reply (1:5–11 [III]), God answers that he is sending the Chaldeans, and he gives a terrifying description of their ruthlessness. The second prayer of the prophet (1:12–17 [IV]) repeats the complaints already lodged in the first prayer, and includes additional points that seem to arise from the response that God gave in Hab 1:5–11. Hab 2:1–2aA (V) contains one of the two narrative passages in the book. This unit is transitional between the prophet's second prayer (1:12–17) and Yahweh's response (2:2aB–20 [VI]). Strictly only Hab 2:2aA is narrative: "And Yahweh answered me and said. . . ." The narrative could hardly be briefer. Hab 2:1 is spoken by the prophet, but he is talking to himself. From his soliloquy we can infer what happened as he waited for Yahweh's response. Yahweh's second speech, which begins inHab 2:2aB, is followed by (or includes) the "woe oracles" (2:6b–20 [VII]).

The connection between the prophet's two prayers in Hab 1:2–4 and Hab 1:12–17 has been explained in various ways.

1. Because of the similarity between Hab 1:2–4 and Hab 1:12–17 in form and mood, some scholars (Nowack 1922; Wellhausen 1892) regarded these pieces as originally a single speech, into which the oracle in vv 5–11 has been ineptly inserted. On this theory, "the wicked one" is the same in both parts, and the situation is the same throughout. To support this argument, it was pointed out that the complaint in vv 12–17 is very little different in content and concern from that in vv 2–4, as if the oracle in vv 5–11 had made no difference—almost as though Yahweh's response had not been given. This reasoning is not entirely cogent. The description of the Chaldeans' action in vv 15–16 has a resemblance to Yahweh's predicted activity in the oracle of vv 5–11—gathering people like fish is similar to collecting people like sand. This is a thematic or rhetorical link, certainly. But the protagonists and the perspective are different. The two developments are theologically connected—Yahweh sends the Chaldeans and is responsible for what they do. The concept is almost a commonplace of the theology of the Hebrew Bible, so its expression in two places does not prove that they belong to a single speech.

2. Hence vv 12–17 can be interpreted as the prophet's horrified response to the answer given by Yahweh in vv 5–11. If the situation described in vv 2–4 is bad, the remedy proposed in vv 5–11 is worse. The complaint in vv 12–17 is then lodged against the atrocities that the Chaldeans will commit among the nations, as described (in anticipation) in vv 5–11, or perhaps have already committed.

3. A different explanation of the connection between vv 5–11 and vv 12–17 is possible if it is supposed that there was a time interval between v 11 and v 12 during which the events forecast in vv 5–11 took place. The second round of complaint and response between the prophet and God (1:12–2:20) can then be dated after the Chaldeans have despoiled Judah. Any justice that might have been seen in God's use of such agents to punish the wicked within Judah is entirely lost in the horrendous scale of their oppressions, and in the fact that the righteous suffer along with the wicked. The following "woe oracles," if they are part of God's second response, make more sense if they are directed against Babylon after Judah has suffered deeply from its cruelty. Accordingly, the time interval between Hab 1:11 and Hab 1:12 could be as much as twenty years. Ralph Smith (1984:94–95) suggests before the Battle of Carchemish (605 B.C.E.) for the first "lament," 597

B.C.E. for the second one. Some such timetable cannot be pronounced impossible. But the description in vv 15–16 still seems somewhat remote; it does not have the flavor of a recent horrifying experience still in memory. The prophet does not say "us." It seems as though the conquest of the world is still in progress, but not complete. Thus the prayer in vv 12–17 could be intended to call a halt to Babylon's world conquest before Judah feels its full force. That is, vv 12–17 are a protest against the plan of God announced in vv 5–11, and an attempt to persuade God to change that plan, similar to Amos's successful intervention in like circumstances (Amos 7). This reading fits in with our suggestion that the whole dialogue is an intercession that takes place in the divine assembly, where such plans are made (again compare Amos and Jeremiah).

To sum up, there is nothing in Hab 1:12–17 that requires a date much later than the date of Hab 1:2–4. In fact, the Exile period is not appropriate because the conquests are evidently still in progress, not complete, to judge from v 17.

The two prayers made by the prophet in Habakkuk 1 are more straightforward and better organized from the literary point of view than are the two responses given by Yahweh. Quite apart from the inclusion in the second divine response of the "woe oracles," which are very different from the rest, Hab 2:2–6a (VI) is not very coherent and contains some passages of great difficulty. The inconsistencies in this section cause readers to lose their way and to miss the connection between Hab 2:2 and Hab 2:6a:

> Write down the vision,
>   and explain it upon the tablets,
> so that he who reads it can run!
>
>   . . .
> And he will say: "Woe to him. . . .

The revelation that is to be recorded plainly on the tablets and read out by the person who delivers the message consists precisely of the "woe oracles." It is even possible that the material in the gap between v 2 and v 6b (vv 3–6a) is not part of Yahweh's response at all, but a parenthetical commentary put in by way of an introduction to the oracles. The extraordinary difficulty of these verses makes it impossible to reach any firm conclusion about them.

The "woe oracles" are related thematically to the supplications of Habakkuk and serve well within the book as part of Yahweh's answer to the prophet's interrogation. The evils against which Habakkuk protests—injustice, rapacity, idolatry—receive appropriate comment in the "woe oracles."

1. The "woe oracle" against plundering (2:6b, 8a) answers Hab 1:6 etc. (note *lō' lô* as catchphrase).
2. The "woe oracle" against greed (2:9) answers Hab 1:4.
3. The "woe oracle" against murder (2:12) answers Hab 1:17.
4. The "woe oracle" against drunkenness (2:15) answers Hab 2:5.
5. The "woe oracle" against idolatry (2:18) answers Hab 1:16.

The individual speeches thus isolated are by no means uniform in texture. Rough places are met from time to time. They may be due to any of several causes. They could reflect a certain ruggedness in the prophet's writing style, to match the turbulence of his thought. However disconcerting to us, and however difficult for the modern interpreter to manage, these features may be left intact, as authentic and original (Andersen 1995b). Other discordant materials may be intrusive comments either by the prophet or by later editors or scribes. The refrain of Hab 2:8b and Hab 2:17b

> from the blood of humankind,
>   and the lawlessness of the land,
> the city, and all who live in it

could be such a comment, because its connection with its context is not easy to discover. But the strategic placement of this refrain (after the first "woe oracle" and before the last one) could contribute to an intentional structural design.

Furthermore, the "woe oracles" contain two statements (2:14, 2:20) that do not fit well with the rest, do not seem to belong to that genre. They are sentchious rather than precatory. But they are not extraneous. They are placed at the junctures of "woe oracles" (after the third and fifth), and they are connected by the key words "earth" and "Yahweh" in chiasm. The bicolon in Hab 2:11 could be another such independent comment because the address changes from second person to third. The scheme is then:

> First "woe oracle" (2:6b–8a)
>   Refrain (2:8b)
> Second "woe oracle" (2:9–10)
>   Refrain (2:11)
> Third "woe oracle" (2:12–13)
>   Refrain (2:14)
> Fourth "woe oracle" (2:15–17a)
>   Refrain (2:17b)
> Fifth "woe oracle" (2:18–19)
>   Refrain (2:20)

The refrain of v 17b marks the interface of the fourth and fifth "woe oracles." This is helpful in finding the overall structure of the whole set of "woe oracles," because the fifth "woe oracle" is the only one that does not begin with the word *hôy.* (This word is delayed to v 19.) But in any case, the theme of idolatry is clearly present in both v 18 and v 19.

What is Habakkuk talking about? In an attempt to find a movement of thought through the entire book, or at least through the first two chapters, an interpretation has been developed and widely accepted. The only firm pivot around which this entire construction revolves is the mention of the Chaldeans in Hab 1:6. Yet the historical reality to which this word might point is far from evident.

Habakkuk's first prayer does not have this people in mind, but is directed against evildoers in his own community. No names are mentioned, such as Israel or Judah; but the reference to the breakdown of Torah points to a domestic situation. Habakkuk is upset by the collapse of law and order, and he holds God responsible for this through neglecting his duties as judge, a neglect doubly reprehensible because he has not heeded the prophet's complaint, calling for redress.

In his first oracular response, Yahweh points out that he is about to deal with the matter. His strategy is to bring "upon the degenerate covenant nation through the medium of the Chaldeans" (Keil 1954:53–54) suitable judgment. But, according to Habakkuk's second prayer, the victims are not Israel; they are all humankind. And they are not the wicked, rightly punished, but the righteous, or at least the innocent, undeserving of chastisement. To this outcry (it is maintained), God replies that the Chaldeans will also be judged when their turn comes. The "woe oracles" anticipate this judgment.

There is much in the prophecy that does not fit into this neat scheme. Some of the "woe oracles" seem to be directed more against social injustice than international militarism. And the application of the key verse—"the just shall live by faith"—to the whole problem is far from clear.

LITERARY STUDY OF THE BOOK OF HABAKKUK

The discipline of form criticism has contributed generously to the appreciation of the literary craftsmanship of the book of Habakkuk. The main ingredients were identified and labeled. In the early stages of this kind of research, the book was read as a collection of short "more or less disconnected" (Pfeiffer 1952:597) prophetic utterances. Many extraneous fragments were eliminated as inauthentic—that is, added by later scribes. Details can be found in the older handbooks. The history of this enterprise has been written in detail by Jöcken (1977; see also Sweeney 1991).

The affinities of the literary categories used by Habakkuk with prayers and hymns used in the cult led some scholars to the conclusion that the book, or at least Habakkuk 1 and 2, was a "prophetic liturgy," a genre already identified by Gunkel (1924). The book of Habakkuk is cult poetry (Engnell 1970:167). This line of research marched with a correlative proposal that Habakkuk himself was a temple official (cult prophet, composer, singer), either hypothesis relying on, or in circular reasoning fostering, the other.

There is no necessary nexus between the two theories. The role of Habakkuk in the religious institutions of his day will be discussed in detail in the COMMENT on Hab 1:1. While various kinds of prayers and hymns had their prime use in the cult, such compositions could also be used in other situations. Prophets used all available resources in the composition of their messages. They not only imitated conventional forms; they could abuse them with "deliberate reversal" (McKane 1979:172).

There is general agreement that Habakkuk's prayers resemble psalms that have been called "complaints" or "laments" (Harris 1973). Some scholars use one term, some the other. Some use them interchangeably, or say "complaint (or lament)." There is no agreement about the components of a composition rightly identified as a complaint. Compare the breakdowns in Hayes (1974:200), Tucker (1988:12), and Haak (1991:13), a few of many.

An additional question is whether any given lament is communal or individual. Scholars who recognize all or part of the book of Habakkuk as a complaint are divided over whether it is communal (Jeremias 1970:76–81), or individual (Ittmann 1981:30, "Frageform,Wortwahl und Aufbau finden ihre engsten Parallelen in den individuellen Klageliedern des Psalters" [The interrogative form, choice of words, and construction find their closest parallels in the individual lament songs of the Psalter]; Baumgartner 1987:88), or both at once (Bellinger 1984:83). Discussing Habakkuk 3, Avishur (1994:112–13) asserts that "this composition is not an individual lament, but a national lament." I do not understand how he can go on to say that "comparison between our psalm [Habakkuk 3] and other biblical psalms reveals no difference between them in terms of structure, style, or constituent motifs" (113). I would argue, on the contrary, that there is very little similarity between Habakkuk 3 and the templates for laments that have been recognized in the classical studies of Gunkel and Mowinckel. Gunkel and Begrich (1933:117) list Hab 1:2–4, 12–17 (but not Habakkuk 3) as a "people's lament" or "prophetic liturgy," or rather an individual prayer ("Gebete Einzelner") made on behalf of the people. While Habakkuk's prayer is undoubtedly personal, there is no petition for the people. There is no trace of the customary *Sitz-im-Leben* (a fasting ritual [Gunkel and Begrich 1933:117]), of the normal cult setting (unless Hab 2:20 is meant to supply that), or of expressions of misery intended to move God to pity (the consternation expressed in Hab 3:2 and Hab 3:16 is the terrified reponse of the prophet to the theophany; the petitioner does not present himself to God as either tortured by illness or tormented by guilt). An opening invocation (3:2a) followed by a prayer for divine intervention (3:2b) is too generic to establish the *Gattung* of Habakkuk 3 as a lament.

The more firmly Habakkuk is located in the cult, the more likely his prayers will be interpreted as communal rather than personal. This is an artificial dichotomy. People in the Bible did make personal prayers; but they would make use of the common stock. Gunkel was more willing than Mowinckel to recognize that such prayers could be secularized and democratized. In this, however, he was probably biased by romantic pietistic individualism that might not necessarily have been present in the religious sensibilities of ancient Israelites (Koch 1969:177).

Habakkuk's prayers were individual, but, since he was a prophet, they were not private. An individual prophet could speak on behalf of the community, even when his intercessions were provoked by personal need. This combination is likely to be found in the circumstance when a prophet (who had a unique role as a person, but who was also, by that very role, a public figure) identified with the predicament of the community that he shared. Because of the prominent use of "I," we are inclined to take Habakkuk's prayers as personal, at least in their salient focus. At the same time, since Mowinckel's (1921–24) classic study of the "I" in psalms, the possibility that the "I" presents himself to God on behalf of all should be kept in mind. This dual role would apply to Habakkuk as an intercessor or as a prophetic covenant mediator on behalf of his people Israel.

The argument for the cultic connection relies more on vocabulary than on form as such. The exhaustive listings in chap. 3 of Humbert (1944:80–248), "The Literary Affinities of Habakkuk's Vocabulary," are sometimes referred to as evidence. But when his conclusions are studied, it is evident that the cultic connection is counterbalanced by a significant amount of affinity with prophetic writings of Habakkuk's period.

In light of Tucker's (1971) arguments for a distinction between "complaint" and "lament", we will refer to Habakkuk's prayers as "complaints," with particular attention to the vocabulary that points to the law courts or at least to legal disputation as supplying the metaphors for Habakkuk's dispute with God. The term "lament" is more suited to a prayer of misery appealing to God's pity, whereas a "complaint" can take the form of a protest and an appeal to God's justice from a person who has been victimized. We are surprised that scholars who call Habakkuk's prayers "laments" have not paid more attention to the term that Habakkuk himself used to characterize them: *tôkaḥtî* "my remonstration," "my rebuke" (2:1).

In this perspective, the attempt by Haak (1991) to fit the whole of Hab 1:2–2:20 into the template of a cultic complaint or lament is forced to make some improbable matches. His use of these terms as though they were interchangeable is not helpful. He concludes that "the entire book of Habakkuk is in the form of a complaint" (19). At the same time he calls Hab 3:1–19 "a Psalm of Lament" (16), an "expansion" of the complaint form already completely present in Habakkuk 1 and 2. This is too much! The distinctiveness of the "woe oracles" is lost when they are equated with the expressions of confidence that are sometimes met in laments. While admitting that woe oracles "are a form not usually associated with a complaint" (16), Haak argues that the motif in woe oracles of the anticipated reversal of fortune expresses confidence that God will set things right. But that is not how confidence in the outcome is expressed in complaints, and both sides of the indicator are not present in Habakkuk's "woe oracles." They denounce and threaten. They do not promise the rehabilitation of victims.

Haak's (1991) claims that the entire book of Habakkuk is a single literary entity, even if overstated and unconvincing, are a remarkable index of how things have changed in biblical studies. Such claims were unthinkable for most of the literary critics of the twentieth century. We are prepared to argue for the *thematic* unity of the book in an overarching literary structure. But none of the familiar genres supplies the model for the whole book. We find it anachronistic that so much faith can still be placed in form criticism long after Muilenburg (1969) inaugurated the age "beyond form criticism."

THE TEXT OF THE BOOK OF HABAKKUK

Textual study of the book of Habakkuk is a classic instance of the paradox that the more we find out, the less we know. If we had only the traditional Masoretic Text and if all the ancient translations, beginning with Greek Septuagint (LXX) and Aramaic Targum, were accurate renditions of the Masoretic Text, there would be only one text for all practical purposes.

Biblical manuscripts among the Dead Sea Scrolls show that, prior to the triumph of the text type preferred and preserved by the rabbis, a variety of Hebrew texts was in use. Manuscripts of Greek translations, almost as old, give a similar picture. There is no reason to believe that the Hebrew and Greek texts of Habakkuk in circulation at the beginning of the present era were any less diverse.

Since the discovery in various caves in the desert of Judea of manuscripts of biblical books in Hebrew, Aramaic, and Greek that were made shortly before and soon after the turn of the era, numerous attempts have been made to fit all this evidence into a coherent picture of the origins, transmission, and development of these diverse texts, traditions, translations, and recensions of the Hebrew Scriptures and of the interconnections among them. There is still no consensus, not even on the basic classification of "text types" or even on whether we should talk about "text types" at all. The textual affiliation of the manuscripts remains unclear, and their relation to the later Masoretic tradition has not yet been worked out. The seminal hypothesis of Albright (1955), postulating three local text types, as sustained by Cross (1964, 1966, 1975, 1979, 1985), with modifying nuances, has been continually criticized, but not yet replaced by a more viable theory. For reviews of the question see Cross and Talmon (1975), Bremmer and García Martínez (1992), and Ulrich (1998).

If more progress could be made in this field of research, we would be able to make more defensible decisions about the Hebrew text that they all derive from and get behind the MT to something ancestral to them all. For the time being, all such work must remain tentative. Our scholarly habit of giving up and falling back on the MT is better than just giving up. Better, too, than patching up by emendation, at least as an interim measure. But that is all it is, and readings remain open to correction whether by assistance from variants in ancient sources (biblical manuscripts and also quotations from Habakkuk in ancient writings) or even by emendation when all else fails.

This work is made difficult by the confusion that exists over terminology, especially when that terminology derives from theories of text transmission that are not accepted by all scholars. The term "Septuagint" (LXX) has so many different referents that intended usage should be carefully defined and strictly adhered to. It is too vague to use LXX indiscriminately when quoting any rendition of a text from the Hebrew Bible that is available in Greek. It is our intention to use LXX when referring to the Göttingen edition, keeping in mind that it is eclectic. We use its apparatus when citing manuscript variants. It is misleading to quote the Göttingen LXX as "Old Greek." That critical edition is simply as close as we can get at present to likely earlier forms of the text of the earliest Greek translations; but the Göttingen LXX should not be quoted as though it were the pre-Christian text. See the cautions in *ABD* (V:1093).

Among the Qumran scrolls is a commentary (*pešer*) on the book of Habakkuk (1QpHab) that reproduces most of the text of Habakkuk 1 and 2. This manuscript dates to the second half of the first century B.C.E. Its date of composition could be earlier. The text of Habakkuk preserved in this *pešer* has been thoroughly studied by Brownlee (1959).

Another manuscript containing text of Habakkuk was found in Wadi Murabbaʿat in 1955 (*DJD* II Mur 88, cols. XVIII–XIX [MurXII is now the standard *siglum*]). It has been dated to the second century C.E. Its text is virtually the same as the Masoretic Text.

The original translation of the Torah into Greek was followed by the rest of the Hebrew Bible, with more than one translation or perhaps revision. A scroll of the Minor Prophets in Greek (8Ḥev XIIgr) was found at Nahal Ḥever in 1952. The official publication did not take place until 1990 (*DJD* 8), but the textual significance of this manuscript had already been fully examined by Barthélemy (1963). Reference to this manuscript as R (initiated by Barthélemy in his provisional first publication of the text and continued by Hiebert [1986] and others) should be replaced by the standard 8Ḥev XIIgr (or 8Ḥev 1 [Flint and VanderKam 1999:784). I have not been able to find out why Barthélemy chose this letter; he simply says: "Dans l'étude qui suit, je désignerai par le sigle 'R' cette œuvre" (1963:179). These sources together supply evidence for nearly all of the book of Habakkuk.

1:3–2:11	MurXII col XVII
1:5–11	8 Ḥev XIIgr col 11
1:6–17	1QpHab
1:14–17	8 Ḥev XIIgr col 12
2:1–8a	8 Ḥev XIIgr col 12
2:1–20	1QpHab
2:13–20	8 Ḥev XIIgr col 13
2:18–3:19	MurXII col XIX
3:9–15	8 Ḥev XIIgr col 14

The textual history of Habakkuk 3 is made more complex by the existence of a divergent Greek translation, attested by six MSS. It is usually referred to as the Barberini version. Because of its unique features, this tradition will receive special attention in our treatment of Habakkuk 3.

The significance of these materials for study of the book of Habakkuk has been reviewed ably by Haak (1991:1–11). Individual readings will be considered on a case-by-case basis in the following discussion.

DATE OF COMPOSITION OF THE
BOOK OF HABAKKUK

Jöcken (1976:3–115) surveyed all the proposals that had been made for dating the book of Habakkuk up to the time of his study. The problem of dating the book has been posed in various ways, depending on whether it is viewed as a single composition or as a collection of loosely related but essentially independent pieces. In one case, the question is simple: When was the whole book written or at least finished? In the other, the question has many parts: When was each portion written, and when were they joined together? Even more elaborate theories purport to trace the growth of the work over a period of many centuries. Beginning with the perspective of Habakkuk 3, which goes back to Creation and deals also with the Exodus, we have here an ancient composition that came down through tradition and was incorporated into the prophecy. The question of the origin and date of this material is distinct from the problem of the literary production of the book of Habakkuk as a whole. It will be enough to say that most of the hymnic material in Hab 3:3–15 could be premonarchical and that some of the Creation passages could go back to very remote Hebrew antiquity.

The prophetic material in Habakkuk 1 and 2 focuses on many moments or situations. In Hab 1:2–4, the prophet is distressed by a situation in which "the wicked surround the righteous." If these characters could be identified, the prayer could be dated. It is our conclusion that the righteous man is the prophet himself, who is suffering persecution. The crisis is private, and nothing is said that enables us to put a date to it. Other researchers have tried to find in the circumstances behind Habakkuk's concerns a crisis more public and political, either domestic (within Judah, so that the wicked and the righteous are Judaeans) or international (so that the righteous [man] is Judah the nation and the wicked is some foreign oppressor). The latter view leads to the earliest proposed dates for Hab 1:2–4: the "wicked" is Assyria (Budde 1930). The scheme is that Assyria is the instrument of God's judgment against his people, an idea found in Isa 10:5. Then, in its turn, Assyria will be the object of God's judgment, with Babylon as the instrument (Hab 1:5). On this theory Hab 1:2–4 could have been produced in the middle of the seventh century B.C.E., and Hab 1:5–11, if a prediction, must have been produced before 612 B.C.E. There is nothing in the book of Habakkuk itself to identify Assyria as "the wicked." If this theology of history had not been present already in Isaiah, it is doubtful whether anyone would have found it in Habakkuk.

An interesting variant of this theory is found in the work of Peiser (1903). He supposed Habakkuk to have been a royal prince of Judah held hostage in Nineveh, writing in anticipation of the assault of the Medes and Chaldeans on Assyria. Such a location makes more sense of the universal perspective of the vision. An invasion of Judah could hardly be described as the conquest of the whole world. But the perspective of Habakkuk nevertheless seems to be that of an observer in the land of Judah, which in the late seventh century B.C.E. had little recent experience of Assyria as an oppressor. In fact, Assyrian suzerainty had become nominal by Josiah's time.

A different historical setting for Hab 1:2–4 has been found in the wickedness that prevailed in Judah before the time of Josiah. The "wicked" need not be any particular individual; the term could refer to the general lawless element within the community. The essential point is that the wrong Habakkuk complains about is done by one Judaean against another. The theory then is that Hab 1:5–11 is the LORD's answer to the prophet's complaint: he will raise up the Chaldeans to punish the wicked Judaeans. Scholars who accept the authenticity of Hab 1:5–11, and, more important, who leave the word "Chaldeans" in place as referring to the Neo-Babylonians, feel that this highly specific prophecy can be dated with some accuracy. Thus Marti (1904:329) considered Hab 1:5–10 and 14–15 to be the oldest part of the book, dated 605 B.C.E. Cannon (1925) interpreted Hab 1:2–4 as an expression of disillusionment over the failure of the Deuteronomic reform after the death of Josiah. Consequently he put this oracle "in the earlier part of the reign of Jehoiakim" (66). This enabled him to turn to Jeremiah 22 and 23 to supply the background of social injustice for the prayer of Habakkuk. The result itself is plausible. It does not need the supporting argument that Hab 2:4 specifically describes the reaction against Josiah's policy. The plausibility of the date, however, does not give any support to the theory that the Torah mentioned by Habakkuk is the book of the law found by Josiah; that is circular reasoning. An unknown consideration here is the extent to which Judah might have suffered oppression from foreigners prior to the Babylonian conquest. It is doubtful that the Assyrians would have been viewed as "the wicked" encompassing "the righteous" at any time. After the accession of Josiah, Assyrian influence was receding; before that, it would have been felt through the rule of Manasseh.

The search for "the wicked" must satisfy two conditions. First, the activities of "the wicked" must have been experienced by the righteous within Judah. The language could describe Manasseh, but not Assyria. Second, "the wicked" must be open to punishment through the agency of the Chaldeans. This identification could apply to Assyria, but not to Manasseh. Yet a combination of oppression on the domestic level with an international setting is needed. This combination is found in the early part of the reign of Jehoiakim (2 Kgs 23:31–37). As an Egyptian puppet, he was obliged to collect tribute. This was regarded as oppressive, and it led to a reaction, with some Judeans looking to Babylon to deliver them from Egypt. And, in the event, the Chaldeans did get rid of the Egyptians who were behind this (2 Kgs 24:7).

Another theory that gives Hab 1:2–4 an international setting identifies "the wicked" as the Chaldeans, who are tyrannizing the whole world, including Judah. The reasoning that leads to this conclusion begins with Hab 2:6b–20, which is appropriately directed against the Babylonians. Assuming that "the wicked" are the same throughout, Hab 1:2–4 as well as Hab 1:12–17 must refer to them. The complaints (1:2–4, 12–17) as well as the "woe oracles" that answer them (2:6b–20) must have arisen after the Neo-Babylonians had conquered Syria-

Palestine—that is, during the Exile, in the mid-sixth century B.C.E. (Wellhausen 1893:161; Duhm 1906:12–13; Nowack 1922:264). In order to maintain this perspective, Wellhausen (1893:162) was obliged to explain Hab 1:5–11 as not belonging to this situation: "It is an older oracle that predicts and describes the first appearance of the Chaldeans." This theory has been criticized on various grounds.

1. The similarity of Habakkuk to Jeremiah, in mood and language, is best explained by a similar date soon before, rather than after, the conquest of Judaea by the Chaldeans—at least for the opening oracle.
2. Marti (1904:326–27) argued in another direction that Hab 1:2–4, 12a, 13; 2:1–4 are the remains of a psalm (he compares Psalm 73 [334]) dealing in more general terms with the problem of the undeserved sufferings of the righteous. On these grounds, he considers any time from the fifth to the second century B.C.E. possible.

Sellin's explanation (in the 1930 edition of his commentary) is similar to Wellhausen's, but he dates it more precisely, and he finds more unity in Habakkuk 1 (381). The Chaldeans are the cause of the distress in Hab 1:2–4; but there is more to come, predicted in Hab 1:5–11. The time is between the first and second attack of the Babylonians on Jerusalem, that is, between 600 and 587 B.C.E.

A much later date was recommended by Duhm (1906). He identified the world conqueror as Alexander the Great, so the time must be between the Battle of Issus (333 B.C.E.) and the Battle of Arbela (331 B.C.E). His main reason for doing this was the word "eastward" in Hab 1:9, which points to an invasion from the west. Duhm finds other details in the text to support this result. There are several reasons for rejecting this theory, or at least to doubt it severely. Among them are these:

1. From the point of view of a Judaean, Alexander, like any other invader, came from the north (or south).
2. The features that are said to apply to Alexander are so general that they would fit almost any aggressor. It is a capital weakness in the theory that Duhm felt obliged to change "Chaldeans" in Hab 1:6 to Kittim (= Greeks). 1QpHab glossed "Chaldeans" (spelled hkśd'ym) as hkty'ym, a reading prompted by the historical circumstances of the Qumran sectaries. Now that the Arad ostraca have shown that kittiyyīm were already present in Judea in preexilic times, it cannot be said that the use of that word by Habakkuk would have been impossible. But if hakittiyyīm were original, why would a scribe change it to hakkaśdîm?

An even later date was suggested by Happel (1900; see Jöcken 1976)—the Seleucid period. The "righteous" are the Jews persecuted by Antiochus Epiphanes. This is impossible because Jesus ben Sirach already knew about a collection of twelve prophets in the early second century B.C.E (Sir 49:10).

Cannon (1925) succeeded in explaining the variety of points of view within the book in terms of development in the prophet's outlook over a period of time. The unity of the book is found, not on the formal level, but in a continuity of experience in the life of Habakkuk himself.

To sum up. There is no sure proof of the date of the book as a whole, or of any constituent part. As long as it is not tampered with, or explained as symbolic, the reference to the Chaldeans in Hab 1:6 points to the Neo-Babylonian period. If this statement is taken in its obvious intention as a prediction, a date before the major incursion of the Babylonians into Judaea is required. The "woe oracles" and the Psalm (Habakkuk 3) could be further reactions to this threat, either in anticipation or after its fulfillment. All could have been done within the lifetime of one person, between, say, 605 B.C.E (Battle of Carchemish) and 575 B.C.E. Rudolph (1975:194) is more precise, settling the latest likely date at 597 B.C.E.

BIBLIOGRAPHY

◆

This bibliography does not attempt a complete listing of the literature on the book of Habakkuk. It provides references to sources used in the preparation of this commentary, most of which are referred to in the NOTES and COMMENTS. For a systematic bibliography, see Adri van der Wal, *Nahum, Habakkuk: A Classified Bibliography*, with a special paragraph concerning literature on the Qumran Commentaries on Nahum and Habakkuk. Applicatio 6 (Amsterdam: Free University Press, 1988).

COMMENTARIES

Achtemeier, Elizabeth R.
   1986   *Nahum-Malachi. Interpretation: A Bible Commentary for Teaching and Preaching*. Atlanta: John Knox Press.
Bič, Miloš
   1968   *Trois prophètes dans un temps de ténèbres: Sophonie–Nahum–Habaquq*. Lectio Divina 48. Paris: Cerf.
Brandenburg, H.
   1963   *Die Kleinen Propheten*. 2 vols. Das Lebendige Wort. Giessen: Brunnen.
Calvin, John
   1846   *Commentaries on the Twelve Minor Prophets*. Vol. 3, *Habakkuk, Zephaniah & Haggai*. John Owen, trs. Edinburgh: Calvin Translation Society. Reprint. Grand Rapids, Mich.: Eerdmans, 1950.
Cohen, A., ed.
   1948   *The Twelve Prophets*. Bornemouth: Soncino.
Craigie, Peter C.
   1985   *Twelve Prophets*. Vol. 2. Daily Study Bible Series. Philadelphia: Westminster.
Davidson, A. B.
   1905   *Nahum, Habakkuk and Zephaniah*. Cambridge Bible. Cambridge: Cambridge University Press.
   1920   *The Books of Nahum, Habakkuk and Zephaniah*, adapted to the text of the Revised Version with some supplementary notes, by H. C. O. Lanchester. Cambridge: Cambridge University Press.
Deden, D.
   1953–1956   *De kleine Profeten uit de grondtekst vertaald en uitgelegd*. Adri-

anus ven den Born, ed. De Boeken van het Oude Testament 12. Roermond: Romen.

Deissler, Alfons
1984   *Zwölf Propheten II: Obadja, Jona, Micha, Nahum, Habakuk.* NEBib. Würzburg: Echter.

Deissler, Alfons, and M. Delcor
1964   *Les petits prophetès: 2: Michée-Malachie.* La Sainte Bible 8:1. Paris: Letouzey & Ané.

Delitzsch, Franz
1843   *Der Prophet Habakuk.* Exegetisches Handbuch zu den Propheten des Alten Bundes. Leipzig: Tauchnitz.

Duhm, Bernhard
1906   *Das Buch Habakuk: Text, Übersetzung und Erklärung.* Tübingen: Mohr (Paul Siebert).

Eaton, J. H.
1961   *Obadiah, Nahum, Habakkuk and Zephaniah.* TBC. London: SCM Press.

Edelkoort, Albertus Hendrick
1937   *Nahum, Habakuk, Zefanja.* Amsterdam: Albertus Hendrik.

Edgar, S. L.
1962   *The Minor Prophets.* Epworth Preacher's Commentaries. London: Epworth.

Elliger, Karl
1964   *Das Buch der zwölf Kleinen Propheten II.* ATD 25/II. Göttingen: Neues Göttinger Bibelwerk.

Ewald, G. H. A. von
1867–1868   *Die Propheten des alten Bundes erklärt.* 2nd ed. Göttingen: Vandenhoeck & Ruprecht. [Habakkuk is Vol. II, pp. 29–51]
1875–1881   *Commentary on the Prophets of the Old Testament.* J. Frederick Smith, trs. London and Edinburg: Williams and Norgate. [Translation of Ewald 1867–1868]

Gailey, James H.
1962   *Micah, Nahum, Habakkuk, Zephaniah, Haggai, Zechariah, Malachi.* Layman's Bible Commentary 15. Richmond: John Knox Press.

Guthe, Hermann
1923   *Der Prophet Habakuk.* HSAT II.⁴ Hg von Franz Feldman. Bonn: Herkenne.

Haak, Robert D.
1991   *Habakkuk.* VTSup 44. Leiden: Brill.

Hailey, M.
1972   *A Commentary on the Minor Prophets.* Grand Rapids, Mich.: Baker.

Hieronymus (Jerome)
1884   Commentarii in Abacuc Prophetam. Cols. 1273–1338 in *Patrolo-*

giae Cursus Completes. Series Latina 25, ed. P. J. Migne. Paris: Garnies Frates.

Hitzig, Ferdinand
1881   *Die zwölf kleinen Propheten.* 4th ed. KEHAT. Heinrich Steiner, ed. Leipzig: Hirzel.

Holland, Martin
1986   *Die Propheten Nahum, Habakuk und Zephanja.* Wuppentaller Studienbibel. Wuppental: Bockhaus.

Hoonacker, Albin van
1908   *Les douze petits prophètes, traduits et commentés.* EBib. Paris: Gabalda.

Jöcken, Peter
1976   *Das Buch Habakuk: Darstellung der Geschchte seiner kritischen Erforschung mit einer eigenen Beurteilung.* BBB 48. Cologne: Hanstein.

Junker, Hubert
1938   *Die zwölf kleinen Propheten II. Hälfte: Nahum, Habakuk, Sophonias, Aggäus, Zacharias, Malachias.* HSAT VIII.3/2. Bonn: Hanstein.

Keil, Carl Friedrich
1866   *Biblischer Commentar über die Zwölf kleinen Propheten.* Biblischer Commentar III/4. Leipzig: Dorffling & Franke.

1954   *Biblical Commentary on the Old Testament.* James Martin, trs. Grand Rapids, Mich.: Eerdmans. [Pp. 44–116 in Vol 2]

Keller, Carl-A.
1971   *Nahoum. Habacuc. Sophonie.* CAT 11B. Neuchâtel: Delachaux & Niestlé.

Kleinert, Paul
1893   *Obadja, Jona, Micha, Nahum, Habakkuk, Zephanja.* 2nd ed. J. P. Lange, ed. Theologisches-homiletisches Bibelwerk. Bielefeld: Velhagen und Klasing.

Knabenbauer, Joseph
1924   *Commentarius in prophetas minores.* 2nd ed. M. Hagen, ed. Cursus Scripture Sacrae, 2nd sec., 24. Paris: Lethielleux.

Koch, Klaus
1980   *Die Profeten II: Babylonisch-persische Zeit.* Stuttgart: Kohlhammer.
1984   *The Prophets.* Vol. 2. *The Babylonian and Persian Periods.* Philadelphia: Fortress.

Lachmann, Paul
1932   *Das Buch Habakkuk.* Eine textkritische Studie. Aussig: Selbstverlag des Verfassers.

Laetsch, Theo
1956   *Bible Commentary: The Minor Prophets.* St. Louis: Concordia.

Lange, J. P.
1865–1919   *Commentary on the Holy Scriptures, Critical, Doctrinal and*

Homilectical with Special Reference to Ministers and Students. Trs. from the German, ed., and with additions by Peter Schaff. 25 vols. New York: Scribner.

Marbury, Edward
  1979   *Obadiah and Habakkuk.* Minneapolis: Klock.
Marti, K.
  1904   *Das Dodekapropheton.* KHAT 13. Tübingen: Mohr.
Nötscher, Friedrich
  1949   *Zwölfprophetenbuch oder Kleine Propheten.* Echter-Bibel. Würzburg: Echter.
Nowack, W.
  1922   *Die kleinen Propheten.* 3rd ed. HAT 3.4. Göttingen: Vandenhoeck & Ruprecht. [First edition 1896]
Orelli, C. von
  1908   *Die zwölf kleinen Propheten.* 3rd ed. Kurzgefasster Kommentar zu den Heiligen Schriften Alten und Neuen Testaments. Munich: Becksche.
Proksch, O.
  1910   *Die kleinen prophetischen Schriften vor dem Exil.* Erläuterung zum Alten Testament. 3 Teil. Calwer & Stuttgart: Vereinsbuchhandlung.
Pusey, E. B.
  1866   *The Minor Prophets.* Oxford: Parker.
Rieszler, Paul
  1911   *Die Kleinen Propheten oder das Zwolfprophetenbuch.* Rottenburg: Bader.
Rinaldi, Giovanni
  1969   *I Profeti Minori, Fascicolo III: Michea Nahum Abacuc Sofonia Aggeo Zaccaria Malachia.* Turin: Marietti.
Roberts, J. J. M.
  1991   *Nahum, Habakkuk, and Zephaniah.* OTL. Louisville, Ky: Westminster/John Knox Press.
Robinson, Theodore H.
  1938   *Die zwölf kleinen Propheten.* HAT 14. Tübingen: Mohr.
Rudolph, W.
  1975   *Micha–Nahum–Habakuk–Zephanja,* KAT 13:3. Gutersloh: Mohn.
Schumpp, Meinrad
  1950   *Das Buch der zwölf Propheten.* Herders Bibelkommentar 10:2. Freiburg: Herder.
Sellin, Ernst
  1930   *Das Zwölfprophetenbuch übersetz und eklart.* 3rd ed. KAT 12:1. Leipzig: A. Dichtersche Verlagsbuchhandlung D. Werner Scholl.
Seybold, Klaus
  1991   *Nahum Habakkuk Zephanja.* ZB herausgegeben von Hans Hein-

rich Schmid, Siegfried Schulz und Hans Weder. Zürich: Theologischer.

Smith, George Adam
1899   *The Book of the Twelve Prophets Commonly Called the Minor*. Vol 1. *Amos, Hosea and Micah*. 6th ed. ExB. London: Hodder and Stoughton.

Smith, J. M. P., W. H. Ward, and J. A. Bewer
1911   *A Critical and Exegetical Commentary on Micah, Zephaniah, Nahum, Habakkuk, Obadiah and Joel*. ICC. New York: Scribner. [Each commentary is separately paginated. *Habakkuk* will be cited as "Ward 1911."]

Smith, Ralph L.
1984   *Micah–Malachi*. WBC 32. Waco, Tex.: Word Books.

Stonehouse, George Gordon Vigor
1911   *The Book of Habakkuk: Introduction, Translation and Notes on the Hebrew Text*. London: Rivington.

Széles, Mària Eszenyei
1987   *Wrath and Mercy: A Commentary on the Books of Habakkuk and Zephaniah*. Trs. George A. F. Knight. ITC. Grand Rapids, Mich.: Eerdmans.

Trinquet, J.
1953   *Habaquq Abdias Joel*. Paris: La Sainte Bible de Jerusalem.

Ungern-Sternberg, Rolf Freiherr von, and Helmut Lamparter
1960   *Der Tag des Gerichtes Gottes: Habakuk, Zephanja, Jona, Nahum*. BAT 23:4. Stuttgart: Calwer.

Vartholomey
1913   Книга Пророка Аббакчма Введеніе и Толкованіе, и.д. Доцента Имрераторской Московской Академіи *ІЕРОМАХА ВАРѲОЛОМЕЯ*. Сергіевъ Посадъ, Москва: ТИПОГРАФІЯ И. И. ИВАНОВА [*Kniga Proroka Abbakuma: Vvedeniye i Tolkovaniye i.d. Dotsenta Imperatorskoĭ Moskovskoĭ Akademii IERO-MAKHA VARTHOLOMEYA. Sergie' Posad', Moskva: Tipografiya I. I. Ivanova.*]

Vischer, Wilhelm
1958   *Der Prophet Habakuk*. BSt 19. Neukirchen: Verlag der Buchhandlung des Erziehungsvereins.

Vuilleumier, Rene, and Carl A. Keller
1971   *Michée Nahoum Habacuc Sophonie*. CAT 11b. Neuchâtel: Delachaux et Niestlé. [2nd ed., 1990]

Wade, G. W.
1929   *The Book of the Prophet Habakkuk with Introduction and Notes*. WC. London: Methuen.

Ward 1911; see Smith, J. M. P., W. H. Ward, and J. A. Bewer

Wellhausen, Julius
1892   *Die kleinen Propheten übersetzt und erklärt, mit Noten: Skizzen und*

Vorarbeiten. Berlin: Reimer. [2nd ed., 1893; 3rd ed., 1898; 4th ed., Berlin: de Gruyter, 1963]

Woude, Adam S. van der

1978   *Habakuk, Zefanja.* POuT. Nijkerk: Callenbach.

OTHER WORKS

Abusch, Tzvi

1990   An Early Form of the Witchcraft Ritual *Maqlû* and the Origin of a Babylonian Magical Ceremony. Pp. 1–57 in *Lingering over Words: Studies in Ancient Near Eastern Literature in Honor of William L. Moran.* Tzvi Abusch, John Huehnergard, and Piotr Steinkeller, eds. HSS 37. Atlanta, Ga.: Scholars Press.

Ackroyd, Peter, and Barnabas Lindars, eds.

1968   *Words and Meanings,* D. Winton Thomas Festschrift. Cambridge: Cambridge University Press.

Aharoni, Yohanan

1967   *The Archaeology of the Land of Israel.* Philadelphia: Westminster.

1968   Arad: Its Inscriptions and Temple. *BA* 31:2–32.

1975   Arad. *EAEHL.* Vol 1. Michael Avi-Yonah, ed. Englewood Cliffs, N.J.: Prentice-Hall.

Ahuviah, A.

1985–1986   "Why Do You Countenance Treachery?" A Study in the Oracle Which Habakkuk Saw. (in Hebrew) *Beth Mikra* 31:307–27.

Akao, J. O.

1990   Yahweh and *Mal'ak* in the Early Traditions of Israel: A Study of the Underlying Traditions of Yahweh / Angel Theophany in Exodus 3. *IBS* 12:72–85.

Albrecht, Karl

1895   Das Geschlecht der hebräischen Hauptwörter. *ZAW* 15:313–25.

1896   Das Geschlecht der hebräischen Hauptwörter. *ZAW* 16:41–121.

Albright, William Foxwell

1922   The Oldest Forms of Hebrew Verse. *JPOS* 2:69–86.

1926   Mesopotamian Elements in Canaanite Eschatology. Pp. 143–54 in *Oriental Studies Dedicated to Paul Haupt.* Baltimore: Johns Hopkins University Press.

1933   More Light on the Canaanite Epic of Al'êyân Ba'al and Môt. *BASOR* 50:13–20.

1934   The North-Canaanite Poems of Al'êyân Ba'al and the Gracious Gods." *JPOS* 14:101–40.

1939   The Babylonian Matter in the Predeuteronomic Primeval History (JE) in Gen 1–11, Part 2 (reply to Mowinckel). *JBL* 58:87–103.

1941a   Two Letters from Ugarit (Ras Shamrah). *BASOR* 82:43–49.

1941b The Land of Damascus between 1850 and 1750 B.C. *BASOR* 83:30–36.

1950a The Psalm of Habakkuk. Pp. 1–18 in *Studies in Old Testament Prophecy: Presented to Prof. Theodore H. Robinson*, H. H. Rowley, ed. Edinburgh: Clark.

1950b A Catalogue of Early Hebrew Lyric Poems. *HUCA* 33:1:1–39.

1955 New Light on Early Recensions of the Hebrew Bible. *BASOR* 140:27–33.

1957a *From the Stone Age to Christianity: Monotheism and the Historical Process.* 2nd ed. Garden City, N.Y.: Anchor Books.

1957b The High Place in Ancient Palestine. VTSup 4:242–58.

1958 An Ostracon from Calah and the North-Israelite Diaspora. *BASOR* 149:33–36.

1961a *Samuel and the Beginnings of the Prophetic Movement.* Goldenson Lecture for 1961. Cincinnati: Hebrew Union College Press.

1961b The Archaeology of the Ancient Near East. Pp. 58–65 in *Peake's Commentary on the Bible*, M. Black and H. H. Rowley, eds. London: Nelson.

1964 *History, Archaeology, and Christian Humanism.* New York: McGraw-Hill.

1968 *Yahweh and the Gods of Canaan: A Historical Analysis of Two Contrasting Faiths.* Garden City, N.Y.: Doubleday.

Alexander, Lovejoy, ed.
1991 *Images of Empire.* JSOTSup 122. Sheffield: JSOT Press.

Alfrink, B.
1933 Der Versammlungsberg in Aussersten Norden. *Bib* 14:41–67.

Alomía B.
1988 Habacuc, el profeta de la justificación por la fe. *Theologika* 3:138–51.

Alonso Schökel, Luis
1988 *A Manual of Hebrew Poetics.* Adrian Graffy, trs. Rome: Pontifical Biblical Institute.

Alt, Albrecht
1959 *Kleine Schriften zur Geschichte des Volkes Israel.* 3 vols. Munich: Beck'sche Verlagsbuchhandlung.

1966 *Essays on Old Testament History and Religion.* Garden City, N. Y.: Anchor Books.

Amiet, Pierre
1953 Les combats mythologiques dans l'art mésopotamien du troisième et du début du second millénaires. *RArch* 42:129–164.

Amsler, Samuel
1981 La parole visionnaire des prophètes. *VT* 31:359–63.

Amusin, I. D.
1966 "Избранник бога" в Кумранксих текстах. Вестник Древней Истории. 1:73–79.

1967   Новый эскатологический текст Кумрана (11QMelchisedek). Вестник Древней Истории. 3:45–62.

1971   Тексты Кумрана Выпуск 1. Перевод е древне-еврейского и арамейского, введениие и комментарий. PPV XXXIII, 1. Moscow: Nauka.

1983   Кумранксая община. Moscow: Nauka.

Andersen, Francis I.

1958   Who Built the Second Temple? *ABR* 6:1–35.

1966   The Socio-juridical Background of the Naboth Incident. *JBL* 85:46–57.

1970a   Biconsonantal Byforms in Biblical Hebrew. *ZAW* 82:270–74.

1970b   *The Verbless Clause in the Hebrew Pentateuch.* JBL Monograph Series 14. New York: Abingdon.

1971   Passive and Ergative in Hebrew. Pp. 1–15 in *Near Eastern Studies in Honor of William Foxwell Albright,* H. Goedicke, ed. Baltimore: Johns Hopkins University Press.

1974   *The Sentence in Biblical Hebrew.* Janua Linguarum, Series Practica 231. The Hague: Mouton.

1986   Yahweh, the Kind and Sensitive God. Pp. 41–88 in *God Who is Rich in Mercy: Essays presented to Dr. D. B. Knox.* Peter T. O'Brien and David G. Peterson, eds. Homebush West, NSW: Anzea.

1987   On Reading Genesis 1–3. Pp. 137–50 in *Backgrounds for the Bible.* Michael Patrick O'Connor and David Noel Freedman, eds. Winona Lake, Ind.: Eisenbrauns.

1992   The Second Book of Enoch. Pp. 516–22 in *The Anchor Bible Dictionary.* Vol. 2. Garden City N.Y.: Doubleday.

1995   Linguistic Coherence in Prophetic Discourse. Pp. 137–56 in *Fortunate the Eyes that See: Essays in Honor of David Noel Freedman in celebration of his seventieth birthday.* Astrid B. Beck, Andrew H. Bartelt, Paul Raabe, and Chris A. Franke, eds. (Grand Rapids, Mich.: Eerdmans).

Andersen, F. I. and A. D. Forbes

1983   "Prose Particle" Counts of the Hebrew Bible. Pp. 165–83 in *The Word of the Lord shall go forth: Essays in honor of David Noel Freedman in Celebration of his Sixtieth Birthday.* C. L. Meyers and M. O'Connor, eds. Winona Lake, In.: Eisenbrauns.

1986   *Spelling in the Hebrew Bible.* BOr 41. Rome: Pontifical Biblical Institute.

1989   Methods and Tools for the Study of Old Testament Syntax, Pp. 61–72 in *Actes de la 2ième conférence de l'AIBI "Bible et Imformatiques: méthodes, outuils, résultats.* Genève: Slatkine.

1992a   *The Vocabulary of the Old Testament.* 2nd ed. Rome: Biblical Institute Press.

1992b   Mapping Clause Boundaries in Biblical Hebrew. Pp. 181–202 in *Les Actes de la 3ième Conférence de l'AIBI.* Geneva: Slatkine.

1995 Syntactic Ambiguity in the Hebrew Bible. Pp. 356–67 in *Les Actes de la 4ième Conférence de l'AIBI*. Geneva: Slatkine.

Andersen, F. I., and David Noel Freedman
1980 *Hosea: A New Translation with Introduction and Commentary*. AB 24. Garden City, N.Y.: Doubleday.
1989 *Amos: A New Translation with Introduction and Commentary*. AB 24A. Garden City, N.Y.: Doubleday.
2000 *Micah: A New Translation with Introduction and Commentary*. AB 24E. New York: Doubleday.

Andersen, Timothy David
1986a Renaming and Wedding Imagery in Isaiah 62. *Bib* 67:75–80.
1986b Problems in Analysing Hebrew Poetry. *EAJT* 4:2:68–94.

Anderson, Bernard W.
1962 Exodus Typology in Second Isaiah. Pp. 177–95 in *Israel's Prophetic Heritage: Essays in Honor of James Muilenburg*. by B. W. Anderson and W. Harrelson, eds. New York: Harper.
1967 *Creation versus Chaos*. New York: Association Press.
1976 Exodus and Covenant in Second Isaiah and Prophetic Traditions. Pp. 339–60 in *Magnalia Dei: The Mighty Acts of God. Essays on the Bible and Archaeology in Memory of G. Ernest Wright*. F. M. Cross, W. E. Lemke, and P. D. Miller, eds. Garden City, N.Y.: Doubleday.

Anderson, George Wishart, ed.
1979 *Tradition and Interpretation: Essays by Members of the Society for Old Testament Study*. Oxford: Clarendon Press.

Archer, Gleason L., and Gregory Chirichigno
1983 *Old Testament Quotations in the New Testament*. Chicago: Moody Press.

Archi, Alfonso
1979 The Epigraphic Evidence from Ebla and the Old Testament. *Bib* 60:556–66.
1990 "The Names of the Primeval Gods." *Or* 59:114–29.

Archi, Alfonso, ed.
1988 *Eblaite Personal Names and Semitic Name-Giving: Papers of a Symposium Held in Rome, July 15–17, 1985*. Archivi reali di Ebla 1. Roma: Missione archeologica italiana in Siria.

Arnold, William R.
1905 The Interpretation of לו מידו קרנים [*qrnym mydw lw*], Hab 3:4. *AJSL* 21:167–72.

Atkinson, K. M. T.
1959 The Historical Setting of the Habakkuk Commentary. *JSS* 4:138–40.

Avishur, Yitzhak
1971–1972 Pairs of Synonymous Words in the Construct State (and in Apposition Hendiadys) in Biblical Hebrew. *Sem* 2:17–81.

1975   Word-pairs Common to Phoenician and Biblical Hebrew. *UF* 7:13–47.

1981   "Parallelism of Numbers in the Bible and in the Ancient Semitic Literature." Pp. 1–9 in *Proceedings of the Seventh World Congress of Jewish Studies.* Studies in the Bible and the Ancient Near East [Hebrew section]: Jerusalem: World Congress of Jewish Studies.

1984   *Stylistic Studies of Word-pairs in Biblical and Ancient Semitic Literatures.* AOAT 210. Neukirchen: Neukirchener Verlag.

1987–88   *Mî-baʿal mišpāṭ yiggaš ʾēlāy* (Isa 50:8)—A Stylistic Biblical Figure or a Calque from Akkadian. *Lešōnēnû* 52:18–25.

1994   *Studies in Hebrew and Ugaritic Psalms.* Jerusalem: Magnes.

Axelsson, Lars Eric
1987   *The Lord Rose up from Seir: Studies in the History and Traditions of the Negev and Southern Judah.* ConBOT 25. Stockholm: Almqvist & Wiksell.

Baars, W.
1965   A New Witness to the Text of the Barberini Greek Version of Habakkuk III. *VT* 15:381–82.

Baer, Y.
1970   ‏פשר חבקוק ותקופתו‎." *Zion* 34:1–42.

Baldacci, Massimo
1982   *Kārâ* III, "far festa." *RivB* 30:225–28.

Balentine, S. E.
1980   A Description of the Semantic Field of Hebrew Words for "Hide." *VT* 30:137–53.

1983   *The Hidden God. The Hiding of the Face of God in the Old Testament.* Oxford Theological Monographs. London: Oxford University Press.

Baloian, Bruce Edward
1994   *Anger in the Old Testament.* American University Studies. Series 7 Theology and Religion 99. New York: Lang.

Baltzer, Klaus
1964   *Das Bundesformular.* WMANT 4. Neukirchen: Neukirchener Verlag.

Balzer, H. R.
1991   Eschatological Elements as Permanent Qualities in the Relationship Between God and Nation in the Minor Prophets. *OTE* 4:408–14.

Bar-Deroma, H.
1964   Kadesh-Barneʾa. *PEQ* 96:101–34.

Barnett, R. D., J. Leveen, and C. Moss
1948   A Phoenician Inscription from Eastern Cilicia. *Iraq* 10:56–71.

Barr, James
1960   Theophany and Anthropomorphism in the Old Testament. VTSup 7:31–38.

1967a   St. Jerome and the Sounds of Hebrew. *JSS* 12:1–36.

1967b   "Vocalization and the Analysis of Hebrew Among the Ancient Translators." Pp. 1–6 in *Hebräische Wortforschung: Festschrift zum 80. Geburtstag von Walter Baumgartner.* VTSup 16. Leiden: Brill.

1968   *Comparative Philology and the Text of the Old Testament.* Oxford: Clarendon Press.

1978   Some Notes on *bên* 'between' in Classical Hebrew. *JSS* 23:1–22.

1981   A New Look at KETHIBH-QERE, *OTS* 21:17–37.

1985a   Why? in Biblical Hebrew. *JTS*, n.s., 36:11–33.

1985b   Why the World Was Created in 4004 B.C.: Archbishop Ussher and Biblical Chronology. *BJRL* 67:575–608.

1989   *The Variable Spellings of the Hebrew Bible.* Schweich Lectures 1986. New York: Oxford University Press.

1995   The Synchronic, the Diachronic and the Historical: A Triangular Relationship? Pp. 1–14 in *Synchronic or Diachronic: A Debate on Method in Old Testament Exegesis.* Johannes C. de Moor, ed. OTS 34. Leiden: Brill.

Barré, Michael L.

1988   Habakkuk 3:2: Translation in Context. *CBQ* 50:184–97.

Barrick, W. Boyd

1982   The Meaning and Usage of RKB in Biblical Hebrew. *JBL* 101:481–503.

Barrick, W. Boyd, and John R. Spencer

1984   *In the Shelter of Elyon: Essays on Ancient Palestinian Life and Literature in Honor of G. W. Ahlström,* JSOTSup 31. Sheffield: University of Sheffield.

Barthélemy, Dominique

1953   Redécouverte d'un chaînon manquant de l'histoire de la Septante. *RB* 60:18–29.

1963   *Les devanciers d'Aquila: Première publication intégrale du texte des fragments du Dodécaprophéton trouvés dans le Désert de Juda: Précédée d'une étude sur les traductions et récensions Greques de la Bible réalisées au premier siècle de notre ère sous l'influence du Rabbinat Palestinien.* VTSup 10. Leiden: Brill.

1978   *Études d'histoire du texte de l'Ancien Testament.* OBO 21. Göttingen: Vandenhoeck & Ruprecht.

1982   *Critique textuelle de l'Ancien Testament: 1. Josue, Juges, Ruth, Samuel, Rois, Chroniques, Esdras, Nehemie, Esther.* OBO 50:1. Fribourg: Editions Universitaires.

1986   *Critique textuelle de l'Ancien Testament: 2. Isaïe, Jérémie et Lamentations.* OBO 50:2. Fribourg: Editions Universitaires.

1992   *Critique textuelle de l'Ancien Testament: 3. Ézéchiel, Daniel et les 12 Prophètes.* OBO 50:3. Fribourg: Editions Universitaires.

1993   Un archétype commun au pré-massorétique, à la Septante et à 1QpHab? Pp. 150–76 in *Philologia Sacra. Biblische und patristis-*

che Studien für Hermann J. Frede und Walter Thiele zu ihrem siebzigten Geburtstag, Vol. 1. Roger Gryson, ed. Freiburg: Herder.

Barthélemy, Dominique, and J. T. Milik
  1955   *Qumran Cave I.* DJD 1. Oxford: Clarendon Press.

Bartlett, J. R.
  1969   The Use of the Word ראש as a Title in the Old Testament, *VT* 19:1–10.

Barton, George Aaron
  1937   *Archaeology and the Bible.* 7th ed. Philadelphia: American Sunday-School Union.

Barton, John
  1980   *Amos' Oracles Against the Nations.* Cambridge: Cambridge University Press.

Bauer, Hans and Pontus Leander
  1922   *Historische Grammatik der hebräischen Sprache.* Halle: M. Niemeyer. Reprint. Hildesheim: Georg Olms, 1965.

Bauer, T.
  1957   Ein Viertes altbabylonisches Fragment des Gilgames-Epos. *JNES* 16:254–62.

Baumgartner, Walter
  1987   *Jeremiah's Poems of Lament.* David E. Orton, trs. Historic Texts and Interpreters in Biblical Scholarship. Sheffield: Sheffield Academic Press. [Translation of *Die Klagegedichte des Jeremia.* BZAW 32. Giessen: Töpelmann, 1917]

Baumgartner, Walter, Otto Eissfeldt, Karl Elliger, and Leonard Rost, eds.
  1950   *Festschrift Alfred Bertholet zum 80. Geburtstag.* Tübingen: J. C. B. Mohr (Paul Siebeck).

Begg, Christopher
  1986   The Non-mention of Amos, Hosea and Micah in the Deuteronomistic History. *BN* 32:41–53.
  1987   The Non-mention of Zephaniah, Nahum and Habakkuk in the Deuteronomistic History. *BN* 38:9:19–25.

Begrich, J.
  1928   Mabbul. Eine exegetischlexicalische Studien 2. *SVG* 6:135–53.
  1934   Das Priesterliche Heilsorakel. *ZAW* 52:81–92.
  1936   Die priesterliche Tora. *BZAW* 66:63–88. Reprinted in Begrich 1964:232–60.
  1964   *Gesammelte Studien zum Alten Testament.* Walther Zimmerli, ed. Munich: Chr. Kaiser.

Béguerie, P.
  1954   Le psaume d'Habacuc. Pp. 53–84 in *Études sur la prophetes d'Israël.* LD 14. Paris: Cerf.

Bellinger, W. H.
  1984   *Psalmody and Prophecy.* JSOTSup 27. Sheffield: JSOT Press.

Bentzen, Aage
  1959   *Introduction to the Old Testament.* 5th ed. 2 vols. Copenhagen: Gad.
Berlin, Adele
  1979a   Grammatical Aspects of Biblical Parallelism. *HUCA* 50:17–43. [Reprinted Pp. 311–48 in House 1992]
  1979b   Isaiah 40:4 : Etymological and Poetic Considerations. *HAR* 3:1–6.
  1981   Motif and Creativity in Biblical Poetry. *Proof* 3:231–41.
  1982   Point of View in Biblical Narrative. Pp. 71–113 in *A Sense of Text: The Art of Language in the Study of Biblical Literature.* JQR Sup. Winona Lake, Ind.: Eisenbrauns.
  1983a   *Poetics and Interpretation of Biblical Narrative.* Bible and Literature Series 9. Sheffield: Almond Press.
  1983b   Parallel Word Pairs: A Linguistic Explanation. *UF* 15:7–16.
  1985   *The Dynamics of Biblical Parallelism.* Bloomington: Indiana University Press.
  1989   Lexical Cohesion and Biblical Interpretation. *HS* 30:29–40.
  1991   *Biblical Poetry Through Medieval Jewish Eyes.* Indiana Studies in Biblical Literature. Bloomington: Indiana University Press.
Beuken, W. A. M.
  1972   *Mišpāṭ:* The First Servant Song and Its Context. *VT* 22:1–30.
Bévenot, Dom Hughes
  1933   Le cantique d'Habacuc. *RB* 42:499–525.
Bezold, Carl
  1926   *Babylonisch-assyrisches Glossar.* Heidelberg: Carl Winter's Universitätsbuchhandlung.
Biran, Avraham, ed.
  1981   *Temples and High Places in Biblical Times.* Jerusalem: Nelson Glueck School of Biblical Archaeology of Hebrew Union College, Jewish Institute of Religion.
Blenkinsopp, J.
  1983   *A History of Prophecy in Israel from the Settlement in the Land to the Hellenistic Period.* Philadelphia: Westminster.
Blommerde, Anton C. M.
  1969   *Northwest Semitic Grammar and Job.* BOr 22. Rome: Pontifical Biblical Institute.
Boadt, Lawrence
  1982   *Jeremiah 26–52, Habakkuk, Nahum.* OTM 10. Wilmington, Del.: Michael Glazier.
Bodi, Daniel
  1990   *The Book of Ezekiel and the Poem of Erra.* OBO 104. Göttingen: Vandenhoeck & Ruprecht.
Boriskovskaya, S.
  1976   Bronze Statuette of a Syrian God. *Trudy Ermitazha Gosudarstvennogo Ordena Lenina* 17:5:5–10.

Bosshard, Erich
      1987   Beobachtungen zum Zwölfprophetenbuch. *BN* 40:30–62.
Bosshard, Martin
      1969   Bemerkungen zum Text von Habakuk I 8. *VT* 19:480–82.
Breck, John
      1994   *The Shape of Biblical Language: Chiasmus in the Scriptures and
                 Beyond.* Crestwood, N.Y.: St. Vladimir's Seminary Press.
Bremmer, Jan N. and Garcia Martinez, Florentino, eds.
      1992   *Sacred History and Sacred Texts in Early Judaism: A Symposium
                 in Honour of A. S. van der Woude.* Contributions to Biblical Exe-
                 gesis and Theology 5. Kampen: Kok Pharos.
Briggs, Charles A.
      1886   *Messianic Prophecy: The Prediction of the Fulfillment of Redemp-
                 tion through the Messiah.* New York: Scribner. Reprint. Peabody,
                 Mass.: Hendrickson, 1988.
Brockelmann, Carl
      1956   *Hebräische Syntax.* Neukirchen: Buchhandlung des Erzie-
                 hungsvereins.
Brockington, Leonard H.
      1973   *The Hebrew Text of the Old Testament: The Readings Adopted by
                 the Translators of the New English Bible.* Oxford: Oxford Univer-
                 sity Press.
Brooke, George J.
      1991   The Kittim in the Qumran Pesharim. Pp. 135–59 in *Images of
                 Empire.* JSOTSup 122. Lovejoy Alexander, ed. Sheffield: JSOT
                 Press.
      1994   The Pesharim and the Origin of the Dead Sea Scrolls. Pp. 339–53
                 in *Methods of Investigation of the Dead Sea Scrolls and the Khir-
                 bet Qumran Site: Present Realities and Future Prospects.* Michael
                 O. Wise, ed. New York: Academy of Sciences.
Brouwer, Arie R.
      1993   Facing Death and Growing in Grace [Habakkuk and Paul]. *Per-
                 spectives* 8:8–23.
Brownlee, William Hugh
      1953   *The Dead Sea Habakkuk Midrash and the Targum of Jonathan.*
                 Durham, N.C.: Duke Divinity School.
      1959   *The Text of Habakkuk in the Ancient Commentary from Qumran.*
                 JBL Monograph Series 11. Philadelphia: Society of Biblical Liter-
                 ature and Exegesis.
      1963   The Placarded Revelation of Habakkuk. *JBL* 82:319–25.
      1971   The Composition of Habakkuk. Pp. 255–75 in *Hommages à An-
                 dré Dupont-Sommer.* A. Caquot et M. Philonenko, eds. Paris:
                 Maisonneuve.
      1979   *The Midrash Pesher of Habakkuk.* SBLMS 24. Missoula, Mont.:
                 Scholars Press.

Broyles, Craig C.
  1989   *The Conflict of Faith and Experience in the Psalms: A Form-Criti-*
          cal Theological Study. JSOTSup 52. Sheffield: Sheffield Academic
          Press.
Bruce, F. F.
  1951   *The Acts of the Apostles: The Greek Text with Introduction and Com-*
          mentary. London: Tyndale.
Bruce, Graham A.
  1990   From Holy Mountains to the New Earth. *TE* 23:27–34.
Bruno, D. Arvid
  1957   *Das Buch der Zwölf: Eine rhythmische und textkritische Unter-*
          suchung. Stockholm: Almqvist & Wiksell.
Buchanan, G. W.
  1989   The Fall of Jerusalem and the Reconsideration of Some Dates.
          RevQ 14:31–48.
Budde, Karl
  1889   Zu Habakuk 2,3ff. *ZAW* 9:155–56.
  1893   Habakuk und Zephanja. *TSK* 66:383–399.
  1930   Habakuk *ZDMG* NF 9, 84:139–47.
  1931   Zum Text von Habakuk Kap. 1 u. 2. *OLZ* 34:409–11.
Bulatov, A. B.
  1963   Bulgarskiye epigraficheskiye pamyatniki XIII–XVI vv. pravober-
          ezh'ya Volgi. *Epigrafiki vostoka* 16:56–71.
Buren, E. D. van
  1934   The God Ningizzida. *Iraq* 1:80–89.
Burgmann, Hans
  1980   "Twkḥt" in IQpHab V,10: Ein Schüsselwort mit verhängnisvollen
          historischen Konsequenzen. *RevQ* 10:293–300.
Burkitt, Frederik Crawfoot
  1915   The Psalm of Habakkuk. *JTS* 16:62–66.
Burrows, Millar, John C. Trever, and William H. Brownlee.
  1950   *The Dead Sea Scrolls of St. Mark's Monastery.* Vol. 1. *The Isaiah*
          Manuscript and the Habakkuk Commentary. New Haven, Conn.:
          The American Schools of Oriental Research.
Butler, James T., Edgar W. Conrad, and Ben C. Ollenburger
  1985   *Understanding the Word: Essays in Honor of Bernhard W. Ander-*
          son. JSOTSup 37. Sheffield: JSOT Press.
Cagni, Luigi
  1969   *L'Epopea di Erra.* SS 34. Rome: Instituto di Studi del vicino Oriente.
  1970   *Das Erra-Epos: Keilschrifttext.* Studia Pohl 5. Rome: Pontifical Bib-
          lical Institute.
Calkins, Raymond
  1947   *The Modern Message of the Minor Prophets.* New York: Harper.
Campbell Thompson, R.
  1937   A New Record of an Assyrian Earthquake. *Iraq* 4:186–89.

Cannon, W. W.
  1925   The Integrity of Habakkuk cc. 1, 2. *ZAW* 43:62–90.
Caquot, André
  1956   Sur quelques démons de l'Ancien Testament: Reshep, Qeṭeb, De-
          ber. *Sem* 6:53–68.
Caquot, André, and M. Delcor, eds.
  1981   *Mélanges bibliques et orientaux en l'honneur de M. Henri Cazelles.*
          AOAT 212. Neukirchen: Neukirchener Verlag.
Caquot, André, S. Légasse, and M. Tardieu, eds.
  1985   *Mélanges bibliques et orientaux en l'honneur de M. Mathias
          Delcor.* AOAT 215. Kevelaer: Butzon & Bercker.
Carmignac, Jean
  1955   Précisions apportées au vocabulaire de l'hébreu biblique par la
          Guerre des Fils de Lumière contre les Fils de Ténèbres. *VT*
          5:345–65.
  1969   Le texte de Jérémie 10,13 (ou 51.16) et celui de 2 Samuel 23,7;
          améliorés par Qumrân. *RevQ* 7:287–90.
  1969–1971   La notion d'eschatologie dans la Bible et à Qumran. *RevQ*
          7:17–31.
Carrez, M.
  1992   Ambakoum Septante. *RHPR* 72:129–41.
Carroll, Robert P.
  1976   A Non-cogent Argument in Jeremiah's Oracles Against the
          Prophets *StTh* 30:43–51.
  1979   *When Prophecy Failed: Cognitive Dissonance in the Prophetic Tra-
          ditions of the Old Testament.* London: SCM Press.
  1981   *From Chaos to Covenant: Uses of Prophecy in the Book of Jeremiah.*
          London: SCM Press.
  1982   Eschatological Delay in the Prophetic Tradition? *ZAW* 94:47–58.
  1992   Night Without Vision: Micah and the Prophets. Pp. 74–84 in *The
          Scriptures and the Scrolls: Studies in Honour of A. S. van der Woude
          on the Occasion of his 65th Birthday.* F. García Martínez, A. Hil-
          horst, and C. J. Labuschagne, eds. VTSup 36. Leiden: Brill.
Casetti, P., Othmar Keel, and Adrien Schenker, eds.
  1981   *Mélanges Dominique Barthélemy. Études bibliques offertes a l'occasion
          de son 60e anniversaire.* OBO 38. Fribourg: Éditions Universitaires.
Cassuto, Umberto
  1943   On the Formal and Stylistic Relationship between Deutero-Isaiah
          and Other Biblical Writers. Pp. 141–77 in *Biblical and Oriental
          Studies.* Vol 1. Bible. Jerusalem: Magnes.
  1975   Chapter III of Habakkuk and the Ras Shamra Texts. Pp. 3–15 in
          Biblical and Oriental Studies. Vol 2. Israel Abrahams, trs.
          Jerusalem: Magnes.
Catastini, Alessandro
  1984   Reminiscenze noachiche in 1QpHab. *AION* 44:483–89.

Cathcart, Kevin J.
1984   A New Proposal for Hab 1,17. *Bib* 65:575–76.
1986   Legal Terminology in Habakkuk 2:1–4. *PIBA* 10:103–10.
Cathcart, Kevin J., and Robert P. Gordon
1989   *The Targum of the Minor Prophets: The Aramaic Bible Vol. 14.* Wilmington, Del.: Glazier.
Cavallin, H. C. C.
1978   "The Righteous Shall Live by Faith," A Decisive Argument for the Traditional Interpretation. *ST* 32:33–43.
Ceresko, Anthony R.
1975   The A:B::B:A Word Pattern in Hebrew and Northwest Semitic, with Special Reference to the Book of Job. *UF* 7:73–88.
1976   The Chiastic Word Pattern in Hebrew. *CBQ* 38:303–11.
1978   The Function of Chiasmus in Hebrew Poetry. *CBQ* 40:1–10.
Cheyne, Thomas Kelly
1908   An Appeal for a More Complete Criticism of the Book of Habakkuk. *JQR*, n.s., 16:3–30.
Childs, Brevard S.
1993   *Biblical Theology of the Old and New Testaments: Theological Reflections on the Christian Bible.* Minneapolis: Fortress.
Chilton, Bruce D.
1994   Aramaic and Targumic Antecedents of Pauline "Justification." Pp. 379–97 in *The Aramaic Bible: Targums in their Historical Context.* D. R. G. Beattie and M. J. McNamara, eds. Journal for the Study of the Old Testament, Sup. Series 166. Sheffield: JSOT Press.
Christensen, Duane L.
1975   *Transformations of the War Oracle in Old Testament Prophecy: Studies in the Oracles Against the Nations.* HDR 3. Missoula, Mont.: Scholars Press.
Clark, David J., and Howard A. Hatton
1989   *A Translator's Handbook on the Books of Nahum, Habakkuk, and Zephaniah.* Helps for Translation. New York: United Bible Societies.
Clements, Ronald Ernest
1982   The Form and Character of Prophetic Woe Oracles. *Sem* 8:17–29.
Clements, Ronald Ernest, ed.
1991   *The World of Ancient Israel: Sociological, Anthropological and Political Perspectives.* Cambridge: Cambridge University Press.
Clifford, Richard J.
1966   The Use of *hôy* in the Prophets. *CBQ* 28:458–64.
1972   *The Cosmic Mountain in Canaan and the Old Testament.* Cambridge, Mass.: Harvard University Press.
1980   The Function of Idol Passages in Second Isaiah. *CBQ* 42:450–64.
Coggins, Richard
1982   An Alternative Prophetic Tradition? Pp. 77–94 in *Israel's Prophetic*

Tradition: Essays in Honour of Peter R. Ackroyd. Richard Coggins, Anthony Phillips, and Michael Knibb., eds. Cambridge: Cambridge University Press.

Cohen, Niami G.
1987   "DBR—BÎ: An "Enthusiastic" Prophetic Formula. ZAW 99: 219–32.

Cohn, Robert L.
1974   The Sacred Mountain in Ancient Israel. Ph.D. diss., Stanford University.

Coleman, Shalom
1964–1965 The Dialogue of Habakkuk in Rabbinic Doctrine. *AbrN* 5:57–85.

Coleson, Joseph, and Victor Matthews, eds.
1996   *Go to the Land I Will Show You: Studies in Honor of Dwight W. Young.* Winona Lake, Ind.: Eisenbrauns.

Collon, Dominique
1972   The Smiting God: A Study of a Bronze in the Pomerance Collection in New York. *Levant* 4:111–45.
1982   *Catalogue of the Western Asiatic Seals in the British Museum. Cylinder Seals II. Akkadian-Post Akkadian Ur III Periods.* London: British Museum.
1985   *Catalogue of the Western Asiatic Seals in the British Museum. Cylinder Seals III. Isin-Larsa and Old Babylonian Periods.* London: British Museum.

Comfort, Philip W., and David P. Barrett
1999   *The Complete Text of the Earliest New Testament Manuscripts.* Grand Rapids, Mich.: Baker.

Condamin, Albert
1898   La forme chorale du ch. III d'Habacuc. *RB* 8:133–40.

Conrad, Edgar W., and Edward G. Newing, eds.
1987   *Perspectives on Language and Text: Essays and Poems in Honor of Francis I. Andersen's Sixtieth Birthday, July 28, 1985.* Winona Lake, Ind.: Eisenbrauns.

Coogan, Michael David
1978   Review of *The Canaanite God Rešep* by William J. Fulco. *JBL* 97:111.

Coogan, Michael David, J Cheryl Exum, and Lawrence E. Stager, eds.
1994   *Scripture and Other Artifacts: Essays in Honor of Philip J. King.* Louisville, Ky.: Westminster / John Knox Press.

Copeland, Paul E.
1992   The Midst of the Years. Pp. 91–105 in *Text and Pretext: Essays in Honour of Robert Davidson.* Robert P. Carroll, ed. JSOTSup 138. Sheffield: JSOT Press.

Cornelius, Izak
1990   The Sun Epiphany in Job 38:12–15 and the Iconography of the

Gods in the Ancient Near East—the Palestinian Connection. *JNSL* 16:25–43.

1994   *The Iconography of the Canaanite Gods Reshef and Ba'al: Late Bronze and Iron Age I Periods (c 1500–1000 BCE).* OBO 140. Fribourg: Universitätsverlag.

Crenshaw, James L.

1971   *Prophetic Conflict: Its Effect upon Israelite Religion.* BZAW 124. Berlin: de Gruyter.

1972   *Wedôrek 'al-bamotê 'areṣ. CBQ* 34:39–53.

Croatto, Jose S., and J. Alberto Soggin

1962   Die Bedeutung von *šdmwt* im Alten Testament. *ZAW* 74:44–50.

Cross, Frank Moore, Jr.

1950   Notes on a Canaanite Psalm in the Old Testament. *BASOR* 117:19–21.

1953   The Council of Yahweh in Second Isaiah. *JNES* 12:274–77.

1964   The History of the Biblical Text in the Light of Discoveries in the Judaean Desert. *HTR* 57:281–99.

1966   The Contribution of the Qumrân Discoveries to the Study of the Biblical Text, *IEJ* 16:81–95. Reprinted in Cross & Talmon 1975:278–92.

1968   The Song of the Sea and Canaanite Myth. *Journal for Theology and the Church* 5:1–25.

1973   *Canaanite Myth and Hebrew Epic: Essays in the History of the Religion of Israel.* Cambridge, Mass.: Harvard University Press.

1974   Prose and Poetry in the Mythic and Epic Texts from Ugarit. *HTR* 67:1–15.

1975   The Evolution of a Theory of Local Texts, Pp. 306–20 in *Qumran and the History of the Biblical Text.* F. M. Cross and S. Talmond, eds. Cambrdige, Mass.: Harvard University Press.

1979   Problems of Method in the Textual Criticism of the Hebrew Bible. Pp. 31–54 in *The Critical Study of Sacred Texts.* Wendy Doniger O'Flaherty, ed. Berkeley Religious Studies Series. Berkeley: Graduate Theological Union.

1983   The Epic Traditions of Early Israel: Epic Narrative and the Reconstruction of Early Israelite Institutions. Pp. 13–39 in *The Poet and the Historian: Essays in Literary and Historical Criticism.* Richard Elliott Friedman, ed. HSS. Chico, Calif.; Scholars Press.

1985   New Directions in Dead Sea Scroll Research. Part I: The Text Behind the Text of the Hebrew Bible, *BRev* 1:12–25.

1994   A Phoenician Inscription from Idalion: Some Old and New Texts Relating to Child Sacrifice. Pp. 93–107 in *Scripture and Other Artifacts: Essays in Honor of Philip J. King.* Michael David Coogan, J. Cheryl Exum, and Lawrence E. Stager, eds. Louisville Ky.: Westminster / John Knox Press.

1998   Palaeography and the Dead Sea Scrolls. Pp. 379–402 in *The Dead*

Sea Scrolls after Fifty Years: A Comprehensive Assessment. Peter W. Flint and James C. VanderKam, eds. Vol. 1. Leiden: Brill.

Cross, Frank Moore, Jr., and Shemaryahu Talmon, eds.
1975   *Qumran and the History of the Biblical Text.* Cambridge, Mass.: Harvard University Press.

Culley, R. C.
1970   Metrical Analysis of Classical Hebrew Poetry. Pp. 12–28 in *Essays on the Ancient Semitic World.* Toronto Semitic Texts and Studies. J. W. Wevers and D. B. Redford, eds. Toronto: University of Toronto Press.

Daalen, D. H. van
1973–1982   The *'ĕmûnāh/pistis* of Habakuk 2,4 and Romans 1,17. Pp. 523–27 in *SE VII: Papers Presented to the Fifth International Congress on Biblical Studies.* E. A. Livingstone, ed. Berlin: Akademie.

Dagut, M. B.
1951   The Habakkuk Scroll and Pompey's Capture of Jerusalem. *Bib* 32:543–48.

Dahood, Mitchell
1979   Two Yiphil Causatives in Habakkuk 3,13a. *Or* 48:258–59.
1982   Hebrew *hapax legomena* in Eblaite. Pp. 439–70 in *Il bilinguismo a Ebla: Atti del convegno internazionale (Napoli, 19–22 Aprile 1982).* Naples: Istituto universitario orientale, Departimento di studi asiatici, Series minor 22.
1983   The Minor Prophets and Ebla. Pp. 47–67 in *The Word of the Lord shall go forth: Essays in honor of David Noel Freedman in Celebration of his Sixtieth Birthday.* C. L. Meyers and M. O'Connor, eds. Winona Lake, Ind.: Eisenbrauns.

Dalley, Stephanie
1990   Yahweh in Hamath in the 8th Century BC: Cuneiform Material and Historical Deductions. *VT* 60:2–32.
1991   *Myths from Mesopotamia. Creation, the Flood, Gilgamesh, and Others.* Oxford: Oxford University Press.

Daniels, Dwight R.
1987   Is There a "Prophetic Lawsuit" Genre? ZAW 99:339–60.

Day, John
1979a   Echoes of Baal's Seven Thunders and Lightnings in Psalm XXIX and Habakkuk III 9 and the Identity of the Seraphim in Isaiah vi. *VT* 29:143–51.
1979b   New Light on the Mythological Background of the Allusion to Resheph in Habakkuk iii 5. *VT* 29:353–55.
1985   *God's Conflict with the Dragon and the Sea: Echoes of a Canaanite Myth in the Old Testament.* Cambridge: Cambridge University Press.
1986   Asherah in the Hebrew Bible and Northwest Semitic Literature. *JBL* 105:385–408.
1989   *Molech: A God of Human Sacrifice in the Old Testament.* Univer-

sity of Cambridge Oriental Publications 41. Cambridge: Cambridge University Press.

Dearman, Andrew
 1988   *Property Rights in the Eighth-Century Prophets: The Conflict and its Background.* Atlanta: Scholars Press.
 1989   *Studies in the Mesha Inscription and Moab.* Archaeology and Biblical Studies 2. Atlanta: Scholars Press.

Decroix, J.
 1972   Le Pesher d'Habaquq. *BTS* 137:19.

Deist, Ferdinand
 1978   Prov. 31:1: A Case of Constant Mistranslation. *JNSL* 6:1–3.

Delaporte, Louis Joseph
 1920   *Catalogue des Cylinders Orientaux: Cachets et pierres gravés du Musée du Louvre.* Paris: Louvre.

Delcor, Mathias
 1953   La geste de Yahvé au temps de l'Éxode et l'espérance du psalmiste en Habacuc III. Pp. 287–302 in *Miscellanea Biblica B. Urbach.* Romualdo M. Diaz, ed. Barcelona: Montisserat.

Delitzsch, Friedrich
 1883   *The Hebrew Language in the Light of Assyrian Research.* [Reprinted from a series of articles originaly published in *The Athenaeum*] London: Williams & Northgate.

Dell'Acqua, Anna Passoni
 1992   Lo scarabeo in Ab 2,11. *RivB* 40:3–66.

Derrett, J. D. M.
 1985   "Running" in Paul: The Midrashic Potential of Hab. 2,2. *Bib* 66:560–67.

Dhorme, Édouard
 1967   *A Commentary on the Book of Job.* Translated by Harold Knight. Nashville: Thomas Nelson. Reprint with Preface by Francis I. Andersen, 1984.

Di Marco, A.
 1975   Der Chiasmus in der Bibel. 1 Teil. *LB* 36:21–97.
 1978   Der Chiasmus in der Bibel. 2 Teil. *LB* 39:37–85.

Diaz, J. A.
 1965   Habacuc o las perplejidades da un Profeta aute la Historia. *CB* 12:195–201.

Dick, M. B.
 1984   Prophetic *poiêsis* and the Verbal Icon. *CBQ* 46:226–46.

Dietrich, Manfred, and Oswalt Loretz, eds.
 1993   *Mesopotamica-Ugaritica-Biblica: Festschrift für Kurt Bergerhof zur Vollendung seines 70. Lebensjahres am 7. Mai 1992.* AOAT 232. Kevalaer: Butzon & Bercker.

Dietrich, Manfred, Oswalt Loretz, and Joaquín Sanmartin, eds.
 1995   *The Cuneiform Alphabetic Texts from Ugarit, Ras Ibn Hani and Other Places (KTU: second, enlarged edition).* Münster: Ugarit-Verlag.

Dietrich, Walter
  1994   "Habakuk—ein Jesajaschüler." Pp. 197–215 in *Nachdenken über Israel, Bible und Theologie: Festschrift für Klaus-Dietrich Schunk zu seinem 65. Geburtstag*. H. Michael Niemann, et al., eds. BEATAJ 37. Frankfurt: Lang.

Dinçol, Belkis
  1994   New Archaeological and Epigraphical Finds from Ivriz: A Preliminary Report. *TA* 21:117–28.

Dockery, D. S.
  1987   The Use of Hab. 2:4 in Rom. 1:17: Some Hermeneutical and Theological Considerations. *Wesleyan Theological Journal* 22.2:24–36.

Donner, Herbert, and W. Röllig
  1968   *Kanaanäische und Aramäische Inschriften*. Wiesbaden: Harrassowitz.

Driver, Godfrey Rolles
  1934   Hebrew Notes. ZAW 52:51–56.
  1936   *A Treatise on the Use of the Tenses in Hebrew*. Edinburgh: Clark.
  1938a   Linguistic and Textual Problems: Minor Prophets II. *JTS* 39:260–73.
  1938b   Linguistic and Textual Problems: Minor Prophets III. *JTS* 39:393–405.
  1943   Critical Notes on Habakkuk III,7. *JBL* 62:121.
  1945–1946 "Mistranslations." *Expository Times* 57:192–93.
  1950   Difficult Words in the Hebrew Prophets. Pp. 52–72 in *Studies in Old Testament Prophecy: Festschrift for T. H. Robinson*. H. H. Rowley, ed. Edinburgh: Clark.
  1951   Hebrew Notes. *VT* 1:241–50.
  1971   Isaiah 6:1: "his train filled the temple." Pp. 87–96 in *Near Eastern Studies in Honor of William Foxwell Albright*. H. Goedicke, ed. Baltimore: Johns Hopkins University Press.

Driver, Samuel Rolles
  1874   *A Treatise on the Use of the Tenses in Hebrew*. Oxford: Clarendon Press.
  1902   *A Critical and Exegetical Commentary on Deuteronomy*. ICC 3. Edinburgh: Clark.
  1906   *The Minor Prophets. II: Nahum, Habakkuk, Zephaniah, Haggai, Zechariah, Malachi*. Edinburgh: Clark.
  1913a   *Introduction to the Literature of the Old Testament*. 9th ed. International Theological Library. Edinburgh: T. & T. Clarke.
  1913b   *Notes on the Hebrew Text and the Topography of the Books of Samuel with an Introduction on Hebrew Palaeography and the Ancient Versions and Facsimiles of Inscriptions and Maps*. 2nd ed. Oxford: Clarendon Press.

Duhm, Bernhard
  1875   *Die Theologie der Propheten als Grundlage für die innere Entwicklungsgeschichte der israelitischen Religion*. Bonn: Marcus.

Dykes, Donna S.
   1976   *Diversity and Unity in Habakkuk.* Ph. D. diss., Vanderbilt University.

Eaton, J. H.
   1964   The Origin and Meaning of Habakkuk 3. ZAW 76:144–71.
   1979   "The Psalms and Israelite Worship." Pp. 238–73 in *Tradition and Interpretation: Essays by Members of the Society for Old Testament Study.* Ed. George Wishart Anderson, ed. Oxford: Clarendon Press.

Ehrlich, Arnold B.
   1912   *Randglossen zur hebräischen Bibel.* Leipzig: Hinrichs.

Eisenman, R. H.
   1986   *James the Just in the Habakkuk Pesher.* SPB 35. Leiden: Brill.
   1991   Playing on and Transmuting Words: Interpreting "Abeit-Galuto" Offered in the Habakkuk Prayer. Pp 177–96 in *Mogilany 1989: Papers on the Dead Sea Scrolls in Memory of Jean Carmignac: Part 2, The Teacher of Righteousness, Literary Studies.* Zdzislaw J. Kapera, ed. Cracow: Enigma.

Eissfeldt, Otto
   1951   The Prophetic Literature. Pp. 115–61 in *The Old Testament and Modern Study: A Generation of Discovery and Research: Essays by Members of the Society for Old Testament Study.* H. H. Rowley, ed. Oxford: Clarendon Press.
   1965   *The Old Testament: An Introduction, including the Apocrypha and Pseudepigrapha and also the Works of Similar Type from Qumran: The History of the Formation of the Old Testament.* by Peter R. Ackroyd, trs. Oxford: Blackwell.

Elliger, Karl
   1950   Das Ende der "Abendwölfe" Zeph 3,3, Hab 1,8. Pp. 158–75 *Festschrift Alfred Bertholet zum 80. Geburtstag.* Walter Baumgartner, Otto Eissfeldt, Karl Elliger, and Leonard Rost, eds. Tübingen: Mohr (Paul Siebeck).
   1953   *Studien zum Habakuk-Kommentar von Toten Meer.* BHT 15. Tübingen: Mohr (Paul Siebeck).

Emerton, John A.
   1977   The Textual and Linguistic Problems of Habakkuk II. 4–5. *JTS* 28:1–18.
   1982   New Light on Israelite Religion: The Implications of the Inscriptions from Kuntillet ʿAjrud. ZAW 94:2–21.
   1989   The meaning of the verb *ḥāmas* in Jeremiah 13,22. Pp. 19–28 in *Prophet und Prophetenbuch: Festschrift für Otto Kaiser zum 65. Geburtstag.* Volkmar Fritz, Karl-Friedrich Pohlmann, and Hans-Christoph Schmitt, eds. BZAW 185. Berlin: de Gruyter.

Engnell, Ivan
   1970   *Critical Essays on the Old Testament.* John T. Willis, trs. London: S.P.C.K.

Erlandsson, Seth
  1970   *The Burden of Babylon: A Study of Isaiah 13:2–14–23.* ConBOT.
          Lund: CWK Gleerup.
Evans, J. Ellwood
  1955   The Song of Habakkuk. *BS* 112:62–67, 164–69.
  1956   The Song of Habakkuk. *BS* 113:57–65.
Eybers, Ian H.
  1971   The Pesher-Commentaries on Habakkuk and Nahum and the Ori-
          gin of the Qumran Sect. *Oud Testamendtiese Werkgemeenskap in
          Suid-Afrika* 12:70–90.
Fabry, Heinz-Josef, ed.
  1977   *Bausteine biblischer Theologie: Festgabe für G. Johannes Botterweck
          zum 60. Geburtstag dargebracht von seinen Schülern.* BBB 50.
          Cologne: Hanstein.
Falkenstein, Adam, and W. von Soden
  1953   *Sumerische und akkadische Hymnen und Gebete.* Züruch /
          Stuttgart.
Fauth, Wolfgang
  1984–1985   Der Morgenhymnus *Aeterne rerum conditor* des Ambrosius
          und Prudentiua Cath. 1 (*Ad Galli Centum*). *JAC Jahrgang* 27/28:
          97–115.
Feltes, Heinz
  1986   *Die Gattung des Habakukkommentars von Qumran (1QpHab):
          Eine Studie zum frühen jüdischen Midrasch.* Würzburg: Echter.
Ferris, P. J.
  1992   *The Genre of Communal Lament in the Bible and the Ancient Near
          East.* SBLDS 127. Atlanta: Scholars Press.
Feuillet, A.
  1959–1960   La citation d'Habacuc II.4 et les huit premiers chapitres de
          l'Épitre aux Romains. *NTS* 6:52–80.
Field, Fridericus
  1875   *Origenis Hexaplorum quae supersunt sive Veterum Interpretum
          Graecorum in totum Vetus Testamentum Fragmenta.* Oxford: Ox-
          ford University Press. Reprint. Hildesheim: Olms, 1964.
Fishbane, Michael A.
  1971   Studies in Biblical Magic: Origins, Uses and Transformations of
          Terminology and Literary Forms. Ph.D. diss., Brandeis University.
  1985   *Biblical Interpretation in Ancient Israel.* Oxford: Clarendon Press.
Fitzmyer, Joseph A.
  1957   The Syntax of *kl, kl'*, "All," in Aramaic Texts from Egypt and in
          Biblical Aramaic. *Bib* 38:170–84. [Reprinted in Fitzmyer 1979:
          205–17]
  1979   *A Wandering Aramean: Collected Aramaic Essays.* SBLMS 25.
          Chico, Calif.: Scholars Press.
  1981   Habakkuk 2:3–4 and the New Testament. Pp. 236–46 in *To Ad-
          vance the Gospel: New Testament Studies.* New York: Crossroad.

1993   *Romans*. AB 33. New York: Doubleday.
1999   Paul and the Dead Sea Scrolls. Pp. 599–621 in *The Dead Sea Scrolls After Fifty Years: A Comprehensive Assessment*. Vol. 2. Peter W. Flint and James C. VanderKam, eds. Leiden: Brill.

Flint, Peter W., and James C. VanderKam, eds.
1998   *The Dead Sea Scrolls After Fifty Years: A Comprehensive Assessment*. Vol. 1. Leiden: Brill.
1999   *The Dead Sea Scrolls After Fifty Years: A Comprehensive Assessment*. Vol. 2. Leiden: Brill.

Floyd, Michael H.
1994   Prophecy and Writing in Habakkuk 2,1–5. ZAW 105:462–81.

Fløysvik, Ingvar
1995   When God Behaves Strangely: A Study in the Complaint Psalms. *CJ* 21:298–304.

Flusser, David
1983   האסיים מלבות רומא בציני בית חשמונאי ובראי *Zion* 48:149–76.

Fohrer, Georg
1951   Neuere Literatur zur alttestamentlichen Prophetie. *ThRu* n.s., 19:277–346.
1952   Neuere Literatur zur alttestamentlichen Prophetie (Fortsetzung). *ThRu* n.s., 20:192–271, 295–361.
1954   Über den Kurzvers. ZAW 66:199–236.
1961   Remarks on Modern Interpretations of the Prophets. *JBL* 80: 309–19.
1962   Zehn Jahre Literatur zur alttestamentliche Prophetie (1951–1960). *ThRu* 27:1–75, 235–97, 301–74.
1967   *Studien zur altestestamentlischer Prophetie (1949–1965)*. BZAW 99. Berlin: Töpelmann.
1968   *Introduction to the Old Testament*. David E. Green, trs. Nashville, Tenn.: Abingdon.
1969   *Studien zur alttestamentliche Theologie und Geschichte (1949–1966)*. BZAW 115. Berlin: Töpelmann.
1974   *Die Propheten des Alten Testaments*. Gütersloh: Gütersloh Verlaghaus.
1975   Neue Literatur zur alttestamentlichen Prophetie (1961–1970). *ThRu* 40:193–209, 337–77.
1976   Neue Literatur zur alttestamentlichen Prophetie (1961–1970). *ThRu* 41:1–12.
1982   Der Tag Jhwhs. *EI* 16:43–50.
1985   Das, Gebet des Propheten Habakuk (Hab 3,1–16). Pp. 159–67 in AOAT 215 [*Mélanges bibliques et orientaux in l'honneur de M. Mathias Delcor*. A. Caquot, S. Légasse, and M. Tardieu, eds. Neukirchen: Neukirchener Verlag.

Follis, Elaine R., ed.
1987   *Directions in Biblical Hebrew Poetry*. JSOTSup 40. Sheffield: University of Sheffield.

Foster, Benjamin R.
    1977   Ea and Saltu, Pp. 79–84 in *Essays on the Ancient Near East in Memory of Jacob Joel Finkelstein*. Maria de Jong Ellis, ed. Memoirs of the Connecticut Academy of Arts and Sciences 19. Hamden, Conn.: Archon.

Fox, Michael V., Victor Avigdor Hurowitz, Avi Hurwitz, Michael L. Klein, Baruch J. Schwartz, and Nili Shupak, eds.
    1996   *Texts, Temples, and Traditions: A Tribute to Menahem Haran*. Winona Lake, Ind.: Eisenbrauns.

Frankfort, Henri
    1934   Gods and Myths on Sargonid Seals. *Iraq* 1:2–29.

Fredericks, Daniel C.
    1989   Chiasm and Parallel Structure in Qoheleth 5:9–6:9. *JBL* 108:17–35.

Freedman, David Noel
    1949   The "House of Absalom" in the Habakkuk Scroll [1QpHab 5:9]. *BASOR* 114:11–12.
    1953   Notes on Genesis. *ZAW* 64:190–94.
    1960a   Archaic Forms in Early Hebrew Poetry. *ZAW* 72:101–7.
    1960b   History and Eschatology: The Nature of Biblical Religion and Prophetic Faith. *Int* 14:143–54.
    1960c   The Name of the God of Moses. *JBL* 79:151–56.
    1961   The Chronicler's Purpose. *CBQ* 23:436–42.
    1962a   The Massoretic Text and the Qumran Scrolls: A Study in Orthography, *Textus* 2:87–102. [Pp. 196–211 in Cross and Talmon, 1975]
    1962b   The Law and the Prophets. *VTSup* 9:250–65.
    1972   Pottery, Poetry, and Prophecy: An Essay on Biblical Poetry. *JBL* 91:5–26.
    1980   *Pottery, Poetry and Prophecy: Studies in Early Hebrew Poetry*. Winona Lake, Ind.: Eisenbrauns.
    1981   Temples without Hands. Pp. 21–30 in *Temples and High Places in Biblical Times*. A. Biran, ed. Jerusalem: Nelson Glueck School of Biblical Archaeology of Hebrew Union College, Jewish Institute of Religion.
    1982   Discourse on Prophetic Discourse. Pp. 141–58 in *The Quest for the Kingdom of God: Studies in Honor of George E. Mendenhall*. H. B. Huffmon, F. A. Spina, and A. R. W. Green, eds. Winona Lake, Ind.: Eisenbrauns.
    1983   The Earliest Bible. *Michigan Quarterly Review* 22:167–75.
    1985   What the Ass and the Ox Know—But the Scholars Don't. *BRev* 1:42–44.
    1986a   Acrostic Poems in the Hebrew Bible: Alphabetic and Otherwise. *CBQ* 48:408–31.
    1986b   Deliberate Deviation from an Established Pattern of Repetition in

Hebrew Poetry as a Rhetorical Device. Pp. 45–52 in *Proceedings of the Ninth World Congress of Jewish Studies: Jerusalem, August 4–12, 1985. Division A: The Period of the Bible.* Jerusalem: World Union of Jewish Studies. [Pp. 205–12 in *Divine Commitment and Human Obligation: Selected Writings of David Noel Freedman.* Vol. 2. *Poetry and Orthography.* John R. Huddlestun, ed. Grand Rapids, Mich.: Eerdmans, 1997]

1987a   Headings in the Books of the Eighth-Century Prophets. *AUSS* 25:9–26.

1987b   Another Look at Biblical Hebrew Poetry. Pp. 11–28 in *Directions in Biblical Hebrew Poetry.* Elaine R. Follis, ed. JSOTSup 40. Sheffield: University of Sheffield.

1987c   Yahweh of Samaria and his Asherah, *BA* 50:241–50.

1987d   The Structure of Isaiah 40:1–11. Pp. 167–93 in *Perspectives on Language and Text: Essays and Poems in Honor of Francis I. Andersen's Sixtieth Birthday, July 28, 1985.* E. W. Conrad and E G. Newing, eds. Winona Lake, Ind.: Eisenbrauns.

1988   Is it Possible to Understand the Book of Job? *BRev* 2:26–33, 44.

1989   The Nine Commandments. The Secret Progress of Israel's Sins. *BRev* 5/6:28–37, 42.

1990   Confrontations in the Book of Amos. *PSB* 11:240–52.

1991   "The Book of Job." Pp. 33–51 in *The Hebrew Bible and its Interpreters.* William H. Propp, Baruch Halpern, and David Noel Freedman, eds. Biblical and Judaic Studies from the University of California, San Diego, 1. Winona Lake, Ind.: Eisenbrauns.

1991   *The Unity of the Hebrew Bible.* Ann Arbor: University of Michigan Press.

1992   Patterns in Psalms 25 and 34. Pp. 125–38 in *Priests, Prophets and Scribes: Essays on the Formation and Heritage of Second Temple Judaism in Honour of Joseph Blenkinsopp.* E. Ulrich, J. W. Wright, R. P. Carroll, and P. R. Davies, eds. JSOTSup 149 Sheffield: JSOT Press.

1994   The Structure of Psalm 119: Part II. *HAR* 14:55–87.

1995   The Structure of Psalm 119: Part I. Pp. 595–628 in *Pomegranates and Golden Bells: Studies in Biblical, Jewish, and Near Eastern Ritual, Law, and Literature in Honor of Jacob Milgrom.* David P. Wright, David Noel Freedman, and Avi Hurvitz, eds.Winona Lake, Ind.: Eisenbrauns.

Freedman, David Noel, A. Dean Forbes, and Francis I. Andersen
1992   *Studies in Hebrew and Aramaic Orthography.* William Henry Propp, ed. Biblical and Judaic Studies from the University of California, San Diego, 2. Winona Lake, Ind.: Eisenbrauns.

Freehof, Solomon Benedict
1941–1942   Some Text Rearrangements in the Minor Prophets. *JQR* 32:306–8.

Friedmann, M.
    1935   L'enigma di Habaquq. *Religio* 11:219–30.
Fritz, Volkmar, Karl-Friedrich Pohlmann, and Hans-Christoph Schmitt, eds.
    1989   *Prophet und Prophetenbuch: Festschrift für Otto Kaiser zum 65.*
            Geburtstag. BZAW 185. Berlin: de Gruyter.
Fulco, William J.
    1976   *The Canaanite God Rešep.* New Haven, Conn.: American Orien-
            tal Society.
Garcia Cordero, M.
    1948   El Càntico de habacuc. *CB* 5:171–74; 254–60.
García Martínez, Florentino
    1979–1980   4QpNah y la Crucifixión. Neuva hipótesis de recon-
            strucción de 4Q 169 i, 4–8. *EstBib* 38:221–35.
    1985   ¿Judas Macabeo, Sacerdote Impío? Notas al margen de 1QpHab
            viii, 8–13. Pp. 169–81 in *Mélanges bibliques et orientaux en l'hon-*
            neur de M. Mathias Delcor. A. Caquot, S. Légasse, and M. Tardieu,
            eds. Neukirchen: Neukirchener Verlag.
    1992   *Qumram and Apocalyptic: Studies on the Aramaic Texts from Qum-*
            ran. STDJ 9. Leiden: Brill.
    1996   *The Dead Sea Scrolls Translated: The Qumran Texts in English.*
            2nd ed. Wilfred G. E. Watson, trs. Grand Rapids, Mich.: Eerdmans.
García Martínez, Florintino, A. Hilhorst, and C. J. Labuschagne, eds.
    1992   *The Scriptures and the Scrolls: Studies in Honour of A. S. van der*
            Woude on the Occasion of His 65th Birthday. VTSup 49. Leiden:
            Brill.
García Martínez, Florintino, and Ed. Noort, eds.
    1998   *Perspectives in the Study of the Old Testament and Early Judaism:*
            A Symposium in Honour of Adam S. van der Woude on the Occa-
            sion of His 70th Birthday. VTSup 73. Leiden: Brill.
García Martínez, Florintino, and E. J. C. Tigchelaar
    1997   *The Dead Sea Scrolls Study Edition: Volume One 1Q1–4Q273.*
            Leiden: Brill.
Gaster, Theodor Herzl
    1937   The Battle of the Rain and Sea: An Ancient Semitic Nature-Myth.
            Iraq 4:22–32.
    1943   On Habakkuk 3:4. *JBL* 62:345–46.
    1950   *Thespis.* New York: Harper & Row.
Gelb, Ignace J.
    1950   Šullat and Ḫaniš. *ArOr* 18:189–98.
Gelston, A.
    1987   *The Peshitta of the Twelve Prophets.* Oxford: Clarendon Press.
Gemser, Berend
    1955   The Rîb- or Controversy-pattern in Hebrew Mentality. Pp. 120–37
            in *Wisdom in Israel and in the Ancient Near East: Presented to Pro-*
            fessor Harold Henry Rowley by the Society for Old Testament Study

in Association with the Editorial Board of Vetus Testamentum in Celebration of his Sixty-fifth Birthday, 24 March 1955. VTSup 3. Leiden: Brill.

Gerstenberger, Erhard
1962   The Woe-Oracles of the Prophets. *JBL* 81:249–63.

Gese, Hartmut
1957   Die hebräischen Bibelhandschriften zum Dodekapropheton nach der Variantensammlung des Kennicott. *ZAW* 69:55–69.

Gevaryahu, H. M.
1975   Biblical Colophons: A Source for the "Biography" of Authors, Texts, and Books. VTSup 28:42–59.

Gevirtz, Stanley
1963   *Patterns in the Early Poetry of Israel.* SAOC 32. Chicago: University of Chicago Press.
1986   Of Syntax and Style in the "Late Biblical Hebrew"—"Old Canaanite" Connection. *JANES* 18:25–29.

Ginsburg, Christian David
1897   *Introduction to the Massoretico-critical Edition of the Hebrew Bible.* New York: KTAV. [Reprint, 1966]

Glueck, Nelson
1936   The Theophany of the God of Sinai. *JAOS* 56:462–71.
1967   ḤESED *in the Bible.* Alfred Gottschalk, trs. Introduction by Gerald L. Larue. Cincinnati: Hebrew Union College.

Goldberg, Jonathan A.
1994   Variant Readings in Pesher Habakkuk. *Textus* 17:9–24.

Good, Edwin M.
1959   The Barberini Greek Version of Habakkuk III. *VT* 9:11–30.
1966   Hosea 5:8–6:6: An Alternative to Alt. *JBL* 85:273–86.

Goodwin, Donald Watson
1969   *Text-Restoration Methods in Contemporary U.S.A. Biblical Scholarship.* Pubblicazioni del Seminario di Semitistica a cura di Giovanni Garbini: Ricerche V. Naples: Instituto Orientale di Napoli.

Gordis, Robert
1938   Some Effects of Primitive Thought on Language. *AJSL* 55:270–84. [Pp. 137–51 in Gordis, 1976.]
1949   Quotations as a Literary Usage in Biblical, Oriental, and Rabbinic Literature. *HUCA* 22:157–219. [Pp. 104–59 in R. Gordis, *Poets, Prophets, and Sages: Essays in Biblical Interpretation.* Bloomington, Ind.: Indiana University Press, 1971]
1965   *The Book of God and Man: A Study of Job.* Chicago: University of Chicago Press.
1976   *The Word and the Book: Studies in Biblical Language and Literature.* New York: KTAV.

Gordon, Robert P.
1995   A Story of Two Paradigm Shifts. Pp. 3–26 in Gordon, ed. 1995.

Gordon, Robert P., ed.
1995 *"The Place Is Too Small for Us:" The Israelite Prophets in Recent Scholarship.* Sources for Biblical and Theological Study 5. Winona Lake, Ind.: Eisenbrauns.

Goshen-Gottstein, Moshe Henry
1960 *Text and Language in Bible and Qumran.* Jerusalem: Orient.

Gossai, Hemchand
1988 Ṣaddîq in Theological, Forensic and Economic Perspectives. *SEÅ* 53:7–13.

Gosse, Bernhard
1986 Le "Moi" prophétique de l'oracle contre Babylone d'Isaïe XXI,1–10." *RB* 93:70–84.

Gottstein, H. H.
1953 A DSS Biblical Variant in a Medieval Treatise. *VT* 3:187–88.

Gowan, Donald E.
1968 Habakkuk and Wisdom. *Perspective* 9:157–66.
1976 *The Triumph of Faith in Habakkuk.* Atlanta: John Knox Press.

Grabbe, Lester L.
1995 *Priests, Prophets, Diviners, Sages: A Socio-historical Study of Religious Specialists in Ancient Israel.* Valley Forge, Pa.: Trinity.

Greenfield, Jonas C.
1959 Lexicographical Notes. *HUCA* 30:141–51.

Grintz, Y. M., and D. Briskin-Nadiv
1971 Habakkuk. Pp. 1014–17 in *EncJud* Vol. 7. New York: Macmillan.

Gross, Heinrich and Franz Mussner
1961 *Lex tua veritas: Festschrift für Hubert Junker zur Vollendung des siebzigsten Lebensjahres am 8. August 1961, dargeboten von Kollegen, Freunden, und Schülern.* Trier: Paulinus.

Grove, Ron
1983 The Interpretation of Scripture in Christian Liturgical Texts: A Case Study of Habakkuk 3:2–3. *Theologia Athēnai* 54:319–46.

Gruenthaner, M. J.
1927 Chaldeans or Macedonians? *Bib* 8:129–60, 257–89.

Gunkel, Herman
1924 Jesaia 33, eine prophetische Liturgie. *Zeitschrift für die alttestamentliche Wissenschaft* 42:177–208.
1933 *Einleitung in die Psalmen.* [completed by J. Begrich] Göttingen: Vandenhoeck & Ruprecht.

Gunneweg, A. H. J.
1986 Habakuk und das Problem des leidenden ṣdyq. *ZAW* 98:400–415.

Gutierrez Herrero, Jesus
1974 *El Problema del mal en Habacuc 1,1–2,4.* Jerusalem: Studii Biblica Franciscani.

Haak, Robert D.
1982 A Study and New Interpretation of qṣr npš. *JBL* 101:161–67.

1988   "Poetry" in Habakkuk 1:1–2:4? *Journal of the American Oriental Society* 108:437–44.

Haberman, A. M.
1981   Habakkuk 3 According to the Genizah Text. *Beth Mikra* 26: 105–107.

Hackett, Jo Ann
1984   *The Balaam Text from Deir-ʿAllā.* Chico, Calif.: Scholars Press.

Hadley, Judith M.
1987   The Khirbet el-Qom Inscription. *VT* 37:50–62.
1987   Some Drawings an Inscriptions on Two Pithoi from Kuntillet ʿAjrud. *VT* 37:180–213.
1993   Kuntillet ʿAjrud: Religious Center or Desert Way Station? *PEQ* 125:115–24.

Haller, M.
1914   *Das Judentum, Geschichtsschreibung Prophetie und Gesetze nach dem Exil.* Göttingen: Vandenhoeck & Ruprecht.

Hamborg, G. R.
1981   Reason for Judgement in the Oracles Against the Nations of the Prophet Isaiah. *VT* 31:145–59.

Hanson, Paul D.
1979   *The Dawn of Apocalyptic: The Historical and Sociological Roots of Jewish Apocalyptic Eschatology.* 2nd ed. Philadelphia: Fortress.

Harder, G.
1939   Die Septuagintazitate des Hebräerbriefs *ThViat* 1939:33–52.

Harris, J. G.
1966   *The Qumran Commentary on Habakkuk.* London: Mowbray.
1973   The Laments of Habakkuk's Prophecy. *EvQ* 45:21–29.

Harvey, Julien
1962   Le "Rîb-Pattern," réquisitoire prophétique sur la rupture de l'alliance. *Bib* 43:172–96.
1967   *Le plaidoyer prophétique contre Israël après la rupture de l'alliance: Étude d'une formule littéraire de l'Ancien Testament.* Studia 22. Bruges: Desclée de Brouwer.

Hayden, Eric William
1958   *Faith's Glorious Achievement: Three Studies in the Book of Habakkuk.* London: Marshall, Morgan and Scott.

Hayes, J.
1968   The Usage of Oracles against Foreign Nations in Ancient Israel. *JBL* 87:81–92.

Hayes, John H., ed.
1974   *Old Testament Form Criticism.* Trinity University Monograph Series in Religion 2. San Antonio: Trinity University Press.

Heidel, Alexander
1951   *The Babylonian Genesis: The Story of Creation.* 2nd ed. Chicago: University of Chicago Press.

Held, Moshe
  1962   The YQTL–QTL (QTL–YQTL) Sequence of Identical Verbs in Biblical Hebrew and in Ugaritic. Pp. 280–91 in *Studies and Essays in Honour of A. A. Neuman*, M. Ben-Horin, B. D. Weinryb, and S. Zeitlin, eds. Leiden: Brill.

Hermann, Wolfram
  1987   Das Aufleben des Mythos den Judaern wahrend des babylonischen Zeitalters. *BN* 40:79–129.

Hertzberg, H. W.
  1963   "Sind die Propheten Fürbitter?" Pp. 63–74 in *Tradition und Situation: Studien zur alttestamentlichen Prophetie. Artur Weiser zum 70. Geburtstag am 18. 11. 1963 dargebracht von Kollegen, Freunden und Schülern*. Ernst Würthwein and Otto Kaiser, eds., Göttingen: Vandenhoeck & Ruprecht.

Hess, Richard S.
  1999   Joshua 10 and the Sun that Stood Still. *Buried History* 35/1:26–33.

Hess, Richard S., and David Toshio Tsumura, eds.
  1994   *"I Studied Inscriptions from before the Flood:" Ancient Near Eastern, Linguistic Approaches to Genesis 1–11*. Sources for Biblical and Theological Study 4. Winona Lake, Ind.: Eisenbrauns.

Hiebert, Theodore
  1986   *God of My Victory: The Ancient Hymn in Habakkuk 3*. HSM 38. Atlanta: Scholars Press.
  1987   The Use of Inclusion in Habakkuk 3. Pp. 119–40 in *Directions in Biblical Hebrew Poetry*, Elaine R. Follis, ed. JSOTSup 40 Sheffield: University of Sheffield.
  1996   "The Book of Habakkuk." Pp. 623–55 in *The New Interpreter's Bible*. Vol. 3. Nashville, Tenn.: Abingdon.

Hillers, Delbert R.
  1964   *Treaty-Curses and the Old Testament Prophets*. BOr 16. Rome: Pontifical Biblical Institute.
  1965   A Convention in Hebrew Literature: the Reaction to Bad News. *ZAW* 77:86–90.
  1983   *Hôy* and *Hôy* Oracles: A Neglected Syntactic Aspect. Pp. 185–88 in *The Word of the Lord shall go forth: Essays in honor of David Noel Freedman in Celebration of his Sixtieth Birthday*. C. L. Meyers and M. O'Connor, ed. Winona Lake, Ind.: Eisenbrauns.

Hirota, K.
  1979   Chasidim and the Wicked [Hab 2,4]. In *Kiristutokyo Gaku* Christian Studies 21. [Special Issue. Thirtieth Anniversary of the Department of Christian Studies and the Retirement of Nakazawa Koki] Tokyo: St. Paul's University.

Hoftijzer, Jacob
  1985   *The Function and Use of the Imperfect Forms with "nun paragogicum" in Classical Hebrew*. SSN 21. Assen: Van Gorcum.

Holt, J. M.
    1964   So He may Run who Reads it. *JBL* 83:298–302.
Hooght, Everard van der
    1867   *Biblia Hebraica.* 2nd ed. Augustus Hahn, ed. Leipzig: Bredt.
Horgan, Maurya P.
    1979   *Pesharim: Qumran Interpretations of Biblical Books* CBA MS 8.
            Washington, D.C.: Catholic Biblical Association.
Horine, Steven
    1989   A Study of the Literary Genre of the Woe Oracle. *Calvary Baptist
            Theological Journal* 5:74–97.
House, Paul R., ed.
    1992   *Beyond Form Criticism: Essays in Old Testament Literary Criticism.*
            Sources for Biblical and Theological Studies 2. David W. Baker,
            ed. Winona Lake, Ind.: Eisenbrauns.
Humbert, Paul
    1944   *Problèmes du livre d'Habacuc.* MUN 18. Neuchâtel: Secrétariat de
            l'Université.
    1958   *Opuscules d'un Hébraïsant.* Neuchatel: Secretariat de l'Université.
    1961   Emploi et portée bibliques du verbe *yāṣar* et de ses derives sub-
            stantifs. Pp. 82–88 in *Von Ugarit nach Qumran* BZAW 77 [Eiss-
            feldt Festschrift]. Berlin: Töpelmann.
Hunter, J. H.
    1989   The Literary Composition of Theophany Passages in the Hebrew
            Psalms. *JNSL* 15:97–107.
Hyatt, J. P., ed.
    1965   *The Bible in Modern Scholarship.* Nashville, Tenn.: Abingdon
            Press. [London: Carey Kingsgate, 1966]
Hymes, Dell H. ed.
    1974   *Studies in the History of Linguistics.* Traditions and Paradigms.
            Bloomington: Indiana University Press.
Irwin, William A.
    1932   Critical Notes on Five Psalms. *AJSL* 49:9–20.
    1942   The Psalm of Habakkuk. *JNES* 1:10–40.
    1956   The Mythological Background of Habakkuk, Chapter iii. *JNES*
            15:47–50.
Isaksson, Bo
    1987   *Studies in the Language of Qoheleth: With special emphasis on the
            verbal system.* AUU: Studia Semitica Upsaliensia 10. Uppsala:
            Almqvist & Wiksell.
Ittmann, Norbert
    1981   *Die Konfessionen Jeremias: Ihre Bedeutung für die Verkündingen
            des Propheten.* WMANT 54. Neukirchen: Neukirchener Verlag.
Jacob, Edmond
    1958   *Theology of the Old Testament.* A. W. Heathcote and P. J. Allcock,
            trs. London: Hodder and Stoughton.

Jacobsen, Thorkild
  1976   *The Treasures of Darkness*. New Haven, Conn.: Yale University.
James, Fleming
  1947   *Personalities of the Old Testament*. New York: Scribner.
Janzen, J. Gerald
  1980   Habakkuk 2:2–4 in the Light of Recent Philological Advances. *HTR* 73:53–78.
  1982   Eschatological Symbol and Existence in Habakkuk. *CBQ* 44:394–414.
Janzen, Waldemar
  1972   *Mourning Cry and Woe Oracle*. BZAW 125. Berlin: Töpelmann.
Jeremias, A.
  1916   *Das Alte Testament im Lichte des Alten Orient*. 3rd ed. Leipzig: Hinrichs.
Jeremias, Jörg
  1965   *Theophanie: Die Geschichte einer alttestamentliche Gattung*. WMANT 10. Neukirchen: Neukirchener Verlag.
  1970   *Kultprophetie und Gerichtsverkündigung in der späten Königszeit Israels*. WMANT 35. Neukirchen: Neukirchener Verlag.
Jöcken, Peter
  1977   War Habakuk ein Kultprophet? BBB 50:319–32.
Johnson, Aubrey R.
  1962   *The Cultic Prophet in Ancient Israel*. 2nd ed. Cardiff: University of Wales Press.
  1979   *The Cultic Prophet and Israel's Psalmody*. Cardiff: University of Wales Press.
Johnson, Bo
  1986–1987   Who Reckoned Righteousness to Whom? *SEÅ* 51–52:108–15.
Johnson, Marshall D.
  1985   The Paralysis of Torah in Habakkuk i 4. *VT* 35:257–66.
Joüon, Paul
  1947   *Grammaire de l'hébreu biblique*. Rome: Pontifical Biblical Institute. [See also Muraoka 1991]
Jung, P.
  1951   Hab 2,5 κατοινωμένος oder κατοιομένος? *Bib* 32:564–66.
Kaminka, Armand
  1928   Studien zur Septuaginta aus der Hand der zwolf kleinen Prophetenbucher. *MGWJ* 72:46–60, 242–73.
Kapelrud, Arvid S.
  1981   Domstanker i jodisk apokalyptik. *NorTT* 82:65–77.
Kaufman, Stephen A.
  1995   Paragogic *Nun* in Biblical Hebrew Hyper-correction as a Clue to a Lost Scribal Practice. Pp. 95–99 in *Solving Riddles and Untying Knots. Biblical, Epigraphic, and Semitic Studies in Honor of Jonas C. Greenfield*. Ziony, Zevit, Seymour Gitin, and Michael Sokoloff, eds. Winona Lake, Ind.: Eisenbrauns.

Kaufmann, Yehezkel
    1961   *The Religion of Israel.* Trans. and abridged Moshe Greenberg. London: George Allen and Unwin.

Keel-Leu, O.
    1978   *The Symbolism of the Biblical World: Ancient Near Eastern Iconography and the Book of Psalms.* T. J. Hallett, trs. New York: Seabury Press.

Keller, Carl-A.
    1973   Die Eigenart der Prophetie Habakuks. ZAW 85:156–67.

Kelley, Fred T.
    1902   The Strophic Structure of Habakkuk. *AJSL* 18:94–119.

Kissane, Edward J.
    1953   *The Book of Psalms.* Dublin: Browne and Nolan.

Klein, Joel T
    1984   "Habakkuk 3:13—a Problematic Verse." *DD* 13:105–10.

Klostermann, E.
    1895   *Analecta zur Septuaginta Hexapla und Patristik.* Leipzig: Deichert.

Koch, Dietrich-Alex
    1985   Der Text von Hab 2,4b in der Septuaginta und im Neuen Testament. ZNW 76:68–85.

Koch, Klaus
    1969   *The Growth of the Biblical Tradition: The Form-Critical Method.* S. M. Cupitt, trs. New York: Charles Scribner's Sons.

Koenig, J.
    1969   Zum Verständnis von Habakuk 2,4–5. ZDMG Supp. 1:291–95.

Kosmala, Hans
    1978   *Hebräer–Essener–Christen: Studien zur Vorgeschichte der Frühchristlichen Verkündigung.* SPB 1. Leiden: Brill.

Kraus, Hans-Joachim
    1973   *hoj* als prophetische Leichenklag über das eigene Volk im 8. Jahrhundret. ZAW 85:15–46.

    1988   *Psalms 1–59: A Commentary.* Hilton C. Oswald, trs. Minneapolis: Augsburg.

Kselman, John S.
    1975   A Note on Isaiah II 2. *VT* 25:225–27.

    1982   The ABCB Pattern: Further Examples. *VT* 32:361–71.

    1985   The social world of the Israelite prophets: A review article. *RelSRev* 11:120–29.

Kuenen, Abraham
    1892   *Historisch-kritische Einleitung in das Alte Testament.* Vol. 2. Leipzig: Hinrichs.

Kugel, James L.
    1981   *The Idea of Biblical Poetry: Parallelism and its History.* New Haven Conn.: Yale University Press.

Kuntzmann, Raymond, ed.
    1995   *Ce Dieu Qui vient: Mélanges offerts à Bernard Renaud.* Paris: Cerf.

Kutler, Laurence
   1984   A "Strong" Case for Hebrew *mar*. UF 16:111–18.
Laato, Antti
   1996   *History and Ideology in the Old Testament Prophetic Literature:*
            A Semiotic Approach to the Reconstruction of the Proclamation
            of the Historical Prophets. ConBOT 41. Stockholm: Almqvist &
            Wiksell.
Labuschagne, Casper J.
   1973   The particles הֵן and הִנֵּה. OTS 18:1–14.
Lambert, W. G.
   1960   *Babylonian Wisdom Literature.* Oxford: Clarendon Press. [The
            standard edition of texts in Akkadian that may be compared with
            biblical wisdom writings.]
   1965   A New Look at the Babylonian Background of Genesis. *Journal of*
            Theological Studies 16:287–300. Reprinted, with two postscripts
            (1991, 1994) pp. 96–114 in *"I Studied Inscriptions from before the*
            Flood": Ancient Near Eastern, Linguistic Approaches to Genesis
            1–11. Sources for Biblical and Theological Study 4. Richard S.
            Hess and David Toshio Tsumura, eds. Winona Lake, Ind.: Eisen-
            brauns.
   1988   Old Testament Mythology in its Ancient Near Eastern Context.
            Pp. 124–43 in *Congress Volume (Jerusalem 1986).* VTS 40. J. A.
            Emerton, ed. Leiden: Brill.
Lambert, W. G., and Alan R. Millard
   1969   *Atra-Ḥasīs: The Babylonian Story of the Flood.* Oxford: Clarendon
            Press.
Lange, Amin
   1995   Wisdom and Predestination in the Dead Sea Scrolls. *DSD*
            2:350–54.
Le Peau, Andrew T., Phyllis J. Le Peau, and John D Stewart.
   1979   *Just Living by Faith.* Downers Grove, Ill.: InterVarsity Press.
Lehmann, Manfred R.
   1954   A New Interpretation of the Term *šdmwt*. VT 3:361–71.
Leivestad, Ragnar
   1972–1973   Das Dogma von der prophetenlosen Zeit. NTS 19:288–99.
Lescow, Theodor
   1995   Die Komposition der Bücher Nahum und Habakuk. BN 77:59–85.
Lichtenstein, M. H.
   1982   Chiasm and Symmetry in Proverbs 31. CBQ 44:202–11.
Lieb, Michael
   1991   *The Visionary Mode: Biblical Prophecy, Hermeneutics, and Cul-*
            tural Change. Ithaca N.Y.: Cornell University Press.
Lim, Timothy H.
   1990   Eschatological Orientation and the Alteration of Scripture in the
            Habakkuk Pesher. *JNES* 49:185–94.
   1993   The Wicked Priests of the Groningen Hypothesis. *JBL* 112:415–25.

Limburg, James
 1969 The Root *ryb* and the Prophetic Lawsuit Speeches. *JBL* 88: 291–304.

Lipiński, E.
 1974 אשבעל [*'šb'l*] and אשיהו [*'šyhw*] and Parallel Personal Names. *OLP* 5:5–13.

Lloyd-Jones, David Martyn
 1953 *From Fear to Faith: Studies in the Book of Habakkuk.* London: InterVarsity Fellowship.

Loewenstamm, Samuel E.
 1962 *yāpēᵃḥ, yāpīᵃḥ, yāpîᵃḥ. Lešōnēnû* 26:205–8.
 1980 *Comparative Studies in Biblical and Ancient Oriental Literatures.* AOAT 204. Kavelaer: Butzon & Bercker.
 1992 *From Babylon to Canaan. Studies in the Bible and its Oriental Background.* Y. Avishur and J. Blau, eds. Jerusalem: Magnes, Hebrew University.

Luckenbill, D. D.
 1928 *Ancient Records of Assyria and Babylon.* 2 vols. Chicago: University of Chicago.

Lund, Nils Wilhelm
 1942 *Chiasmus in the New Testament: A Study in the Form and Function of Chiastic Structures.* Chapel Hill: University of North Carolina Press Reprint. Peabody, Mass.: Hendrickson, 1992.

Lys, Daniel
 1962 *"RÛACH" Le souffle dans l'Ancien Testament: enquête anthropologique à travers l'histoire théologique d'Israîl.* Paris: Presses universitaires de France.

Marcos, Natalio Fernandez
 1976 El Texto Barberini de Habacuc III reconsiderado. *Sef* 36:3–36.
 1985 *La Septuaginta en la Investigacion Contemporarea.* V Congresso de la IOSCS. Madrid: Textos y Estudio "Cardenal Cisneros" de la Biblia Polyglota Matrintense Instituto "Arias Montano."

Margolis, Maximillan Leopold
 1908 The Character of the Anonymous Greek Version of Habakkuk, Chap. 3. Pp. 133–42 in *Old Testament and Semitic Studies in Memory of William Rainey Harper.* R. F. Harper, F. Brown, and G. F. Moore, eds. Chicago: University of Chicago Press.

Margulis, Baruch
 1970 The Psalm of Habakkuk: A Reconstruction and Interpretation. *ZAW* 82:409–42.

Mattiae, P.
 1979 Princely Cemetery and Ancestor Cult at Ebla during Middle Bronze: A Proposal of Interpretation. *UF* 11:563–69.

May, Herbert G.
 1955 Some Cosmic Connotations of *Mayim Rabbim* Many "Waters." *JBL* 74:9–21.

Mays, James Luther, et al., eds.
  1995   *Old Testament Interpretation: Past, Present, and Future: Essays in Honor of Gene M. Tucker.* Nashville, Tenn.: Abingdon.
Mazar, Benjamin
  1981   Yahweh came out from Sinai. Pp. 5–9 in *Temples and High Places in Biblical Times.* Avraham Biran, ed. Jerusalem: Nelson Glueck School of Biblical Archaeology of Hebrew Union College, Jewish Institute of Religion.
McAdams, R.
  1982   Property Rights and Functional Tenure in Mesopotamian Rural Communities. Pp. 1–14 in *Societies and Languages of the Ancient Near East. Studies in Honour of I. M. Diakonoff.* J. N. Postgate, ed. Warminster: Arris & Phillips.
McAlpine, Thomas H.
  1987   *Sleep, Divine and Human, in the Old Testament.* JSOTSup 38. Sheffield: JSOT Press.
McCarthy, Carmel
  1981   *The Tiqqune Sopherim and Other Theological Corrections in the Massoretic Text of the Old Testament.* OBO 36. Göttingen: Vandenhoeck & Ruprecht.
McGann, Jerome J.
  1992   *A Critique of Modern Textual Criticism.* Charlottesville: University Press of Virginia.
McKane, William
  1979   Prophecy and the Prophetic Literature. Pp. 163–88 in *Tradition and Interpretation: Essays by Members of the Society for Old Testament Study.* G. W. Anderson, ed. Oxford: Clarendon Press.
Meier, Samuel A.
  1992   *Speaking of Speaking: Marking Direct Discourse in the Hebrew Bible.* VTSup 46. Leiden: Brill.
Melamed, Ezra Zion
  1961   Breakup of stereotype phrases as an artistic device in Biblical Poetry. Pp. 115–53 in *Studies in the Bible.* C. Rabin, ed. ScrHier 8. Jerusalem: Hebrew University Press.
Mendenhall, George E.
  1955   *Law and Covenant in Israel and the Ancient Near East.* Pittsburg: Biblical Colloquium.
  1958   The Census Lists of Numbers 1 and 26. *Journal of Biblical Literature* 77:52–66.
  1973   *The Tenth Generation: The Origins of the Biblical Tradition.* Baltimore: Johns Hopkins.
du Mesnil du Buisson, Robert
  1973   *Nouvelles Études sur les Dieux et les Mythes de Canaan.* EPRO 33. Leiden: Brill.

Mercati, G.
   1955   Osservazioni preliminari circa la versione barberiniana del Cantico di Abacuc. Pp. 155–80 in *Studi in Memoria di Ipp. Rossellini*. Vol. 2. Pisa.

Meyers, Carol L., and Eric M. Meyers
   1987   *Haggai, Zechariah 1–8*. AB 25B. Garden City, N.Y.: Doubleday.

Michaelson, Peter
   1989   Ecstasy and Possession in Ancient Israel. A Review of Some Recent Contributions. *SJOT* 2:28–54.

Miller, Patrick D., Jr.
   1964   Two Critical Notes on Psalm 68 and Deuteronomy 33. *HTR* 57:240–43.
   1967   El the Warrior. *HTR* 60:411–31.
   1973   *The Divine Warrior in Early Israel*. Cambridge, Mass.: Harvard University Press.
   1979   *yāpîaḥ* in Psalm xii 6. *VT* 29:495–501.
   1994   *They Cried to the Lord: The Form and Theology of Biblical Prayer*. Minneapolis: Fortress.

Miller, Patrick D., Paul D. Hanson, and S. Dean McBride, eds.
   1987   *Ancient Israelite Religion: Essays in Honor of Frank Moore Cross*. Philadelphia: Fortress.

Molin, Georg
   1952   Der Habakukkommentar von ʿEn-Fešḫa in der alttestamentlichen Wissenschaft. *TZ* 8:340–57.

Moody, R. M.
   1981   The Habakkuk Quotation in Romans 1:17. *ExpT* 92:205–08.

Moor, Johannes de, ed.
   1995   *Synchronic or Diachronic: A Debate on Method in Old Testament Exegesis*. OTS 34. Leiden: Brill.

Moran, William L.
   1961   The Hebrew Language in its Northwest Semitic Background. Pp. 59–84 in *The Bible and the Ancient Near East: Essays in Honor of William Foxwell Albright*. G. E. Wright, ed. Garden City, N.Y.: Doubleday.
   1962   Some Remarks on the Song of Moses. *Bib* 43:317–27.

Morgenstern, Julian
   1911   Biblical Theophanies. *ZA* 25:139–93.
   1913   Biblical Theophanies. *ZA* 28:15–60.

Mowinckel, Sigmund
   1921–1924   *Psalmenstudien*. 6 vols. I–VI. SNVAO kapsselskapets Skrifter. II Hist.Filos. Klasse. Kristiania. [Reprinted in two volumes, Amsterdam: Schippers, 1961]
   1925   "Zwei Beobachtungen zur Deutung der פִּצְלֵי אָרֶן." *ZAW* 43:260–62.
   1928   Mikaboken. *NorTT* 29:3–42.
   1933   Die Komposition des Jesajabuches Kap. 1–39. *ArOr* 11:267–92.

1934–35   Ecstatic Experience and Rational Elaboration in Old Testament Prophecy. *AcOr* 13:264–91.

1939   The Babylonian Matter in the Predeuteronomic Primeval History (JE) in Gen 1–11. *JBL* 58:87–103.

1947   *Prophecy and Tradition: The Prophetical Books in the Light of the Study of the Growth and History of the Tradition.* Oslo: Dybwad.

1951   *Offersang og Sangoffer.* Salmediktningen i Bibelen. Oslo: Aschenoug.

1953   Zum Psalm des Habakuk. *ThZ* 9:1–23.

1957   *Real and Apparent Tricola in Hebrew Psalm Poetry.* SNVAO. II Hist. Filos. Klass 1957. No. 2. Oslo: Aschehoug.

1961   "Ich" und "Er" in der Ezrageschichte. Pp. 211–33 in *Verbannung und Heimkehr: Wilhelm Rudolph zum 70. Geburtstage.* A. Kuschke, ed. Tübingen: Mohr.

1962   Drive and / or Ride in the OT. *VT* 12:278–99.

Muilenburg, James

1953   A Study of Hebrew Rhetoric: Repetition and Style. VTSup 1: 97–111.

1966   The Office of Prophet in Ancient Israel. Pp. 74–97 in *The Bible in Modern Scholarship.* J. P. Hyatt, ed. London: Carey Kingsgate. Nashville, Tenn.: Abingdon Press, 1965. [Pp. 127–50 in Muilenburg, 1984]

1968   The Intercession of the Covenant Mediator: Ex 33:1a, 12–17. Pp. 159–81 in Ackroyd and Lindars, 1968. [Pp. 170–92 in Muilenburg, 1984]

1969   Form Criticism and Beyond. *JBL* 88:1–18.

1984   *Hearing and Speaking the Word: Selections from the Works of James Muilenburg.* Thomas F. Best, ed. Homage Series. Chico, Calif.: Scholars Press.

Mullen, E. Theodore

1980   *The Divine Council in Canaanite and Early Hebrew Literature.* HSM 24. Chico Calif.: Scholars Press.

Müller, Hans-Peter

1985   Ergativelemente im akkadischen und althebräischen Verbalsystem. *Bib* 66:385–417.

1995   Ergative Constructions in Early Semitic Languages. *JNES* 54: 261–71.

1998   Punische Weihinschriften und alttestamentliche Psalmen in religionsgeschichten Zusammenhang. *Or* 67:477–96.

Muntingh, L. M.

1969   "Teman and Paran in the Prayer of Habakkuk." Pp. 64–70 in *Ou-Testamentiese Werkgemeenskap van Suid Africa.*

Muraoka, Takamitsu

1975   The *Nun energicum* and the Prefix Conjugation in BH. *AJBI* 1:63–71

1991   *A Grammar of Biblical Hebrew.* subsidia biblica 14/I, II. Trans. and revision of Joüon, 1947. Rome: Pontifical Biblical Institute.

1998   *Hebrew / Aramaic Index to the Septuagint Keyed to the Hatch-Redpath Concordance.* Grand Rapids: Mich.: Baker Books.

Murray, D. F.
1987   The Rhetoric of Disputation: Re-examination of a Prophetic Genre. *JSOT* 38:95–121.

Murray, R.
1982   "Prophecy and the Cult." Pp. 200–216 in *Israel's Prophetic Tradition: Essays in Honour of Peter R. Ackroyd.* Richard Coggins, Anthony Phillips, and Michael Knibb, ed. Cambridge: Cambridge University Press.

Newton, Thomas
1826   *Dissertations on the Prophecies which have remarkably been fulfilled, and at this time are fulfilling in the world.* London: Tegg.

Niditch, Susan
1980   *The Symbolic Vision in Biblical Tradition.* HSM 30. Chico, Calif.: Scholars Press.

Niehaus, Jeffrey J.
1995   *God at Sinai: Covenant and Theophany in the Bible and the Ancient Near East.* Grand Rapids, Mich.: Zondervan.

Niehoff, Maren
1992   A Dream Which Is Not Interpreted is Like a Letter Which Is Not Read. *JJS* 43:58–84.

Nielsen, Eduard
1952   The Righteous and the Wicked in Habaqquq. *ST* 6:54–78.

Nielsen, Kirsten
1978   *Yahweh as Prosecutor and Judge: An Investigation of the Prophetic Lawsuit (Rîb-Pattern).* F. Cryer, trs. JSOTSup 9. Sheffield: University of Sheffield Press.

1979   Das Bild des Gerichts (rib-pattern) in Jes I-XII: Eine Analyse der Beziehungen zwischen Bildsprache und dem Anliegen der Verkundigung *VT* 29:309–24.

Nitzan, Bilhah
1986   *Pesher Habakkuk: A Scroll from the Wilderness of Judaea (1QpHab).* Jerusalem: Bialik.

1994   *Qumran Prayer and Religious Poetry.* Jonathan Chipman, trs. Leiden: Brill.

North, Christopher R.
1961   The Essence of Idolatry. Pp. 150–60 in *Von Ugarit nach Qumran* BZAW 77 [Eissfeldt Festschrift]. Berlin: Töpelmann.

Noth, Martin
1928   *Die israelitischen Personennamen im Rahmen der gemeinsemitischen Namengebung.* Beiträge zur Wissenschaft vom Alten und Neuen Testament, III, 10. Stuttgart: Kohlhammer Reprint. Hildesheim: Olms, 1966.

Obermann, Julian
  1929   Yahweh's Victory over the Babylonian Pantheon. The Archetype
          of Is 21:1–10. *JBL* 48:307–28.
O'Connell, Kevin G.
  1979   "Habakkuk—Spokesman to God." *Currents in Theology and Mis-
          sion* 6:227–31.
O'Connor, Michael Patrick
  1980   *Hebrew Verse Structure.* Winona Lake, Ind.: Eisenbrauns.
  1987a   The Pseudosorites in Hebrew Verse. Pp. 239–53 in Conrad and
          Newing, 1987.
  1987b   The Pseudosorites: A Type of Paradox in Hebrew Verse. Pp. 161–72
          in Follis, 1987.
  1987c   Irish Bull and Pseudosorites: Two Types of Paradox in English. *Ars
          Semeiotica* 10:271–85.
  1995   War and Rebel Chants in the Former Prophets. Pp. 322–37 in *For-
          tunate the Eyes That See: Essays in Honor of David Noel Freed-
          man in Celebration of His Seventieth Birthday*, Astrid B. Beck, An-
          drew H. Bartelt, Paul R. Raabe, and Chris A. Franke, eds. Grand
          Rapids, Mich.: Eerdmans.
Oded, Bustenay
  1979   *Mass Deportations and Deportees in the Neo-Assyrian Empire.*
          Weisbaden: Reichert.
Ohmann, H. M.
  1989   Some Remarks on the Use of the Term "Theophany" in the study
          of the Old Testament. Pp. 2–12 in *Unity in Adversity: Studies Pre-
          sented to Dr. Jelle Faber on the Occasion of His Retirement.* Riemer
          Faber, ed. Hamilton, Ont.: Senate of the Theological College of
          the Canadian Reformed Churches.
Oldenburg, Ulf
  1969   *The Conflict Between El and Ba'al in Canaanite Religion.* Leiden:
          Brill.
Oppenheim. A. L.
  1959   A New Prayer to the "Gods of the Night." *AnBib* 12:282–301.
Orlinsky, Harry M.
  1965   The Seer in Ancient Israel. *OrAnt* 4:153–74. [Parts of this paper
          in Chap. 12 in *The World History of the Jewish People*. B. Mazar,
          ed. Vol. 3. Reprinted as "The Seer-Priest and the Prophet in An-
          cient Israel," Pp. 39–63 in *Essays in Biblical Culture and Bible
          Translation.* H. M. Orlinsky, ed. New York: KTAV, 1974]
Osswald, Eva
  1956   "Zur Hermeneutik des Habakuk-Kommentars." *ZAW* 58:243–
          56.
Oswalt, John N.
  1977   The Myth of the Dragon and Old Testament Faith. *EvQ*
          49:163–72.

Otto, Eckart
  1977   Die Stellung der Wehe-Worte in der Verkundigung des Propheten
          Habakuk. ZAW 89:73–107.
  1985   Die Theologie des Buches Habakuk. *VT* 35:274–95.
Otzen, Benedikt
  1954   Die neugefundenen hebräischen Sektenschriften. *ST* 7:125–57.
Palumbo, Arthur E.
  1993   1QpHab 11:2–8 and the Death of James the Just. *Qumran Chron-
          icle* 3:139–53.
  1994   1QpHab 5:8–12: The "Pillars" and Paul. *Folia Orientalia* 30:
          125–37.
Pardee, Dennis
  1978   *yph* "Witness" In Hebrew and Ugaritic. *VT* 28:204–13.
Parente, Fausto
  1995   ΤΟ ΜΥΣΤΗΡΙΟΝ ΤΗΣ ΒΑΣΙΛΕΙΑΣ ΤΟΥ ΘΕΟΥ. 2 "פשר di
          Habaqquq" (1QpHab) ed il problema del cosidetto "Segreto mes-
          sianico (Mc 4,10–12)." *Aug* 35:17–42.
Parker, Simon B.
  1978   Possession Trance and Prophecy in Pre-Exilic Israel. *VT*
          28:271–85.
  1989   KTU 1.16 III, the Myth of the Absent God and 1 Kings 18. *UF*
          21:283–96.
Parmentier, Roger
  1979   Livre du prophète Habaquq. *ComViat* 22:205–22.
Peake, A. S.
  1904   *The Problem of Suffering in the Old Testament.* London: Kelly.
Peckham, Brian
  1986   The Vision of Habakkuk. *CBQ* 48:617–36.
Peiser, F. E.
  1903   Der Prophet Habakuk. *MVAG* 8:1–38.
Petersen, David L.
  1977   *Late Israelite Prophecy. Studies in Deuteroprophetic Literature and
          in Chronicles.* SBLMS 23. Missoula, Mont.: Scholars Press.
  1981   *The Roles of Israel's Prophets.* JSOTSup 17. Sheffield: University
          of Sheffield.
Petersen, David L., and Kent Harold Richards
  1992   *Interpreting Hebrew Poetry.* Minneapolis: Fortress Press.
Pfeiffer, Robert H.
  1924   The Polemic against Idolatry in the Old Testament. *JBL*
          43:229–40.
  1952   *Introduction to the Old Testament.* London: Black.
Podella, Thomas
  1993   Der "Chaoskampfmythos" im Alten Testament. Eine Proble-
          manzeige. Pp. 283–329 in *Mesopotamica-Ugaritica-Biblica:
          Festschrift für Kurt Bergerhof zur Vollendung seines 70. Lebens-*

jahres am 7. Mai 1992. Manfred Dietrich and Oswalt Loretz, eds. AOAT 232. Kevalaer: Butzon & Bercker.

Pope, Marvin H.
1955 *El in the Ugaritic Texts.* VTSup 2. Leiden: Brill.

Porath, Renatus
1993 Profetas, Interlocutores Indispensàveis Neste "Fim da História:" Um Diàlogo com o Profeta Habacuque. *EstTeo* 33:26–36.

Prinsloo, W. S.
1979 Die boodskap van die book Habakuk. *NGTT* 20:146–51.

Propp, William H.
1987 The Skin of Moses' Face—Transfigured or Disfigured? *CBQ* 49:375–76.
1988 Did Moses Have Horns? *BibRev* 4:30–37.

Rabin, C., ed.
1961 *Studies in the Bible.* ScrHier 8. Jerusalem: Hebrew University Press.

Rad, G. von
1967 *Die Botschaft der Propheten.* Munich: Siebenstern-Tachenbuch.

Rast, Walter E.
1983 Habakkuk and Justification by Faith. *Currents in Theology and Mission* 10:169–75.

Reiner, Erica
1960 Plague Amulets and House Blessings. *JNES* 19:148–55.
1965 Dead of Night. Pp 247–52 in *Studies in Honor of Benno Landsberger on His Seventy-Fifth Birthday.*

Reiterer, F. V.
1976 *Gerechtigkeit als Heil.* "ṣdq" bei Deuterojesaja. Aussage und Vergleich mit der alttestamentlichen Tradition. Graz: Akademische Druck and Verlangsanstalt.

Renz, Johannes & Wolfgang Röllig
1995 *Handbuch der althebräischen Epigraphik.* Darmstadt: Wissenschaftliche Buchgesellschaft.

Richter, Georg
1914 Erläterungen zu dunkeln Stellen in den kleinen Propheten. *BFCT* 18:275–473.

Ringgren, Helmer
1981 Yahvé et Rahab-Léviatan. Pp 387–93 in *Mélanges bibliques et orientaux en l'honneur de M. Mathias Delcor.* André Caquot, S. Légasse, and M. Tardieu, eds. AOAT 215. Kevelaer: Butzon and Berker. [Neukirchen: Neukirchener Verlag, 1985]

Roberts, J. J. M.
1972 *The Earliest Semitic Pantheon.* Baltimore: Johns Hopkins University Press.

Robertson, David A.
1972 *Linguistic Evidence in Dating Early Hebrew Poetry.* Missoula, Mont.: Society of Biblical Literature.

Robertson, O. Palmer
    1983   " 'The Justified (by Faith) Shall live by His Steadfast Trust'—Habakkuk 2:4." *Presbyterion* 9:52–71.

Robinson, Theodore H.
    1921   "The Ecstatic Element in Old Testament Prophecy." *The Expositor* 8th series 21:217–38.

Roche, Michael de
    1980   Zephaniah I 2–3: the "Sweeping" of Creation. *VT* 30:104–09.
    1983   Yahweh's *rîb* against Israel: A Reassessment of the So-Called "Prophetic Lawsuit" in the Pre-exilic Prophets. *JBL* 102:563–74.

Roth, W. M. W.
    1975   For Life, He Appeals to Death (Wis 13:18): A Study of Old Testament Idol Parodies. *CBQ* 37:21–47.

Rothstein, J. J. Wilhelm
    1894   Über Habakkuk Kap.I u. II. *TSK* 67:51–85.

Roussel, Bernard
    1982   La 'Bible d'Olivétan' [mieux de Neuchatel 1535]: la traduction du livre du prophète Habaquq. *ÉTR* 57:537–57.

Rowley, H. H., ed.
    1950   *Studies in Old Testament Prophecy: Presented to Professor Theodore H. Robinson.* Edinburgh: Clark.
    1951   *The Old Testament and Modern Study: A Generation of Discovery and Research: Essays by Members of the Society for Old Testament Study.* Oxford: Clarendon Press.

Ruiz, Gregorio
    1984   El clamor de las piedras (Lk 19:40; Hab 2:11): el Reino choca con la ciudad injusta en la fiesta de Ramos. *EstEcl* 59:297–312.

Saggs, H. W. F.
    1978   *The Encounter with the Divine in Mesopotamia and Israel.* London: Athlone Press.

Sahlin, Harald
    1951   Tva messianska profetiori det fordolda. *STK* 27:272–75.

Sanders, H. A., and C. Schmidt
    1927   *The Minor Prophets in the Freer Collection and the Berlin Fragment of Genesis.* New York: Macmillan.

Sanders, James A.
    1959   Habakkuk in Qumran, Paul, and the Old Testament. *JR* 39:232–44.
    1993   Habakkuk in Qumran, Paul, and the Old Testament. Pp. 98–117 in *Paul and the Scriptures of Israel.* Craig A. Evans and James A. Sanders, eds. JSOTSS 83. Sheffield: JSOT. [A "slightly revised" version of Sanders, 1959]

Sasson, Jack M.
    1968   Bovine Symbolism in the Exodus Narrative. *VT* 18:380–87.

Satran, David
  1995   *Biblical Prophets in Byzantine Palestine: Reassessing the Lives of the Prophets.* SVTP 11. Leiden: Brill.
Schmidt, Hans
  1949–1950   Ein Psalm in Buche Habakuk. ZAW 62:52–63.
Schnutenhaus, Frank
  1964   Das Kommen und Erscheinen Gottes im Alten Testament. ZAW 76:1–22.
Schreiden, Jacques
  1955–1957   Le regne d'Hyrcan II et les allusions historiques du Commentaire d'Habacuc. A propos de la thèse récente de M. Dupont-Sommer. *La Nouvelle Clio* 7–9:247–60.
Schreiner, Stefan
  1974   Erwägungen zum Text von Hab 2,4–5. ZAW 86:538–42.
Scott, James M.
  1985   A New Approach to Habakkuk II 4–5a. *VT* 35:330–40.
Segert, Stanislav
  1953   Zur Habakkuk-Rolle aus dem Funde vom Toten Meer I *ArOr* 21:218–39.
  1954   Zur Habakkuk-Rolle aus dem Funde vom Toten Meer II *ArOr* 22:99–113.
  1954   Zur Habakkuk-Rolle aus dem Funde vom Toten Meer III *ArOr* 22:444–59.
  1955   Zur Habakkuk-Rolle aus dem Funde vom Toten Meer IV *ArOr* 23:178–83.
  1955   Zur Habakkuk-Rolle aus dem Funde vom Toten Meer V *ArOr* 23:364–73.
  1955   Zur Habakkuk-Rolle aus dem Funde vom Toten Meer VI *ArOr* 23:575–619.
Selms, A. van
  1982   Job 31:38–40 in Ugaritic Light. *Semitics* 8:30–42.
Seux, Marie-Joseph
  1976   *Hymnes et prières aux dieux de Babylonie et d'Assyrie: Introduction, traduction, et notes.* LAPO 8. Paris: Cerf.
  1981   Šiggayôn = šigû. Pp. 419–38 in *Mélanges bibliques et orientaux en l'honneur de M. Henri Cazelles.* André Caquot and M. Delcor, eds. AOAT 212. Neukirchen: Neukirchener Verlag.
Siebsma, P. A.
  1991   *The Function of the Niph'al in Biblical Hebrew in Relationship to Other Passive-Reflexive Verbal Stems and to the Pu'al and Hoph'al in Particular.* SSN 28. Assen: Van Gorcum.
Simian-Yofre, Horacio
  1980   Exodus en Deuteroisaias. *Bib* 61:530–53.
  1981   La teodicea del Deuteroisaias. *Bib* 62:55–72.

Sinker, Robert
1890   *The Psalm of Habakkuk.* Cambridge: Deighton Bell.
Sjöberg, Erik
1952   The Restoration of Col II of the Habakkuk Commentary of the Dead Sea Scrolls. *STL* 4:120–28.
Smith, John Merlin Powis
1920–1921   Some Textual Suggestions: ii. Hab 2:17. *AJSL* 37:239.
Smith, Mark S.
1991   *The Origins and Development of the Waw-Consecutive: Northwest Semitic Evidence from Ugarit to Qumran.* HSS 39. Atlanta: Scholars Press.
Smitten, W. Th. in der
1977   Habakuk 2,4 als prophetische Definition des Gerechten. *BBB* 50: 291–300.
Snyder, G.
1975   Sayings on the Delay of the End. *BR* 20:19–35.
Soden, Wolfram von
1992   Der Genuswechsel bei *rûaḥ* und das grammatische Geschlecht in den semitischen Sprachen. *ZAH* 5:57–63.
Sollamo, Raija, ed.
1992   *Roullen meren kirjakääröt. Qumranin tekstit suomeski.* Helsinki: Yliopistopiano.
Sorg, Rembert
1969   *Habaqquq III and Selah.* Fifield, Wis.: King of Martyrs Priory.
Southwell, P. J. M.
1968   A Note on Habakkuk 2:4. *JTS*, n.s., 19:614–17.
Speiser, E. A.
1960   "People" and "Nation" of Israel." *JBL* 79:157–63. [Pp. 160–70 in Speiser, 1967]
1967   *Oriental and Biblical Studies: Collected Writings of E. A. Speiser.* Ed. and Intro. J .J. Finkelstein and Moshe Greenberg. Philadelphia: University of Pennsylvania Press.
Sperber, Alexander
1962   *The Bible in Aramaic.* Vol. 3. Leiden: Brill.
1966   *A Historical Grammar of Biblical Hebrew: A Presentation of Problems with Suggestions to Their Solutions.* Leiden: Brill.
Sprenger, Hans Norbert
1977   *Theodori Mopsuesteni Commentarius in XII Prophetas: Göttinger Orientforschungen veroffentlichen des sonderforschungsbereiches Orientalistik an der Georg-August-Universität Göttingen 5. Reihe: Biblica et Patristica. Band I1.* Weisbaden: Harrassowitz.
Stade, Bernhard
1884   Miscellen: 3. Habakuk. *ZAW* 4:154–59.
1895   Beiträge zur Pentateuchkritik. *ZAW* 15:157–78.

Staerk, W.
    1933   Zu Habakuk 1,5–11, Geschichte oder Mythos? ZAW 51:1–28.
Stager, Lawrence E.
    1996   The Fury of Babylon: Ashkelon and the Archaeology of Destruc-
            tion. BARev 22:56–69, 76–77.
Starkova, C. B.
    1998   Понятие тайа в кумранских текстах. Палестинский Сборник
            98:9–13.
Stenzel, Meinrad
    1952a   Habacuc 2,1–4,5a. Bib 33:506–10.
    1952b   Zum Vulgatatext des Canticum Habacuc. Pp. 25–33 in Colligere
            Fragmenta: Festschrift Alban Dold zum 70. Geburtstag am 7. 7. 52.
            B. Fischer and V. Fjala, eds. Beuron: Beuroner Kunstverlag.
    1953   Habakkuk II 15–16. VT 3:97–99.
Stephens, Ferris. J.
    1924   The Babylonian Dragon Myth in Habakkuk 3. JBL 43:290–93.
Streck, M.
    1916   Assurbanipal und die letzen assyrischen Konige bis zum untergange
            Niniveh's. Vorderasiatische Bibliothek. Leipzig: Hinrichs.
Strobel, August
    1961   Untersuchungen zum eschatologischen Verzogerungsproblem;
            auf Grund der spätjudisch-urchristlichen Geschichte von Habakuk
            2,2ff. NovTSup 2. Leiden: Brill.
Sweeney, M. A.
    1991   Structure, Genre and Intent in the Book of Habakkuk. VT 41:63–83.
Talmon, Shemaryahu
    1951a   Yom Hakkippurim in the Habakkuk Scroll. Bib 32:549–63. [Pp.
            186–99 in Talmon 1989]
    1951b   Notes on the Habakkuk Scroll. VT 1:33–37. [Pp. 142–46 in Tal-
            mon, 1989]
    1989   The World of Qumran from Within: Collected Studies. Jerusalem:
            Magnes Press.
Tantlevski, Igor R.
    1995   The Two Wicked Priests in the Qumran Commentary of Habakkuk.
            Cracow: Enigma.
Taylor, Joan E.
    1995   The Asherah, the Menorah and the Sacred Tree. JSOT 66:29–54.
Teixeira Sayao, Luiz Alberto
    1993   Habacuque e o problema do mal. Vox Scripturae 3:3–18.
Thackeray, H. St. John
    1911   Primitive Lectionary Notes in the Psalm of Habakkuk. JTS
            12:191–213.
    1923   The Septuagint and Jewish Worship: A Study in Origins. Pp. 47–55
            in The Schweich Lectures 1920. 2nd ed. London: Oxford Univer-
            sity Press.

Thompson, Michael E. W.
1993   Prayer, Oracle and Theophany: The Book of Habakkuk. *TynBul* 44:33–53.

Thorion-Vardi, Talia
1986   MWR' in Pešer Habaquq VI, 5. *RevQ* 12:282.

Torczyner, H.
1947   A Hebrew Incantation against Night-demons from Biblical Times. *JNES* 6:18–29.

Torrey, C. C.
1925   Alexander the Great in the Old Testament Prophecies. BZAW 41:281–86.

1935   The Prophecy of Habakkuk. Pp. 565–82 in *Jewish Studies in Memory of George A. Kohut*. S. W. Baron and A. Marx, eds. New York: Alexander Kohut Memorial Foundation.

1936   The Foundry of the Second Temple at Jerusalem. *JBL* 55:247–60.

1942   The Evolution of a Financier in the Ancient Near East. *JNES* 2:295–301.

Trever, John C.
1972   *Scrolls from Qumrân Cave I: The Great Isaiah Scroll, The Order of the Community, The Pesher to Habakkuk.* intro. Frank Moore Cross. Jerusalem: Albright Institute.

Tromp, N. J.
1969   *Primitive Conceptions of Death and the Netherworld in the Old Testament.* Rome: Pontifical Biblical Institute.

Trudinger, Paul
1995   Two Ambiguities in Habakkuk's "Unambiguous" Oracle. *DRev* 113:282–83.

Tsumara, David Toshio
1982   Hab 2,2 in the Light of Akkadian Legal Practice. ZAW 94:294–95.

1985   An Exegetical Consideration on Hab 2:4a. *Tojo* 15:1–26.

1986   Niphal with an Internal Object in Habakkuk 3:9a. *JSS* 31:11–16.

1989b   Ugaritic Poetry and Habakkuk 3. *TynBul* 40:24–48.

1996   The "Word Pair" *qšt* and *mṭ* in Habakkuk 3:9 in the Light of Ugaritic and Akkadian. Pp. 353–61 in *Go to the Land I Will Show You: Studies in Honor of Dwight W. Young.* Joseph Coleson and Victor Matthews, eds. Winona Lake, Ind.: Eisenbrauns.

Tucker, Gene M.
1971   *Form Criticism of the Old Testament.* Philadelphia: Fortress.

1988   The Law in the Eighth-Century Prophets. Pp. 201–16 in Tucker, Peterson, and Wilson, 1988.

Tucker, Gene M., David L. Petersen, and Robert R. Wilson, eds.
1988   *Canon, Theology, and Old Testament Interpretation: Essays in Honor of B. S. Childs.* Philadelphia: Augsburg / Fortress Press.

Tuttle, Gary A.
1973   Wisdom and Habakkuk. *Studia Biblica et Theologica* 3:3–14.

Tuttle, G. A., ed.
  1978   *Biblical and Near Eastern Studies: Essays in Honor of William San-*
          ford LaSor. Grand Rapids, Mich.: Eerdmans.
Ulrich, Eugene
  1998   The Dead Sea Scolls and the Biblical Text. Pp. 79–100 in *The*
          Dead Sea Scrolls after Fifty Years: A Comprehensive Assessment. Pe-
          ter W. Flint and James C. VanderKam, eds. Vol. 1. Leiden: Brill.
Ulrich, Eugene, J. W. Wright, R. P. Carroll, and P. R. Davies, eds.
  1992   *Priests, Prophets and Scribes: Essays on the Formation and Heritage*
          of Second Temple Judaism in Honour of Joseph Blenkinsopp. JSOT
          Sup 149 Sheffield: JSOT Press.
Ungerer, W. J.
  1976   *Habakkuk: The Man with the Honest Questions.* Grand Rapids,
          Mich.: Baker.
Urbach, Ephraim E.
  1975   *The Sages: Their Concepts and Beliefs.* Trans. from the Hebrew by
          Israel Abrahams. Jerusalem: Magnes Press, Hebrew University.
Vanel, A.
  1965   *L'Iconographie du dieu de l'orage.* CahRB 3. Paris: Gabalda.
Vanhoozer, Kevin J.
  1998   *Is There a Meaning in this Text? The Bible, the Reader and the*
          Morality of Literary Knowledge. Leicester: Apollos.
Vaux, Roland de
  1969   Téman. Ville ou région d'Edom. *RB* 79:379–85.
Vegas Montaner, Luis
  1989–1990 Computer-Assisted Study on the Relation Between 1QpHab
          and the Ancient (Mainly Greek) Biblical Versions. *RevQ*
          14:307–23.
Volck, W.
  1896–1913 Habakuk. Pp. 278–80 in *Real-encyklopadie für protestantische*
          Theologie und Kirche 7. Johann Jacob Herzog, ed. Leipzig: Hin-
          richs.
Vollers, K.
  1883   Das Dodekapropheton der Alexandriner. ZAW 3:219–72.
  1884   Das Dodekapropheton der Alexandriner (Schluss). ZAW 4:1–20.
Vries, Simon J. de
  1978   *Prophet Against Prophet. The Role of the Micaiah Narrative (I Kings*
          22) in the Development of Early Prophetic Tradition. Grand Rapids,
          Mich.: Eerdmans.
Vriezen, Theodor Christian [*Fs.*]
  1966   *Studia Biblica et Semitica Theodoro Christiano Vriezen qui munere*
          Professoris Theologiae per XXV annos functus est, ab amicis, col-
          legis, disciplinis dedicata. Wageningen: Veenman Zonen.
Waard, J. de
  1966   *A Comparative Study of the Old Testament Text in the Dead Sea*

Scrolls and in the New Testament. STDJ. J. van der Ploeg, ed. Leiden: Brill.

1977   The Chiastic Structure of Amos V,1–17. *VT* 27:170–77.

Wakeman, M. K.

1969   The Biblical Earth Monster in the Cosmogonic Combat Myth. *Journal of Biblical Literature* 88:313–20.

1973   *God's Battle with the Monster: A Study in Biblical Imagery.* Leiden: Brill.

Wal, A. J. O. van der

1988a   *lō' nāmût* in Habakkuk 1:12: a suggestion. *VT* 38:480–82.

1988b   *Nahum, Habakkuk: A Classified Bibliography, with a special paragraph concerning literature on the Qumran Commentaries on Nahum and Habakkuk.* Applicatio 6. Amsterdam: Free University Press.

Waldman, Nahum M.

1976   A Comparative Note on Exodus 15:14–16. *JQR* 66:189–92.

1979   God's Ways—A Comparative Note. *JQR* 70:67–72.

Walker, H. H., and N. W. Lund

1934   The Literary Structure of the Book of Habakkuk. *JBL* 53:355–70.

Walsh, J. P. M.

1979   Exegetical Method in the Qumran Habakkuk "Pesher" Ph D. diss., Harvard University.

Waltke, Bruce K., and M. O'Connor

1990   *An Introduction to Biblical Hebrew Syntax.* Winona Lake, Ind.: Eisenbrauns.

Ward, Benedicta

1993   "In medium duorum animalium:" Bede and Jerome on the canticle of Habakkuk. Pp. 189–93 in *StPatr 25: Biblical et Apocrypha, orientalia, ascetica: Papers, 11th International Conference on Patristic Studies, Oxford, 1991.* Elizabeth A. Livingstone, ed. Louvain: Peeters.

Watson, Wilfred G. E.

1976a   Puzzling Passages in the Tale of Aqhat. *UF* 8:371–78.

1976b   The Pivot Patterns in Hebrew. *ZAW* 88:239–53.

1977   Reclustering Hebrew *'l yd-. Bib* 58:213–15.

1983   Further Examples of Semantic-Sonant Chiasmus. *CBQ* 45:31–34.

1984a   *Classical Hebrew Poetry: A Guide to its Techniques.* JSOTSup 26. Sheffield: JSOT Press.

1984b   Allusion, Irony and Wordplay in Micah 1:7. *Bib* 65:103–5.

1988a   More on Metathetic Parallelism. *WO* 19:40–44.

1988b   Some Additional Wordpairs. Pp. 179–201 in *Ascribe to the Lord: Biblical and Other Studies in Memory of Peter C. Craigie.* Lyle M. Eslinger and Glen Taylor, eds. Journal for the Study of the Old Testament Supplement 67. Sheffield: University of Sheffield Press.

1989a   Internal or Half-Line Parallelism in Classical Hebrew Again. *VT* 39:44–66.

1989b   The Unnoticed Word Pair "eye(s)" // "heart." *ZAW* 101:398–408.

1989c   Internal or Half-Line Parallelism Once More. *LASBF* 39:27–36.

1990   Abrupt Speech in Ugaritic Narrative Verse. *UF* 22:415–20.

1993   Problems and solutions in Hebrew verse: a survey of recent work. *VT* 43:372–84.

1994   *Traditional Techniques in Classical Hebrew Verse.* JSOTSup 170. Sheffield: University of Sheffield Press.

Weimar, Peter

1973   Formen frühjüdischer Literatur, eine Skizze. Pp. 123–62 in *Literatur und Religion des Frühjudentums.* Johann Maier and Josef Schreiner, eds. Würzburg: Echter.

Weiser, Artur

1961   *Introduction to the Old Testament.* London: Darton, Longman & Todd.

Welch, John W.

1981   *Chiasmus in Antiquity: Structures, Analysis, Exegesis.* Hildesheim: Gerstenberg.

Wellhausen, Julius

1893   *Skizzen und Vorarbeiten* 5. 2nd ed. Berlin: Reimer.

Westermann, Claus

1960   *Grundformen prophetischer Rede.* Munich: Kaiser.

1966   Jesaja 48 und die "Bezeugung gegen Israel." Pp. 356–66 in *Studia Biblica et Semitica Theodoro Christiano Vriezen qui munere Professoris Theologiae per XXV annos functus est, ab amicis, collegis, disciplinis dedicata.* Wageningen: Veenman & Zonen.

1967   *Basic Forms of Prophetic Speech.* Hugh C. White trs. Philadelphia: Westminster Press.

1986   Zur Erforschung und zum Verständnis der prophetischen Heilsworte. *ZAW* 98:1–13.

1989   Bedeutung und Funktion des Imperativ in den Geschichtsbüchern des Alten Testaments. Pp. 13–27 in *Der Weg zum Menschen. Für A. Deissler.* Rudolf Mosis and Lothar Ruppert, eds. Freiburg: Herder.

1991   *Prophetic Oracles of Salvaton in the Old Testament.* Keith Crim, trs. Louisville Ky.: Westminster / John Knox Press.

Wever, T.

1977   *Habakuk, dertien brieven aan een profeet.* VerkBG. Kampen: Kok.

Whitley, C. F.

1975–1976   A Note on Habakkuk 2,15. *JQR* 66:143–47.

Williams, Nolan, Jr.

1995   The Book of Habakkuk. Blessings Denied? Pp. 57–62 in *Many Voices: Multicultural Responses to the Minor Prophets.* Alice Ogden Bellis, ed. Lanham, Md.: University Press of America.

Williamson, H. G. M.

1977–78   The Translation of 1QpHab V, 10. *RevQ* 9:263–65.

Willis, John T.
1979 The Expression *bĕʾaḥărîth hayyāmîm* in the Old Testament. *ResQ* 22:54–71.
1979b The Juxtaposition of Synonymous and Chiastic Parallelism in Tricola in Old Testament Hebrew Psalm Poetry. *VT* 29:465–80.

Winton Thomas, David
1956 "The Use of נֶצַח as a Superlative in Hebrew." *Journal of Semitic Studies* 1:106–09.

Wolfe, Rolland E.
1935 The Editing of the Book of the Twelve. *ZAW* 53:90–129.

Woude, Adam S. van der
1966 Der Gerechte wird durch seine Treue Leben. Erwägungen zu Habakuk 2.4–5. Pp. 367–75 in *Studia Biblica et Semitica Theodoro Christiano Vriezen qui munere Professoris Theologiae per XXV annos functus est, ab amicis, collegis, disciplinis dedicata*. Wageningen: Veenman & Zonen.
1970 Habakuk 2,4. *ZAW* 82:281–82.
1978 *Habakuk, Zefanja*. Prediking O.T. Nijkerk: Callenbach.
1981 Bemerkungen zu einigen umstrittenen Stellen im Zwölfprophetenbuch. Pp. 483–99 in *Mélanges bibliques et orientaux en l'honneur de M. Henri Cazelles*. André Caquot and M. Delcor, eds. AOAT 212. Neukirchen: Neukirchener Verlag.
1982 Wicked Priest or Wicked Priests? Reflections on the Identification of the Wicked Priest in the Habakkuk Commentary. *JJS* 33:349–59.

Wright, David P., David Noel Freedman, and Avi Hurvitz, eds.
1995 *Pomegranates and Golden Bells. Studies in Biblical, Jewish, and Near Eastern Ritual, Law, and Literature in Honor of Jacob Milgrom*. Winona Lake, Ind.: Eisenbrauns.

Yadin, Yigael
1963 *The Art of Warfare in Biblical Lands*. 2 vols. New York: McGraw-Hill.

Zalcman, Lawrence
1979 Di sera, Desert, Dessert. *ExpT* 91:311.

Zemek, George J.
1980 Interpretive Challenges Relating to Habakkuk 2:4b. *GTJ* 1:43–69.

Zevit, Ziony, Seymour Gitin, and Michael Sokoloff, eds.
1995 *Solving Riddles and Untying Knots. Biblical, Epigraphic, and Semitic Studies in Honor of Jonas C. Greenfield*. Winona Lake, Ind.: Eisenbrauns.

Ziegler, J.
1943 *Septuaginta: Vetus Testamentum Graecum vol. XIII, Duodecim prophetae*. Göttingen: Vandenhoeck & Ruprecht.
1952a Konjektur oder überlieferte Lesart? Zu Hab 2,5 κατοινωμένος / κατοιομένος. *Bib* 33:366–70.
1952b Ochus und Esel en der Krippe. Bibilschpatristische Erwagungen zu Is 1,3 und Hab 3,2 (LXX). *MTZ* 3:385–402.

Zimmerli, Walter
    1979   Vom Prophetenwort zum Prophetenbuch. *TLZ* 104:481–96.
Zorell, Fr.
    1927   Canticum Habacuc. *VD* 5:234–37.
Zuurmond, R.
    1985   De rechtvaardige zal door geloof leven. Habakuk 2:4 bij Joden en
            Christen voor het jaar 135. *Amsterdamse Cahiers voor exegese en
            Bijbelse theologie* 6:162–73.
Zwickel, W.
    1987   Zu Habakuk 1,15f. *BN* 38–39:72–74.

NOTES AND COMMENTS

◆

I. TITLE (1:1)

◆

1:1   The burden that Habakkuk the Prophet saw.

INTRODUCTION

The titles of the various prophetic books have been studied in detail in connection with Hos 1:1. (Andersen and Freedman 1980:143–45).

NOTES

1. *burden.* This name for a revealed oracular message is derived from the verb *nāśā'*, "to lift up (in order to carry)." This verb commonly describes the transport of a load of merchandise by a pack animal (Exod 23:5; 2 Kgs 5:17; 8:9; Jer 17:21–27; etc.). The verb lends itself to rich figurative use. The fullest discussion is by Freedman in *TDOT* (X:24–40). In prophetic writings *maśśā'* becomes a technical expression for the message brought by the prophet (Isa 14:28). Such an oracle is called "the LORD's burden" (belonging to him) in the phrase *maśśā' yhwh* to match *dĕbar-yhwh*. The former is a rare variant, found only in Jeremiah (23:33, 34, 36, 38). The composite phrase *maśśā' dĕbar-yhwh* is found in Zechariah (9:1; 12:1) and Malachi (1:1). Prov 30:1 refers to the words of Agur as the "burden" that he uttered as a teacher.

The message (or the book) is not called the prophet's "burden" (carried by him). Here it is qualified only as the burden "that Habakkuk the prophet saw"(cf. Isa 13:1). Otherwise, *maśśā'* may be qualified by the name of a country that is the object of a hostile prophecy, but not necessarily the direct recipient of the message. Phrases like "the burden of Babylon" and "the burden of Egypt," are characteristic of Isaiah's oracles against the nations (Isa 15:1; 17:1; 19:1; 21:1, 11, 13; 22:1; 23:1) (Barton 1980; Erlandsson 1970; Hamborg 1981).

The designation of an utterance as a *maśśā'* could derive from the idiom *nāśā' qôl*, "lift up the voice (in speech)." In this association, *maśśā'* can refer to utterances of various kinds, delivered by people in different roles. With this connotation, the meaning of *maśśā'* overlaps that of *māšāl*. The idiom *nāśā' māšāl* occurs in Hab 2:6 and eleven more times in the Hebrew Bible, notably in connection with the activity of Balaam, the prototypical visionary (Num 23:7, 18; 24:3, 15, 20, 21, 23). In Isa 14:4, *maśśā'* refers to a taunt prophecy against the king of Babylon, much in the vein of Hab 2:6–20, and in Mic 2:4 it has similar intimations of impending disaster. In Job 27:1 and 29:1, the usage is neutral;

it is a conventional introduction to a (poetic) speech with no implications about the character and purpose of the discourse.

The title of the book of Habakkuk describes the *maśśā'* as something seen in a vision, rather than heard. It should be remembered, however, that the prophetic vision was an experience in which the prophet typically saw the LORD in the divine assembly (1 Kgs 22:19; Isaiah 6; Jer 1:11; Ezekiel 1; etc.) and so was able to hear what the LORD said. The report of the LORD's proclamation is then the burden to be carried by the prophet to the people from his meeting with Yahweh. Even so, the message could be conveyed in the form of a physical object actually carried. In the present case, the prophet is told to write down the vision onto the tablets (2:2). This instruction was intended to provide a permanent record, in case there was a delay in its fulfillment (2:3, cf. Isa 8:16). This provision also enabled the person delivering the message to run with it and to read it out when he reached his destination (2:2b; there are other explanations of this curious expression [see the NOTE]). If this eventual proclamation is precisely the "woe oracles" in Hab 2:6b–20, then that composition is the actual "burden" received, the message to be proclaimed. Such a denotation would match Isaiah's use of *maśśā'* as a title for his oracles against the enemy nations, which are in a similar vein to Habakkuk's "woe oracles."

The title *maśśā'*, "oracle" (RSV), while more appropriate for the "woe oracles" in Hab 2:6b–20, serves as the name of the whole book. At the same time, the "woe oracles" are identified as the main matter of the prophecy. The remainder of the book supplies the context and circumstances from which this "burden" emerges. It is the outcome of a visionary encounter between Habakkuk and Yahweh. If the "vision" comprehends this experience in its entirety, it would include all the dialogue in Hab 1:2–2:6a, which seems to concern the prophet himself more personally, as well as the special material for public proclamation. The main content of Habakkuk 3 is a theophany that could equally well be called a vision, whether in the prophet's ecstasy (the normal meaning of *ḥāzôn*) or as seen in the mind's eye of an Israelite who knew his nation's traditions. The theophany in Habakkuk 3 is a variant of the historic theophany of the Exodus.

On the relation Habakkuk 3 to other biblical theophanies, see Akao (1990), Barr (1960), Glueck (1936), Hunter (1989), Jeremias (1965), Morgenstern (1911), Niehaus (1995), Ohmann (1989), and Thompson (1993).

Habakkuk describes what he saw and repeats what he heard. His combination of seeing and hearing is expressed in the phrase "to see what he will say" (2:1). Seeing and hearing are combined in the psychology of perception. We read body language, and we listen to speech. In common idiom, while "I hear you" recently had some vogue, when we understand what someone *says* we say "I see."

Habakkuk. Nothing is known about this person except what might be inferred from his book. The meaning of his name is not known, and there is no wordplay in the book to suggest that it has symbolic significance. Sane scholarship has now reached a point where nothing new, at least nothing useful, can be said about the word *Habakkuk.* There is nothing to be gained from groping after the "meaning" of a person's name in its etymon. It is fatuous to spin from such thin material explanations of the personal character, temperament, or professional style of any biblical prophet. There might be some grounds for this kind of commentary when the circumstance of giving a name (at birth, for instance) or replacing a previous name (to commemorate an event) or augmenting it with a sobriquet is reported as part of the biography (T. D. Andersen 1986a). No such clues are available in the case of Habakkuk.

Not only is the word unique, the form is unparalleled in Hebrew. There is a root *ḥbq*. The verb, in both *Qal* (2 Kgs 4:16; Qo 3:5; 4:5) and *Pi'el* (ten times) means "enfold," "clasp," "embrace." In the three instances in Genesis (29:13; 33:4; 48:10) the verb refers to the greeting of male kin in a kissing embrace. These affectionate gestures (or at least "kindly," in the old sense) are the basis of Jerome's suggestion that the name commemorates a like embrace between the prophet and God (*PL* 25: col. 1273; Rudolph 1975:199). Similarly fanciful is Davidson's (1905:45) proposal to gloss the name as "darling or delight." The cognate noun occurs only in the phrase *ḥibbuq yādayim*, "folding the hands" in sleep or sloth (cf. Prov 6:10; 24:33. There is a LXX manuscript [𝔊⁶¹³] that glosses *Abbakoum* with *ho patēr anestē*, "the father stood up," as if from Aramaic (but why indicative rather than imperative?). A curiosity, that's all. There is a full discussion of such speculations in Vartholomey (1913:15–19).

It is possible in Semitic languages to make an artificial word by duplicating the final consonant of a root or even the last two, but the vocalization of Habakkuk does not follow the pattern of alleged analogies: *na'ăṣûṣ*, "thornbush"; *ša'ărûr*, "horrible"; *na'ăpûpîm*, "adulterers" (Noth 1928:231). The peculiar doubling of the first *q* could be the outcome of assimilation in a form made by doubling the second and third consonants of the root to yield **ḥăbaqbûq*. The only Biblical Hebrew noun with this form is *'ăsapsûp*, "mixed multitude" (Num 11:4), but there is no analogy to the back assimilation of *b* to *q*. The Akkadian word *ḥambaqûqu* resembles *ḥăbaqqûq* to some extent. There is, however, no Hebrew word with similar syllable structure. Akk. *ḥambaqûqu* is the name of a plant of some kind, perhaps a tree (*CAD* 6:13). It is also attested as a personal name in Mesopotamia; but it does not seem to be a Semitic word, and it throws no light on the use of such a word as the name of an Israelite.

The LXX *Ambakoum* resembles that Akkadian word a little more closely, both pointing to *Ḥabbaquq*. If based on the Akkadian *ḥambaqûqu*, the Hebrew must have rearranged the syllable structure, even though the Hebrew language has no words of the same shape to provide a model. Furthermore, one must hypothesize that this restructuring took place within Hebrew after the bridge form had yielded the Greek. The Akkadian *ḥambaqûqu* as a source for the Greek, whether directly or indirectly, could account for the difference between the Greek form and the Hebrew form in syllable shape; but if Hebrew **Ḥabbaquq* is the bridge, the Greek has recovered -*mb*- by dissimilation, coincidentally restoring a feature of the supposed Akkadian original! The rendition of the final *q* as Greek *m* is puzzling, however. Helbing, as reported by Vartholomey (1913:17), drew attention to the similar puzzle of Beelzeboub for Beelzebul, with assonance between the ending consonant and one in the word. Neither of these adjustments is forced on the pronunciation by inner-Greek phonetic constraints, such as the evocation of two *m*'s through consonant harmony.

The Hebrew–Akkadian equation was first pointed out by Friedrich Delitzsch (1883:24). Peiser (1903) made curious use of this fact. He supposed that Habakkuk found himself a hostage in Assyria in 625 B.C.E., and studied cuneiform texts in the famous library of Ashurbanipal. Peiser found many traces of this influence in the prophecy and concluded: "All these quotations and allusions now show that the author was acquainted with Assyrian literature" (10). In particular, the language of Hab 2:2 ("inscribe it upon the tablets") "permits the conclusion that he had studied this literature in its distinctive script" (10; see also Jeremias 1916:642). In spite of this bizarre theory, Peiser's paper has some interesting comments on the poetic features of the book of Habakkuk compared with Assyrian.

Commentators have inferred from the liturgical setting of the final prayer that Habakkuk was a priest-prophet like Jeremiah and Ezekiel. There is a tradition that the stories of Bel and the Dragon were taken from "the prophecy of Ambakoum, son of Jesus, of the tribe of Levi" found in Origen's texts (for details, see AB 44:132). Habakkuk comes into the Daniel tradition because, while Daniel was in the den of lions, Habakkuk was transported from Judea by an angel, along with a luncheon of bread and stew that the prophet had prepared for the reapers in the field. After he had given the food to Daniel, the prophet was taken back to Judea (Add Dan 14:33–39 [NAB]: separate book in NEB, REB, NRSV). This and the other legends that grew up around Habakkuk's name are of no historical value. The hagiographical treatment of the life of Habakkuk in *The Lives of the Prophets* is in OTP (2:393–94). The *Zohar* (I:7b; II:44a), on the basis of the expression *'attî hōbeqet bēn*, "you will embrace a son" (2 Kgs 4:16), but with no sense of history, identified the Shunammite of the Elisha story as Habakkuk's mother. The unique reference (*Qal*) is to a mother enfolding a child (the first embrace of the newborn?). Other legends about Habakkuk are reviewed by Vartholomey (1913:24–30).

the prophet. The same designation is used in Hab 3:1. Whereas Theodotian introduces Habakkuk to the Daniel cycle as "Habakkuk the prophet" (*Bel and the Dragon* v 33), with the story following *Susanna* without a break, in LXX the story has been given a title: "From the prophecy of Ambakoum, son of Jesus, of the tribe of Levi." The grounds for this larger name have never been ascertained, and this datum can hardly be used for inferences about Habakkuk's status as a cult prophet.

The abundant use of the construction "PN* the prophet" (at least ninety times in the Hebrew Bible) serves to identify the person and takes the place of the customary patronymic. It is standard for such notables as Gad, Nathan, Elijah, Elisha, and Jeremiah ("Jeremiah the prophet" is used abundantly from chapter 20

---

*PN = proper noun.

onwards in the book of Jeremiah); but not Ezekiel, whose name, curiously, occurs only twice in his book. The fuller "PN *ben*-PN the prophet" is, however, found sometimes—Jehu (1 Kgs 16:12), Jonah (2 Kgs 14:25), and Isaiah. The title also indicates the role in which Habakkuk produced his book.

It is surprising, at least to us, that no further personal details are given about Habakkuk. This is disappointing to modern readers, brought up on literary theory or biblical hermeneutics that look for the significance of texts and for aids to their interpretation in the biography and psychology of biblical authors. For this enterprise, the book of Habakkuk supplies nothing whatever. Speculations about Habakkuk's personality are reviewed by Vartholomey (1913:19–24), with negative results.

saw. The verb and the cognate noun *ḥāzôn* have definite connotations of a visionary perception, such as would come to a prophet in a state of ecstasy. It would seem that such an experience often took the form of participation in the divine assembly. In this context, the more everyday verb *rā'â* can also be used for prophetic seeing; but *ḥāzâ* is not often used for normal physical seeing. In early times, the title "seer" was *rō'eh*, and 1 Sam 9:9 notes that this term was later supplanted by *nābî'*. Now Habakkuk is called the "prophet," not the "seer" (whether *ḥōzeh* or *rō'eh*). The verb *ḥāzâ*, however, along with "burden," highlights the visionary aspects of his prophetic experience. (For a fuller discussion of the connotations of *ḥāzâ*, see the NOTE on Mic 1:1 [Andersen and Freedman 2000:119–25].) The influence of such an experience on the eventual literary presentation of the prophecy that comes out of the experience is discussed in Andersen (1995).

COMMENT

There are two main opinions about the title to the book. Some scholars find it appropriate for Habakkuk 1–2, Habakkuk 3 not being part of the prophecy. Others (Rudolph 1975:199) accept it as a title for the whole book, giving weight to the term "vision" in Hab 2:2–3 and the visionary features of Habakkuk 3.

Habakkuk is called "the prophet." The use of the definite article could suggest that at any one time, only one person was chosen by Yahweh to function as "the prophet." Compare the use of "the priest," meaning "the chief priest" (1 Kings 1), and the usual meaning of "the king." While "the prophet" identifies a person's status and role (Petersen 1981), there were plenty of occasions when there was more than one in action. The early communities of "the sons of the prophets" did not last long. The massed choruses of prophets found in Ahab's entourage were bureaucrats and timeservers. By contrast, the classical prophets of Yahweh were solitary figures, and even when more than one was around at the same time, they did not operate in concert. No two prophets ever worked conjointly, except for Haggai and Zechariah. Elisha was Elijah's servant, not his associate, as long as he was only his anointed successor. Micah and (First) Isaiah were contemporaries, and there is much general similarity between their prophecies; yet neither refers to the other. Habakkuk was probably a contemporary of Jeremiah, along with Nahum, Zephaniah, Obadiah, and Ezekiel. Yet only Jeremiah names other prophets operating at the same time—Uriah (Jer 26:20–21) and Hananiah (Jereremiah 28).

The use of a term such as "ministry" to describe the activity of biblical prophets carries too much association with latter-day clerics to be of any use. As fashions in prophecy studies have changed with the intellectual climate of the past two centuries, so the prophets have been characterized as theologians, moralists, cult officials, mystics, social activists. The first modern scholarly book on the theology of the prophets was published 125 years ago (Duhm 1875). Even so, in spite of the use of the word "theology," the prophets were not seen as teachers of doctrine, but rather as moralists whose great breakthrough was the recognition of "ethical monotheism" and of the worth of the individual, in contrast to the formal, ritualized, communal religion of the cult. This naturally led to interest in the "personality" of each prophet, often with psychological analysis or with claims for their "religious genius." The last full-scale study along these lines was James (1947).

In reaction against the one-sided characterization of the prophets as critics outside and against institutionalized religion, evidence in the prophetic writings of an affirming attitude to the cult suggested to some scholars that an Israelite prophet could be an officer of a shrine, available to worshipers who wished to inquire of the LORD. The presence of a considerable amount of oracular material in the Psalter pointed in this direction, first appreciated by Gunkel (Bellinger 1984; Johnson 1962, 1979). As a counterpoise to this mixture, hymnic materials were no longer considered out of place in the prophetic writings; rather, they showed that the prophet could be at home in the Temple. Mowinckel, in particular, devoted the third volume of his *Psalmenstudien* (*Kultprophetie und Prophetische Psalmen* [1922]) to this theme. He saw the book of Habakkuk as "another not-so-common corroboration of the link between prophets and temple singers and psalm composers" (27). For Mowinckel, the hymnic motifs and the forms of lament, prayer, assurance, and divine response were not sufficiently explained as the outcome of the influence of cult motifs on Habakkuk's prophetic composition; they indicated that Habakkuk 1 and 2 was a "Prayer-day Liturgy" composed by a prophet. The evidence of Habakkuk 3 is even more compelling: "And this Psalm was employed in the cultus and indeed was even composed for cultic use" (27). Mowinckel (1951) subsequently identified Habakkuk as a Temple prophet (316) and psalm composer (356), along with Nahum ("among temple prophets in Jerusalem both *Nahum* and *Habakkuk* composed hymns" [405]).

In the same year Eissfeldt (1951:159) reviewed "The Prophetic Literature" and objected that "the new point of view has taken much too much upon itself, in regarding all the prophets without exception as cult prophets, and explaining as many as possible of their sayings and acts accordingly" (159). There is no evidence that there was a school for the training of prophets attached to the Temple in Jerusalem, as claimed by Jeremias (1970:139). In spite of counterarguments, the belief that a writing prophet might be a cult official has held on.

Supporting evidence is found in four features of the book of Habakkuk: (1) the liturgical character of the prayers and oracles in Habakkuk 1; (2) the appropriateness of a cult setting for the "prayer" in Habakkuk 3; (3) the convulsions described in Hab 3:16 —the incidents of the prophet-Levite Jahaziel (2 Chr 20:14) and Zechariah (2 Chr 24:20) are often quoted in this connection—whether they are routine dramatics (antics) intended to impress and convince the audience (Jeremias 1970:107) or whether Habakkuk was grabbed by the Spirit on the occasion of a cult festival and in connection with the prayer liturgy of Habakkuk 1 (Eaton 1964:168); and (4) the "lookout point" (2:1) from which Habakkuk awaited a response from God is a place in the Temple allocated to this purpose (Humbert 1944:280; Jeremias 1970:104).

The history of research on the question of Habakkuk's possible involvement in cultic ceremonial, along with the correlative issue of the identification of the book of Habakkuk as some kind of temple liturgy, has been fully reviewed by Jöcken (1976, 1977). Rudolph (1975:194) rejected the theory that Habakkuk was a cult prophet as having no basis at all. None of the points is compelling.

1. While many personal and private prayers in the narrative portions of the Hebrew Bible are in prose, some are more formal, and doubtless benefit from liturgical models. But that does not prove that all such prayers could be said only in a cult ceremony, let alone by cult officials only. While prophets could meet God through the cultus like anybody else (Isaiah 6), they could also talk to God anywhere. There is much in the content of Habakkuk's prayers that is more personal than set forms. There is a spontaneity about them that suggests the sincerity of a profound emotional disturbance, with impromptu expression. Furthermore, in the absence of narrative framework for the claimed procedure for securing an oracle and in the absence of rubrics for the oracle in Hab 1:5–11, there is nothing "priestly" in the reply. And what, then, is Habakkuk's role—the suppliant speaking vv 2–4 or the consultant speaking vv 5–11? Unlike the replies given to Hezekiah by Isaiah or to Josiah by Huldah (these are personal, addressed to the king in his capacity as head of state), the plural verbs in v 5 imply a public audience.

2. The cultic character of Habakkuk 3 can be freely recognized; but, as part of the national epic heritage, the use of that ancient poem would not be confined to cultic settings, and its literary use in the book of Habakkuk is clearly derivative.

3. As for the syndrome of Hab 3:16, the conventional literary features in its publication do not impeach its authenticity. The "watchtower" of Hab 2:1 is part of a metaphorical description of the role of the prophet as sentinel, and its use in other places makes it almost a cliché. There is no evidence of such an architectural feature in the Temple to support a literal reading, putting Habakkuk in that location.

The role of the Israelite prophet as "messenger" of Yahweh as royal deity goes a long way toward explaining much of the language and behavior of the genuine prophets. This identification yielded insight into some of the formulaic speech forms used by prophets. Here Westermann's (1967) study has had a lasting influence. This emphasis came to a climax in von Rad's *Die Botschaft der Propheten* (1968:18), in which he said: "Prophecy ultimately employed the 'messenger formula' as the most direct means of expressing its function."

One could argue with equal cogency that the use by prophets of the language of litigation and of the forms of disputation (there is some of this in Habakkuk, too) shows that a prophet was a juridical official, functioning in the law courts.

A better explanation of the presence of forensic imagery in the speeches of the prophets, whether in prayers of reproach directed against God or in accusations leveled against the people, was offered by scholars, notably Muilenburg (1966, 1968), who argued that some of the most outstanding prophets stood in succession as covenant mediators in the line and style of Moses. The visionary element in the attested experiences of some prophets and the mythopoeic imagery in many of their messages can be understood as going with this role, which was nurtured by the established traditions of Israel's origins.

Unlike other prophets, Habakkuk does not use conventional formulas like "Thus said the LORD" to introduce his oracles. But he stands squarely in the main tradition all the same. His visionary experience, which allowed dialogue with God himself, is comparable to those of a long succession beginning with Moses, if not Abraham. His remonstrations with the LORD, his disputatious questions, have a mediatory, intercessory character resembling those in Genesis 19, Exodus 32–34, Amos 7–8, Isaiah 6, and Jeremiah 15–18 (Hertzberg 1963). The narrative details are not supplied in the book of Habakkuk, as in those other instances, and the trappings of the divine assembly are not in open evidence. The language of Hab 2:1a strongly suggests this setting, however. With *'e'ĕmōdâ* compare 1 Kgs 22:19 and Isa 6:2; with *'etyaṣṣĕbâ* compare Job 1:6; 2:1. In the light of more ample "prophetic call narratives," the "holy temple" of Hab 2:20 could be where the theophany takes place (Isa 6:1; Ps 29:9) and where all present cry "Glory" (Ps 29:9) or "Holy" (Isa 6:3). "Glory" occurs once in Hab 2:20, while the threefold "Glory" of Ps 29:1–3 matches the Trishagion of Isa 6:3. Both Psalm 29 and Isa 6:4 feature the voice of Yahweh, "the voice that calls out [*haqqōrē'*]" in Isa 6:4, "the voice of the LORD" in Isa 6:8. Note the same succession of *qōrē'* in Isa 40:3 and *qôl 'ōmēr* of Isa 40:6. Compare *qōrē'* in Amos 7:4. The theophany of Isaiah 40 also has affinities with that in Habakkuk 3. In the divine assembly, Isaiah both sees and hears the LORD (Isaiah 6) (Cross 1953). The autobiographical "I said" (Isa 6:5) recurs in Isa 40:6. There is a consistent picture of the prophet as present in the divine assembly, while the deliberations take place and decisions are made. The LORD raises such questions as what to do and whom to send (1 Kgs 22:20; Isa 6:8). In the assembly described in 1 Kings 22, Mikayhu seems to be only a silent observer. The discussion takes place within the ranks of "the whole retinue of heaven" (v 19). "One said this and another said that" (v 20). Amos, however, intervenes successfully and persuades the LORD to alter his plans (Amos 7). A similar intercession is represented by Isaiah's question "How long O LORD?" (Isa 6:11). Habakkuk's almost identical question (Hab 1:2) points to a similar circumstance. The dialogue takes place in the divine assembly to which the prophet has been admitted by his prophetic "call."

Isaiah 6 records another important development. From the assembly in 1 Kings 22, the LORD dispatches as his agent "the Spirit." The definite noun *hārûaḥ* indicates a distinct personage, a member of the assembly, male gender. He goes out to be "a lying spirit in the mouth of all the prophets" (v 22). In Isaiah 6, it is the prophet who offers his services in exactly the same way: "Here am I, send me" (v 8). The LORD's agent and messenger is now a man, not a celestial spirit.

Habakkuk's status in the divine assembly is similar to Isaiah's. He sees, hears, and takes part. Compare Jer 23:18 with the verbs "stand," "see," and "hear," the same as in Hab 2:1; 3:2, 16. Then, when a decision has been reached, and declared as a divine decree, it is recorded "on the tablets" and the messenger runs to proclaim it (2:2).

This analysis also leads to an explanation of the definite and plural form of *hallûḥôt* in Hab 2:2. These are the heavenly tablets of destiny of which Mesopotamian myths speak so often. (The discussion in Saggs [1978:64–91], however, cautions restraint in making this kind of comparison.) They may be compared with the "tablets" on which the Ten Commandments were written. Once more, there has been an encounter between God and the prophet as a result of which the divine decrees are brought to the people and proclaimed. From Moses' tradition, we can trace a similar transference of the heavenly functions to a man. The first set of tablets was written by God himself (Exod 31:18; 32:15–16), and so was the second (Exod 34:1). God says to Moses "I will write the words on the tablets." He says to Habakkuk, "You write it on the tablets" (2:2)—*ktb. . .ʿal-hallûḥôt* in both places.

In the later apocalypses, this motif is remythologized, and once more it is a heavenly messenger (an eagle) who brings the heavenly scroll and reads from it the "Woes" (Rev 8:13).

Having said all this, it should be admitted that this comparative evidence for the prophet's role is only partial. It points to cult official, royal messenger, and court advocate, but in each instance the arguments are tenuous, and the analogies are weak. Gordon (1995:15) asks, perhaps tongue in cheek, whether composing a dirge makes a prophet "a professional wailer." Reviewing prophecy studies in the mid-twentieth century, Fohrer (1967) came to quite negative conclusions about the usability of form-critical arguments to reach conclusions about the place and function of the prophet in Israelite society. Fohrer's points are well taken in that classification of oracles through a mechanical application of the forms of speech that prophets were supposed to have used as templates for their messages was frustrated by a failure of the extant texts to match the reconstituted models. The method discredited itself when it had to resort to heroic rewriting of the oracles to make them better fit the models, with departures from "pure" forms blamed on inept redactors or scribes. But to rubbish form criticism just because it overreached itself in its youthful enthusiasm would be a great loss to prophecy studies. The affinities of prophetic oracles with numerous identifiable forms cannot be gainsaid. And, as Westermann (1967) and others have insisted, it is precisely the recognizability of the chosen form by people in the community who know how it is supposed to work that enables the prophet to communicate with them. At the same time, the prophets were eclectic, versatile, and creative, even to the point of perversity, like all original poets. According to McKane (1979:168–69), "There is, perhaps, something ultimately unsatisfactory in the reduction of prophetic speech to stereotypes and in the denial that it has anything of the momentous character of a new creation. Even if it is necessarily an amalgam of traditional linguistic resources, it has elements of freedom and eclecticism to which a thoroughgoing form criticism does not do justice."

The frequent exhibition by prophetic oracles of elements that seem to belong to different forms (a blatant instance, not infrequent, is the co-occurrence of a message of doom and a message of salvation in the same speech) is not the only difficulty confronting an interpreter of a prophetic text. On a larger scale, similar inconsistencies (contradictions to our logical minds) are found among the constituents of a whole book. The book of Habakkuk is no exception. Both features — mixed forms and logical contradictions — call for a fresh understanding of prophetic texts as compositions, rhetorical and artistic, in which the total effect of a pericope or of the whole book requires acceptance of the unresolved tension between the opposing parts. Reducing such disturbing literature to something that is simple and clear trivializes the "message," imagining that the prophet (to say nothing about the God who sent him) can be pinned down to some easily comprehended point of view.

There are as many differences as similarities among the prophets of Israel. They affect multiple roles, just as they exploit the manifold resources of the speech forms current in their culture. There is a common tradition in which they all stand. To be sure, all biblical prophets delivered messages from God, and some of them wrote books that might have some autobiographical material (or had books written about them that preserved some of their oracles). Yet the "occasional" character of their messages, and each prophet's unique historical circumstances and individual personality prohibit all but the most bland generalizations. The book of Habakkuk itself tells us nothing about the man, his times, and his "experience" apart from what might be inferred (all too tentatively) by reading between the lines.

The best inference from this seemingly inconsistent evidence is that prophets were protean operators, able to interact with all of the community's institutions, without belonging to any of them, certainly without needing legitimation by them. All too often, the prophet combined acceptance and affirmation along with criticism and rejection, threats of destruction (nothing was immune) along with hopes and promises of restoration.

II. Habakkuk's First Prayer (1:2–4)

◆

1:2 How long (will it be), Yahweh?
      I have called out (for help);
         and thou didst not listen.
      I protested to thee (because of) lawlessness.
         and thou didst not rescue.
3 Why didst thou make me see iniquity,
      and look at wretchedness,
         and the devastation and lawlessness that are before me?
      And there was disputation,
         and contention rose up.
4 Is that why the Torah has become paralyzed,
      and justice never came forth?
         In fact the wicked restricted the righteous!
      Is that why the verdict came out twisted?

Scansion of Habakkuk's First Prayer (1:2–4)

		BEATS	SYLLABLES	SYLLABLES
2aA	*ʿad-ʾānâ yhwh šiwwāʿtî*	3	8	
2aB	*wĕlōʾ tišmāʿ*	2	4	
2bA	*ʾezʿaq ʾēleykā ḥāmās*	3	6	
2bB	*wĕlōʾ tôšîaʿ*	2	4	41
3aA	*lāmmâ tarʾēnî ʾāwen*	3	6	
3aB	*wĕʿāmāl tabbîṭ*	2	5	
3bA	*wĕšōd wĕḥāmās lĕnegdî*	3	8	
3bBα	*wayĕhî rîb*	2	4	
3bBβ	*ûmādôn yiśśāʾ*	2	5	
4aA	*ʿal-kēn tāpûg tôrâ*	3	6	41
4aB	*wĕlōʾ-yēṣēʾ lāneṣaḥ mišpāṭ*	4	8	
4bA	*kî rāšāʿ maktîr ʾet-haṣṣaddîq*	4	9	
4bB	*ʿal-kēn yēṣēʾ mišpāṭ mĕʿuqqāl*	4	9	

INTRODUCTION

The Language of Hebrew Poetry

The prophet's first prayer (vv 2–4) consists of thirteen clauses, each of which can be taken as a unit (a colon) in a poetic composition. The poetic intention of the author is evident in several features. First, the language is that of Hebrew poetry insofar as the so-called "prose particles" (definite article, *nota accusativi*, and "relative" pronoun) are sparsely used. In forty-one orthographic words there are only two prose particles: *'et* and *ha-* (both in the same construction) in v 4bA. The raw percentage (5%) is only a crude index of this poetic property, but the low score is within the range characteristic of most poetry in the Hebrew Bible (Andersen and Forbes 1983; Freedman 1987b).

Of more significance is the nonuse of such items when there was an opportunity to use them, when normal prose syntax required them. There are twelve nouns in the poem, and it is likely that some of them are definite in their reference. Yet only one has the definite article.

It is possible that the definiteness of some of these nouns, grammatically unmarked for definiteness, should have been indicated by means of a possessive pronoun; yet not one of them was marked in this way. Comparison with the usage of possessive pronouns in other languages can help to clarify this point. In English it would be ungrammatical to say "I raise hand." It would be acceptable to say "I raise a hand," or "I raise the hand," or "I raise my hand." In a language such as Latin, which has no articles, the definiteness or indefiniteness of a noun is usually indicated by cohesive devices in the text surrounds. By default it is understood, even in English, that if I raise a hand it is most likely my own. In fact, in a language such as Russian, it would be "incorrect" to say "I raise my hand"; simply "I raise hand" is "correct" (Russian has no definite article). If a possessive pronoun were used, it would secure contrast—"I am reading *my* book" (that is, not someone else's).

In other words, in sentences of these kinds, when an object, clearly definite, has no indicator of definiteness, the default reading is that the defining element is co-referential with the subject. So in Hebrew *nāśā'tî qôl*, literally "I-lifted-up voice," means "I lifted up *my* voice." One could hardly lift up someone else's voice. Speiser (AB 1:51) has further pointed out the inverse usage: "[T]he possessive pronoun of Hebrew often corresponds to our definite article." In v 4 the words *tôrâ* and *mišpāṭ* are not general in reference (indefinite in grammatical state). The prophet is concerned about a concrete situation that demands a special and particular response from God, an oracle appropriate for the occasion, a verdict on the issue that Habakkuk is arguing. Translations recognize this, supposing that *tôrâ* means "the law" in some sense. Similarly, the *mišpāṭ* that has not gone out is "the verdict," "thy verdict," or "my verdict"—all of them meaning "thy decision in my case." 1QpHab already has *hmšpṭ* in v 4a.

There is a methodological moral in these observations. When reading Hebrew poetry or poetic prophecy, one must deliberately search for the implicit signals from the context that a noun, formally indefinite, might have a definite reference.

Double-duty Items

The sparse use of prose particles and pronoun suffixes is not the only or even the main indicator of poetic language. Poetic composition is lean and laconic. Other items besides prose particles and pronoun suffixes, required for complete grammatical expressions, may be missing. It is often possible to supply what is missing from one position because the functional item is already in place nearby—the item is supplied once but operates twice. This principle of "double duty" has been increasingly recognized in recent Hebrew poetry studies, but it is usually invoked only as a means of getting out of a tight corner and as a last resort. It would be better to expect the device of double-duty items to be used almost routinely in poetry. We need a new sensitivity to Hebrew poetic art. Often the use of various kinds of ellipsis has not been appreciated either because literal-mindedness has forced some kind of interpretation onto the surface features of the text (and then that reading becomes canonized in the scholarly tradition) or because the text is deemed to be corrupt since it is evidently ungrammatical (there is something missing) and attempts are made to repair the damage by emendations following the rules of grammar worked out for Hebrew prose.

Such corrective rewriting of the text has been a main preoccupation of critical scholars in modern textual studies of Hebrew poetry, but the drift had already begun in antiquity. One illustration should be enough at this stage in the discussion. Ps 47:7 contains a nice instance of the retroactive use of a double-duty preposition. We adduce this example because the scope of the double-duty function, to say nothing of making it work backwards, is scarcely recognized in current scholarship:

zammĕrû	*'ĕlōhîm*	*zammĕrû*	Sing [to] God, sing!
zammĕrû	*lĕmalkēnû*	*zammĕrû*	Sing to our king, sing!

The first colon is routinely translated "Sing praises to God, sing praises!" There are even Hebrew manuscripts that read *l 'lhym* (BHS). This adjustment is so obvious that commentators do not trouble to report the implied emendation. Long before the theory of parallelism legitimated such adjustments, the Greek translators leveled, not only the preposition, but also the pronoun suffix:

psalate tō theō hēmōn, psalate	Sing to our God, sing!
psalate tō basilei hēmōn, psalate	Sing to our king, sing!

According to BHS, there is even one Hebrew manuscript that reads *l 'lhynw*. It does not follow, however, that this reading was already present in the *Vorlage* of LXX; the analogical leveling could have taken place independently in the two lines of transmission. A few scholars, trying to account for the Masoretic Text as it is, identify *'ĕlōhîm* as vocative (Gaster 1950:421; Dahood AB 16:283). Too literalistic! The obvious reading is "correct," but the text does not have to be changed.

In calling for restraint on emendations intended to make Hebrew poetry more like prose, and recommending that the text as it is might yield up its secrets to more patient attention to poetic practices, we are not going to the other extreme and claiming that the text is immaculate. Here and there, it is almost certainly blemished by mistakes made in copying. Indeed, the very obscurity of poetry makes it vulnerable to copyists' errors, as the faulty recitation of many well-known poems continually betrays. The oral performance of Longfellow's *"The Day is Done"* often ends:

Shall fold up their tents like the Arab,	< Shall fold their tents, like the Arabs,
And silently steal away.	< And as silently steal away.

Three mistakes, mainly the outcome of turning Longfellow's "irregular" rhythms into a jingle!

Idiomatic expressions and clichés are self-perpetuating, and it is the business of poets to fracture them. Thus the idiom behind v 3bA is "I engaged in litigation," "I had a lawsuit," literally "And it was to me a *rîb*" (*wayĕhî lî rîb*). The usual *lî* is missing from Hab 1:3. There is no way now of telling who left *ly* out—the original author or a scribe (haplography through homoeoteleuton of *wyhy ly*). The literal translation "and there is strife" is mistaken. It is too general; it loses the technical reference of *rîb* and it loses the intensely personal content of the outburst.

There are some transitive verbs whose objects have to be understood. Comparing v 2aB with Jonah 2:3b shows that "my voice" is the implied object of "thou didst heed" (*tišmā ʿ*). The matching verb *tôšîa ʿ* in v 2bB likewise requires an object, possibly "me." Even if the verb was deliberately left vague ("thou has not saved [anyone]"), some kind of object has to be understood.

The syntax of Hebrew poetry is likely to be parsimonious in the use of prepositions. The verb *z ʿq*, "cry out," is usually intransitive; Hos 8:2 is a rare exception where what is uttered is the object of the verb:

*lî yizʿāqû * ʾĕlōhê yĕda ʿānûkā yiśrāʾēl*

They cried out to me, "We know you, God of Israel"

We recognize "God of . . . Israel" as a discontinuous construct phrase.

Hab 1:2bA would be the only other instance of transitive *z ʿq* in the Hebrew Bible. Exod 2:23 is more typical, and its vocabulary uses the same roots as Hab 1:2: "And the children of Israel groaned because of [*min-*] their slave-work, and they protested [*z ʿq* (no modifiers)], and their outcry [*šw ʿ*] went up to God because of their slave-work." If the construction of Hab 1:2aA is similar, but laconic, *ḥāmās*, "lawlessness," is not the word uttered (Haak 1991:30); it is the cause of Habakkuk's outcry. The preposition *min*, which usually marks this adverbial function, is simply not used here. (Such use of a noun alone with an adverbial function has been recognized by grammarians as "adverbial accusative"

[Waltke and O'Connor 1990:169–77]; but the terminology of "case" is not appropriate for Hebrew.)

If *ḥāmās* has an adverbial rather than an accusative role, then the string of nouns of which *ḥāmās* is the first have similar roles in the ongoing discourse. Habakkuk expected Yahweh to see and hear him in his plight, a righteous man encompassed by the wicked (v 4bA), by *ḥāmās, ʾāwen, ʿāmāl, šōd, ḥāmās,* all of which confronted the prophet (*lěnegdî*). These nouns describe a concrete situation, and Habakkuk expected God to look at him "(in my) *ʿāmāl*," not just to "look upon trouble" (RSV).

Another device that contributes to the sparse use of small vocabulary items is the continued operation of some item without repetition—the so-called "double-duty" item. A simple and obvious instance is in v 3a, where the pronoun suffix "me" serves as a common object for the two parallel verbs, so that *tabbîṭ* means "thou dost look at [me]." Recognition of *-ēnî* as the object of both verbs

3aA   *lāmmâ tarʾēnî ʾāwen*
3aB   *wěʿāmāl tabbîṭ*

entails confirmation also that *ʿāmāl,* as already discussed, is one of a set of nouns with similar functions in successive clauses. Similarly, the opening interrogative *ʿad-ʾānâ,* "How long . . . ?" applies to *ʾezʿaq ʾēleykā ḥāmās* as well as to *šiwwāʿtî.* The interrogation, in fact, continues through the whole poem. It is reactivated by *lāmmâ* in v 3, and this interrogative blankets the rest of the speech. So v 4aB means "And [why] has (my) judgment never come forth?"

Negation can likewise continue to operate in successive clauses without the repetition of *lōʾ.* After the repeated use of this particle in v 2, its absence from v 3 seems to imply that Yahweh doesn't listen or rescue, but that, on the contrary, he makes Habakkuk see the misery, while he looks at the wretchedness, devastation, and lawlessness that are before the prophet. Our translation follows the Masoretic Text exactly, but there is dissonance between the two *Hipʿil* verbs in v 3a. The first is causative (the prophet sees iniquity); the second is not causative (there is no attested *Qal* of this root) (Yahweh looks at wretchedness).

If, however, the negation continues from v 2 to v 3, Habakkuk is reproaching God for not listening and not looking—for not noticing the iniquity, the wretchedness and all the other bad things listed in v 3. Ps 94:9 affirms that God does both listen and look, using the same verbs as Hab 1:2–3.

hǎnōṭaʿ ʾōzen	Did he plant the ear?
hǎlōʾ yišmāʿ	Will he not listen?
ʾim-yōṣēr ʿayin	Did he mold the eye?
hǎlōʾ yabbîṭ	Will he not look?

Habakkuk 1 can be brought into line with Psalm 94 and the apparent discrepancy between Hab 1:2 and Hab 1:3 (Yahweh is watching, but not listening) can be resolved once it is realized that the negation of the two matching verbs in v 2 (*tišmaʿ* // *tôšiaʿ*) continues for the two matching verbs in v 3—Yahweh didn't listen and he didn't even look, or so it seemed to Habakkuk. Furthermore, the prophet's distress is caused by Yahweh's unresponsiveness to *his* plight. He wants God to look at him and listen to him. This reading requires a small adjustment to the verb *tarʾēnî* (> *tirʾēnî*) so that it is synonymous with its parallel *tabbîṭ*, with -*nî* as its only direct object, and *ʾāwen* as adverbial.

Four double-duty influences thus feed into *wĕʿāmāl tabbîṭ* (v 3aB): (1) interrogation, (2) negation, (3) adverbial function for *ʿāmāl* in line with *ḥāmās* and *ʾāwen*, (4) the pronoun object from *tirʾēnî*. When all these elliptical elements are made explicit, the clause means "And [why] hast thou [not] looked [at me] [in] [my] trouble?"

This is an extreme instance, and the argument might seem strained. A reader unfamiliar with the conventions of Biblical Hebrew poetry and the practices of Hebrew poets might not sense the cumulative effect of filling out such a brief clause (two words only!) with four double-duty items from the preceding context. These four double-duty items have been introduced one by one in the preceding text: (1) interrogation in v 2aA (reactivated in v 3 by *lāmmâ*); (2) negation twice in v 2 (to be understood in v 3); (3) the adverbial noun *ḥāmās* (v 2bA), which controls the grammar of the string of similar nouns that follow; and (4) the object "me" in v 3aA. The effect is paradoxical, because the thematic continuity of the composition is secured by grammatical cohesion between one clause and the next mainly through the flow-on of double-duty items. It is easy for the reader to miss the artistry. The result is very dense and formally ambiguous. And, because of the high level of formal ambiguity, it is not possible to prove one disambiguation against another. We recognize a certain amount of obscurity, even incoherence, in this highly emotional outburst, but we opt all the same for an underlying unity in the accumulated statement as a whole.

Such a holistic literary approach to the reading of the text permits v 3aB to be tied into the preceding discourse. It is not an independent statement: "Destruction and lawlessness are before me" (RSV). Verse 3aB is not parallel to v 3b (BHS), which is actually the first clause in the second part of the speech. Habakkuk is complaining about all the wrongs that he has experienced and that God hasn't noticed. To preserve the cohesion of the list of nouns that itemize these wrongs, *šōd wĕḥāmās* has to be coordinated with *ʾāwen . . . wĕʿāmāl*, all governed by the same two parallel verbs: "[Why haven't you noticed] the destruction and lawlessness [that] confront me?" In other words, v 3aB is a phrase, not a clause, and the relative pronoun that would be normal in prose is simply not used in poetry.

The Use of the Verb Forms in Poetry

In addition to the sparse use of "prose particles," and the use of double-duty items, Hebrew poetry often shows a preference for archaic usage of verb forms. The biggest difference between ancestral Hebrew and the standard language of the classical (monarchical) period is the splitting of the meaning of *yiqṭōl* forms into "imperfect" (mainly future tense) and preterite (in the specialized

Tenses that render the Hebrew verbs in Hab 1:2 in selected
English translations

	NRSV	REB	NAB	NJB	NIV	NJPS
2aA *šiwwā'tî*	fut.	noun	pres.	pres.	pres.	fut.
2aB *tišmā'*	fut.	fut.	pres.	fut.	pres.	(fut.)*
2bA *'ez'aq*	fut.	pres.	pres.	pres.	pres.	fut.
2bB *tôšîa'*	fut.	pres.	pres.	fut.	pres.	(fut.)*

*Implied.

wayyiqṭōl). (The literature on this matter is so vast that we refer to only Isaksson [1987], outstanding for its treatment of the coexistence of diachronic and synchronic factors and for the superiority of its use of modern linguistic theory.) When the poetic use of *yiqṭōl* with its archaic past-tense meaning is misread as the prose use with future meaning, what was intended to be a story of past events is wrongly read as a prediction of coming events. If the verb usage in a text is a mix of the archaic preterite *yiqṭōl* with the classical "perfect" (*qāṭal*), the outcome can be very confusing. If the presence of *yiqṭōl* is accepted as evidence of prediction, the co-occurrence of *qāṭal* has been explained as "prophetic perfect," describing predicted events as though they had already occurred. All too often, however, the seeming clash of future *yiqṭōl* and past *qāṭal* is resolved by translating all the verbs with a neutral and pallid present tense. Thus Haak (1991), like many others, translates the only perfect verb form (*šiwwā'tî*) as future and all the imperfect verbs as present! The versions are every which way as shown in the table below. We have yet to come across a commentary that even notices this problem, let alone discusses it in order to justify the choice of English tenses to translate these Hebrew verbs. None of them opts for the salient past-tense meaning. In Hab 1:2–4 the occurrence of an opening *qāṭal* form (*šiwwā'tî*) and a later *wayyiqṭōl* (*wayĕhî*) anchors the discourse in past-time reference and coerces the *yiqṭōl* forms into the same tense. Thus *šiwwā'tî* has as its parallel *'ez'aq*; yet the first is commonly translated future tense ("shall I cry out" [NJPS]), or present; the second as present or future tense, along with the other *yiqṭōl* forms in the quatrain ("you do not hear . . . I call . . . you do not deliver" [Haak 1991:23]). Throughout this commentary, we shall be especially alert to this problem.

Chiasmus

Hebrew poetry often arranges similar or matching items in chiastic patterns (Breck 1994; Ceresko 1975, 1976, 1978; de Waard 1977; Di Marco 1975, 1978; Fredericks 1989; Lichtenstein 1982; Lund 1942; Welch 1981; Willis 1979b). This device has often been waved aside as merely stylistic, and James Barr (1995:10, n. 10) has recently said that chiasmus is "a practice which seems to me not to betoken a profound degree of skill." In other words, anyone could write poetry as good as Milton's. What has not been sufficiently noticed in the use of chiasmus is the way in which it secures thematic connections and even

grammatical relations between chiastically placed items (Andersen 1974). Hab
1:2 is a tetracolon in which alternate colons are parallel:

2aA   *ʿad-ʾānâ yhwh šiwwāʿtî*
2aB   *wĕlōʾ tišmāʿ*
2bA   *ʾezʿaq ʾēleykā ḥāmās*
2bB   *wĕlōʾ tôšîaʿ*

The matching verbs *šiwwāʿtî* // *ʾezʿaq* are placed chiastically, and the congruence of the unit requires that they have the same time reference, which we think
is past. The nouns and verbs are chiastic in v 3a, supporting our claim that the
pronoun object on the first verb does double duty on the second:

3aA   *lāmmâ tarʾēnî* [> *tirʾēnî*]   *ʾāwen*
3aB   *wĕ*   *ʿāmāl*   *tabbîṭ*

A similar pattern in v 3bB invites the recognition that the two verbs have the
same past-time reference:

3bBα   *wayĕhî*   *rîb*
3bBβ   *û*   *mādôn*   *yiśśāʾ*

In v 4, the modifiers *lāneṣaḥ* and *mĕʿuqqāl* are placed chiastically with the repeated idiom *yēṣēʾ mišpāṭ*, requiring an integrated reading of the unit:

4aB   *wĕlōʾ-yēṣēʾ*   *lāneṣaḥ*   *mišpāṭ*
                        . . .
4bB   *ʿal-kēn yēṣēʾ*   *mišpāṭ*   *mĕʿuqqāl*

The opportunity to set *tôrâ* and *mišpāṭ* in chiasmus in v 4a was not taken.
   So far, we have not mentioned directly the one thing that everybody knows
about Hebrew poetry—parallelism. The complex interweaving of themes and
verbal patterns and the dependence (sometimes at long range) of one colon on
one or more other colons because of double-duty items results in very few of the
contiguous clauses in Hab 1:2–4 fitting the simple parallelistic patterns of the
bicolon that are usually shown in textbooks on Hebrew poetry. As examples of
such extended linkage, we note that *ʾāwen* in v 3aA is parallel to the preceding
ḥāmās (v 2bB) and the following *ʿāmāl* (v 3aB); and that *mišpāṭ* in v 4aB is parallel to both the preceding *tôrâ* (v 4aA) and the repeated *mišpāṭ* in v 4bB.

Poetic Scansion

Finally, we note that the rhythms of Hab 1:2–4 do not have the regularity of
classical Hebrew verse, whether scanning by beats or measuring length by counting syllables. The thirteen colons we have recognized have 82 syllables—mean
6.3 syllables per colon—with a range of 4 to 9.

The fresh onset marked by the use of *wayĕhî* in v 3b divides the poem into two equal strophes: vv 2–3a (seven colons and 41 syllables) and vv 3b–4 (six colons and 41 syllables). In the first strophe, long (3-beat) and short (2-beat) colons alternate; the second strophe has one 2:2 bicolon followed by two 3:3 bicolons.

The arrangement of the colons is symmetrical:

Strophe 1   Tetracolon (v 2 — 3:2 3:2 — 22 syllables)
            Bicolon (v 3aA — 3:2 — 11 syllables)
            Colon (v 3aB — 3 — 8 syllables)
Strophe 2   Bicolon (v 3b — 2:2 — 9 syllables)
            Tetracolon (v 4 — 3:4 4:4 — 32 syllables)

A balance of a different kind can be seen in an introverted arrangement of four constituent units:

Strophe 1   Questions: Hexacolon (vv 2–3aA — 3:2 3:2 3:2 — 33 syllables)
            Colon (v 3aB — 3 — 8 syllables)
Strophe 2   Bicolon (v 3b — 2:2 — 9 syllables)
            Questions: Tetracolon (v 4 — 3:4 4:4 — 32 syllables)

Each strophe begins with an indubitably past-tense verb (*šiwwā'tî* [v 2aA] and *wayĕhî* [v 3bA]) and these openers take all the following *yiqṭōl* verb forms with them into past-tense reference. The balance between the strophes is enhanced by the fact that the major theme of each is expressed by four different nouns, one repeated to make five in all:

Strophe 1 — *ḥāmās, 'āwen, 'āmāl, šōd, ḥāmās*
Strophe 2 — *rîb, mādôn, tôrâ, mišpāṭ, mišpāṭ*

This structural and thematic symmetry does not match the quantitative symmetry of the two strophes; the central single colon belongs to the first strophe. The two strophes have quite different rhythmic patterns when each major stress is counted as a beat, accepting MT.

The structure of the first tetracolon is clear: parallel colons alternate. The structure of the last tetracolon is more complex. The first and fourth colons are linked by the repeated *'al-kēn*, while the first and second are linked by the match of *tôrâ* and *mišpāṭ*. The second and fourth colons are clearly parallel (with chiasmus). So these three colons are all tightly linked. The third colon *kî rāšā' maktîr 'et-haṣṣaddîq* (v 4bA) has no semantic parallels with the rest of the second srophe, but the reference to the "wicked" connects it with the violent crime that is the theme of the first strophe.

This discussion has attempted merely to describe the literary features of Habakkuk's first prayer. We cannot penetrate beyond a formal analysis of the text itself to enter the consciousness or the intent of the author in order to claim that he was deliberately applying certain rules to his craft. Contrary to the preoccupation of many textbooks with the bicolon as the characteristic (almost the only) unit in Hebrew poetic composition, this prayer of thirteen colons has only one stand-alone bicolon. The piece is unique in its structure; it cannot be certified as a model or canon. We are content to leave it at that, recognizing the achievement of spontaneity, originality, and creativity within the wide freedom of equally acceptable possibilities for composing Hebrew prophetic discourse.

The integrity of the entire unit need not be doubted, despite the combination of a variety of poetic features. The overall structure is harmonious; there is thematic continuity; the whole is dominated by a single experience and is pervaded by a consistent, albeit complex, emotion—a turbulent combination of faith and perplexity, of expectation and misgiving.

NOTES

2. *How long . . . ?* The phrase used here— *ʿad-ʾānâ*—appears to be synonymous with the more frequent *ʿad-mātay* (2:6). There is a difference between *ʾānâ* and *mātay*, however. While *mātay* without a preposition asks "When . . . ?" (always about a point in future time, with a *yiqṭōl* verb form [Gen 30:30; Amos 8:5; Pss 41:6; 42:3; 94:8; 101:2; 119:82, 84; Prov 6:9; 23:35; Job 7:4]), *ʾānâ* on its own means "Where . . . ?" Yet *ʿad-ʾānâ* is always temporal. The syntactic uses of *ʿad-ʾānâ* and *ʿad-mātay* are similar.

1. Either, followed by a *yiqṭōl* verb form (perhaps with a vocative before the verb [Prov 1:22; 6:9]), asks about the duration of a situation that already exists: "How much longer . . . ?" (with *ʿad-ʾānâ* [Num 14:11, 11; Pss 13:2–3 (4 times); 62:4; Job 18:2; 19:2], with *ʿad-mātay* [Exod 10:7; 1 Sam 1:14; Jer 4:14, 21; 12:4; 31:21; 47:5 (but note *ʿad-ʾānâ* in v 6); Ps 82:2]).

2. Instead of asking "When [*mātay*] will you do something?" one can use negation to ask "How much longer will you not do [*yiqṭōl* verb form] it?" (with *ʿad-mātay* [2 Sam 2:26; Hos 8:5; Zech 1:12], with *ʿad-ʾānâ* [Jer 47:6]).

3. When the clause is constructed with a second person pronoun and a participle (Josh 18:3 [*ʿad-ʾānâ*]; 1 Sam 16:1; 1 Kgs 18:21 [*ʿad-mātay*]), the focus seems to be on the present situation, and the purpose of the question is to disapprove and rebuke, not to seek information.

4. Rare and problematic is the use of these interrogatives followed by a suffixed verb (Exod 16:28; Hab 1:2 [*ʿad-ʾānâ*]; Exod 10:3; Ps 80:5 [*ʿad-mātay*]).

5. Sometimes the interrogative is the complete utterance (Isa 6:11; Hab 2:6; here in Hab 1:2 also, we think), and there are a few disjointed occurrences (Num 14:27; Jer 23:26). It is only in Neh 2:6, Dan 8:13, and Dan 12:6 that questions framed in this way receive an answer. The usage is predominantly rhetorical.

The distribution of these equivalents *ʿad-mātay* and *ʿad-ʾānâ* in the Hebrew Bible does not permit either to be associated with any particular period or regional dialect. Note their occurrence side by side in Jer 47:5–6.

The verb following the interrogative usually asks something about the activity of the person addressed, or inquiry is made about the conduct of a third party.

In Hab 1:2 the following verb refers to activity of the questioner himself. This is almost unique, although all three kinds of referent are combined in Ps 13:2–3.

עַד־אָנָה יְהוָה תִּשְׁכָּחֵנִי נֶצַח	How long, Yahweh, wilt thou utterly forget me?
עַד־אָנָה תַּסְתִּיר אֶת־פָּנֶיךָ מִמֶּנִּי׃	How long wilt thou hide thy face from me?
עַד־אָנָה אָשִׁית עֵצוֹת בְּנַפְשִׁי	How long must I put advices in my soul,
יָגוֹן בִּלְבָבִי יוֹמָם	misery in my heart all the day long?
עַד־אָנָה יָרוּם אֹיְבִי עָלָי׃	How long will my enemy be superior to me?

The parallelism of "in my soul" // "in my heart" keeps 'ēṣôt and yāgôn in line; but the dogma that poetic parallels should be synonyms has forced on the first word a meaning unsupported elsewhere: "pain" (RSV, NRSV), "anguish" (REB), "sorrow" (NAB) to match "grief." The Syriac apparently already felt the pressure to level the meaning. The proposal of Driver (1945–1946) to explain the problematic collocation of 'ēṣôt by linking it to an Arabic cognate meaning "rebel" lies behind NJB "rebellion" and is sponsored by *HAL* (821) as II * 'ēṣâ, with eight examples. The suggestion, however, remains dubious (*NIDOTTE* 3:485); even *HAL* expresses reservations about Ps 13:3. Casting off the spell of synonymous parallelism, the construction 'ēṣôt . . . yāgôn can be recognized as a discontinuous construct. The psalmist has reached the point where the only advice he can give himself is to grieve. This diversion to Psalm 13 has been valuable not only to demonstrate this less recognized kind of parallelism, in order to be on the lookout for it in other poems, but also to appreciate the flow of thought. The series of "How long . . . ?" questions does not follow the unfolding of the experience in time. It begins with a situation in which the wicked has got the better of the righteous (Hab 1:4bA = Ps 13:3b). The victim has cried out to God (1:2a), but the insufferable delay, indeed the lack of any indication that God has even seen or heard, leads to despair. The threat to faith is terrible; the temptation to give up—"What's the use?"—leads to even more profound questionings of the ways of God.

When there is a battery of questions, the interrogative particle can be repeated (Num 14:11; Ps 13:2–3). Ps 94:3 begins by using the interrogative 'ad-mātay twice in step parallelism, but the interrogation continues through v 6:

> How much longer the wicked, O Yahweh,
>> How much longer will the wicked exult?
> [How much longer] will they prate?
>> [How much longer] will they talk insolence?
> [How much longer] will the doers of iniquity talk to one another?
>> [How much longer] thy people, O Yahweh, will they crush?
> And [how much longer] thine heritage will they oppress?
> [How much longer] widow and alien will they slay?
>> And [how much longer] orphans will they murder?

Many translations make Ps 94:4–6 statements of fact (present tense). The use of one interrogative to blanket five questions in Ps 80:5–7 is of interest because the series begins with three past-tense verb forms, followed by two *yiqṭōl* forms, a development like that in Hab 1:2. The whole litany refers to the same situation, with emphasis on what has already happened in the past rather than on what might happen in the future. Dan 8:13 contains a threefold question; REB repeats "How long . . . ?" three times. Ps 74:10–11 resembles Hab 1:2–3 in having a double question, with one *'ad-mātay* followed by a pair of questions with one *lāmmâ* blanketing both. Applying this insight to Hab 1:2–3, we conclude that *'ad-'ānâ* blankets all four clauses in v 2, just as *lāmmâ* blankets both clauses in v 3. With *šiwwatî* in the lead, the focus is on what has already happened, not on how long it will continue in the future. It would be out of the question to translate the *yiqṭōl* verb forms as future: "I will call out . . . and you won't save. . . ." If the *yiqṭōl* verb forms were chosen to secure some aspectual nuance, it would be durative—"You haven't been listening!"

In the rhetoric of such prayers in the literature of the biblical world, the interrogative "How long . . . ?" can be repeated several times before the evil whose duration is intolerable is named. There is a prayer to Enlil that begins "Resplendent Lord! Take me by (my) hand!" This is followed by nine invocations, such as "Lord of all lands, how long?" through "Lord of Nippur, how long?" The question is completed in the eleventh line: "Lord, how long will a strong enemy have dominion over your country?" (Seux 1976:147–48). Similar use of suspense in Hab 1:2–4 could mean that the prophet is not asking how long he must keep on praying, but how long will the evils he deplores be allowed to continue with no response from God.

Questions asked with *'ad-mātay* or *'ad-'ānâ* are requests for information only in postexilic works (Nehemiah, Daniel); elsewhere they are always rhetorical and, moreover, accusatory. If there is a note of exhortation as well as rebuke, it is an attempt to get someone to desist from current reprehensible conduct. It is therefore natural that a human would chide another human in this way (Exod 10:7; Josh 18:3; 1 Sam 1:14; 2 Sam 2:26; 1 Kgs 18:21; Ps 62:4; Job 8:2; 18:2; 19:2). It is understandable that God would denounce a human with such language, directly (Exod 10:3; 16:28; Num 14:11a, 11b, 27; 1 Sam 16:1; Ps 85:2), or in an oracle (Jer 4:14; 23:26; 31:22; 47:5; Hos 8:5), or as Wisdom speaking to the fool (Prov 1:22; 6:9). What is startling is that a human would dare to talk to God like that, mostly in Psalms (6:4; 13:2a, 2b, 3a, 3b; 74:10; 80:5; 90:13; 94:3a, 3b), but prophets pray that way too (Isa 6:11; Jer 12:4; Hab 1:2). Compare the intercession of the angel in Zech 1:12 and the question to the Sword of Yahweh in Jer 47:6. Unique is Jer 4:21—God asks himself a question in this form, in deliberation.

Habakkuk's question thus has its closest analogy in liturgical prayers of complaint (Broyles 1989:95–99). Isaiah's question "How long?" is asked in dialogue in the Temple (perhaps in the divine council). This affinity does not, however, warrant the inference that these prophets, praying thus, were operating as officials in the formal cult. As the human-to-human instances show, such questions had ordinary functions too.

Hence it is likely that the focus of the question is on the inactivity of God: "How much longer will you refuse to listen to me, even though I have cried out for help?" Such questions always express vexation, even exasperation, over someone's persistent misconduct that has become intolerable, and that shows no sign of coming to an end. So here Habakkuk's question is not so much an expression of uncertainty about how long he has to keep on praying. The problem would then be his own lack of spiritual stamina, the prayer would be a plea for strength, and the appropriate response would be encouragement to be persistent. Rather, the focus is on the unresponsiveness of God. God is reproached, "impeached" (Driver 1913: §8). The prophet has prayed more than long enough, and it is already too late. The urgency of the call for swift action has given way to a deeper anxiety. A late response will no longer set matters right, for the question then requiring an answer is: Why did the response not come sooner? The timing of God's actions must make sense. The question "How long?" becomes "Why?" (v 3) (Barr 1985a).

In Hebrew, there is considerable semantic overlap among interrogatives, negatives, and exclamations. A common example is the use of a rhetorical question to make a positive assertion. In *hălō'*, "is not?" the interrogative and the negative cancel each other. The interrogative *mî*, can mean "nobody", the interrogative *mâ* can mean "how (very) much" in the superlative sense. So here "How long?" is an expostulation rather than an inquiry—"It has been altogether too long." As such, the opening words could be detached grammatically from what follows, as the phrase is used by itself in some Psalms (6:3, for example). This usage then accounts for the unusual suffixed verb—"I have called out"—unusual if it is part of the interrogative clause, but not so unusual if it stands apart as a narrative statement that describes what has happened. The prophet's prayer is thus a complaint, rather than an inquiry. But the question (or outburst) does not express disbelief about the justice of God. A person who has lost that faith does not pray any more. Hence George Adam Smith's (1899: chap. X) designation of Habakkuk as "sceptic" is quite inappropriate. The freedom with which the prophet has the matter out with God shows how deep is the bond between them. His agony is caused by the very strength of his theological convictions. There is no doubt that God has really heard Habakkuk's prayers. He is quite sure that God has seen everything that happened (v 3), and at the same time he is convinced that God's eyes are too pure to look at evil (Hab 1:13). It is unthinkable for him that God could find evil tolerable. Hence he cannot understand why God has done nothing, why he has delayed so long. By his insistence on an explanation, the prophet takes up the position that he has a right to know. While he recognizes that the response of God (both its timing and its manner) arises from the inscrutable mystery of his sovereign will, he is not deterred by any cant that "it is not for us to question the ways of the Almighty." By his prayers, he expects to be taken into the secrets of the divine council.

Yahweh. Although the whole book is called a "burden," meaning a prophetic message from God, it begins with a prayer. Like other preexilic prophets,

Habakkuk addresses God directly by his personal name. The invocation is abrupt. Honorifics and other formalities are not used (cf. Hab 3:2). Habakkuk's language lacks the courtesy of address to a superior that customarily contains a title defining the role in which the deity is being supplicated ("my God" or "my Lord"). Elsewhere in the Hebrew Bible, "(my) Rock" is used in the interests of parallelism, often associated with deliverance (*qeren-yiš'î* [2 Sam 22:3 = Ps 18:3]), while the triple name "Yahweh, my God, my Holy One" in Hab 1:12 adds intensity to the prayer. Habakkuk as suppliant does not delineate the social distance between lord and slave, as when the petitioner uses the self-designation "thy slave" to express humility or servility. Nor does the prayer have the buildup of honorifics (cf. Ps 62:7–8) that give dignity to formal prayers.

I have called out. The verb describes a cry for help. Habakkuk's choice of this verb could have been influenced by his preference for sibilants and laryngeals in combination—š-'...š-'...z'...ḥ-s...š-'—all in this verse. But the precise meaning of the verb also expressed Habakkuk's predicament. It is a cry for help. The verb is past tense, and common translations as future (KJV, ASV) have no justification. They have been influenced in part by the normal translation with "How long?" and in part by the prefixed verb *'ez'aq* in parallel. But the parallelism could just as well make the latter past tense, in line with *šiwwa'tî.*

We shall find throughout this prophecy that its verb usage is in line with archaic standards. Both suffixed and prefixed are past tense, except where future is absolutely required and indicated explicitly by the pragmatics of the text or by temporal adverbs with future-time reference. Certainly with first-person forms there is no confusion. For the future tense, the lengthened form, the so-called cohortative, is regularly used.

This verb ("I have called out" [√ *šw'*]) describes an appeal usually made to God. It is used mainly in psalms (twelve times, in Psalms, including Jonah 2, and Lamentations). Its poetic character accounts for the eight occurrences in Job. It occurs twice in Isaiah, and here. Its prominence in the Psalter does not mean that Habakkuk's prayer is cultic in the formal liturgical sense. Poetic diction is the common ground; the use of the verb in Job shows that it could have purely secular associations. Other verbs with similar connotations are √ *ṣ'q* , √ *z'q* , √ *qr'*.

The grounds of Habakkuk's appeal to Yahweh are not disclosed. The note of lamentation is struck only indirectly if the misery and suffering mentioned in v 3a are the prophet's own. There is no explicit appeal to God's compassion toward the pitiable, nor to his just anger toward the wicked, nor to his personal honor in keeping his promises. The language of v 4, however, suggests that Habakkuk expects God to be concerned for justice. Only later does he mention holiness and purity as relevant attributes (1:12, 13). Job 19:7 has a similar bicolon, with the verbs in reversed sequence:

hēn 'eṣ'aq ḥāmās	Behold! I protested because of lawlessness!
wělō' 'ē'āneh	but I was not answered;
'ăšawwa' wě'ēn mišpāṭ	I called for help, but there was no judgment.

This passage and Jeremiah 20:8 show that "lawlessness!" or "rapine!" is the reason why the oppressed person cries out in an appeal for help:

kî-middê ʾădabbēr	For whenever	I spoke
ʾezʿāq ḥāmās	(whenever)	I cried out (because of) lawlessness!
wāšōd ʾeqrāʾ	and (whenever)	(because of) devastation I called out.

The Masoretic punctuation of Jer 20:8 makes *ḥāmās wāšōd* one phrase, hendiadys, the sequence the reverse of that in Hab 1:3aB; but the display above recognizes the chiastic parallelism that gives each verb a noun adjunct. The three matching verbs have similar *grammatical* functions, obscured in the usual banal translation, such as "For, whenever I speak, I cry out, I shout, 'Lawlessness and destruction!' " (RSV). The whole of this tricolon is integrated by double-duty effects, and, as a whole, it is linked by the opening conjunction into a complex sentence with v 8b. More work needs to be done on these passages to show how the syntax, the prosody, and the rhetoric are integrated to achieve the total effect. The main benefits of the comparison for the elucidation of Hab 1:2 are the similarities among these pieces in the sparse use of prepositions to indicate the relation of nouns to verbs (not just the absence of *nota accusativi ʾet*) and in the poetic use of prefixed verb forms when telling the story of a spiritual experience. The old explanation that the future tense was used in reports of this kind to secure vivid visual presentation (Brockelmann 1956, § 42e) is not needed. The proverbial use of prefixed verb forms "to express facts known by experience, which occur at all times, and consequently hold good at any moment" (GKC § 107f), while appropriate for generalizations, takes away their highly personal and specific autobiographical reference when detected in prophets' confessions.

The experiences of "the law's delays" by Job, Jeremiah, and Habakkuk are essentially the same, no matter what the artistry of their expression. The generic nouns leave unspecified the exact nature of this "lawlessness." The cryptic language does not show who the victim is (the "righteous one" in v 4 is similarly general), whether the suppliant himself (as with Job and Jeremiah) or some unfortunate on whose behalf the prophet is making intercession. LXX *adikoumenos* has the prophet identify himself as the one who has suffered injustice. Targum *ʿal ḥaṭôpîn*, "on account of violent crimes," leaves it general, but the presence of the preposition supports our arguments for the adverbial function of the nouns.

Job's complaint that there has been no *mišpāṭ* resembles Habakkuk's complaint that *mišpāṭ* has not gone out (v 4aB), and it shows that the "verdict" is the favorable decision that the just have a right to expect from God. It is not simply that justice has disappeared from the dealings of human with human.

thou didst not listen. This should not be translated as the future "thou wilt not hear" (KJV). For the argument that the verb is past tense, see the preceding NOTE. Since Held's (1962) watershed paper on this matter, there should be no need to argue for it all over again.

To listen in Hebrew involves much more than the mere act of hearing. There is no suggestion that God is deaf, has not heard. He has not heeded the prophet. The verb means "to hear with attention and to respond." Hence its common translation "obey." The pronoun objects are not supplied; such brevity is usual in poetry of this sort. The indirect object "to you" in v 2b serves both verbs, and the object "me" could be supplied in translation for both *tišma'* and *tôšîa'*.

protested (or "shouted"). The verb has a wide range of meaning, but it mainly expresses a protest about mistreatment. When directed to God, such a cry becomes an appeal for redress, with some of the verbs of prayer as poetic parallels. In addition to Job 19:7 quoted earlier, Job 35:9 and Lam 3:8 use *šw'* in parallel.

lawlessness. Although *ḥāmās* is usually translated "violence," it would be misleading to give it a denotation of crime committed by force and with physical assault on people. NEB "Murder!" in Job 19:7 is altogether too specific. Speiser (AB 1:51) calls *ḥāmās* "a technical legal term" that he translates "lawlessness." Its use in Job 6:11 is significant, for it covers wickedness of all kinds, ranging from evil thoughts to uncontrolled sexual lust. More specifically, it can describe political atrocities (Gen 49:5; Judg 9:24) that involve the *violation* of oaths and treaties. Habakkuk uses the word six times, but does not give it any specific connotation. Presumably it applies to all the things he complains about, and particularly to the crimes listed in the five "woe oracles." Brownlee (1979:38) glosses *ḥāmās* as "the anguished outcry of the oppressed."

rescue. The verb *hôšîa'* is usually transitive, and some object must be understood here. What that object is depends on the concrete circumstances and intention of the prophet's prayer. Keil (1954:55) suggests that the prophet laments "in the name of the righteous." But there is nothing in the prayer itself to indicate that, unless *haṣṣaddîq* (v 4; cf. v 13b and Hab 2:4) is collective or generic. The "woe oracles" in Hab 2:6b–20 provide a catalog of evils that permits interpretation in terms of individual, national, or international wrongdoing. If individual, the object of "rescue" is to be understood as the prophet himself; if national, it is the righteous group within Israel; if international, it is Israel itself as the covenant people of God. The key to the solution of this problem is the correct identification of "the wicked" and "the righteous" in Hab 1:4 and 13 (Nielsen 1952). An assured result is not possible because the words are ambiguous (singular or collective?) and lacking in concreteness—wicked or righteous with respect to what specific actions? Because the plurals can be used to make a community reference certain, as in Psalm 1, we suggest that an individual is in mind here. Compare Noah and Job, both designated *ṣaddîq*. Such conspicuously righteous individuals can be symbolic and representative. But, because of the prominence of "I" in the first prayer, and the intensely personal character of the resolution in Habakkuk 3, we suggest that the book of Habakkuk enshrines the Job-like experience of a righteous sufferer—the prophet himself. The fact that he expects an answer from God "concerning my protest" (Hab 2:1) shows that a personal dispute with God lies at the heart of this book. But Habakkuk's private distress arises from his status as a prophet and from his involvement in public and international events, and the response of God, when it comes in due time, has corresponding scope and serves the needs of the community as well as the prophet's more immediate crisis of faith. In this context, *hôšîa'*, "Rescue!" means "Vindicate me!" as well as "Save me!" One can use this verb in appealing to a magistrate for justice, as well as in appealing to a protector for safety. In a good ruler, the offices of vindicator and savior are combined. So the widow of Tekoa, pretending to have a problem, said to David, *hôšî'â hammelek*, "Rescue [me], O King!" (2 Sam 14:4), with the absence of an explicit object, as in Hab 1:2b. She wants a favorable verdict in a quasi-legal petition, and she wants in addition that the king should see that his decision is carried out, by force if necessary. This is what Habakkuk expects from God: he wants an answer (2:1), and he wants action.

3. *make me see*. The *Hip'il* of √ *r'y* usually has two objects. Hence the usual translation: "Why dost thou make me see wrongs?" (RSV). This question could imply that God, in his providence, has brought Habakkuk into contact with much evil in the world. But this is too commonplace. To judge from *yar'ēnî* in Num 23:3, God might have shown Habakkuk *'āwen* in a prophetic vision. But this is not appropriate either, because Habakkuk blames the desperate situation on the failure of the Torah in the real world.

Hebrew poetic language is economical. Not only is it uncommon to use the definite article, *nota accusativi*, and the relative pronoun, but prepositions and pronouns are often omitted or used only once, doing double duty, as in v 2. The idiom in v 13 also points to the condensed character of v 3aA, where the preposition *'el* is not used as expected. Once v 3aA is recognized as laconic, the usual interpretation, as old as LXX and the Masoretes, can be revised.

The poetic character of v 3aA is unmistakable. The words *'āwen* and *'āmāl* are conventional parallels (Job 4:8; 5:6), sometimes coordinated (Pss 10:7; 55:11; 90:10). The word *'āmāl* describes the agony of body or mind that is humanity's inevitable lot (Job 5:7), especially the troubled state of a person worn out by work and the cares of this life. The possibility that this association makes *'āwen* mean "misery" rather than "iniquity" has been influenced (wrongly, we think) by form-critical classification of Habakkuk's prayer as lament rather than complaint. In v 13, *ra'*, "bad," takes the place of *'āwen*, and other near synonynms referring to bad experiences, and experiences of bad are used in matching pairs in numerous combinations.

In the poetic bicolon of v 3aA, the verbs (suffixed // prefixed) and nouns are in chiasmus. A similar collocation of words with chiasmus is found in Ps 10:14:

rā'îtâ kî-'attâ 'āmāl	You, even you, have watched suffering,
wāka'as tabbîṭ	and gazed on grief.

Nearby in the same Psalm (v 11), belief in the indifference of God is considered to be an impious opinion. It is the wicked who thinks

šākaḥ 'ēl,	God has forgotten,
histîr pānāyw	he has averted his face,
bal-rā'â	he has seen nothing

Hab 1:13a follows as a counter-assertion of the believer, the basis of further prayer, a significant link between Habakkuk's two prayers:

ṭĕhôr ʿênayim   *mērĕʾôt*   *rāʿ*
wĕ-   *habbîṭ*   *ʾel-ʿāmāl lōʾ tûkāl*

The two verbs are conventional parallels. In nearly half its OT occurrences, *hibbîṭ* is parallel to *rāʾâ*. Nineteen times *hibbîṭ* comes first. It follows *rāʾâ* seven times, three in Habakkuk. The others are Isa 38:11; Ps 10:14; Lam 1:11; 2:20. In every instance *rāʾâ* is *Qal*, except in Hab 1:3. This is enough to throw doubt on the *Hipʿil* of the MT. The pointing as adopted by the Masoretes is readily explained by the unusual suffix *-nî*. The consonants *trʾny* were pointed *tarʾēnî* rather than *tirʾēnî* to make the verb capable of two objects, *ʾāwen* being the second. This was necessary, because the Masoretes no longer recognized the poetic syntax in which the pronoun suffixed to a verb might be referential or an indirect object, or might anticipate a noun object in apposition. An example of the latter, with the same verb (!) is found in Exod 2:6: *wattirʾēhû ʾet hayyeled*, "and she saw him (namely) the boy." By analogy, Hab 1:3 means "You watch me, misery," that is, "You watch me (in my) misery" or "You watch my misery." The imposition of a *Hipʿil* on Hab 1:3 seems to flout the poetic usage and the conventional parallelism with *tabbîṭ*. Only in a formal sense are the two *Hipʿils* parallel, because the second is only singly transitive. *Hipʿil* does not always have to be causative or doubly transitive. Furthermore the *Hipʿil tarʾēnî* of the MT deviates from Habakkuk's own use of *Qal* in vv 5 and 13. The verbs refer to the scrutinizing activity of God, as Num 23:21 shows.

lōʾ-hibbîṭ ʾāwen bĕyaʿăqōb
wĕlōʾ-rāʾâ ʿāmāl bĕyiśrāʾēl

This poem celebrates the Exodus, and the interpretation of *lōʾ* is problematic, as also in the preceding lines. Could it be asseverative? Then the clauses can be read as statements, not questions:

He is the one who	said (it)
and he will certainly (*lōʾ*)	do (it);
and he	promised,
and he will certainly (*lōʾ*)	make it stand;
and he	blessed,
and he will certainly (*lōʾ*)	bring it about.
He certainly (*lōʾ*)	beheld the misery in Jacob
and he certainly (*lōʾ*)	saw the suffering in Israel.

The validity of the point we are making about *rāʾâ* does not depend on showing that *lōʾ* is assertive in Numbers 23. The questions could be rhetorical. The tradition attested in Num 23:21 cannot mean that God regards his people as sinless. That is contradicted on every page of the Hebrew Bible, especially the book of Numbers. God saw the misery of his people and responded to their cry for help (Exod 2:23; 3:7). Habakkuk knows the LORD's reputation (3:2), but his similar plea has gone unheeded (compare Hab 1:2 with Exod 2:23, 3:7, 4:31, with a different word for "misery"). This emphasis on the plight of the righteous rather than on the criminal activities of the wicked supports our claim that the prayer is a complaint (against God) following a failed protest (a demand for punitive justice against the wrongdoer). The complaint is that God *has not rescued* (v 2). And it is precisely "rescue" that is the purpose of God's spectacular intervention in Habakkuk 3 (see v 13). In casting his prayer in the language of the old traditions, which he has heard (3:2), Habakkuk expects the LORD to do the same thing again "in the midst of the years."

These idioms in other places in the Hebrew Bible probably explain why the Qumran *pešer* took v 3aB to mean "God looked upon oppression and treachery."

me. The (indirect) object of the first verb goes with the second verb as well, by double duty. Again, this structure is best viewed as a poetic attachment of the possessive pronoun on the verb rather than on the noun. It means "Why do you look at my suffering of iniquity?"

iniquity . . . wretchedness. Several of the passages studied earlier contain *'āwen //'āmāl*. Translators who want to make them synonyms are not sure which should dominate the other. *DCH* (I:154) gives *'āwen* the meaning of "misfortune" when it is associated with *'āmāl* at Num 23:21; Hab 1:3; Job 5:6; Pss 55:11; 90:10, but not in other instances. No reason is given for this selection; indeed, the very proposal is a fallacious application of the dogma of synonymity for poetic parallels. *TDOT* (I:142) does not recognize "misfortune" as a possible meaning for *'āwen*, explaining the collocation satisfactorily as the logic of the figurative "conceive // bring forth" and "plow // reap." Trouble (*'āmāl*) is the outcome of iniquity (*'āwen*). *NIDOTTE* (I:313), however, pushes the point, inferring from the parallelism at Num 23:21; Job 4:8; 5:6; 15:35; Pss 10:7; 55:11; 90:10 (but not Hab 1:3) that *'āwen* "signifies not only the immediate act but also the resulting troubles"; hence the meanings "misfortune / trouble / adversity." This has not been thought through. Trouble (*'āmāl*) is experienced by a victim of the iniquity (*'āwen*) of a wrongdoer (NRSV). Two different things.

NEB and REB bring *'āmāl* into line with *'āwen*: "wickedness // wrongdoing." I have not found the meaning "wrongdoing" for *'āmāl* in any work of reference. It is not easy to glimpse behind the scenes the source of some of the eccentric renderings of these translations. It is often the case that published emendations of G. R. Driver turn up as the text, without identification as emendations. Brockington's (1973:259) notes do not indicate that a different Hebrew text was the basis of this translation. In the present case, it would seem that the meaning "wrongdoing" comes from **m'l*, the supposed reading of the text in 1QpHab. That *commentary* glosses *'wn w'ml* as *'šq wm'l*. The supposition that *m'l* occurred rather than *'āmāl* in the Hebrew text used by the Qumran interpreter was possible because there is a lacuna at this point, with the letter *'ayin* only partly legible. Brownlee (1959:5–6) reports van't Land and van der Woude as favoring this reading over MT, but Brownlee's meticulous measurement of the space available shows that the suggestion is unlikely, unless there was crowding. In any case, the first word *'wn* is clear. There is no suggestion that MT *'wn* should be replaced by *'sq*. The commentator gave a comment on each noun, with sound play on the second, even though "treachery" (done) is different from "trouble" (experienced).

devastation and lawlessness. This is like what Jeremiah said (Jer 20:8; cf. Amos 3:10; Jer 6:7; Ezek 45:9). By hendiadys: "devastating lawlessness."

before me. Again, the personal reference highlights the evil experienced by the righteous man, not the crimes done by the wicked. The thing that is supposed to move God to action is not the sight of the bad doing wrong so much as the sight of the good suffering wrong.

disputation . . . contention. Both *rîb* and *mādôn* can have the meaning of "contention" in general. The etymology of the latter is closer to the language of the law courts, and the problem is how much forensic connotation there is in v 3b and how much this connotation colors the whole speech, making it a covenant lawsuit (against God!). Although derived from the root *dyn*, "judge," *mādôn* is frequently used in Proverbs (which accounts for the most of its biblical occurrences) to describe "strife," not necessarily litigation. This nuance is secured by 1QpHab (col. i, line 9) in glossing *rîb* as *mĕrîbâ*, which not only moves it from juridical reference (the word is used in the Hebrew Bible only in Gen 13:8 and Num 27:14, contentions with no merit), but also arouses the negative association of the notorious rebellion at Meribah in the wilderness. These stories of Israel's apostasies under Moses provided the Qumran people with paradigms that are not evident in Habakkuk's language.

The problem of the structural connection of v 3b has already been discussed. As a continuation of vv 2–3a, "quarrel" and "argument" could be two more ills of society that distress the prophet but do not move the LORD to action. But the juridical language of v 4 is unmistakable, and v 3bB could connect with either the preceding or the following text. If the following, *rîb // mādôn* is a formal lawsuit. The new beginning of discourse with *wayĕhî* supports the second reading. But recognizing this break still leaves open the question of whether the prophet is exasperated by the breakdown of justice in human courts or whether it is the LORD who has failed to do his job as judge. This question is hard to settle when the verbs are so unclear and apply equally well to either scenario.

The traditional interpretation of v 3bB as "contention arises" is difficult to accept: *nāśā'* is transitive in *Qal* (see the NOTE on Hos 13:1 [AB 24:629]). If *mādôn* is the required object, no subject is identified. If *mādôn* is the subject, what is the (implied) object? If the meaning were middle—"contention lifts itself up"—the *Nip'al* would be used, although one could surmount this problem with a *Qal* passive (see the NOTE on Hos 1:6 [AB 24:193]). To be the subject of the active verb, as vocalized, *mādôn* would have to be personified. There are common idioms in which the object of the verb *nāśā'* is an organ of the body: foot, hand, head, face, voice. Such an object is often omitted. Similar ellipsis here would require a paraphrase "contention raises (its voice)" or the like. Such an idiom could lie behind "clamorous discord" (NAB; cf. "discord raises its head" [NEB]).

Verse 3bA is similarly terse. "And a *rîb* took place" could mean several things. It could be subordinate to what follows: "when there was a lawsuit . . . the verdict came out perverted." But it is more likely that it is a principal clause. A full statement would be "X has a *rîb* with Y" (cf. Mic 6:1–2). An attempt to fill out Hab 1:3b in this way will be influenced by any general conclusion reached about the prayer as a whole. It could be a general complaint about lawlessness: "There is quarreling." Or it could be describing corruption in the courts of the land. We suggest that the reference to *tôrâ* in v 4 requires the involvement of Yahweh in some capacity, and the arguments already given that the speech as a whole is a complaint made to and against God suggest that v 4 describes something that the prophet is deploring. Greater cohesion in the speech is secured once it is recognized that the collapse of *tôrâ* and the nonappearance of *mišpāṭ* are due to the unresponsiveness of God described in v 2. The prophet has already stated his case, and he is waiting for the LORD to reply to "*my* remonstration" (*tôkaḥtî* [2:1]). Now the roots *ykḥ* and *ryb* are frequent parallels, almost synonyms. This association suggests that the *rîb* in Hab 1:3 is also the prophet's own, and that v 3bA means *wayĕhî lî rîb*, "I have conducted my argument (or presented my case)." It is the presentation of this *rîb*, prior to the present prayer, that is described by the verbs "I called out // I protested" in v 2. We are now at a later stage of Habakkuk's experience, where the indifference of God to the prophet's *rîb* has created a deeper anguish. This is supported by the collocation of *rîb* and *mādôn* in Jer 15:10, and the association persists in the *Hodayoth* (1QH 13:22–24), which supplies the further correlatives *qn'h w'p*, "jealousy and anger," and *rgn wtlwnh*, "impudence and grumbling."

w 'ny hyyty	*'l [wmdy*	*wt'my]dny*
	lryb wmdnym	*lr'y*
	qn'h w'p	*lb'y bryty*
	wrgn wtlwnh	*lkwl nw'dy w['w]kly lḥmy*

and I have become. . .	
contention and litigation	to my neighbors
jealousy and anger	to those who have entered into my covenant
and challenge and insubordination	to all who joined me and have eaten my bread

The echoes of biblical language are unmistakable, with original and elaborate pairing of related items. The language shares with Habakkuk the perception of being the victim of hostility that throws the suppliant upon the protection of God. Nitzan (1994:325), drawing attention to the psalms' parallels, comments on how "the author [of the Thanksgiving Psalms] identifies with the feelings of the persecuted and suffering biblical poets." While it might be true that, drawing inspiration from the Psalter, the author "to some extent abandoned the conventional anonymity of the biblical psalms in order to articulate the unique troubles he experienced as a member of the Qumran sect" (325), insofar as Jeremiah and Habakkuk supplied some of the language quoted earlier, inspiration was drawn from perceived similarity to known prophets. This connection makes the use of the book of Habakkuk by the group understandable, especially if the same person wrote the *Hodayoth* and the Habakkuk *pešer*.

When conventional word pairs like these are split up and distributed over parallel colons, discontinuous hendiadys may be suspected. In such cases, the second item in the pair is attributive, sharpening the focus of the first noun, which is more general. While *rîb* can cover any kind of quarrel in many settings, *mādôn* has more legal associations, pointing to some kind of court as a likely location for the dispute. This conclusion, however, does not warrant the use of the formalities of a properly conducted trial to control the interpretation. In the rhetoric of prophetic discourse, the speeches may be composed in the manner of juridical oratory, and allowance should be made for the figurative language of poetry when a dispute with a human antagonist provides a metaphor for disputation with God.

The statement "I have a quarrel" (that is, with Yahweh) could apply more generally to the book of Habakkuk as a whole. It is a record of his "dispute" (*rîb, mādôn, tôkaḥat*) with Yahweh. This is shown not only by its argumentative tone, but also by the disposition of the protagonists. The lawsuit is not one conducted in human courts. Nor is Habakkuk's quarrel with the wicked whom he accuses before God as judge. The culprit is God, who looks on "while the wicked devours the righteous" (1:13). Habakkuk is not directly invoking the judgment of God on the wicked. The gravamen of his complaint is that by his negligence God must now bear responsibility for the spread and perpetuation of evil. He argues with God to find out "Why?" This reading is borne out by the fact that the response of God is not to judge the wicked (this is not described in historical terms), but to explain his strategy to the prophet in terms that will require faith and much patience if he is to survive (Hab 2:4).

4. *Torah.* Considering that Habakkuk may have lived in the time of the Deuteronomic Reformation under Josiah, his statement that the *tôrâ* "is benumbed" suggests an opinion that the movement had been a failure. Yet there is no indication that he has in mind a written body of instruction—the Law of Moses or a portion of it—that served as the primary means of access to the mind of God. Habakkuk's concerns, theological or ethical, are not those of Deuteronomy. They are more in the tradition of Isaiah and Micah.

paralyzed (or "effete"). The root *pwg* is rare, and most of its occurrences are accompanied by textual difficulties. Applied to a bodily organ, such as the heart, it means "grows numb and useless." Applied to the *tôrâ*, it would be a fanciful metaphor, but the intended reference eludes us: "loses its grip" (NJB). To interpret the "numbness" of the *tôrâ* by saying "the sacred fountain was frozen" (Cannon 1925:65) might imply failure by God to supply Torah. We think that this is close to the point. Cannon blames the priests for not delivering *tôrâ*, quoting Deut 33:10; Jer 2:2, 18:18; Ezek 7:25; Mic 3:11. LXX has *dieskedastai,* "is frustrated."

The insinuation in Habakkuk's complaint that God is ultimately accountable for this ineffective *tôrâ* was unthinkable to the author of the Qumran *pešer.* For him, the text was talking quite specifically about events in which he was involved, and he referred to the "dribbler of the lie" and the men of his community who had rejected the *torah* of El (1QpHab col. i, line 11).

The matching use of the verb *yṣ᾿* in connection with *mišpāṭ* and the use of the latter in parallel with *tôrâ* invites comparison with Mic 4:2 (= Isa 2:3; cf. Amos 1:2):

kî miṣṣiyyôn tēṣē᾿ tôrâ	Because from Zion goes out Torah,
ûdĕbar-yhwh mîrûšālēm	And the word of Yahweh from Jerusalem.

Agreement between Habakkuk and this oracle in the use of *tôrâ* without the definite article, which is a great rarity, is an important feature, inviting the use of one to clarify the other. The parallelism of Mic 4:2 shows that the *tôrâ* of Yahweh is issued in Jerusalem as a prophetic "word," and the *mišpāṭ* in Hab 1:4 is the same. In the commentary on Hos 6:3 and 6 (AB 24a:423) it was shown that the *mišpāṭ* of God comes out (from his mouth) like the rising sun. So it is more likely that what Habakkuk calls the slackening of the *tôrâ* is not the neglect of their teaching duties by the priests (Jer 18:18; cf. Hos 4:6), or the failure of human judges to apply *tôrâ,* but the silence of God. Habakkuk's prayers have not been answered. What he expected was not so much an act of destruction against the wicked as a word of explanation or guidance from God. Nevertheless, the use of the term "verdict" rather than, say, "word" shows that he wanted a "decision" about his *rîb.* The *mišpāṭ* is the judge's announcement of his decision on a case, and this the LORD has not given. The combination *rîb ûmišpāṭ* is equivalent to *dînum wapurusam* in the terminology of Babylonian jurisprudence (CH VI:§ 5:7–10). This connotation casts the LORD in the dual role of defendant and judge, an accused judge! This still does not resolve the contradiction between the statement in v 4aB that *mišpāṭ* never came out, and the statement in v 4bB that *mišpāṭ* came out twisted.

never. The translation "is defeated" (REB) is probably intended to secure a nuance in *lāneṣaḥ* because that term expresses the superlative (Winton Thomas 1956:106), or has connotations of "power" (HAL), because the verb *yṣ᾿* is taken in its military sense, or because we have here another of Habakkuk's juxtapositioning of a word with its negated antonym: "paralyzed // ineffective." The notion that *lāneṣaḥ* can mean "victoriously" is ancient. Even LXX *eis telos,* "to completion," has the same flavor. The idiom can be compared with *le᾿ĕmet yôṣî᾿ mišpāṭ* (Isa 42:3), which turns up in Matt 12:20 as "bring justice to victory." The verb √*nṣḥ* has the meaning "to be victorious" in Northwest Semitic (DNWSI 751). LXX renders *lāneṣaḥ* as *eis nikos* in 2 Kgs 2:26; Jer 3:5; Amos 1:11; 8:7; Lam 3:18; 5:20. Even so, the range of Greek glosses on this expression (Muraoka 1998:99) suggests that it was interpreted rather freely to match the context, and it seems more likely that in these instances *eis nikos* is equivalent to *eis telos*, "to the end," rather than meaning "unto victory." Lampe's *Patristic Lexicon* glosses *eis nikos* simply as "utterly," which approximates Winton Thomas's notion of the superlative. But some Fathers reliteralized the expression homiletically.

The difficulty with the Hebrew lies in its placing the adverbial *lāneṣaḥ* between the verb and the subject and in its attachment of the negative to *lāneṣaḥ*, so that *lō' . . . lāneṣaḥ* means "never," when simple negation would secure the idea that justice hasn't been coming out at all. When *lō' lāneṣaḥ* is followed by a prefixed verb with future-time reference, it means that something now happening will sometime stop (Isa 28:28; 57:16; Ps 103:9, with prohibitive negation it means "stop what you are now doing" [Pss 44:24; 74:19]; cf. Jer 3:5), or that something that is not happening now will never happen (Isa 33:20; Ps 9:19), or that a change to be made in the future will never be altered (Isa 13:20; Jer 50:39). Hab 1:4 does not match any of these constructions. It does not mean that justice is coming out now, but will sometime cease; it does not mean that justice is not coming out now and never will (Habakkuk does not know that; he certainly doesn't want to believe that, even if it is beginning to look that way); it does not mean that justice will cease permanently some time in the future. The construction nearest to v 4aB is Ps 10:11b, *bal rā'â lāneṣaḥ*, where inapplicable reading of *lāneṣaḥ* as "for ever" has yielded a misreading of the perfect verb as future. All the suffixed verbs in parallel are past tense. The fool thinks to himself, "God forgot; he hid his face, he didn't see (anything) *at all*." So here, in a context where we have already demonstrated that the verbs have past-time reference, v 4aB means "justice did not come forth *at all*."

came forth. The significance of the verb *yṣ'* has been examined partly in the preceding NOTES. Vocabulary used in Isa 2:3; Mic 4:2; Amos 1:2; Hos 6:3, 6 is found again in Isa 51:4, where the use of *tôrâ*, once more without the definite article, and of its parallel *mišpāṭ*, is decisive for our claim that Habakkuk is speaking about a revelation, an oracle of promised deliverance, or at least some kind of determination by God as judge:

kî tôrâ mē'ittî yēṣē'	For [my] torah will come forth from me,
ûmišpāṭ lā'ôr	and [my] judgment [will come forth] to the light.
'ammîm 'argîa'	I will shine brightly on the peoples.
qārôb ṣidqî	My victory is at hand.
yāṣā' yiš'î	My deliverance has gone forth,
ûzšrō'ay 'ammîm yišpōṭû	And my arms will judge the peoples.

Habakkuk's thought has the same background, as his use of *yeša'* in Hab 3:13 shows.

The slackening of Torah, then, is an aspect of the unresponsiveness of God. There is no need to look for a criticism of the priests for not doing their duty (Cannon 1925:65). Such a fault does not appear elsewhere in the book as a matter for criticism or judgment. Nor is Habakkuk's complaint about the nonobservance of *tôrâ* in the community. It is easy to suspect something like this, when Jeremiah is allowed to supply the missing background. An incident like that recorded in Jeremiah 34 is used as evidence that Josiah's Deuteronomic Reform was superficial and short-lived. But any kind of immorality, such as that denounced in Habakkuk's "woe oracles," could be described as nonobservance of *tôrâ*, and there is no indication that by *tôrâ* Habakkuk has in mind a written code like Deuteronomy. Indeed, his choice of the unusual verb *pwg* suggests something dysfunctional in the *tôrâ* itself, not delinquency on the part of the priests. To see this breakdown as unresponsiveness in God is in keeping with the rest of Habakkuk's prayer. The remedy is not to work for the restoration of respect for an available Torah. What would meet his need is a fresh word from God (2:1–2). Interpretation should not suppose that here *tôrâ* is a technical term for the traditional teaching of Moses, written or otherwise. Such tradition certainly existed, and had authority. But in Habakkuk's time Israel was still at a stage where living *tôrâ* could be given through priests (Jer 18:18). If Habakkuk's complaint is not that priests have relaxed *tôrâ* and magistrates have perverted justice (he does not identify "the wicked" with either of these professions), but that God has failed to supply him with *tôrâ* and *mišpāṭ*, then these terms could be included under the broad heading of "prophecy." Prophecy is the communicating to people of the directions and decisions made by God, through Moses in the first paradigmatic instance. The "guidance" (*tôrâ*) that Habakkuk hoped to receive from Yahweh was a "decision" (*mišpāṭ*) of "deliverance" (*yešaʿ*). He complains that it has not come.

Habakkuk's audacity is very revealing of his integrity as a prophet. There is no indication that an honest prophet of Yahweh would dare to concoct oracles to suit his own taste or to please his audience. The false prophets did that (Jereremiah 23). Much as he longed for a hopeful message, he knew he had not been given one. But this does not mean that the loyal Yahweh prophet bowed unquestioningly to the divine fiat, good or bad. As Habakkuk's prayers showed, he was prepared to argue with God, to wrest from him a word of assurance, and to wait until he knew he had been answered (2:2).

restricted. The participle *maktîr* is a rare word. There is no need to emend to *makrît,* "cut off." If it means "surround" in a hostile (Ps 22:13) or military (Judg 20:43) sense—these occurrences are *Piʿels*—it is hard to see how the verb could describe a miscarriage of justice in the courts, unless it is the opposite of the situation in Ps 42:8. More likely, it describes the success of criminals in society. To interpret it as "gets around" (that is, circumvents the law) is really another picture. LXX reads *katadynasteuei,* "oppresses," an attempt at interpretation.

the righteous. The opposite number, the wicked, has no definite article. Is it generic? Compare v 13. Largely due to its frequent use in poetry, "wicked" rarely has the definite article; in the Hebrew Bible, the singular form of *rāšāʿ* lacks the definite article 97 times out of 116 occurrences (*ṣaddîq,* 138 out of 142); the plural, 117 times out of 125 (*ṣaddîqîm,* 52 out of 58). The majority of the definite forms occur in prose (Deuteronomy, Ezekiel). The imbalance in this verse between two terms that occur so frequently in correlation throws doubt on the correctness of *nota accusativi* and the definite article in this passage, the only exceptions to the purely poetic syntax of the prayer. 1Qp Hab confirms these details, however. So the text is best left as it is; "the righteous" (one) is a specific individual.

The righteous one is the person in the right. In contrast to the wicked, he is the one who should win his case (Deut 25:1) as the one who had been wronged. In a civil suit, being "right" has nothing to do with virtue or morality. It has to do with only the specific charge in the action. At most, it would affirm the innocence of a victim in relation to the charges of that case or give acquittal in the merely negative sense of "not guilty." Once more, in settling its exact connotation here, we must decide if the term is forensic, almost secular, or whether it carries ideas of intrinsic righteousness, even godliness. Abraham's intercession, which arose from a concern resembling Habakkuk's, argued that "the judge of the whole world" would not be doing *mišpāṭ* if he destroyed *ṣaddîq* and *rāšā'* alike (Gen 18:25). Abraham's logic creates Habakkuk's problem. Whatever God does is open to objection, unless he can succeed in punishing each individual strictly in accordance with his or her deeds. The historical disasters that are God's main instruments for judgment in the Bible are not so discriminating. Either the righteous perish with the wicked, or the wicked are spared for the sake of the righteous. These matters are not argued so nicely in the book of Habakkuk; for example, the author does not resort to the idea that a righteous remnant—even a minimum quota of ten (Genesis 18)—can immunize a whole city. Nor does the prophet see that there is merit in the patient sufferings of the righteous, although the crucial statement in Hab 2:4 approaches this insight, expressed so poignantly in Isaiah 53.

Although 1QpHab col. 1 line 13 is almost completely lost, the surviving *hw' mwrh hṣdq*, "he (is) the teacher of righteousness," is enough to show that this person was identified as "the righteous one" and that the wicked priest was "the wicked one." In the hermeneutic of the Qumran community, this equation revealed the secret meaning of the ancient text as a precise prediction, not just the application of prototypical figures to later specimens. For a long time, modern criticism searched for the original historical references of these terms in Habakkuk's contemporaries and disdained the sectaries' preoccupation with their own struggles as paranoid. Yet the application of the passage to the players in their own drama at Qumran brought the prophecy to life, and might even be accepted as a valid option for recycling "the wicked" and "the righteous" as the good and bad of our own day.

perverted (or "twisted"). The last line of the prayer is climactic, but, unfortunately for us, obscure. It could be parallel to v 4bA. When the wicked surrounded the righteous, the verdict came out "twisted." But the parallelism is not evident, and the conjunctions have to be explained. The subordinating conjunction *kî*, "because," at the beginning of v 4bA could link that colon to v 4aB, leaving the two colons beginning *'al-kěn*, "therefore," as parallels. (The translation on p. 97 records the possibility that *kî* is an asseverative adverb "indeed" or "in fact.") There could be congruence in the ideas that *tôrâ* is benumbed and that the *mišpāṭ* is twisted. Note the chiasmus in the placement of *mišpāṭ* in lines 4aB and 4bB, which suggests some connection between the two occurrences.

Perhaps we need not be very concerned about the logical contradiction between vv 4aB and 4bB. This kind of thinking is often met in the Bible. The best resolution is to see here another instance of pseudosorites:

> The verdict never comes forth;
> (but, if it does come forth,)
> the verdict comes forth twisted.

See the discussions of pseudosorites in AB 24A and O'Connor (1987a, 1987b, 1987c).

This is the only place in the Hebrew Bible where the verb *ʿql* is used. Derivatives are *ʿăqalqāl* (Jdg 5:6; Ps 125:5) and *ʿăqallātôn* (Isa 27:1). The root *ʿwt* is synonymous in meaning, and specifically describes the apparent perversion of justice *mišpāṭ* by God in Job 8:3; 19:6; 34:12 (cf. Amos 8:5). The twisting of judgment and the collapse of "law" are not traced simply to the superior strength of the wicked, who hamper the just "so that the righteous cannot cause right to prevail" (Keil 1955:57). The repeated *ʿal-kēn* links back to the two negative statements in v 2: "you haven't heeded . . . you haven't rescued . . . that's why. . . ." It is not the triumph of the wicked, but the inactivity of God that tests Habakkuk's faith. His "argument and case" (v 3b) are his outcry and appeal (v 2) against the lawlessness, misery, suffering, and destruction that confront him (vv 2–3). Yahweh just looks on (v 3), but how he can bear to do so is beyond the prophet's comprehension. If the prophet himself is the "righteous" man (v 3) who expects a favorable response from the one who gives *tôrâ* and *mišpāṭ*, then that response would be more than a word of condemnation; it would be some saving act, in which the righteous is visibly vindicated, and the wicked, frustrated. The opposite happens (v 4bA).

If we have correctly recognized vv 2–4 as the prophet's complaint against God, then there is no basis for the theory that the LORD's response that follows in vv 5–11 is a plan for punishing the injustice within Judah by sending the Chaldeans against the corrupted people of God. We shall immediately see that this is not at all what God says. The Chaldeans' victims are not Judah, but the whole world. And the victims are not identified as wicked, deserving punishment. If this were so, God's pure eyes could look on with satisfaction. Habakkuk does not see it this way, as his second prayer will show.

COMMENT

This unit is the passionate prayer of a desperate man. From the form-critical point of view, it combines features of accusation and complaint. In form-critical terms, Hab 1:2–4 has been described as "a complaint expressed in the tone of the individual song of lament" (Eissfeldt 1965:417). Roberts (1991:88) says that it has "the form of an individual lament." The prayer is perhaps too short to display all the components that are likely to be present in a well-made formal psalm.

Miller (1994:68) recognizes the need to distinguish "lament" from "complaint." His use of the term "dimension," however, suggests that he is using "lament" and "complaint" to refer to themes or motifs in psalms rather than as labels for distinguishable form-critical categories. On the one hand, Miller says that "lament and complaint are dimensions of the prayer for help" (382). On the other hand, he says that "the complaint against God does in fact belong to the dimension of lament generally" (69).

Miller (1994:73) states that "Habakkuk's anguished prayers are almost nothing but complaint to God in challenging questions." God is criticized, even blamed. The questions express "human rage against heaven" (72). There is nothing defiant in a true lament. The author of Lamentations presents himself to God in brokenness. What God has done is accepted; it is not questioned. The topic of a complaint is some external wrong that is brought to God's attention. The theme of lament is the misery of the suppliant in bodily pain or spiritual distress. The plea in a complaint is for the God of justice to do something about those causing the injustice; in a lament, someone pleads with the God of compassion to bring relief to the sufferer (Bentzen 1959 I:157). A complaint can be querulous, expressing anger in a litigious setting. A lament can be plaintive, describing the speaker's suffering of illness or injustice; it can be sorrowful, grieving over some loss, such as bereavement. But if the loss is, say, the impoverishment of a victim of violent crime, all these moods can be present at once in the same person and in the same prayer. Hence the difficulty of form critics in classifying mixed forms. In some compositions, the two genres flow together, as when the author of Lamentations feels that the punishment, although deserved, is excessive and too prolonged.

The suppliant sometimes includes vows in anticipation of a good outcome. In either case, laments in the Psalter characteristically conclude with expressions of confidence, representing a change of mood that is often so abrupt that some researchers have felt either that we must suppose that a favorable response had been given at the transition point in the form of an oracle of assurance or deliverance (Begrich 1934, 1936), or that the two pieces do not belong together, that the happy ending was added by an inept scribe. The second explanation of abrupt mood changes associated with quite different kinds of prayer was dominant in much Hebrew prayer studies, especially in Psalms, in the first part of the twentieth century. Interestingly, it was form criticism, which you might think was concerned mainly with literary formulas and expressions, that turned attention to the liturgical use of such pieces, and so highlighted the cultural and cultic function of biblical prayers in various institutional or ritual settings. The reviews of Psalms research in Rowley (1951), Hayes (1974), and Anderson (1979) showed little interest in the literary "unity" of the biblical Psalms, despite mixed genres. The same can be said of form-critical analysis and classification of prophetic oracles. So the presence of a prayer in the book that purports to be prophecy need not be problematic.

The prophet's prayers in Habakkuk 1 contain no affirmations of confidence, no vows, no direct appeals for God to look favorably on him, no requests for deliverance. God is not reminded of past promises, or exhorted by the recital of past deeds to emulate them in order to meet Habakkuk's present need. Habakkuk's prayer sounds a single note and is driven by one mood—moral outrage and perplexity.

The *Gattungen* of *Strafrede* (judicial sentence) and *Scheltrede* (reproachful reprimand) have been recognized as kinds of confrontational speech. Classification of individual specimens has proved difficult because tone and motivation might be more significant than form in determining the intended *function* of any particular utterance. The written text has lost this living timbre. The prominence of questions in Habakkuk's prayers, and the absence of moving descriptions of the prophet's inner state of mind (contrast the "confessions" of Jeremiah), place his prayers in the category of "complaint." Bentzen (1959 I:157) sees the "reproachful questions" as a determinative part of the complaint, but Habakkuk's prayer is nothing but questions and outright accusation of God. It has gone beyond complaint. It is an indictment.

As we have seen (NOTE on v 2), the question "How much longer . . . ?" can be used in addressing a human or God. To settle the literary genre of Habakkuk's prayer in Hab 1:2–4, notice should be taken not only of distinctive language, of structural components and their sequence, of the emotional tone, but also of the place of that unit in the larger composition of which it is a part. The kind of answer given to a question in ongoing dialogue will provide an idea of what kind of question it was, at least what the answerer thought it was. If there is continuity with vv 5–11, we can look at question and answer together, each clarifying features of the other. But God's response might not have been the kind of answer that Habakkuk was expecting.

What kind of prayer is this? In whose interests? Is the prophet praying for personal deliverance from persecutors whom he calls "the wicked"? Or is he making intercession as a covenant mediator on behalf of the community? In favor of the private character of Habakkuk's appeal is the intensely personal tone of the whole book. "You make me see wickedness." Habakkuk himself is "the righteous" man of Hab 1:4, 13 and Hab 2:4. In Hab 2:1 he calls his appeal *tôkaḥtî*, "my complaint." This prayer is not a lamentation in the sense of bewailing one's misery in order to move God to compassion, although there is a reference to "pity" in Hab 3:2. Habakkuk's outburst is more like a protest, an accusation that Yahweh has failed to live up to his covenant commitment. However distressed Habakkuk may be about the wickedness rampant in his day, it is the inactivity of God that exasperates him even more.

In support of the highly personal character of the opening prayer, and of the whole prophecy, we note, on the one hand, such additional features as the intimate address "My God, my Holy One" (1:12) and the powerful *wa 'ănî*, "and I," in the climax at Hab 3:18. On the other hand, the crimes against which woes are uttered in Habakkuk 2 are social, and the impression is given that they are widespread. Habakkuk is not the only one suffering the double abuse—victimization by oppressors and marginalization by the justice system. Habakkuk's personal concerns are inseparable from his membership in the covenant community of Israel. The scope of the prophecy enlarges from a private situation to embrace the world scene, and in Hab 3:13 Yahweh comes to rescue his people as well as his messiah.

But even if Habakkuk's vehemence shows that he has been personally injured by the lawlessness of his day, with his own faith severely tested, because his hopes in Yahweh have been disappointed, his prayer shows that the public breakdown in the *tôrâ* has become widespread and has already reached an advanced stage. His complaint thus combines the misery and audacity that we find in both Job and Jeremiah. The affinities between Habakkuk and Jeremiah in this respect are seen in their use of similar language for similar purposes:

v 2a	*'ez'āq*	*'ēleykā*	*ḥāmās*	
	'ez'āq		*ḥāmās*	(Jer 20:8)
v 2b	*wĕlō'*		*tôšîa'*	
	lō'-	*yûkal*	*lĕhôšîa'*	(Jer 14:9)
v 3a	*tar'ēnî*		*'āwen*	
	mašmîa'		*'āwen*	(Jer 4:15)
v 3aA	*wĕ'āmāl*		*tabbîṭ*	
	lir'ôt	*'āmāl*	*wĕyāgôn*	(Jer 20:18; it distressed Jeremiah)
v 3aB	*šōd*		*wĕḥāmās*	
	ḥāmās		*wĕšōd*	(Jer 6:7; 20:8)
v 3b	*rîb*		*ûmādôn*	
	'îš rîb		*wĕ'îš mādôn*	(Jer 15:10)

The considerable amount of legal terminology (*rîb, mišpāṭ, ṣaddîq*) gives the prayer a forensic character, as a plea for justice. The protest has moved from complaining about "the wicked" to blaming God. The prophet has already got beyond intercession; he has tried that without result (v 2). We have argued that the "misery" (v 3) is the prophet's own, made worse by perplexity about God's apparent indifference to the situation. The question "How long?" is not a request for information; it is the complaint of a very desperate person who cannot endure much longer.

The compactness of the language makes it difficult to be specific about the reference of some of the key terms in the prayer. The statement "and there was a *rîb*" raises the question "Who is having a quarrel with whom about what?" unless we take it to be a general complaint: "There is quarreling going on (among everyone about anything and everything)." Even if we supply an implied pronoun suffix and read "And I have a *rîb*," the question remains whether the suppliant himself is the victim, deprived of justice in the human courts (he is the righteous person wronged by the wicked [v 4bA], for whom justice was perverted); whether he is speaking on behalf of that righteous victim, taking his case to a higher court, namely God; or whether in his laconic language he is saying obliquely that his immediate *rîb* is with God himself.

All these possible connotations of the term *rîb* are not necessarily mutually exclusive. It does not have to be a choice between the prayer as individual (Habakkuk's personal altercation) or communal (Habakkuk speaks in solidarity with his people). In Psalms studies, discussion has long continued over whether the "I" of some Psalms is an individual (citizen, prophet as intercessor, or king as representing the nation) or the community. (The history of research into the "I" of the Psalms is reviewed by Eaton [1979:255–60].) Habakkuk's prayer makes no mention of national or communal entities ("people," for instance), and we are inclined to interpret the dialogue as essentially private. But Habakkuk is a prophet, and, like Jeremiah, his personal struggle is inseparable from the problems of Israel in his time. Making intercession on behalf of the community does not exclude deep personal involvement of the prophet himself. In compassion, he identifies with the victims on whose behalf he prays. More than that, he is a member of that community, possibly a fellow sufferer of the wrongs against which he protests (Bellinger 1984:27–31).

In keeping with the artistic expression of such emotions, the thought of the prayer does not develop logically, step by step. It is not analytical; consequently, much of it is not clear to us. The effect of the outburst is to charge Yahweh with the ultimate responsibility for the mess that the world is in. There is "devastation and lawlessness." In a world ruled by a just God, there should be some reassuring signs that he reigns in justice. Those who are loyal, those who are in the right, cry out to God to keep his promises. Yet he does nothing. This encourages the wicked to be even more unrestrained. Those who are supposed to teach God's ways (*torah*) relax his demands. Those who are supposed to enforce justice in God's name pervert it. The wicked have the better of the righteous, who seem to be helpless. Doubly so: they cannot help themselves, and the LORD does not come to their aid.

This is only a general impression of what the prayer is about. When we come to the details, there are many difficulties. There are indications that an archaizing style has been deliberately cultivated. The most striking of them is the sparsity of the "prose particles"—relative pronoun (not present), object sign, and definite article (only in v 4bA). The nonuse of the definite article is particularly startling in the case of *tôrâ*, "the law." This completely unmodified form of the noun is a great rarity, found mainly in poetry (Deut 33:4; Isa 2:3; Mic 4:2). The indefinite *rāšā‛*, "wicked," is notable, because the definite is doubtless intended.

It is possible that some of these apparently indefinite nouns should be modified by pronoun suffixes. Habakkuk's complaint is that "(my) *mišpāṭ* never comes forth," as he would expect in response to his call for help. Alternatively, an implied definite article ("the *mišpāṭ*") would make the reference more general in scope—the machinery of law does not work for anyone. The choice between these alternative possibilities depends to some extent on how much the prophet's plea is personal and on how much he is interceding on behalf of the people. Most likely, the object to be supplied for the transitive, but elliptical verbs "heed" and "save" in v 2 is "me." This is indicated by the suffixes "me" in v 3, especially the poetic *lĕnegdî*.

There is no mistaking the archaic use of the verb forms. The so-called imperfect ("prefixed" *yiqtōl*) predominates—nine in all. One clause has a participle predicate (v 4bA); one is verbless (v 3aB). The *wāw*-consecutive is used only once (v 3b), and there is only one "suffixed" form (v 2aA). These two undoubtedly past-tense forms are used in strategic points at the onset of the two halves into which the whole speech naturally divides; *wayĕhî* (v 3b) obviously marks a new beginning. Division into two halves at this point receives support from the fact that there are forty-one syllables in each of these two sections. The past-tense forms at the head of these two parts fix the time reference of the whole. The "prefixed" verbs can hardly be translated as future tense (RSV). We could have rendered them by the neutral present tense (NAB), but this choice washes out the urgency and the particularity of the prayer. Habakkuk's outburst is not a reflection on abstract generalities; it is the desperate expression of a crisis for faith. This existential horror, however acute in one particular "moment," can find relief only when the whole of a person's life makes sense—its memories, the present crisis, and the prospects for the future. So past tense is more appropriate for such probing reflections.

The poetic sequence of suffixed // prefixed verb forms, both with the same time reference, whether past or future, as in v 2 is now widely recognized in Hebrew poetry (AB 17A:420–22).

The parallelism in v 2 is well developed, whether it is construed as two long colons or as four short ones. The interrogative "How long?" or "Until when?" embraces the whole verse, so that the second part means: "Until when? I have cried out to you because of lawlessness, and you didn't rescue me." The rhythmic compensation for the omission of *'ad-'ānâ* in v 2b is supplied by *'ez'aq . . . ḥāmās* as the parallel of *šiwwa'tî*. Although "Yahweh" is vocative, it is matched by *'ēleykā*, and these words are placed in chiasmus with the verbs.

The two other very short colons in v 2 are identical in grammatical structure:

but you didn't listen
but you didn't rescue

Verse 3aA similarly consists of two parallel questions, with "Why?" doing double duty for both. Possibly the question extends to v 3aB as well. The double questions in vv 2–3a are linked further by the series of nouns —"lawlessness," "iniquity," "wretchedness," "devastation," "lawlessness." The same word *ḥāmās* opens and closes the list, unless the list continues further with "disputation" and "contention" in v 3b. It is possible that v 3aB is a circumstantial clause: "while desolation and lawlessness are in front of me." In that case, v 3aB ties in with the preceding text, and v 3b begins something new. It is likely that v 3aB is more integral to v 3aA than that. The repeated pronoun suffix "me" is one strong link. If all four nouns are seen as the objects of the verbs "watch," then v 3 means "Why do you look at the misery and wretchedness, the desolation and lawlessness (that are) before me?"

The reproachful words in v 2 should be attached equally to the question in v 3a: "Why have you looked at misery . . . and did not rescue?"

The second part of Habakkuk's first prayer (vv 3b–4) is unified by the language of legal disputation, but the poetic organization is harder to find. The general idea seems to be that, because the LORD has been so unresponsive to the prophet's cry for redress, the Torah itself has become slack, judgment is not given (by God? through oracles?), and what comes out (from human courts?) is twisted. In short, the wicked have the better of the righteous in the law courts, giving final success to their crimes.

The difficulty with this kind of paraphrase is that the logical connections among the various parts have not been demonstrated. The poetry of the second part of Habakkuk's first prayer is not well formed. The first and last colons of v 4, each beginning with 'al-kēn, could express similar ideas; at least tôrā and mišpāṭ are good parallels. By the same token, v 4aB has affinities with both of these. This leaves v 4bA without a companion, unless it is found in v 3b. But v 4bA does not present the usual *parallelismus membrorum* with v 3b, which can be construed as a bicolon of two short colons with good parallelism of their own.

The verbs in v 4b are hard to relate to each other, but the use of the prefix form yiśśā' after wayĕhî is poetic. All the pieces are brought together by the chiasmus.

We have not been able to establish the line of argument within vv 3b–4. We have not been able to find the logical connections among the three or four statements of fact (vv 3bA, 3bB, 4aB, 4bA [?]) and the two or three subordinate clauses (vv 4aA, 4bA [?], 4bB).

The prayer contains three kinds of statements. First, vv 3b and 4bA, and perhaps vv 3aB and 4aB, describe a situation in which desolation and lawlessness are manifest (v 3aB): there are quarrels (or lawsuits) (v 3b), and the wicked suppress the righteous. The logical connection between these assertions is less evident. It depends on whether rîb and mādôn in v 3b describe disputation in a general sense or whether they refer more specially to formal litigation and, if so, who the litigants are. This problem is complicated by the apparent contradiction between v 4aB and v 4bB. Verse 4aB says that mišpāṭ never comes out at all, and this suggests that the judicial process has broken down. Yet v 4bB says that mišpāṭ does come out, but it comes out twisted; and this suggests that the courts are operating, but that they are corrupt. Harmonization could be achieved by glossing the first mišpāṭ as "true judgment." In the light of v 4aB, v 4bA would mean that the evil suppress the good because there are no restraints; the Torah itself has become useless. In the light of v 4bB, v 4bA would mean that when a court case takes place (v 3b), the wicked win the suit (it is not certain that maktîr can mean this) because the courts are corrupt—a common enough abuse. But this interpretation does not account for 'al-kēn, "therefore." If anything, the logical sequence in v 4b is that mišpāṭ comes out twisted because the wicked surround the righteous, not the other way around. Both interpretations are far from satisfactory.

One way out of this perplexing series of statements is to recognize a pseu-dosorites: the wicked rich obstruct and deny the righteous poor access to the due processes of law; but, if the latter do make it to trial, there is no verdict (*mišpāṭ*); but, if a decision is given, it comes out crooked.

The second kind of statement is found in v 4aA and v 4bB, both beginning with *'al-kēn*. This subordinating conjunction introduces a logical consequence; it usually follows the explanation of the statement of affairs: A exists; *that's why* B exists. We have already observed that the suppression of the righteous by the wicked can hardly be the *explanation* of the perversion of justice, unless the wicked are the judges themselves. Similarly, the mere occurrence of strife (v 3b) can hardly be the *explanation* of the relaxation of the *tôrā*. It would, in fact, be more logical to argue the other way: the collapse of the *tôrā* has led to lawless-ness and injustice.

A decision has to be made about the meaning of *kî* in v 4bA. If it is the sub-ordinating conjunction "because," then we have two subordinate clauses in a row. This compounds the difficulty. Hebrew can say "A, *therefore* B" or "B, *be-cause* A," but not "*because* A, *therefore* B." Verse 4b cannot be construed as a single complex sentence. For these reasons, it is better to take *kî* as assertative "indeed."

The third kind of statement is the more personal outcry of the prophet him-self. Verses 3b–4 seem to be more objective than vv 2–3a, in that there are no personal pronouns—"I," "me," "my." If, however, v 3bA means "I have made my argument,"—that is, presented my case—then this statement supplies a link with vv 2–3a, and the prophet's outcry becomes more specific. In the first part of the prayer (vv 2–3a) we noticed that the interrogatives *'ad-'anâ* and *lāmmâ* apply to parallel statements in which they are not explicitly present—the prin-ciple of double duty. If *'al-kēn*, "therefore," in v 4 does multiple duty, applying equally to all the statements in v 4, then these statements describe the conse-quences of the situation that was laid out in vv 2–3a. The logical connections are these:

The prophet is aware of desolation and lawlessness (v 3aB). He is himself the righteous person (v 4bA; cf. Hab 2:4), it is his own misery and suffering he be-wails (see the NOTE on v 3a). He has cried out to God (v 2bA) and called for help (2aA). But God has done nothing. He did not listen (v 2aB); he did not rescue (v 2bB). The inactivity of God is the reason for *all* the ills listed in the second part of the prayer. The whole prayer is a powerful impeachment of the deity. The position of v 3b in all this is less clear. Because of the juridical vo-cabulary, v 3b could be connected with v 4. The quarrels and disputes break out because God does not restrain the wicked or rescue the just. But it is one thing to recognize that *'al-kēn* brackets all four statements in v 4. It is strained to extend its influence to preceding statements that begin with *wayěhî*. It is pos-sible that *rîb* and *mādôn* continue the list of nouns in vv 2–3a. More precisely, vv 3aB and 3b make a good bicolon, with *šōd* and *ḥāmās* matching *rîb* and *mādôn*. If v 3b is part of the prayer that begins with v 2, the opening and clos-ing verbs match:

I called out. . . .	I shouted. . . .
(I) made (my) argument	(I) presented (my) case

These are matters that concern the prophet himself. The difficulties in the over-terse statement *wayĕhî rîb* can be overcome if we recognize that *lî*, "[belonging] to me," is understood, so that it means "I have (conducted) my *rîb*." The role of Habakkuk here is exactly like that of Jeremiah (Jer 15:10): he is disputing with Yahweh, complaining that the LORD has not fulfilled his covenanted promises to his people and, more particularly, to his prophet. Jeremiah's statement that he has rolled his *rîb* on Yahweh (Jer 11:20; 20:12) means more than handing over for God's judgment his quarrel with those who persecuted him. When he calls on God to "listen to the voice of my disputes" (*qôl yĕrîbay* [Jer 18:19]; on the textual problem, see AB 21A:123), he is reminding God of his promise to deliver him (Jer 1:19; 15:20). There were many times in Jeremiah's life when this promise must have seemed empty; for at one point Jeremiah desperately accuses Yahweh of deceiving him in this matter (Jer 20:7). The distress of Habakkuk is similar to that of Jeremiah. Their sense of desertion, like that of Job, Jesus, and countless others, arises from the failure of God to protect or rescue those who trusted him. In the case of Habakkuk, the resolution of this crisis for faith, expressed in Hab 3:17–18, provides a tangible link between the closing hymn and the opening prayer. And it shows the whole book to be an intensely personal "passion" of the prophet himself.

In focusing the explanation on the predicament of one person (Habakkuk himself), we have in mind the concern of the Hebrew Bible for specific situations and concrete events rather than concern to discourse on universal generalizations. This does not mean, however, that oracles for the occasion are just whimsical and arbitrary responses of the deity. Habakkuk expects consistency in God's behavior to match his reputed character as just. So each event in which God is involved has lasting value as a revelation of God's true being and as an expression of his holiness and righteous that people can trust (2:4). Hence the preservation and continual reuse of the old stories (Habakkuk 3 is a splendid example). The records of God's notable deeds in history are memorials and monuments from the past. But can they be used as paradigms for the present and future?

Yahweh is the living God, not to be controlled by humans. The precedents recited as the story of God's people do not become patterns and programs for every future development of a similar kind. They do not permit predictions, by analogy, of God's response that people can count on. There is a consistent inconsistency in Yahweh's behavior, as recorded in the Hebrew Bible, that has always been disturbing for those who believe that Yahweh is the one and only real God, always free and interacting freely with human freedom, so that nothing is determined, everything is unpredictable. You never know where you are with the living God.

It is precisely the attempt to gain understanding of God's ways (so that we know where we stand with him) by means of generalizations (such as that God routinely rewards the righteous and punishes the wicked) that caused Habakkuk such perplexity and vexation. This bewilderment, even frustration, continually turns up in the Bible, for it is the unavoidable consequence of faith in God's justice that often does not match the way things are in this world.

In the Bible, there are bold spirits who dare to indict God for his failure to manage this world in a way that a good, just, and competent Creator should. Moses and Jeremiah were remarkably outspoken on this subject; but their audacity rises from a core faith that God is just. Similar criticisms of God's regime can be made speciously, for paradoxically, the dismissal of such a God is vacuous if there is no such God! This kind of comment can be mere sophistry. There are many profound, sensitive, and morally serious persons who find the way things are unacceptable and reject with understandable loathing and justifiable indignation the trite demands of some religious people to believe in a good God blindly, in spite of everything. It is to the credit of the Bible that it faces that dilemma. The best exemplar of such honesty is Job, and Habakkuk is very much like him.

The intensity of their agony (it is painful for them to keep on believing in God) and the genuineness of the moral concern that drives their criticism of God shows that their seeming doubt arises from a deeper ground of faith. This sets such men and women apart from the superficial or skeptical or cynical commentators who ease that pain by ceasing to believe. The fact that Job prays, and persists in prayer, makes all the difference. Habakkuk is the same.

The prayer of Habakkuk is a complaint. He has already pleaded and petitioned—for too long, he thinks. God's unresponsiveness is not only intolerable, it is irresponsible. The energy with which the prophet struggles against God, to force a blessing, is characteristic of biblical prayers. Abraham long ago had dared to disagree with God's proposal to destroy the Cities of the Plain. Indeed, God opened himself to such discussion, as if he wanted (needed?) Abraham's support and approval before going into action. In that instance, the outcome was a standoff. Concessions were made; the quota of righteous persons needed to exempt a community from divine punishment was lowered, almost to a minimum. Readers have wondered why Abraham quit when he was doing so well. Why not try for one? Perhaps Abraham thought he had pushed as far as he dared. After all, ten would have been a very small fraction of the population, and even the most depraved community should have at least that many. Jeremiah was sent on a futile search for just one righteous person in the Jerusalem of his day, and Ezekiel was told that even the presence in the city of the three most righteous persons of all time would not save anyone besides themselves. A psalmist recorded the dismal opinion that God was searching for at least one righteous person, without success: "There is none righteous, no, not one!"

The ground of Abraham's negotiations for moderation of God's severity was a belief that the judge of the whole world must do what is right (Gen 18:25). And what he does must satisfy the human ombudsman, in this case Abraham. God is morally accountable to Abraham.

The notion that God's moral government of the world must meet human standards of morality pulls in two directions. If God is not seen to be just, how can we believe that he *is* just? If questions about God's justice are silenced by quoting good biblical texts that remind us of the immense (infinite) difference between humans and their Creator, does this mean that our primal, indestructible notions of fairness and rightness, even in our behavior with one another, have no validity for God? Isaiah 55 can be quoted perversely to claim that God operates with a system of morality quite different from ours. We can find just as many good biblical quotations that close the gap, that affirm identical standards for God and humans. If we are required to be holy because God is holy, we are equally required to do *ṣedeq*, and nothing but *ṣedeq*, because that is what God does. So when, to all appearances, God has failed to do *ṣedeq*, the very least that a human might expect is some kind of explanation. And tormented souls are forever sending up to God the anguished cry, "Why?" (Job 3).

There is no occasion in the Bible in which God forbids or rebukes such a question. When God does respond, as in the case of Job, he might not give the kind of answer that Job was hoping for. And many readers have been uncomfortable, puzzled, even outraged, by the devious, even irrelevant, way in which God deflects the debate away from moral issues to a grand tour of his zoo (Job 38–41). Yet Job is our hero. He was right to talk as he did, and even God affirms that in the end (Job 42:7, 8). It is appropriate for a human to hold God accountable.

There is a kind of philosophical piety that is horrified by the presumption of people like Job, who protest to God against God. Ivan Karamazov is one of the most vehement and unanswerable of those voices. It does them no good for believers to affirm the sovereignty of God and the inscrutability of God's ways.

Prayer often seems futile. There is no identifiable response from God (vv 2aB // 2bB). God continues to look at (and to show the prophet) iniquity, trouble, destruction, and lawlessness (v 3a). The three parts of v 3a cover all facets of the situation; it's in front of me (v 3aB); you see it (v 3aAβ); you show it to me (v 3aAα).

This has been going on for a long time, and there is no sign of letup.

Verses 2–3 lay the blame squarely and exclusively on God. And it is precisely because of God's delinquency that humans get away with so much wrongdoing. There are two ways in which Yahweh might have been expected to intervene in situations of this kind, especially when his people appeal to him for redress in their prayers, and most of all when a prophet makes intercession. Elsewhere, the Bible encourages such negotiations with assurances that God can be depended on to hear and answer. The first kind of response would be through an oracle (various techniques were available), with a message of doom for the wrongdoer, of deliverance for the oppressed. The second kind of response would be some overt act of judgment against the wicked, its main purpose being to rescue and vindicate the one in the right.

Traditions from earlier times included numerous stories about both kinds of divine response, the deliverance from Egypt under Moses being the great paradigm. But nothing of the kind had happened recently. Yahweh has been equally heedless of the people's plight and of the prophet's prayers. He said nothing; he did nothing. It is possible in the total context of the prayer that v 4 records Yahweh's failure to pronounce the verdict that Habakkuk has sought. As discussed in the NOTES, *yṣ' mišpāṭ* can describe divine speech (cf. Ps 109:7). The slackening of *tôrâ* could be another way of describing the silence of God. If v 4 is a restatement of vv 2aB // 2bB, then the related conjunction *'al-kēn* argues that God does not speak *tôrâ* // *mišpāṭ* because he doesn't even listen to the prophet's *rîb*. This reading implies that *tôrâ* is not an established body of revealed instructions for life and, especially, for the administration of justice (that would be part of the nation's heritage), but a fresh ruling for the occasion, such as was granted to Moses in situations of crisis.

This is how the book begins. Hab 2:2 indicates that the LORD did respond. Even though vv 5–11 do not have a similar heading, we identify them as spoken by God. They begin the dialogue that continues through the rest of the book.

III. YAHWEH'S FIRST RESPONSE (1:5–11)

◆

1:5aA	Look among the nations and gaze!
5aB	And be astonished, be astounded!
5bA	For I am doing a deed in your days;
5bB	you won't believe when it is reported.
6aA	For behold I am raising up the Chaldeans,
6aB	the bitter and impetuous nation,
6bA	that marches over the breadth of the earth,
6bB	to seize territories not its own.
7a	Dreadful and terrifying is he.
7b	His justice and status proceed from himself.
8aAα	And his horses are swifter than leopards,
8aAβ	and they are more savage than evening wolves.
8aB	And his cavalry dashes ahead,
8bA	and his cavalry gallops vast distances.
8bB	They swoop on their prey like a swift eagle to devour.
9aA	All of them come for violence.
9aB	The *mgmt* of their faces is to the front.
9b	And he gathered prisoners like sand.
10aA	And he, he ridiculed kings,
10aB	and rulers were a laughingstock for him;
10bA	he, he laughed at every fortress.
10bB	And he heaped up earth and captured it.
11a	Then the spirit swept on and passed by;
11b	and he was guilty—he whose strength is his god.

Scansion of Yahweh's First Response (1:5–11)

		BEATS	SYLLABLES	BICOLON
5aA	rĕʾû baggôyīm wĕhabbîṭû	3	9	
5aB	wĕhittamměhû tĕmāhû	2	8	17
5bA	kî pōʿal pōʿēl bîmêkem	3	8	
5bB	lōʾ taʾămînû kî yĕsuppār	4[1]	8	16
6aA	kî-hinĕnî mēqîm ʾet-hakkaśdîm	4	10	
6aB	haggôy hammar wĕhannimhār	3	8	18
6bA	hahôlēk lĕmerḥăbê-ʾereṣ	2[2]	8	
6bB	lārešet miškānôt lōʾ-lô	3	7	15
7a	ʾāyōm wĕnôrāʾ hûʾ	3	6	
7b	mimmennû mišpāṭô ûśĕʾētô yēṣēʾ	4	12	18
8aA	wĕqallû minnĕmērîm sûsāyw	3	9	
	wĕḥaddû mizzĕʾēbê ʿereb	3	8	17
8aB	ûpāšû pārāšāyw	2	6	
8bA	ûpārāšāyw mērāḥôq yābōʾû	3	10	16
8bB	yāʿūpû kĕnešer ḥāš leʾĕkôl	4	8	
9aA	kullōh lĕḥāmās yābôʾ	3	7	15
9aB	mĕgammat pĕnêhem qādîmâ	3	9	
9b	wayyeʾĕsōp kaḥôl šebî	3	7	16
10aA	wĕhûʾ bammĕlākîm yitqallās	3	9	
10aB	wĕrōzĕnîm misḥāq lô	3	7	16
10bA	hûʾ lĕkol-mibṣār yiśḥāq	3	7	
10bB	wayyiṣbōr ʿāpār wayyilkĕdāh	3	9	16
11a	ʾāz ḥālap rûaḥ wayyaʿăbōr wĕʾāšēm	5[3]	10	
11b	zû kōḥô lēʾlōhô	3	7	17

[1] Each word has a Masoretic accent. The two particles are stressed; maqqef is not used.

[2] The construct noun has no Masoretic accent in BHS—an error in L. Other editions (for example, van der Hooght / Hahn [1867]) have mûnaḥ but no maqqef, three beats.

[3] We accept the Masoretic placement of ʾatnaḥ.

INTRODUCTION

The poetic features of Yahweh's first response (1:5–11) are markedly different from those of Habakkuk's first prayer (1:2–4).

1. The language is more ample and a little closer to the usage of prose. The presence of six "prose particles" (five the definite article) in a unit of eighty words (7.5 percent) is not high on the differentiating scale. But the gross incidence is not the best measure, and they are all concentrated in v 6. As far as the rest of the unit is concerned, there are places where "prose particles" might have been used, but were not. The definite article, normal for prose, could have been employed in the construct phrases in vv 6bA and 8aA. If every possible "prose particle" had been used, there would have been 16 or 20 percent, well above the average for standard Biblical Hebrew prose.

The parallelism of *bammĕlākîm* // *rōzĕnîm* is revealing in this connection. The Masoretes sensed that the nouns were definite and were able to supply the definite article to the first because it rides on the inseparable preposition. But they were unable to match *rōzĕnîm*, for that would have required alteration of the consonantal text. Note the similar inconsistency between *kšnešer* (v 8) and *kahôl* (v 9). In poetry, a noun can have a definite reference without using the definite article; an instance is *rûah*, "like the wind" (v 11a [RSV]). The relative "pronoun" *'ăšer* was not used where it might (should) have been in vv 5bB, 6bB, 8bB. Note the archaic determiner or relative "pronoun" *zû* in v 11b.

Another prose feature is the use of *wāw*-consecutive verb forms (*wayye'ĕsōp, wayyiṣbōr, wayyilkĕdāh, wayya'ăbōr*). But they are intermingled with *yiqtōl* verb forms that clearly have the same time reference, namely past, so the *wāw*-consecutive pointing is probably a Masoretic artificiality. Coupled with this feature, we note a number of *qātal* forms preceded by *wāw* (*wĕqallû, wĕhaddû, ûpāšû, wĕ'āšēm*). In normal prose, this construction has future tense as its salient reading. In a few places in the verb paradigm, the distinction between the past and the future reference of a *qātal* verb form is secured by a difference in the stress pattern (penultimate for past, ultimate for future), but for most attested instances there is no formal differentiation. The ambiguity can be resolved only by congruence with other unambiguous verb forms in a coherent text. This principle of congruence suggests that the three different verb forms in v 11a (*'āz hālap rûah wayya'ăbōr wĕ'āšēm*) all have the same tense value, namely past. Thus the two *yiqtōl* forms in v 10 should likewise be accepted as past tense. These clauses should be read as narrative.

The policy of refocusing the time frame from past to future was already in place by the time the Hebrew Bible was translated into Greek, doubtless brought about by a belief that prophecy was prediction. So LXX made all the verbs in vv 7–11 future, even those pointed by the later scribes as *wāw*-consecutive. The same was done in Hab 2:6b. Admittedly, the difference between *wĕ-* and *wa-* in pronunciation of the conjunction would have been almost imperceptible in living speech. Yet the distinction was carefully preserved, and, while always open for reconsideration, the judgment of the rabbinic scribes has first claim. In some instances, reading a past-tense verb as future betrays thoughtlessness. Even in

Hab 1:14 LXX renders *watta'áśeh* "and thou didst make" as *kai poiēseis* "and thou shalt make." Impossible!

2. The prosody of vv 5–11 is more regular than that of vv 2–4. The twenty-four colons come as twelve bicolons, with a fair amount of internal parallelism. But the syntax of these bicolons rarely fits the simple formula supplied by many writers on Biblical Hebrew poetry. The preferred unit is said to be "a relatively short sentence-form that consists of two brief clauses" (Kugel 1981:1), the second one matching, repeating, echoing the first in some fashion. In Hab 1:5–11, there are not twenty-four clauses—one per colon. Some clauses, such as v 5b, are so long that one clause is enough for a bicolon (so-called "synthetic parallelism," a misnomer because there is no parallelism at all). Verse 6a, whose language we have already noted as prose-like, is one long clause shaped by its natural prosodies into a quatrain. Other clauses are so short (some just one word) that there can be more than one clause in a colon (for example, vv 5aA, 5aB, 10bB; three clauses in v 11a, according to the Masoretic accentuation).

In terms of rhythmic scansion, the unit is quite regular. Measuring length by the number of syllables, the bicolons are slightly longer, on average, than the standard sixteen-syllable bicolon of Hebrew lyrical and cultic poetry, with a range from fifteen to eighteen syllables among individual bicolons. The individual colons spread over a wider range (six to twelve syllables). In other words, although the bicolons are pretty uniform in total length, the caesura comes at various positions, so that the colons in one bicolon are sometimes quite unequal. In fact, only one bicolon fits the ideal of 8:8 (v 5b). By contrast, the bicolon in v 7 is quite lopsided, and, moreover, with the second colon twice as long as the first, it violates the rule set by some writers on the theory of Biblical Hebrew poetry that the first colon can be longer than the second, but never the reverse.

There is very little conventional parallelism in this unit; v 10 has a standard word pair, but that is as far as it goes. Each has a different role in the syntax (object, subject). That switch enables the poet to put the two pronominal references to the Chaldean nation ("and-he . . . to-him") in a chiastic inclusion:

10aA   *wĕhû' bammĕlākîm yitqallās*
10aB   *wĕrōzĕnîm miśḥāq lô*

Verse 8aA has parallel similes. Sometimes there is parallelism *within* a colon (Watson 1989a), either by repeating a root (v 5aB; cognate object [the diction here is poetic]) or by assonance (vv 8aB, 8bA).

3. Finally we note a moderate use of chiasmus:

8aB	*ûpāšû*	*pārāšāyw*		
8bA		*ûpārāšāyw*	*mērāḥôq*	*yābō'û*
8bB	*yā'ūpû*	*kĕnešer*	*ḥāš*	*le'ĕkôl*
9aA		*kullōh*	*lĕḥāmās*	*yābô'*
10aA	*wĕhû'*	*bammĕlākîm*	*yitqallās*	
10aB		*wĕrōzĕnîm*	*miśḥāq*	*lô*

There is no introduction to this unit to identify it as a speech of God using a standard formula, such as "Thus said Yahweh. . . ." It is the content that clearly marks it as a divine proclamation.

Yahweh's first response to Habakkuk's prayer is simple; it announces one coming event. The message, however, is not addressed to the prophet personally, however personal his prayer might have been. The opening imperative verbs and matching pronouns are plural. It sounds like an oracle for public proclamation. In other words, Habakkuk's opening prayer is ignored or, rather, the response is not supplied as an answer that explicitly takes up the issues in that prayer. Habakkuk is told to carry on with his work as a prophet, however arduous and perplexing. If this oracle is an answer to his prayer, it is devious. Hence the impression gained by many previous scholars that there is no connection between vv 2–4 and vv 5–11 at all.

There is something remorseless in the tone of Yahweh's response that makes it shocking for listeners, an effect that Yahweh himself clearly intended (v 5aB).

In response to the prophet's query "How much longer . . . ?" Yahweh promises action. He is about to raise up the Chaldeans (v 6aA). That is all. The participle in v 5bA and, especially, the construction *hinĕnî mēqîm* (v 6aA) announce impending action. The remainder of the speech (most of it) is dedicated to a description of the Chaldeans, "the bitter and impetuous nation" (v 6aB), with no attempt to conceal the horror of their policies and the cruelty of their practices. If the evident reading of the verbs as past tense is valid, this is a recital of the deeds the Chaldeans have already performed, as the audience can confirm by gazing around among the nations (v 5aA).

Although the oracle begins with a prediction of what Yahweh is about to do, it is mainly about what the Chaldeans have already done. What they might do next, as Yahweh's agent (the language of v 6aA is clear on that point), is left to the imagination, already horrified and terrorized by knowledge of the established reputation of the Chaldeans for aggression and atrocities.

NOTES

5. *Look.* The same verbs are used in God's response as in Habakkuk's prayer, and in the same poetic sequence (see the NOTE on v 3). Habakkuk saw only distressing lawlessness in the world. God invites him to look at it so as to see justice in that violence, not in spite of it. BDB (907b) suggests that *rā'â* with *b-* means "gaze at (a spectacle)." The idiom *rā'â b-* is attested forty times, and the command to inspect the nations is appropriate; Habakkuk's sights are being raised. The idea is similar to that in Exod 34:10: "And he [Yahweh] said, Behold, I make a covenant: before all thy people I will do marvels, such as have not been done in all the earth, nor in all the nations [*hgwym*]; and all the people among which thou art shall see [*rā'â*] the work of the LORD: for it is a terrible thing that I will do with thee."

The verbs are plural. The message is not a private one for Habakkuk's personal benefit. It is an oracle for public proclamation. But, apart from the plural

verbs, there is no hint as to the identity of the intended audience. This is not
the case, however, with some ancient versions, whose evidence for v 5a is mixed:

MT   *rĕ'û baggôyīm   wĕhabbîṭû   wĕhittammĕhû tĕmāhû*
LXX   *idete hoi kataphronētai kai epiblepsate kai thaumasate thaumasia
            kai aphanisthēte*
      Look, you despisers, and gaze and wonder with wonder and disappear!

NT   *idete hoi kataphronētai   kai thaumasate   kai aphanisthēte*
      Look, you despisers   and wonder   and disappear! (Acts 13:41)

V   *aspicite in gentibus   et videte   et admiramimi et obstupescite*
      Look carefully among the nations and see and wonder and be
            astounded!

the nations. Habakkuk has said nothing about the nations. He gave no indication that he was concerned about world events. The reading *baggôyyīm*
is, accordingly, a surprise. While Aquila, Symmachus, and Theodotion have
translations that match MT "in the Gentiles," along with Vulgate *in gentibus*,
LXX *hoi kataphronētai*, "you scorners!" (quoted in Acts 13:41), and Syriac
mrḥ', "supercilious ones," can be retrojected to *bōgĕdîm*, because LXX *kat-
aphronountas* matches *bôgĕdîm* at Hab 1:13, and *kataphronētēs* matches *bôgēd*
at Hab 2:5.
    This evidence points to a variant *(hab)bôgĕdîm* in v 5a. The change *bgwym*
⟷ *bwgdym* could have taken place in either direction. On the one hand, if
bgwym is original, reading *bwgdym* for *bgwym* within the transmission of the
Hebrew text requires the transposition of *w* and addition of *d*. It is possible
that the change was motivated by the need to know whom Yahweh is addressing
(the verbs have no subject in the MT). To judge from Jerome's comments (not
the Vulgate text), he saw Hebrew manuscripts with this variant. The choice
of *bwgdym* could have been prompted by its similarity to *bgwym* and by influence from words with √*bgd* that occur later in the book (the spelling of the
participle is *plene* in Hab 1:13 and Hab 2:5). Retrojection of the Greek vocative might require the restoration of *hbwgdym* in the *Vorlage*, the definite article making it a bit more difficult to accept the derivation of this variant from
bgwym. Even so, leveling influences are more likely to flow forward than backward. And it should be remembered that *bwgdym* is not the only candidate to
be the source of *kataphronētai*. Were it not for the root *bgd* in the MT of
Habakkuk, one could suspect roots *bwz* or *bzh* in the *Vorlage*. Hebrew *bôgēd*,
"deceiver," "traitor," is not the same as Greek *kataphronēs*, "despiser," and this
semantic shift complicates things somewhat. Bruce (1951:272) says that *hoi
katafronētai* "would represent Heb. *ha-bōzīm*." While it is true that in LXX the
verb *katafronein* renders both √*bwz* and √*bgd*, the noun matches only √*bgd*,
and of the six occurrences in the MT of the participle of √*bzh*, only one (Prov
19:16) is rendered in LXX by the participle of *katafronein*. So Bruce's retrojection is too confident.

On the other hand, if (*h*)*bwgdym* was original, we have to explain how it became *bgwym*. That word is common and might have been written by pure carelessness. A third possibility (suggested by David Noel Freedman) is that both words were originally present (in either order), and one was lost by word haplography.

It is highly likely and generally accepted that the Qumran *pôšēr* read *bwgdym* in his source text, but we cannot be certain because the line containing the biblical text is missing from the bottom of the first column. The commentator has much to say about traitors who violated the covenant (1QpHab col. ii, lines 6–7)—that is, they are apostate Jews—and nothing to say about the "nations." Even so, just as we did not allow the language of the *pešer* at v 3 as evidence for replacing MT *'ml* with *m'l*, so it would be going too far to declare *bwgdym* superior to *bgwym* in v 5. Rather than seeing *m'l* as an inner-Hebrew variant by metathesis that came to the Qumran commentator ready-made, it is more likely that he felt free to play on the sounds and talk about *m'l*, without having to change the original. He could have done the same thing with *bgwym*.

In the context of the book, the MT is a suitable reading. Habakkuk's vision is set on the world stage; the Qumran interpreter shrank it to sectarian squabbles within Judaism.

The request for an explanation was not made by "despisers" or "traitors," so there is no reason why the response should be addressed to them. If the Neo-Babylonian Empire had already risen up and was active on the international stage, it would be appropriate to direct attention to this development by asking the (Judean) listeners to "look among the nations."

By the time the end of the book is reached, Habakkuk's vision has expanded to cosmic proportions. The progression is like that in the book of Job, where questions that arise from one man's personal anguish are answered by an apparently irrelevant excursion into the realms of nature. The purposes of God for one person or one nation can be understood only in terms of the whole world. This means that God alone understands it all, while humans get glimpses. The purpose of God for one period of time ("your days" [v 5bA]) can be understood only in terms of eternity (v 12) and eschatology.

be astounded. The arrangement of the verbs in v 5a presents problems for analysis. With *zāqēp qāṭôn* on *habbîṭû* and *'atnāḥ* on *těmāhû*, the MT groups the verbs in two pairs. There is no problem with the first pair, but the second two are curious. There is no "and" before the last verb. Normally two pairs of items in Hebrew would be coordinated "A and B, C and D," not "A and B and C, D," as here. This asymmetry could be rectified by a slight textual change, supplying a third "and" (*wāw*- lost by haplography with the terminal -*wāw* of *whtmhw*) and even by deleting the middle *wāw* (added by dittography from the terminal *wāw* of *whbyṭw*). More problematic is the progression from *Hitpa'el* to *Qal* in the two verbs based on the root *tmh*. Both mean "be astonished." If the *Hitpa'el* (found only here in the Hebrew Bible) is more intensive, we would expect it to come second for the sake of climax. But the same progression of *binyānîm* is used in Zeph 2:1. It would be more climactic if a new sentence begins with *těmāhû*, and this would also explain the pattern of "and."

By joining all the verbs with "and," the versions escape the awkwardness of MT's lack of "and" with the final verb. LXX is more ample than MT, with an additional word: "Behold, you despisers, and look, and marvel marvellously, and perish!" It is difficult to recover the textual development from *wěhittamměhû těmāhû* (MT) to *kai thaumasate thaumasia kai aphanisthēte* (LXX). The match of MT's cognate verb with LXX's cognate noun suggests that *kai aphanisthēte* (found also in Acts 13:41) is an extra, with no evident basis in MT, unless it points to an infinitive absolute *tāmôah*, lost by haplography. But the latter is a match for the final verb in MT, at least in being a verb, so LXX possibly has a conflate reading of originally alternative renderings of the final verb. Or else "LXX may simply be an attempt to give a fuller rendering to the longer hithpalel form" (Roberts 1991:91). The Vulgate confirms MT, except for the additional "and," which makes for smoother reading. NT's lack of a match for *wěhabbîṭû*, which comes through in both LXX and V, marks Acts 13:41 as inferior. It lost the first word by haplography through double homoeoarcton. Archer and Chirichigno's (1983:159) judgment that NT "is therefore closer to the MT in leaving out *kai epiblepsate*" is doctrinaire.

Isa 29:9 contains a similar construction — *htmhmw wtmhw*. If these verbs were cognate, we would have the same transition from complex to simple. The ensuing pair of verbs in Isa 29:9 have a similar pattern *hšt῾š῾wš῾w*. It is more likely that Isa 29:9 should be brought into line with Hab 1:5 by reading *htmhw* ($\sqrt{tmh}$) in both places. Habakkuk knows the *Hitpa῾el* of *mhh* (2:2), but a command to linger would be inappropriate in both places, unless it means "Gaze on the nations, and take your time!" The construction in Isa 29:9 provides further clarification of the progression from the complex to the simple verb forms of the same root. It describes a transition from the iterative aspect to the stative:

> Become more and more astounded until you are quite stupefied;
> become more and more blind until you are quite blind!

Isa 29:9 also contributes to Hab 1:5 an argument for adding "and" to the fourth verb.

The LXX command *kai aphanisthēte*, "and perish!" has moved further from this idea and, in spite of its use in NT to address a hostile audience, must be set aside as interpretive.

In addition, the continuation of Isa 29:9 shows that the state of stunned amazement described by the root *tmh* is like advanced intoxication. The verb describes astonishment at some unexpected and inexplicable event (Gen 43:33), accompanied by confusion and anguish (Jer 4:9; Ps 48:6, also in association with *rā῾â*).

Habakkuk had hoped that the LORD would do or say something to relieve his distress. This response is intended to be devastating, not comforting. Hence suspicion that this unit could be a prior oracle that is the cause of his opening prayer. As a response to his questions in vv 2–4, vv 5–11 can only make matters worse. There is going to be more lawlessness (note *ḥāmās* again in v 9) and on a global scale. No attempt is made to soften the horrors of the Chaldean world conquest. No explanation in terms of moral purpose is advanced. The inference so frequently made by commentators that the Chaldeans are God's chosen instrument for judgment on the deserving wicked (Assyria, Egypt, or the godless in Judah) finds no support in the passage itself.

deed. The noun *pō'al* will be picked up in Hab 3:2, an important link between the two parts of the prophecy. The conquest of the world by Babylon was actually an act of God.

I am doing. The construction is succinct. The subject "I" is not present. Cannon (1925:67) and Budde (1931:410) favor the restoration of *'ănî* on the basis of LXX *egō ergazomai*. The pronoun may be rightly understood from the parallel participial clause in v 6a. This double action of *hinĕnî* is important evidence that the principle of double duty can operate retroactively (NJB). Other examples of a participle predicate without the expected pronoun subject are Jer 38:23 (relieved in one MS by reading *Hoph'al*) and 1 Sam 6:3, without benefit of a nearby parallel. First Sam 2:24 is sometimes adduced, but Driver (1913b:34) raises weighty objections. Ps 7:10, adduced by Keil (1954:78), is not a certain example because the participle could be a title (NAB), or perhaps "Just God" is the subject (AB16:40) in spite of the abnormal word order. Recognizing in this way the grammatical cohesion between v 5bA and v 6aA rules out any need for improving or adjusting the text by supplying a pronoun subject *'ănî*, by reading *'ep'al* (gratuitously preferred by BHS), or by following V (*opus factum est*) and Tg (*'t'byd*) to make the participle passive (Roberts 1991:91): "a work is being done" (NAB, NEB, NRSV; RSV had "I am doing a work"). No passive of *p'l* seems to be attested in the MT, but Budde (1931:410) suggests *pō'al* ("or better *yĕpō'al* or *yippā'ēl*") as a possible emendation. This emendation distances God as the doer of the deed, and makes v 5bA inconsistent with v 6aA. Unnecessary, indeed implausible. Applying the word *hinĕnî* to both participles shows that God's astounding deed is precisely the active raising up of the Chaldeans and that the action is impending, not yet current.

in your days. The pronoun is plural; the people are addressed, not just the prophet. Because *yāmîm* can mean a "life span," God promises to do this deed within the life span of those who hear the oracle or one generation at the most. On the expectation that everyone now living will be dead in seventy years (or most adults in forty years), fulfillment would not have to be immediate (Hab 2:3). The impression is that it will take place soon, but the time reference is not precise enough to be used for dating this oracle or the prophecy as a whole. Keil (1954:51), for example, infers that it was written during the reign of Josiah, rather than during one of his successors, so as to make room for delayed fulfillment in the next generation.

you won't believe. If the inactivity of God (vv 2–4) is incomprehensible, the activity of God (vv 5–11) is incredible. The verb used here (root *'mn*) has an intellectual component (confidence in the truthfulness of the report) as well as the element of trust. You rely on God because you are convinced that he is reliable. There is a similar problem in Isa 53:1, and the same root is used again in the word "faith" in Hab 2:4. In Hab 1:5, as a parallel to astonishment, this expected disbelief is not so much a difficulty in accepting the reported facts (Gen 45:26), as in acknowledging (*h'mn* means "affirm") the events as acts of God perceived to have a just purpose. Far from countering the temptation to unbelief that drives Habakkuk's opening prayer, God's response adds to the strain, and God openly says that he doesn't expect the people to believe what he says he will do. The anticipated disbelief is not the same as the unbelief of Manasseh's heedlessness (2 Chr 33:10; cf. 2 Kgs 21:12). This "deed" of God constitutes a crisis of faith for the believer, not an invitation to faith for the unbeliever. The real cause of that crisis is not explained. The idea that God raises up a foreign nation to accomplish his purpose was not new and should not have surprised any Israelites who knew their traditions, as old as the Exodus. Why should this act be astounding? Is it incredible that a just God could use wicked foreigners to punish wicked Judeans? If the "deed" is the spectacular rise of Babylon, and the sudden dramatic collapse of the Assyrians, does the difficulty lie in believing that such distant events are acts of Israel's God? If so, the world stage (v 6b) might dwarf the problems in Judah as but a small part of God's domain.

reported. The use of √*spr* points to storytelling, not preaching. The "deed" will not be "believed," even after it has happened and the report is given. It does not mean that the prediction will be disbelieved. In any case, the prophecy is not given by way of a warning from which the listeners might profit. Yet this is not the main point. The problem for faith in the prophetic word at this time was not just the credibility of the prophet in his speech, it was the credibility of Yahweh in his acts. If the situation in Judah that is disclosed more fully in the book of Jeremiah is any guide to the mood of the times, Habakkuk is himself struggling with the acute crisis in Judah as to whether they were still God's favored people. Having survived the Assyrian threat at the time of Hezekiah—an astonishing miracle—Judah was convinced that no power on earth could harm them. The holy Temple in Jerusalem was the focal point of this false trust (Jeremiah 7, cf. Hab 2:20). The Chaldeans could not be worse than the Assyrians, and the power of Yahweh would be a match for the one as for the other. Habakkuk does not enter a polemic against this self-deceiving faith the way Jeremiah does. But then he does not simply transpose the earlier faith of Isaiah into his own times. He is caught in the middle. This oracle does not say explicitly that God is now sending the Chaldeans against Jerusalem (Jer 34:22), but because the Chaldeans are going to conquer the whole world, Judah will not be excluded. The state of stunned disbelief predicted in Hab 1:5 was expressed in the book of Lamentations, after the event.

English translations usually connect vv 5bA and 5bB by making the latter a relative clause modifying "deed," although there is no relative pronoun in the source text. The result is awkward, as in "a work . . . that you would not have believed were it told" (NAB). Indicatives are better than subjunctives. But both clauses in v 5b are probably covered by the opening conjunction "because," and these two subordinate clauses correspond, each in turn, to the two commands given in v 5a:

Look around,
because the LORD is about to perform a deed
Be astounded
(because) you will not believe it!

6. *raising up.* The divine intention was announced several times in this form:
2 Sam 12:11; Amos 6:14 (this does not warrant the addition of "against you" to
Hab 1:6); Zech 11:16. All these passages are referring to impending judgments.
For the idiom, compare Mic 5:4 and Jer 5:15 (contemporary, with *mēbî'*). Jer
5:15; 6:22 similarly describe the calling up of an invader by Yahweh. Unlike
some of these examples, in which the oracle is addressed to the intended victims of the punitive action, Hab 1:6 does not specify whom the LORD is raising
up the Chaldeans against. And, unless we emend v 5, the audience of the oracle is not identified either. Such warnings are found elsewhere in Scripture as
the culmination of judgment speeches that spell out the moral justification for
the impending action by presenting it as punishment of the deserving wicked.
That inference does not fit the present context. Such a plan would cause satisfaction, not astonishment. No attempt is made to ease the anticipated strain on
the listeners' faith by justifying the actions of the Chaldeans as agents of God
by pointing out the guilt of their victims. The announcement emphasizes the
ruthlessness and wickedness of the conquerors, especially their idolatry (the
supreme wickedness), in contrast to the innocence and helplessness of their victims. In particular, it cannot be maintained that the Chaldeans are to chastise
"the wicked" about whom Habakkuk complained in v 4, for in v 13 he is still
complaining that the wicked swallow "the righteous."

Chaldeans. The term is characteristic of the Neo-Babylonian Empire, whose
rise can be dated to the accession of Nabopolassar (626–605 B.C.E.). It lasted until the fall of Babylon to Cyrus in 539 B.C.E. After its first attestation early in the
first millennium B.C.E., the word *kaśdîm* (better *kaśdiyyîm*) designates an ethnic
group located in the southern part of Mesopotamia. A typical early notice is
found on the "Black Obelisk" of Shalmaneser III (859–825 B.C.E.). In his eighth
year, he was obliged to engage in a punitive expedition into Babylon. (*ARAB*
I:203–4). The king of Babylon, Marduk-zakir-shumi, was an Assyrian vassal. His
brother, Marduk-bel-usate, evidently led an anti-Assyrian faction and rebeled
against the king. Shalmaneser marched forth "to avenge" his protégé. It needed
another campaign in his ninth year to complete the subjugation of the rebel.
For good measure, the Assyrian king proceeded as far as the Persian Gulf:

I went down to Chaldea
Their cities I captured
The gifts of the kings of Chaldea I received.
The terror of my arms overpowered (the enemy)
as far as the Bitter Sea. (*ARAB* I:204)

Judah's first substantial contact with the Chaldeans came in the reign of
Hezekiah. The cause of Babylonian nationalism was in the hands of Merodach-

Baladan, who sought alliance with Jerusalem (2 Kgs 20:12–21). Isaiah's condemnation of such politics included a prophecy that Jerusalem itself would be despoiled by the Babylonians in due time (Isa 39:4–7). Habakkuk's similar forecast a century later was not entirely new. For the time being, Sennacherib was able to subdue Merodach-Baladan. This pattern was repeated in 647 B.C.E., when Ashurbanipal quenched a similar rebellion by his brother Shamash-shum-iskun. Finally, the governor of Babylon, Nabopolassar (626–605 B.C.E) declared his independence. In concert with Medes and Scythians, he captured Nineveh in 612 B.C.E. At this point, Egypt moved in to support what remained of Assyrian strength and, for the time being, claimed Palestine. But in 605 B.C.E., the Egyptian army was defeated in the Battle of Carchemish. So the new Babylon was virtually master of the former provinces and vassals of Assyria "from the brook of Egypt to the river Euphrates" (2 Kgs 24:4). The Chaldeans under Nebuchadrezzar did not arrive in force in Judah until after 600 B.C.E. The prediction in Hab 1:5 could have been made any time before then. The vivid description of their army (1:5–11) suggests a time when their conquests had already created terror in nearby lands. If the Battle of Charchemish provides the description in vv 8–11, then the oracle can be dated precisely between 605 and 600 B.C.E.

Some such conclusion is so irresistible that scholars who build their interpretation around another date are forced to the desperate step of changing the word "Chaldeans" to something else or explaining it as purely symbolic.

Cannon (1925:77–83) gave nine distinct arguments against tampering with the word "Chaldeans" in Hab 1:5. Briefly summarized they are:

1. The leading word of a passage should never be changed in the interests of a theory. This argument can be made with even greater force. An emended reading should never be adduced as *evidence* for anything. Only in a most diffident way should an emendation—shown to be plausible itself on quite other grounds—be included as marginal, corroborative evidence. We are willing to acknowledge that the agreement of a proposed emendation with a plausible theory can be mentioned—taking the chain of reasoning backwards—as part of the argument for an emendation, but never as part of the main argument. In the case of *kaśdîm*, the only cogent argument would be that Habakkuk's language does not fit the Chaldeans, but does fit some other nation.

Let us state the logic in a somewhat extreme form. It is admitted (1) that a case can be made that what is said in this unit about the Chaldeans is not always easy to attach to what we know about these people or to what Habakkuk (near 600 B.C.E.) may have known about them. It is conceded further (2) that some other people might be nominated as fitting the description. This is not enough. It is precisely the lack of clarity in the picture that permits us to imagine identifications other than Chaldeans. But to settle the issue, it must be shown (3) that there is something in the picture that *cannot* fit the Chaldeans and (4) that there is something in the picture that can fit *only* the rival candidate. A major argument for identifying the enemy with the Greeks, and changing *kaśdîm* to *kittîm*, is the word *qādîmâ*, "eastwards," in Hab 1:9. This is not compelling for several reasons:

a. The word *qādîmâ* does not necessarily mean "eastwards." It depends on where you are looking at the situation. It can mean "forwards."
b. The Greeks did not come from the West, so far as their approach to Israel is concerned
c. The verse is too problematic in itself to bear the weight of such an important conclusion.

Cannon drew attention to other passages in which an enemy is described but not identified, such as Jeremiah 4–6 and Zeph 1:14–18. If only they had included the name—or even if an ancient copyist had added the name—the task of modern interpreters would be set up quite differently. They would not simply have to guess with an open field, but would have a candidate with first claim on credence.

2. Cannon pointed out that the proposed substitute *kittîm*, or *kittiyyīm*, is not used to describe a nation *haggôy* in the political sense, as here. It generally modifies a word like "coast" or "islands" or "land" so that it is geographic or at most gentilic (Num 22:24; Isa 23:1; Jer 2:10; Ezek 27:6), and this usage continues into the Greek period. In 1 Macc 1:1, it refers to the island of Cyprus or more western Greek regions. (The occurrence of *ktym* in the Arad ostraca can now be added to this evidence.) Cannon argued further that the more likely Hebrew term for Greeks as such was *bĕnê hayyĕwānîm* (Joel 4:6; Zech 9:13). In fact, the reading *hyyn* in Hab 2:5 has been corrected by some scholars into *hayyĕwānîm*, "the Ionians," to give another reference to the Macedonian Greeks. Yet it is unlikely that the writer would refer to the same nation by two different names and that both would then be lost.

3. The proposed reconstructed change to *hkśdym* from *ktym*, which never has the definite article, can hardly be due to a copying error. But, if intentional, what could have been its motivation? In later times, as in the book of Daniel, *hkśdym* no longer refers to a nation, but to a professional class of scholars. As such, the word "Chaldean" had a long afterlife, down into late antiquity. If the book is dated so late as to make an original reading *ktym* conceivable, it is altogether too late for the substitute *hkśdym* to be acceptable.

4. Cannon argued further that the Macedonians (in anticipation, or in experience) would not have been described with the horror that troubled Habakkuk so deeply.

5. Idolatry was a burning issue for the prophets (2:19), until the time of exile. After that the polemic moved into a new phase. Cannon does not think that this problem would have occupied the mind of a writer of 331 B.C.E. or later in this form.

6. A difficulty in the way of accepting the term "Chaldeans" as authentic is the further statement of Hab 1:5 that the observers will find this action of God incredible. On the one hand, Duhm (1906) argued that the Babylonians were so well known that no one would have been surprised that in due time they overcame their age-old enemies, the Assyrians. On the other hand, the Macedonians were newcomers to the scene in the fourth century B.C.E., and Alexan-

der's rapid advance must have caused astonishment and disbelief. There are several weak links in this chain of reasoning. The NOTES on v 5 have shown that it is not at all clear what it is about the LORD's action that will not be believed. In fact, what the LORD will do is mentioned in a single statement: "I am raising up the Chaldeans." The rest of the speech is taken up with a description of the character of the Chaldeans. Some of that description seems to refer to known actual achievements that have already given them their reputation. What it amounts to is world conquest—sudden, ruthless, irresistible. Why should this be incredible? Why should it be incredible when applied to the Greeks, but not incredible when applied to the Chaldeans?

7. The adjectives "bitter," "hasty," "terrible," "ruthless" are said to be more applicable to the Greeks than to the Chaldeans. More precisely, these qualities go with the use of cavalry (v 8), and there was a time when it was believed that the Chaldeans did not make much use of soldiers mounted on horseback (as distinct from chariotry). Such words are so general that they could apply to any dramatic change in world powers. The transition from Assyrian to Babylonian domination, as far as Judah was concerned, took place in little more than a decade. Everything changed. The successive capture of Asshur (614), Nineveh (612), and Haran (610) represented as spectacular a series of events as any in history. And, as though the total destruction of Assyria was not enough, Nebuchadrezzar in 605 B.C.E. inflicted utter defeat on Egypt. From that moment, any in Judah who knew about world politics must have recognized that their little state lay open and helpless before the Chaldeans. Already, to all intents and purposes, they had conquered the whole world.

8. As to the use of cavalry, the Assyrian monuments show horseback riders as well as charioteers in the army. The combination "horse(s), chariot(s), and riders" describes the Babylonian besiegers of Tyre in Ezekiel 26, a passage that has several affinities with Habakkuk 1. In any case, the argument for cavalry versus chariotry in Habakkuk 1 is slender. It rests on the absence of the word "chariot." But the word "riders" is ambiguous (see the NOTE on v 8), leaving the matter quite open.

9. It is true that Alexander the Great became a legend largely through the prowess of his cavalry, combining swiftness and impetuosity with discipline. But his conquests in the East were so swift that there was hardly time for his reputation to grow, let alone precede him. It should also be emphasized that "raise up" does not mean "bring a new nation into existence." It means "appoint to a task." So identification of the Kasdim as Greeks cannot be used to settle the date of Habakkuk. The equation could be considered only if the date of Habakkuk could be determined on other grounds.

bitter and impetuous. The second adjective repeats the consonants of the first. The sound play continues in *mrḥby* in the next colon. Hebrew *mar* usually means "bitter," the taste that is the opposite of "sweet" (Prov 2:7) or the wretchedness and resentment of a person struggling with lasting sorrow (1 Sam 1:10; Ruth 1:20). Such persons have good reason for their sadness, for life has ill-used them. They say that "God" has embittered them; Job said that, too. It is, accordingly, strange that a vicious aggressor should be called "bitter." BDB (600b) points to Judg 18:25 and 2 Sam 17:8 to support the meaning of "fierce." But the bitterness of a she-bear robbed of her whelps is the rage of loss, the desire for revenge. It is provoked. There is no hint here that the Chaldean world conquest was provoked. Perhaps the analogy, which the ensuing comparisons with other wild animals encourage us to suspect, arises from the savagery of an animal that will attack anything. The victims of the bereaved bear on the rampage are likely to be quite innocent, and it is this part of the simile, not the cause of the animal's fury, that applies to the Chaldeans.

As a parallel, "impetuous" might refer to the hot temper of the Chaldeans, but it could anticipate the description of the speed and efficiency of their troop movement, as described in v 8. The *Nipʿal nimhār* suggests energetic, impatient haste rather than impulsiveness. That it is morally neutral is shown by IQH (39:22–23): *ʿm nmhry ṣdq*, "people (?) eager for righteousness (or victory?)."

marches. The common participle "walking," which covers all kinds of locomotion, including swimming and sailing.

breadth (or "extremities"). A *merḥāb* is a broad expanse, a place of liberty (2 Sam 22:20; Pss 18:2; 31:9), where there is plenty of room (Hos 4:16). Although the expression "the vast surfaces of the earth" might suggest the huge area of the Chaldean empire, the verb "march to" highlights the enormous distances traveled by the Babylonian expeditions. The plural, used only here in the entire Hebrew Bible, brings out further the multiplicity of the Chaldean invasions. There is a similar semantic flux between distance and area in the use of *gĕbūl*, which can mean "territory" as well as "frontier." The parallel term *miškānōt*, "dwelling places," suggests inhabited regions, and the qualification "not his own" emphasizes that these conquered territories are outside the natural bounds of Chaldean soil, so that their conquests are robberies. God's agent is a thief. No limit is set for Neo-Babylonian expansion, so we could translate "march to the extremities of the earth" rather than "march through the breadth of the earth" (RSV). RSV "through" is not satisfactory as a translation of *l-*, and "breadth" misses both the plural of *merḥābê* and also the meaning of "large open area." Nevertheless, if "unto" were meant, *ʾel* or *ʿad* might have been expected. So it is possible that *l-* is a more general preposition of reference (there is no need to make it a lexical polysememe with "from" as one of its meanings). The movement is described not from the perspective of an observer in Babylon, who sees the army marching out to the most distant places of the earth, but from the viewpoint of an observer on the frontier, who sees them coming. The plural, however, might suggest an army coming from many distant places for mobilization rather than traveling the great distance from Babylon. This, and the use of the plural "nations" in v 17, supports the nuance in our alternative translation, which tries to include the idea of distance covered as well as area conquered.

seize (or "take possession"). The verb, based on √ *yrš*, is used frequently in the Hebrew Bible, especially in the Deuteronomic writings, to describe the Israelite occupation of the promised land. It implies dispossession as well as seizure and settlement. The original population was either exterminated or absorbed by Israel. The Neo-Babylonian policy was more imperialistic, with deportation and resettlement of whole populations. The imagery of catching nations like fishes in a net describes this very well. For Israelites, such a prospect—total deprivation of their traditional way of life (3:17)—would be nothing short of the shattering of the covenanted arrangement between Yahweh and his people. Because Yahweh himself is now raising up the Chaldeans to dispossess Israel, Israel has become like Canaan of old. Such connotations, however, are not developed in the explicit language of the prophet, and we should be cautious about importing them. We cannot be sure to what extent the choice of a traditional word like *lārešet* was intended to evoke such ideas. The analogy does not go very far. No one land is assigned to this new nation, and they are God's instrument, not his people. Even so, Jeremiah does use language to describe Yahweh's relation to Nebuchadrezzar similar to the traditional talk about Yahweh and Israel. So does Daniel. A limit is put to the analogy by the qualification that the lands are "not his own." But in the Deuteronomic theology, the promised land was Israel's only in the divine gift, and there is a biblical tradition that the country was always "Yahweh's land" (see the COMMENT on Hos 9:4 [AB 24A:528]; cf. Hos 2:25 ["my land"]).

territories. A *miškān* is a residence or shrine. In the P tradition, the *miškān* of Yahweh is the tent shrine (cf. *'ōhel mô'ēd*). In the plural, this noun can describe the encampments of a seminomadic people (Num 24:5; Ps 78:28; Song 1:8) or the tombs of the dead (Ps 49:12). There are many such terms of pastoralists that undergo a semantic shift with urbanization. Semitic *'uhlum* becomes *âlu*, "city," in Akkadian, *'ōhel*, "tent," in Hebrew. *Miškān* is a synonym of *'ōhel* (Job 21:28). *Nawum / nāweh* is another such word, and *byt*, "house," can similarly extend to "estate" and "realm" as well as "residence." This kind of transition is nicely illustrated by comparing Num 24:5 (pastoral) with Isa 54:2 and Jer 30:18 (urban). The parallelism of *nāweh* and *miškānōt* in Isa 32:18 is a metaphor that retains the nomadic memories as idyllic. The plural *miškānōt*, "habitations," can describe all the houses in a city such as Babylon (Jer 51:3) or, as a plural of majesty, the splendid Temple of Yahweh (Pss 43:3; 84:2; 132:5)—the latter being the whole of Zion as the LORD's residential complex (cf. Ps 46:5, with the masculine form of the plural). The meaning "territories," with no suggestion of houses or cities, is attested in Job 39:6. The wild ass has the salty wastelands as his *miškānōt*. The meaning in Hab 1:6 lies somewhere along this semantic spectrum—tents, houses, cities, (inhabited) regions. But where? The question is worth pursuing because parallelism with *mibṣār* in v 10bA, where the idea of capturing is present, should be considered. This need not conflict with its association with *merḥābîm* if it refers to cities as political (territorial) units as well as fortresses, because the verb √*yrš* describes the military seizure of lands rather than of individual buildings.

This review leaves several matters for further discussion, including the meaning of "house" in Hab 2:9–11. The statement "he passed on" in Hab 1:11 is a further point against the scenario of permanent occupation of conquered lands. The purpose of the expeditions seems to be spoil of human captives (vv 9b, 15).

Another question is whether the cult associations of *miškān* point to the shrines of foreign gods, held in contempt by the conquerors who acknowledge no god but their own might. As against this possibility, Hab 2:20 calls Yahweh's temple a *hēkāl* (but this "holy temple" is more likely to be Yahweh's heavenly dwelling, beyond the reach of any human foe).

not its own. From the very beginning, the Highest God had allocated to each people a territory with well-marked boundaries (Deut 32:8; cf. Acts 17:26). This arrangement was an ordinance of Creation. In another tradition, "the land" was assigned to Abram as part of an activity of God through a covenant intruded into history at a later stage. In either view, when Israel eventually took possession of this land, it was a God-given right, but a right only in relation to other human claimants, never a right vis-à-vis God. The conquest traditions never make the point that the Canaanites were trespassing, usurpers to be justly dispossessed. Rather, the Canaanites had forfeited their right to dwell in the land by defiling it. Thus they became an object lesson for Israel, made explicit in prophetic warnings, especially by Ezekiel. If there was a doctrine for this policy, it was that the LORD gives the countries to anyone he likes, and historical changes are not violations of a natural order intended by God to be permanent, but revisions made by the living Sovereign himself in the constitution of his realm, changes made however he might please. Such adjustments were not whimsical, however; they had moral justification, formerly with the Canaanites, now with Israel.

Israel's relationship to the land was consequently ambivalent, at once secure and precarious. This paradox matches the mixture in the covenant (original formulations and subsequent reviews and revisions) of absolute and conditional terms. No attempt is made in Scripture to harmonize by formal logic the contradiction between the immutability of the divine counsels and the frequent changes in the plans of God. The same paradox is found here. The LORD raises up the Chaldeans to take possession of lands they have no right to. As with the Assyrians before them, in one and the same act (destroying Samaria in the case of the Assyrians, Jerusalem in the case of the Chaldeans), they (unwittingly) carried out the plan of God by punishing his people and (reprehensibly) violated God's law (at least humane ethics) by their lawlessness and cruelty. The repetition of the phrase "not his" in Hab 2:6, even to the dagesh in the first *l*, shows that the activity of the Chaldeans is considered to be reprehensible. Yet God organized it. No wonder he expected people to be puzzled.

Habakkuk interprets the situation somewhat differently from Jeremiah and Ezekiel, however, if we are correct in our reading that his "woe oracles" in Hab 2:6–20 are not directed against people in Judah, but against a foreign tyrant.

For Israel, dispossession constituted a crisis in which their standing with God became equivocal. They have not lost tenure in Yahweh's covenant, but he has now decreed that the Chaldeans be the agents of his covenant disciplines. The sovereignty of Yahweh is found not in the immutability of his decisions and the irresistibility of his power, but in his freedom to revise the project that began with the call of Abram in the light of the conduct of his descendants.

7. *he.* With *haggôy,* "the people" (v 5), as antecedent, rather than "the

Chaldeans" (plural), all the anaphoric pronouns are singular. Note the repeated *hû'* in v 10. The literal translation "he" gives the impression that an individual person is in mind—one particular Neo-Babylonian king. This could be so; but the pronoun objects are likewise singular, so it is more likely that the nation is viewed as a collective entity.

Dreadful. The adjective is used only here and in Song 6:4, 10. The corresponding noun *'êmâ* is used more often. It describes terror in the face of a strong and cruel enemy, as well as the paralyzing effect of the overwhelming frightfulness of the LORD.

terrifying. *'êmâ* is a synonym of *nôrā'*. The latter is used characteristically as an attribute of Yahweh—majestic and fear-inspiring.

justice. This word provides a link with the opening prayer, where it was used twice. Its significance in the present context is far from clear. The traditional interpretations of this verse imply that the Chaldeans acknowledge no master but themselves: "from himself derive his law and his majesty" (NAB). LXX has a more ample text:

eks autou to krima autou estai	From himself his judgment will come,
kai to lemma auto eks	and his gain from himself will come out.
auto ekseleusetai	

Symmachus, a little more succinctly:

autos heauto dikasei	He will decide for himself
kai dogmati heautou	and by his own decision he will march out
epekseleusetai	

This reading is a preferable recognition of the military connotations of *yṣ'*. There is, then, an ironic contradiction between the Chaldean's belief that he plans his own campaigns and the truth of the matter, which is that Yahweh is raising him up. Yet the Babylonian monarchs did not suppose that they were autocrats. Like his predecessors, Nebuchadrezzar II carried out all his enterprises under the authority of Marduk. It may be doubted that v 7b is an ancient statement of the doctrine that "might makes right." It could be that, in relation to Yahweh, the new Babylon was a political power that recognized no moral authority higher than itself and worshiped its own strength as its only god (v 11b). But the Hebrew Bible is not likely to make this concession, and this oracle has already established the point—vital and characteristic for the Hebrew Bible—that it is the LORD who is raising up this power (v 6a). It could be that the prophet takes no account of the mighty Marduk. He represents Babylonian religion as puerile; under the figure of fishing nets, he speaks contemptuously of these pagans making sacrifices to their implements of war (v 16), and idolatry is attacked in more conventional terms in Hab 2:18–19.

There are other difficulties in the usual interpretation of v 7 besides the abstractness of the idea. As usually taken, v 7b is rather long—the longest colon in this speech. Its twelve syllables provide enough for two poetic colons of ac-

ceptable length. In favor of the usual translation is the fact that the idiom *mišpāṭ*
. . . *yēṣē'* has already been used twice in v 4, but the issuing of a verdict by a
judge is not the same as the autonomy of a tyrant. There is also the problem of
discord between the plural subject ("law and majesty") and the singular verb
("goes out"). If it were not for the influence of v 4, the military context would
associate *yēṣē'* with the meaning "go out (to war)."

   status (or "dignity"). From the root *nś'*, *śē'ēt* is a kind of verbal noun that
means "lifting up." Except when it is used in a physical sense to describe the
swelling of a diseased organ (Leviticus 13), its exact denotation is obscure in all
other occurrences. In Job 13:11, it describes the terror inspired by God's majesty,
and the same parallelism with *paḥad* occurs in Job 31:23. The problematic *mś'tw*
in Ps 62:5 has been solved by Gunkel (AB17:92) by reading *maśśū'ōt*, "crafty
schemes." Perhaps something similar should be read in Hab 1:7 as a better parallel to *mišpāṭ*. But the idea of terror fits in with v 7a, and this can be combined
with the idea of marching out to war by paraphrasing:

7bA   He makes its own decisions;
7bB   And in his self-exaltation he sets out (on military expeditions).

This interpretation also encourages connecting v 7bB with v 8, even though this
linkage leaves v 7bA in isolation. There are also structural advantages in regarding vv 7bB–8 as a small unit. The three clauses that begin with consecutive
suffixed verbs (v 8a) are flanked by clauses that end with prefixed verbs—*yēṣē'*
in v 7bB and *yābō'û* in v 8bA. And these verbs are a natural pair for describing
going out to war and coming back. By the same token *yābō'* in v 9aA is an even
better parallel for *yēṣē'*. If vv 7bB–9aA is a complete unit, then *yābō'û* is parallel and chiastic to *yā'ûpû*.

   Verses 8–9. The eight colons of these verses are unified by numerous poetic
and rhetorical devices. The bicolon in v 8aA is unified by the similar verbs and
by the animal comparisons. The bicolon in vv 8aB–8bA is unified by the similar verbs and by chiasmus. The bicolon in vv 8bB–9aA is similar. These six
colons in vv 8–9aA can also be construed as two tricolons. The initial verb in v
8aB continues the series of v 8aA. The repeated *pārāšāyw* links v 8bA to the following bicolon. The bird simile in the last colon of v 8 is a further link with the
animals in v 8aA. These six colons, as a unit, are distinguished from the rest of
the speech by the plural verbs. Unfortunately, both v 7 and v 9 are so unintelligible (see the NOTES) that no further progress seems possible.

   8. *swifter.* 1QpHab apparently read singular *wqwl*, but it agrees with the MT
in having plural verbs in the rest of the verse. This colon is quoted exactly in
Jer 4:13. Compare "the wolf of the desert" in Jer 5:6. The Neo-Babylonians in-
herited from their predecessors a skill in blitzkrieg tactics in which the chariot
was the main mobile equipment. The chariot is not mentioned here. Because
cavalry was also used, it remains unclear whether *pārāšāyw* is a synonymous parallel to *sûsāyw* (stallions // mares), or whether *pārāšāyw* refers to "riders." Compare *sûs wĕrōkēb* in the Exodus story. If the latter, these "horsemen" could be
mounted (cavalry) or drivers (chariotry). In any case, the comparison of "his

horses" with "leopards" and "wolves" must be a transferred epithet because it is the ferocity of the troops, not of the mounts, that is like the savagery of beasts.

leopards. There is a similar problem of connecting the simile in Deut 32:11.

savage. LXX reads *oksus*; Keil (1954) has "sudden" for *ḥdd* — "a hasty precipitate dash." This is congruous with the eagle simile.

wolves. The attribute "evening" for wolves must have been already puzzling in antiquity, because LXX read *tes Arabias* (cf. Zeph 3:3). But is "Arabian wolves" any clearer? Or "desert wolves" (reading *ʿārābâ*), for that matter? Might a possible geographic reference here throw light on the problematic *qādîmâ* (east?) in v 9aB? Jer 5:6 has *zěʾēb ʿārābôt*), "desert wolf" (in parallel with "forest lion"), and this throws more doubt on *ʿereb*, "evening," in Hab 1:8. See Elliger (1950).

dashes. Budde (1931:410) repunctuated and repointed to

pôš yāpūšû pārāšāyw
mērāḥôq yābōʾû yāʿûpû

This certainly improves the rhythm, and the assonance is marvelous. But a solution that rewrites every word in a bicolon has to be treated with great caution. The deletion of one of the duplicated *pārāšāyw* is supported by a few MSS and by the readings of both Greek and Syriac versions. BHS suggests that the MT has dittography, but with reserve. In general, haplography is more likely than diplography (AB21A:885–87). 1QpHab *pšw wpršw pršw* agrees in principle with the MT although differing in some details.

The description of swift horsemen has been compared with that in Jer 4:13, and both referred to the Scythian horsemen who were allied with Nabopolassar. Whether they still had contingents in Nebuchadrezzar's army is another matter.

vast distances (Heb. *mērāḥôq*, "from afar"). The emphasis here on the distance traveled matches the reference to "the extremities of the earth" in v 6b. A strict interpretation of *yābōʾû* as "return (from war)," to balance *yēṣēʾ* in v 7b, would complete the balance with v 6b, where the corresponding verb is √*hlk*. The emphasis, then, is not on the long distance from Babylon to Judah — no factor in the safety of Judea — or on the distances from which Babylon recruits its multinational (?) army (it is called only one *gôy*). It depends on whether the point of reference for the verbs of movement is Babylon or Jerusalem. They go out from Babylon and come back to Babylon. But if √*bwʾ* in vv 8–9 means "arrive" at Jerusalem, the perspective has switched. It could be argued that *yābōʾû* in v 8 cannot mean "return" to Babylon, for then the expedition would be over and there is still more action to follow in vv 9 and 11. It could be, however, that the use of different verb tenses in vv 9b–11 shows that this unit reports a distinct episode.

swoop (literally, "fly"). NEB (following Budde 1931) reaps a certain advantage from dropping the second *pršyw*. It secures the bicolon:

mērāḥôq yābōʾû yāʿûpû   from afar they come they fly
kěnešer ḥāš[û] leʾěkōl   like vultures swoop[ing] to devour (the prey)

The double verb—"they come they fly"—is good, although Habakkuk does not use double verbs much. The image is apt because the vulture is swift, rapacious, and frightening. But all in all, we think that the smaller colons we have recognized are better.

9. *All.* Keil (1954) interpreted *kullōh* as "all at once." This meaning does not seem to have been established in Semitic (Fitzmyer 1957). Note the use of this word again in v 15, in the same strategic position. There is a confusion of grammatical number at this point. All the referential pronouns in vv 6–11 are singular except in "their faces." If "his all" goes back to v 8, it refers to the faces of the horses or of the horsemen. More progress is not possible as long as the meaning of *mgmt* remains unknown. "A sea of faces rolls on" (NEB) is one of many conjectures. Emendation is another way out, easier to propose than to prove, such as Keil's "endeavour." LXX has *anthestēkotos,* "resisting understanding," for *mgmt,* and the idea of opposition seems to be in the Boharic as well. What is the Hebrew behind this? *Měgôrat,* "the *terror* of their faces"?

to the front (literally "eastward"). The cry *qādîmâ!* "Onward!" familiar in modern Hebrew, is hardly appropriate here. But why should the Chaldeans be advancing eastward? To Elam? This problem may be enough to account for the divergences in ancient texts and versions at this point, for all of them may be guessing. Budde (1931:410) suggested (with all due reserve) *měqaddēm kanpê haqqādîm.* Duhm's (1906) celebrated emendation is *miggōmer pěnêhem qēdmâ,* "from Cappadocia they advanced eastward." Wellhausen (1893), for once, admitted defeat at this point, concluding that the colon was so corrupted that emendation was impossible. (Not in his notes, where his translation [1893:34] excludes vv 5–11.) In his commentary, Wellhausen (1983:162) guessed that the meaning of *mgmt* is *Streben* ("ambition") but admitted that this has "too feeble a meaning"—*ein viel zu schwachen Sinn.* Cannon (1925:82) prefers to read *qiddēmâ,* "The terror of their faces goes before them."

1QpHab *qdym* has some claim to be taken seriously, and the versions that read "east wind" need attention. Emendation might not be necessary to arrive at such a result, for the needed word "wind" is present in v 11a, and can be related to *qdym* once the introverted structure is recognized. Gender is not a problem. The clue is supplied by the symmetrical placement of the verb forms, and the result is similar to that obtained in the eight-colon unit vv 7–9aA.

The next seven colons are built on a symmetrical pattern of certain key words and constructions:

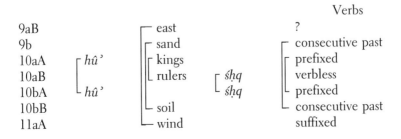

			Verbs
9aB		east	?
9b		sand	consecutive past
10aA	*hû'*	kings	prefixed
10aB		rulers	verbless
10bA	*hû'*	*śhq*	prefixed
10bB		soil	consecutive past
11aA		wind	suffixed

The repeated (and unusual) construction of *hû'* with a prefixed verb, in clauses with identical word sequences (vv 10aA, 10bA), encourages belief that there is an introverted pattern, as shown above. The verbless clause in the middle (v 10aB) is not a monocolon unconnected with the rest; rather, it has parallelism with what precedes ("kings" // "rulers") and with what follows (*mišḥāq* // *yišḥāq*). So vv 10aA, 10aB, and 10bA are a tricolon. It was easier to accept v 10bB as a parallel to v 10bA in the days when biblical scholars saw parallelism in a very narrow field of view, were willing to recognize only bicolons in Hebrew poetry, and expected all pairs of parallel colons to be contiguous. Now that we are aware of wider patterns of parallelism, the superior claims of vv 10A, 10aB, and 10bA to be recognized as a tricolon threaten to leave v 10bB as an unmatched colon. The match of "sand" // "soil," however, shows that vv 9b and 10bB are another split bicolon. And the match of the consecutive past-tense verbs fixes the time reference of the whole unit (unless we revise the pointing and follow LXX), which continues in v 11. This connection does not rule out the long-recognized link of v 10bB with v 10bA through sound play on *mbṣr* and *yṣbr*. On the contrary, the richness of the poetry is appreciated even more when it is recognized that one colon (v 10bB) might be shared between two bicolons. The central unit clearly consists of the five colons in vv 9b–10, with v 10bB a partial match for v 10bA and an inclusion for v 9b.

Appreciation of this extended pattern of introversion also suggests a solution for the problem of v 9aB; vv 9aB and 11aA could be another split bicolon around the central pentacolon. There is, however, no verb in v 9aB to match either of the verbs in v 11aA. This result is less firm. The connections of v 9aB are quite obscure. And because *'āz* could mark the transition to a new moment in the narrative, the thematic development could be arrival (through v 9aA), engagement (vv 9b–10), departure (v 11). This would leave v 9aB stranded. But the strange verb sequence in v 11, with a *wayyiqṭōl* construction followed by a coordinated suffixed verb *wĕ'āśēm*, permits the analysis shown in the diagram, with *wayya'ăbōr* as the onset of the last scene.

This analysis leads to important new results, with better controls for interpretation of small details in the larger structure. The three colons in vv 10a–bA constitute a well-formed tricolon whose numerous unifying devices have already been described. If we have correctly identified v 9b and v 10bB as a bicolon, split and wrapped around these three colons, then several inferences follow:

1. Verse 9b is no longer left stranded as a colon without a parallel.
2. We do not have to bring v 9aB into parallel with v 9b, or try to use v 9b (which is clear) to solve the problems of v 9aB. Putting it another way, it would be illicit to rewrite v 9aB in order to supply v 9b with a suitable parallel.
3. We do not have to bring v 10bB into line with v 10bA by finding in v 10bB a description of the capture of the fortress referred to in v 10bA, as is usually done:

They despise every fortress,
they raise siege-works and capture it. (NEB)

Such a result has to smooth over several problems. First, the emphatic "every fortress" is followed by the singular "it" rather than the expected "them." The singular could, however, be distributive—one at a time. Second, the plurals "kings" and "rulers" similarly clash with the description in v 10bB of one citadel. Third, there is a clash of gender in the pronoun object: "And he . . . captured her" (the city?). The discord had already been removed in antiquity, for both 1QpHab and LXX read "him" and the MT could have been pointed -*ōh* (cf. *kullōh* [vv 9, 15]).

Bringing the results together depends in part on another observation. Hebrew poetry made little or no use of the particles *h-*, *ʾăšer*, and *ʾet*. This feature was explained as a legacy from the early history of the language when these items were not yet in use. It has been recognized to a lesser degree that compactness in poetry was achieved by similar omission of other "particles," notably conjunctions and prepositions (*k-*, "like," in v 9b; see the NOTES on v 3). It is commonly recognized that the word "wind" in v 11a is part of a simile ("like the wind" in many translations), but there is no need to restore *k-* to the text (BHS). Once the same thing is recognized in v 10bB, its parallelism to v 9b is seen to be even closer:

9b   And he collected captives like sand,
10bB   And he heaped (them) up (like) dust.

10. *And he, he.* The pronoun is *hûʾ*, "he," which we have taken as collective, the Chaldean nation. The use of the free form of the pronoun subject with the prefixed verb is very striking, and its repetition even more so. Another unusual feature of the construction is the use of the conjunction with the first, but not with the second, *hûʾ*. The opposite would have been expected, and some Hebrew manuscripts, including 1QpHab, as well as ancient versions, have "and he" in both places. The loss in MT could have been due to haplography in **lw whwʾ*.

kings . . . rulers. These words are a stock poetic pair. The contempt of the Chaldeans for foreign rulers, whom they can subdue with the greatest of ease, is exactly like that of their predecessors, the Assyrians (2 Kgs 18:33–35, where they ridicule the gods).

laughed. 1QpHab reads *yqls* rather than the *Hitpaʿel* of the MT.

captured. Verse 10bB links with v 10bA through sound play on *mbṣr* and *yṣbr*: the operation is aimed at the fortress. The verb *ṣābar* in its biblical occurrences always describes the accumulation of a great quantity of something, such as food (Gen 41:35), frogs (Exod 8:10), and wealth (Ps 39:7). The conventional similes are used: "And Joseph heaped up grain like the sand of the sea" (Gen 41:49; the same as Hab 1:9b). Job speaks of heaping up silver "like dust" (Job 27:16; also Zech 9:3, the same idiom as Hab 1:10bB, except that it lacks the preposition). The verb *ṣābar* always describes the acquisition of goods, never the construction of a siege ramp (unless here, of course). Hence the object, which is missing, as in Ps 39:7, must be recognized as *šĕbî* in v 9b. The two similes used with *ṣābar* elsewhere (*kĕḥōl* and *kĕʿāpār*) are both used here, with *k-* in v 9b doing double duty (see also Gen 16:16; 28:14; Num 23:10; Ps 78:27; Job 27:16). This completes our argument that vv 9b and 10bB constitute a discontinuous bicolon. A sinister and gruesome inference can be made. Jehu displayed the heads of the seventy "sons of the King" in "two heaps" (ṣibbūrîm) in the gateway of Jezreel (2 Kgs 10:8). The picture is clear, and it is the same in every case when the verb is used. It is not just the gathering of prisoners of war (v 9b), it is the slaying of whole nations without restraint (v 17b) and the piling up of the corpses like the dead frogs of Exod 8:10.

The feminine pronoun object suffix of the MT has no obvious antecedent. The MT "her" could be retained if some suitable feminine noun can be found for it to refer to. Keil (1954) suggested that mibṣār really means "fortified city," and 'îr is feminine. Budde (1931:410) thought that the restoration of 'îr was desirable, although not strictly necessary. This is oversubtle.

The masculine suffix of 1QpHab is probably intended to secure agreement with mibṣār (the obvious antecedent); but it is not certain that the capture of a fortress is in mind. In its other occurrences, the verb can describe the seizure of places or persons or animals. So the masculine pronoun could be a distributive reference to "captives," or a singular referring to a collective noun. If we are correct in recognizing v 10bB as a parallel to v 9b, then both refer to the numerous prisoners taken by the Chaldeans, and "he heaped (them) up (like) dust" comes between "he laughed at every fortress" and "and he captured her." The translation "heaps up a ramp" (NAB) finds siege warfare in the image, and this supplies continuity to the three clauses in v 10b. We have already questioned this reading. The problem now is this: Does "and he captured her" go with v 10bA ("her" = a city)? Or does it go with v 10bB ("her" = ?)? If v 10bB goes with v 9b, the object is ṣĕbî. This noun is usually masculine, but in Isa 52:2 it is feminine. So it is possible that both verbs in v 10bB describe the taking of captives. This, rather than the conquest of territory as such, is a major cause of the prophet's anguish, for he dwells on it again (v 15) and again (2:5bB, 8, 13).

fortress. In sixteen of the twenty-two occurrences of the singular noun it is the nomen rectum of "city" or "cities." So on its own, mibṣār means "fortress city." The plural occurs only twice with "city" or "cities"; 'ārê mibṣār and mibṣārîm are equivalent, and Habakkuk's unique kol-mibṣār is equivalent to kol-'îr mibṣār (2 Kgs 3:19). The rarity of the definite article with this noun, singular or plural—it occurs only five times, always in 'ārê hammibṣār (Num 32:17; Josh 10:20; Jer 4:5; 8:14; 2 Chr 17:19)—suggests that it is a frozen archaic expression (cf. 'ōhel mô'ēd, likewise definite, but never with the definite article).

11. swept on . . . passed by. Two verbs, near synonyms, in tandem. The noun between them, "wind" or "spirit," is a major problem. Because this noun is taken to be feminine it has been rejected as the subject. It is sometimes masculine, however, so this possibility is not excluded (see the EXCURSUS). Another and more general difficulty is to work out what this wind might be and what it is doing in the story. One solution is to take "wind" as a simile (RSV, NEB, NAB). There are five reasons for this:

1. The pericope abounds in comparisons, with leopards, wolves, eagle, sand, dust.

2. A simile can be made without *k-*, "like," as with "(like) dust" in v 10bB.
3. By structural analysis, we have already linked v 9aB with v 11aA, as the first and last colons in an introverted unit.
4. "East wind" is a well-known phrase, and the adjective shows that *rûaḥ* has its usual gender. It is, however, straining the language to its limit to have an attributive adjective not only before its noun, but separated from it by such a distance. It could be, all the same, that it was the very familiarity of the usual phrase *rûaḥ qādîm* that invited splitting it up and spreading it. This is not the only specimen of this trope. In Job 15:2, it is the stock phrase *rûaḥ . . . qādîm* that is broken up, with one of the words in each of two colons in parallel. On the general phenomena of the breakup of stereotype phrases, see Melamed (1961).
5. The simile is apt; the east wind is swift and destructive, like the Chaldeans. The picture of the Chaldean army, swooping on its prey "like an eagle" is completed when it rushes "like the wind." But even if this is the trope, there is no need to touch up the text by restoring *k-*. A preposition can be omitted in poetry.

guilty. The MT is difficult. The punctuation *'atnāḥ* isolates "and he became guilty" from v 11b. The verb form is ambiguous; but after a *wayyiqṭōl* form, the past-tense option is indicated. LXX, which made all the verbs future, leans the other way: "and he will make propitiation." The use of the term *'āšēm*, with its cultic connotations (hence LXX's choice of vocabulary), compounds the problem. The kinds of deeds listed do not make a person "guilty" in this sense; certainly, there is no hint of admission of guilt requiring ritual remedies. The obscurity of the rest of the verse makes it difficult to secure any further assistance from coherence with that context.

An emendation proposed in modern times received grateful endorsement from the Dead Sea Scrolls. 1QpHab reads *wyšm* or *wyśm*, "and he made his strength his god." Yet the statement remains obscure. What did he do? It is possible that both words are original. They co-occur in Isa 53:10. Each tradition has lost one word through haplography.

he whose. LXX *hautē hē iskhys*, "this power," took *zû* as demonstrative before its noun. But there is no antecedent for the demonstrative to refer to. An emendation that uses the *z* is Ward's (1911:11)—*wyśm mizbḥw l'lhyw*, "and he set up his altar to his god." This is banal, but it makes sense. The changes in the text, however, are too substantial to be accepted as a likely restoration of the original. All the same, the proposal is on the right lines, and shortly we shall arrive at a similar result, but without the emendation.

strength. The word "strength" is confirmed by LXX, but it is particularly troublesome. A paraphrase—"he is guilty because his strength is his god"—turns the thought in a different direction. There is no indication that Babylonians thought that way or were accused of thinking that way, making a deity out of an abstract idea. Up to this point, the focus has been the arrogance and cruelty of the Chaldeans in their military activites. If v 11 completes the scenario of vv 9–10, the reference to the Chaldeans' "strength" could cover the military might by which the conquest was accomplished. He sacrificed what he had acquired by his strength.

Another possible solution is suggested by the use of *kōaḥ* in Gen 49:3. Jacob calls Reuben "the first[-born] of my strength" (see the discussion of this discontinuous construct phrase in Andersen 1970b:37, 57). If *zû* has its normative function as a determiner, *zû kōḥô* means "the one of his strength." A literal translation would then be "and he made a guilt-offering of [or, following 1QpHab, he appointed] the one of his strength to his god." This would refer to the ritual dedication of a firstborn son in sacrifice to a god (Cross 1994; Müller 1998; AB24E:532–39).

his god. LXX reads "my god," but this has been influenced by the next colon. Hab 1:11 is the only place in the Hebrew Bible where the noun *'lwh* has a pronoun suffix and the only place where it is spelled *defective*. The obvious emendation to *'lhyw* assumes a rare *defective* spelling of the ubiquitous plural suffixed form. While this plural *'ĕlōhîm* is the usual name for "God," it serves equally as the common (generic) noun, at least in appelatives. As such, it is freely modified by a suffix pronoun or *nomen rectum*. The shorter *'ēl* has the same dual function, but *'lwh* in all its other occurrences (56 times, 41 times in Job) is a proper noun; it never takes the definite article. Its form in v 11 remains unexplained.

The presence of the preposition *l-* is a major obstacle in the way of the interpretation "he whose strength is his god." Comparison with v 9 suggests transferring *l-* in *l'lhw* to the preceding word, thus eliminating the troublesome "his strength" and retrieving the familiar *kḥwl*, "like the sand"—"and he made his god(s) (as numerous) as the sand." This adjustment would enhance the structural analysis presented earlier; but it also requires a rereading of the final word.

It is simpler to take *l'lhw* literally: "and he set (offered) [the captives] as an *'āšām* (sacrifice) to his god." This is what Mesha of Moab said he did. Josiah "sacrificed" (*wayyizbaḥ*) the priests at Bethel (2 Kgs 23:20). Gruesome scenes on the walls of Assyrian palaces show that executions followed victories. Whether they were religious ceremonies is not clear. Nor are we aware of any documentation of similar Babylonian practices.

There is another reference to Babylonian religion in v 16 (see the NOTE). If the Babylonian army had a cult of adoration of their weapons, it is scarcely attested in their own remains and can hardly be said to have dominated their religion.

EXCURSUS: Grammatical Gender of *rûaḥ*

The use of dubious grammatical information to make an exegetical point is illustrated by the interpretation of 2 Sam 23:2 proposed by O'Connor (1995:323). In the text "The Spirit of Yahweh spoke in me and his word was upon my tongue," O'Connor argues that, since *rûaḥ* is feminine, it cannot be the subject of the masculine verb *dibber*. O'Connor's explanation is that *rûaḥ* is "an accusative of specification." Another way of explaining away the apparent masculine gender of *rûaḥ* is to argue that "[w]hen the subject is composed of a nomen regens (in the construct state) [in this instance, *rûaḥ*] with a following genitive [in this instance, *yhwh*], the predicate sometimes agrees in gender and number not with the nomen regens, but with the genitive, when this represents the principal idea of the compound subject" (*GKC* § 146). *GKC* does not cite 2 Sam 23:2 as an instance of this "exception," but Albrecht (1896) refers to this paragraph in *GKC* in order to explain away the masculine gender of *rûaḥ* in this and several other texts. This explanation does not work with Hab 1:11. Other instances of apparently masculine *rûaḥ* Albrecht disposes of by exegesis or by declaring the text corrupt. In spite of these measures, however, there still remain enough instances that resist such treatment for Albrecht to end by declaring *rûaḥ* to be "common gender" (44).

These are not the only possible readings of texts in which *rûaḥ* seems to be masculine. The most natural reading of Hab 1:11 is that *rûaḥ* is the subject of the preceding and following masculine verbs. In Mic 2:7, likewise, the Masoretic vocalization (*qāṣar*) makes the first word a verb and the punctuation makes *rûaḥ* a construct. Since a subject usually agrees with its verb in number and gender, the masculine verb in Mic 2:7 shows that in this instance the noun *rûaḥ* is masculine. The error of doubting such texts lies in the assumption that grammatical gender is an intrinsic feature of a word such as *rûaḥ*, that it is feminine, and that it should manifest that gender in all its occurrences. The remedy in Hab 1:11 is to take *rûaḥ* as a simile and even to "restore" the preposition "like" (BHS).

Like all other features of natural languages, the allocation of the word stock to the grammatical categories of gender is purely arbitrary. Gender has no intrinsic or essential referential logic. It has no ontological meaning. The feature of gender is most familiar in the taxonomy of nouns and derivatively by coreferentiality in adjectives, pronouns, verbal nouns, and verbs. How this is done is language specific. Being arbitrary, a language might make no use of gender distinctions at all, and there is no upper limit to the number of genders that might be invoked. We do not know which of the world's more than 5000 known natural languages holds the record for the greatest number of genders. The gender-like "classes" of some African languages run into the dozens. To have gender at all, there must be at least two categories.

Historically, the scientific study of language originated with Indo-European languages (Panini studied Sanscrit [ca. 400 B.C.E.], and the foundations of classical philology were laid by the Greeks [Hymes 1974]) and with the Semitic languages (here the Arab grammarians led the way). It was not until after the Renaissance that language became an object of study in its own right by European scholars. As a consequence of this background, the concept of gender in language has been dominated by the fact that the families of languages first studied scientifically have simple gender systems (three genders in Indo-European, two in Semitic). It so happens that the vocabularies of these languages have a partial correlation between grammatical gender and biological sex. Hence the conventional names for the gender categories. The grammatical gender of nouns that were names of organisms with (or that were perceived as possessing) male sexual organs and functions was *masculine*; many names of females had *feminine* gender. Languages with more than two grammatical genders can reduce the scale of arbitrariness by classifying nouns that are names of nonsexual entities as "neutral" or neuter. Another device is to have a third category of "common" gender, that is, a noun that is the name of members of a species, used for individuals of either sex. Such common-gender nouns can map onto biological sex in any of three ways:

1. The common-gender noun is accompanied by special nouns for male and female ("sheep," "ram," "ewe"; "child," "boy," "girl").
2. There is a special noun for one of the sexes. This system involves "markedness." The unmarked form can be used either as common gender or, in contexts where it contrasts with the marked form, as the polar opposite of the marked form, by default. So "dog" is common, but in the question "Is it a dog or a bitch?" the implication is that "dog" means "male." Italian distinguishes the genders—*cane, cagna*.
3. The language has only the common-gender noun. Gender distinctions must be secured by modifiers or referentials that correlate with biological sex—"male camel," "female camel." This precise usage is attested for *rûah* in a Jewish magical text: *rwh zkr wnqbh*, "male and female spirit" (AMB 4:15; cf. Gen 1:27).

Languages that retain gender distinctions in their morphology (commonly with suffixes) have more scope for coping with biological distinctions. The English use of the feminine endings, such as "-ess" and "-ix," as morphological markers is cumbersome, and these suffixes have now fallen into disfavor as sexist, at least in their use for designating human females in social roles. "Tigress" is still acceptable, but not "poetess."

The correlation between grammatical gender and biological sex in Hebrew is partial in two respects. First, there were "exceptions" among the names of male and female organisms—males whose names were feminine in form, and females whose names were masculine in form. Second, since every noun in a two-gender language must have either masculine or feminine gender, names of entities that do not have biological sex (the majority of the vocabulary) have grammatical gender assigned to them arbitrarily. An ancient philosophical tradition enlarged the analysis of sexuality to embrace all ranks of being, projecting maleness or femaleness onto entities on the basis of the grammatical gender of their names. In reverse, the assigment of masculine or feminine grammatical gender to everything that had a name was explained by recognizing in everything stereotypical maleness or femaleness. These "explanations" now strike us as ludicrous, or perhaps offend us by their sexism.

As the outcome of some kind of analogy, various semantic sets of nouns have acquired the same gender. The well-known rule for Hebrew that names of body parts that occur in pairs ("hand," "eye," "ear") are feminine ("nostril," however, is evidently masculine), even without the otherwise ubiquitous markers of feminine gender in Hebrew nouns, such as *-â* or *-t*, has nothing to do with biological sex. The category of grammatical gender is merely grammatical. Among certain sets of words in Hebrew that might be thought to belong to the same semantic domain, some are masculine, some feminine. Why are some names of geographic features masculine, and some, feminine? This arbitrariness can be illustrated by names for abstract notions, mental states, and moral qualities. There is no evidence of complementary distribution that would associate masculine nouns with conventional masculine psychology or male virtues, and feminine nouns with conventional feminine psychology or female virtues. There is no linguistic warrant for supposing that in Hebrew thought there was something masculine about "peace," something feminine about "wisdom." There are four patterns:

1. Masculine noun with no attested feminine equivalent, such as *mśwś*, "joy"; *qṣr*, "anguish"; *l'g*, "derision."
2. Feminine noun with no attested masculine equivalent, such as *ḥrph*, "scorn"; *bwšh*, "shame"; *'nwh*, "humility."
3. A masculine and feminine pair with the same root, identical in meaning, such as *rš'*, *rš'h*, "wickedness"; *ṣdq*, *ṣdqh*, "righteousness"; *tbwn*, *tbwnh*, "understanding."
4. A noun that is sometimes masculine, sometimes feminine, with the same meaning: *rûaḥ*.

Works of reference have not handled the fourth category very well. Lexicons feel obliged to declare a noun as having one gender or the other. The best that they can do for such a noun is to say that it is (usually) masculine "less often" feminine (*derek* [BDB 202]) or that it is (usually) feminine "less often" masculine (*rûaḥ* [BDB 924]; cf. *meist fem., selten m.* [HAL:1117]). Such pairs are given one entry in the lexicon, but when the gender distinctions are morphologically marked (case 3 above), two entries. Daniel Lys (1962) pays practically no attention to the gender of the word *rûaḥ*.

When a word such as *rûaḥ* has two attested genders, it is poor method to report only one gender (in this instance, feminine) as normative, and the other (masculine) as exceptional. It is mischievous to absolutize this classification as a grammatical rule: *rûaḥ* (feminine) is correct, *rûaḥ* (masculine) is incorrect. Then the theory is defended by declaring texts in which *rûaḥ* is evidently masculine to be corrupt and in need of emendation or to resort to some other parsing that makes *rûaḥ* feminine.

The methodological issues opened up in this discussion can be illustrated in more detail and tested by examining more closely the grammatical gender of *rûaḥ* "spirit, wind, breath." It is widely believed to be a feminine noun. The one "exception" of apparent masculine gender (Num 11:31) reported in BDB (924) leaves the impression that *rûaḥ* is feminine in all other occurrences. Naive users of BDB, and even mature scholars who should know better, proceed to use this

"fact" as a basis for all kinds of textual, philological, and even theological inferences and conclusions.

   To lay the groundwork for this study, it must be emphasized that grammatical gender of nouns is a *syntactic*, not a semantic, category. The gender system is more clearly embodied in pronouns, finite verbs, participles, and adjectives. While there is a rule that says that related words must "agree," it is
really the other way around. We work out the gender of a noun by its agreement with the more unequivocal attributive participle or adjective, with the
gender of a finite verb when the noun is its subject, or with the gender of a referential pronoun. The agreement diagnostic is not surefire, all the same. Two
indeterminacies characteristic of Hebrew grammar can coincide and cancel
each other in phrases in which *rûaḥ* is followed immediately by a substantive.
Hebrew is short on adjectives, and a noun used attributively can be either in
apposition or *nomen rectum*. And *rûaḥ* has the same form, whether it is absolute
or construct. So when it is followed immediately by another noun, that noun
will determine the gender of *rûaḥ* in that instantiation if the two are in apposition, but not if it is a construct phrase. In Ps 107:25, the phrase *rûaḥ sĕʿārâ*
is the object of the verb, and *rûaḥ* is the *nomen regens*, so *rûaḥ* has undetermined gender here. In Ezek 1:4, its gender is determined by the following feminine participle (cf. Ps 148:8).

   Hebrew grammar lacks the amenity of concord between a verb and its object,
so unless *rûaḥ* as object has an attributive adjective, its gender in that instance
remains indeterminate. *It is not possible to say what the gender of a noun is in an
instantiation that lacks such evidence.* By this test, more than half of the occurrences of *rûaḥ* in the Hebrew Bible are indeterminate as to gender (Table 1).

   The distribution of the data shows that the phenomenon of *Genuswechsel*
(gender fluctuation) is found all over the Hebrew Bible. When *rûaḥ* has explicit
grammatical gender, there are four kinds of usage:

1. *rûaḥ* is consistently feminine. All twenty-seven references to the spirit from
   God (good or bad) in Judges and 1 Samuel are feminine gender. This is,
   in fact, the only block of text in the entire Hebrew Bible in which *rûaḥ* is
   consistently one gender.
2. *rûaḥ* is consistently masculine. The most remarkable instance is 1 Kgs
   22:21–24, where the occurrence of five masculine verbs makes the evidence unassailable, a feature that persists in the duplicate in 2 Chronicles
   18. It is not as "singular" as von Soden (1992) asserts. The older criticism
   resorted to desperate ploys to eliminate this evidence. Albrecht (1896:43)
   recommended replacing *rûaḥ* in vv 21–22 with "Satan" and striking out
   rûaḥ in v 24, thus removing the word *rûaḥ* completely from the text! The
   proposed emendation was placed in the apparatus of BH³, no longer in
   BHS. Yet few commentators even report this fact, let alone discuss it.
3. Both masculine and feminine gender are attested in the same context (even
   in the same idiom), referring to the same spirit. Joshua's courage (Bern-

hard Stade 1895) is feminine in Josh 2:11, masculine in Josh 5:1. The "spirit of jealousy" is masculine in Num 5:14, feminine in Num 5:30. Blaming the confusion on a redactor is the explanation advanced by Stade (1895:173). If this were the only place where the word is "erroneously" masculine, the dismissal of the evidence might have some point. But with so much attestation, the data pointing to *rûaḥ* masculine should be accepted as authentic. A particularly remarkable instance is 1 Kgs 19:11, where *rûaḥ* is the subject of two masculine participles, but has two attributive adjectives, one masculine, the other feminine. Equally startling is Hos 4:19, where the verb is masculine, but the genitive pronoun suffix is feminine. These patterns restrain us from normalizing the gender of all the occurrences of *rûaḥ* in any given passage.

4. Even when the evidence that *rûaḥ* has both masculine and feminine gender is taken seriously, no correlation of the genders with lexical distinctions has been found (Jacob 1958:123). It is possible, however, that Qoheleth uses masculine *rûaḥ* to refer to "wind," feminine for the life-breath of animals and humans. In his favorite phrase—"striving after wind"—*rûaḥ* is neutral. The recognition of both male and female spirit in the magical text quoted earlier could be reflected also in the Dead Sea Scrolls, where nonbiblical texts have the masculine form of the plural (Carmignac 1955). In the Hebrew Bible, the only plural is *rûḥôt*, mainly of the four winds (cardinal points), but also "the spirits of all flesh" (Num 16:22; 27:16).

TABLE 1. Gender of רוּחַ in the Hebrew Bible

GENDER	INDETERMINATE	FEMININE	MASCULINE	TOTAL
Hexateuch*	23	10	11	44
Judges–1 Samuel	2	27	1	30
2 Samuel–Kings	10	1	7	18
Isaiah	32	11	7	50
Jeremiah	13	3	2	18
Ezekiel	30	18	5	53
Minor Prophets	23	5	6	34
Psalms	25	12	2	39
Job	17	10	4	31
Proverbs	16	4	1	21
Qohelet	17	4	3	24
Other Writings	19	11	5	35
Total	227	116	54	397

*Instead of the traditional divisions into Torah, Prophets, and Writings, portions have been recognized in which the gender allocation is distinctive. To illustrate: the domination of Judges–1 Samuel by feminine usage with reference to the charismatic leaders would obscure the quite different treatment in 2 Samuel–Kings if the Former Prophets were taken as one text. The text with which we began this excursus (2 Sam 23:2) is out of line with Judges, but in line with Kings.

COMMENT

A response from God begins with v 5, although the usual formula of quotation is not used to mark the change of speaker, as it is in Hab 2:2. The prophet is manifestly talking to God again in v 12. Apparently, all the intervening material (vv 5–11) constitutes a single speech by God. Because the change to the prophet as speaker is not marked by a formula of quotation either, the boundaries of the speeches are not marked with certainty. The description of the world conqueror given by the prophet in vv 15–17 resembles that given by God in vv 9–11. The curious use of *kullōh* at the commencement of vv 9 and 15 is another indication that the themes of both speeches are the same.

Haak (1991:14) suggests that vv 5–6 correspond to the "oracle of salvation" that many form critics consider to be an essential component of a psalm of lament. This is strained. Many pieces identified as lament psalms lack this ingredient (it is circular reasoning to say it was "omitted" from them). The program announced in vv 5–6 does not predict the rescue of the suppliant, except possibly in the oblique sense that the Chaldeans will punish the wicked on behalf of God, but that is not stated. It is even more strained to identify vv 7–11 as the petitioner's "expression of confidence" such as is found in some laments, rather than as a report given by God to astound people. By doing so, Haak is obliged to make Habakkuk, not Yahweh, the speaker of vv 7–11, recognizing that the Chaldeans have the capability to carry out Yahweh's plans. But the words are hardly an expression of hopeful expectation. Of course, the prophet could be echoing God's words, so that the terrifying description of the Chaldeans in vv 7–11 expresses the prophet's horror at what has already happened (hence the past tense). If that is the case, then only vv 5–6 would have been spoken by God.

If the change of mood detected between v 6 and v 7 requires a break at that point, assigning vv 7–11 to Habakkuk makes it even harder to find continuity between v 11 and v 12. The question and the invocation in v 12 sound like the beginning of a prayer.

The unity of vv 5–11 can be established only by evidence of its internal coherence, and this is not forthcoming to complete satisfaction. Our present difficulties in connecting all of vv 5–11 together do not drive us to the quite different explanation that they consist of several short statements that were not originally part of the same discourse. Nor is there any indication that any of the materials have come from later editors or scribes. Such possibilities cannot be denied a priori, but they should be invoked only as a last resort, and then bashfully.

As it now stands, the speech moves through four phases. It begins (1) with a summons to look among the nations (v 5a), because (2) God is about to do an astounding thing (vv 5b–6). His prediction that he is about to raise up the Chaldeans is followed (3) by a description of this nation that begins in general terms (vv 7–8) and then goes on to describe (4) what sounds like more particular events (vv 9–11). So there seems to be a single theme throughout. Yet the form and intention of the speech are not easy to find.

Form criticism is of little help. Yahweh's response is not a typical oracle of doom or rescue. God announces his plan, but does not explain its purpose in a way that makes it sound like an answer to Habakkuk's opening prayer. He does not say that he is sending this nation to carry out his judgments on deserving sinners, and it is certainly not a message of salvation. What the Chaldeans have done and will do is clearly wrong. This is hardly a fitting response to the prayer that Habakkuk has just offered in vv 2–4, unless one reads a great deal between the lines, as commentators usually do. Hence one may gravely doubt that vv 5–11 are intended to be a response to Habakkuk's prayer in any cogent sense.

Further progress in literary analysis is hampered by obscurities at certain places—vv 7b, 8b, 9aB, and all of v 11.

Our study of the verb forms of vv 5–11 in the INTRODUCTION indicated that vv 5–6 are future, and vv 7–11 are past. The idiom of v 7 (*hinnēh* + participle) usually introduces a prediction of an imminent event (Labuschagne 1973; especially Humbert 1958:54–59). By the same token, the participle *hōlēk* in v 6b continues the construction and should be taken as future tense. When v 6 at least was originally uttered, the Babylonian invasions had yet to take place; or if some such events had already occurred, there was more to follow. The participle *pō'ēl* in v 5b is likewise future, and the astonishment predicted in v 5aB and the incredulity forecast in v 5bB will result from the news of the impending events of v 6 after they have happened, not simply from the announcement of the predictive oracle of v 5 before they happened. The people will be astounded not by the word of the LORD, but by the activities of the Chaldeans as described in vv 7–11 and by the knowledge that they will gain by gazing on the world scene (v 5aA), not by prophetic revelation.

Budde (1931:410) made the time reference of the verbs in vv 5–11 uniform by insisting that the conjunctions in v 10bB are *wĕ*-, not *wāw*-consecutive. He similarly normalized the following verse to future tense, changing

'āz ḥālap rûaḥ wayya'ăbōr wĕ'āšēm zû kōhô

to

'āz yaḥălōp kārûaḥ wĕya'ăbōr 'aššûr śām kōhô

Only the first and last words survive. Such extensive remodeling obliges the scholar to explain how the MT came to be the way it is. On this problem, Budde offers not one word. The one clear example of a simple suffixed verb—*ḥālap* in v 11—supports the impression that this part at least is past tense, for no tinkering with conjunctions can change its plain meaning. There are six clauses in which prefixed verbs are used. A notable feature of the syntax is the placement of five of these verbs at the end of their clause—an unusual pattern that shows that we do not have normal prose. Colons that end in a verb give the composition an epic quality. Unless controlled by other, clearer instances, such prefixed verbs are neutral in the matter of tense and decide nothing for the time orientation of the whole passage. Finally, there are three clauses containing *wāw*-consecutive constructions with suffixed verbs (v 8). These are normally future tense, but they can be used consecutively with prefixed verbs with past continuous meaning. Exod 15:1–18 has the same usage. Everything in vv 7–11 can be read as past, and vv 7–11 all hang together as an account of what the Chaldeans have already done to give them their reputation for being "dreadful and terrifying."

Another cause of nonuniformity in the passage is variation in the grammatical number of the verbs. The clearest passage is the description of the Chaldean cavalry in v 8. Here all the verbs are plural, consistent with the subjects "horses" and "riders." The narrative in vv 9–10 is also quite straightforward, with singular verbs. All the verbs in vv 7, 9–11 are singular, with *haggōy*, "the nation," as subject throughout. This is true also in v 8, where the singular-possessive pronouns in "his horses," and "his riders" refer to the Chaldeans as a nation. The singular ("nation") and plural ("horses" and "riders") passages are then interleaved:

Plural	v 6aA	Chaldeans
Singular	vv 6, 7	*haggōy, hû'*
Plural and singular	v 8	"his horses," "his riders"
Collective	v 9aA	"his all" with singular verb
Plural	v 9aB	their faces
Singular	vv 9b–11	no plural forms

Hab 1:5–11 is not a smooth composition, but it is difficult to explain as a collection of smaller pieces. Most of it can be accounted for as a description of the Chaldeans, now plural, now collective, with a warning that their world conquests, although well advanced, are not yet complete. From the perspective of Judah, this would put the date toward the end of seventh century B.C.E.

To sum up. After the opening command (imperative) in v 5a, there are six colons (vv 5b–6) whose future (predictive) reference is clear from the participial constructions, especially *hinnēh* plus participle. The remaining seventeen colons are a sustained description of the Chaldeans.

This result enables us to date Hab 1:5–11 to a time when the Chaldeans have already emerged on the world scene and have accomplished much. But their conquests are not yet complete. The most obvious date is after the destruction of Assyria, but before the invasion of Judah. Thus the purpose for which the LORD will raise up the Chaldeans is not to deal with Assyria. That is over. So Assyria is not the "wicked" of v 4. It could be Egypt or Judah—the next victim. If Egypt has already been defeated (605 B.C.E.), Judah is now exposed helplessly to the menace.

IV. Habakkuk's Second Prayer (1:12–17)

◆

1:12aA Art thou not eternal, Yahweh,
12aB my God, my Holy One, who never dies?
12bA O Yahweh, for judgment thou didst appoint him;
12bB and, O Rock, for accusation thou didst establish him.
13aA Thine eyes are too pure to look on evil,
13aB and to watch wrong thou art not able:
13bA why then didst thou watch cheats,
13bB and (why) wast thou silent when the wicked swallowed someone
more righteous than himself?
14a And thou didst make humankind like fishes of the sea,
14b like reptiles, who have no ruler.
15aA All of them with a hook he brought up;
15aB and he dragged each one out with his net;
15aC and he collected each one with his mesh.
15b That's why he was happy and celebrated.
16aA That's why he made a sacrifice to his net,
16aB and burned incense to his mesh;
16bA because with them his portion was fat,
16bB and his food was plump.
17a Will he therefore empty his net,
17b and for ever slay nations without qualms? ס

Scansion of Habakkuk's Second Prayer (1:12–17)

		BEATS	SYLLABLES	BI(TRI)COLON
12aA	hălō' 'attâ miqqedem yhwh	4	8 ⎫	
12aB	'ĕlōhay qĕdōšî lō' nāmût	4	9 ⎭	17
12bA	yhwh lĕmišpāṭ śamtô	3	7 ⎫	
12bB	wĕṣûr lĕhôkîaḥ yĕsadtô	3	8 ⎭	15
13aA	ṭĕhôr 'ênayim mērĕ'ôt rā'	4	8 ⎫	
13aB	wĕhabbîṭ 'el-'āmāl lō' tûkāl	4	9 ⎭	17
13bA	lāmmâ tabbîṭ bôgĕdîm	3	7 ⎫	
13bB	taḥărîš bĕballa' rāšā' ṣaddîq mimmennû	5	12 ⎭	19
14a	watta'ăśeh 'ādām kidĕgê hayyām	4	10 ⎫	
14b	kĕremeś lō'-mōšēl bô	3	6 ⎭	16
15aA	kullōh bĕḥakkâ hē'ălâ	3	8 ⎫	
15aB	yĕgōrēhû bĕḥermô	2	7 ⎬	[24]
15aC	wĕya'aspēhû bĕmikmartô	2	9 ⎭	
15b	'al-kēn yiśmaḥ wĕyāgîl	3	7 ⎫	
16aA	'al-kēn yĕzabbēaḥ lĕḥermô	3	8 ⎬	[23]
16aB	wîqaṭṭēr lĕmikmartô	2	8 ⎭	
16bA	kî bāhēmmâ šāmēn ḥelqô	4	8 ⎫	
16bB	ûma'ăkālô bĕrî'â	2	7 ⎭	15
17a	ha'al kēn yārîq ḥermô	4	7 ⎫	
17b	wĕtāmîd lahărōg gōyim lo' yaḥmōl	5	11 ⎭	18

INTRODUCTION

This unit is composed along the same lines as the two preceding sections. No change of speaker is indicated, but the manner of the opening address makes it clear immediately that this is a prayer to Yahweh. Like Habakkuk's first prayer, this speech is dominated by interrogatives: opening with hălō', "Is it not a fact that . . . ?" (v 12aA), followed by "Why . . . ?" in the middle (v 13bA), and ending with ha'al kēn (v 17a)—an inclusion. As with the analysis of Habakkuk's first prayer, the issue arises as to how far the sustained influence (multiple duty) of these interrogatives extends to adjacent clauses. In any case, the presence of these interrogatives shows that Habakkuk is still asking questions or, more likely, complaining to God that his policies and practices are unintelligible and unacceptable. In the first prayer, the search for explanations was expressed similarly by questions that blanketed the whole speech, culminating in two statements beginning with 'al-kēn, "That's why . . . ." (v 4). There is a similar pair in vv 15b–16aA. Perhaps they should all be read as "Is that why . . . ?"

A number of details in vv 12–17 are hard to explain apart from cohesion within the larger dialogue—that is, semantic signals from what one person says into what another person says. In these verses the most striking detail of this kind is

the prophet's account of the oppressions and cruelties of an agent who is identified only as *rāšā*, "wicked person" (v 13bB). The subject "he" of the nine third-
person-singular masculine verbs and the referent of the seven third-person-
singular masculine pronoun suffixes "his" are not identified. This agent is
undoubtedly the Chaldeans (v 6aA). After their introduction with the plural gentilic, they are immediately called a "nation," and the singular number prevails
in the rest of the chapter.

It is precisely because Habakkuk's position in this second prayer has not
changed significantly from his position in his first prayer that some scholars have
felt that the intervening material (vv 5–11) is intrusive. We suggest, on the contrary, that Habakkuk's persistence indicates that the response from Yahweh has
not been found satisfactory; indeed, it has made things worse.

Although the mood of perplexity and reproach continues from the first prayer
into the second, the tone is not so strident, and the poetic composition is more disciplined. The structure is evident, the scansion is regular, and the meaning is clear.

The language of vv 12–17 is that of poetry. There are seventy-one orthographic
words, but only one "prose particle"—the definite article in *hayyām* (v 14). Even
in poetry it is likely that a definite article will be used in a construct phrase, if
nowhere else. There are many nouns here that are formally indefinite, that is,
without the definite article. Literal translation would give the impression that
the discourse is quite general: *mišpāṭ*, "judgment"; *rā*, "evil"; *ʿāmāl*, "trouble";
rāšā, "wicked person" (even if generic, *the* wicked man of gnomic discourse);
ʾādām, "humankind" (collective, generic, does not usually have the definite article [7 out of 134 occurrences in Psalms–Job–Proverbs; 58 out of 103 in the
Pentateuch]). In many instances, it is clear that a definite referent is in mind,
requiring a pronoun suffix or another modifier: *ʿênayim*, "thine eyes"; *bôgĕdîm*,
"these cheats"; *ṣaddîq mimmennû*, "*the* man (who is more) righteous than him";
gôyīm, "*the* nations"; *remeś lōʾ-mōšēl bô*, "like *the* crawling creatures (that) have
no ruler"; *ḥakkâ*, "*his* hook" (the following nouns do have the expected pronoun
suffix: *ḥermô, mikmartô, ḥermô, mikmartô, ḥelqô, maʾăkālô, ḥermô*). Habakkuk
is not discussing abstract questions about the existence of evil in the world. He
is speaking out of a concrete and intensely personal situation.

The *nota accusativi* has been avoided completely. All pronoun objects are suffixed (there are four of them). Object nouns, even if definite in meaning, are
not marked as objects by using *nota accusativi*. There are at least two relative
clauses (vv 12aB, 14b) that are not marked as such with the relative ("pronoun").
The difference between the language of poetry and the language of prose is inescapable, yet most interpreters approach the text as though it is Standard Biblical Hebrew of narrative prose.

The poem does not make much use of double-duty prepositions. The preposition *ʾel-* with the object of the infinitive *habbîṭ* in v 13aB can be supplied to
the object of the cognate verb in the next colon. Otherwise, prepositions are repeated with parallels: *l-* (vv 12b, 16a); *b-* (v 15); *k-* (v 14). The pronoun object
is repeated for successive verbs in v 15, and the pronoun suffix with nouns is
used six times in vv 13–17, making more conspicuous its absence from the first
noun of the series (*ḥakkâ*), which clearly requires it. It is instructive to note how

the versions have responded to the nonuniformity in the three connected nouns "hook," "net," "mesh." LXX has the possessive pronoun with the third noun only; Tg Jonathan and V confirm the MT.

In v 16, the instrumental *bāhēmmâ* does double duty. It is more difficult to demonstrate that modal particles continue to function from clause to successive clause without being overtly repeated. The reader (or listener) is used to expecting each bicolon to be a whole grammatical unit, with no change of mood from one colon to the next. A double question is usually easy to detect within the parallelism of a bicolon, as in vv 13b and 17. It is not so easy to determine when such an influence shuts down. NJB and NEB, for example, continue the interrogation into v 14: "Why treat people like fish of the sea . . . ?", a translation that has lost the identity of the subject of the verb ("Thou"!).

And it is harder still to decide when double duty works backward. The syntactic connections of v 13a with its text surrounds are not easy to track. While v 13aB can be read as a complete clause ("Thou art unable to gaze on trouble"), v 13a is grammatically just one complex noun phrase, part of which (*rĕʾôt rāʿ*, "to see evil") is in chiastic parallelism with *habbîṭ ʾel-ʿāmāl*. But "pure of eyes" is not in synonymous parallelism with *lōʾ tûkāl*. In the past, this puzzle has been untangled in two ways. One is to make the whole bicolon an elaborate vocative, in preparation for the question in v 13b:

> You whose eyes are too pure to look upon evil,
> > Who cannot countenance wrongdoing (NJPS)

The other is to make v 13a a statement of fact, telling God something about himself. This reading goes back to LXX: "The eye [singular!] is (too) pure to see wicked things." Recognizing the ways in which all parts of the text are connected up, we suggest that the noun phrase "too pure of eyes to see (a) wicked (man)" is a predicate whose subject is supplied, long-distance, by *hălōʾ ʾattâ* from v 12aA. In terms of compositional technique, this observation shows that one colon may have more than one parallelistic connection; the poem is not just a string of discrete bicolons. As statements about Yahweh in the form of rhetorical questions, vv 12aA and 13aA are closer to each other, while vv 12aB and 13aB resemble each other with a negated verb at the end of the colon. This similarity is enhanced if we cancel the *tiqqûn sōpĕrîm* and restore the preserved original reading: *lōʾ tāmût // lōʾ tûkāl*. Verses 12a and 13a together thus constitute a complex tetracolon, all blanketed by *hălōʾ*, in which the second and fourth colons are matching negative statements against the positive implications of the preceding rhetorical questions, the whole a mix of question, vocative, and assertion:

> Are you not from antiquity, O Yahweh?
> > [Yes, you are eternal]
> > O my God, O my Holy One, you will *not* die!

> > > . . .

[Are you not] too pure of eyes to see evil?
[Yes, you are too pure . . .]
And to look at trouble you are *not* able.

The reading is not greatly different if the second member of each bicolon is caught into the first colon as part of a double question: "(Is it not also true that) you will never die?"

As already seen in vv 2–11, the verb usage in vv 12–17 is mixed. The *wāw*-consecutive verb form *watta ʿăśeh* at the beginning of v 14 dominates the rest of the speech, so that the following *hē ʿălâ* is likewise past tense. It would be a jolt in the middle of the recital if the subsequent *yiqṭōl* verb forms—*yĕgōrēhû, wĕya'aspēhû, yiśmaḥ, wĕyāgîl, yĕzabbēaḥ, wîqaṭṭēr, yārîq,* and *yaḥmôl*—were read as future. The abruptness of the switch is usually softened by translating the *yiqṭōl* verb forms as present tense, but students of the problem have not agreed on where the switch occurs.

The narrative is almost allegorical; the world conqueror is a fisherman. But at what temporal point in the enterprise does the prophet stand? God's creation of humankind is in the past (v 14), and the final question about the continuation of the fishing expeditions looks to the future (v 17). Are vv 15–16 as a whole a prediction like that in v 6 (LXX), so that the pres-ent moment from which the prophet speaks comes between v 14 and v 15? Or are vv 15–16 a review of the fulfillment of that prediction (as we suggest), so that the present moment from which the prophet speaks comes between v 16 and v 17? Or does that the moment of speech come between v 15 and v 16 (NJPS), or are the celebrations going on while Habakkuk prays? Finally, does the choice of English present tense

TABLE 2. Tense of verbs in various translations of Hab 1:14–17

MT	LXX	NJPS	REB	NJB
watta ʿăśeh	wilt thou make	You have made	You have made	Why treat . . . ?
hē ʿălâ	he brought up (aorist)	he has fished	(they) haul	(they) haul
yĕgōrēhû	drew out (aorist)	pulled	or catch	they catch
wĕya'aspēhû	gathered (aorist)	and gathered	or drag	they sweep
yiśmaḥ	will rejoice	he rejoices	make merry	make merry
wĕyāgîl	will be glad	is glad	rejoice	rejoice
yĕzabbēaḥ	will sacrifice	he sacrifices	offering sacrifices	offer a sacrifice
wîqaṭṭēr	will burn incense	makes offerings	burning offerings	burn incense
yārîq	will cast	shall . . . keep emptying	are they to draw	are they to go on emptying
yaḥmôl	will not spare	(without) pity	pitilessly	without pity

for all the verbs in vv 15–16 imply that the prophet is not talking about specific events, but general practices?

Attempts have been made to locate the various portions of Habakkuk 1 in a time frame with a view to establishing the date of composition. Some commentators have the impression that all the activities of the Chaldeans described in Habakkuk 1 are anticipated, pointing to a date of composition no later than 600 B.C.E. Others have the impression that the language of vv 15–16 is retrospective, requiring a date after 600 B.C.E., or even during the Exile. It is usually observed, in this part of the discussion, that the language is elusive in that it is somewhat specific, but not precise enough to be attached to any identifiable historical event; at the same time, it is somewhat general, but not abstract enough to be detached altogether from historical particulars. That's poetry for you!

We have taken the middle ground, supported by a more scrupulous attention to the choice of verb forms, with the proviso that once the unequivocal past-tense form at the beginning of v 14 has set the time reference, the integrity of the following account keeps it all in the past. The *yiqṭōl* verb forms are pulled into their archaic past-time reference by discourse cohesion. A future-time reading is more problematic. A present-time reading can be accepted if it is an historic present. And a present-time reading for v 16 can be accepted if it means that the conquests (v 15) are over, but the celebrations (v 16) are still going on when Habakkuk asks (v 17) how much longer this cycle of conquest and celebration will continue, a question that takes us back to his opening complaint (v 2).

The syntax of vv 12–17 is also poetic in places. The verb is placed at the end of the clause in vv 12bA, 12bB, 13aB, 15aA, 17b. In v 13, this pattern puts the infinitives in chiasmus (it is rare in normal Hebrew for an infinitive to precede a verb whose argument it is). The names of God are chiastic in v 12a, as are the two similes in v 14, the two complements in v 15a. In other places, however, the opportunity to put matching items in chiasmus was not taken (vv 13b, 16a, 16b).

Most of the twenty colons in vv 12–17 have been composed as contiguous pairs. Many of these bicolons have synonymous parallelism of a familiar kind (vv 12b, 13b, 15aB–15aC, 15b–16aA, 16b, 17). In others, the parallelism is less well developed (vv 12a, 13a, 14a). In vv 15–16, we have to recognize two tricolons. Verse 15a is unified by the set of three fishing implements; vv 15aB and 15aC are closely parallel, with patterns chiastic with the opening colon v 15aA. The Masoretes recognized this unit in their placement of *'atnāḥ*. The repeated *'al-kēn* links the introductory v 15b to the following bicolon (v 16), which has simple synonymous parallelism, without chiasmus.

From the quantitative point of view, the twenty colons in vv 12–17 have a mean length of just above eight syllables per colon, the standard. The spread of bicolon length is not great, fifteen to nineteen syllables, even though individual colons range from six to twelve syllables. The two tricolons, with twenty-four and twenty-three syllables, are also normal in this regard. Keeping in mind the margin of uncertainty that is always present—whether about the text itself (we cannot assume that it is immaculate), about the Masoretic identifications enshrined in the vocalization (for example, we cannot rule out entirely the possibility that *'ĕlōhay qĕdōšî* might have been *'ĕlōhê qodšî*; but cf. LXX *ho theos ho hagios mou*), or about the rules for recovering the pronunciation that might have been in vogue in Habakkuk's time—keeping all that in mind, the rhythmic regularity of vv 12–17 is really quite impressive. This regularity is not displayed when the scansion is based on a count of stresses or beats; some colons have only two beats (but then the words are longer), and some have more than three beats (but then the words are shorter).

To sum up, vv 12–17 are a well-made and well-preserved poem, and the poetic nature of this unit has to be kept in mind when making all text-critical or exegetical judgments.

NOTES

12. *Art thou not.* The construction *hălō'* is used 272 times in the Hebrew Bible, least frequently in the Pentateuch (362 per one million words), most frequently in Job (1798 per one million words), as befits its argumentative tone. God does not ask many rhetorical questions in the Primary History, but he is the speaker of most of the eighty-six occurrences of *hălō'* in the Latter Prophets. Such questions are called rhetorical because they do not function as a request for information, but rather to make an incontrovertible assertion. The *hă-* and the *lō'* cancel each other. When the Ziphites said to Saul *hălō' dāwîd mistattēr 'immānû*, "Isn't David hiding with us?" (Ps 54:1), they were telling him, not asking him. In most instances, however, the fact asserted is usually one that the hearer already knows, and the interrogative form amounts to a rebuke, chiding the hearer for overlooking an important fact. Most of Yahweh's rhetorical questions in prophetic oracles have this tone. Understandably, most of the ninety-six occurrences of *hălō'* in the Former Prophets are in vigorous human altercations. It is a different matter for humans to take God to task like that—too risky. Psalmists are restrained from talking to God in such an argumentative way, but *hălō'* is used from time to time to reproach God in prayers of complaint.

Nothing could be more abrupt than the beginning of Habakkuk's second prayer. There is nothing like it anywhere else in the Bible. God is not approached with courtesy and respect by reverent invocation, as in more decorous prayers. Psalm 85, for example, softens the reproach of the rhetorical questions in v 5 by a buildup of adulation in vv 1–3. Habakkuk's question, while reminding Yahweh that he is eternal, holy, immortal, nevertheless betrays, even if it does not openly express, a doubt that is part of the prophet's anguish. The attributes chosen do not include the justice and power that one might expect Yahweh to display in governing the world and destroying the wicked. The attributes chosen are more fundamental, dealing with character and ultimate being rather than activity. It is declared that God made humankind (v 14), and he has appointed "him" (the Chaldean nation [v 6a]) for judgment (v 12b). Because God is supposed to be holy and immortal, why are humans unprotected, and why has God's rule of the world been usurped with impunity by tyrants?

eternal. The word *qedem* does not strictly mean "eternity," an idea not yet within the range of Israelite speculative thought. It refers to the earliest times, going back to stories about the creation of the world. Israelite tradition contains no trace of any myth about how Yahweh came into existence: biblical thought does not engage in speculation about absolute existence as timeless. Indeed, in the strictest sense of myth as a story about a divine being or divine beings concerned with their affairs with little, if any, involvement of humans, there is no mythology about Yahweh. All the stories about Yahweh involve humans, but never any other gods. This feature of Israelite religion has no parallel in the ancient world.

The contribution of Habakkuk's opening remark to the prayer that follows is not clear. No argument is based on the fact of Yahweh's antiquity, as such, but both sections of the following prayer begin with statements about creation.

my God, my Holy One. In the opening words of the prayer, there are three titles for God in a row. The Masoretic punctuation makes the second and third title a single phrase, and LXX translates "My holy God." Alteration to *'ĕlōhê qodšî* has suggested itself, or to the "Holy One of Israel" (Budde 1931:410). The former emendation requires no change in the consonants of the text, but replaces the unique *qĕdōšî*, "my holy one," with the familiar *qodšî*, "my holiness." The latter expression is met most commonly in attributive phrases such as "the name of my holiness" (= "my holy name") (attested twelve times) and "the mountain of my holiness" (= "my holy mountain") (attested thirteen times), where "my" refers to God. These phrases account for nearly all the occurrences of *qodšî*; *'ĕlōhê qodšî* is not attested.

A difficulty with *qĕdōšî*, "my holy one," is that the pronoun suffix "my" here refers to the prophet. But Yahweh is called "Israel's Holy One" in Isa 10:17; 43:15; 49:7, where the *plene* spelling requires *qādōš*. The Masoretic vocalization of Hab 1:12 can therefore be retained, even though it is rare for this word to be spelled defectively. The title *qādōš* occurs again in Hab 3:3, where its parallelism with *'ĕlôah* makes it possible to read *'ĕlōhî* in Hab 1:12, supported by *'ĕlōhô* in v 11. Were it not for this singular form in Hab 1:11, the more familiar pseudo-plural *'ĕlōhay* could stand. The difference is slight in any case. "Yahweh my God" is a better phrase, but the Masoretic punctuation makes the two colons nearer to equality in length.

At this point in the book, invocation of Yahweh as holy, whatever the locution, prepares for the reference to Yahweh in his holy temple (2:20) at the end of the first part of the book. Verse 13 implies that the Holy One cannot even sully his eyes with the sight of evil.

never dies. The MT is literally "we shall not die" (KJV). Such a statement is quite out of place here. We would expect a parallel assertion about God's immortality. Indeed, immortality for a human in any absolute sense is nowhere asserted in the Hebrew Bible. Death followed by resurrection is a human's lot. The present reading is not original. It is a *tiqqûn sôpĕrîm* replacing *lō' tāmût*, "you won't die," widely restored in modern versions. Ginsburg's (1897:358) notes show that the old scholars were unanimous that *tāmût* is the proper reading. Because the *sôpĕrîm* did not argue their case, we are not sure what they felt to be the problem at this point. See the full discussion in McCarthy (1981: esp. 105–111). This classical rabbinic "emendation" (*tiqqûn*) cannot be disposed of by saying that the corrected text is "almost meaningless" (Cannon 1925:72, n. 2). "We shall not die" is quite meaningful, but we cannot see its point in this prayer. The *tiqqûnê sôpĕrîm* were made either because the variant had textual attestation or because a completely unacceptable reading demanded some change, usually for pious reasons. The latter does not seem to apply here. Yahweh is "the living God," an epithet that must have meant "ever-living" in the sense of "never-dying," in contrast to a dying–rising god who could be considered immortal only in a conditional sense. In spite of the Canaanite story of Baal, who dies and is restored to life, the main tradition of the ancient Near East is that the gods, unlike humans, do not die at all.

The reminder of Yahweh's immunity to death is poignant in a text that is so concerned with the huge scale of human casualties in war. One is reminded of the opening lines in Arabic on tombstones (Bulatov 1963):

| *huwa 'alḥad 'al-ḥay la' namūt* | He alone, the Living One, does not die |
| *wakul ḥayu namūtu* | and all that live die |

It is hard to see what the Jewish readers found objectionable in the statement that Yahweh does not die, unless simply to say that it might raise the thought that it might not be true, and harder to see how they thought that "we shall not die" is an improvement. The mortality of humans is described with pathos in v 17, but life is promised to the righteous in Hab 2:4. In the *tiqqûnê sôpĕrîm*, the scribes did not emend the original away. In spite of indications that they found the genuine text disrespectful of deity, they preserved the original. Their preference was not for one out of two attested variants, but for a reading that, they must have persuaded themselves, was the "true" meaning. Even if motivated by reverence, in such a *correctio scribarum* reverence for the text competed with reverence for God, and the scribes often compromised by concealing the offensive words under a euphemism. This is hardly the case in this verse. "We shall not die" is hardly a euphemism for "you will not die."

In Israelite thought, the attributes of God are not approached primarily through negation, as in later scholastic theology. The Hebrew Bible prefers strong positive adjectives, such as "holy," "just," "terrible," "kind," "living." Privatives are sometimes used, all the same. God is "not a man" (Num 23:19; for the opposite case, that man is not God, see Isa 31:3). Habakkuk has several examples of such paired antithetical assertions.

1:13	His eyes are pure; he cannot look at evil
1:15	Humankind is like fish; they have no ruler
1:17	He kills the nations; he does not spare
2:3	He hurries; he won't deceive
2:3	He is coming; he won't be late

2:4   His soul is twisted, not straight
2:5   Presumptuous; not reliable
2:5   Like death, never satisfied
2:19   Gold and silver outside, no spirit inside

It is possible that *lō' tāmût* is intended to be the counterpart of *miqqedem*. If the first member of this pair of expressions is equivalent to *mē'ôlām wě'ad-'ôlām*, "from eternity and unto eternity," the second means "you will never die."

It is possible that *nāmût* is a genuine alternative reading with the same meaning: not first person, but a *Nip'al* with middle meaning. While no *Nip'al* of √*mwt* has been recognized, and a passive of a stative verb like *mēt*, "he is dead," is not to be expected (the only attested passive form of this root is that of the transitivized *Hip'il*), nevertheless the existential *hāyâ* has a *Nip'al*, scarcely distinguishable from the *Qal* in meaning. A significant number of its occurrences are in the negated *lō' nihyeh*, "it never existed" (Joel 2:3; Zech 8:10; Neh 6:8; Exod 11:6; Judg 19:30; Dan 12:1) or questioned (Deut 4:32, where interrogative is tantamount to negative). By analogy, a negated middle *Nip'al* of √*mwt* is not impossible. In the present context, an adjectival use of the participle ("the one who does not die") serves better than a verb, for *lō' mēt* is "the one who is not dead"—that is, has not died—and *lō' tāmût* is "(thou art the one who) will not die." A divine attribute is needed. The meaning "we will not die" could, then, be a misinterpretation of the intention of the scribes.

appoint. The rhetorical *hălō'* probably continues its effect into v 12b. Yahweh is still being addressed with misgiving: "Isn't it supposed to be true, Yahweh, that you appointed him for judgment? Why then has that judgment not been carried out?" The prophet is irked by the delay in the fulfillment of a specific prophecy that had been given, dooming the Chaldeans. Hence the call to patience (2:3) and the need to live by faith (2:4; 3:17–18).

Budde (1931:410) considered v 12b a gloss and at the same time proposed some emendations. The verb *śām* means "put" in all kinds of ways. With more abstract things as its object, it means "determine" or "designate." One can "put" an accusation against someone (Deut 22:14). The verb can refer to issuing statutes or decrees (Deut 4:44) or handing down an administrative decision (2 Kgs 18:14). As such, the verb can be used in creation stories to describe the ordering of the cosmos (Job 38:5, 33; Ps 104:9; Jer 5:22). The parallel verb *ysd* and the divine name *ṣûr*, (a creator title; cf. Deut 32:4, 30) support such a connotation here. But this does not mean that the Chaldeans were predestined to judgment from the creation (as one of the decisions of the original creation). Rather, the decisions to judge in history come from the sovereign will of Yahweh the Rock as history moves along, just as the decisions to create.

The idiom is used in an unusual way. Normally *śm* X *lě*-Y means "to turn X into Y." Thus Judg 1:28 means "they committed the Canaanites to forced labor." A following infinitive indicates the purpose of the decision: "All Israel designated me to reign" (1 Kgs 2:15). In the present instance, this idiom would mean that Yahweh appointed him "to judge and to rebuke"; *lāḥôkîaḥ* is active, and *lĕmišpāṭ* is parallel to it. Hence the conclusion of commentators that Yahweh has appointed the Chaldeans to carry out his judgment. This conclusion derives support from the use of the title *ṣûr*, for it could come from an ancient song and bring quite specific associations with it. A likely source is Deut 32:4, which states that the *ṣûr*'s deed (*poʿŏlô*, the same word as in Hab 1:5 and 3:2) is perfect; or Deut 32:30, which explains the victory of a non-people over Israel by saying

The(ir) Rock sold them
and Yahweh delivered them up

This connection would mean, then, that Yahweh, the Rock, has similarly appointed the Chaldeans for corrective judgment—that is, to apply corrective judgment to Judah—by handing Judah over to them. Because this device was well known in Israel's thought, in itself it could not have been objected to. What Habakkuk is complaining about must be the disproportionate scale or a belief that his circumstances are different from those behind the events reported in the Song of Moses. Yet he does not say this; so v 12b does not clarify the prayer, and in what follows it is the event itself, not simply its scale, that he complains about.

Far from being a key to the pericope, the supposition that v 12b is based on ancient tradition throws it all into distorted perspective. If the prophet believes that Yahweh is using the Chaldeans to accomplish his righteous purposes, by judging the wicked on his behalf, why does he not consent? He is not protesting against this arrangement; he is not asking for its justice to be explained to him. He does not accept the fact while denying its justice. There is no indication in Yahweh's first speech (vv 5–11) that he is sending the Chaldeans to judge anyone; that can only be inferred from the prayer (vv 2–4) that it is the response to. The usual interpretation of v 12b finds no support in the rest of the prophecy. There are no grounds for importing into it the theology of Isaiah (the Assyrian is the rod of Yahweh's anger [Isa 10:5]) or of Jeremiah (Yahweh commands the Babylonians to attack wicked Jerusalem [34:2]). In vv 12–17, Habakkuk does not find anything right in what the Chaldeans are doing. At no point does he discover any justification for their wholesale and indiscriminate conquest and slaughter in the argument that some of their victims at least (the wicked element in Israel?) deserve to be punished. If the Chaldeans are the object, or the prime object of the statements in Hab 2:6–20, their condemnation is unqualified. The only identifiable wicked in the prophecy are the Chaldeans, and the justice Habakkuk is looking for is their destruction. Their judgment has been determined, but it has not been carried out. On the contrary, their conquests continue unabated (v 17). Habakkuk is not disagreeing with Yahweh about the decision to judge (Judah?) by means of the Chaldeans. To do that he would have to argue, like Abraham, that the judge of all the earth must not destroy the righteous along with the wicked. Or he would appeal to the covenant promises as an argument that Israel must be preserved, in the tradition of all the prophetic covenant mediators. Habakkuk's prayer follows neither of these lines. It is the apparent indifference of God (v 3b), in spite of his decree of judgment (v 12b), that perplexes the prophet. His essential problem is delay in the fulfillment of a prophecy (2:3).

for accusation. The Qumran reading *lmwkyḥw* makes another noun to match *mišpāṭ*. It has little claim for being original. This nominal form is the *Hip̄ ʿil* participle meaning "critic," "accuser." The variant reflects the interpretation that the LORD has set up the Chaldeans to be the accuser of some third party, presumably Judah. But, as we have seen, the victims of Chaldean aggression are represented as righteous (vv 2–4b, 13b) and they are all nations.

Rock. A proper noun, as in Deuteronomy 32, not just a title, as in Psalm 18. There is no need to emend to "my rock," as in BHS. The series of titles—"Yahweh," "my God," "my Holy One," "Rock"—is reminiscent of the profusion of similar vocatives that begins David's great victory ode (Ps 18:2–3). The exultation in that hymn, however, contrasts with the gloom of Habakkuk's prayer. David called out to Yahweh and was delivered (*ʾiwwāšeaʿ* [Ps 18:4]). Habakkuk cried out and was not delivered (v 2). So the prophet's use of this ancient name Rock has a somewhat bitter flavor. At the same time, Yahweh is not disowned. The ancient titles serve to arouse and reaffirm the ancient faith. They are part of the "report" of Yahweh that Habakkuk has heard (3:2). The recitation of such ancient poems, which become creedal in the liturgy, provides the basis for Habakkuk's present and persistent prayers.

Two distinct words could be involved. BDB recognizes four homonymous roots *ṣwr*. The main contrast is between the description of God as a "rock" in a military context, which could derive from the geological term (*ṣûr* — "cliff" or "crag"), and the use of the name Rock in creation statements. The latter derives from √*yṣr*, "form," "shape," and is undoubtedly the one used here. Perhaps it should not be translated as "Rock," but as something like "Shaper" (Andersen 1970a).

establish. The root *ysd* is another creation verb. Hebrew creation stories use a wide range of figurative language carried by verbs with specific technological connotations. Verbs with √*ysd* are primarily architectural and usually describe the construction of the lower portions of the cosmos as a vast edifice. It would be more suitable for describing the foundation of a city than the appointment of a person or nation. For its geological and architectural meaning see Andersen (1958), and Meyers and Meyers (1987:63).

If the leading verb of the parallel pair in the bicolon

yhwh lĕmišpāṭ śamtô
wĕṣûr lĕhôkîaḥ yĕsadtô

dominates the following verb, so that the connotations of the first are definitive and the associations of the second are figurative, the √*śm* implies purpose and assignment to a particular task.

13. The logical connections of v 12 with its context are not clear. Its state-

ments of facts are not grounded in any information about where such knowledge comes from. The source cannot be simply the general truth that Yahweh is judge of the world; the passage refers to a more specific decree that the Chaldeans are marked off for judgment. This belief would most likely come from an oracle of judgment given previously, whose background is not supplied here, unless vv 11–12 are such an oracle, as suggested by some scholars.

In any case, the statement is not developed; the judiciary role of Yahweh is not exploited by presenting his dealings with the Chaldeans as a *rîb*-dispute. We suggest that the accumulation of titles and attributes and acts of God at this point is part of a long invocation, and that all six colons in vv 12–13a are vocative. The prominent positions of the names Yahweh and Rock are in keeping with this reading. And v 13aA is not well construed as an assertion because it is not a clause. KJV supplies a subject "Thou art." NASB breaks up the construct phrase: "Thine eyes are too pure . . ." (cf. JB, NAB). NEB makes vv 12bB and 13aA vocative, but it breaks up the parallelism within v 12b by making v 12bA an assertion. RSV makes all of v 13a vocative, but all translations fail to highlight the noun *ṭāhôr* as a title for God—"O Pure One!" The parallelism within v 13a is not close, as in the usual practice, although the ideas are similar and the colons are almost identical in length. There is chiasmus, because "look at evil" is parallel to "gaze on agony." The preposition *'el* does retroactive double duty in these constructions. The final verb makes the whole of v 13a second person and combines with the opening phrase to give the explanation "You can't look on evil because you are too pure in (your) eyes." Another indication of the unity of vv 12–13a as an elaborate invocation is the balance between *lō' tāmût* and *lō' tûkāl*, discussed earlier.

pure. God's inexplicable behavior is brought out by the contradictory statements that he cannot look on wrongdoing (v 13aB); yet he does look on cheats (v 13bA, same verb!). The word "pure" implies that God's eyes would be defiled by the sight of evil and that he would have to cleanse himself. The choice of this word matches "Holy" in v 12 and they have assonance (*qādôš // ṭāhôr*).

look. The use of the same vocabulary in this verse and in v 3 shows that there is little difference between the prophet's problem in both prayers. The same idiom *'āmāl tabbîṭ* and the same parallelism of *rā'â* and *hibbîṭ* indicates that *'āwen* in v 3 is like *rā'* in v 13. By the same token, we have another reason for reading *rā'â* as *Qal* in both places. It is God who is looking at evil. Similar questions are asked:

3   Why do you look at me in (this) iniquity?
13b   Why do you look at (these) deceivers?

The same problem is described in v 4b in the statement that the wicked surround the righteous, and in v 13 in the statement that the wicked swallow the righteous—using the same nouns. The inactivity of God in the face of such wickedness and, more exactly, his silence (v 13b) are described in v 4aB by saying that *mišpāṭ* never comes out, that is, God does not even pronounce a verdict of condemnation. (We recognized, in the NOTE on v 4, that it is unclear whether it is the divine judge or a human court that is inoperative in this way; but, because Habakkuk complains to God, it is more likely that he holds God to blame.)

evil. The masculine singular noun can be taken as a reference to an evil person (= *rāšāʿ* [v 13bB]). The connections among the four colons in v 13 support this reading. Verse 13bA asks why God looks at "deceivers" when his eyes are supposed to be too pure to see (an) evil (man). An evil deed or evil in the abstract is usually referred to by the feminine noun *rāʿâ*. LXX *ponēra* could be feminine singular or neuter plural.

The supply of the preposition *b-* to mark the object in 1QpHab is most likely a move away from the leanness of poetic diction in using prepositions in the original text. Whether the attestation of the same reading in medieval sources (Gottstein 1953) is evidence for the authenticity of the Qumran reading or whether it is independently due to similar pressures is a tricky text-critical call. The rarity of the idiom is a point in its favor. The object marker with the verb √*rʾh* is commonly *nota accusativi ʾet*, but *b-* is not infrequently used, particularly when the object is a noun referring to misery (Gen 29:32; 1 Sam 1:11 [but *ʾet* in 2 Kgs 14:26]), evil (Num 11:15; Gen 44:34; Est 8:6), or death (Gen 21:16; Isa 66:24). See also Jer 29:32; Ezek 21:26; Mic 7:9.

wrong. Recognizing that v 13b matches v 13a suggests that the wrong so offensive to God's sight is the action of the wicked swallowing the righteous (v 13bB).

cheats. A *bôgēd* is a person who deceives by wearing a disguise. The idea is close to "hypocrite," a person who conceals a wicked self under a mask of goodness. The point is not elaborated here, although doubtless the prophet had some concrete cases in mind. These traitors are the same as the wicked who engulf the righteous, so *rāšāʿ* and *ṣaddîq* could be representative singular (generic), perhaps collective. The only plurals in the prayer are "cheats" (v 13b), "fishes" (v 14), and "nations" (v 17). Otherwise, "evil," "wicked," "man," and "reptile" are collective, and all the verbs and pronouns referring to the Chaldeans (presumably, the word is not actually used in this unit, but who else could he be referring to?) are singular. The plural *bôgĕdîm* is, accordingly, out of line with the rest of the prayer. Wellhausen (1892) tried to bring this word into parallelism with *bblʿ* by reading **bibgôd.*

The question is whether *bôgĕdîm* was chosen deliberately, so that its specific meaning is important for the passage as a whole, or whether any word meaning "miscreant" would have done equally well. The participle *bôgēd* is used again in Hab 2:5 — "wine is a cheat" — but once more the significance of that statement in its context is quite elusive. The theme of drunkenness recurs in the fourth "woe oracle," which is directed against a person who used intoxicating drinks as an aid to the gratification of sexual lusts. The verb *habbît*, so prominent in Habakkuk 1, is used again in Hab 2:15b. The sin of idolatry is another obvious connection between the second prayer and the "woe oracles." The gloating gaze of the depraved "deceivers" is contrasted with the uncaring gaze of God, who looks on, but says nothing.

silent. This verb is all the more powerful because it has connotations of deafness as well, with the *Hip'il* used here meaning "to act like a deaf person, and so make no response." The unresponsiveness of God to prayer was a cause of distress to several Psalmists (Ps 35:2), especially when they are crying out against wickedness (Ps 83:2), and when the silence of God contrasts with the insolent speech of the wicked (*rāšā'*) (Ps 109:1). Silence is ominous because it implies either tacit acquiescence (Numbers 30) or admission of guilt (Job 6:24).

wicked. The stock terms for a good and bad person in opposition are *ṣaddîq* and *rāšā'*. They turn up in poetic parallelism in a wide variety of genres in biblical literature—prayers, moralistic wisdom, juridical texts. They have already occurred in v 4bA:*kî rāšā' maktîr 'et-haṣṣaddîq*, where the second noun has the definite article. LXX has the same assymetry in v 13 (*ton dikaion*). The reactivation of this vocabulary in v 13bB is a significant link between Habakkuk's two prayers, and the simplest approach is to assume that the reference is the same in both places.

Psalm 1 is the classic analysis of the conduct and destiny of these two opposing types. There all the nouns are plural, except for the opening *hā'îš*, and all lack the article but two (*hā'îš* [v 1] and *hārĕšā'îm* [v 4, marking the onset of the second part of the poem]). The usage in Habakkuk is similar. Here, however, the singular number dominates. Plural nouns appear once each for the wicked (*bôgĕdîm*) and their victims (*gôyīm*). In the first prayer, there is nothing to indicate that Habakkuk has in mind anything more than injustice between one person and another in his own community. It is only when *gôyīm* is used at the very end of his prayer (v 17) that it becomes clear that Habakkuk has been analyzing international imperialism, at least in the second prayer.

This change of focus has already been made in Yahweh's first response (1:5–11), which speaks quite clearly about world conquest by the terrible Chaldeans. That was supposed to rectify the injustice that Habakkuk had complained about. Yahweh's agent was supposed to punish the wicked in Judah or to punish Judah for the wickedness in it. What, then, happens to the righteous on whose behalf Habakkuk has sued Yahweh? By the end of his second prayer, he seems to be maintaining that all the nations oppressed by the Chaldeans are "righteous"!

swallowed. The metaphorical use of this word for greedy eating prepares for the elaborate figure that follows, where the nations are seen as a fat and juicy meal for the Chaldeans (v 16b). There does not seem to be any difference between the meaning of the *Qal* and the *Pi'el* of the verb. Sperber (1966:10) quotes Num 16:13 and Isa 25:8 as illustrations of their similarity.

than himself. LXX lacks this phrase. But other Greek translations and the Vulgate have it. Budde (1931:410) did not think that this evidence, in spite of the exceptional length of the colon, was any reason for deleting the words. Yet it must be admitted that it overweights the construction and actually weakens the impact. For "the righteous" (absolutely) is a stronger expression than "the one who is more righteous than he" (relatively). The nouns are definite in meaning in this verse as in Hab 1:4 (where "the righteous" does have the definite article). This terminology implies direct personal litigation between two persons, one of whom is in the right, one in the wrong—in respect to each other. So *ṣaddîq* means "righteous in relation to the wicked in this particular suit"—that is, "more righteous than he" whether *mimmennû* is expressed or not.

14. *thou didst make.* The nonapocopated form "is so frequent, especially in the first person singular, that it can hardly be considered erroneous" (Muraoka 1991:208). NEB interprets this statement as a continuation of the question. Either way, the fact that God created humankind is the basis of the question that emerges in v 17. The ultimate responsibilities for human history lie with God, who created all.

humankind. This general reference to the creation of the human race gives further support to our contention that the concern of the prophet is universal, not just national. The victims are not the chosen people Israel, even less the righteous within Judah at that time. They are "the nations" (v 17) without restriction.

Habakkuk reminds God of his obligation to look after everybody, not because of covenant promises, but because of the fact of creation as such. An additional appeal arises from the helplessness of humankind because they have no ruler, no protector. By comparing them with the "fishes of the sea" and the "swarming things," Habakkuk highlights the teeming population of the earth. Both terms are used in the creation story of Genesis 1 and with the same parallelism in Gen 1:28, except that it has *děgat hayyām.* The verbs "make" and "rule" are also part of the vocabulary of Genesis 1; that is, every word in Hab 1:14 is found in Genesis 1.

In the rest of the poem, however, it is not God, but the world conqueror, who treats humankind like the fish of the sea. Hence Budde (1931:410) proposed to interpret **wt ʿśh* [*lô*] as "and (why) did you make humankind [for him!] like the fish of the sea?" God is blamed for providing the world conqueror with so many victims.

ruler. In Isaiah 63 there is a complaint in which God is charged with neglect of his people, exposing them to the ravages of the heathen. At the end the prayer says (v 19):

hāyînû mēʿôlām	We have always been (yours)
lōʾ-māšaltā bām	you never ruled them
lōʾ-niqrāʾ šimkā ʿālêhem	your name was never pronounced over them

Habakkuk does not point up the contrast between Israel and other nations in this matter, so it is not clear whether they "have no ruler" means that the helplessness of the nations is due to absence of leadership, or whether it is only part of the simile and refers to the fish.

15. The eight colons in vv 15–16 are unified by the imagery of the world conqueror as a fisherman. It is interesting that the Akkadian word *bāʾiru* means "fisherman," "hunter," and "soldier." Perhaps knowledge of this usage suggested the image to the prophet.

The first three colons constitute a tricolon in which the words "hook," " net," and "mesh" are parallel. The Masoretic punctuation recognizes this pattern. The first colon is introductory, and the second and third make the better bicolon because they have identical structure. They are linked by "and," whereas v 15aB has no "and." 1QpHab does have "and."

All of them. That is, all humankind. Compare *kullōh*, with the same archaic spelling, in v 9.

hook. The word *ḥakkâ* is a general name for a fishing hook (Isa 19:8; Job 40:25). The *ḥerem* is a throwing net used for hunting (Mic 7:2; Qoh 7:26) or fishing. This is the only place where the word *mikmeret* is used in the Hebrew Bible. (There is also a masculine form.) There is no way of telling if this term refers to a more specialized piece of equipment, such as a drag net (*seine, sagēnē* [LXX]) or whether the words are interchangeable.

he brought up. The verb is probably suffixed in poetic parallelism with the following prefixed verb forms. The unique vocalization is inexplicable. 1QpHab has the easier reading *yʿlh*, already proposed by Budde (1931:410).

collected. The same verb was used in v 9 to describe the gathering of prisoners of war.

That's why. Verse 15b and v 16a constitute another tricolon. The first colon contains the conventional parallels "happy" and "jubilant." LXX reads

heneken toutou eufranthēsetai	Therefore he will rejoice
kai kharēsetai hē kardia autou	and his heart will be glad

Restoration of *libbô* would make v 15b a bicolon. The first two colons are joined by the repeated *ʿal-kēn* (see Hos 9:1). The second and third colons are similar in structure and repeat the nouns from v 15a.

16. *made a sacrifice.* The four verbs in this tricolon are all cultic in association. We need not suppose that this description was intended to describe any actual ceremony in Babylonian religion, because the fishing tackle is only a metaphor. The analogy could be acts of devotion to weapons of war. LXX has *amphiblēstron* and *sagēnē* in chiastic order when they are repeated in v 16.

his portion. Budde (1930:146; 1931:410) suggested that the apparent disagreement in the gender of subject and predicate can be resolved if *bĕrîʾâ* is virtually neuter and that the "adjectives" are the subject:

(a) fat (thing) (is) his portion
and (a) plump (thing) (is) his food

Verse 16b picks up the image of the tyrant, swallowing his victim (v 13b). The images are incongruous. Fish are caught to be eaten. The nations are slain (v 17b); the corpses are piled up (v 10bB).

plump. 1QpHab reads *brʾ*, which is apparently the correct adjective to modify *maʾăkāl*. Otherwise, this would be the only place in the Hebrew Bible where this noun is feminine. In v 16b, the nouns and adjectives are arranged in chiasm.

17. *Will he . . . ?* The MT has a question. 1QpHab and the versions don't have this problem. In fact, the two difficult *he*'s—in *brʾh* and *hʿl*—are both absent from 1QpHab, which weakens the theory that one is a dittograph of the

other. This is the fifth time that Habakkuk has used ʿal-kēn, "That's why?" This alone should be enough to prohibit alteration to hă ʿōlām, proposed by Giesebrecht, followed by Wellhausen (1893:163) and others. There is no obvious logic in the question in v 17. It makes sense to worship the fishing nets, because by their means he is well fed. But this is not *why* he empties his net. This difficulty was overcome by Giesebrecht's emendation to hă ʿōlām, "Will he for ever . . . ?" (Budde 1931:410). This adjustment achieves excellent parallelism with tāmîd. But this kind of argument is never sufficient to justify a substantial emendation; parallelism of that mechanical kind cannot be assumed.

It is worth pointing out that most of the differences between 1QpHab and the MT at this place obviate the difficulties of the latter. In all the following pairs, 1QpHab is the easier reading:

VERSE	MT	1QpHab
13	rʿ	brʿ
	thryš	whryš
14	wtʿšh	wtʿš
15	hʿlh	yʿlh
	ygrhw	wygrhw
	brʾh	brʾ
17	hʿl	ʿl
	hrmw	hrbw
	wtmyd	tmyd

1QpHab is probably secondary and inferior in these more difficult cases:

VERSE	MT	1QpHab
13	tbyt	tbytw
	lʾ	wlwʾ

Because 1QpHab tends to add the conjunction wāw, the "and perpetually" of the MT is probably to be preferred as the more difficult reading. For a full assessment, consult Brownlee (1959, 1979).

The 1QpHab reading "brandish his sword" rather than "empty his net" is probably due to the influence of the common idiom. It is remarkable that this reading had already suggested itself as an emendation before the Dead Sea Scrolls were discovered. One late Greek minuscule in the Vatican Library reads *ekkenōsei makhairan autou*, "he will empty [!] his sword," partly accommodating MT. The sword makes a good parallel to the verb "slay" in v 17b. And "he does not desist" is a good parallel for "perpetually." If the imagery has changed, v 17 might not have anything at all to do with the fishing figure, and hermô might have come into the Masoretic Text under the influence of its two preceding occurrences.

The interrogative form of v 17 can be salvaged if it is seen to be a conclusion to the second part of the prayer (vv 14–17), matching the question that concludes the first part of the prayer (vv 12–13). Swallowing the righteous and slaying the nations unsparingly are similar ideas. The prophet's central question is "Why do you look on silently?" (v 13aA). What God sees—the wicked swallowing the righteous—is described in detail in vv 15–16. And all this happens in spite of the fact that humankind is a special creation of God and they have no ruler (but God?). So Habakkuk asks, "Is that why . . . ?" Is it because God looks on silently that he (the tyrant) does not spare to slay nations?

slay nations. The archaic style accounts for the absence of the definite article; the noun should be understood as definite. If *yaḥmôl* is the auxiliary for the infinitive, its placement at the end of the clause is irregular, but not impossible. It is easy to clean this up by reading *wĕtāmîd yaḥărōg gôyīm lōʾ yaḥtôl* (Wellhausen 1893:163) but neatness as such can never prove that an emendation is correct. Nevertheless, v 17b, whether *wĕtāmîd* is included or not, is awkward. The reference to "nations" constitutes an inclusion with Yahweh's opening words (v 5), and the last four words would make an excellent parallel to v 6bB:

| to take possession of | dwellings | not his |
| to slay | nations | not sparing |

At the very least this similarity points to the stylistic unity of Habakkuk 1.

COMMENT

Habakkuk's second prayer is twice as long as the first. The colons are more numerous and generally longer. The prayer is similar to the first; it contains the same kinds of expressions—questions (13b, 17), statements of fact, and logical inferences introduced by subordinating conjunctions (*ʿal-kēn* and *kî*). The way in which these materials are arranged resembles that in vv 2–4. Common vocabulary points to a common theme and to the same author.

habbîṭ ʾel-ʿāmāl	(v 13; cf. v 3)
mišpāṭ	(v 12; cf. v 4)
rāšāʿ, ṣaddîq	(v 13; cf. v 4)

We have already reported the suspicion of some scholars that these similarities show that originally vv 2–4 and 12–17 were parts of a single prayer.

The interconnections among the constituent parts of vv 12–17 are not easy to find. The argument is not developed step by step along a straight line.

The problem that causes Habakkuk's anguish arises from what he believes about God and what he sees in the world. Habakkuk believes, on the one hand, that the LORD is the living, never-dying God; yet in the world there is death. On the other hand (it is implied, if not said), there are no limits to God's knowledge. So he must know what is going on in the world. How, then, can he possibly be so indifferent to it all? Again, Habakkuk believes that God's eyes are too pure to look on evil; he is unable to gaze on trouble (v 13a). Why, then, does he look on while treachery flourishes (v 13bA), while injustice triumphs (v 13bB)? There seems to be a contradiction in these representations of God's omniscience. He sees everything. That cannot be doubted. At least he can see everything if he wants to. So why does God's inaction make it seem as though he hasn't noticed? Does he wait until somebody draws his attention to what is going on? Does God intervene in human affairs only when he is invited? Has he averted his eyes to protect them from contamination? Can Habakkuk really believe that God is prudish? Or does his statement that God's eyes are too pure to look on evil (v 13aA) insinuate that the appropriate measures would be to remove the offending spectacle by wiping out what is wrong?

Another belief of Habakkuk is that God created humankind "like fishes of the sea" (v 14a). So, if God is the sole creator, did he also create the Chaldeans? If so, why? These statements provide the starting point for an elaborate figure that occupies half the speech (vv 14–17). The teeming multitudes of people are all caught by the world conquerer with as little compunction as a fisherman pulling in his catch; indeed, he does it with glee (vv 15–16). The scale of his success makes the indifference and unresponsiveness of God all the more intolerable. Just as Habakkuk began by asking "How long . . . ?" (v 2), now he asks whether this slaughter and enslavement will ever come to an end (v 17).

The last question does not simply ask how long this lawlessness will prevail in the world. It asks, "Is this the reason [*hă'al kēn*] . . . ?" (v 17aA). The suggested reason is that humankind, like the reptiles, has no ruler (v 14b). This could mean that God is not doing his job as ruler of humankind; his inactivity is the explanation of the unrestrained wickedness in the world. This charge is made in both of Habakkuk's prayers. It could mean that most of humankind lacks leadership; they are as helpless as fishes in the face of organized militarism. Or it could mean that the Chaldeans acknowledge no ruler but their own might—their weapons, represented as their fishing equipment (v 11b). Their worship is directed to these things (vv 15b–16a). Their gluttony (16b), ruthlessness (17b), and idolatry are all an affront to a person who believes God to be just.

Another statement made by Habakkuk is that Yahweh has appointed "him" for judgment (v 12). The relationship of this assertion to the whole speech is not clear. It could mean that God has already marked out the Chaldeans for retribution that will fall on them in due course. This act would then represent the verdict of God as judge of the world in the light of their conduct in history. If God has reached such a decision, and issued such a verdict, it could be represented by the long catalog of woes that follows in Habakkuk 2. (But such a speech is not the normal form of a verdict from a judge.) If Habakkuk is supposed to believe that this is God's purpose for the Chaldeans, we are at a stage later than that of v 6. There God announces his intention of raising up the Chaldeans to conquer the world. It could be that v 12b is saying the same thing in another way. God has appointed the Chaldeans for the judgment of the other nations, to rebuke or chastise them (*hôkîaḥ*). Israel as the people of God is not specifically mentioned as the object of this corrective punishment; the picture is general and universal. Because the vocabulary of creation is used in v 12b (the title *ṣûr* for God, and the verb *ysd*) the language implies that from the very beginning of history the Chaldeans were made and marked for this task. The tradition that God (or the gods) determined the course of history in such an absolute way from the very beginning (even before creation) does not emerge until we reach the more formal theological determinism (predestination) of later Judaic and derivative Christian tradition. In the ancient Near East, the gods met in congress (regularly on New Year's Day, but also in emergency session) to "determine the fates." In the Hebrew Bible, God acts freely as history moves along, continually changing his mind in response to historical developments and, especially, as provoked by human prayers. Prophetic intercession frequently influences these changes of policy. The appointment of the Chaldeans for judgment need not be primeval and is certainly not fixed.

But whatever the nuance, God's policies for running the world impose an impossible strain on Habakkuk's faith. If the Chaldeans are God's instruments for punishing the rest of humankind, then it is too much; it is excessive for it to go on so long. The injustice of the punishment is greater than the injustice it is supposed to punish. In fact, compared with the Chaldeans, their victims are righteous, and it cannot be an act of justice for the wicked to swallow someone who is righteous by contrast (v 13bB). This was Habakkuk's concern in his first prayer also (v 4b). The *mišpāṭ* that comes out (from God!) in these historical events is "twisted."

Habakkuk's analysis of the politics of his day as the destruction of the righteous nation by the wicked, while God is silent, is a point against the theory that the Chaldeans (although admittedly godless) find their place in the purposes of a just God, ruler of the world, because they are being used to punish wicked Israel. This is the usual theory, influenced too much, perhaps, by the theology of Isaiah in relation to the Assyrians. The movement through the dialogue has been traced by saying that in the first speech Habakkuk is complaining about the triumph of the wicked within Israel. In response to this, God says:"You haven't realized it, and you won't believe it when you hear about it, but I'm raising up the Chaldeans to deal with precisely that problem." But the Chaldeans don't punish only the wicked Israelites (such a group is nowhere identified in the book). They conquer the whole world, without discrimination. And their victims are called "righteous"; there is no recognition that any of them deserve the treatment they receive from the Chaldeans as punishment from God. Nor is the moral problem stated in the form of the suffering of the just along with the unjust, when such retribution takes place en masse (Genesis 18). Nor is there a trace in Habakkuk's prayers of the insight found in the book of Lamentations (after the very same events that are supposed to be the background of this book), that the nation accepts the justice of God in what he did through the Chaldeans, and the undeserving righteous, in particular, accept their role of suffering along with, or even on behalf of, the deserving wicked. We might say that the believers of the next generation (Lamentations) moved toward a resolution of this problem, of which Habakkuk's agonized prayers are the early struggles.

The opening question (v 12a) is the hardest part of this prayer to fit in with the rest. It is rhetorical, and so is an assertion of fact in its effect. The repetition of the name Yahweh at the beginning of v 12b (cf. v 2) shows that there is a fresh beginning here. The fact of the eternity and immortality of the holy Creator God, Yahweh, is recognized. His holiness is a quality more essential (that is, of his essential being) than righteousness. Habakkuk's first words sound like an act of adoration at the commencement of a prayer unrelated to the statements that follow, but Habakkuk's unique use of a rhetorical question to begin a prayer has the flavor of reproach, of perplexity, of doubt. His prayer is a complaint against God rather than a lament of a sufferer. Verse 12a does, however, create a long perspective in time that will permit the righteous to cultivate the patience enjoined in Hab 2:3. The same perspective is found again in Hab 3:2.

The human drama viewed in the concluding verses (vv 15–17) represents the Chaldeans as a fisherman, with the nations as fish. This elaborate figure grows out of the creation simile in v 14. The nouns referring to these participants are both singular and plural. If there are only two participants, the presence of the plural nouns indicates that the singular nouns are collective, representative, or distributive.

The composition of Habakkuk's second prayer is clearer and the form is more regular than those of his first prayer. Even so, some of his perplexity, even anger, continues. Habakkuk's problem is that he is horrified at the atrocities, whereas God is apparently indifferent, unresponsive. Is God's aloofness due to revulsion and desertion? Has he turned his eyes away from the offensive sight of human cruelty? This is not a thought that Habakkuk arrives at and remains with. He has lodged his protest. He still expects a more satisfactory answer and will remain at his post until Yahweh replies (2:1). By reminding God of his purity, Habakkuk could have had in mind the provisions made in the Israelite cult for defilements to be removed so that people could venture into the holy precincts and not contaminate them. Clearly Yahweh wanted his people to be holy because he was holy, to be pure because he was pure, to be just because he was just.

By going right back to creation and recognizing Yahweh's supreme power as Creator, Habakkuk intimates, reminds God, that there must be a purpose in the original act and an ongoing commitment to created things. By comparing humankind to fishes, the poet brings out both their huge population and also their helplessness, making the image even more pathetic and appealing by adding they "have no ruler" (v 14b). This is not true! God is supposed to be their ruler, so once more there is a reproach for the negligent sovereign and an appeal to his compassion.

V. HABAKKUK'S RESPONSE (2:1)

◆

2:1aA Upon my lookout I will stand;
  1aB   I will stand on guard on the tower:
  1bA and I will look out to see what he will say in me,
  1bB   and what I will reply concerning my protest.

Scansion of Habakkuk's Response (2:1)

		BEATS	SYLLABLES	BICOLON
1aA	'al-mišmartî 'e'ĕmōdâ	2	7 ⎫	
1aB	wĕ'etyaṣṣĕbâ 'al-māṣôr	2	8 ⎭	15
1bA	wa'ăṣappeh	1	4	
	lir'ôt mah-yĕdabber-bî	2	8 ⎫	
1bB	ûmâ 'āšîb 'al-tôkaḥtî	3	8 ⎭	16

INTRODUCTION

In this little poem, we have one of the two brief passages in which Habakkuk recounts his experience, or a small part of it. This speech uses the language of resolution ("cohortative" verb forms). It is a soliloquy because he refers to Yahweh in the third person. The other autobiographical passage is Hab 3:17–19, the conclusion of the whole matter.

From a structural point of view, we could, perhaps, add the opening prayer (1:2–4) as part of Habakkuk's "confessions." These three passages trace a painful journey of faith from outrage in Hab 1:2–4 to patience in Hab 2:1 to equanimity in Hab 3:17–19.

This little transitional piece is too brief to permit significant remarks about the kind of language it uses, whether that of prose or poetry. There are no opportunities to use any of the "prose particles," so nothing can be inferred from their absence. It is obvious from the match of the phrases 'al-mišmartî // 'al-māṣôr that the suffix "my" does double duty. This is confirmed by 1QpHab mṣwry. The verb forms have meanings salient for Standard Hebrew.

The five colons we have recognized consist of two well-formed bicolons around a short hinge colon of one beat (four syllables). The two bicolons feature conventional parallelism. The parallelism of v 1a is synonymous; in v 1b, it is progressive and complementary. These bicolons are of standard length (fifteen and sixteen syllables). The rhythms are different when measured by beats.

191

Accepting the Masoretic accentuation, in which proclitic particles have no stress, three of the colons have only two beats. Remarkable is the ligaturing of *mah-yĕdabber-bî*, with only one stress.

The three phrases with the same preposition— *'al-mišmartî*, *'al-māṣôr*, and *'al-tôkaḥtî* — make a unifying pattern.

NOTES

1. *lookout* (or "guard post"). There are a number of Hebrew nouns derived from the root *šmr*. The commonest, *mišmār* and its feminine form *mišmeret*, can refer to the guarding of a captive (*bêt mišmeret* = *mišmār*, "prison"), but the latter also refers widely to any responsible job that requires watchfulness. The word commonly refers to priestly tasks, "looking after" things. This usage does not warrant the inference that Habakkuk was a priest-prophet who received his vision while on duty in the sanctuary, but it is quite possible that his vision was granted in a temple without this circumstance implying that he had professional status in that institution. Such an event could be another instance of the ancient procedure for seeking and receiving a divine revelation in some shrine, perhaps sleeping there overnight. Verse 20 would then constitute an inclusion with v 1, embracing the whole chapter. Tracing the tradition from Samuel (or even Jacob) to Zechariah (Luke 1), a shrine would be a suitable place to wait for the hoped-for revelation (see the NOTE on Hab 2:20).

stand // stand on guard. We don't know how long the prophet had to wait before he received the reply that begins in v 2. This verb and its immediate parallel, both cohortative in form, express resolve; *hityaṣṣēb* specifically indicates the respectful posture of a courtier attending on a king or of the heavenly hosts waiting on the LORD. It could be the posture of prayer, often made standing. We are not to suppose that Habakkuk maintained this stance indefinitely; *'āmad* (v 1aA) can also mean "continue." So v 1a probably intends to say, "I will remain on duty, waiting at my post."

Later on, the rabbis were in two minds over Habakkuk's attitude to God in his prayers. Some considered his forthrightness to be admirable; others found it impudent. Far from reading Hab 2:1 as an expression of patient resignation, Jewish legend made Habakkuk the model for Honi the Circle-Drawer, who vowed to remain in his circle until God answered his prayer for rain (*Ta'anit* 23a).* There is no hint that Habakkuk was in a position to twist God's arm, to force a response. Habakkuk's diffidence is at the other pole from this kind of impudence, tainted as it is with magic. The pathetic helplessness of his preceding prayers bespeaks otherwise. Yet somehow Habakkuk was cited in the Talmud along with Moses, David, and Jeremiah as one who prayed out of bounds (*Tehillim* 90:385). Disapproval, however, was tempered by compassion, most im-

---

*Babylonian Talmud (London: Soncino), 115–16.

portantly because of God's willingness to excuse him. A basis for this was found
in the wordplay—it can hardly be taken as a scientific etymology—between the
sound of *šigyōnôt* (3:1) and words with roots *šwg* and *šgg* that mean "stray." His
overstepping the bounds was classified as inadvertent and therefore pardonable
(see the discussion on Hab 3:1).

tower (or "strong point"). The parallel to "guard post" has a more exact and
material denotation. It refers to a strong place capable of withstanding a siege.
The verb "keep watch" (v 1b) also has military associations, but it would be going too far to cast Habakkuk in the role of a sentry, unless only as a metaphor
for the prophet as watchman (Ezekiel 3, 33). The prophet as watchman is already an idea in Hosea (9:8). The analogy of a military observation post holds
to some extent, for the prophet will proclaim what he sees to prepare the people for coming events. Even so, the figure is not developed. The prophet does
not go on to warn the people about coming danger. He is not looking out for
an enemy. He is waiting for the answer to his earlier prayers, and, if the "woe
oracles" are the warning, they are addressed to the enemy. Whether the textual
variants that read "my strong-post" are right or the Masoretic indefinite noun is
modified by the pronoun suffix in the preceding line, the statements are personal, even private. Habakkuk is not functioning as a public figure, on duty in
either a shrine or a military fortification. He is keeping his own watch, as part
of "my dispute" (v 1b). This is in line with the impression gained already from
preceding prayers, that Habakkuk is engaged in an intensely individual altercation with God.

look out (or "keep watch"). The connotations of √ *spy* are usually military.
The *Qal* participle denotes a sentry or a spy as well as a watchdog (Isa 56:10).
The *Pi'el* is the preferred form for finite verbs, apparently the same in meaning
as *Qal*. As often as not, the participle describes a lookout who hopes to see a relief force coming to a beleaguered garrison (Mic 7:7). The imagery of Isa 21:6
is typical, and its sequence of verbs—"stand . . . look . . . see . . . report . . ."—is
similar to that in Hab 2:1. But Habakkuk's case is unique. He is on the lookout
for Yahweh, as though hoping for his return after a long absence or at least for
speech after a long silence. Rudolph (1975:193) interprets *'aṣappeh*, "I will be
on the lookout," as an expression of Habakkuk's concentration of all his senses
in preparation for the revelation.

to see what he will say. This mixture of verbs is true to the combination of visionary and auditory experience in the prophetic encounter with God. Habakkuk
sees the LORD; he hears him. The same paradox is met in Habakkuk 3, where
a theophany that is wholly visionary (no speech of God accompanies the
epiphany) is reported as "I heard" (3:16).

through me. Literally, "in me." Hardly "to me." The difficulty of *bî* as adjunct
of "say" is shown in the various translations. The same problem is met in Hos
1:2 (cf. Num 12:2). In 2 Sam 23:3, the idiom is explicated by the parallel "and
his word was on my tongue." Even though the prophet's immediate concern is
his own troubled mind, his experience will result in an oracle for wide application.

I will reply. Verse 1bB is difficult. On the surface, it is not in synonymous parallelism with the preceding expression; it seems, rather, as though Habakkuk is wondering what he might say in response to the as-yet-unspoken reply by Yahweh that he is waiting for. The repetition of *mh*, "what," encourages emendation of *ʾāšîb*, "I will return," to *yāšîb*, "he will return" (Wellhausen 1893:163), supported by Syriac and widely accepted. This reading would quite suitably describe the LORD's addition of a second speech to his earlier one. The text would then mean "What he will say in reply concerning my dispute," that is, in response to the complaint that Habakkuk had lodged against the LORD's apparent mismanagement of the world. Budde (1931:410) resolved the difficulty by reading a passive *ʾûšab*.

If, however, we try to retain the MT, then what the LORD will say through Habakkuk is what he will take back and repeat as the answer to the complaint he has lodged against the wicked. The "woe oracles" that follow would suit this purpose quite well.

my protest ("argument"). Compare "case and suit" in Hab 1:3, which we identified as the prophet's own dispute, as expressed in the two preceding prayers.

COMMENT

From the formal point of view, the narrative framework of the book of Habakkuk is as simple as can be. It all hangs on the two verbs at the beginning of Hab 2:2—"And Yahweh answered me and said. . . ." This fragment is autobiographical, but it is not all the narrative there is. The final event is reported in Hab 3:19aB, using a *wāw*-consecutive verb form *wayyāśem*:

And he made my legs like does,
and he made me trample on my high places.

That part of the story reports the final action of God, who replied to Habakkuk in deed as well as word.

Verse 2aA documents an experience in which Habakkuk is addressed by God. The first verb *wayyaʿănēnî*, when it is simply *wayyaʿan*, could be no more than a conventional and lexically empty lead-in to *wayyōʾmer*, a familiar biblical cliché. But with the pronoun suffix object ("me"), the expression implies that Yahweh is responding to an inquiry already made, so that what Yahweh now says should answer a prayer or match a request or Habakkuk's "protest" (*tôkahtî*). As such, *wayyaʿan* is similar to *wayyišmaʿ*. Verse 2aA thus shows that the painful situation described in Hab 1:2 has been relieved and that the content of the response, recorded in Habakkuk 2, is a reply to the prayers made in Habakkuk 1.

The soliloquy of Hab 2:1 serves as a transition from the prayers of Habakkuk 1 to the response of Habakkuk 2. To complete the report of dialogue, the reflective speech in v 1 implies that "And I said (to myself)" is autobiographical narrative to carry the reported speech. Habakkuk 3 is titled "The prayer of

Habakkuk the prophet." This heading matches and balances the title at the beginning of the book (1:1). While these editorial details have been taken by some scholars as an indication that here we have two independent literary compositions, each with its own title, we are working with an analysis that accepts the whole book as a dialogue consisting of prophetic prayers and oracular responses. There is no narrative framework in Habakkuk 1, identifying the alternating speakers. The prayers of Habakkuk (1:2–4, 12–17) are delineated clearly enough to permit the other material to be identified as oracular, even without the benefit of the usual introductory formulas.

If Habakkuk 2 contains an oracle (or oracles) from Yahweh in response to the prayers in Habakkuk 1, the final prayer in Habakkuk 3 can be understood as the prophet's response to the vision in which the message of the "woe oracles" was revealed to him. Without going into a detailed analysis of Habakkuk 3 at this point, we notice briefly that it consists of a theophany report (vv 3–15), which we believe to be ancient, framed in two personal statements coming from the prophet himself, one a prayer (3:2) and the other more reflective (3:16–19aA). This final unit can be recognized as a soliloquy that matches Hab 2:1.

This brief soliloquy (no audience is identifiable) gives us a fleeting glimpse of Habakkuk's self-understanding of his status and role as a prophet. The content of his prayers in Habakkuk 1 suggest that he was ardent and sensitive, attached to his God and concerned about the LORD'S reputation. Habakkuk is caught in an agony peculiar to Israelite prophets and characteristic of their experience. The "confessions" of Jeremiah give the fullest disclosure of the suffering that a prophet might have to endure. The first prayer in the book of Habakkuk (1:2–4) is by no means the beginning of the struggle. Its language implies that Habakkuk had already prayed much and had expected results that had not yet come to pass. The grounds of this expectation were in all likelihood his privilege as a prophet with special intercessory rights and duties. To judge from other "lives" more amply reported, to be a prophet required a "call." No such episode is recorded of Habakkuk. But the forthrightness of his first recorded prayer (1:2–4), and the argumentative tone of his second prayer (1:12–17) match the audacity of Moses and Amos, who speak to God in peremptory tones that would not be tolerated in ordinary persons. And they match the intimacy of Jeremiah. All these prophets dare to reprove and reproach God for some kind of shortcoming, as the prophet sees it. Habakkuk addresses God—with *tôkaḥtî,* "my remonstration" (v 1). He prays as though he has a right to be heard and a right to an explanation from God. Here the prophet sees himself as an intimate, almost an associate, of God. Elijah had said, "There will be no dew or rain these years, unless I say so." Amos was of the belief that God did nothing without disclosing his secret to his servants the prophets (Amos 3:7). On this side of the equation, the genuine prophet, as God's authorized spokesman and agent, was the purveyor of the authority of God himself. Toward humans, that is.

Toward God it was different. The prophet had no proprietary rights over divine oracles. He could not requisition them. Kings thought otherwise. They considered that prophets, whether on the palace staff or not, could be summoned and required to inquire of the LORD concerning some matter on which guidance was needed. Prophets accepted this role, even if they often came out with a message quite different from what the king wanted. Micaiah's disagreement with Ahab (1 Kings 22) is the classic instance. Most disconcerting of all, the credibility of a prophet could be sabotaged when God canceled or reversed a message that the prophet had recently delivered in categorical terms. In two instances, unambiguous doom pronounced against a king was mitigated when the king went into mourning (Ahab in 1 Kgs 21:27) or turned his face to the wall and wept (Hezekiah in 2 Kgs 20:2–3). In the latter case, Isaiah had not even left the precincts when he had to go back with an opposite message. In these instances, as with Moses' dramatic success in getting Yahweh to change his mind about the apostasy at Horeb (Exodus 32–34), it is clear that no word from God can be final when it interacts with human freedom. The rationale of all these stories is that Yahweh prefers to be gracious and compassionate and forgiving, even on the slenderest shows of penitence or on the weakest counterarguments (such as Amos' appeal to Jacob's littleness as grounds for reversing a decision to punish him). It was this side of God's character that caused Jonah's exasperation.

Considerations of these kinds do not enter into Habakkuk's altercation with Yahweh. The prophet's concern is for justice, not mercy. As we have observed in the COMMENTS on Habakkuk 1, God's response to Habakkuk's first prayer only makes things worse for him. His stance in Hab 2:1 shows that he is expecting something different, and is still waiting for an acceptable answer to his "remonstration."

Habakkuk's extraordinary honesty is seen in the fact that he is unable to rationalize away the startling prediction of Hab 1:5–11 (God would never do a thing like that) or concoct out of his own conscience a more conventional and acceptable prophecy. He knows the word of Yahweh when he gets it, and he has to wait until it comes. Rudolph (1975:193) sees in Habakkuk's expectancy evidence that he is not one of those prophets who can make up an oracle when they feel like it: *ḥăzôn libbām yĕdabbĕrû lōʾ mippî yhwh*, "a vision of their own heart they speak, not from Yahweh's mouth" (Jer 23:16). Habakkuk knew when Yahweh gave an oracle and, by the same token, he knew when he wasn't receiving one. We do not know how he could tell. We have only his word for it. Delay irked him. The silence of God vexed and grieved him, but he knew that there was nothing he could do about it. Or rather, all he could do was keep on praying, keep on waiting, keep on watching.

The helplessness of the genuine prophet contrasts with the guarantees of assured service that would make a prophet a valued community resource, like a shaman who had the hidden powers at his disposal and under his control. There were always plenty of operators ready to cater to this need, presenting and selling themselves as proprietors of the word of God, not just purveyors. It is now the practice to label this second kind of prophet "false." No such term is ever used in the Hebrew Bible. All such practitioners are simply "prophets," whether their messages came actually from God or were merely invented. The time lag of ten days reported in the case of Jeremiah when the people requested him to secure guidance for their future (Jer 42:10) was made all the more telling by the urgency of the situation. It advertised with the greatest clarity that it did not lie in any person's power to requisition an oracle. There was no way for a human to coerce God. By resorting to a known prophet, however, the people acknowledged that not just anybody could access God and extract the needed guidance. To judge by the sparse attestation, God was silent most of the time.

By using the same term "prophet" for all the claimants to have a vision or an oracle, the Bible recognizes that they are indistinguishable both in their behavior and in the forms of their messages. It was different, of course, with prophets of an alien god (such as the numerous prophets of Baal) or prophets who preached immorality. The problem lay with professed prophets of Yahweh, all using the same techniques and making speeches that all sounded alike. The reluctance of the authentic prophet might contrast with the alacrity of the phony who could prophesy at the request of a client. But the time it took was not an infallible mark of the real thing. Nothing about God could be predicted. You never know what God will do or say next, or if he will remain hidden and silent. In some stories, God's response is instantaneous, with true as well as with false prophets. Delay can increase suspense, raise the stakes. Once delay is considered to be a mark of genuine prophecy, it would be easy enough for a bogus prophet to simulate, pretending to wait and then producing his own homemade message.

The freedom of God to do whatever he pleases (or nothing) in unpredictable ways is not exercised in such an arbitrary fashion that there is no way of telling that some deed or word is not God's. Because he is a prophet, because he has been praying, and because he has heard from God before, Habakkuk readies himself for God's next move.

VI. YAHWEH'S SECOND RESPONSE (2:2–5)

◆

2:2aA	And Yahweh answered me and said:
2aB	Write down the vision,
2aC	and explain it upon the tablets,
2b	so that he who reads it can run!
3aA	For the vision is still for the appointed time.
3aBα	And he is a witness to the end,
3aBβ	and he will not deceive.
3bA	If he delays, wait for him;
3bBα	for he will certainly come,
3bBβ	he won't be late.
4a	Behold, swollen, not straight, is his throat in him,
4b	and the righteous person by its trustworthiness will survive.
5aA	And yet indeed the wine is treacherous,
5aB	the man is presumptuous and he will not endure,
5bAα	who enlarged his throat like Sheol,
5bAβ	and he is like Death, and he will not be satisfied.
5bB	And he gathered to himself all the nations,
5bC	and he collected to himself all the peoples.

Scansion of Yahweh's Second Response (2:2–5)

		BEATS	SYLLABLES	BI(TRI)COLON
2aA	wayyaʿănēnî yhwh wayyōʾmer	3	9	
2aB	kĕtôb ḥāzôn ûbāʾēr ʿal-hallūḥôt	4	11	
2b	lĕmaʿan yārûṣ qôrēʾ bô	4	7	25
3aA	kî ʿôd ḥāzôn lammôʿēd	3	7	
3aB	wĕyāpēaḥ laqqēṣ wĕlōʾ yĕkazzēb	4	10	
3bA	ʾim-yitmahmāh ḥakkēh-lô	2	7	25
3bB	kî-bōʾ yābōʾ lōʾ yĕʾaḥēr	3	8	
4aA	hinnēh ʿuppĕlâ	2	5	12
4aB	lōʾ-yāšĕrâ napšô bô	3	7	
4b	wĕṣaddîq beʾĕmûnātô yiḥyeh	3	10	
5aA	wĕʾap kî-ḥayyāyin bôgēd	4	7	14
5aB	geber yāhîd wĕlōʾ yinweh	4	7	
5bAα	ʾăšer hirḥîb kišʾôl napšô	4	9	17
5bAβ	wĕhûʾ kammāwet wĕlōʾ yiśbāʿ	4	8	
5bBα	wayyeʾĕsōp ʾēlāyw kol-haggôyīm	3	9	18
5bBβ	wayyiqbōṣ ʾēlāyw kol-hāʿammîm	3	9	

INTRODUCTION

By all appearances, and in accord with the general character of the book of Habakkuk, this unit is another poem. It exhibits many of the usual features of Biblical Hebrew verse, but, compared with some elegant specimens, it seems rather rough and unfinished. Another explanation of the untidiness of this unit could be that it has suffered damage in transmission. Perhaps it has a bit of both, with the ruggedness of the original composition contributing to the difficulties encountered by scribes.

There is only one "prose particle" in the first thirty-five words (vv 2–4a): the definite article in *hallūḥôt*. There are more in the last thirty-four words—four in all: the relative once, the definite article three times. The definite articles in the parallel construct phrases *kol-haggôyīm // kol-hāʿammîm* (v 5b) are no surprise, but *hayyāyin* (v 5aA) attracts close scrutiny. These few "prose particles" are enough to show that the discourse is not general, but is referrring to specific topics and concrete objects. Other nouns are definite in reference, even without the definite article, as translations are forced to recognize: *ḥāzôn*, "*the* vision" (vv 2aB, 3aA; as a grammatical object in v 2aA, it would be *ʾet-heḥāzôn* in prose), *qōrēʾ*, "*the* one who reads," and, of course, "*the* righteous person" in v 4b.

It is difficult to be sure about the rhythmic patterns of this unit. The constituent clauses vary considerably in length and do not fit a rhythmic grid of one clause per colon, as is often the case with lyrical Biblical Hebrew poetry. On the one hand, there are some complex sentences in which the subordinated clause makes the second colon; in such instances (v 2aB // 2b, 3b), there is no parallelism of the conventional kind. On the other hand, there are some short clauses, some in pairs with the second containing a negation: *wĕyāpēaḥ laqqēṣ wĕlōʾ yĕkazzēb* (v 3aB); *kî-bōʾ yābōʾ lōʾ yĕʾaḥēr* (v 3bB); *geber yāḥîd wĕlōʾ yinweh* (v 5aB); *wĕhûʾ kammāwet wĕlōʾ yiśbāʿ* (v 5bAβ). This pattern is a feature of Habakkuk's style. The constraints of well-formed bicolons, especially when their identity is made certain by complete parallelism (as with vv 5bA and 5bB), forbid the analysis of these clause pairs as bicolons with antithetical parallelism. Each is retained as one colon in the display on p. 198, except possibly for v 4a. The scansion shown in the display on p. 198 leaves two unmatched colons (vv 2aA and 4b). The climactic and vital v 4b is unmatched within this part of the reply. The quotation formulas (vv 2aA, 6bA) make an inclusion, or rather v 6bA continues the idiom of v 2aA and shows that the "woe oracles" are given in the vision. So v 6 is transitional. It is a segue to the "woe oracles" so that it is not appropriate to make a clean break between the units.

As a result of this rough style, the individual colons in vv 2–5, according to Masoretic punctuation, vary in length, whether measured by beats (two to four) or syllables (five to eleven). In spite of this range, the mean colon length for the whole unit (sixteen colons, 130 syllables) is eight, the standard value.

There is enough good parallelism in vv 1–6a to enable a fair amount of the poetic design to be perceived. The most easily recognized bicolons are v 3a (*lammôʿēd // laqqēṣ*), v 4a (two feminine singular perfect verbs in parallel), v 5bA (parallel similes), v 5bB (complete synonymous parallelism), and v 6a (*māšāl // ḥîdôt*). Starting with pairs of adjacent colons that constitute well-formed bicolons, it becomes more likely that other materials less amenable on first glance will be seen as parts of larger structural patterns when examined more carefully.

The following are well-formed bicolons. Complete synonymous parallelism:

5bB   *wayye'ĕsōp 'ēlāyw kol-haggōyīm*
      wayyiqbōṣ 'ēlāyw kol-hā'ammîm

This bicolon contains such prose features as the *wāw*-consecutive and the definite article, but the definite objects do not have the *nota accusativi*. The two colons of the bicolon are grammatically complete and grammatically identical. All the other bicolons fall short of this kind of symmetry.

Synonymous parallelism with chiasmus:

1a   *'al-mišmartî 'e'ĕmōdâ*
     wĕ'etyaṣṣĕbâ 'al-māṣōr

The noun in the second colon is "(my) strong point"; the pronoun suffix in the first colon does double duty. 1QpHab has seen fit to supply the pronoun suffix.

When we attempt to give an account of bicolons that seem to be less well formed, we do not know how much they seem opaque because the text has suffered damage or because we have the tightly packed constructions of laconic poetry. Verse 1a has a minimal difference between the two colons, with one pronoun suffix doing double duty. If this kind of ellipsis is resorted to on a larger scale, the result can become very laconic indeed, both colons in a bicolon lacking material to be supplied from the other, or simply "understood." Verse 2aB supplies an example:

Write (the) vision,
    and explain (it) on the tablets

In v 5bA, the parallelism of "like Sheol" and "like Death" is unmistakable. There is no matching balance quantitatively, and the use of *hû'* is difficult. Perhaps the pronoun is resumptive of the preceding relative clause and is intended to assist identification of the "proud" with the Chaldean (Hab 1:10), and the language of v 5b agrees:

who enlarged his throat like Sheol
    and he (enlarged his throat) like Death.

The missing parallels are left out to leave room for the expansion of the idea with the negative "and he is not satisfied." From the point of view of rhythm, there are two colons, almost equal in length. From the point of view of parallelism, there are three statements. Similar devices are used in v 3a. There are

two colons in parallel, but three statements that the vision is speeding to fulfillment. Here the verb is withheld until the second colon (retroactive double duty).

> For the vision is still (hurrying) to the appointed time
> And (the vision) is still hurrying to the end,
> and it won't deceive.

A further difficulty is the use of very short clauses as well as those of a length
suited to be single colons of poetry. Notable in this connection are the clauses
in which a prefixed verb is negated:

wĕlō' yĕkazzēb	and it will not deceive
(*wĕ*)*lō' yĕ'aḥēr*	and it will not delay (1QpHab has the conjunction)
wĕlō' yinweh	and it will not endure
wĕlō' yiśbāʿ	and it will not be satisfied

The fact that there are four of these negations encourages belief in the unity of
the whole section. Furthermore, in each instance, this construction seems to be
part of the second colon of a bicolon.

Although v 3b has four clauses, it has exactly the same rhythmic pattern as
the others. This pattern points to the need for a revision of the Masoretic punctuation of v 5a, even though the second colon is a little short. Another bicolon
can be recognized in v 1b, even though the first colon is short and the second
has difficulties of its own:

> What he will say through me,
> and what I will return concerning my complaint.

The poetic structure of v 4 is harder to discern. There is no obvious parallelism
between v 4a and v 4b. An embarrassment is the fact that each half of the verse
is of a length too great for a single colon. Verse 4b cannot possibly be two colons,
and it is difficult to see where v 4a might be divided into two. If v 4 has internal parallelism, it must be of a general kind, contrasting the righteous person
with the one whose soul is not straight. The language of v 4a is so obscure that
many scholars have concluded that it has been badly damaged in transmission,
and they either give up or try to repair it. Perhaps that is the situation, but neither alternative is a happy one. Some progress can be made when we recognize
that the two feminine singular verbs have the same subject, but the subject ("his
soul" or "throat") has been delayed until the second clause.

Some of the difficulties in the interpretation of this unit are due to the terse-
ness of the language. This is often the case with Hebrew poetry. Some expressions are laconic because of ellipsis. In some short colons, the missing items are
supplied by the double-duty function of some nearby item. Thus the object of
the verb *bāʿēr* is "the vision"; in fact, we might have expected "Write the vision
upon the tablets and expound it" (orally?; see the NOTE on v 2). In some colons,

there is a verb with no explicit subject, and in some instances it is quite hard to work out what the implied subject is. Is it possible that "the vision" is the continuing subject of all the verbs in v 3?

In contrast to the usage in Habakkuk 1, the verbs in Hab 2:2–5 seem to be employed with the salient references of prose—*qāṭal* past tense, *yiqṭōl* future.

Throughout the poem, contrasts are developed by negation of opposites: the vision is dependable, it won't deceive; it will be on time, it won't be late; his soul is crooked, not straight. These contrasts are worked out for various kinds of human character, in contrast with the "righteous person" (v 4b), and with the reliability of either that person, or the vision, or God himself (see the NOTE on v 4b).

NOTES

2. *answered*. This verb is used to introduce the favorable response, in word (salvation oracle) or deed (rescue act) by the Deity to an appeal from a devotee in distress (cf. Hab 1:2 with Jonah 2:3). The precision with which the prophet specifies "he answered me" shows that this is exactly an answer to his prayer, and not just another case of "the word of the LORD came to me." The prophet does not tell us here that the response took the form of a vision.

Write. The vision itself is not described. If the vision itself is to be recorded in writing, it is possible that this is where Habakkuk 3 fits in. But more likely, Habakkuk is here instructed to record the oracle given in the vision. Verse 3 speaks of the vision hastening to its fulfillment, which is probably a reference to the set of judgments announced in the "woe oracles."

Other cases are on record where prophets were instructed to write down their messages, sometimes after delivery. Isaiah and Jeremiah thus made provision for a possible delay in the fulfillment of some of their predictions. This idea is present here as well (v 3), but the main purpose in inscribing the vision is to enable the person who has to read it to run with it.

explain. The verb *bē'ēr* is usually taken to mean "expound" in public delivery (the speeches of Moses [Deut 1:5]). With this connotation, the verb would anticipate *qôrē'*, which follows. But as a more immediate parallel to "write," "explain" probably describes the initial production of the recorded message. It is not certain that the prophet himself is scribe, courier, and herald. Possibly so. But if he used an amanuensis, *bā'ēr* could mean "dictate" rather than "preach" and gives a bit more detail of the process of writing the vision. The language is comparable to that in Deut 27:8, which is a similar command to Moses to write "all the words of this Torah" "upon the stones" (*'al-hā'ăbānîm = 'al-hallūḥôt*), and *bā'ēr* is specified further with *hêṭēb* (dictating it correctly or inscribing it legibly).

tablets. Literally "upon the tablets." LXX uses the singular *pyksion*, but makes the object of "read" plural. Considerable importance has been attached to this detail by some commentators. We are not told whether these tablets were made of clay or of stone. The discovery of an ancient biblical text on silver foil opens up another possibility. The idea that the words were to be inscribed on large slabs to be set up in a public place so that they could be easily read, even by someone running past, is a fancy—"and engrave it so plainly upon tablets that everyone who passes may be able to read (it easily and quickly) as he hastens by" (*The Amplified Bible*). This reading assumes hendiadys ("read swiftly" [BDB 91a]).

Nevertheless, this idea has generally held the field in interpretation. Passages such as Isa 8:1 and 30:8 have been adduced "to show that prophets were in the habit of setting up in public places tablets or plates containing short pregnant oracles, a sort of publication" (Cannon 1925:74). It is supposed furthermore that these were clay tablets similar to those in use in Mesopotamia (Peiser 1903; Ward 1911:13). There are several reasons for disbelieving this theory.

1. The very small number of inscribed clay tablets found in Palestine shows that this medium never came into general use for communication on the domestic in contrast to the international scene. With the tablets discovered at Aphek, the number of cuneiform inscriptions found in the entire country as a result of all excavations ever done is fewer than twenty. Ostraca, such as those uncovered at Samaria, Lachish, and Arad, are another matter. But their use was occasional and personal; no one has ever suggested that writing with ink on a piece of broken pottery gives any parallel to the recording of an oracle by a prophet.

2. Commemorative inscriptions, such as the Moabite Stone, erected by Mesha in the ninth century B.C.E., may have had their counterpart in Israel. The text of the covenant set up by Joshua could have been displayed in such a form. Archaeology has not yet recovered any Israelite inscriptions of this kind. The discovery of a stele at Tel Dan, erected by Hazael, king of Damascus, and inscribed in Aramaic, and the dedication plaque from Eqron, in Phoenician, have raised hopes that something similar in Hebrew might yet turn up.

3. The destruction of Jeremiah's written prophecies, which is described in such vivid detail in Jeremiah 36, shows that a scroll of any scope would be written on some inflammable material, almost certainly papyrus. Such a practice would also explain why so few written records have survived from what must have been quite a literate civilization in Israel in preexilic times. Apart from the destructions wrought by Assyrians, Babylonians, and other invaders, natural conditions in Israel are not favorable to the survival of such a perishable material as papyrus. The case of the Dead Sea Scrolls is exceptional, and most of them are animal hide, which is more durable than papyrus.

4. A distinction should be made between a short memorandum and a large formal public document. The record made by Isaiah (8:1) consisted of only four words. It was "written" upon "a large *gillāyôn*. This document may have included the names of witnesses. Unfortunately, we do not know what a *gillāyôn* is. The word occurs only there in the Hebrew Bible. The related plural word in Isa 3:26 has suggested that it was some kind of fabric rather than polished metal. The record made in Isa 30:8 was intended to be durable, for it was to last "for ever and unto eternity." The writing material there is described by the words

lûaḥ and *sēper*. The action is described by the verbs *ktb* and *ḥqq*. The latter corresponds to *bʾr* in Hab 2:2, and means "incise." We do not know what material such a *lûaḥ* was made of. While a metal plate cannot be completely ruled out, the most eligible candidates are clay, stone, and wood, with probability increasing in that order. In other passages, the writing implement for use with such tablets is a *ḥeret*, "stylus," as distinct from a pen (*ʿēṭ*). The latter was probably a piece of reed that could write (or brush) ink onto a potsherd or papyrus. The stylus could make impressions in soft clay, or a sharp point would scratch letters on stone, wood or brick. The word *bʾr*, "dig," could describe cutting or incising, and *ḥqq* similarly means "engrave." The material, size, and shape of the "tablets," and the mode of inscription cannot be determined among these possibilities.

The possibilities could be narrowed a little if we could settle two related points. First, how long was the text of the "vision"? If, as we suggest, what was revealed and had to be read from the tablets, was "the woe oracles" (vv 6–20), two or three tablets of average size would have sufficed. The second question is their subsequent use. If they were to be set up in public so that they could be read easily by anyone running past (the popular interpretation), then big stone slabs with big letters would be needed. Cannon (1924:71) is of the opinion that only v 4 was to be published in this way. If, however, they were to be carried by a running herald, small bricks or soft stones would do.

Why is the definite article used with "tablets" as though they were special or well-known tablets? We would expect "write it on tablets" (indefinite). Now the usual object of *bʾr* is formal teaching, notably the Torah (Deut 1:5). The giving of the vision is the answer to the complaint about the Torah in Hab 1:4. Hab 2:2 is similar to Deut 7:8, and the tablets are like the plastered stones used there. In Deut 27:8, there seems to be some confusion between the stones with writing on them and the stones of the altar. In any case, they were fixed on Mount Gerizim for regular public use in the cult. The tablets of Hab 2:2 are portable.

it. The word *bô*, "in it," is admittedly difficult; the sense of the preposition is hard to establish. It could be "from it" or "by means of it." However that particular matter is settled, the pronoun is an object of some kind for the participle *qôrēʾ* and must refer to "vision" (masculine singular) not to "the tablets" (feminine plural). LXX has neuter plural.

run. Why bring a runner into it as the intended reader of the vision? Is he the extreme case of a busy person, intent on some other matter, yet still unable to miss the plain inscription? But it is not a runner who reads; it is the reciter who runs—not reading as he runs, but running in order to read. The participle *qôrēʾ* is virtually a title. The absence of the definite article is no problem, considering how rarely it is used in this prophecy, even with nouns that are clearly definite, such as "vision." And it does not mean "read to oneself." The *qôrēʾ* reads aloud; he is the herald, the announcer of an oracle. The vision is written down in order to be conveyed and proclaimed. It is a prophet who runs (Jer 23:21).

All the activity could be carried out by one person: the prophet, who sees the vision, writes it down, runs with it, and reads it out. As many as three persons could be involved: the prophet, his scribe to whom he dictates (*bʾr*) the mes-

sage, and the courier who is also the herald. That the runner at least is different from the prophet is suggested by the change in person of the verbs—"you
write the vision so that he may run."

3. *still.* The awkwardness of *ʿôd* has been resolved by changing it to *ʾiwwāʿēd*,
with *môʿēd* as a cognate modifier: "For the revelation will be fulfilled in its time"
(Budde 1931:411; see the following NOTE on the proposed emendation to *ʿēd*
"witness"). All such suggestions are dubious.

appointed time. Because a time fixed for a festival is a *môʿēd*, it is possible that
a time as portentious as the day of the LORD is in mind, and the word "end" has
an eschatological ring. The statement that the vision is still for the appointed time
is followed by five staccato statements, each containing a third person masculine
singular reference, "it," presumably the vision, possibly "he," one of the participants in the scenario. It will hurry; it won't lie; it might delay; wait for it; it will
come; it won't be late. It is hard to get the picture. Haak (1991:57) says, "To a
large extent the problems of interpretation of the prophecy could be solved if the
antecedents of the various ambiguous pronouns within the book could be determined." Apart from the contradiction between hurry and delay, how can all these
things be true of a vision? Can a vision "hurry" or "delay," "come" or "be late"?
Can a vision "deceive"? And, most curious of all, why is Habakkuk told to wait
for the vision if he has already received it and written it down? Can personifica-
tion be carried that far? The language would be suitable for a living agent, the announcer. As Janzen (1982:404) says, "Grammatically, of course, the antecedent
of the third person pronoun elements in the couplet is unclear: it may be the vision, it may be the *moʿed / qeṣ*, or it may be God." The LXX used *horasis* (feminine) for "vision," but its anaphoric pronoun in v 3b is masculine—"wait for him!"
It would make sense if the subject of the verbs is Yahweh. Such a reading would
fit into the tenor of the whole prophecy. Habakkuk has been irked by Yahweh's
apparent indifference to what is going on and his unresponsiveness to the prophet's
protracted prayers. Now, at last, Yahweh has given him a vision, told him in a vision, and it is what the vision contains that will arrive on schedule. What can this
be but a vision of the long-awaited intervention of Yahweh along the lines set forth
in Habakkuk 3? The certainty of its fulfillment comes from the reliability of Yahweh (*ʾĕmûnātô*, "his dependability"), who never lies.

witness. The earlier interpretation of *yāpēaḥ* as "hurries" followed by "delay"
put opposite ideas side by side in a strange way. The certainty of the vision, in
spite of apparent delay, requires hope. The verb *yāpēaḥ* seems to be the *Hipʿil*
of *pwḥ*, "breathe, blow." None of the meanings that this root has in other biblical occurrences seems to fit the present context, although Humbert
(1944:146–47) was able to stretch the meaning through a chain of near synonyms: "souffler, répandre, exhaler, affirmer, proclaimer quelque chose" [to
pant, to spread/scatter, to exhale, to proclaim something]. Hence some English
translations have "speaks" (NIV, NRSV). Verbs from √*pwḥ* occur twice as *Qal*,
and thirteen times as *Hipʿil*. Half the occurrences are in Proverbs, two in Psalms,
three in Canticles, so its poetic character is evident. It seems to describe all kinds
of breathing. In Canticles it describes the pleasant breeze. In other occurrences

√*pwḥ* describes a destructive wind that stirs up fire (Ezek 21:36; Ps 10:5). The cliché *yāpîaḥ kĕzābîm* occurs five times in Proverbs, and the occurrence of the same two roots together in Hab 2:3 cannot be an accident. In Prov 29:8, the expression is associated with scorn, while Prov 12:17—"He who breathes truth [*ʾĕmûnâ*] proclaims righteousness [*ṣedeq*]"—contains two words with cognates that are conjoined in Hab 2:4. The interpretation that here *yāpēaḥ* means "pant" because the vision is breathless with hurry (BDB:806) is too fanciful to be taken seriously. Similarly, the meaning of *yĕkazzēb* is "he tells lies"; the weaker alternative "disappoint" is marginal and poorly attested (Isa 58:11). The collocation of *pwḥ* and *kzb* in Hab 2:3 points to the same antithesis that we have in proverbs—*yāpîaḥ ʾĕmûnâ*, "he breathes truth," versus *yāpîaḥ kĕzābîm*, "he breathes lies" (= *yĕkazzēb*). Furthermore, because it is either a faithful or a deceitful person who "breathes" in these opposite ways, the "reciter" of the vision would be a better antecedent subject than "the vision" for the verbs in v 3aB.

The difficulty of making sense of *yāpēaḥ* if derived from *pwḥ*, "breathe, blow," prompted many attempts to find an alternative reading assisted by the evidence of the versions. LXX *kai anatelei eis peras*, "and it will rise up unto completion," suggested emendation to *yiprāḥ*, "it will spring up."

The puzzle of the word *yāpēaḥ* has now been solved, to the satisfaction of many scholars, by evidence from Ugaritic (Haak 1992:55–57; Roberts 1991:106). The potential of the Ugaritic word *ypḥ* "witness" (*UT*, #1129) for supplying a better meaning for Hebrew cognates was pointed out by Loewenstamm (1962) and applied by Dahood to Ps 27:12 (AB 16:169). Pardee (1978) and Miller (1979) found that the meaning "witness" fitted other passages better than the traditional "breathe." This meaning has now been accepted: "it will testify" (REB).

The parallelism of *ypḥ* with *ʿd*, "witness," in Hebrew clinched the identification of the synonyms, both nouns:

yāpîaḥ ʾĕmûnâ yaggîd ṣedeq	a witness of truthfulness will report righteousness
wĕ ʿēd šĕqārîm — mirmâ	and a witness of falsehoods—deceit (Prov 12:17)
ʿēd šĕqārîm lōʾ yinnāqeh	A witness of falsehoods will not go unpunished
wĕyāpîaḥ kĕzābîm lōʾ yimmālēṭ	and a witness of lies will not escape (Prov 19:5)

Prov 19:9 is almost identical: *wĕyāpîaḥ kĕzābîm yōʾbēd*, "and a witness of lies will perish." It is pushing synonymous parallelism too far, however, to bring Hab 2:3 into line with these bicolons by emending *ʿôd* to *ʿēd* (Pardee 1978). The evidence for *ʿôd* is solid: 1QpHab *ʿwd*; LXX *eti* (cf. Dan 10:14).

It needs to be emphasized that in all these passages the terms *yāpîaḥ* // *ʿēd* refer to a person, not a document or an announcement. Looking ahead to v 4b, the point can also be made that *ʾĕmûnâ* is a quality of a truthful, reliable witness. So it is better to look for an agential reference for the following pronominal elements, rather than to connect them all with the vision. This person will "witness" (*yāpēaḥ*), and not lie; he will declare the whole vision ("to the end") and not distort it in any way. A further grammatical comment is needed. In the instances discussed above, *yāpēaḥ* is nominal. This parsing permits the syntax of v 3aBβ to be construed so that the verbal function of the stative form *yāpēaḥ* comes into play—a suffixed form with *wāw*-consecutive.

deceive. The poetic structure assists the diagnosis just given. Rather than inaugurating a new series of statements about the vision, the repetition of *ḥāzôn* in v 3aA completes the quatrain (vv 2aB–3aA) with an inclusion. The similar construction of vv 3aB and 3bB suggests that the verbs in these colons have similar relations to one another, all having the same subject.

he will witness to the end	he will surely arrive
he won't deceive	he won't be late

Searching for the common subject of these clauses, the completeness of the quatrain in vv 2aB–3aB and the completeness of the pentacolon in the rest of v 3 loosens the continuity between v 3aA and v 3aB, a structural reason for doubting that *ḥāzôn* is to be taken as the grammatical subject of the verbs in v 3: "it" (six times in RSV). It might just make sense to say that a vision will not deceive, although it would be more appropriate and more in line with biblical thought to say that the message given in a vision is not a lie (false prophecies, that is, messages not really from God, but fraudulently spoken in God's name are "lies"). It is even better to say that the speaker of the oracle (God himself) will not lie (Num 23:19). After all, the vision has already been given, so why say that it will certainly come? What is awaited now is the fulfillment of the predictions presumably made in the vision. We say "presumably" because vv 1–3 tell how Habakkuk waited for Yahweh to reply and the reported response tells Habakkuk to write the vision on the tablets and wait some more. But where is that text? The best we can do is to identify the visionary component of the book (Habakkuk 3) as the vision and the oracular component (the "woe oracles") as the message.

Another way of working out the content of the vision is to read between the lines. When Habakkuk says "And Yahweh answered me" (v 2aA), an acceptable answer would be a response to the complaints, protests, and questions addressed to Yahweh in Habakkuk 1. Both the "woe oracles" of Habakkuk 2 and the theophany of Habakkuk 3 can be interpreted as that response: the oppressors are doomed to woe; Yahweh will come again, just as he did in the olden days, to bring the day of trouble on these invaders (3:16b). That revelation—vision of Habakkuk 3 and oracles of Habakkuk 2—if it is believed, can give the prophet hope for the future; but it is still only a promise. It is a promise that Yahweh will come, and v 3 makes sense if Yahweh, not the vision, is the grammatical subject of all the verbs:

He will not deceive.
If *he* should (seem to) delay, wait for *him!*
For *he* will certainly come; *he* won't be late.

That "vision" was not an appropriate subject for the verbs in v 3 was already felt by the Greek translators, for LXX rendered *ḥāzôn* as *horasis* (feminine), "vision," but *lô* in v 3b as *auton* (masculine)—"wait for *him*." They seem to have taken v 3a as a description of the vision, while v 3b talks about the activities of an unidentified person.

A grammatical accident enabled the Christian writer to the Hebrews to make the needed identification. Greek translators did their best with the Hebrew infinitive absolute construction *bō' yābō'*, "come he will come," by using a participle—*erkhomenos hēksei*, "coming, he will come." Add the definite article and *ho erkhomenos* is a messianic title in Heb 10:37. This adjustment permitted the text to be developed eschatologically, beyond what Habakkuk could possibly have had in mind, but not necessarily untrue to the potentiality of his latest thoughts. If we are correct in identifying the theophany in Habakkuk 3 as part of the vision given in Hab 2:2, then the archaic preterite *yābō'* of Hab 3:3 is matched by the future tense *yābō'* of Hab 2:3. Yahweh will come once again, as he already did in the past (3:2).

late. The five colons of vv 3aB–3b are interwoven. The first two and the last two make reasonable bicolons with the same inner design. This analysis assumes that each clause constitutes a colon. But the colons are short, and the count of twenty-five syllables suggests a tricolon. The same can be said of vv 2aB–3aA, also twenty-five syllables.

4. his throat. Traditionally "soul." A psycho-spiritual interpretation of this word is altogether improbable. The continuity in the passage suggests that repeated vocabulary has the same meaning in both occurrences. In the next verse, *napšô* is "his throat." If the prepositional construction *bô* means the same in vv 2 and 4, it refers to the vision. The preposition *b-* probably means the same in both parts of v 4, both referring to the vision. Verses 2–4 are concerned throughout with the response to the word of the LORD in the vision. Verse 4 then contrasts the two opposite reactions to the vision—presumption and perversion versus trustfulness. The righteous man will live by means of its (the vision's or God's) reliability. The person with a crooked throat defames the vision. Hence *napšô bô* does not mean "his soul (that is) in him," but "his throat is twisted against it" (that is, the vision). He speaks crookedly.

swollen. The *hapax legomenon* '*uppĕlâ* is the only known instance of the verb form, usually parsed as *Pu'al*. The fuller orthography of '*wplh* in 1QpHab confirms the passive of the MT. There is a noun '*ōpal*, "tumor." The word '*uppĕlâ* is often considered corrupt (Eissfeldt 1965:417) and is changed to *(he)'awwāl* or *(hen)ne'ĕpal* or *(hā)'appāl*. The former is due to Wellhausen (1893:164), who translated it *der Frevler*, "one causing malicious mischief" (34), to be identified with the Chaldeans (164). That emendation receives textual support from Syriac and Tg. The second is due to Budde (1931:411), who added also *hanne'ĕlāp* (not attested). Aquila *nōkheleuomenou*, "being sluggish," is given a slight edge for literalness because he has *idou* for *hinnēh* whereas LXX has *ean*. Aquila's reading could have come from '*ullĕpâ*, "covered over, confused" (cf. Isa 51:20). LXX has a completely different reading, reflected also in Heb 10:38—"If he should draw back, my [*sic*] soul has no pleasure in him." In the face of such chaos, all one can do is resign to the likelihood that the original text is irretrievably lost or else struggle to make the best of the MT as it is.

Because there is no attested *Pi'el*, *Qal* passive is just as likely as *Pu'al*. The difference is subtle. If any exegetical nuance is to be extracted from it, apart from the *Qal* passive as a sign of archaic usage, it would be that *Qal* passive describes a condition, *Pu'al* would suggest an induced condition, and *Nip'al*, self-induced. Reference to a tumor (*'ōpal*) could be intended in the physical sense, which implies a disease. But the word here could have the same connotation as the same root in Num 14:44—presumptuous defiance of the LORD's command, arising from self-trust and leading to death. Traditional "proud" or "arrogant" is probably the best that can be done.

crooked. Literally "not straight." The *metheg* in the manuscripts makes it clear that this word is the suffixed verb *yāšĕrâ*, not the noun *yošrâ*; the omission of the *metheg* in BHS reproduces a blemish of L. Only the masculine form *yošer*, "uprightness," is attested in the MT, but such nouns often have a feminine synonym, for example, *ṣdq~ṣdqh*, "righteousness." Yet 1QpHab reads *ywšrh*, apparently the noun. But the vowel letter in *ywšrh*, in correlation with *'uppĕlâ*, has suggested to some scholars that the similar spelling points to an analogous formation of a *Qal* passive. They translate "not made straight" (Amusin 1971:182, who draws attention to the evidence in Mishnaic Hebrew that *ṣaddîq* and *yāšār* are virtual synonyms).

The verb *yāšĕrâ* is feminine to agree with "his soul." The idea that the wicked person has a crooked soul might have some appeal, but no metaphysical meaning can be given to it. Either it means the whole person or it refers to the throat, the organ of sinful speech (connected somehow with the word *ykzb*, "lie" [v 3a]), or the organ of sinful greed or gluttony (connected with "wine" in v 5a).

The syntax of this colon is curious in several ways. The grammatical function and hence the meaning of *bô* are indeterminate; is it adverbial or adjectival? This is one of the commonest kinds of structural ambiguity in Hebrew (Andersen and Forbes 1995). It is unusual to have two verbs with a common (delayed) subject, although it sometimes happens with coordinated verbs. There is an extreme example in the mourner's Kaddish, admittedly Aramaic:

yitbārak wĕyištabbaḥ wĕyitpāʾar wĕyitrômam wĕyitnaśśāʾ
wĕyithaddar wĕyitʿalleh wĕyithallal šĕmēh dĕqûdĕšāʾ bĕrîk hûʾ

Blessed, and praised, and glorified, and exalted, and raised high,
and honored, and elevated, and lauded be the Name of the Holy One
      (blessed is he!)

In Hab 2:4a, however, the second verb is a negated antonym (or at least a word with contrasted meaning) of the first. If *hinnēh* has its usual function of drawing attention to something actually present, the person whose soul is "swollen, not straight," should be identifiable as a participant in the situation. We probably have here an instance of delayed identification of the participant. The reference of the pronoun suffix is cataphoric, the nearest eligible noun being *bôgēd* (see the following NOTE). The feminine stative verb refers to "his soul (or throat)." The suffixed verbs could be past tense, or they could be perfective, describing a present state. In v 5bB, the verbs are certainly past; v 5bA has a mixture. If all are referring to the wicked in contrast to the righteous in v 4b, then v 5a, which is probably future, forecasts the consequences—"he will not endure," unlike the righteous man who will live (v 4b).

More startling is the divergence of LXX from the MT in its rendition of v 4a. There does not seem to be any hope of recovering a viable alternative Hebrew text by back-translation. Notable is the similarity of the change in the possessive pronoun in each half verse, "my" for "his." LXX was on the right track to find in the two parts of the verse a contrast between two kinds of person. Because one of them is the *ṣaddîq*, the other must be the *rāšāʿ* who stands over against the *ṣaddîq* elsewhere in the book, harassing him (1:4), devouring him (1:13). The biggest switch is with the word "soul." In the MT this is the swollen, crooked soul of the wicked person. In LXX, it is God's soul.

The Greek rendition must be recognized as free interpretation, not accurate translation. At least, if an attempt is made to recover a different *Vorlage*, it could hardly oust the MT, the more so because the four words that caused LXX most trouble are extant in 1QpHab: *hnh ʿwplh lwʾ ywšrh*.

righteous. As in Hab 1:13, the noun has no definite article (but see Hab 1:4). The usage in Hab 2:1–5 is mixed in this regard. There are two nouns whose definite article is carried by the preposition—a doubtful vocalization. Four have the definite article: "tablets," "wine," "nations," and "people." Six nouns are indefinite in form, but definite in meaning. This feature should be accepted as authentic. Perhaps no definite articles at all were used in the original composition. But if the four definite nouns now present required a scribal addition of *h-*, why these and not the others? The definite articles in v 5 concur in its prose-like language usage. The relative pronoun and the *wāw*-consecutive occur there, too. By contrast, v 4 is more poetic, as we have already noticed in the laconic style of v 4a. In v 4b, the poetic construction is immediately apparent in the word order. The verb is at the end, an unusual position, although not uncommon in Habakkuk. The grammatical connections among the words in this clause are less apparent. Because of the contrast implied between life by faithfulness and disaster through perversity, the conjunction *w-* should be translated as "but" (*de* [LXX]). As far as the other words are concerned, syntax and semantics must go hand in hand.

Not surprisingly, such a capital text is vulnerable to being taken in various directions, and the Greek tradition presents four distinct forms.

1. The Göttingen LXX reads, following MSS S, B, Q, V, and W*:

> *ean huposteilētai, ouk eudokei hē psukhē mou en autǭ*
> *ho de dikaios ek pisteōs mou zēsetai*

If he should draw back, my soul has no pleasure in him;
   but the righteous from my faith will live.

This is the oldest Greek translation that can be recovered, perhaps the first ever made (Koch 1985).The Greek translators already confronted the obscurity of the Hebrew text of v 4 and were evidently baffled. Assuming that they were honest workmen, who did their best, they were obliged (as all who try their hand at it still are) to come up with some kind of paraphrase. Even though LXX cannot be used to recover a text that might hope to compete with the MT as more original, the Greek translators have grasped the general sense. The reading "my faith" for "his faith" need not be queried as interpretive; it could be a sincere reading of the final consonant *waw* as *yod* from a Hebrew MS in which these two letters were hard to distinguish from each other. The ambiguous suffix is in tension with the ambivalence of *'ĕmûnâ*, which could refer to the steadfastness of the righteous person (that's how the NT and later the rabbis took it, followed by the Reformers), or to the reliability of the vision (connecting v 4b with v 3—this is our preference), or to the fidelity of God (which is how the earliest Greek translators understood it). The Old Greek resolved the suffix in the direction of "my," an option that would appeal because "by his faithfulness" seemed wrong when God himself is the speaker. (This difficulty vanishes if God is continuing to affirm the reliability of his revealed plan, along the lines already present in v 3.) In any case, the Old Greek interpretation has resolved the ambiguity of *'ĕmûnâ* in the right direction, away from man to God. By translating "his *'ĕmûnâ*" as "my *pistis*," LXX correctly identified the *'ĕmûnâ* as God's faithfulness. The guarantee of life for the righteous is grounded in the reliability of God.

   Quotations in the NT either represent the authors' own translations from the Hebrew to suit their exegetical needs or else are evidence of a variant Greek translation in circulation in the first century C.E.

   2. Heb 10:38 has the variant:

ho de dikaios mou ek pisteōs zēsetai,
ean huposteilētai, ouk eudokei hē psukhē mou en autǫ

But my righteous one from faith will live;
   if he should draw back, my soul will have no pleasure in him

The earliest attestation of this text is in the mid-second century A.D. papyrus 𝔓46 (P. Chester Beatty I + P. Mich. Inv. 6238), which varies at two points: *ho de dikaios mou ek pisteōs zēsetai kai ean huposteilētai, ouk eudokei mou hē psukhē en autǫ* (Comfort and Barrett 1999:231), with the pronoun "my" even more conspicuous before the noun—a distinctively Greek style. The most notable details in this tradition are the inversion of the colons and the migration of the possessive pronoun *mou* from "my faith" to "my righteous one." Because God is the speaker, "his soul" was changed to "my soul," and this could also explain "my righteous one."

The same detail is attested in two LXX traditions (A, catenae of family C). It is a fine judgment whether the latter readings have been influenced by the NT (de Waard 1966:20). Quotations of Heb 10:38 matching either LXX or Paul's citations understandably have either been brought into line or drifted to these other traditions by quotation from memory. The original treatment of Hab 2:4 by the writer to the Hebrews is in the tradition of the Qumran *pešer* in that it finds the text applicable to the situation of the writer and his community. Like the Teacher of Righteousness, the Christian author read the contrast between wicked (the twisted person of v 4a) and righteous (the steadfast person of v 4b) with the "we" versus "they" mentality of the sectarian (see Hans Kosmala's essay "Das wir" im Hebräerbriefes" [1959:1–3]). The quotation of Hab 2:3–4 in Heb 10:37–38 is supplied as a proof-text for the preceeding exhortation: "Do not throw away your confidence, which has a great reward. For you have need of endurance, so that you may do the will of God and receive what is promised" (vv 35–36). The quotation is followed by a Christian *pešer*: "But we are not of those who shrink back (recede) and are destroyed, but of those who have faith and keep their souls" (v 39). Here *pistis* is the virtue of holding on (*hypomonē*, "endurance") and not apostatizing. This is a fair reading of Habakkuk's words.

3. Different again are Paul's quotations:

ho [de] dikaios ek pisteōs zēsetai (Rom 1:17; Gal 3:11 [the latter omits *de*])

[But] the righteous one from faith will live.

The identical wording of Hab 2:4 in MS 763* is probably due to adjustment to Paul's version. In Paul's exegesis, the term *pistis* has been given a radical new definition, focused on trust in a Savior-Messiah.

4. The fourth variation is found in 8 ḤevXIIgr 17:29–30:

[kai di]kaios ev pistei autou zēset[ai]

And a righteous one in (by) his faith will live

This is a literal translation of MT and represents a revision of the Old Greek toward the Hebrew. As such, it is important evidence for the originality of MT.

Some Fathers quoted the text with "his faith." LXX "from my faith," indicates faith as source, rather than instrument. The righteous person will not live "in (or by) his own faith" (Hebrew), but will derive life "from" the faithfulness of God. It is more appropriate to recognize the faithfulness of God as the source of life, rather than to ascribe such power to the faith of a human.

trustworthiness. The word *'ĕmûnâ* occurs forty-nine times in the Hebrew Bible. It is used to refer to a human quality twenty times, mainly in the historical books and prophets, three times in Proverbs. LXX renders these instances seventeen times as *pistis*, twice as *alētheia*. In the narratives, *(be)ʾĕmûnâ* describes entrustment with a task or satisfactory performance of a duty. The word is used in prophecy to condemn human failure in this regard (Isa 59:4; Jer 5:1, 3; 7:28). In view of the use of *bôgēd* in Habakkuk, Jeremiah's characterization of *bōgĕdîm*, "treacherous ones," as speaking *šeqer* and not *ʾĕmûnâ* (Jer 9:3), falsehood, not truth (LXX *pistis*) identifies *ʾĕmûnâ* as a quality of authentic revelation, in contrast to fake oracles. Apart from referring to the steadiness of Moses' hands (Exod 17:12) and "truth" as the girdle for the loins of a descendant of Jesse (Isa 11:5), the other twenty-seven occurrences refer either to the character of God, whether *pistos* / *pistis* (Deut 32:45; Lam 3:23; Isa 33:6 has lost the connection, but V literally *et erit fides in temporibus tuis*) or *alēthinos*, or, with the twenty-two occurrences in Psalms, to the certainty of God's works (LXX *en pistei* [Ps 33:4]) and words. The word *ʾĕmûnâ* often occurs in parallelism or hendiadys with *ḥesed*. Apart from Ps 33:4, *ʾĕmûnâ* is uniformly rendered *alētheia* in the LXX Psalms.

The faithfulness of the righteous human, which will gain him life (*b-* of price?), is identical with his righteousness and defines it. This is clearly expressed in David's protestation of self-righteousness, an appeal to God's justice in the spirit of Ps 62:13 that follows on David's deliberate choice of right conduct and his assiduity in its performance:

wĕyhwh yāšîb lāʾîš ʾet-ṣidqātô wĕʾet-ʾĕmûnātô

And Yahweh will return to the man his righteousness and his faithfulness

Here the collocation of *ṣidqātô* and *ʾĕmûnātô* is a virtual hendiadys.

To summarize. While *ʾĕmûnâ* is used almost as often to refer to human virtue as to divine virtue, and translated almost as often by *pistos* / *pistis* (faithful / faith) as by *alēthinos* / *alētheia* (truthful / truth), human references are restricted almost entirely to narrative and Proverbs; divine, to Psalms (mainly Psalms 89 and 119). For humans, according to LXX, the word *ʾĕmûnâ* is mainly *pistis*, "trustworthiness." For God likewise, *pistos* is a personal attribute "trustworthy" (4 times). Otherwise, divine *ʾĕmûnâ* is *alētheia*, "truth," as an attribute of God's pronouncements and promises. This is clearly the case with Psalm 89, a piece which is important for understanding Hab 2:4b, not only because of the concentration of *ʾĕmûnâ* (7 times) in that poem, but also because the author of Psalm 89 is grappling with a problem similar to Habakkuk's. The occurrence of *ʾĕmûnātî*, "my (that is, God's) *ʾĕmûnâ*," in vv 25 and 34 warrants the LXX translation of Hab 2:4b as *pisteōs mou*. The reiterated theme of Psalm 89 is *ḥesed weʾĕmet*, "true loyalty," by hendiadys. The poem rings the changes on the parallelism of *ḥesed* and words with root *ʾmn*, and reaffirms, after agonizing spiritual struggles, Yahweh's *ḥesed* sworn in his *ʾĕmûnâ* (v 50). In v 29, Yahweh identifies his *ḥesed* as *bĕrîtî neʾĕmenet*, "my dependable covenant."

There are, then, three associations of *ʾĕmûnâ* in the Hebrew Bible: human dutifulness (*pistis*), divine reliability in deeds (*pistis*), and divine truthfulness in words (*alētheia*). By translating *ʾĕmûnâ* as *pistis* in Hab 2:4, LXX made it clear that it was God's *pistis* by adding "my." But, to judge by the statistics, it is more likely that *'ĕmûnātô*, "his / its reliability," refers to the dependability of the vision or the message given in the vision, guaranteed by the reliability of the God who gave the vision or to God's dependability in fulfilling a promise (the ideas are not much different). Haak (1991:59) understands the antecedent of the suffix on *'ĕmûnātô* as "the vision, since it is the reliability of the vision that is in question (cf. Hab 2:3a)" and continues: "It is difficult, and probably not desirable, however, to draw too sharp a distinction between the vision, the content of the vision (the Chaldeans), and the author of the vision (Yahweh). Their reliability is interdependent" (1991:59). (It would be better to recognise the "woe oracles" as the message in the vision.)

This connotation establishes that the vision is the theme of vv 2–4. The antithetical parallelism of v 4 predicts two possible responses to the message. The righteous will accept the message and rely on it; the wicked will pervert it (it will get stuck in his crooked throat). The message is received favorably by one who is already righteous. He does not become righteous by receiving it. It is part of the righteous person's mentality to trust God. Human faith (trust) is included in *'ĕmûnātô* only indirectly. If "his" refers to God's reliability, it is his consistent upholding of justice, punishing the guilty, delivering the innocent. It is valid for humans to act in the same way, for then they are like God, or, rather, they are righteous only if their righteousness is underwritten by the righteousness of God.

The prophet's complaints in Habakkuk 1 arose from the unrestrained, unending slaughter of humankind, so pathetically helpless like fish (1:17). Yet God created humankind as though he were willing life for them (1:14). In particular, the wicked swallows the righteous (1:13): his throat is as wide as Sheol; his appetite, as insatiable as death (2:5). The affirmation of life is God's answer to all that, and this assurance enables the prophet to contemplate the loss of everything and still rejoice in God (3:16).

The Qumran *pešer* gave as the interpretation: "It refers to all the doers of the Torah in the house of Judah whom God will rescue from the house of judgment on account of their suffering [*'āmāl*] and their faith [*'ĕmûnātām*] in the Teacher of Righeousness." Here is a complex representation of "the righteous" under three marks: (1) performance of Torah; (2) endurance of suffering; and (3) *'ĕmûnâ* as a human virtue, more like "faith" as belief, not trust in God or his word, but acceptance of the authoritative leadership of the Teacher of Righeousness, including his inspired interpretations of sacred Scriptures. In respect to the third point (trust in a leader) Fitzmyer (1999:606) comments that: "such a [*sic*] interpretation related to a person is transitional and enables Paul to apply his understanding of Hab 2:4 to Christ Jesus." In respect to trust in an interpretation, Starkova (1998) has discussed the significance of this passage in relation to the Qumran notion of "mystery."

Driver (1913a) and Davidson (1920) were not far from the truth when they found in v 4 a contrast between the arrogant Chaldeans (whose soul was inflated) and the faithful Judeans. According to Driver (1913a:§8), "the soul of the Chaldæan is elated with pride." After the terrifying picture of the Chaldeans given in Hab 1:12–17, it could be a weak characterization to say "his soul is not upright in him." Nor can it be claimed that all the Judeans were characterized as "righteous." The oracle is addressed to God's people and will evoke disbelief or trust. Only those who have faith (or who trust in the reliability of God or of his word) will live. To that extent, the Greek versions, including Heb 10:38, have the gist of it.

In any case, *ʾĕmûnâ* does not mean "trustingness" as a spiritual virtue of which a human being is capable. As ascribed to a human being, *ʾĕmûnâ* describes reliability in carrying out a task, steadfastness in relationships, being worthy of someone else's trust. This same quality of "trustworthiness," so often celebrated as an attribute of God, is the object of human faith and the ground of confidence that God will accomplish what he has promised (Ps 89:34; 50; etc.), will do what the vision predicts: "It is closely associated with the divine *ḥesed*, mercy (Pss 89:25; 92:3; 98:3; Hos 2:22); with the divine righteousness (Pss 56:13; 143:1; Isa 11:5); and salvation (Ps 40:11)" (BDB 53a). Thus the dependability of God is inseparable from the certainty of his word. This is the emphasis of v 3. The vision (or God) will not deceive or fail. The righteous will live because the vision is certain, God is reliable. The referent of "its," the pronoun in "in its (his) faithfulness," is "the vision," not "the righteous man." The topic of discourse in v 3a is probably "the vision" (or indirectly God); it is the subject of all the verbs and the referent of the pronoun in "wait for it." God is the most natural referent for the pronouns that follow in v 4. The person whose outlook is perverted twists his throat "against him" (*bô*); the righteous man will live because of his reliability.

Further consideration of the syntax of v 4b enables the meaning to be focused a little better. The sequence of the three items—subject, adverbial, verb—is remarkable. As a statement of fact—that the righteous person will live by means of "his" (whoever) dependability—it simply says what the righteous one, in contrast to the crooked one, will do. The characterization of the righteous has moved to different ground. In Habakkuk 1, the righteous one was contrasted with the wicked (v 13) with reference to morality. In Hab 2:4 the contrast is found in the responses of the wicked and righteous, respectively, to the vision, to revelation, and this produces a different definition of the righteous person. He is manifested now in the person of the prophet as one who is prepared to wait (v 3) because of his trust in the dependability of God's announced plan.

We have already noticed that the generic article is missing from the noun, in keeping with poetic usage. If the relative pronoun also is missing, but implied, then the placement of the verb last rather than first shows that v 4b is a nominal sentence (verbless clause): "(The) righteous (person) (is) (the one who [*ʾăšer*]) lives by means of the reliability of the oracular vision."

survive. Survival is promised. The person destined to live is not made righteous (right with God) by his trustful attitude. His righteousness, at least as far as the book of Habakkuk is concerned, is a matter already established vis-à-vis the wicked (1:4) and is the ground of the appeal to God for salvation—vindication. The righteousness of God, his holiness (1:12), and his purity (1:13) guarantee that no just cause will suffer terminal frustration and that no righteous person will be permanently deprived of justice. This intrinsic rightness of God has been affirmed in assurances that the endless wickedness of men (1:17) will come to an end and that the lawlessness of men will come to its proper retribution (3:16b). The righteous person believes this; he is right in the rightness of God himself.

There is no hint in Hab 2:4b that an evil person can be set right by the gracious forgiveness of God, accepted by faith. There is no call to repentance, which is an essential part of such a transaction. The validation of the use to which later Christian interpreters put this verse (Rom 1:17; Heb 10:38) is not part of our present task (see the COMMENT). Habakkuk's quest, to which this word is the answer, is not faith or righteousness, but life.

A lexical text from Dhibāʿî (AOAT 25:1–12) has incorporated what seems to be a Sumerian proverb:

nig-gina-ta a-na-am eb-ta-sa nam-til-la ù-tu (IM. 70209 III:15–16)

Abdul Hadi Al-Fouadi translates:

What will you attain from justice?
It generates life.

This association of justice with life is not an abstraction. Literary analogies from proverbs and hymns show that it is the performance of justice in human action that brings life as a gift that remains the sole prerogative of the gods. So the idea in Hab 2:4 could be a very ancient one, almost a commonplace.

Christians were not the only ones who seized on Hab 2:4 as an affirmation of the essence of true religion. Its weight was felt also by the rabbis. In a famous exposition by Rabbi Simlay (a Palestinian rabbi of the third century C.E.) in *Makkoth* 23b–24a the question is how many rules a person has to keep:

but Moses received 613 precepts;
but David reduced them to eleven (Psalm 15)
but Isaiah reduced them to six (Isa 33:15–16)
but Micah reduced them to three (Mic 6:8)
but Isaiah reduced them to two (Isa 56:1)
but Amos reduced them to two (Amos 5:5)

Hab 2:4 is then adduced as another way of comprehending all God's commandments in one aphorism.

5. Because of the finality of v 4, and the new beginning with *wě'ap kî-*, some scholars have found a major break in the book at this point. Budde (*EB* II 1923) inserted Hab 1:5–11 here. This makes the promise of judgment of the wicked (Assyrians) by the Chaldeans a more conclusive and satisfactory answer to Habakkuk's question, rather than a cause of his perplexity. Cannon (1924:75) explained the break as due to a time interval between the dialogue in Hab 1:2–2:4

and the "woe oracles" that follow. But *wĕ'ap kî*- is better taken as a link that secures continuity between v 4 and v 5.

The tone of disapproval in v 5a (after the ringing affirmation of v 4b) has suggested to more than one critic that the "woe" series begins here (Wellhausen
1898:168; Elliger 1953:40, 42) or even earlier (Weiser 1961:262). While admitting the intractable incoherence of vv 2–5, we feel that we are on fairly firm
ground when we take the thematic connections between v 2b and v 6a as a kind
of inclusion around the unit, so that the series "he will run, read [v 2b] . . . and
say (v 6a)" describes the promulgation of the riddle-like "woes" that come out
of the vision. That leaves the material in between (vv 3–5) as a unit.

yet indeed. Verse 4b is climactic. The onset of the next section is marked by
a plethora of conjunctions. The initial "and" shows that v 5 continues something, but it need not be coordinated with the immediately preceding clause.
The meaning of *'ap kî* continues to evade. The most famous instance (Gen 3:1)
suggests that it need not be subordinative, unless it is a very clever use of a protasis without an apodosis (see AB1:23). A possible meaning of "even though"
has been proposed. The present construction is made more problematical by
the use of the definite article, so rare in Habakkuk, and the participle. In association with *'ap, kî* is probably asseverative: "indeed."

wine. Verse 5 goes on to describe the insatiable greed of the tyrant, drawing
on the iconography of the god of Death, the monster that eventually swallows
down everything. It is not clear how wine comes into the picture. The difficulty
of calling "the wine" a deceiver has led to suggestions about a better word to replace it. One proposal is Bredenkamp's ingenious *wĕ'epes kĕ'ayin* (Budde
1931:411). Wellhausen (1893:164) and Nowack (1922) dismissed "the wine" as
"quite impossible" and replaced it by *hôy*, increasing the number of "woe oracles" to six. LXX already read *ho . . . katoiomenos*, "the conceited person." Cannon (1925:84, n. 4) suggested *hayyôneh*, "the oppressor," as in Jer 25:38; 46:16;
Zeph 3:1. The last instance is of interest because it occurs in a "woe oracle."

There could be a gnomic touch in the reference to wine. The definite article is used in exactly the same way in proverbs, such as in Prov 20:1:

lēṣ hayyayin	the wine is a deceiver
ḥōmeh šēkār	liquor is riotous
wĕkol-šōgeh bô	and anyone who wanders in it
lō' yeḥkām	is not wise

The concluding negation also compares with Hab 2:4. But the good syntax of
lēṣ hayyayin (predicate, subject) shows up the abnormal subject, predicate sequence *hayyayin bôgēd*. Even if we ignore that difference in word order and accept "the wine is a deceiver" as a kind of proverb, how does *geber yāhîr* fit in?
In prophecy, wine is often the instrument of God's judgment, infuriating the
wicked to self-destruction. The Chaldean's madness for conquest is like intoxication. Drunkenness figures in the fourth "woe oracle," and this message could
be presaged here. The choice of poetic *geber*, which has connotations of great

strength and also military associations, gives more impact to the following statement that he will not endure.

Criticism of *hyyn* took a new turn with the variant *hwn*, presumably "wealth,"
in 1QpHab, along with *ybgyd*, "wealth will make the *gbr yhyd* a traitor." The
Hip̄ʿil of √*bgd* is otherwise unattested, and other readings of *hwn* are possible.
Some recent translations accepted "wealth," but read the verb as *Qal*, or at least
as intransitive: "wealth is treacherous" (NRSV, NJB, NAB). Qumran scholars
are no longer comfortable resorting to the idea that *wāw* and *yōd* were indistinguishable in Qumran scribal practice: "In Hasmonaean times the tops of both
waw and *yod* become an angular hook, often shaded, so that a triangular effect
is produced. In late Hasmonaean times the right down-stroke of *yod* lengthens
and straightens, and in the early Herodian period *waw* and *yod* become virtually, if not actually, indistinguishable. Finally, in the late Herodian period, *waw*
and *yod* again are increasingly distinguished, with *waw* becoming slightly longer
and *yod* tending to shorten" (Cross 1998:390). Early researchers were divided
over *ybgyd* or *ybgwd*. Brownlee still preferred the *Hip̄ʿil* in 1979 (p. 132). But
Elliger already preferred *Qal* in 1953 (p. 197), and this is now generally accepted (Horgan 1979:40). García Martínez and Tigchelaar (1997:16) concur,
but their translation "Surely wealth will corrupt the boaster" is debatable because the verb is stative, meaning "be treacherous," and Ps 73:15 is the only possible attestation of its transitive use.

treacherous. The participle *bôgēd* has already been used in Hab 1:13, where
it refers to the wicked man. Here it is wine that is treacherous. These statements
need not be incongruous, for the fourth "woe oracle" denounces the person who
deceives his neighbor, making him drunk in order to abuse him sexually. Note
the similarity of *wĕ ʾap kî-hayyayin* and *wĕ ʾap šakkēr* (2:15). The miscreant will
receive the same treatment when the cup comes around to him (2:16; note the
verb *śbʿ* there and in Hab 2:5), and v 5 already predicts his decay. This does not
fully explain what "the wine" is doing in v 5, but is enough to restrain us from
relinquishing the word.

The simplest explanation is that the "hero" draws deceptive inspiration from
wine, which can only ruin him.

the man. The Masoretic punctuation makes *geber yāhîr* a phrase—"proud
man" (KJV, which has to supply a subject and resort to paraphrase: "because he
transgresseth by wine, he is a proud man"). This reading is very loose. The syntax of this word order is better if *bôgēd* is verbal. Hence our translation, supported by Prov 20:1.

presumptuous. The poetic parallelism within v 5a suggests that the two similar nouns are placed chiastically. The word *yāhîr* occurs only here and in Prov
21:24. The presumptuousness of this crooked person has already been exposed
in v 4a. The last three words in v 5a make a good poetic colon, as soon as the
"and" is recognized as a postpositive, a Hebrew construction that should not
need argument. The examples adduced by Dhorme in his commentary on Job
(1967:45) should be enough. See also the literature on so-called emphatic or
pleonastic *wāw* in Blommerde (1969).

If it is considered that the analysis proposed here results in poetic colons of unequal length, we could heed *zāqēp qāṭôn* on *bôgēd* and translate:

And yet indeed the wine deceives;
And the arrogant man will not endure.

not endure. This prediction contrasts with "will live" or "survive" in v 4. The difficulty of this word has led to emendations, ancient and modern. 1QpHab confirms the MT. There are several Hebrew words with the root *nwy*, and perhaps more than one homonym behind them, and this is the only place where a *Qal* verb meaning "abide" has been identified. Hence the emendation to *yānûaḥ* (Budde 1931:411) (cf. *'ānûaḥ* [3:16]). This reading could gain some support from LXX *peranē*, "he won't finish anything." Because of this precarious claim, Wellhausen (1892) wanted to read *yirweh*, "he will be satiated," which matches the last word in v 5bA. A related adjective meaning "beautiful" occurs in Jer 6:2, and the prediction that the arrogant man will not be beautiful agrees with the forecast of shame instead of glory (2:16).

who. The use of the relative ("pronoun") is itself remarkable; it occurs only four times in the book (once in the [prose] title). A frequency density of this order (0.6 percent) is characteristic of poetry (only Job, Proverbs, and Hosea have lower scores). Given the authenticity of the particle, the problem is its grammar, its antecedent, if it has one. There is no noun antecedent immediately preceding it, as in standard prose. Discontinuous or delayed use of a relative clause is not unknown in Biblical Hebrew (Goshen-Gottstein 1960), but the construction is cumbersome, found only in very long clauses, while in Habakkuk's poetic prophecy the clauses and the colons tend to be short. It is in keeping with the confused condition of this pericope that the connections (thematic and grammatical) of v 5b with its text surrounds are elusive, and to suspect corruption of the reading has a particularly strong allure. With v 5b, we have a piece of firmer ground, surrounded by the soft sand of vv 4–5a and 6a. Verse 5bB presents the paradox that it is almost the only portion of vv 2–6a that is easy to read, and the synonymous parallelism of its bicolon is almost banal. The price paid for this relief is poetry of little merit, written in language whose grammar is essentially prose (it uses *wāw*-consecutive and the definite article). The imagery of v 5bA is congruous with that of v 5bB, and reminds the reader of the aggressor of Habakkuk 1. And v 5bA has its own parallelism, albeit not well developed (the two similes match, and possibly *'ăšer* has *hû'* as its parallel). All these considerations suggest that v 5b is a quatrain. All four masculine third-person-singular verbs have the same grammatical subject, even though no noun is immediately present. The most eligible candidate in the vicinity is *geber*, the presumptuous person whose throat is opened wide and whose appetite is never satisfied. At the same time, the similar clauses (negated prefixed verbs, presumably with the same subject) at the ends of vv 5a and 5bA serve as an indicator of continuity between these two bicolons. In other words, v 5 is a six-colon unit. In spite of the awkwardness, the deceiving proud strongman of v 5a (the crooked man of v 4a) is the topic, the antecedent of *ʾăšer*, and the subject of all the verbs in the verse. The picture of the wide-open throat points to the wicked man of Hab 1:13 who swallows down the righteous, like Sheol. If v 5bB continues the figure, it provides the additional clarification that it is all the nations of the world that are being engulfed.

Death. Because the imagery is quite concrete, it is death as a monster that opens its maw, and mythology is not far away (Oldenburg 1969:35). The insatiable hunger of death is shown by the fact that its meal of the living never ends. For discussion of the god Mot feeding on the dead, see Tromp (1969).

gathered . . . collected. The two verbs are stock parallels. The recapitulation here of a theme that occurs several times in Habakkuk 1 makes v 5bB a kind of coda before the "woe oracles." LXX confirms the singular number of the verbs, but reads the conjunction as coordinating, not consecutive as in MT. That made it a prediction rather than a fragment of narrative. The V agrees with LXX, but Tg and Peshitta took the verbs to be past tense. This is another instance of the propensity of the versions to read prophetic texts as predictive rather than narrative. 1QpHab, however, has made the verbs plural, so that "all the nations . . . // all the peoples" become the subjects of these verbs, which have to be read as *Nipʿal*. Yet the *pešer* itself goes on to quote the verbs as *Qal* singular, with *wāw*-consecutive, applying them to the Wicked Priest: "and he abandonned God and he betrayed the statutes for the sake of riches [*hwn* (the variant reading of 1QpHab in v 5aA)] and he robbed and he gathered [*wyqbwṣ*] riches [*hwn*] . . . ."

Students of 1QpHab disagree over the *Nipʿals*. Brownlee (1979:131) renders them as passive and past: "All nations have been gathered to him," essentially the same meaning as MT. Elliger (1953:197) takes them to be middle present. García Martínez and Tigchelaar (1997:17) understand that they express hostile acts (anticipating Hab 2:8): "All the peoples ally against him, all the nations come together against him."

The orthography of 1QpHab is remarkable at this place in preserving the archaic *ʾlw* (MT *ʾlyw*).

COMMENT

The material we have isolated as Habakkuk's response and the LORD's second reply (2:1–5) can be identified as a unit by exterior clues. Verse 1 is clearly transitional. Along with v 2aA, it constitutes the only narrative material in the whole book. The five "woe oracles" (2:6b–20) can be isolated as a distinct unit by their introductory formula (v 6a), by their consistent content, and by their internal organization.

Verses 2aB–5 present none of these helpful features; they seem to be disorganized and it is hard to find any coherent structure or continuous thematic development. The onset of the LORD's speech is clearly marked by imperative verbs after the quotation formula of v 2aA. The speech itself is not unified by a consistent theme or by internal organization. Some pairs of contiguous colons can be recognized as bicolons, but the connections between one such unit and the next are harder to find, perhaps impossible. It is no wonder that many commentators have given up the search for coherence and have explained the passage as a gathering place for bits and pieces.

Without pretending to have made much progress, we are nevertheless hopeful that something can be salvaged. Some general observations may serve as a guide:

1. The passage is redolent of terms that occur elsewhere in Habakkuk. This general feature suggests that some of the themes of the book continue to receive attention in these verses and that the meaning of such vocabulary elsewhere will help to explain its use at this point. Such words are "righteous," "deceive" (cf. Hab 1:13), and "wine" (cf. Hab 2:15). The insatiable appetite of the greedy person in v 5bA is like that in Hab 1:16–17, and the language of v 5bB is found in Hab 1:9–10.

2. The apparent confusion in the presentation of these materials—the sudden breaks and abrupt transitions—could be due to discontinuities deliberately introduced for stylistic effect. The thought is arrested and kept in suspense; then, after other material is supplied, the thought is resumed. "And he will say" (singular), the first word of v 6b, cannot be the continuation of "they will raise a proverb" (plural), unless the switch from plural to singular is distributive. Some witnesses level to "and *they* will say." We suggest, however, that v 2 is followed naturally by v 6b. The reciter will run . . . and *he* will say. . . .

More careful work needs to be done in order to arrive at identifications of the participant references of the various pronouns, however tentative this must remain. To illustrate: Who is the one against whom "these" will lift up the proverb? And who are they? The nearest referent is the nations in v 5b. In due time, they might ridicule their former oppressors, when the roles are reversed. But they are not likely to be cast in the role of proclaiming prophecies. Linking v 6b with v 2 makes better sense of the language in v 2. The LORD's answer, which is called a "vision" (cf. Hab 1:1), is to be written down, taken by a runner, and read out. The oracle becomes a message and a proclamation. Only after their fulfillment will the "woe oracles," which are announced as a prediction and a warning, be turned into a chorus of derision in which the victim nations might join.

On the one hand, the material in vv 3–5 (perhaps 6a as well) is manifestly not oracular; it includes remarks about the vision (v 3a) and exhortations about responding to it (v 3b), as well as other comments that may or may not be connected with this (vv 4–5). On the other hand, vv 6b–20 are eminently suitable for announcement as the word of Yahweh in this situation. As such, they are not left dangling, as they are when v 6b is felt as a too abrupt transition from v 6a. But there is no need to isolate vv 6b–20 as an independent composition, with no place in the dialogue between Habakkuk and Yahweh, just because of the break between v 6a and v 6b. The connection between v 2 and v 6b shows that the five "woe oracles" are the product of the vision; they are the content of the LORD's second reply. They are the saving answer for which the prophet has hoped, even though they do not have the conventional form of a salvation oracle; and, as such, they are integral to the dialogue.

3. This analysis leaves vv 3–6a as intrusive or transitional. These verses are best viewed as an exhortation and a commentary on the message that is to fol-

low. The imperative verbs in v 2 are singular (contrast the plural in Hab 1:5) and are addressed to the prophet himself. This mood continues in v 3, an indication of continuity in vv 2–5. As such, this more personal word is, in part, the LORD's answer to Habakkuk's own spiritual needs, an answer that receives further amplification in the final chapter. By contrast, the "woe oracles" are for the public. They are what is to be written on the tablets and recited by the *qôrē'*.

4. This analysis of vv 2–6a does not solve all the problems. The word of exhortation lasts only through v 3. Verses 4–5 contain assertions that contrast the righteous with the wicked. Verse 5b reverts to a concrete narrative form in the past tense and is so similar in thought, and even in vocabulary, to what has been said in Habakkuk 1, as to suggest that the proud deceiver is the Chaldean nation. Verse 5b is then an inclusion for Hab 1:5–17.

The words of encouragement in vv 2–3 are addressed to the prophet, who, we suggest, is himself the righteous person of v 4b. The continuity of what follows requires identification of the person whose rapacity is described in v 5, and against whom the proverb is raised in v 6a. The most probable identification is with the perverted person of v 4a, who is also the person, deceived by wine, who will not endure (v 5a). Verse 5bB shows that this person is the Chaldean of Hab 1:9–10, and Hab 2:15–16 indicate that he is also the future victim against whom all these (v 6a)—that is, all the nations and all the peoples of v 6bB (the word "all" links them)—will take up the taunt; the wine of v 5 matches the strong drink of v 15, bringing about desolation as judgment from God.

It is therefore possible to say that vv 2–5 refer to the righteous (vv 2–3, 4b) and his opposite (vv 4a, 5). They are interlocked by the central affirmations of v 4, confirming a long-standing impression that v 4 is the heart of the speech.

Our demonstration that vv 2aB–5 constitute a well-wrought quasi-poetic unit leaves v 6a to be accounted for. The contrast between its plural verbs and the singular "he will say" makes it difficut to identify the taunting proverb(s) taken up "against him" with the five "woe oracles" that follow. 1QpHab and LXX resolved this by reading "and they will say," but this easier, obviously harmonizing reading does not have the same claim as the MT, especially as the subject of "he will say" can be identified as the "reciter" in v 2. In any case, v 6a does not yield to poetic analysis. The nouns at least are parallels, and "against him" matches "for him"; but, as already said, it need not be the same "him." The transition from the vision to the "woe oracles" may be explained as follows. The nations, victims of the tyrant described in vv 4a and 5, will have their revenge when they raise their voice against him, echoing the woes of v 6b–20 in derision after his downfall. This is the LORD's message written on the tablets, and the reciter of the tablets proclaims this message as prediction.

COMMENT ON Habakkuk 1:2–2:6a

The interaction between Habakkuk and Yahweh documented in Hab 1:2–2:6a retains in its literary presentation some of the liveliness and untidiness of actual experience. The language remains rough and rugged, as in living speech. The dialogue does not proceed logically by systematic debate in which each speech argues with the preceding one. It is not conversation in which alternating remarks are usually shorter, but it is not a series of formalized speeches either.

One can appreciate the opinion of scholars such as Pfeiffer (1952:597) that "[t]he first two chapters are a series of five short and more or less disconnected prophetic utterances." One can appreciate also the temptation to reduce the incoherence of the available text by smoothing out some of the rough places or by more drastically rearranging the material. Or, leaving the text as it is, to harmonize it by forced exegesis. It requires sensitive critical judgment and much restraint to balance the mix of continuity and discontinuity that the text exhibits.

We have analyzed the book so far as a dialogue between the prophet and Yahweh, with a prayer (1:2–4) followed by an oracle (1:5–10) that provoked a second prayer (1:12–17). After an interval (2:1), Yahweh replied once more (2:2–20, in which the suite of "woe oracles" [2:6b–20] is embedded).

The fact that Hab 1:2–4 and Hab 1:12–17 can be read as a single speech has long been recognized. Several attempts have been made to recover what is believed to be the original state of this composition. Wellhausen's (1892) explanation was that Hab 1:5–11 is an oracle predicting the Babylonian expansion that climaxed in the Battle of Carchemish in 605 B.C.E. or a *vaticinium ex eventu* of the same. It has nothing to do with Habakkuk's complaint. It has been quite unsuitably inserted in the middle of what was once a continuous speech and should be removed. Wellhausen (1893:162) states the problem thus: *Wie kann die Ankündigung, daß die Chaldäer erscheinen werden, die Antwort auf die Klage sein, daß sie seit lange das Volk Jahves bedrücken?* (How can the announcement that the Chaldeans will put in an appearance be the answer to the complaint that they have been oppressing the people of Yahweh for a long time?).

The question becomes unnecessary if Hab 1:2–4 does not complain about the Chaldeans, but about lawlessness within Judah, as we have maintained, along with many commentators.

The solution of van Hoonacker (1908) was less drastic. He recognized both of Habakkuk's prayers as a fitting response to the LORD's announcement in Hab 1:5–11. So he placed this oracle at the beginning of the book. The wicked whose excesses are deplored in both of Habakkuk's prayers are then the Chaldeans, whose activities are described in Hab 1:5–11. But the prophet's first protest is directed not against the LORD's forecast, but against his silence; and it would seem from the language of vv 15–17 that the predictions made in vv 9–11 had already come about when that second prayer was made.

Attempts have been made by other scholars to give the prophecy a more extended view of history. George Adam Smith (1899 II:123–24) conjectured that the wicked against whom the prophet cries out are the Egyptians, responsible for the death of Josiah, the righteous king. Hab 1:4b then describes the events of 609 B.C.E. The LORD's response to this is that Babylon will destroy Egypt, and this assurance is given in Hab 1:5–11, which should come after Hab 2:1–4. The book is thus simplified into two parts—prayers by the prophet (1:2–4,

12–17) and replies by the LORD (2:1–4; Hab 1:5–11; 2:5–20). George Adam Smith's views were adapted from a theory of Budde, who cast the Assyrians in the role of the wicked. It is their tyranny that evokes the prophet's outcry in Hab 1:2–4, 12–17. The simple response is that the Chaldeans will bring about their downfall, so that all of Habakkuk 2 (with Hab 1:5–11 inserted) is intended to reassure the righteous of that outcome. The "woe oracles" were directed against Assyria. Budde supposed furthermore that the removal of Hab 1:5–11 to its present place was an attempt by a later reviser of the book to cast the Chaldeans in the role of oppressor, rather than avenger. For a detailed criticism of these and other similar theories, see Stonehouse (1911:148–63).

The justice of the observations can be appreciated without resorting to such drastic solutions. It is not uncommon for mediatorial prophets, when making heated intercessions, to incorporate into their arguments quotations of speeches previously made by God. Such statements might be disputed (to get God to change his mind) or affirmed (to get God to keep his promise). Such quotations are not necessarily marked by the usual formulas, and so they have to be identified by purely structural or internal arguments. This general problem has been investigated by Gordis (1949, 1965).

If Hab 1:5–11 is such a quotation within Habakkuk's own words (1:2–17), it may be left where it is. Habakkuk has then built his prayer around an earlier oracle of Yahweh that is partly the cause of his present distress.

By the very character of the evidence, not much certainty can be hoped for in solving a problem of this kind. Too much weight should not be attached to logical coherence within speeches or logical development between speeches as an aid to literary criticism. It should not be supposed that a certain lack of logic in the present arrangement can be blamed on the disorganization of the text by a careless scribe. It is not to be supposed that the reorganization of the text into a more logical pattern by a modern scholar means the recovery of the original plan. We have already noticed that the logical connections among the several colons in the first speech are hard to find, and the same applies to the oracle in Hab 1:5–11.

One reason for the difficulty in finding the connection between one part and another of this speech is caused by the limited development of poetic designs. The parallelism that is always such a helpful guide to analysis and interpretation is not used much, and we do not have the opposite compensations of clear and straightforward prose. In view of these uncertainties, we have adopted a straightforward reading, in line with mainstream scholarship, taking the first two chapters as the report of verbal exchanges (they can hardly be called dialogue) between the prophet and Yahweh, Habakkuk's prayers answered with oracular messages.

VII. THE WOE
ORACLES (2:6–20)

♦

The set of five "woe oracles" constitutes the speech to be delivered by "the reciter" from the vision written on the tablets. These denunciations could be made appropriately by the victim nations as a mocking byword against their former oppressor (v 7b), but it is more likely that the prophet is making this speech on their behalf, at least in the first instance.

The set is unified by more than the fact that the five "woe oracles" have been strung together editorially in one place in the finished book. They have been unified into a single composition and in their whole effect are a suitable response to Habakkuk's prayers. They have links with the rest of the book. Some of these links are clearer than others. Some are verbal; some are thematic.

There are five "woe oracles" in all, as shown by the occurrence of the word *hôy* (vv 6, 9, 12, 15, 19). Apart from this common feature, no two of the "woe oracles" are the same in literary design.

It is not certain that all the material in vv 6b–20 is to be distributed among the five "woe oracles" in their proper identity. There is no regular pattern into which all the statements can be put, and some of the components could be extraneous. Thus v 20, although contrasting aptly with the preceding remarks about idolatry, could be a pious remark on the side or a scribal gloss. (The "temple" does not otherwise figure in the prophecy.) Verse 14 could also be another such comment that is not part of the third "woe oracle."

The five "woe oracles" are of different lengths, whether estimated as colons or syllables. The shortest (the third, vv 12–14) has seven colons and sixty-five syllables. The longest (the fourth, vv 15–17) has eleven colons and ninety-one syllables.

The prosody is quite mixed. There are enough recognizable, indeed well-formed, bicolons to suggest that the author was aspiring to poetic expression, but many of the passages are prosaic (for example, v 15) and have no parallelism of the kind met in lyrical or cultic Hebrew verse compositions. The colons range in length from four to thirteen syllables.

The matter is complicated by the presence of several very short phrases that have little or no connection with their context. They could be random expostulations, fragments of incoherent speech, or the debris of a corrupted text. The most obvious ones are

6   *How long?*
9   *Evil to his house*

225

10   *Shame to thy house*
13   *Behold!*
19   *He instructs*

Notwithstanding such problems, the main thrust of the "woe oracles" is clear. Similar ingredients turn up in all of them, even though no two have either the same elements or the same sequences. As many as six different constituents might be found, as shown in Table 3. The classification of many of the individual ingredients remains problematic because of textual difficulties.

All the "woe oracles" begin with *hôy* except the fifth, which has a question first. The first, second, and fourth contain statements in which the culprit is addressed as "thou" (singular). It is possible that quite different persons are the targets of these several objurgations. But because v 6a speaks of all the nations taking up derisive sayings "against him," it is more likely that one and the same reprobate is having the several aspects of his wickedness itemized one by one.

Each of the reproaches is composed as *hôy*, "woe," followed by a singular active participle. In all but the fifth "woe oracle," there is a second participle in parallel, and even here one may be restored. In the second "woe oracle," this parallel participle is delayed, creating the impression that "sinning fatally" is a floating fragment. However, it is the second participle that supplies the clue to the structure of that difficult "woe oracle" (see INTRODUCTION to 2:9–11).

Three of the "woe oracles" contain questions, which could be why the speeches can be called taunts, and some have imprecations.

TABLE 3. Components of the Woe Oracles*

Woe Oracle	*hôy* + participle	question	What he [thou] did	His [thy] fate	imprecation	comment
1	6bA 8b	How long? (6b) Is not? (7a)	8aA [thou]	7b [thou] 8ab	6bB	—
2	9 . . . . . . 10bB	—*	10 [thou]	11(?)	9 (?)*	—
3	12	Is not? (13a)	—	13	13 (?)	14
4	15	—	16aA	16b [thou] 17a [thou]	16aB [thou]	17b (?) [imperative]
5	19a	What? (18a)	18b 19b	—	—	20

*— means that the component is not present; (?) means that the classification is not certain.

Common to all the "woe oracles" are predictions of the fate of the wrong-doer, sometimes linked appropriately to a reminder of the deeds that deserve such just rewards. The punishment will match the crime. The spoiler will be despoiled; the racketeer will be defrauded; the empire builder will be devastated; the pervert will be abused. The one exception is the idolater, whose penalty is not specified.

The exposure and condemnation of human failing can take many forms, ranging from "Woe!" pronounced against the wrongdoers to reproaches (intended to shame), denunciations, warnings (to deter), invitations to amend, and, in the last resort, announcements of doom and pronouncements of punishment.

In spite of the variety in the shape of the "woe oracles," the prophet's poetic intention is clear throughout. There are enough bicolons of familiar design to prove that. And it is the identification of these indubitable bicolons that assists analysis of the overall structure of each "woe oracle." In the first "woe oracle," the first bicolon (v 6bAβ // 6bB) has two *Hip'il* participles in parallel. The second bicolon (v 7a) has two *yiqṭōl* verb forms in parallel. Verse 8a contains the stock parallels *gôyīm* // *'ammîm*, and v 8b is clearly a unit. It is encouraging from the outset that these four bicolons are also regular in these scansion (16, 16, 16, 17 syllables). This leaves v 7b as an unmatched colon in the very center of the unit. Verse 7a is the judgment, spoken directly to the culprit.

The second "woe oracle" also has nine colons, arranged in the same symmetrical pattern with the monocolon in the center addressing the culprit directly. The rhythms in the second "woe oracle," however, are quite different from those in vv 6–8. The colons are quite short (mean 5.9 syllables). Whereas v 6b has the participle that follows *hôy* followed immediately by a parallel participle, in the second "woe oracle" the initial participle in v 9aA is not given its mate until v 10bB. Recognizing this long-range connection takes care of the otherwise problematic v 10bB, which has no grammatical or thematic connections with its immediate context, but which serves well as the parallel to v 9aA. In a similar fashion, the apparently stranded infinitival construction in v 10bA is in discontinuous parallelism with the parallel infinitives in v 9b.

The seven colons in the third "woe oracle" (mean 9.3 syllables) are longer than the standard eight-syllable colon. If we detach the refrain (v 14), there is once more a single colon flanked by two well-formed bicolons. The first (v 12) is a typical "woe" utterance, with matching participles. Verse 13b has the stock parallels *'ammîm* // *lĕ'ummîm*.

In terms of the overall structure of the five "woe oracles," the monocolon that is the middle of the middle "woe oracle," "Isn't this—Behold!—from Yahweh Sebaoth?" with its arresting language and the impressive title for God, must be regarded as the climax of the entire set and the key theological statement of the whole.

In the fourth "woe oracle," the eleven colons are closer to the standard length (8.3 syllables). Once again there is a single colon symmetrically placed between two tricolons of identical length (twenty-six syllables). This subunit is followed by two bicolons in v 17, the last being a refrain already used in v 8b.

The final "woe oracle" is quite regular in its scansion. There are ten colons

TABLE 4. Scansion of the Woe Oracles

WOE ORACLES	COLONS	SYLLABLES	MEAN (syllables per colon)
1 (vv 6bB–8)	9	75	8.3
2 (vv 9–11)	9	53	5.9
3 (vv 12–14)	7	65	9.3
4 (vv 15–17)	11	91	8.3
5 (vv (18–20)	10	84	8.4
Total	46	368	8.0

and eighty-four syllables, close to the standard colon length. Again there is symmetry, this time with a bicolon flanked by two quatrains of comparable length. This time it is the "woe" formula itself that is placed in the center. So all five "woe oracles" have their most important statement in the middle. This common design feature is clearly intentional. If it had been noticed and appreciated, scholars would not have worried about the deviation of the fifth "woe oracle" from the usual pattern of having the word *hôy* first. It is also useful, in this connection, to recall the "law" discovered by David Noel Freedman (1986b) of deliberate departure (once) from the template when a pattern is used many times.

Although there is variety all through the suite of five "woe oracles" the aggregate effect evens out the range of colon lengths so that the mean for the whole is standard (see Table 4).

Recognition that the "woe oracles" are composed as prophetic poetry is confirmed by an examination of the language used. There are thirty-five words in the first "woe oracle," and only one prose particle, the definite article with the first participle (Table 5). That already shows two things: (1) that the language is that of poetry, (2) that the definite participle has a distinct rhetorical function in this lead position. The low percentage of prose particles is the more impressive when we note that more "prose particles" could have been used. In prose, the object *lō'-lô* "that which does not belong to him" would normally be nominalized by *'ăšer* and governed by *nota accusativi 'et*. Parallelism suggests that the participle in v 6bD should have the definite article. The noun *qiryâ* in

TABLE 5. Prose Particles in the Five Woe Oracles

WOE ORACLE	WORDS	*'ăšer*	*'et*	*hē'*	TOTAL	PERCENT
1	35	0	0	1	1	
2	26	0	0	0	0	
3	31	0	1	1	2	
4	41	0	0	0	0	
5	42	0	0	1	1	
Totals	175	0	1	3	4	2.3

v 8aB is probably definite in reference ("the city" or "his city"), and in each of the three construct phrases in v 8 the *nomen rectum* would normally be definite. If all opportunities to use prose particles had been taken, the percentage would have been 26 percent, high even for prose.

Other linguistic features characteristic of poetry are *lāmô* and the use of *bô* as *nomen rectum* in v 8bB, rather than *yôšěbeyhā*. Note also how the preposition *min* governs a coordinated noun phrase in v 8bA instead of being repeated with the second noun phrase.

There are twenty-six words in the second "woe oracle," but no prose particles. The provision of a pseudo-article in *bammārôm* was possible only because the vowel point could ride on the inseparable preposition. The vocalization shows that the Masoretes felt the pressure for definiteness in the reference, but they did not feel free to make any nouns explicitly definite by changing the consonantal text with the addition of *hē'*. There are at least eight places where prose particles could have been used in the second "woe oracle": (1, 2) to show that the participles are definite, (3) *nota accusativi 'et* to show that *qinnô* is the object, (4) in the construct phrase "the paw of the evil one," and (5–8) the nouns in v 11 are definite, as translations recognize ("For the stone in the wall will cry out, and the beam in the woodwork shall answer it" [NAB]). Thus thirty percent of the words presented opportunities for using prose particles.

There are thirty-one words in the third "woe oracle," and two prose particles (both in v 14a). As in the previous units, the message is not a shot at random; it is delivered against a specific person for specific crimes: not "anyone who builds a town with bloodshed" (NJB). In the second "woe oracle," this is made clearer by the address to the culprit in the second person. The definiteness of the person who built his city with blood could have been shown explicitly by using the appropriate "prose particles."

There are forty-one orthographic words in the fourth "woe oracle," but no prose particles. The extreme opacity of the language due to the sparsity of particles, including prepositions, makes it difficult to determine how many of the nouns are definite. As many as eight prose particles could be supplied, and they are implied by the translations.

There are forty-two orthographic words in the fifth "woe oracle," and one prose particle (v 20b). More could have been used. It is the language of poetry.

VII.1. INTRODUCTION TO THE WOE ORACLES (2:6a)

6aA   Will not these—all of them—raise a proverb against him,
6aB   and derision, enigmas for him?

6bA   And he will say:

Scansion of the Introduction to the Woe Oracles (2:6a)

		BEATS	SYLLABLES	BICOLON
6aA	hălô'-'ēlleh kullām 'ālāyw māšāl yiśśā'û	5	13 }	
6aB	ûmĕlîṣâ ḥîdôt lô	3	7 }	20
6bA	wĕyō'mer . . .			

INTRODUCTION

The connections of this half-verse are not obvious, so uncertainty remains in any suggestion about how to fit it into the context. It is best seen as transitional between the portrait of the world conqueror in v 5 and the forecast of his doom in the "woe oracles." In the MT the problem lies in the singular verb "And he will say," which introduces the "woe oracles." This verb has a strong claim as the more difficult reading. 1QpHab and LXX, which read plural, have smoothed the transition. As a result of that adjustment, the "woe oracles" are to be declared by all the nations as in mockery of their former tyrant. But, as we have seen, it is more probable that the "woe oracles" are announced by the "reciter" of v 2, either the prophet or the person who runs with the tablets. This is why the first verb in v 6b is singular. Thus verse 6b has only loose links with what immediately precedes it, because the subject changes from colon to colon: in v 5, the conqueror, in v 6a, the nations, in v 6b, the "reciter." As pointed out above, there is a more distant link of v 6a with the language of v 2.

NOTES

6a. *all of them.* The phrase is unusual; *kol-'ēlleh* is normal. "These, all of them" is a more emphatic construction, widely attested (for a fuller discussion of the syntax of *kullām* see AB24E: 150–51). "All" links back to v 5bB, where it occurs twice. This evidence makes emendation unnecessary. Nevertheless, the strain of the construction "these, them all" instead of "all these" can be relieved if *'ēlleh* is not the demonstrative pronoun but a mispointing of the noun *'ālâ*, "curse"—an incantation with oaths of conjuration to be used against an enemy (Torczyner 1947:20–21). This reading suits the purpose of the "woe oracles" and supplies another related noun in the colon with *māšāl*, *mĕlîṣâ*, and *ḥîdôt*. Even without emendation of *'ēlleh* to *'ālâ*, the other three words referring to kinds of speech encourage the search for some kind of poetic parallelism in this half-verse. Yet, as it now stands, the text is simply one long cumbersome prose clause: "Will not these all of them against him a proverb raise and derision enigmas for him?" 1QpHab lacks *'ēlleh* (haplography? [Rudolph 1975:219]). At first, Brownlee (1959:52) was inclined to accept 1QpHab as "the more primitive reading," with *'ēlleh* in MT as a gloss to secure more firmly the link with v 5b. But "all of them" (especially after the double *kol* in v 5b), along with the plural verb, should have been more than enough for that. And if such reinforcement were needed, it could have been secured by the original author. The clause is extraordinary for having five words before the verb. This, and the consequent inequality of the colons in length, as well as the absence of parallelism (the second half has no verb), throws doubt on the present text at several places. Procksch (BH^3) shortened v 6aA by omitting *ʿālāyw*, but this diminishes the parallelism with *lô* in v 6aB. Elliger (1953:53), taking v 6a as "obviously redactional," was not worried by its length, and explained the absence of *ʾelleh* from 1QpHab as accidental: "hinter הלוא freilich leicht [אלה] übersehen werden konnte" (following הלוא, to be sure, [אלה] could easily be overlooked [1953:53]). Another verb is needed, preferably in the earlier part of the colon. An ingenious way of supplying another verb is to find the root *klm*, "shame," instead of the syntactically awkward "all (of) them." Even then, the boundaries of the clauses are not easy to chart.

The three nouns are an additional difficulty, and all translations have to paraphrase. If the three nouns are the object of the verb "raise," it is strange, to say the least, to have one noun before, two after the verb. Furthermore, because *kullām* has an obvious referent ("all the nations"), the need for a verb to parallel "will . . . raise" can be met if some derivative of the verb √*ʿly* can be recovered from *ʿālāyw*. This is the thinking behind emendation to a *Hipʿil* form: "Will not all of them *send up* a curse, raise a by-word?" The more drastic solution of Budde (1931:411) restores cognate verb-object constructions: *yimšĕlû māšāl* // *yiśʾû mĕlîṣâ* // *yāḥûdû ḥîdâ*, "they will compose a proverb // they will raise a taunt // they will devise a riddle." Only two of the original words survive unscathed, two are changed slightly, two new words are introduced. Budde did not emend the text; he composed a new text.

raise. The idiom *nāśāʾ māšāl*, "utter a proverb," is well attested (Budde [1931] lost the collocation) and is characteristic of prophetic utterance in poetic form. The oracles of Balaam are the best known instances introduced by this formula. They share with Habakkuk's "woe oracles" the feature of denunciations with international scope. This idiom, in spite of the inverted sequence, has provided the only firm foothold in the colon.

proverb. All three words—"proverb," "mockery," and "enigmas"—are more at home in wisdom literature, but they could be stretched to cover the "woe oracles."

and. The difficulty in the MT lies with the conjunctions, literally: "proverb . . . and derision riddles." Only by taking liberties do we obtain "a taunt . . . satire and epigrams" (NEB). Partial relief is secured by emending the noun to a verb *yhwdw*: "A proverb they will raise // and a taunt they will concoct."

derision. In between "proverb" and "enigmas," one would expect *mĕlîṣâ* to have similar connotation. The noun *mĕlîṣâ* occurs in the Hebrew Bible only here and in Prov 1:6. The verb means "scorn." The combination with "enigmas" represents a grammatical and a lexical problem. The grammaitcal problem at this point has usually been identified as the juxtaposition of two absolute nouns with no readily discovered relation between them. If the two nouns are coordinated, why no "and"? To solve the lexical problem, Haak's (1991:60) translation "and his ambassador (will lift up) a 'riddle' " derives from parsing *mlyṣh* as the *Hip'il* participle with the archaic third-person-singular masculine suffix (used in Hab 1:9, 15). This will not get us very far until we can work out who that ambassador might be and how he fits into the scenario. 1QpHab apparently read a participle *mlyṣy*: "and those who make scornful epigrams" or "those who interpret riddles." The 1QpHab variant *mlyṣy* (plural construct participle) was seen by Elliger (1953:53) as a trite softening of the hiatus between the two nouns. The resultant construct phrase was parsed as complement of the subject of the preceding verb, so that those who railed at the proverb were also explainers of riddles (García Martínez and Tigchelaar 1997:17). Segert (1953) took a hint from the *defective* spelling of the suffixed preposition *'lw* twice in v 5 in 1QpHab to read *mlyṣw* with the same spelling. By supplying a verb to the second colon, Segert, according to Brownlee (1959:55) arrived at:

> Shall not they all take up a parable against him?
> And his scorners speak riddles with regard to him?

Haak (1991:60), however, takes the participle as singular, normalizes the verb to singular number, and takes the second colon as gapped:

> Upon him a 'mashal' he will lift up,
> and his ambassador (will lift up) a 'riddle'

Brownlee (1979:130) took the antecedent of this supposed suffix to be the *mashal*:

> Will they not all intone a burden concerning him?
> and its composers taunt him with riddles / as they sing:

Qumran scholars are now less impetuous in considering *waw* and *yod* to be interchangeable, and the reading *mlyṣy* is now preferred. Even if 1QpHab is to be preferred to MT for this word, the translations already given show that there is no agreement about what it means: scoffer, ambassador, composer? The participle itself enjoyed some currency at Qumran, enough to explain its replacement of *mlyṣh*. At Qumran, it meant "interpreter" rather than "slanderer."

Apart from all that, the word *mĕlîṣâ* cannot be impeached, since the same trio, in the same sequence, occurs in Prov 1:6. There the phrase *māšāl ûmĕlîṣâ* supports the retention of MT in v 6b. The grammatical problem is solved once it is recognized that the object *māšāl ûmĕlîṣâ* is a discontinuous coordination noun-phrase wrapped around the verb. Since the other terms are generic, it is probably pushing the etymology too far to say that a *mĕlîṣâ* is "a saying laden with satire, sarcasm, and innuendo" (*NIDOTTE* 2:799).

enigmas. These utterances are called *ḥîdôt*, "riddles." In wisdom literature, a *ḥîdâ* is an enigma (Prov 1:6), an obscure saying that the listener is challenged to unravel (1 Kgs 10:1). Riddles are found in stories (Judg 14:13). This set of "woe oracles" does not have the traditional form of *ḥîdôt*, so the use of the term here could be a hint that these "woe oracles" are not to be taken literally, but are in some kind of code. It is recognized in Num 12:8 that the LORD's oracles might be couched in enigmas, plain speech being reserved for a privileged person, such as Moses. In a loose sense, straightforward moral teachings might be called *ḥîdôt* because of their poetic form (Ps 49:5), just as the companion word *māšāl* can mean "simile," "proverb," "poem," or "poetic oracle"—almost any literary composition.

COMMENT

In trying to understand the accumulation of the vocabulary of wisdom discourse when referrring to prophetic messages, we might ask if the cycle of "woe oracles" is an anti-Babylonian manifesto, subversive in character and, like later apocalypses, dangerous to whoever wrote and circulated it. The Chaldeans themselves are not named, as they are in Hab 1:6. Cannon (1925:83) suggested that Hab 2:5–20 was written by Habakkuk and added to the previous vision some time after the shattering events of 597 B.C.E., when Jehoiakin had been deported to Babylon and the Chaldean triumph was complete. To make the message a little safer, its true intent was veiled under mysterious and oblique language. If this was intended to prevent the oppressive Babylonians from seeing the real point, we also, as outsiders, are likewise ignorant of the code.

   This indirect strategy could be why, on the surface, many of the "woe oracles" seem to be denunciations of persons who do things that are described as individual crimes. The fourth "woe oracle" is a good example, for most of it can be explained in terms of the abuse of one individual by another. But underneath this language, it is easy to make the metaphorical application to a nation as an oppressor. This scholarship raises the question of whether specific historical individuals are in mind in these vituperations and whether the atrocities described in the "woe oracles" can be identified with any known historical events. Perhaps such a quest is bound to be futile; for if it succeeds, it shows that the attempt to conceal the accusations under "riddles" has failed. Some examples may be given. The reference to "the lawlessness of Lebanon" (v 17) is not clear, in spite of the familiarity of the name. And what does it mean to say that "the lawlessness of Lebanon will cover thee" (v 17)? Can we identify the city whose builder is execrated in the third "woe oracle"? Or the city whose massacred inhabitants are bewailed in vv 8b and 17b? Does the pillaging described in the first "woe oracle" refer to the removal of royal and temple treasures from Jerusalem in 597 B.C.E.? And so on.

   The difficulty of making these "woe oracles" fit what we know about the Chaldeans in any convincing way has led some scholars to declare that they do not apply to the Chaldeans at all or at least only in part. Kuenen (1892:373) eliminated all but the first "woe oracle" as later additions, not applicable to the Chaldeans, and subsequent scholars have argued the point in other ways. The consensus seems to be that the whole set can be applied to the Chaldeans as the Judeans experienced them in the early sixth century B.C.E. more readily than it can be fitted into any other situation. But they need not have been freshly composed for this application. These "woe oracles" are so general, the crimes that they denounce are so perennial, that they could be appropriate in many times and situations. They could have been available as set pieces, part of the stock-in-trade of moralists, and in this sense "proverbs" already familiar to the hearers. In this regard, the "woe oracles" are a mix of bywords about individuals (such as the person who makes his friend drunk) that the prophet, in his comments, can extend by analogy to nations (v 8).

Apart from these details, the question remains unanswered: Who is saying the words of v 6a? They could be editorial, that is, spoken to the reciter as an explanation of what is happening. It is not likely that these taunts are to be uttered defiantly against the tyrant by the conquered nations in his hearing. It is more likely that they predict that the downfall of the tyrant will provide material for bywords and clever sayings. In particular, great calamities provided similes for later times. The destruction of Sodom and Gomorrah is a pertinent example. Compare Hos 10:14, which reports an event remembered only in the proverb. The prophets anticipate a time when the old clichés will be replaced by new ones, because even more spectacular events have occurred (see Jer 16:14–15).

VII.2. THE FIRST WOE ORACLE (2:6b–8)

6bB Woe to him who accumulated what is not his!
6bC   — for how long? —
6bD   and got rich with unpaid debts!
7aA Won't thy creditors suddenly rise up,
7aB   and (won't) those who agitate thee wake up?

7b   And thou shalt be loot for them.

8aA Because thou, thou didst plunder many nations,
8aB   all the other peoples will plunder thee;

8bA   *from the blood of humankind,*
      and the lawlessness of the land,
8bB   *the city, and all who live in it.*   ס

Scansion of the First Woe Oracle (2:6b–8)

		BEATS	SYLLABLES	BICOLON
6bAβ	*hôy hammarbeh lō'-lô 'ad-mātay*	4	9 ⎫	
6bB	*ûmakbîd 'ālāyw 'abṭîṭ*	3	7 ⎭	16
7aA	*hălô' peta' yāqûmû nōšĕkeykā*	4	9 ⎫	
7aB	*wĕyiqṣû mĕza'zĕ'eykā*	2	7 ⎭	16
7b	*wĕhāyîtā limĕšissôt lāmô*	3	10	
8aA	*kî 'attâ šallôtā gôyīm rabbîm*	4	9 ⎫	
8aB	*yĕšollûkā kol-yeter 'ammîm*	3	7 ⎭	16
8bA	*middĕmê 'ādām waḥămas-'ereṣ*	3	9 ⎫	
8bB	*qiryâ wĕkol-yōšĕbê bāh*	3	8 ⎭	17

INTRODUCTION

"Woe oracles" are characterized by the use of an interjection like *hôy* or *ʾôy* (or, less frequently, *hô* or *ʾăhâ*). This formal clue does not take us very far in getting a handle on any given "woe oracle." There are four distinct dimensions to be investigated.

1. Content: What kind of person is the target of a "woe" pronouncement?
2. Affect: What emotions does the speaker express?
3. Performative speech act: What does a "woe oracle" *do?*
4. Time perspective.

A whole range of emotions can be expressed by such words—self-pity, commiseration or, in imprecations, a wish that another might suffer, or, in the event, a vindictive jeer at the wicked as they receive their deserts. To discern which of these moods prevail in Habakkuk's "woe oracles," we have to decide whether it predicts woes with sorrow or rejoices gleefully in their anticipated accomplishment. Or whether they are kept ready for the time when one can say, "It serves you right!"

Good (1966:279) explains *hôy* utterances as accusations lodged by the prophet in "a dialog in litigation form" to which Yahweh responds with a sentence of doom. Now it is true that "woe oracles" are often spoken out in the name of God; but here they are uttered by "all of them"; their use will be widespread. Hence the "woe oracles" would seem to be oracles supplied by God, but taken up to be used later after the prophet has published them. The victims thus deriding the fallen tyrant could be either all the Judeans or all the conquered nations.

Verse 8 of the first "woe oracle" shows that it stands at a point in time between when the tyrant plundered the nations and when the residual nations will plunder the tyrant.

There are nine colons in the first "woe oracle." Verse 6b is a bicolon (sixteen syllables); v 7a is a bicolon (eighteen syllables); v 8a is a bicolon (eighteen syllables); v 8b is a bicolon (seventeen syllables). This leaves only v 7b as an unpaired colon. Its central position is confirmed by the symmetrical arrangement of the other material around it. The quantities before and after are equal, measured by colons or syllables. Verse 7b is the only clause with a consecutive future verb in it, and this describes the ultimate outcome.

The four bicolons differ in the neatness of their internal parallelism. It is notable that the central block of five colons contains references in the second person. This further indication of symmetry suggests that the first and last bicolons go together, thus supplying v 8b with a connection that it would otherwise lack.

NOTES

6b. *accumulated.* There are ten participles in the cycle, two for each "woe oracle." This feature itself is enough to indicate that the composition is well planned and well preserved. Only the first participle in the series has the definite article.

Its genuineness should not be doubted just for that reason. Indeed, it probably secures an important effect. A definite article on each of the participles would make them into a list. But only one culprit is in mind in each "woe oracle." The participles within each "woe oracle" are synonymous or correlative in pairs. The definite article on the first participle blankets all ten, showing that all five woes are addressed to the same person. This observation agrees with v 6a, which says that the sayings are "about him."

how long? It is understandable that these words have been deleted by many scholars, for they have no evident grammatical or thematic connection with their context, and they spoil the rhythm. As an interjection, they echo the concern expressed in the opening prayer.

got rich. The root *kbd* is associated with ideas of heaviness, glory, or wealth. The *Hipʿil* is not common. It can be used intransitively as elative: A becomes excessively rich (much the same as reflexive: A makes himself [ʿālāyw] rich). As a monotransitive causative, it would mean "make heavy": A makes B rich. If doubly transitive: A makes B rich with C. The prepositional phrase "upon himself," if reflexive, would indicate that this person "loads himself down with debts"—that is, with other people's indebtedness to him. If, however, the root *kbd* retains more of its literal meaning of "heavy," v 6bD could be referring to the injustice of weighing people down with heavy debts. There could be a subtle double entendre here, laying the foundation for the working out of *jus talionis.* The idea is that the plunderer, enriching himself through his victims' pledges, becomes a debtor to his victims. The victims are called his "creditors" in v 7. What is "not his" is not seen as stolen property to be returned, but as a debt to be paid. A major objection to this interpretation is that the primary reference of *ʿabṭîṭ* is a pledge. The metaphor does not work if plunder is equated with a pledge (security for a loan), for there is nothing matching the loan. BDB (p. 716a) recognizes both possibilities. Hence JB renders "loads himself with pledges." This reading suggests that the target of the first "woe oracle" is (figured as) a very successful moneylender, and even that he finds ways of retaining the pledges indefinitely, making them his own property.

debts (or "pledges"). The word *ʿabṭîṭ* occurs only here in the Hebrew Bible, but other words with the same root show that it has to do with property mortgaged in lieu of payment of debt. Budde (1931:411) suggested *ʿăbōṭôt.* If the creditor enjoys perfect usufruct as interest, the owner is totally deprived of his livelihood. Such an antichretic mortgage was abhorred in Israelite social ethics. It would represent the last stages of destitution. In ancient imperialism, the relationship of a vassal state to a suzerain was viewed in a similar way. The subject people was considered a tenant of its creditor on its own farm. The complaint that the foreigner "eats" our substance discloses this, for "eat" is the technical term for "have the usufruct of" (*akālu* [CAD]). This connection enables us to see more exactly that the culprit here becomes rich, not so much by holding on to pledges, as by enjoying the produce of mortgaged lands. At least we can say that the abuse is not just economic exploitation distinct from the imperialism of v 8a, or even a simile for the annexation of territory. The heavy trib-

ute did in fact reduce conquered nations to bankruptcy. What was called rent
(the imperialists described it as a "gift"!) was just long-term plunder.

7. *thy creditors.* In this verse the speaker addresses the tyrant. The *nešek* is the
"bite," a crippling initial payment (or a deduction from the capital of the loan), distinct from the loan (Driver 1902:266). This has the effect of making the interest
effectively higher. The *nôšēk*, "biter," is the one with all the money. The activity
of a *nôšēk*, "one who requires interest on a loan," was forbidden to an Israelite, at
least as far as his compatriots were concerned. Loans were to be interest free. This
meaning of the root is not entirely certain (BDB 675). The parallel "agitators" is not
a synonym. It would be better if these avengers were identified as former victims of
Babylonian oppression. They cannot be called "those who make thee infirm" until
after they have reduced Babylon to debility (Ecc 12:3). Passives would serve:

> Those whom thou hast forced to pay interest will rise up,
> And those whom thou hast caused to tremble will wake up.

Haak (1991:64), following Dahood, plays with the possibility that *nšk* has its literal meaning with the parallel *měza'zě'eykā* supplying the bark that goes with
the bite:

> Will not those who are biting you . . . get up,
>   those who are howling at you awake? (60)

He even speculates that the avengers are the forces of the underworld. There is
no need to grow metaphors out of metaphors in this way.

loot. This is the only occurrence of the plural *měšissôt*, which is probably intended to be majestic. The picture is more coherent if the plunderers of Babylon are to be the former victims, and not, as it proved in the event, the Persians.
And they did not plunder Babylon. Verse 8a does not settle this point, for "all
the left-over of peoples" could mean either nations that Babylon did not conquer or the survivors of nations that Babyon did conquer.

8. *plunder . . . plunder.* The repeated verbs bring out the poetic justice in the
events. It is not usual to use the free form of the pronoun with a perfect verb.
The effect is to emphasize "thou." The plunderer himself will be plundered by
his victims. The imperfect verb at the beginning of the second clause could be
jussive: "let the nations plunder thee!"

other peoples. The meaning of *yeter* is not clear. It might seem appropriate
for roles to be reversed. It is possible that those robbed by Babylon become its
creditors (v 7) and those Babylon plundered will plunder it. "All the surplus of
peoples" would then be the remnant population of conquered nations. But the
"left-over" peoples could be the nations that Babylon did not conquer.

blood. The connections of v 8b remain undetermined. The same problem occurs in v 17b. The introverted structure of the first "woe oracle" suggests that v
8b goes with v 6b. In this context, "blood(s)" in parallel with "lawlessness" probably means "murder" (cf. Hab 1:17). There is no way of telling what this "land"

and "city" might be. It is stretching the grammar a bit to make "lawlessness" govern all three following nouns. The sequence "humankind," "land," "city," and "inhabitants" is chiastic. This list suggests that the city and its inhabitants are the objects of murder and lawlessness. It is possible that the thought of v 8b is echoed in v 12, but there the city is built with murder, not destroyed.

COMMENT

The first "woe oracle" is a typical case of poetic justice. Verse 7 seems to be part of the same prediction. Nevertheless, the connections among the several parts of this "woe oracle" are not easy to trace. This difficulty has several aspects. First, there is an incongruity between the image of plundering by conquest (v 8a) and that of getting rich on unredeemed pledges (v 7b). Second, there is a difference between the statement in v 8 and the question in v 7. Third, the connections of "How long?" are not plain; the words in v 6b make a good (a better) bicolon without them. There is a change from third to second person. Finally, v 8b, which is only a long noun phrase, has no obvious connection with anything else.

These difficulties are not insuperable. Although they cannot all be resolved with equal satisfaction, some progress can be made. The sin that is condemned has two aspects. The person denounced has grown rich by plunder and fraud. The looting of the nations (v 8a) is a theme closer to the prayers in Habakkuk 1 than getting rich on pledges. The punishment also fits the former and not the latter. This match suggests that the reference to getting rich on pledges (v 6b) is a figure for plunder by conquest. The catchphrase "not his" is common to both images (cf. Hab 1:6b with Hab 2:6b). The *mashal* is, then, "A nation that accumulates territories not its own is like a person who gets rich on unredeemed pledges." If the pledge is real estate (the commonest asset in the ancient Near East), then both parts of the comparison contain the idea that land is inalienable. If the reference to debt is a figure for an international sin, then there is no reference within this "woe oracle" to domestic wrongs in Judah.

VII.3. THE SECOND WOE ORACLE (2:9–11)

9aA   Woe to him who becomes rich with fraudulent profits . . . †→
9aB   — Let evil come to his estate! —
9bA   to put his nest on the height,
9bB   and to make himself secure from the fist of evil . . . ‡→

10aA   Thou didst scheme!
10aB   — Let shame come to thine estate! —

10bA   →‡ . . . to cut off many peoples.
10bB   →† . . . and thy soul is sinful.

11a   *For a stone from the wall will cry out,*
11b   *and a beam from the woodwork will echo it.*   פ

Scansion of the Second Woe Oracle (2:9–11)

		BEATS	SYLLABLES	BICOLON	
9aA	*hôy bōṣēaʿ beṣaʿ . . . † →*	3	4 ⎫	8 + 5	
9aB	*rāʿ lĕbêtô*	2	4 ⎭		
9bA	*lāśûm bammārôm qinnô*	3	7 ⎫	14 + 6	
9bB	*lĕhinnāṣēl mikkap-rāʿ . . . ‡ →*	2	7 ⎭		
10a	*yāʿaṣtā bōšet lĕbêtekā*	3	6		
10bA	*→ ‡ . . . qĕṣôt ʿammîm rabbîm*	2	6		
10bB	*→ † . . . wĕḥôṭēʾ napšekā*	2	5		
11a	*kî-ʾeben miqqîr tizʿāq*	3	6 ⎫	14	פ
11b	*wĕkāpîs mēʿēṣ yaʿănennâ*	3	8 ⎭		

INTRODUCTION

On first reading, this "woe oracle" seems to be incoherent. It is impossible to find continuous sense in it. Investigators might do one of three things in such a case. They could abandon the text as incorrigibly corrupt; they could try to repair it; or they could take it as it is, making as much sense as they can and accepting the incoherence as an artistic effect, as befits the emotional, almost hysterical character of such an outburst. When such similar outcomes might result from such diverse causes, it is well-nigh impossible to work out which of the causes was at work in each particular instance. Any one explanation by itself is not likely to solve all the problems. All three responses to the problems of the text can be combined. Some corrections could be ventured, and some corruptions left because they are now beyond recovery. Then we must make the best we can of what we have.

The best clue to understanding the composition is supplied by the fact that every statement has a parallel, but many of the matching pairs are not contiguous. And two staccato curses are inserted into other clauses.

The parallelism in v 11 is evident, although there are problems when it comes to details, and its connections with the rest of the "woe oracle" are unclear. Verse 9b is also a good bicolon, making a single complex idea. The main difficulties lie in v 10, which differs from the rest in being addressed to the miscreant in the second person.

The accusation is: "Thou didst scheme." There seems to be two sides to this:

1. He planned to cut off many nations, a concern of the entire prophecy.
2. He tried to make himself secure by building a nest on a high point.

The language of v 11 suggests that a material edifice is in mind; it is not a metaphor for something abstract, and the "woe oracle" expects this structure to be destroyed. We suggest that the corresponding imprecation is found in the colons:

Evil to his house!
Shame to thy house!

These ejaculations have no grammatical connection with their context.

The opening reproach (v 9) speaks of the acquisition of unjust gain. This would be a social crime, and perhaps a domestic, not an international, one, if it were just a matter of violent exploitation. Such an interpretation seems to owe too much to the belief that Habbakuk is concerned about social wrongs within Judah. This could be so, or at least part of the larger picture. The word "house" is quite ambiguous in this respect. But the building of a secure "house" could be a way of describing imperialistic aggression, whereas cutting off many nations could hardly be an image for the acquisition of unjust gain within Judah. We conclude that only one matter is in mind and that the "woe oracle" is directed against a foreign conqueror. The poetic justice in his fate is seen in the fact that his attempts to escape the paw of the evil one will not succeed. Evil will come to his house. Because *mārôm* has connotations of pride, shame will come to his house.

The recognition that "Evil to his house!" and "Shame to thy house!" are parenthetical eases the strain on the text considerably. It does not make sense to say "Thou didst scheme shame for thy house." It does make sense to say "Thou didst scheme . . . to cut off many nations." Similarly, v 9a is improved when *bōṣēaʿ beṣaʿ* is recognized as a complete statement, and "Evil to his house!" is parenthetical.

In every "woe oracle" in Habakkuk 2, there are two participles in parallel. Here the second participle has to be found in the later phrase "sinning (against) thine own life," which has completely baffled commentators.

In the second "woe oracle," then, we have poetry that is neither lyrical nor classical in form, but, contrariwise, nervous, disjointed, and rough in its grammar. There are no indications, however, that these features are either defects in composition or blemishes caused by careless scribes. At least, there is now no obvious way of improving or correcting what we have.

NOTES

9. *fraudulent profits*. The cognate object is used several times with the verb √*bṣ ʿ*. This language need not necessarily be a reference to dishonest business practices. The associations of the root are with both greed and lawlessness, often with money as the gain. The only specific statement in the "woe oracle" is the reference to "many peoples." The first "woe oracle" is similar to this one in using the exploitive imposition of excessive interest payments on the indigent as a metaphor for the crippling imposition of tribute on conquered nations. Calling tribute "profits" is a sarcastic metaphor. The parallel "sinning fatally" to "gaining gain" shows that this is not legitimate commerce.

estate. The word "house" could refer to the conqueror's empire or to his personal residence. We choose "estate" to allow for either possibility.

nest. The nest on the height could be a continuation of the image of the eagle (1:8). The figure is used in other places in the Hebrew Bible. It can describe a mountain stronghold (Num 24:21; Jer 49:16; Obadiah 4), and v 9bB suggests that this is what is meant here.

fist. The choice of *kap* rather than *yad* reflects a detail in Hebrew anatomical terminology that is not always appreciated. While conventionally translated as "hand," *yad* includes the forearm, with *kap* distinguished by the conventional "palm." The *yad* is used to deliver a blow. It suggests strength and is often translated as "power." The *kap* is used for clutching. To deliver from someone's hand can be protective; to deliver from the "palm" or "paw" is to rescue captives and to recover stolen property. The word "evil" is used twice in this verse, but the thought runs backward if "evil to his house" is a curse. He puts his nest on a height, in order to be safe from harm, but harm will come to his house just the same. Verse 11 then describes the destruction of this stronghold.

10. *Thou didst scheme.* As already pointed out, it is not likely that anyone would scheme "shame" for his house. But the plan to conquer many nations was the intention of the Chaldeans throughout Habakkuk 1.

to cut off. The infinitival form *qĕṣôt* is difficult. Is it a gerund (Driver 1874: § 205)? LXX retrojects to a finite verb *qāṣîtā* or even *qāṣôtā.*

11. *stone.* The usual correlate of *'eben* is *'ēṣ;* but these words are not matched in this verse unless there is chiasmus. This could be claimed were it not for the *mem*'s in *miqqîr* and *mē'ēṣ,* for the meaning *'ēṣ,* "woodwork," is strained. The difficulty lies in the word *kāpîs,* which is *hapax legomenon* in the Hebrew Bible. It is apparently a solid piece of dressed timber. While "rafter" is possible, it could refer to a strengthening crossbeam in a wall structure. The phrase then means "beam (made) from a tree."

cry out. As in Hab 1:2, this verb expresses a call for redress, not a cry of exultation over the downfall of the tyrant. If the building materials plead for justice, the idea is quaint. They are witnesses to the unjust gains of the condemned; what he meant for splendor is proof of his rapacity (cf. v 12). If a Judean is in mind, Shallum (Jehoahaz) or perhaps his successor, Jehoiakim, is a good candidate (Jer 22:11–17).

echo. It is God who should answer a cry for justice. Here the rafter is not responding to the stone; it is joining in, making an antiphon. The wood and stone bear united witness against the tyrant.

VII.4. THE THIRD WOE ORACLE (2:12–14)

12a   Woe to him who built a town with blood,
12b   and established a city with iniquity!

13a   Isn't this—Behold!—from Yahweh Sebaoth?

13bA   And peoples labored only for fire,
13bB   and nations only for nothing exhausted themselves.

14a   *But the earth will be filled with the knowledge of the glory of Yahweh,*
14b   *as the waters cover the sea.*   ◌

Scansion of the Third Woe Oracle (2:12–14)

		BEATS	SYLLABLES	BICOLON
12a	*hôy bōneh ʿîr bĕdāmîm*	4	7 ⎫	
12b	*wĕkônēn qiryâ bĕ ʿawlâ*	3	8 ⎭	15
13aA	**hălôʾ hinnēh mē ʾēt yhwh ṣĕbāʾôt**	5	11	
13bA	*wĕyîgĕ ʿû ʿammîm bĕdê ʾēš*	3	9 ⎫	
13bB	*ûlĕ ʾummîm bĕdê-rîq yī ʾāpû*	3	10 ⎭	19
14a	*kî timmālēʾ hā ʾāreṣ lāda ʿat ʾet-kĕbôd yhwh*	6	13 ⎫	
14b	*kammayim yĕkassû ʿal-yām*	3	7 ⎭	20 ◌

INTRODUCTION

This is the shortest and simplest of the "woe oracles." It is possible that v 14 does not belong in it at all. Its ideas are not used elsewhere in Habakkuk—the earth (meaning the whole world), the knowledge of God, the glory of Yahweh—and its weight is entirely eschatological. Verse 14 has no obvious connection with the rest of this "woe oracle"; thus it is hard to think why anyone would have put it in at this point. It is identical in content with Isa 11:9, but there are numerous small verbal differences. Verse 20 might be a similar comment intended to give finality to the "woe oracles" as a whole. Verse 14 is the least poetic of all the materials in the "woe oracles" as far as rhythms are concerned, although it has a majestic effect of its own.

The remaining five colons consist of two well-made bicolons, with v 13a in the middle. Verse 12 has complete synonymous parallelism with a perfect ABC // A′B′C′ pattern. Verse 13b also has complete synonymous parallelism, with the pattern ABC // B′C′A′. The placement of the verb at the end of the second colon strikes a note of finality for the whole and is a further reason for regarding v 14 as not part of this "woe oracle" proper. The question in v 13a is unintelligible, even if *hnh* can be read (with the versions) as "this" or "these." For what are "these" things that are "from Yahweh *ṣĕbāʾôt*"?

The third "woe oracle" indicts the one who builds a city by murder. This culprit could be a tyrant king in his own realm or a world conqueror. For the first, "house" is a palace; for the second, an empire. The reference to "nations" in v 13b points to the latter, so the city in question would be Babylon. Yet no corresponding destruction of this city is forecast; the burning of the peoples is described in v 13b, but this cannot be their just punishment. The sympathies of

Habakkuk are entirely with these victims (1:17; 2:8, 10). The implied punishment would be the burning of the bloody city. Only in a general manner can this "woe oracle" be made coherent, and then a lot has to be supplied. Even the wickedness of the tyrant (v 12) is under the sovereign rule of Yahweh (v 13a). In due time, all nations will come to the same end, and beyond the wreckage of history (v 13b) the glory of Yahweh will wash over it all (v 14).

NOTES

12. *built a town.* The foundation of a city was often seen in the Hebrew Bible as an act of political arrogance, the act of a person who lives away from God, such as Cain (Gen 4:17) and Nimrod (Gen 10:11). The oppressive Pharaoh was a city-builder (Exod 1:11). God's disapproval of such enterprises is revealed in the Babel story (Genesis 11).

with blood. The preposition is instrumental. The plural "bloods" points to murder.

iniquity. The word translated as "iniquity" can refer to a wide range of wickedness. The same parallelism is met in Mic 3:10, where the city is Jerusalem. The blood could be that of a foundation sacrifice:

Mic 3:10a	*bōneh ṣiyyôn bĕdāmîm*	He who built Zion with blood,
10b	*wîrûšālēm bĕ 'awlâ*	and Jerusalem with wickedness.
Hab 2:12a	*bōneh 'îr bĕdāmîm*	He who built a city with blood,
12b	*wĕkônēn qiryâ bĕ 'awlâ*	and who founded a city with wickedness.

13. *this.* It requires no change in the consonants to read *hēnnâ,* "they," instead of *hinnēh,* "behold." But it is still difficult to find a feminine plural referent for the pronoun in the context. If it were not for the use of *hălō'* to make a rhetorical question, *hinnēh* could serve as a predicator, meaning "it is." There is a familiar formula in the historical books—"And the rest of the deeds of X, *behold* they are written" (*hinnām kĕtûbîm* . . . [1 Kgs 14:19; 2 Kgs 15:11, 15, 26, 31]) or "are they not written . . ." (*hălō' hēmmâ kĕtûbîm* . . . [1Kgs 11:41; 14:29; 15:7, 23, 31; 16:5, 14, 20, 27; 22:39]).

Two formulas are used in the books of Kings and Chronicles to refer to sources. *Hinnām* is used preponderantly in Chronicles. The combination *hălō' hinnām* occurs once (2 Chr 25:26). This could be enough to endorse the same combination here. Nevertheless, emendation to *hēnnâ,* "these things," is widely favored.

In the most general terms, what has come "from Yahweh *ṣĕbā'ôt*" is the set of "woe oracles" in which this question is embedded. But because Habakkuk does not otherwise use this name for God, the clause is rightly suspected of being a gloss.

peoples. Verse 13b has a perfection in its poetic form rarely met in prophetic writing. In itself, it is perfectly clear. As a statement of fact, it could be a merely sententious observation that all the efforts of humankind come to nothing in the end. As a prediction, it forecasts the fate of all nations. Yet what this bicolon is doing in the rest of the "woe oracle" is unclear. Throughout the prophecy, "the peoples" are seen as the helpless victims of Chaldean aggression. The burning of all their achievements is an injustice, not a punishment. It would be necessary to supply many missing links in the chain of argument to join v 13b with v 12. Babylon has been built by slaying nations (1:17)—"with blood" (v 12a). Captives as numerous as the sand (2:9) have been used in the construction projects (v 12b), wearing themselves out. The "iniquity" in v 12b would then be the slave labor of v 13bB. All for nothing. Babylon will be burned, not to punish the "peoples" mentioned in v 13, but the "builder" of v 12. Only in this indirect sense will the nations get their own back on their oppressor. Some support for this kind of interpretation is gained from the similar relationships between the opulent conqueror of the first "woe oracle" and the *gôyīm // 'ammîm* he has plundered (with mention also of "bloods" and a city [*qiryâ*]) and in building projects that involve the destruction of "many peoples" in the second "woe oracle."

There is a development in the vocabulary:

 5   *kol-haggôyīm // kol-hā'ammîm*
 8   *gôyīm rabbîm // kol-yeter 'ammîm*
10   *'ammîm rabbîm*
13   *'ammîm // lĕ'ummîm*

This progression provides links among the first three "woe oracles."
Hab 2:13b is almost identical to Jer 51:58:

Hab 2:13bA   *wĕyîgĕ'û 'ammîm bĕdê 'ēš*
             and labored peoples only for fire

Jer 51:58bA   *wĕyīgĕ'û 'ammîm bĕdê rîq*
             and labored peoples only for nothing

Hab 2:13bB   *ûlĕ'ummîm bĕdê-rîq yî'āpû*
             and nations only for nothing were exhausted

Jer 51:58bB   *ûlĕ'ummîm bĕdê-'ēš wĕyā'ēpû*
             and nations only for fire and were exhausted

The verbal variations are interesting. The verbs and nouns come in the same sequence in both places. The parallel *lĕ'ummîm* is a poetic word, usually plural, and usually a B parallel to *gôyīm* or *'ammîm*. The verbs similarly are synonyms. Neither of them is exclusively poetic, but they are often used as a poetic pair, with *yg'* usually first, as here. Isa 40:28–31 is a famous example. In that text the sequence varies, and the variations secure a more extended rhetorical pattern.

These variations restrain normalization of the final verb in Jeremiah to the easier reading of Habakkuk. There is no need to invoke a separate clause for this verb in Jeremiah: Habakkuk's version shows that. The *wāw*-consecutive with the suffixed verb at the end of Jer 51:58 makes a good parallel with the prefixed verb. Literal translation, as in KJV, is unnecessary. The *wāw*-consecutive goes with the verb (it is part of its morphology) and does not have to be first in the clause. It is notable that *y'pw* is spelled defectively in Habakkuk, while *yg'w* is defective in Jeremiah. Here the evidence of the Habakkuk *pešer* from Qumran is important, for it reads *yg'w*. This is so different from Qumran practice of going for *plene* spellings that a strong tradition may be suspected. Of course, a reading *yy'pw* could lie behind Jeremiah's reading. But it is also possible that it was the *defective* spelling of the prefixed form that led to its wrong identification as suffixed.

While certainty is unattainable in instances like this, the appearance of such a nice bicolon in two distinct contexts suggests that both Habakkuk and Jeremiah are quoting a byword, not that one is quoting the other. If each quotation is apt, Jeremiah's clearer association of the saying with the fall of Babylon supports our suspicion that Habakkuk is talking about the same thing.

14. The difficulty of finding a place for v 14 in the third "woe oracle," or in the whole cycle for that matter, has already been noted. It sounds like a slogan that could be put in anywhere. Another version occurs in Isa 11:9:

Isaiah	*ky-ml'h h'rṣ d'h 't-yhwh kmym lym mksym*
	For the earth is full of the knowledge of Yahweh as the waters cover the sea.
Habakkuk	*ky-tml' h'rṣ ld't 't-kbwd yhwh kmym yksw 'l-ym*
	For the earth will be full of knowledge of the glory of Yahweh as the waters cover the sea.

The eschatological setting of Isa 11:9 is more appropriate for such a scenario than the "woe oracles" of Habakkuk. Habakkuk's version is amplified, and the grammar is less poetic. Driver (1874: §135.7) has an interesting observation on the use of the definite article with the participle. When it is lacking, as in Isa 11:9, the participle is more verbal, allowing the "object" to precede. He considers Hab 2:14 to be an "imitation" that "is satisfied to use an ordinary Hebrew idiom." All the verb forms have been changed to commoner usage, and the word "glory" has been added.

A place for Hab 2:14 in the book as a whole can be found once the occurrence of the same verbs (in chiasmus) is noticed in Hab 3:3. There, however, it is the sky that is covered with the LORD's splendor (*hôd* matches *kābôd*). If v 14, embedded in the "woe oracles," is intended to supply a point to which Habakkuk 3 could be attached, then the fulfillment of the "woe oracles" is to be achieved by a theophany of the kind described in the ancient poem that is reworked in Habakkuk 3.

VII.5. THE FOURTH WOE ORACLE (2:15–17)

15aA	Woe to him who made his neighbor drink,
15aBα	who poured out his anger,
15aBβ	and even made him drunk —
15b	so as to gaze on their nakedness!

16aA Thou didst satiate thyself with shame instead of glory.

16aB	Drink, thou also! And expose thy nakedness!
16bA	The cup in Yahweh's right hand will circulate to thee,
16bB	and shameful vomit upon thy glory.
17aA	For the lawlessness of Lebanon will cover thee,
17aB	and the devastation of beasts will terrify thee —
17bA	*from the blood of humankind,*
	and the lawlessness of the land,
17bB	*the city, and all who live in it.* ☐

Scansion of the Fourth Woe Oracle (2:15–17)

		BEATS	SYLLABLES	BI(TRI)COLON
15aA	*hôy mašqēh rēʿēhû*	3	6	
15aB	*mĕsappēaḥ ḥămātĕkā wĕʾap šakkēr*	4	11	26
15b	*lĕmaʿan habbîṭ ʿal-mĕʿôrêhem*	3	9	
16aA	*śābaʿtā qālôn mikkabôd*	3	7	
16aB	*šĕtēh gam-ʾattâ wĕhēʿārēl*	3	9	
16bA	*tissôb ʿaleykā kôs yĕmîn yhwh*	5	9	26
16bB	*wĕqîqālôn ʿal-kĕbôdekā*	2	8	
17aA	*kî ḥāmas lĕbānôn yĕkassekkā*	4	9	17
17aB	*wĕšōd bĕhēmôt yĕḥîtan*	3	8	
17bA	*middĕmê ʾādām waḥămas-ʾereṣ*	3	7	15 ☐
17bB	*qiryâ wĕkol-yōšĕbê bāh*	3	8	

INTRODUCTION

The fourth "woe oracle" is in several respects the best organized of the five. The sin is clearly identified, and the appropriate punishment is a familiar instance of poetic justice. He who makes his neighbor drunk in order to expose his nakedness for lewdness or worse, will have the same done to him. This pattern unifies vv 15–16 at least. The contrast between glory and shame receives special attention in v 16. The connection with v 17 is less obvious. The formula in v 17b has already been used in v 8b and could be extraneous. The use of the verb "cover" in v 17 could contrast with the theme of exposure in vv 15–16. A contrast is secured in the use of the preposition ʿal in the phrases "upon their nakedness" and "upon thy glory."

There are connections with the rest of the prophecy. The lawlessness and destruction that will cover the tyrant correspond to the destruction and lawlessness about which Habakkuk complained in his first prayer (1:3). The similarity of the phrase *'ap šakkēr* (v 15) and *'ap kî hayyayin* (v 5) cannot be a coincidence; regrettably, both phrases are obscure. The verb "gaze" (*habbîṭ*) supplies an important theme in Habakkuk 1: the vileness of human eyes contrasts with the purity of God's eyes (1:13).

From the poetic point of view, the best bicolon is v 17a; it is a classic example of synonymous parallelism. Verse 16 is best construed as four colons. The first and fourth colons go together, with the same words "shame" and "glory." The second and third colons are clearly parallel, even though the verbal correspondences are not exact. The rhythms of v 15 are less clear. The two participial constructions constitute a bicolon, although the colons are quite short. The parallelism suggests that *ḥēmâ* is some kind of liquor, not "wrath," and from this it follows that *'ap* is "even," not "wrath," a parallel to *ḥēmâ*. The construction *wĕ'ap šakkēr* can then be joined to v 15b as its parallel, even though the two colons are quite unequal in length. The use of the conjunction "and" points to similar results. There are, nevertheless, many minor problems when it comes to details. The pronouns do not agree between "his neighbor" and "their nakedness."

NOTES

15. *neighbor.* The additional *yod* in 1QpHab could be leveling the noun to agree with the plural pronoun suffix in v 15b. But, as Horgan (1979:48) points out, the MT could have *defective* spelling of the plural stem and 1QpHab could be a Qumran *plene* spelling of the singular.

drink. This verb is used almost exclusively in *Hip'il*. The beverage is the second object of the doubly transitive verb, but the second object is often not specified, as here. In this verse the understood object can only be wine (cf. Hab 2:5). The following root *škr*, which also secures assonance in the consonants, confirms this.

It is easy to see why the sin denounced in this "woe oracle" has been considered personal and domestic rather than political and international. Taken literally, it applies to the depravity that the Israelites saw at its worst in Canaanite custom and the twin vices of drunkenness and homosexuality (Genesis 9), which gained such a hold on Samaria prior to its downfall (Isaiah 28). The Canaanite background might be the basis of the reference to Lebanon in v 17a. The use of the word "neighbor" takes us to the language of the law codes, for it means "fellow citizen." Condemnation of such activities among the Judeans of Habakkuk's day might well be intended, but the whole could be a metaphor of nation and nation. That this level of meaning is uppermost is proved by the use of the familiar image of the cup of judgment in the LORD's right hand (v 16). The making of one's "neighbor" drunk is, then, another way of describing the

Chaldeans' abuse of their victims, not perhaps to be taken literally. But the image of the fishing net is close to ancient picture of war captives in large hunting nets.

When the difficulties met in individual words and constructions in v 15 are compounded, heroic measures can reshape the text into something more manageable. The translation in NEB—"Woe betide you who make your companions drink the outpouring of your wrath, making them drunk, that you may watch their naked orgies!"—reflects the work of G. R. Driver (1951). MT *hôy mašqēh rē'ēhû měsappēaḥ ḥămātěkā wě'ap šakkēr* becomes *hôy mašqēh rē'ēyhû šēkār missepaḥ ḥămātěkā wě'appěkā*. Four words were changed, and one was moved.

poured out. If this is the meaning of √*sph*, it is the only occurrence of this verb. Elsewhere, √*sph* means "join." There are other words containing √*sph*; the noun *sāpîaḥ* refers to what grows uncultivated during the sabbatical year (Lev 25:5–11). If this growth comes from grain accidentally spilled, the idea might be extended to the spilling of a liquid. The apparent cognate *sěpîḥeyhā* (Job 14:19) is commonly emended to *sěpîḥâ*, understood by comparison with Arabic *safaḥa* to refer to a torrential downpour, even though "her outpouring" is acceptable. This is a long chain of inferences with weak links to carry the unique meaning √*sph*, "pour out." It is, however, appropriate in this context. But "pouring out wrath" is not such a good parallel to "make his neighbor drink." The pouring out of wrath is more typically an act of God than of a human king. An ingenious solution to this problem (Wellhausen 1893:165) is to delete the final *h* from *msph* (as dittograph with the next word) to obtain "from the basin of your fury." With *sap ḥēmâ* compare *sap-ra'al* (Zech 12:2), *kôs hattar'ēlâ*, "cup of staggering" (Isa 51:17–22), and *yayin tar'ēlâ* (Ps 60:5)—all to be identified with the cup in Yahweh's right hand mentioned in v 16. It would be premature and out of place to transfer this picture to the tyrant. Wellhausen's emendation is forbidden because each of the five "woe oracles" has two participles in parallel, so the participle *měsappēaḥ* should be retained. The same applies to Driver's (1951) emendation. If the oppressor is pouring out wine, not wrath, then *ḥēmâ* can be retained with its secondary meaning of a "hot liquid" or "poison." The whole may then be paraphrased: "He makes his neighbor drunk by pouring out drugged wine." The suffix "thy" does not seem to fit in with this, because elsewhere the participle constructions in the "woe oracles" are third person. But note "thy soul" in v 10. 1QpHab reads *ḥmtw*, "his wrath."

even. The vocable '*ap* can be an adverb meaning "even" or a noun meaning "anger." The first identification gains a little support from '*ap* in v 5, where "wine" is mentioned. The second is supported by the presence of *ḥēmâ*, "wrath," as a possible parallel, because these two words are a common pair. But '*ap* is usually first, as in Isa 63:3, 6:

wě'ābûs 'ammîm bě'appî	And I trod on them in my anger;
wa'ăšakkěrēm baḥămātî	and I stamped on them in my wrath. (Isa 63:6)

The collocation of *'ap* and *škr* in both Isa 63:3, 6 and Hab 2:15 should restrain emendation of both. The parallelism in Hab 2:15 can be explained if the third colon is very laconic. Parallel to *ḥēmâ*, *'ap* shares its suffix by double duty. (Driver [1951] wanted to supply it.) Parallel to a participle, *škr* could be an infinitive absolute. Comparison with Isa 63:3, 6 suggests that *ḥēmâ // 'ap* are instrumental, but the preposition *b-* has not been used in Habakkuk as it was there. They are not the objects of the verbs. None of the three verbs in v 15a has an explicit object. This result is not significantly altered if *'ap* means "even." A more serious difficulty arises because this common biblical image—intoxication as punishment inflicted in anger—is traditionally used to describe an act of God. This is less certain in this verse, where it seems to be the act of a wicked oppressor, not of a righteous judge, and a "woe oracle" is pronounced against him for it.

The intoxication is intended to lead to other vile acts of abuse. But if this is the motive, why does Habakkuk say it is done in "wrath"? Perhaps there is a hint, in the use of this language, that the oppressor is acting as though he were God. It would, however, probably be oversubtle to see in the tension in such opposite connotations of the chosen language an insinuation that the tyrant is taking upon himself a role reserved for God—that is, inflicting global disasters in wrath.

gaze. The gazing on "their" nakedness could be gloating over the humiliation of naked prisoners of war, taken off as slaves, but something closer to sexual licentiousness seems to be in mind. It is not captivity, but similar exposure that punishes such a sin. The language of v 16aA confirms this. Indeed, we suggest that vv 15b–16aA are a bicolon. It is satiation with such lasciviousness that is well called exchanging glory for shame.

16. *Thou didst satiate.* The past tense shows that this has been done. Scholars have not been comfortable with the parallelism of a suffixed verb *śāba'tā* followed by imperative *śēteh*, hence the alteration of the MT to *śĕba'* (Budde 1931:411). If that kind of parallelism is insisted on, it can be found if *śāba'tā* is a precative suffixed verb with the same force as an imperative. This is probably carrying parallelism too far; it assumes that Hebrew poets composed rather mechanically. Even so, a precative sense for a suffixed verb is acceptable when it has *wāw*-consecutive following an imperative verb. A *Vorlage* with the consecutive *wāw* would be sufficient and less drastic reconstruction, although this construction usually continues rather than precedes an imperative. The logic, however, is the wrong way around. Drink first, and then be satiated. The salient reading of the perfective aspect and indicative mood of the suffixed verb can be retained if v 16aA is the reason ("[Because] thou hast become glutted with inflicting shame on your victims instead of their glory") why the guilty one must now experience the same kind of humiliation. LXX *plēsmonēn. . . .* points to a noun, making the whole of v 16aA the object of the verb "drink!"

We conclude that 16aA is indicative; the words are not a warning, but a condemnation. The penalty comes as the word of command in vv 16aB–16bA, mak-

ing the verb that begins v 16b jussive. This leaves v 16aA as transitional between
v 15b and v 16aB.

shame. The noun *qālôn* is a general term for ignominy in contrast to "honor."
But it has associations with the shameful exposure of the sexual organs (Jer 13:26;
Nah 3:5). The language does not become more specific than this; there is no
way of telling what the prophet has in mind when he gives the enemy such a
reputation for depravity. A different word for "shame" (*bōšet*) is used in v 10. On
the exchange of glory for shame, see the NOTE on Hos 4:7 (AB 24:357).

drink. In this verse, the potion is certainly administered by God (cf. Jer 25:15,
27).

thou also. With *gam-'attâ*, compare *kî-'attâ* in v 8.

thy nakedness. If the verb is taken as it is, it means precisely "reveal the fact
that you are uncircumcized." This is the only occurrence of the *Nip'al* of this
root, so a rearrangement of the same consonants has been suggested: *h'rl → hr'l*,
"stagger!" a reading already present in 1QpHab and supported by LXX and other
versions (cf. Isa 51:17–22; Zech 12:2; Ps 60:5). This verb describes the staggering of an inebriate and so fits the imagery. Logically, the circulation of the cup
(v 16bA) should come before the drinking and exposure (or staggering). Either
the natural sequence of events is reversed or this is a distinct taunt.

vomit. The word *qîqālôn*, written as one word in the MT, is unique. No explanation of its derivation is to hand. The suggestion that it comes from √*qll*,
"curse" (BDB 887a), is not convincing; the morphological differences are too
great. Another proposal, that the first consonant is duplicated for intensification,
is equally unconvincing. In Semitic, it is the later, not the initial, radicals that
are so repeated. LXX reads *kai synēkhthē atimia epi tēn doksan sou*, "and shame
has (been) gathered upon your glory." This suggests a *Vorlage wayyiqqāwû qālôn*.
Because *qālôn* has already been used in this verse (v 16aA), in association with
kābôd (its common antonym), the same association could be present here. LXX,
using *atimia* twice, encourages this reading. The point can be conceded without changing the MT. The choice of *qîqālôn* clearly echoes *qālôn*, but with a
twist. We suggest that *qî* is a distinct word, "vomit," normally spelled *qy'* or *q'*.
The context of its use in Isa 28:8 supports this result, the more so if we accept
the emendation *h'rl → hr'l* in v 16aB. Perhaps an imperative verb √*qy'* should
be identified, to make a companion colon to v 16aB:

> Drink, you too, and stagger!
> Vomit shame over your glory!

This result invites a further look at the overall structure of v 16. Verses
16aB–16bA are closely linked by the theme of drinking, although the logic of
the action runs backward. If they are closely parallel, *tissôb* is probably jussive:

> Let the cup in Yahweh's right hand circulate to you!
> Drink (it), you too, and expose yourself (or stagger)!

Verses 16aA and 16bB are connectd by the ideas of shame and glory. Gluttony (*šābaʿtā*) is followed by nausea. The *qālôn* is first consumed (v 16aA), and then vomited (v 16bB).

17. Verse 17a seems to be a well-formed bicolon, but the details refuse to disclose their secret. "Lawlessness" and "devastation" are good parallels (Hab 1:3), but "beasts" is not a good match for "Lebanon." Indeed, neither of the phrases—"the lawlessness of Lebanon," "the devastation of beasts"—yields any clear meaning. If Lebanon is the mountain region, then *běhēmôt* could be a by-form of *bāmôt*, meaning "peaks." The etymology of both words supports this. Even so, there has been no mention of Lebanon, and there is no perceptible connection between Lebanon (let alone beasts) and the motif of drunkenness.

The reference to Lebanon has a plausible explanation in the activities of Nebuchadrezzar in taking cedar from Lebanon for his building projects. This is alluded to in Isa 14:8, where the cedars are relieved when the King of Babylon stops chopping them down:

Yes, the fir-trees rejoice over you,
and the cedars of Lebanon:
since you have been laid low,
no feller has come up against us.

Verse 17b is similarly extraneous, throwing doubt on the authenticity of the entire verse (see the NOTES on v 8b). The finishing touch in incomprehensibility is the unique form *yěḥîtan*. It is easy to emend it to something more normal, from the point of view of textbook grammar; *yěḥitteḳā* (cf. LXX and Syriac), "it will terrify you," enjoys wide favor and is, perhaps, the best we can do. 1QpHab is different again—*yḥth*, "he will terrify him"—and the general meaning is confirmed by the versions. The problem is the morphology. No hollow root *ḥ-t* is known, and the terminal *-n*, while possible (energic), is curious.

The two colons in v 17a share the unusual syntax of having the verb last in the clause. This suggests deliberate thought in the composition and restrains emendation until all other critical resources have been exhausted. The combination of *ḥms* and *šd* is unobjectionable and secures the combination of *lbnwn* and *bhmwt*. These two words are not semantic parallels, but a rare instance of an inverted construct chain: "the monstrous beasts of Lebanon." The mythic associations of Lebanon are wide and ancient. They are prominient in the *Epic of Gilgamesh*, as well as in Canaanite traditions, including the Hebrew Bible (cf. Behemoth in the book of Job). The matching verbs make hendiadys: "overwhelm you with terror."

It is understandable that the theme of lawlessness has suggested to some investigators the removal of this verse to one of the other "woe oracles"—near v 14, for instance—a proposal that also brings the two occurrences of the verb "cover" together.

VII.6. THE FIFTH WOE ORACLE (2:18–19)

VII.7. CONCLUSION (2:20)

VII.6. *The fifth woe oracle (2:18–19)*

18aA	How does an image benefit?
	For its craftsman has carved it;
18aB	a metal casting, and a teacher of lies.
18bA	For he who shapes his own shape has trusted in it,
18bB	to make dumb false gods. ס

19aA	**Woe to him who says to a tree, "Wake up!"**
19aB	**"Get up!" to a dumb stone!**
19bA	**He gives instruction.**

19bBβ	Behold it is overlaid with gold and silver;
19bBβ	and there is no breath inside it.

VIII.7. *Conclusion (2:20)*

20a	*But Yahweh is in his holy temple;*
20b	*be silent in his presence, all the earth!* פ

Scansion of the Fifth Woe Oracle (2:18–19) and Conclusion (2:20)

		BEATS	SYLLABLES	BICOLON	
18aA	*mâ-hôʿîl pesel kî pĕsālô yōṣĕrô*	6	11 }	18	
18aB	*massēkâ ûmôreh šāqer*	3	7 }		
18bA	*kî bāṭaḥ yōṣēr yiṣrô ʿālāyw*	5	9 }	18	ס
18bB	*laʿăśôt ʾĕlîlîm ʾillĕmîm*	3	9 }		
19aA	*hôy ʾōmēr lāʾēṣ hāqîṣâ*	4	8 }	17	
19aB–bA	*ʾûrî lĕʾeben dûmām hûʾ yôreh*	5	9 }		
19bB	*hinnēh-hûʾ tāpûś zāhāb wakesep*	4	9 }	16	
19bC	*wĕkol-rûaḥ ʾēn bĕqirbô*	3	7 }		
20a	*wĕyhwh bĕhêkal qodšô*	3	8 }	15	פ
20b	*has mippānāyw kol-hāʾāreṣ*	3	7 }		

INTRODUCTION

The fifth "woe oracle" is different from the others in that it does not begin with *hôy*, but with a question. The question would seem to be addressed not to the idolater himself in derision, but to the faithful, by way of edification. The final call to worship Yahweh in silence is addressed to the whole world.

The obvious parallelism of several pairs of colons encourages belief that the poetry is well made and well preserved. But many details present difficulties, and it is not clear whether they are caused by the sophistication of the author (requiring subtlety in the interpreter) or by corruption in the text (requiring ingenuity in the emender).

The bicolon with *hôy*, the hallmark of a "woe oracle," is located in the center of the poem, with symmetrical placement of two bicolons before and after it. While individual colons range in length when measured by beats (three to six), length by syllable count is, with one exception, restricted to seven, eight, and nine, with the mean (8.4 syllables per colon) not much above the standard eight-syllable length. These structural features validate the recognition of v 20 as part of this "woe oracle." At the same time, v 20 serves as a fitting conclusion to the entire series, indeed, to Habakkuk 1–2 as a unit.

The three bicolons in vv 19–20 have a measure of internal parallelism, but not of the familiar synonymous kind (except v 19a, partially, and with chiasmus: "tree wake up // get up stone"). The two bicolons in v 18 go in more for alliteration: *pesel . . . pĕsālô; massēkâ . . . šāqer; yōṣēr yiṣrô; ʾĕlîlîm ʾillĕmîm.*

The evident chiasmus in the middle of v 19a suggests that the problematic *hûʾ yôreh* completes a more elaborate introverted structure (palindrome).

Woe to —
> him who says
>> to a post
>>> "Wake up!"
>>> "Get up!"
>> to a dumb stone
> him who instructs

The poetic structure of v 18 is more intricate, looser than the usual neat parallelism. The grammatical problem is to work out the function of the two subordinate clauses that follow the three words of the opening question. The logical answer is not given until v 19bB, which completes the explanation of the derogatory terms applied to idols in the earlier part of the oracle. These things are stupid, helpless, and dumb because there is no spirit in them. If the match between the two *kî* clauses indicates that v 18 has a chiastic structure, v 18bB completes the question: "What is the use . . . of making dumb idols [*ʾĕlîlîm ʾillĕmîm*]?"

The final "woe oracle" is directed against the worshipers of idols (v 19a). The theological attack on idols as such is a secondary theme. Those who make idols, those who pray to idols, those who speak for idols are all denounced. In the other "woe oracles," there are usually two participles in parallel, not always in contiguous colons. Either *môreh* or *yôreh* would do as the parallel to *ʾōmer* in v 19. The latter is the better candidate, both because of proximity, and also because it makes a nice chiasm and contrasts the presumption of the idolater with the proper confidence of the righteous person in the vision granted by Yahweh (2:4).

NOTES

18. *benefit*. Idols are called "unprofitable" (*lō' yô'îl* [Jer 2:8, 11; 16:19]). The same word-field is used in Isa 44:9–10 and 1 Sam 12:21. The doctrine is explicit that the idols cannot save because they are "nothing" (*tōhû, hebel*); they are "not gods" (Jer 2:11). In human relationships *lō' yô'îl* refers to an unreliable ally (Isa 30:5) who cannot deliver on a promise. Jeremiah's characterization of the oracles of the false prophets as "useless" (Jer 23:32) resembles Habakkuk's point that the idol (or its agent) is a "teacher of falsehood."

image. The verb √*psl* describes the work of a stonemason or sculptor; the noun *pesel* can refer also to wood carving. It is always implied that this image, in human or animal form, is made for use in worship. It has become the generic term for "idol," so even a casting (*massēkâ*) can be called a *pesel* or *pāsîl* (North 1961). The phrase *pesel ûmassēkâ* could be hendiadys (Deut 27:15; Judg 17:3–4; Nah 1:14). With such loose terminology, we cannot insist that the mention of silver and gold in connection with idol making—even a *massēkâ*—means that the object was crafted in these metals. The same goes for the root *yṣr*, used three times here. It could mean "shape out of clay," but it extends to other handicrafts. Any manufacturer is a *yôṣēr* (for arguments that *yôṣēr* means "founder → assayer → banker," see Torrey 1936, 1942). Hence there is no contradiction in the use of both roots—*psl* and *yṣr*—in making an idol by any technique whatsoever.

teacher. In Isa 9:14, "the teacher of falsehood" is a prophet, and Jeremiah constantly uses *šeqer* to characterize the utterances of false prophets.

shape. The word *yiṣrô* is ambiguous (Humbert 1961). The cognate object ("shaping his shape") would seem to be redundant, the construction being no different from *yōṣĕrô*, already in v 18a. The referent of the noun *yēṣer*, meaning "shape" or "form," can be material, such as clay (Ps 103:14; Isa 29:16) or abstract (an idea that takes shape in the mind [Gen 6:5; 8:21]). Either sense would suit here, but in view of the other materials mentioned, we suggest that *yiṣrô* means "his clay (object)."

dumb false gods. The play on the sound of the word "God" (*'ĕlōhîm*) is unmistakable. But the word *'ĕlîlîm* was probably not coined just for that, although it is possible that the root *'ll* was developed from the negative *'l*. These gods are "not-things"—that is, things of negation (non-existence), not just things of nought (no value). The word is not used exclusively of idols, but it is impossible to tell which reference is primary. The paronomasia continues in the word *'illĕlîm*; *'illēm* is the ordinary adjective "dumb," literally, not necessarily insulting. The same characteristic of idols is asserted in v 19, using a different root. There is pathos in Habakkuk's emphasis on this point, because much of his own agony is caused by the silence of Yahweh (Hab 1:13) (Roth 1975).

19. *tree . . . stone*. The same words as were used in v 11, where they are building materials. Wood and stone are conventional parallels in polemics against idolatry. Jer 2:27 is typical:

saying to the ʿēṣ, "You are my father!"
and to the ʾeben, "You gave birth to me!"

This tradition is ancient and widespread, but precise theology should not be distilled from it. It is possible in cult installation that the wooden object of veneration was a living tree (Taylor 1995), not just a carving of a god. The contrast in grammatical gender between tree (masculine) and stone (feminine) reflects the worship of deities of both genders that was ubiquitous in the polytheistic religions of the ancient Near East, but identification of wood and stone with particular gods is not possible. We cannot infer that the material used depended on the gender of the deity. Either material could be used for any god. Nor can we discover whether "stone" means "material" (= a statue made out of stone) or "object" (a piece of stone venerated as [representing] a god). All it means is that gods were acknowledged as parents by worshipers. The language is not necessarily mythological. Although stories of creation by divine procreation are known, they do not carry with them a claim to divinity on the part of the devotee. The case of Gudea illustrates the custom. He is called "Gudea, son of (the god) Ningizzida" (Cyl. B. 24:7) or, more fully, "Your god is the lord Ningizzida, the offspring of Anu; your mother is Ninsun, the mother who bore a pure stock" (Cyl. 23:19). Yet, in spite of the intimacy of this language, which is often met in the monuments of Mesopotamian rulers, they were very much aware of their status as mortals and rarely aspired to the status of gods.

"Wake up!" There must have been something in Canaanite religion about a sleeping god, for Elijah taunted the prophets of Baal that their god was asleep (1 Kgs 18:27), and the Psalmist makes the counterpoint that Yahweh never sleeps (Ps 121:4). Perhaps some form of the Telepinus myth is in mind (ANET 127; see also McAlpine 1987). Yet the same figure can be used of Yahweh: the question "Why are you sleeping, LORD?" joined together the exhortations "Get up!" (ʿûrâ) and "Wake up!"(hāqîṣâ), exactly as here (Ps 44:24; cf. Ps 35:23; in Ps 59:5–6 the verbs are used in the same sequence as in Hab 2:19). So the language might not be derisive—laughing at people whose god falls asleep. Rather, the blasphemy lies in addressing sticks and stones with language properly used for Yahweh.

This irony does not seem to have occurred to the idol worshipers themselves. Perhaps they took it for granted that time and chance happen to idols, just as to all things human. A tablet found in the temple of Ishtar at Nineveh (Campbell Thompson 1937) is a letter to the king reporting an earthquake:

15. É DINGIR *gab-bu i-ta-aw-rid*	The house of God, all of it, has come down.
16. *up-ta-ta-ṣi-iḫ*	I rejoice (that)
17. DINGIR^mēš-*ni ša* LUGAL	the gods of the king,
18. *gab-bu* DI-*mu*	all of them, are safe and sound (*šulmu*).

dumb. The morphology of *dûmām* is not clear. It is not the adverb from the root *dwm* (Isa 47:5; Lam 3:26). The roots *dwm* and *dmm* have similar meanings, and *dûmām* could be the result of fusion of their patterns. Because "stone" is feminine, *dûmām* is more likely to be a noun—"silence"— than an adjective. The point being made is that it is futile, absurd, to shout instructions to a stone, so "deafness" could be the transferred epithet here: "They are more deaf than men" (Isa 44:9).

gives instruction. In the giving of Torah (God tells the people what to do), God instructs a priest. In heathen religion, the priest gives instruction (*hû' yôreh*) to worship a false god.

overlaid. Statues of gods might be adorned with gold foil. It is not certain that *tāpûś,* "seized by," "held by," means that. The statues made of wood, stone, or metal might be adorned with clothes and jewelry. Yet the statement is intended to be derogatory, to prove that "there is no spirit inside it."

20. The place of this verse is very fitting as the conclusion of the last "woe oracle," as the conclusion of all the "woe oracles" together, and as the conclusion of the entire dialogue between Habakkuk and Yahweh. It is full of irony. The whole matter began with the frantic prayers of the prophet to his silent God. Now the whole world is reduced to silence before the majesty of Yahweh. Like Job (Job 40:4), Habakkuk ends by putting his hand on his mouth.

holy temple (cf. Ps 11:4). The presence of Yahweh in his holy temple, in which he resides, is contrasted with the absence of "all spirit" from the idol; it is likely that the Temple in Jerusalem, not its heavenly counterpart, is in mind. This would affirm Israelite belief that Yahweh was in their midst. He doesn't need a statue as a receptacle for his manifest presence in the world. But there is little indication in this book that Habakkuk's professional activity, or even the experience embodied in his prophecy, was located in the formal cult. Hence it remains possible that the temple is the heavenly shrine. This likelihood receives support from two other features. The universal scope of v 20 suggests that God in heaven sees everything on earth. It is from heaven that God "looks" (1:3, 13) at events in the world and from these headquarters that he sallies forth into the world to set things to rights (Habakkuk 3).

The two identifications of the holy temple are not incompatible. There was a nexus between the heavenly shrine and its earthly replica. The construction of the latter according to the plan or model of the former was intended to symbolize and to facilitate this combination. Both loci are recognized in Solomon's great prayer. The people pray toward the Jerusalem Temple and God hears in heaven.

silent. Waldman (1976) has gathered a lot of examples of "dumbstruck horror" as part of the conventional reaction to the divine presence. In other places the call to silence in the context of worship suggests the hushed reverence of the cult (Reiner 1965):

> *has mippĕnê 'ădōnāy yhwh* (Zeph 1:7)
> *has kol-bāśār mippĕnê yhwh* (Zech 2:17)

COMMENT

This is the most intelligible of all the "woe oracles." The theme is a familiar one, and the polemic against idolatry is stated in traditional terms. Yahweh is the only God, God of the whole world (v 20). The idol is not a god; it does not even represent anything; it has no resident spirit (v 19b). It is foolish to pray to wood and stone (v 19b). The things are useless (v 18). They are not gods (*'ĕlōhîm*); they are worthless (*'ĕlîlîm*) and dumb (*'illĕlîm*).

The view of idolatry given by the fifth "woe oracle" is widespread in the Hebrew Bible. The materials used to make idols are wooden poles and stone pillars, overlaid with silver and gold or even figurines made out of these metals. The word "casting" is used, but it probably refers to a bronze statue adorned (*tpś*) with gold leaf. The vocabulary points to several techniques of idol manufacture—casting (*nsk*), sculpting (*psl*), molding (*yṣr*), encasing (*tpś*), and the common verb "make" (*ʿśh*). Wood and stone are often associated in denunciations of heathen gods and refer most immediately to the Israelite practice of erecting wood posts (Asherot and Asherim) and monoliths (*maṣṣēbôt*) to represent, respectively, the female and the male participants in fertility religions.

It is simplest to take the person who makes the idol (v 18) and the person who invokes it (v 19) as the same. The traditional Israelite ridicule of idolatry often points out the absurdity of a person regarding as a god something that he himself has manufactured (Isa 44:9–20).

It is not clear whether this "woe oracle" is intended to be wholesale denunciation of idolatry in every shape and form. The variety of materials and techniques mentioned and the plural ("dumb nothings") suggest polytheism. But many terms are singular, and the prominent *hû'*, "it," in v 19b suggests that one particular god is prominent in the argument. Nevertheless, the language remains general; there is no hint about the identity or location of the god or gods. So again, we do not know if this "woe oracle" is hurled against idolaters within Israel or against those of some more distant heathen power.

The fifth "woe oracle" moves logically from stage to stage—the manufacture of the idols (v 18), prayer to the idols (v 19a), the refutation of the idol (v 19b), and the affirmation of Yahweh as the only real god (v 20). All the parts are closely linked. There is a powerful contrast between the futility of crying out to deaf and dumb gods and the silent adoration of the worshipers of Yahweh—silent because it is Yahweh who speaks. The presence of Yahweh in his holy temple (v 20) contrasts with the absence of spirit from the idol (v 19bB). The impact of this juxtaposition is lost when the sequence of vv 18 and 19 is reversed (as in NAB) in order to have the fifth "woe oracle" begin with *hôy*, like the others. This obvious adjustment is widely accepted by scholars, supported by the dogma that a "woe oracle" "must" (Cannon 1925:88) begin with *hôy*. And, apart from its connection with v 20, v 19bB is very effective as the final word on idolatry when it comes at the end of this section, as an answer to the opening question. The technological details in v 19bB continue the description of v 18, leaving v 19a as the "woe oracle" proper.

The last two words of v 19a constitute a problem. They seem to mean "he gives an oracle." It refers to the idol, and *hû'* has the same referent in both its occurrences in v 19b. The Masoretes evidently thought so when they placed the *'atnāḥ* before this phrase. A solution of the problem by deleting these words as a gloss is too drastic. A linkage between the two occurrences of *hû'* is weakened by the use of *hinnēh*, which suggests that a new statement begins here. The editorial display of BHS recognizes this, and v 19b, without *hû' yôreh*, makes a good bicolon. Because v 19a is similarly well formed, this leaves *hû' yôreh* in complete isolation. Hence the suggestion that it is a gloss. But this explains nothing; the origin of such a gloss is unaccountable. As an independent statement, "He gives instruction" contradicts the preceding statement that the stone is "dumb." NAB and other translations resolve this contradiction by making a rhetorical question: "Can such a thing give oracles?" This has the virtue of matching the opening question.

If *hû' yôreh* is to be retained, it might match in some way the description of the idol (or its maker or its user) as *môreh šāqer*, "giver of false teaching." Because the idols are twice said to be dumb, the contradiction can be resolved if the instruction from an idol is not untrue, but spurious. But it is very doubtful if *môreh* refers to the idol at all. The term *šeqer* refers characteristically to false prophecy, fraudulently concocted. The *môreh šeqer* in Isa 9:14 is a prophet. If Hab 2:18 calls an idol a *môreh*, it is a unique instance.

VIII. THE PSALM OF
HABAKKUK (3:1–19)

◆

INTRODUCTION

The prayer (or hymn) proper is framed by a title (v 1) and a colophon (v 19b) of the kind typical in biblical psalms. These annotations show, at the very least, that scribes recognized the distinctively poetic, if not liturgical, character of the piece. How ancient this presentation is cannot be ascertained at this late time. As with similar annotations in the Psalms, there is no attestation of precanonical recensions that lack these kinds of notes. They could be as original as anything in the book (Gevaryahu 1975).

A priori arguments that a psalm is out of place in a prophecy, or in a history for that matter, have no weight whatsoever. Much hymnic material is found in the Hebrew Bible outside the Psalter. Some songs have been incorporated bodily into prophecy (Amos 4:13; 5:8; 9:5–6) and narrative (Jonah 2). Hymnic material has been developed as a medium for sustained and exalted discourse (Second Isaiah) whose exact genre has never been established with certainty, except that it is both liturgical and prophetic. Actual Psalms are quoted, in part or fully, in the books of Chronicles.

When the Qumran *pešer* (1QpHab) was found, the fact that the commentary was apparently restricted to Habakkuk 1–2 was seen as evidence that Habakkuk 3 was not then part of the book (or at least not part of the copy used by that commentator). This argument is not strong. The MS of 1QpHab we now have is not the original autograph, so we cannot be sure that this copy is complete. Furthermore, "[a]mong the *pesharim* from Qumran, no commentaries on complete books have been found" (Haak 1991:7–8). The next earliest evidence (MurXII and 8 ḤevXIIgr) indicates that Habakkuk 3 was part of the book.

Humbert (1944:247–48) argued for the integrity of Habakkuk 3 with Habakkuk 1–2 on the basis of shared vocabulary; and Fohrer (1985:162–63) maintained that shared content indicates unity of composition. We carry these observations further by noting that there are literary structures spanning the whole book. Hiebert's (1987) contention that multiple use of inclusion in Habakkuk 3 is not only evidence for its planned composition but also a major aid to its interpretation can be extended to the book as a whole. Hiebert himself was not able to arrive at this conclusion because he still accepted the theory that Habakkuk 3 was added after the Exile and brought the whole book into a more eschatolog-

ical frame of reference. That's possible, of course; but it is less likely that vocabulary in both parts was revised in the last stages of redaction to enhance the
thematic cohesion.

We are not persuaded that Habakkuk could not have produced the whole
work (the ascription in Hab 3:1 is historically true; he did pray this prayer). Like
Jonah 2, Habakkuk 3 purports to be a personal prayer of the prophet himself,
and the "confessions" of Jeremiah, although quite a mixture of genres from the
literary and liturgical point of view, have the same intense personal character.

While absolute proof either way is out of reach in such matters, and dogma-
tism is a disservice to scholarship, we believe that the balance lies in favor of
the authenticity of the composition and of its integral place in the prophecy as
a whole. Not that we think for a moment that Habakkuk himself wrote it. It is
not original in that sense. But even if he did, it is unreasonable to expect a hymn
to be done in the same style as an oracle. It bears all the marks—or most of it
does—of being an ancient poem. Very ancient indeed, perhaps it is one of the
oldest in the entire Hebrew Bible. The work of Cassuto (1975) on its mythopo-
etic background; the similar observations of Albright (1950a), along with the
prosody itself; its affinities with the oldest poems of the theophany (Deuteronomy 33; Judges 5; Psalms 68, 77 and others)—all these supply some of the arguments that a traditional poem has been taken over with very little change:
"The original text, linguistic features, literary form, historical allusions, and religious motifs all suggest that this poem was composed in the premonarchic era
as a recitation of the victory of the divine warrior over cosmic and earthly enemies" (Hiebert 1986:1). The argument against its authenticity that emphasizes
how different it is from the rest of the book, is, in fact, an argument for its existence and currency before Habakkuk's time. Insofar as this old poem was suited
for this use, its integrity with the rest of the book does not depend on whether
the prophet himself appropriated it and worked it in, or whether a later scribe
saw how well it would fit and ascribed it to the prophet. Most of the poem shows
little sign of having been reworked for this use. To that extent it is intact, but
not necessarily complete. It might even consist of extracts from more than one
ancient poem, a fresh composite in which the sources are carefully preserved,
as Albright (1950b) observed in Psalm 68. For understanding the complete book
in its present form, we do not have to recover the history of its redactional development. In the end, our readings do not come out very differently from
Hiebert's (1986).

Numerous special studies have been dedicated to this remarkable composition. Among the most noteworthy are Albright (1950a); Avishur (1994); Béguerie
(1954); Cassuto (Italian original in 1935–37 [published 1938]; English translation in 1975); Delcor (1953); Eaton (1964); Evans (1955); Garcia Cordero
(1948); Hiebert (1986); Irwin (1942, 1956); Margulis (1970); Mowinckel (1953);
Schmidt (1949–50); Stenzel (1952); Stephens (1924); Zorell (1927).

We follow the general practice of scholarship in using the term "theophany"
to refer to a visible manifestation of the presence of a deity or a report of such
an event (Akao 1990; Barr 1960; Glueck 1936; Hunter 1989; Jeremias 1965;

DIAGRAM 1. Structure of Habakkuk

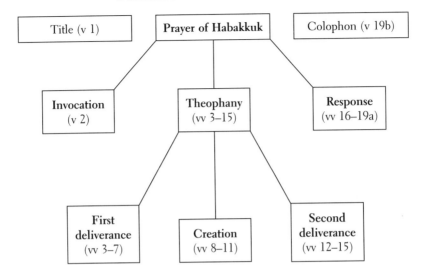

Niehaus 1995; O'Connell 1979; Thompson 1993), even though, curiously, the word *theophania* is not found anywhere in the Greek Scriptures (Ohmann 1989).

As with other early theophanies from the age of the Holy Wars of Yahweh, this poem recites the conflict and victory of Yahweh over hostile powers. The struggle begins with Creation, but it is recapitulated in later confrontations and interventions, notably the Exodus. The cleavage of the waters is a theme common to Creation and Exodus, and the Deluge may have made its contribution to the imagery and vocabulary. The recitation also kindles an eschatological hope, so that memory and expectation nurture the present faith of the righteous man (2:4).

The hand of the prophet (or scribe) himself is more evident in the colons that do not have these archaic features, notably vv 2 and 16–19b. These are the poet's own invocation of God and his meditation on the significance of the vision that is granted him in his recapitulation of the ancient creed. Enclosed in this framework is the primeval account of the destructive-redemptive-creative activity of Yahweh (vv 3–15).

The structure of Habakkuk is shown in the diagram above. Thus the poem has four stupendous moments. The distinctions among them are clearly shown by changes in the mode of address, in the subject matter, and in the poetic style.

1. The opening invocation and closing response are more personal and more subjective.

2. The first account of a mighty deliverance (vv 3–7) is a recital in the third person. The geographic setting established by the place-names in the opening and closing bicolons determines the historical occasion to be the Exodus. Yet Egypt is not in plain view; the stage is cosmic in its expanse; the spectators are the nations; Israel is not named as either the locus or the beneficiary of this dis-

play of power. The strophe has a high mythological component, obvious in the reference to the two associate "gods"—Plague and Pestilence.

3. In the middle strophe (vv 8–11), the mode of address changes to apostrophe in the second person. In this respect, it is more like a continuation of the opening invocation of v 2. The occasion is not evident. God is presented as a chariot-riding warrior, armed with bow and arrows and other weapons; but his combat is with cosmic elements, not historical enemies. His hostility focuses on water, but the mountains are also assailed, and combat extends from the underworld to the heavenly lights. The poem evokes memories of stories of creation, but also of the Exodus and the battles of the early days. And it could just as well be a vision of the eschaton.

4. In the third strophe (vv 12–15) God is involved in history. The setting is the world (v 12); the purpose is deliverance (v 13); the enemy (unnamed) is almost represented as an individual (v 14); and a final reference to the waters makes the Exodus the most likely referent, although this is far from proved.

The state of the text and the character of the poetry place limits on the recovery of the rules of prosody that governed the composition of this poem. A provisional analysis identifies sixty-four colons. They vary in length from four to nine syllables, but most of them have six, seven, or eight syllables, with seven as the average. It could be significant that the four main chunks of the poem are almost identical in size, whether measured by colons (sixteen each) or syllables.

	SYLLABLES
The personal response (vv 2, 16–19b)	109
The first deliverance (vv 3–7)	111
Creation combat (vv 8–11)	112
The second deliverance (vv 12–15)	119

It is emphasized that a considerable margin of uncertainty exists in these estimates.

The prosody is dominated by the usual kinds of parallelism. Although they tend to primitive patterns, there is considerable variety. The bicolon is the commonest unit, but there is a significant incidence of tricolons, as Albright (1950a) pointed out. Albright's pioneering research was an important breakthrough in the study of Habakkuk 3, but it has not been followed up to any significant extent until the work of Hiebert (1986). Further progress, attempted here, requires acknowledgment that the Hebrew poet has a much wider repertoire of patterns of parallelism to draw on than earlier critics recognized. The use (we must suppose it to have been deliberate) of so many devices in the same poem puts a restraint on the criticism that trims and tidies such a poem into greater uniformity of design. One familiar practice is to eliminate a third colon as a gloss or doublet through unwillingness to recognize the tricolon. We have now come a long way from the time when Irwin (1942:18) could say that "the occurrence of an isolated tristich in a series of distichs unless marking the conclusion of a strophe . . . is an almost infallible mark of corruption." Mesopotamian literature also, it is now realized, used "single lines or groups of three as units" (*BWL* vi) as well as bicolons. But acceptance of variety within one and the same poem (that is, several kinds of bicolon and tricolon) means that Albright's (1950a) method of stylistic sequence dating does not get us very far. It is not only that the poem lacks a paramount or distinctive style that places it clearly at some point in time along a hypothetical typological sequence, but also that smaller portions of the poem (for example, bicolons with repetitive parallelism) cannot be singled out for individual dating. Even if they could, the more important consideration would be how the poet has transplanted such units into the new poem we now have.

That it is indeed a creation, not a miscellany, is indicated by the closely woven texture of the larger patterns when units bigger than bicolons and tricolons are recognized. The bicolons and tricolons retain their identity in these larger units; for this reason we shall describe them one by one, including even bicolons that are found in well-formed tricolons.

We need to talk about texture as well as hierarchy, about pattern as well as structure. The point may be illustrated by the tricolon in v 8. The second and third colons constitute a bicolon of classical perfection. It realizes complete synonymous parallelism: "rivers" // "sea"; "rage" // "fury."

The conjunction (= interrogative) (*'im*), the preposition (*b-*) and the suffix (*-kā*) are repeated (no double-duty patterns are used here). It would be possible to regard the first two colons of v 8 as a bicolon, equally classical. The pattern is incomplete synonymous parallelism, with the archaic feature of repetition of the lead word "rivers." The sequence *hă-* // *'im* is canonical. "Yahweh" is an opening vocative with no counterparts, except in the anaphoric pronoun suffixes "thy" in the following colons. But they more properly go with "anger" doing retroactive double duty as a modifier of *ḥārâ*, which parallelism would indicate to be a noun, thus softening the strain of an apparently third person verb in the midst of second person pronouns. On this analysis, the second colon is seen to function simultaneously as the second colon of one bicolon (with one parallelism pattern) and as the first colon of another bicolon (with a different parallelism pattern)—Janus parallelism. But because the constructions of the second and third colons are identical, the third is just as qualified as the second to be parallel to the first. It might seem trivial to add to our description an examination of the first and third colon as another bicolon in the complex. But this important fact is lost sight of if we meet a tricolon in which the first colon is parallel to only the second and the third colon is parallel to only the second. The second and third colons are not simply successive parallels to the first. In this kind of tricolon, the relationships among all the colons can be established in more wholeness by saying that colons 2 and 3 constitute a bicolon that, as a whole, is the parallel to the first colon. This should be enough for now. Discussion of the other poetic units will be presented in the INTRODUCTION and NOTES on each section.

It is in keeping with the archaic character of the poem that prefixed and suffixed verb forms are intermingled, with no distinction in tense. These forms are about equal in number, about sixteen each. We cannot be certain of the exact tally because many obscure forms defy classification.

Nowack (1896:266–67) stated the issue that confronts translator and interpreter:

> Die hier gebrauchten modi der Verba lassen die eine wie die andere Auffassung zu: zum Perf. sowie Impf. consec. wechselnd mit Impf. von der Zukunft . . . ; zum Impf neben dem Perf. von der Vergangenheit. Eine völlig sichere Entscheidung ist kaum möglich, das hängt zum Theil damit zusammen, dass wir hier ein künstl. archaisirendes, mit Rücks. auf vorhegende Litteratur—erzeugnisse verfasstes Lied vor uns haben, zum Theil aber auch damit, dass der ächte Schluss des Liedes wohl nicht erhalten ist.

> The modes of the verbs that are used here permit either of two possible interpretations. Either the perfect along with the consecutive imperfect is future in alternation with the imperfect . . .; or the imperfect in association with the perfect is past. A completely certain resolution is hardly possible. It depends in part on the fact that here we have the result of deliberately composing a song with artifical archaizing that looks back to previous literature, but in part also to the fact that the original ending of the song has probably not been preserved.

This perplexity is ancient. The earliest versions range over the possibilities. The Tg used past tense throughout in vv 3–15, making it all historical narrative. Mechanical translation of all, or most, prefixed forms as future tense produces a mixed translation (Greek, Latin, Syriac), but there is a tendency to cast the whole as future. This policy implies an interpretation of the psalm as a prediction of the LORD's coming that is expected to imitate the traditional historic theophanies.

With the exception of the personal framework, which is obviously contemporary, we can now be confident that all of the core of the poem (vv 3–15) is intended to be past tense. The use of both prefixed and suffixed verbs with this meaning is now better understood (Robertson 1972), and this makes clearer the archaic, not merely archaizing, character of the composition.

TEXT OF HABAKKUK 3

Habakkuk 3 must surely be the most rewritten chapter in the Hebrew Bible. Almost every word has been found unacceptable, touched up, replaced, or given a more appropriate meaning. Hiebert (1986) has ninety textual notes on his translation; Roberts (1991), ninety-eight, treading once more the already well trodden.

To take note of every detail of such work would bloat our presentation, with little hope of having anything better to show at the end of it. We do not mean to imply that what we leave out does not merit serious attention. On the contrary, because so many of the problems cannot be considered solved, given the fine quality of previous work, we are reaching the limits of our resources. The problems have been clearly identified, but it is beginning to look as though they will never be solved.

We recommend that the most competent and thorough previous work on the text of Habakkuk 3 (Albright 1950a; Avishur 1994; Barthélemy 1992; Bévenot 1933; Delcor 1953; Eaton 1964; Good 1959; Hiebert 1986; Humbert 1944; Irwin 1942; Margolis 1908; Margulis 1970; Mowinckel 1953; Roberts 1991; Rudolph 1975; Sellin 1930) be reviewed side by side with our own proposals, so that the reader can see the larger picture and make independent judgments. It is always worthwhile to revisit Wellhausen (1893), the master.

All this work shares an attitude of respect toward the MT; its stated aim is to remedy the flaws in the MT. But deference towards the MT is often more pious than scientific. Often the MT provides a fallback position that, by default, gives relief to the defeated. It is interesting that some scholars, after saying that the MT holds the field, still make numerous changes to it.

The prestige of the MT has been enhanced by finds from the Judean desert, both Hebrew and Greek texts. When using the text of 1QpHab, allowance has to be made for the possibility that the author has moved some details of the text in order to better serve his interpretation. Unfortunately, that *pešer* (or what survives of it) does not extend to Habakkuk 3. It is different with MurXII.

In March 1955, a scroll of the Minor Prophets was found in the Wadi Murabba'at by a shepherd named Kalef Ismail (*DJD* II: 50). Three years before, four caves in the wadi had yielded various finds. Two of the twenty-two columns of MurXII provide much of the text of Habakkuk. It is uncanny how precisely this scroll agrees with the MT in all but a few details. It even attests the antiquity of the traditional paragraphing; it has the *ktyb przw* in v 14. For Habakkuk 3 (not attested in 1QpHab), MurXII differs from MT only in having two *plene* spellings (*mrkbwtyk* [the first hand of D[62] had this, but it was later corrected by erasing the right leg of the *taw* and making the *waw* part of the *taw*] in v 8; *zbwlh* in v 11), and two different words. Verse 10 reads *zrmw mym 'bwt*. It is remarkable when an ancient text comes up with a previously unattested reading that had been hit on by a modern text critic. This reading has a lot to be said for it intrinsically. It was first suggested by Wellhausen (1893:172, taking a lead from Ps 77:18) and followed by many since him. Even so, this unexpected support for a modern emendation has not persuaded everybody. Hiebert (1986:6–7) and Roberts (1991:140) adopt it. No recent translations have accepted it. We share this hesitation because the versions line up with the MT, and it is possible that the prompt from Ps 77:18 already suggested the same adjustment to an ancient scribe as it did to Wellhausen.

The virtual identity of MurXII and the MT has validated what has been long supposed, that the MT is a faithful preservation of an ancient text, at least as old as the turn of the eras. This imposes additional restraint on solving the problems of the MT by emending its text. At the same time, it should be emphasized that the availability of MurXII does not ease in the least the difficulties encountered in the MT. They are just as insoluble as ever; indeed more so, if we are reluctant to attribute the difficulties to errors made by scribes. If the Hebrew text of Habakkuk is corrupt, it was already corrupt two thousand years ago.

Knowledge of the Hebrew text of Habakkuk 3 has not been enlarged by Qumran finds, but interesting variants in Greek manuscripts partly compensate for this lack. Besides the familiar LXX, there is a divergent tradition attested by six manuscripts. The first symbol is the *siglum* used in the Göttingen LXX.

V   Venice, Marciana Library, Gr. 1 (eighth century)
62   Oxford, New College Library 44 (eleventh century)
86   Rome, Vatican Library Barbarini gr. 549 (ninth–tenth century)
147   Oxford, Bodleian Library, Laud. gr. 30 (twelfth century)
407   Jerusalem, Patriarchal Library, Τάφου 2 (ninth century)
        MS fondo San Salvatore 118 (eleventh century) (Baars 1965)

This tradition or recension is usually referred to under the name of the Barberini manuscript in Rome (Albright 1950; Baars 1965; Bévenot 1933; Good 1959; Haak 1991:1–11; Hiebert 1986:10–11; Kaminka 1928; Klostermann 1895; Margolis 1908; Margulis 1970; Mercati 1955; Thackeray 1910/1911, 1923. Margolis (1908) referred to it as "the anonymous Greek version." Thackeray (1923:48) preferred the designation "Oxford."

The Greek translators evidently found as many difficulties in the Hebrew text as we still do, and modern scholars have not been able to resist the temptation of the curious variants of the Barberini–Oxford family as possible evidence of ancient Hebrew readings now otherwise lost.

Thackeray (1923:48) was of the opinion that these copies, in the main, represented an older text, "a precious relic from the first stage in the Greek version of the prophets." Albright, in particular, was inclined to resort to their variant readings when it suited him, but the results were not often persuasive. Bévenot (1933:503) was of the opinion that Barberini does not represent a version (the elusive "seventh"), but is an isolated translation of this one poem made for use in a synagogue of Hellenized Jews. He suggested that its Hebrew *Vorlage* was purer than that of LXX (507).

In contrast to Thackeray's belief in the antiquity of this *Vorlage*, Margolis (1908) had already recorded the impression that this "anonymous" translation was "modern" in thought. It was highly tendentious after the manner of a targum.

Margolis's observation that the anonymous version "strives after idiomatic Greek construction, while LXX affects a hebraizing literalness" (136) calls for caution, for there is no way in which the existence of a curious Greek version can impeach the MT as such, to its own advantage. Certainly not in a sweeping manner, since each individual reading must be assessed on its own merits. We don't know how literal a translation might have been when we no longer have the text it was translated from. At the same time, the sensitive art of "weighing" an individual variant has to factor in a coefficient for the general quality of the MS in which it is found. Hence the influence of opinions about the over-all value of the Barberini–Oxford family, one way or another.

The reexaminations of the text of Habakkuk 3 in Hiebert (1986:10–57) and Roberts (1991:128–48) in the light of all the available evidence supply a fresh starting point for work on this composition. Hiebert's aim throughout is to re-cover what he calls "the original text." But because in his own view, the ancient poem that provides the bulk and core of the poem was likely premonarchical, and because the oldest physical evidence for the text cannot be much earlier than the turn of the era, we have to reckon with a transmission history of one thousand years before that, for which we have no tangible evidence whatsoever. It is too much to hope that we might recover (with any certainty that makes the enterprise worthwhile) individual readings as they existed in the originating poem, let alone intact stretches of text. The best we can hope for, and the most we can claim, is plausible reconstruction of a hypothetical "original" that ac-counts as fully as possible for all the textual evidence now extant. So much un-certainty besets this exercise that we are reluctant to override the MT or set it aside completely.

Haak (1991:10) states that his goal is "to understand the consonantal text of Habakkuk as it was understood in the late 7th–early 6th century B.C.E." This is somewhat optimistic. We can only hope (assume) that either the MT or the best reconstruction we can venture for the originating text that accounts for all the texts we now have is near enough to the book that Habakkuk (or somebody) wrote centuries before. We can hardly proceed otherwise. But recovering how it was *understood* then is even more venturesome, an enterprise declared to be utterly impossible and futile by postmodernists.

This is not the place to justify our continued pursuit of historical–grammati-cal interpretation, in spite of postmodernist bans (Vanhoozer 1998). We will, however, take the present crisis in literary epistemology seriously and be mod-est in the claims we make for recovering, not only original texts, but even more so original meanings. It is still possible, all the same, to say a few things about the literary form, grammatical meaning, and historical background of ancient texts.

There are two aspects of recent literary approaches to the Prayer of Habakkuk that permit modest hopes for progress in the study of the text—if not for solving old problems, at least for discarding old solutions that have lost their appeal. We mention as the first weakness in earlier method the overreliance on poetic par-allelism for the solution of problems. Roberts's (1991) decisions are often guided by this consideration. Thus while admitting that *těhillâ* (v 3) means "praise," he judges it a "weak parallel" to "majesty" in the preceding colon and translates it as "glory." He is not sure, however, whether to replace *těhillâ* with a different word or to give it the required meaning (133, n. 17). This kind of argumenta-tion is obviated once it is recognized that vv 3b–4aA constitute a tricolon in which the third colon is closer to the first (envelope construction or mini-in-clusion) so that the *middle* colon is complementary to the outer bicolon. It is the splendor of Yahweh in the sky that evokes admiration on the earth.

A second procedure in which our method differs from that of earlier work is to study units larger than the tricolon in order to find the connections among the various parts. Hiebert (1987) wrote a fine article on inclusion as the organizing principle in the composition of the Prayer of Habakkuk, but in his monograph (1986) he did not sufficiently exploit this structural fact to narrow the options for text-critical judgments.

VIII.1. TITLE (3:1)

1a   A prayer of Habakkuk the prophet
1b   (upon Shigyonoth).

INTRODUCTION

The difficulty of the Prayer of Habakkuk is univerally recognized. Almost every word constitutes a problem. This state of affairs is reflected in the versions, our oldest evidence for possible textual variants. But many of the deviations attested in ancient translations and quotations could be no more than emendations, and, like their latter-day counterparts, their claim must be heavy indeed to outweigh the principle of *lectio difficilior potior*. If there is one chapter in the Bible where difficult readings are the norm, this is it.

And, without getting into the deep waters of text criticism, it is still legitimate to study the MT as a text in its own right. This will be our main concern in the NOTES.

NOTES

1. *prayer.* The term *tĕpillâ* is a general word for prayer. It appears, as here, in the title of several psalms, most of which represent personal supplications in times of distress. The ascriptive *l-* could indicate authorship ("written by Habakkuk"), or purpose ("written for Habakkuk"), or subject matter ("written about Habakkuk"), or "appropriated by Habakkuk."

If the poem is genuinely archaic, as we believe, none of these readings can be true; the original poem had nothing to do with Habakkuk. But if the prayer is now integral to the prophecy, as we also believe, it is entirely possible that Habakkuk himself found this ancient composition appropriate for personal use and as a vehicle for his timely message.

Habakkuk the prophet. See the NOTES on Hab 1:1.

Shigyonoth. This Hebrew word is not otherwise attested. Habakkuk 3 has already been titled *tĕpillâ*, "for/by/about Habakkuk," so the additional qualification "upon Shigyonoth" resembles the annotations found in the headings of many psalms after the title proper. The preposition *ʿal* suggests that Shigyonoth is the name of a melody (the first word of a lyric that names a melody?). In that case, it does not follow that the meaning of that word or the content of that lost song—which can hardly be recovered from one surviving word—provides any clue to the Prayer of Habakkuk.

Attempts to establish the meaning of *shigyonoth* proceed along three paths: biblical usage, etymology, and ancient translations. The best outcome is when these three approaches converge on the same result.

Biblical Usage

If *šigyōnôt* is the plural of *šiggāyôn* (Ps 7:1), itself *hapax legomenon*, the meaning of both words should be sought together. The usage of the cognate words is not the same in these occurrences. In Ps 7:1, *šiggāyôn lĕdāwîd* is a conventional title. If that heading is intended to characterize the kind of psalm that follows, this does not take us very far, for the two compositions do not have much in common apart from being prayers. Nor does it help to proceed in the other direction, first working out the form-critical classification of the prayers, and then taking that to be the meaning of the title.

The form-critical classification of Psalm 7 is hampered by doubt about its compositional and liturgical integrity. The petitioner's plight seems to be that of an individual falsely accused by an enemy, but Yahweh is appealed to as judge of the nations (Kissane 1953: I 29). Mowinckel (1921:173), however, pointed out that troublemakers could be referred to as singular or plural in one and the same psalm. There was considerable agreement with Gunkel's (1933:172) classification of Psalm 7 as an individual's lament.

There is a curious difficulty in the use of the word "lament" as a label for a form-critical genre. The term *qînâ* clearly characterizes a song or poem used by a bereaved person to express grief, and the words are addressed to the deceased or to bystanders, never to God, who, strangely, is not even mentioned. The inclusion of various prayers in the Psalter and prophetic books under the same term "lament" is entirely due to modern scholars, who even call such a composition a *qînâ* (even though that word does not occur in the book of Psalms) and expect it to conform to the so-called *qînâ* meter (3:2). For a review of the problems of characterizing and classifying prayers and psalms that might be considered laments of one kind or another, see Broyles (1989). While the term *maśkîl* is used in the title of some psalms that are considered to be laments, it is also used for others that are quite different. Such headings are of limited help for form-critical classification.

Eissfeldt (1965:115) listed Psalm 7 among forty "lament" psalms. There is not much agreement about what the suppliant is lamenting about in Psalm 7. Because of the protestation of innocence in vv 3–5, Psalm 7 has been identified as a prayer of the victim of false accusation or malicious prosecution; but the language of juridical investigation could be used metaphorically, especially in poetry, in a prayer to God for justice. In any case, the prayers of Habakkuk do not dwell on his personal misery through illness or deprivation. The argument for identifying Habakkuk 3 as an individual's lament was stated succinctly by Mowinckel (1953:7). Looked at closely, however, the alleged matches between Habakkuk 3 and individual's psalms in the book of Psalms are not firm. In particular, as far as Psalm 7 is concerned, Kraus (1998:168–69) concluded that the "individual lament . . . does not really conform to the distinctive shape and form of expression of the psalm [7]." Krause apparently did not know what to call Psalm 7. The exercise — Habakkuk 3 is the same category as Psalm 7, because they have the same title — fails if Psalm 7 cannot be classified.

Mowinckel (1953) claimed that the mention of the former mighty deeds of Yahweh (Hab 3:2) corresponds to the invocation at the begining of a lament, while vv 18–19 correspond to the confidence of being heard that is expressed at the end of some laments. Although Avishur (1994:113) follows Mowinckel, stating that "comparison between our psalm and other biblical psalms reveals no differences between them in terms of structure, style, or constituent motifs," he concludes that Habakkuk 3 is not an individual's lament, but a national lament. The conclusion that there are "no differences" holds only if the comparisons are so general that the genre of a distinctive psalm cannot be pinpointed.

Mowinckel's (1953:7) position is more nuanced. He tries to balance the references to "I" (vv 2, 16, 18, 19), the prophet is praying by and for himself, and "us" (v 16b, after the first person has been used seven times!), the prophet is praying in solidarity with and on behalf of the community.

One of the reasons that there is so little agreement among Psalms scholars who have addressed independently the task of genre analysis and classification (we exclude the spurious consensus that results when writers simply recycle the work of others) is that so many of the individual psalms seem to be of mixed types. Not many fit the template of a pure specimen. The overlap in form and content between laments and thanksgivings is well recognized, yet their functions are quite different. There are also superficial resemblances between laments and complaints, which is why Habakkuk's prayers have been called by either or both these names. With more careful use of criteria and terminology, a lament expresses the sorrows of a grieving person or community suffering illness or misery through drought, famine, plague, defeat in war, or any kind of disaster or oppression. The primary appeal of their prayers is to God's compassion. As Gunkel said, their aim is to touch God's heart ("Jahves Herz zu treffen" [Gunkel and Begrich 1933:129]). Its hope is deliverance or recovery. A complaint is argumentative. It expresses outrage or indignation at an injustice that has not been restrained or corrected or punished by God. It appeals to God as judge. This is the dominating mood of Habakkuk's prayers. He is hoping for the day of trouble to come upon the wrongdoers (Hab 3:16b).

The emotions expressed in Hab 3:3 and Hab 3:16 are not the sorrows of a grieving person, but the horror experienced by a person on the receiving end of a theophany. With so many differences between Habakkuk 3 and Psalm 7, the two words šigyōnôt and šiggāyôn cannot be accepted as equivalent names for their genres.

Etymology

Other Hebrew roots containing š-g- are šgg ~ šwg, šgy, and šgʿ. The connotations of šgg ~ šwg and šgy overlap: šgg "to err," hence šĕgāgâ "inadvertent sin"; šgy "stray," sometimes helplessly, hence mišgeh "oversight" (Gen 43:12). The root šg is best known for the use of the *Puʿal* participle to refer to the ravings of a prophet considered to be crazy. Speculation from the root šgy, "to stray," concluded that a šiggāyôn is a "wild, passionate song, with rapid changes of rhythm" (BDB 993b). I have not not been able to ascertain how firm is the foundation for the statement made by Mowinckel (and repeated by Roberts 1991:130) that the Akkadian word šēgu, which according to Roberts means "a type of lament prayer," is the source of Hebrew šiggāyôn. Rudolph (1975) likewise quotes šēgu as the Akkadian form, but there is no evidence for the long /ē/ in the texts quoted by von Soden (*AHw*). Nor does *CAD* attest šēgu. More careful scholarship is called for. Avishur (1994:112, n. 6) cites šigu, but the long final vowel is a vital clue for etymology in Akkadian. Bezold (1926:265) has three šegū entries: (1) √ šg, attribute of a mad dog, and evidently cognate with Hebrew šg; (2) šegū " 'Toben' [raving madness], ein Klagegebet mit bestimmtem monatlichem Ritus"; (3) šegū, šugū, Hierodule, a Sumerian loanword. In *AHw*, šegû(m) (1208), adjective and N verb, is the attribute of a rabid dog, extended also to people and gods, and is carefully separated from šigû, šegû, an interjection, "ein Klageruf" (1231). The latter word can be used in a colophon to name a type of prayer in which this kind of cry occurs. An example is in Falkenstein and von Soden (1953:44).

A prayer to Marduk containing the word šigû is found in Seux (1981: 425–29). It begins

[ᵈMarduk] rēmēnû muballiṭ mīti	Marduk the compassionate, reviver of the dead
[pāṭir] kasî	the one who unbinds the bound
ṣābit qāt naski	the one who grasps the hand of the prostrate
[lēqi] teslītiu ikribi atta	the one who receives request and prayer—(art) thou.

After some transitional words, the suppliant states the reason for his presence: [ana] šigû errub, which is code for "I have entered (the temple) to (recite) a šigû" (*CAD* 4:260). A clue to the nature of this kind of prayer is supplied by the verb šasû, which usually has šigû as its object. The whole expression describes the whimpering of a sick child, so that šigû is either the name of that sound or a conventional ritualization of it. If the word is merely onomatopoeic, there is no point in searching for its root (Seux 1981:420). The word is probably "an exclamation appealing for (the god's) pity" (Seux 1981:421). The coincidence of Marduk's attribute "compassionate" in the invocation just quoted with the use of the same root to describe Yahweh's character as "the kind and sensitive God" (ʾēl raḥûm wĕḥannûn) (Andersen 1986), if we have interpreted *rḥm* in Hab 3:2 correctly, suggests that the prayers may also have in common the mood of the suppliant and the rationale of the petition. But these two tenuous equations (*šigû* = *šiggāyôn* and *rēmēnû* = *rḥm*) may not be enough to force Habakkuk 3 and Akkadian *šigû* prayers together. The mood of *šigû* is sorrow, not even contrition (so there does not seem to be any basis for Dhorme's glossing *šigû* as "confession" [*Bible de la Pléiade* II (1959), p. 811]), while the mood of Habakkuk's complaints is outrage. The purpose of many Babylonian and Assyrian prayers is to calm down an irritated deity (often when the worshiper has no idea why the god is upset) (Seux 1976:139–68), whereas Habakkuk is the one who is irked by the apathy of his God. The content of an Akkadian *šigû* does not match either of the suspected Hebrew counterparts (Psalm 7, Habakkuk 3) (Seux 1981).

Mowinckel (1921: IV 7) already pointed out the difficulty of an etymological connection and had to suppose that the Akkadian word had been borrowed into Canaanite and mistakenly interpreted as having a III'*yod* root. The different connotations of the Akkadian words do not seem to have been distinguished by scholars who have sought in them the background of the Hebrew terms; hence the notion that these are hysterical prayers or "giddy" poems (Kraus in *BK* XV⁵, p. 20).

Ancient Translations

The LXX rendered *šiggāyôn* of Ps 7:1 as *psalmos* (for David) and this is reflected in the Old Latin *Psalmus David*. Vulgate read the Hebrew as though it were connected with √*šgg pro ignoratione David*. In Hab 3:1, LXX has *meta ōdēs*, "with (a) song." Comparison of Hab 3:1 with LXX cannot be used to restore an original *šîr(â)* (Irwin 1932:15), for the corruption of a clear word into an obscure word is unlikely. Vulgate of Hab 3:1 lines up with Ps 7:1. None of this evidence assists the recovery of the original meaning of *šiggāyôn* or *šigyōnôt*.

All the same, the endless attempts to make sense of unaccountable catastrophes found pathetic expression in ancient Mesopotamian blanket confessions to sins that the victims feel they must somehow have committed without knowing it. In Israelite religion, too, a distinction was made between deliberate transgression and accidental violation of some rule. Numbers 15 classifies sins as high-handed or unintentional. Theoretically, intentional sin could not be forgiven, but unwitting infringement could be pardoned as long as the innocent fault was acknowledged (once it was brought to the person's attention) and proper steps were taken to repair the damage by means of appropriate cleansing rituals. Inevitably, an elaborate apparatus of casuistry was needed to tell the difference between the two kinds of sin, but the important principle was put in place that intention rather than action was what determined guilt. This distinction also defined the jurisdiction of divine and human magistrates. Humans could try deeds; only God could try the heart. At the same time, a scrupulous or troubled person would like to know where he or she stood, and the terror of suspecting that one might have committed that dreaded "unpardonable sin" could be relieved somewhat if the distinction between mortal and venial sin could be spelled out.

One of the much-sought services of the divination industry in the ancient world was to answer the baffled person's question, "What did I do wrong?" Or, to make sure that everything was covered, there could be global confessions to every sin in the book, with catalogs that continue to turn up in Christian penitential checklists.

While it is always best for human beings to take no chances with the gods and to resort to all the techniques for cleaning the slate, their best hope was to believe that the preference from the divine side was for mercy. In the Hebrew Bible, certainly, the belief was frequently expressed that God's gut feelings of compassion were stronger than his anger and could be aroused by the sight of human misery (hence the prayer "Look at me!") or by even minimal expressions of contrition. The effectiveness of repentance as sufficient grounds for canceling God's disapproval of bad conduct became more prominent in Jewish spirituality when the ceremonial remedies for human sins were no longer operative after the abolition of Temple worship. The conviction emerged that there was no sin that could not be forgiven. This belief was harmonized with the rigor of Numbers 15 and other teachings of the Hebrew Bible by the theory that if a person repented of any sin, however serious, God would reclassify intentional sin as inadvertent, and so be able to forgive it without compromising the rules he had laid down in holy writ.

This is the thinking behind the V translation of *šigyōnôt* as *pro ignorationibus,* "for inadvertent faults." In the Tg this interpretation is expanded into a fuller theological exposition of the power of repentance:

> The prayer which Habakkuk the prophet prayed when it was revealed to him concerning the extension of time which he gives to the wicked [*lršyy'*], that if they return to the torah [*l'wryt'*] with a perfect heart [*blbb šlym*] it shall be forgiven them and all their sins which they have committed before him shall be as sins of ignorance [*kšlwt'*].

VIII.2.i. THE INVOCATION IN HABAKKUK'S PRAYER (3:2)

2aAα Yahweh! I heard the report about thee.
2aAβ   I was frightened, Yahweh, by thy deed.
2aAγ In (our) midst, once more, by the life of Yahweh,
2aB   in (our) midst, once more, thou didst reveal,
2b In (my) distress thou didst proclaim (thy name)—Compassionate.

Scansion of the Invocation in Habakkuk's Prayer (3:2)

		BEATS	SYLLABLES	BICOLON
2aAα	*yhwh šāma 'tî šim 'ăkā*	3	7 }	14
2aAβ	*yārē 'tî yhwh po 'olkā*	3	7 }	
2aAγ	*běqereb šānîm hayyêhû*	3	7 }	13
2aB	*běqereb šānîm tôdîa*	3	6 }	
2b	*běrōgez raḥēm tizkôr*	3	5	[8]

INTRODUCTION

The invocation (v 2) is a stanza of five colons with intricate parallelism that connects all five colons in many different combinations. The first two colons constitute a bicolon with complete synonymous parallelism. The vocative "Yahweh" is in chiasmus with the verbs, and, if we are right, this name is repeated a third time in the midde colon. The third and fourth colons have repetitive parallelism. The third and fifth colons have in parallelism the attributes "life of Yahweh"(?) and "compassionate." The fourth and fifth colons have prefixed verbs similarly placed at the end.

The classical patterns of climactic parallelism achieve their effect by a combination of redundant and laconic expressions. Redundancy is achieved by synonymous parallelism (saying the same thing twice) and, most of all, in repetitive parallelism (saying the same thing again in the same words). Laconism rcsults whcn a complctc colon of poetry is less than a complete clause grammatically, when this elliptical colon has to wait for the climactic element in a later colon, before its significance can be fully grasped. By means of climactic parallelism, a fairly long clause can be realized. The total statement is built up stage by stage, with suspense in the early colons, and resolution in the last colon. In vv 2aAγ-2b the statement, as prose, would be: (A) In the midst (B) once more (C) by the life of Yahweh (D) when I was distressed (E) you declared your name (F) "Compassionate." (This translation is speculative in places; the lexical problems will be discussed in the NOTES.) These six items are distributed over the three colons as follows:

A   B   C
A   B   E
D   F   E

The climax is reached in the name "Compassionate" (F), which has no parallel. The first two colons are unified by repetitive parallelism. The last two are linked by synonymous parallelism between *tôdîa'* and *tizkôr*. In one respect (in the use of the preposition), *běrōgez* is a synonymous parallel to *běqereb*.

The laconism of these terse colons is not fully relieved, and the resulting opacity has misled interpreters. If *rḥm* is, as we have suggested, the common object of both *tôdîaʿ* and *tizkôr*, there is no need to supply an implied object ("make [yourself] known" or "make [your work] known"), as is usually done. Another laconism, characteristically archaic, results from the omission of pronouns. The great affirmation "I (Yahweh) am in your midst" usually has the pronoun suffix *bĕqirbĕkā*. Here the construction is abbreviated. The noun *qereb* is never used as a preposition for time. Unless here, of course. Hiebert accepted a suggestion of Frank Cross, and glossed "Through the years." "In (our) midst" is more likely than the unexampled "in the midst of years," which has been made intelligible only by the most contrived exegesis. Similarly, *rōgez* has to be referred to something, and the wrath of God (*rgz*) has been contrasted with his mercy (*rḥm*) in order to explain *bĕrōgez*. We suggest that *bĕrōgez* refers rather to the prophet's agitation, or to the disturbances in the world into which God proclaims his name (see the NOTE).

The five colons of v 2 are unified by another device used frequently in bicolons in other parts of the poem. This device is the sequence suffixed verb // prefixed verb, both past tense in reference.

The same feature has already been noted in the discussion of the poem in Hab 1:8–11. It is common for the suffixed verb to begin its colon, while the prefixed verb ends its colon. So here the opening pair of colons have matching suffixed verbs at their beginning, and the closing pair of colons have matching prefixed verbs at their end.

2aAα	*yhwh šāmaʿtî*			*šimʿăkā*	
2aAβ	*yārēʾtî*	*yhwh*		*poʿolkā*	
2aAγ	*bĕqereb šānîm*	*ḥayyêhû*			
2aB	*bĕqereb šānîm*				*tôdîaʿ*
2b	*bĕrōgez*		*raḥēm*		*tizkôr*

This five-colon unit exhibits the regular rhythm that is sustained though the entire prayer, with three beats (three words) per colon. Counting segholate nouns as monosyllabic (the old articulation), the colons fall short of the standard eight-syllable colon. The mean length is 6.4 syllables per colon.

NOTES

2. **Yahweh.** The unit 2aAα–2aAβ is the first of several bicolons that use archaic repetitive parallelism. The Greek versions are more ample and would make Hebrew verse more pleasing for those who might find simple repetition mechanical and jarring. The Barberini version differs from LXX in preserving the repeated "Yahweh":

Lord, I heard the report of you, and I became wary [LXX "frightened"];
Lord, I comprehended your works, and I became distraught.

This rendering could be accounted for by a text such as

yhwh šm ʿty šm ʿk wyr ʾty (?)
[*r ʾyty*] *yhwh p ʾlk wyr ʾty* (?)

Because Greek *eksistān* translates twenty-nine different Hebrew verbs, we cannot suggest what the original Hebrew verb might have been here. Torrey (1935) restored *ḥāradtî*. If the original Hebrew used the verbs *yr ʾ* and *r ʾh* in sequence, either one could have been lost by haplography. That *r ʾyty* should be read is suggested by the use of the same verb in v 6 of the Barberini version (Ziegler 1943:273). (LXX uses a different verb.) Irwin (1942:17), who thought that any alteration of the Hebrew verb is "trifling with the evidence," nevertheless reconstructed *wayyārē ʾtî* [sic!] — an unattested form.

Both occurrences of *yhwh* should be retained. The deletion of one as a dittograph is not warranted. Albright (1950a) went to the other extreme, restoring the text in order to increase the amount of repetitive parallelism and the number of tricolons.

The name Yahweh is used at least five times in the poem. We suggest that it occurs again in v 2aAγ. Other names for God are *ʾĕlôah*, *qādôš*. The direct address of God by this mysterious name (*yhwh*) is both intimate and archaic (cf. Hab 1:12).

I heard. This intensely personal response of the poet (Habakkuk himself?) could be explained if a dramatic recital of a traditional credal poem — an ancient account of Yahweh's achievements — stimulated an ecstatic vision. This report about Yahweh is called "thy report," but the suffix is not the subject of the verbal root. It does not describe an account of himself given by God in an oracle; it is a report about God. It is best to identify this "report" with the recital in vv 3–7, a fragment of an epic poem dealing with the Sinai theophany or, rather, with the triumphal march of Yahweh from Sinai through the desert. The same activity is appropriately called "thy deed." Or the "report" could be the whole of vv 3–15.

report . . . deed. By hendiadys, this is a discontinuous construct chain, "the report of your deed." Does this refer to Yahweh's general reputation, the cumulative effect of all his famous achievements, or does it refer precisely to one great deed, which is also the sole subject matter of this poem, such as "the great victory of Yahweh over the demon of chaos" (Irwin 1942:17)? Now *šēma ʿ* can refer to the report of any newsworthy event, good or bad tidings. The fame of Yahweh, which causes dismay among the nations (vv 6, 7, 12), is the defeat of Pharaoh at the Reed Sea (Num 14:15; Deut 2:25). The verb *rgz* is found also in Habakkuk 3, and the same sequence "hear . . . tremble" is found in Exod 15:14. The "work" or "works" of God can describe almost anything he does — works of creation, judgment, and redemption. In Hab 1:5, this language refers to an impending deed. In Ps 44:2, it is the Conquest. In Ps 95:9 the "work" that "they saw" was the desert discipline. It can hardly be said that any one event qualifies as Yahweh's distinctive deed, and it is not certain that the following poem is restricted to any one moment. Nevertheless, at least two of the three occasions in the past that were recounted in terms similar to those of the theophany in Habakkuk 3—Creation, Exodus, Occupation—can be discerned in Habakkuk 3.

was frightened (or "took fright," to bring out the perfective aspect of the suffixed verb). The Masoretic word is widely rejected, replaced by (*w*)*r'yty*. The initial *y* is either read as *w* or else deleted, to yield "(and) I saw," following LXX. But many scholars accept the MT.

LXX differs substantially from the MT. It has four verbs in v 2:

> Lord, I heard [*eisakēkoa*] thy report,
>> and I became afraid [*efobēthēn*];
> I regarded [*katenoēsa*] thy works,
>> and I was beside myself [*eksestēn*].

Barberini agrees with LXX, apart from having *eulabēthēn* rather than *efobēthēn*, with a nuance of pious fear.

The poetic balance of LXX is excellent, but retrojection of the whole to Hebrew does not necessarily recover a text with any superior claim to be a text that actually existed. For then we would have to explain how this fuller text, if more original than the MT, got cut back or, if derived from a (proto-)Masoretic text, how the derivative expanded. The puzzle is compounded by the detail that LXX has *Kyrie* once against *yhwh* twice in the MT. (There is abundant evidence for a second *Kyrie* in other Greek sources and versions [Ziegler 1943:268], accommodation to the Hebrew.)

The more material question is whether the double reading "I feared I perceived" was an inner-Greek development or whether it originated in a Hebrew *Vorlage* that already had two verbs. If an inner-Greek development, it could be a conflation of versions made by independent translations from two distinct Hebrew sources, one with *r'yty*, "I saw," and the other with *yr'ty*, "I feared." In another scenario, both verbs could have been present in LXX's Hebrew *Vorlage*, a conflate reading created there when some scribe preserved the variants *r'yty* ~ *yr'ty* attested by different exemplars. It is also possible that both verbs were juxtaposed by the Hebrew poet for sound play and that one was lost by a kind of haplography. Whichever way, the Greek sources point to variant readings. Which is more likely to have been original? The similarity of the Hebrew verbs (same consonants in both) suggests that one was the source of the other. But which?

In the context of a theophany, either verb makes sense. The Hebrew attests only *yr'ty*, and this is a slightly more difficult reading. That is, if, on the one hand, *r'yty* was original, it is harder to work out why a scribe would have thought that *yr'ty* was better. Rudolph (1975:233) found the motivation for "correcting" *r'yty* to *yr'ty* in a false understanding of v 16, where *šāma'tî* occurs again and where the response is fear. Albright's (1950a:13, n. a) argument that the superfluous *y*- came in under the influence of "two adjacent words [he does not identify them] beginning with it" has little force. More cogent would be the argument that *r'ty* is *defective* (not archaic) spelling wrongly taken as a mistake, with *yr'ty* rather than *r'yty* as the correction. If, on the other hand, *yr'ty* is original, it is understandable that a scribe may have felt that "see" was a more natural correlate of "hear" than "fear," anticipating the reasoning of modern text critics. The same idea could have occurred to a Greek translator, whose (mental) "correction" of *yr'ty* to *r'yty* would have brought out further the visionary side of the poet's experience.

The modern predilection for synonymous parallelism in adjacent bicolons, driven by the observation that *šm'* and *r'h* frequently match (in either sequence [Job 13:1; 29:1]), emends *yr'ty* to *r'yty*. Rudolph (1975:233) says that parallelism "demands" (*verlangt*) this. Too strong, since *yr'* can parallel *šm'* (Ps 76:9). There is more to it than that, however. While "report" (cognate) is a suitable object for "hear," "deed" is a more suitable object for "fear" than for "see." Habakkuk did not see the deed(s) described in the following poem(s). He heard the report of those events when the epic poems were recited. His agitated reaction has already been recorded in *rgz* (v 2b), which is repeated in v 16. The resumption of this combination of seeing and fearing from v 2 in v 16 is another inclusion that is part of the original shape of the composition, and not the outcome of later touch-up by a scribe. Appreciation for inclusion has not turned around the earlier text-critical judgments (still in Rudolph), validating the MT.

Deut 2:25 contains a prediction that the nations will hear of Yahweh's fame (*yišmě'ûn šimăkā*) and will tremble (*wěrāgězû*). Deuteronomy uses the same sequence of roots as Habakkuk, but does not include the verb *yr'*.

In any case, the verb "saw" as expected parallel for "heard" does turn up, but not until v 7a, at the end of the strophe, a reminder that parallels do not have to be in continguous colons. (But the verb *yr'ty* at that point in the poem could be due to an original eyewitness report of the event [by Moses?].)

In (our) midst. The extraordinary difficulty of the MT has been dulled by familiarity and by highflown theological interpretation. It is taken to be a prayer: "In the course of the years revive it" (NAB); "in our time" (NRSV). That would be a request that the ancient deeds be repeated "in the midst of the years." Insuperable difficulties can be urged against this traditional reading. First, there is no proof that the stream of time was called "years" so that an intervention by God in the course of history takes place "in the midst of years." The word "year" has two plural forms in Hebrew. The masculine form, as used here, is nearly always used with numerals. The more abstract idea of a stretch of time is expressed by the *feminine* plural. Second, the idea of "the midst of the years" is a rather abstract one for a highly concrete and mythological composition such as this. If a decisive act of God is expected, matching the deeds of the *Urzeit*, we would expect the time reference to be eschatological, such as "the end of days."

The Greek translations, although various, give support to *qěrōb* "approach." Irwin (1942:18) found that the military imagery that comes later in the poem is already present in *bqrb*, which he translated "in battle."

The so-called doublets of repetitive parallelism are present in nearly all MSS of LXX. (The few exceptions are noted by Bévenot 1933:504, n. 2.) But each *qrb* is translated differently:

en mesō duo zōōn gnōsthēsē
In the midst of the two living creatures you will be known.

en tō eggizein ta etē epignōsthēsē
In the approach of the years you will be acknowledged.

en tō pareinai ton kairon anadeikhthēsē
In the arrival of the time you will be displayed,

> *en tō tarakhthēnai tēn psykhēn mou*
> in the disturbance of my soul,

> *en orgē eleous mnēsthēsē*
> in wrath, mercy you will remember.

The choice of future tense for the verbs makes the whole verse a prophecy. This more ample text has been attributed to two doublets (Margolis 1908:135). The matter is not so simple. The first three colons of Greek correspond to two colons of Hebrew, no one of which is simply reproduced. While there is repetition of the verb in the first colon, there are no individual words in the Greek that do not match words in the Hebrew. The original Hebrew would need the addition of the words shown inside brackets:

2aAγ	*bqrb šnym ḥy*[*wt*][*twdy*ʿ]	→	*bqrb šnym ḥyyhw*
2aB	*bqrb šnym* *twdy*ʿ	→	*bqrb šnym twdy*ʿ
[2aC]	[*bqrb šnym tiwwādēa*ʿ]		
[2aD]	[*brgz rḥy*]		
2b	*brgz rḥm tzkwr*	→	*brgz rḥm tzkwr*

See Bévenot (1933:504). This is not very firm ground on which to reconstruct the Hebrew text.

The bicolon in vv 2aAγ–2aB is satisfactory as it is, so its expansion to a tricolon is not compelling. The odd colon in v 2b, however, is not very satisfactory. It is possible that only one of the five colons in LXX is a doublet. If *brgz rḥm* is a gloss—it looks like a fragment—then there are three repetitive colons, with v 2b as the variant and climax. But if the shortness of *brgz rḥm* as a colon is not a disqualification, then its repetitive parallelism matches that of v 2aB of the Hebrew, and the elimination of one of the first three colons of the Greek as a midrash would produce a regular tetracolon:

bqrb šnym ḥywt	2aAγ	7 syllables
bqrb šnym *twdy*ʿ	2aB	7
brgz rḥy	2bC	4
brgz rḥ[*y*]*m tzkwr*	2b	7

In the midst of the years of my life,
In the midst of the years [of my life] make yourself known!
In the turbulence of my spirit
In the turbulence of my spirit remember (me)!

The *mem* of the last colon is explained as enclitic, producing the spurious "Compassion." If the first colon is a construct phrase, there is an enclitic *mem* there as well. The main flaw is the shortness of the third colon.

A further remark is in order about the LXX reading "in the midst of the two living beings," found also in the Old Latin. If this was a solution to a difficult translation problem, the idea must have come from somewhere. The most obvious source is the two cherubs of the Ark. A more immediate source could be v 5, which speaks of the two attendant deities Deber and Resheph. The text became a conundrum, and the two creatures were variously interpreted as the Ox and the Ass at the Nativity; Moses and Elijah at the Transfiguration, or the two thieves at the Crucifixion.

On the basis of reading "two animals," the fulfillment of the prophecy was connected with the ox and the ass, which became a fixed motif in Nativity scenes, as in *The Gospel of Pseudo-Mathew* (14):

And on the third day after the birth of our Lord Jesus Christ, Mary went out of the cave and, entering a stable, placed the child in the manger, and an ox and an ass adored him. Then was fulfilled that which was said by Isaiah the prophet, 'The ox knows his owner and the ass his master's crib' (Isa 1:3). Therefore the animals, the ox and the ass, with him in their midst, incessantly adored him. Then was fulfilled that which was said by Habakkuk the prophet, saying, 'Between two animals thou art made manifest' (Hab 3:2) (ANT(E):95).

once more. The difficulty of *šānîm*, when it is not numerical, but read as "years," has already been discussed. There are other possibilities. The root meaning "two" suggests itself and came through in the old versions, as already noted. Perhaps the word means "a second time." Habakkuk hopes that God will do in his time deeds like those which made him famous of old. Albright (1950a) rightly abandoned the traditional interpretation of v 2aAγ as a complete clause. The prosody of repetitive parallelism is classical and points to a climactic development. Albright's reference to Judg 5:2 and 4 is relevant (although there the parallel infinitives are not identical), but not enough to prove that *qrb* is an infinitive. Albright's examples with "days" and "years" are really different from those in Hab 3:2; they describe the approach of a definite time ("the time of mourning for my father" [Gen 27:41]), whereas "as the years advance" seems to mean "as time rolls by."

life. The pointing of *ḥyyhw* as an imperative verb, "give him life," is the only thing that makes this statement a prayer. But a prayer at this point contrasts with the indicative mood of the context—two suffixed verbs in the preceding bicolon and two prefixed verbs in the following bicolon. As a command, "Revive him!" is quite obscure. The idea that God will revive his "work," in spite of its vogue in "revivalist" circles, is marginal to biblical thought. Even so, Hiebert (1986) overstates his argument for not recognizing *poʿolkā* as an acceptable antecedent of the object -*hû* because the usual object of *Piʿel* √*ḥyy* is a living creature. Humbert (1944:59) already had drawn attention to the exception in Neh 3:34 ("stones"). Two other parts of his argument are more germane. A second-person-singular masculine suffixed verb is incongruent with the nearby second-person-singular masculine prefixed verbs, all preterite. And the Tg reads like a *pešer* (v 2 has forty-eight words for fifteen in MT): *w'ynwn mrgzyn qdmk bgw šny' dyhbt lhwn ḥyy'*, "and they were not distressed in your presence in the years when you gave them life."

To make the verb indicative, Hiebert (1986:12) emends to *ḥiyyîtā*, "you sustained life" (through the years). But the parallels he cites (Deut 32:29; 1 Sam 2:6 [1986:152]) mean "restore to life." As an act of God, the verb "revive" describes the resuscitation of a dead (or dying) person. This theme is absent from Habakkuk, except perhaps at Hab 2:4. While it is true that the only version that directly corroborates the MT is Jerome's Vulgate, the other versions supply no support for Hiebert's emendation. He has to postulate **ḥyyt → ḥywt* as the source of "animals" in the versions. The plural *ḥywt* is found at Ezek 1:5, 13, 15; 3:13. But how did **ḥyyt → ḥyyhw*?

Albright (1950a) was close to a solution, but took a wrong turn when he omitted one of the *yods* as "superfluous." The example that Albright gave for the use of the *Pi'el* from the Samaria ostraca—*yḥw'ly*—which is a theophoric name, supplies the needed analogy. This word in Habakkuk could point to *ḥy-yhw*, "(by the) life of Yahweh," which is attested in the Lachish Letters as *ḥy . yhwh* (LL 6:12), *ḥ]y yhwh* (LL 12:3), *ḥyhwh* (LL 3:9; cf. *ḥyh[wh* [Arad 21:5]), and possibly a person name *ḥyhw*. A long shot, admittedly. Compare Avishur's (1994) repointing of *ydyhw* in v 10. In the MT, the phrase *ḥy-yhwh* is always written with each word separate.

reveal. We cannot be certain about the tense and mood of this verb. If the imperative *ḥayyêhû* is retained, the two following verbs could be jussive. In poetry of this kind, however, it is possible—indeed more probable, we think—that they are past tense, matching the suffixed verbs in the first bicolon. If the last two verbs have preterite tense, then these references to past events identify the famous feat, so that the first bicolon and the last bicolon make an envelope construction around the central prayer. The object of the verb "know" is either "your fame" or "your name." The LXX passive probably arose because it was not recognized that the verb has an implied object or one more distant ("your report"). There is no need to read "you will be known" or "you will make yourself known."

This solution obviates the need to emend the MT to *Nip'al* (Wellhausen 1898:36, 171), deleting the *yod* (Hiebert 1986:13). The analogous texts to which the emendation conforms Hab 3:2 are plausible in themselves, but that is precisely what makes the MT *lectio difficilior*. With the meaning of *Nip'al *twd'*, "you made yourself known," so familiar (Exod 6:3; Isa 19:21; Ezek 20:5; Pss 9:17; 48:4) and straightforward, why would anyone change it to (apparently intransitive) *Hip'il* by adding *yod*?

distress. The noun is rare. Albright (1950a) preferred to read an infinitive, which would imply "when you are angry." His case depends in part on reading infinitives at the beginning of the previous two colons, as in LXX. The versions are divided. Or, rather, the Greek recensions are expansive or conflate, with both infinitive and noun phrase:

When my spirit is upset [infinitive]
in (thy) wrath, mercy thou shalt remember.

Modern translations still take *rgz* as referring to the wrath of God. They remain with a long tradition that finds a contrast between wrath (*rgz*) and mercy (*rḥm*). In the Hebrew Bible, √*rgz* is rarely used to refer to the wrath of God (Baloian 1994). *HAL* (1104) gives it the meaning "anger" only in Hab 3:2.

The parallelism of "see" and "quake with fear" in v 7 and *rgz* again in v 16 suggests, rather, that *rōgez* is not God's wrath, not "the disruption caused by the theophany" in the world (Hiebert 1986:14), but the prophet's trembling. This is confirmed by the sequence "I heard and I trembled" in v 16 (cf. Exod 15:14; Deut 2:25). That is, v 16 constitutes an *inclusio* with v 2 (see the structural diagram and Hiebert 1987:128). Avishur (1994:115), while giving full weight to the repetition of "I heard" in vv 2 and 16 as evidence that these verses constitute an *inclusio*, does not permit the use of the root *rgz* twice in v 16 to determine that it has the same reference in both places—the poet's agitation. Instead, *rgz* means "trembling" when applied to humans, but "anger" when applied to God. Avishur admits that "[t]his is the only biblical passage where this meaning [*rgz* = "wrath"] is attested" (151). Avishur defends neither this meaning, nor his interpretation of the preposition *b-* "in" as concessive. *DCH* cites only four instances of *b-* with the meaning "despite": Lev 26:27; Deut 1:32; Isa 9:11; Ps 78:32. If *rgz* refers to God's anger, which the suppliant hopes will be replaced by compassion, this implies that the poet feels threatened by God's wrath. The book gives no hint that this is a motive for Habakkuk's prayers. In v 8, God's wrath is directed against various waters. For these several reasons, then—this once giving *rgz* the meaning "anger" rather than the usual "disquietude"; invocation of the rare concessive meaning for *b-*; not following through on the coherence of the two parts of the inclusion—we reject the traditional reading and recognize that vv 2 and 16 both record the prophet's agitation caused by what he heard. His state of mind resembles that of the author of Psalm 77, who describes his distress at length, with details about a number of his body parts, similar to Hab 3:16. Such agitation is presented to God to incite pity. The Psalmist recalls God's marvels of old and recites all his deeds (Ps 77:12–13) and wonders if God has forgotten how to be gracious. Will he show wrath (*'ap*) or compassion? Why was not *'ap* similarly used in Hab 3:2, if that poet wanted to plead for compassion to replace wrath?

The enigmatic character of the root *rgz* is made worse by its semantic ambivalence. At least at some stage of its development, its meanings are polar opposites (Gordis 1938:278). The ideas of painful or pleasurable excitement could indicate that *rgz* is actually neutral. But fear and fascination would be combined when God reveals his majesty, and the beholder is in conflict. He wants to flee from the inescapable; he wants to draw near to the unapproachable.

proclaim. The meaning "remember" for *tizkôr* (in the sense of keep in mind or recall to mind) is in line with biblical prayers that remind God of his covenant commitments. But that meaning is not such a good parallel to "make known." The fame of Yahweh is proclaimed as his name—*šēm* or *zēker*. The latter refers to what is remembered about God. The proclamation of the Name includes not only "Yahweh" and *'ēl qannā'*, "El [the] Passionate," but also *'ēl raḥûm wĕḥan-*

nûn, "El [the] Compassionate and Gracious." We suggest that what we have in v 2b is the former attribute, spelled defectively.

"*Compassionate.*" The Masoretic reading is traditionally an infinitive absolute. We suggest that a noun is a better object for *tizkôr*. "You declared (your name) 'Compassionate'" rather than "Remember to be compassionate." Greek readings are double, with "my soul" (from *rḥy*) and *eleous* (from *rḥmym*). It is a much longer step to change to *rḥb*, as Irwin (1942:18) did. By this kind of overkill, he sabotaged his own attempts to recover the lost mythology of the poem.

By taking "Compassionate (one)" as a virtual name for God, here vocative, the double name has been split to make an inclusion for the whole of this opening invocation.

To sum up. A possible reconstruction, using evidence from all the text traditions, is

> O Yahweh, I heard your fame.
> I revered, O Yahweh, your feat.
> In (our) midst repeat it, O Life-giver
> O Yahweh, in (our) midst repeat it.
> You made yourself known when we were upset.
> You remembered us, O Compassionate one.

VIII.2.ii. THE MARCH IN THE SOUTH (3:3–7)

3aA	Eloh came out from Teman	A
3aB	even Qadosh from Mount Paran. [Selah]	B
3bA	His glory covered the sky,	C
3bB	and his praise filled the earth.	D
4aA	And his radiance was like the sun.	E
4aB	He had horns (coming) from his hand,	F
4b	and there he (un-)veiled his power.	G
5a	In front of him marched Plague;	H
5b	and Pestilence came out behind him.	I
6aAα	He stood and spanned the earth;	J
6aAβ	he looked and made the nations tremble.	K
6aB	And the primeval mountains were shattered,	L
6aC	the ancient peaks dissolved;	M
6b	the ancient highways were ruined.	N
7aA*	Under iniquity I saw [it].	O
7aB	The tents of Kushan were agitated,	P
7bA	the curtains of the land of Midian.	

---

*This division does not match the Masoretic punctuation, which has *zaqef gadol* on "iniquity."

Scansion of the March in the South (3:3–7)

		BEATS	SYLLABLES	BICOLON	
3aA	*ĕlôah mittêmān yābô'*	3	7 ⎫		
3aB	*wĕqādôš mēhar-pā'rān*	3	7 ⎭	14	*selâ*
3bA	*kissâ šāmayim hôdô*	3	6 ⎫		
3bB	*ûtĕhillātô mālĕ'â hā'āreṣ*	3	10 ⎭	16	
4aA	*wĕnōgah kā'ôr tihyeh*	3	6		
4aB	*qarnayim miyyādô lô*	3	6 ⎫		
4b	*wĕšām ḥebyôn 'uzzōh*	3	6 ⎭	12	
5a	*lĕpānānyw yēlek dāber*	3	7 ⎫		
5b	*wĕyēṣē' rešep lĕraglāyw*	3	7 ⎭	14	
6aAα	*'āmad | wayĕmōded 'ereṣ*	3	7 ⎫		
6aAβ	*rā'â wayyattēr gôyīm*	3	7 ⎭	14	
6aB	*wayyitpōṣĕṣû harĕrê-'ēd*	2	9 ⎫		
6aC	*šaḥû gibĕ'ôt 'ôlām*	3	7 ⎭	16	
6b	*hălîkôt 'ôlām lô*	3	6		
7a	*taḥat 'āwen rā'îtî 'ohŏlê kûšān yirgĕzûn*	5	13 ⎫		
7b	*yĕrî'ôt 'ereṣ midyān*	3	6 ⎭	19	

INTRODUCTION

This unit is readily identified by the change to detailed narrative description and by the change from second to third person. The ending of this unit with v 7 is marked by a return to second-person address in v 8. The MT has a *setuma* break at this point. (It could be pointed out, however, that the *petuḥa* break at the end of v 13 does not make comparable sense.) The opening (v 3a) and closing (v 7) bicolons have place-names as parallel pairs. This design makes a frame around the description of the action (Hiebert 1987:123). Avishur (1994:120), however, transposed v 7 to between v 13a and 13b, an emendation that, he claims, yields "perfect symmetry." The placement of v 7 as an inclusion for v 3a is itself symmetrical. Emendations that shunt portions of text around are intrinsically dubious. This one loses as much as it gains and is quite unnecessary. That the starting point (or scene) of the march (Midian) is placed at the end of the recital shows that orderly chronological narration is not to be expected. These opening and closing bicolons also provide a foothold, a much-needed piece of firm ground, from which to venture into the more treacherous places of the intervening text.

This unit is markedly different from vv 8–15, in which Yahweh is more active, or, rather, he acts more directly on things. In vv 3–7, the victims are devastated by the mere sight of his glory. In vv 8–15, Yahweh uses weapons to inflict injuries. This literary effect is achieved, in part, by the way the verbs are used, passive at first, and active later. Verse 6 does not say "He shattered the mountains," but "The mountains were shattered." Verse 9 does not say "The rivers were divided," but "You divided the rivers." Theologically, it might be said that in vv 3–7 God is more transcendent; but this would be misleading. There is still a high level of mythology, or at least a marked use of mythopoeic imagery. The key verse (v 5) could be taken as virtually polytheistic (Deber and Resheph are real beings) or merely poetic (Deber and Resheph are personifications of features of God's destructive power, like *ṣedeq* in Ps 85:14).

The contrast between vv 3–7 and 8–15 should not be forced into a contradiction. They are different pieces of tradition; that is all.

The several literary features of this poem are its standard orthography, false archaisms, poetic language, complex prosody, parallelism, double-duty items, and strophic structure.

1. The orthography is entirely classical; that is, there is little or no trace of archaic spellings. The use of standard orthography is most conspicuous in the consistently *plene* spelling of long /ō/ within the stem of words; to be more precise, this trend is late in the development of Biblical Hebrew spelling. The only palpable archaism is the spelling of *ʿuzzô* as *ʿzh*, not *ʿzw* (v 4). This ancient spelling of the pronoun suffix, however, occasionally survived the normalization of the majority of its occurrences in the Hebrew Bible (Andersen and Forbes 1986:83–84). The generally "modern" spelling cannot be used to disprove the antiquity of the content, or even of the poem itself. But it does make it unlikely that this piece was copied unchanged from an ancient *written* version of this poem. Of course, such a copy could have been made and the spelling normalized. Or it could have been normalized in later scribal transcription (by Habakkuk himself or by the editor of the book or by any later scribe). But in such cases, we would expect at least a few of the older forms to survive.

2. The poem is archaic in many of its ideas and images. A form like *yirgĕzûn* does not have to be suspected, although it is the only verb with nunation in the piece. Remembering the habits of the Deuteronomist in this matter (Driver 1902:lxxxix; Hoftijzer 1985; Kaufman 1995; Muraoka 1975), such a form can be taken either way—archaic or archaizing. But it is not demonstrably an affectation of an antiquarian of limited scholarship.

3. This unit shares with the rest of the "prayer" the poetic features of not using *ʾet*, *ʾăšer*, and the definite article. In fact, each of these elements occurs once in the entire poem, and each is very suspicious. We shall deal with *ʾet* (v 13) and *ʾăšer* (v 16) in the NOTES. The one occurrence of the definite article in v 3 is so exceptional as to invite deletion of *h-*, for four reasons besides the general poetic considerations just mentioned. First, because the other occurrences of *ʾereṣ*, where it is certainly definite (vv 6, 9, 12; in v 7 it is construct), do not have the definite article. Second, the colon is a bit long. Third, the consonant could easily have been repeated by dittography. Fourth, the idiom "the earth is full of (something)," which has the definite article in other occurrences in the Hebrew Bible, would attract normalization in the mind of a scribe. The point is moot.

By the same token, the places where the Masoretes have been able to supply a definite article, because there is a preposition to carry it, can be dismissed as an orthographic artificiality. And the vocalization of *wāw* plus a "prefixed" verb as "consecutive" similarly has no claim, because "prefixed" verbs without *wāw* are equally past tense in the old language.

4. The prosody itself is somewhat neutral as to its possible date, at least so far as patterns of parallelism are concerned. The poem seems to display sixteen colons. Fourteen colons have three beats, a regularity that raises doubts about the Masoretic accentuation of v 6aB (it has three words) and even more about the text itself in v 7a. The length of the colons by syllable count is not so regular, ranging from six to thirteen. Perhaps the dubious v 7a should not be included in the calculations; with so many colons having six or seven syllables, v 7a is long enough to make v 7 a tricolon. But where to put the caesura? We have already adjusted the Masoretic versification in a perhaps futile attempt to make more sense of *taḥat ʾāwen*. The aggregate of 117 syllables gives a mean length of 6.9 syllables per colon, again less than the standard.

Our analysis displays seven bicolons. A long colon usually goes with a short one (vv 3b, 7) keeping the range of bicolon length within reasonable limits. Two single colons are left (vv 4aA, 6b). Perhaps they should be attached to an adjacent biciolon to make a tricolon, because there are several other tricolons in the poem.

We cannot be confident about the identity of every colon. There is no assurance that the section, if an extract from an old poem (as we believe) has survived intact or was reproduced unchanged by the person who wrought it into the "Prayer" of Habakkuk. And it may have suffered damage in subsequent transmission. Nevertheless, its regularity and intelligibility at most points encourage belief that it is well preserved. The main difficulties lie in vv 4b, 6b, and 7aA.

In our display of the text (p. 283), the Masoretic punctuation has been revised at several points. The reasons for this will be given when the time comes. For ease of reference, the colons we have identified are marked by letters of the alphabct.

The sixteen or so colons in the unit can be grouped into poetic periods or "lines," mostly bicolons. The exact count of colons cannot be determined with confidence because of difficulties in the text at several points. The fact that our display has three words in each colon has a certain neatness, but this in itself is not enough to carry the point. Colons F, G, and N are recalcitrant. The abundance of verbs in colons J and K invites a different analysis, especially if one is influenced by an expectation of "one verb (or one clause), one colon." Or colons J and K might be arranged as three two-word colons:

ʿāmad wayĕmōded	6 syllables
ʾereṣ rāʾâ	3
wayyattēr gôyīm	5

This display could be no more than a paper exercise. In favor of our preferred scheme (two colons) is the retention, *within* these two individual colons, of the verb sequence ("suffixed" and "prefixed," both past tense) found elsewhere *between* pairs of individual colons that constitute a bicolon. And the two colons are equal in length, seven syllables each.

The recognition of the constituent bicolons arises from considerations of both poetry and grammar; and it is attained with varying degrees of confidence. Of the sixteen colons we are working with, twelve contain verbs (two have two each), and these are the easiest to manage. Of the fourteen verbs, six are "suffixed" and eight, "prefixed." Of the four colons without verbs, two (B and P, as we have re-punctuated the latter) are in incomplete synonymous parallelism (gapping) with the preceding colon and present no problem. The structural similarity of the opening and closing bicolon in this regard, as well as the four geographic names, contribute to the inclusion effect. The other two colons without verbs (F and G) are the most difficult ones.

Three of the best examples of bicolons (A–B, C–D, and H–I) have a pattern in which the first colon has no conjunction, while the second has "and." In other words, clauses are joined together within a bicolon by "and," but bicolons are not linked to one another by "and." If colons F and G constitute a bicolon, it is similar to them in this detail. Colons J and K have a similar pattern inter- nally; each has two verbs, the second in each instance with "and." This is not a rule, but it does weigh against Albright's (1950a) omission of "and" from the be- ginning of D and Hiebert's deletion of all such "ands." The pattern does not op- erate in the last five colons. The parallelism in L–M is good, except for the pat- tern of verbs and conjunctions at the beginning of the colons. Nevertheless, the individual clauses in L–M are true to type, for there is a complementary distri- bution in the use of the verb forms.

	SUFFIXED	PREFIXED
Clause-initial verb without "and"	C, J, K, M	
Clause-initial verb with "and"		I, J, K, L
Verb not clause-initial without "and"	Nb (?)	A, H, O, Na (?)
Verb not clause-initial with "and"	D	E

The preference is to use a suffixed verb as the opening word in independent clauses (C, J, K, M), where prefixed verbs are never so used, and a prefixed verb as the opening word in co-ordinated clauses (I, J, K, L), where suffixed verbs are never so used. It is this distribution that accounts for the syntax of the two bi- colons (C–D and H–I) in which the parallel verbs have the same form. These are the only two bicolons that have verbs of the same form, and both are chias- tic. They have

	a	b	c	C
"and"	c′	a′	b′	D
	c′	a′	b′	H
"and"	a	b	c	I

The relationship of colon I to colon H is the same as that of colon C to colon D. The proportion C:D::I:H is a chiasm of colon patterns. This symmetry points to integral connections among these four colons, and it explains the choice of verb forms (all narrative past tense), for the sequence "suffixed" (in C–D) // "prefixed" (in H–I) is normal. These four colons describe the retinue—above, below, in front, behind—of Yahweh (see the NOTES on this verse).

Returning to the table on p. 283, the preference for the suffixed verb at the beginning of a clause is in favor of the Masoretic punctuation of v 7a ("I saw the tents of Kushan"), rather than our presentation of colon N. This analysis leaves colon E with the unique combination of "and" with a non-initial prefixed verb. Albright's (1950a) emendation, which makes the verb begin the next clause (without "and"), is too drastic because it involves the alteration or reinterpretation of nearly every word in the verse and creates a clause type otherwise unattested in this poem. The problem of colon E is compounded by the difficulties in colons F and G. At least colons F and G are candidates for recognition as a bicolon by virtue of the sequence "independent clause // coordinated clause." If colons E and F were joined in the pattern "coordinated clause // apposition clause" (the pattern of bicolon L–M), this would leave colon G as a coordinated clause in need of some connection, and we would still be in the same predicament. In favor of retaining F as the lead-colon in the bicolon F–G rather than the dependent colon of the bicolon E–F is its resemblance to colon N, which is isolated as a colon not by any coherence that can be detected in it (for it is utterly opaque), but by the unequivocal status of the flanking bicolons L–M and O–P. The detachment of colon E from colon F is all the more likely once we have abandoned the interpretation of *qarnayim* as "rays," an interpretation that gained its support from the assumption of parallelism between colons E and F. At least some parallelism can be perceived between colons F and G, for "horns" are a symbol of "power." And "glory," "praise," and "radiance" make a good set if C–D–E is a tricolon.

Two final remarks about the table of verb-form patterns. The nonuse of a clause-initial suffixed verb in a colon beginning with "and" weighs against emendations that reconstitute such a construction in colon G (*wśm* or *wśmḥ*). And the nonuse of a clause-initial "prefixed" verb without "and" points to a revision of the punctuation of v 7, as in our bicolon O–P.

5. Colons L and M constitute the only bicolon that has complete synonymous parallelism of the kind a:b:c // a':b':c'. Colons J and K have a similar pattern, although "looked" is not exactly a synonym of "stood." The parallelism of C and D and of H and I (complete synonymous parallelism with chiasmus) has already been described. The bicolons A–B and O–P (which strategically frame the whole unit) have identical parallelism: a:b:c // a':b'. In each of them, "c" is a "prefixed" verb, narrative past tense. In each of them, "b" has rhythmic compensation of a routine kind.

In bicolons like these, with incomplete synonymous parallelism (gapping), the verb that does double duty comes first in the first colon, the normal position for a verb in Hebrew syntax. The unusual placing of the verb *last* in the first colon in A–B and O–P puts it as near as possible to the following gapped colon in which it functions by double duty. This pattern has been amply studied by Watson (1976b; 1984a:214–21), who aptly calls it "pivot parallelism."

This leaves four colons (E, F, G, and N) with no evident parallels, although the identical use of *lô* in colons F and N suggests a tie-up of some kind and cautions against altering these readings without good reason. But further progress can hardly be made without resorting to emendation. It would be wrong, however, to insist on finding parallelism everywhere. The author might have been content to use his good bicolons as stepping stones through some looser patches (F–G and N). Structural considerations on a broader front that recognizes strophes encourage the search for a tricolon in v 6, to match the one in C–D–E. The repetition of *ʿôlām* in colons M and N points in that direction, and Albright's (1950a) emendation to *l(w) tḥtʾn* (*la-tēḥāte ʾnā,* "indeed were shattered"), although somewhat of a tour de force, deserves consideration.

6. The suffixes on "his glory" and "his praise" continue as modifiers of "(his) radiance" in v 4, doing double duty. It is possible that *taḥat* in v 7 means "beneath him" or "his underparts" to match "in front of him" and "behind him" in v 5.

7. The event has two moments—the emergence of God (vv 3–5) and his impact on the world (vv 6–7). These two strophes are not equal in length. The first strophe emphasizes the splendor of God as he comes out with his retinue. The verbs *yābôʾ, yēlēk,* and *yēṣēʾ* constitute a trio that embrace and unify the first strophe. By contrast the verb *ʿāmad,* "he stood (still)," marks an abrupt change, and the verbs—"shake," "tremble," "shatter," "collapse" ("disintegrate"?), "agitate"—describe the violent dissolution of the world and unify the second strophe. The narrative itself is thus quite simple: God comes out and the universe falls apart. (This scenario contrasts with the belief, expressed in other places, that if God should go away, or even look away, the world would go to pieces or even cease to exist.)

The two strophes are unified into a single poem by various structural devices, but the result is not fully symmetrical. The unmanageable colons F–G and N interfere with the introverted pattern:

Location	A–B
Celestial elements	C–D–E
	[F–G]
Movement	H–I
Rest	J–K
Terrestrial elements	L–M
	[N]
Location	O–P

NOTES

3. *Eloh . . . Qadosh.* The ancient names for God used in this verse point to a stage before the widespread or at least dominant use of Yahweh. There seems no warrant for Albright's (1950a) restoration of "Yahweh" at the beginning of v 4. Apart from the lack of textual support, this maneuver goes with extensive re-

construction of the entire bicolon, with emendation and/or reinterpretation of every word in it. In particular, the displacement of the verb to the beginning of the second colon is most undesirable, in view of the consistent pattern pointed out in the INTRODUCTION. The name *qādôš*, "Holy One," is absolutely required by the parallelism. It is a prominent appellative for Yahweh (cf. Hab 1:12). Irwin's (1942) identification of this word with Qadesh (Barnea) gains a third geographic reference at this point. Compare the suggestion that *ʾwn* in v 7 is a reference to the city "On" discussed in the NOTE on v 7. But this is not needed. Additional location is secured by the two place-names in v 7.

came. The imagery of this epiphany is like the iconography of the rising sun god. Many indications point to this.

1. He had a brightness like the sun (v 4aA). For evidence and argument that *ʾôr* here means "the sun" and not simply "light," see the NOTE.

2. He is wearing the horned crown of deity (v 4aB). This point stands whether the "horns" are considered to be those of a bull (Albright 1950a) or those of a wild ox (Num 23:22). The evidence is not greatly affected if *qarnayim* means "rays." The flashing of these rays "from his hand" paints a different picture, more like that of the storm god hurling thunderbolts. The sun does not project his beams in this way. (But compare the classical tradition of Sun as an archer.) In the old glyptic art, the streams of light come from the arms and shoulders of UTU (Shamash), and *yād* with the meaning of "side" could fit this picture. In favor of *yād* meaning "forearm (to the elbow)" is the statement in a similar context in Deut 33:2 that fire flashed from his right hand. In subsequent discussion, we will refine this idea.

3. In glyptic art, the sun is shown as rising between two mountain peaks, with rays shooting out from his arms. The poetic parallelism here suggests that Teman and Paran are to be visualized in this way. A similar parallelism of "Seir" and "the mountain of Edom" is found in Judg 5:4 (cf. Zech 6:1).

4. The verb *yābôʾ*, "he came" can describe sunrise, especially when it has the idiom "he came from . . . ," but does not specify the goal of movement ("he came to . . .") (cf. Genesis 15; and with this Genesis 19, 33, and other predawn events). The root *bôʾ* is neutral in the matter of direction in relation to objects or from the point of view of the narrator. The verb denotes neither "go" (movement away) nor "come" (movement toward) nor "go out" (*yṣʾ*) nor "go in" except when it is the correlative of *yṣʾ* (Ps 121:8). The verb *bôʾ* can connote any of these movements, depending on the situation and especially the preposition that governs any associated noun. The verb generally means "come" (to some place or person). Hence it often means "arrive" rather than "approach." Included in this range is the possibility that it means "come out" (movement away from a point of departure, but toward the speaker.) This possibility is not often realized, but it is attested. The verb *bôʾ* is then the synonym rather than the correlative antonym of *yṣʾ*. Clear examples are Num 14:24 (*šām*, in contrast to the commoner *hennâ*) and 1 Sam 12:8 ("went" is required by the perspective). As far as the sun is concerned, *bôʾ* can mean "go in," that is, "set," but it can also mean "come in," that is, "rise." So Isa 60:1:

Your sun (*'ôr*) has risen (*bā'*)
and Yahweh's glory has dawned upon you.

In the other fragments of poems of this genre preserved in Judg 5:4 and Ps 68:8 the verb is *yṣ'*. This verb also describes the emergence of the sun, but in these poems it has taken on military connotations: "set out on an expedition." Ibn Ezra recognized this, as also in Deut 33:2 (Avishur 1994:154). In Deut 33:2, however, there are four verbs, and two of them (*zrḥ, yp'*) beyond cavil denote the sunrise, clinching our interpretation of Hab 3:3:

	SYLLABLES	
yhwh missînay [yā]bō'	7	Yahweh came from Sinai
wĕzāraḥ misśē'îr lāmô	8	and he himself dawned from Seir
hôpîa' mēhar pā'rān	6	He shone out from Mount Paran
*wĕ'ātâ mērībĕbōt *qādōš*	9	And Qadosh came from Meribeboth

In terms of syllable count and in the use of the conjunctions, the stanza consists of two bicolons (fifteen syllables each) in succession. But the vocabulary groups the colons chiastically. The middle two have excellent synonymous parallelism, and the synonyms [*yā*]*bō'* and *'ātâ* show that the first and last colons have affinity. The question is then how much of the problems of the last colon can be solved by clues from the first colon. One obvious possibility (encouraged by Hab 3:3) is to read *qādōš* as a parallel to Yahweh. The inclusion is excellent. This leaves *mrbbt* to be brought into line with "from Sinai." Traditional "with myriads" is in keeping with the military connotations of the language, but *min* is not the preposition of choice for accompaniment. The *min*, "from," in the other three colons could be doing extra duty in the final colon; but there is also a phonological rule that the first of two word-initial labial consonants dissimilates to zero. Identification of a fourth geographic name in *mrbbt* is plausible.

In terms of word order, the first colon differs from the other three. The first colon is the odd one out (cf. Hab 3:3aA). This detail suggests that the remainder of the stanza is a tricolon expounding the first colon. In that case, *mrbbt* might be closer to the places in the middle colons. But this does not mean that here we have a tradition that places Sinai in Edom. The first two colons do not inevitably contain synonymous parallels. The usual harmonization is to say that Sinai and Seir are in the south for an Israelite in the heartland. But Yahweh is "the one of Sinai," who comes down on Mount Sinai (Exodus 19; 33). There is no clear story of a triumphal march from Sinai, unless the Israelite trek is so interpreted. But see Judges 5, with its comparable references to Edom.

5. The "glory" of God that covers the sky (v 3b; cf. Pss 8:2; 148:13) is the light that God wears as a garment (Ps 104:1, a poem whose affinities with Egyptian sun worship are now widely recognized).

6. The pathways followed by the deity are called *hălîkôt ʿōlām*, "ancient orbits" (v 6). As shown by Albright (1950a:14, n. t), this term describes the paved
roads along which the heavenly beings make their circuits.

In a poem extravagant in imagery, it is not to be expected that all the metaphors
will be congruent. But the description of Yahweh as a chariot-riding warrior (vv
8–15) probably belongs to a distinct and originally independent poem. Nevertheless, the response of the sun to the terrifying aspect of the chariot-riding Yahweh
(v 11) shows that this imagery has nothing in common with later iconography of
Apollo or Sol Invictus. Yahweh the warrior is not a slightly demythologized sun
god. The imagery of the rising sun used in v 3 is no more than a metaphor. Nevertheless, there is one feature of metaphor that can be explained, once it is perceived that it represents the rising sun and not the march of the armies of Israel
under Yahweh's leadership from the Southland to Canaan. Psalm 29 provides
a parallel case. There the geographic references to Lebanon, the mountains of
Qadesh, and the desert describe the progress of a storm that comes in from the
sea, spends itself in the mountains, and moves on to the east. All this is in the
perspective of a resident of the Phoenician coastland. This setting has been retained, even though the psalm was adapted to Yahwism. It does not fit the perspective of a worshiper in Jerusalem.

With the imagery of sunrise, the perspective of Hab 3:3 is that of a resident
of the Negeb or farther south. It describes the progress of Yahweh from the east
westward, not a march from the south northward. The apparent contradiction
between references to Sinai // Horeb, and to Teman // Paran // Edom // Seir
can be resolved. The revelation of the splendor of Yahweh at Mount Sinai is
like that of the rising of the sun between the peaks of Edom as viewed from
Sinai. Because Edom and, more particularly, Teman are northeast of Sinai, a
movement from Teman would not correspond to the movement of the sun, unless to a person in the Negeb. But it is just as problematic to postulate a march
of Yahweh from the south to the promised land (following Moses' historic route),
for Teman (although on the King's Highway) was not on that line of march.
That is, there is no history of Yahweh marching through or from Teman, or
Edom itself for that matter.

Some of the poems in this tradition say equally that God came "from Sinai."
The language of Habakkuk 3 is so shrouded in mythological imagery that historical statements are hard to nail down in it. But its historical memories are
closer to the Exodus than to any other known event. It does not describe the
conquest of Canaan. The March of Yahweh is, accordingly, a march from the
desert into Egypt via Sinai to rescue his people (v 13). The sequence from the
first strophe (vv 3–7) to the second (vv 8–15) is chronological.

Targum has *'tgly*, "revealed himself," instead of "came"—a move from
mythology to theology.

Teman. This is a place-name, required here by the historical setting of vv 3–7.
LXX has *Thaiman.* The use of *têmān* to denote a point of the compass explains
the preference for that meaning in the versions (*mdrwm'* [Tg]; *deus ab austro
veniet* [Latin]; *apo notiou* [Theodotion]; *apo Libos* [Barbarini]). The directional

meaning is clear when other points, such as north, are correlative. The frequent use of Teman = south in liturgical texts (P and Ezekiel) points to a later, literary usage, although BDB (412b) says it is "chiefly poetic" otherwise. Note the parallelism in Ps 78:26, which shows that Teman could be considered as east. The version of this incident in Num 11:31 says that the quail came "from the sea" ("west?"). "Southeast" is a harmonizing interpretation (Gray in *ICC*:118). But for the people in Sinai, Teman would be literally in the east, so Ps 78:26 indirectly supports our suggestion that Hab 3:3 was originally written from the same perspective. The connection with the root *ymn*, which has given Teman an etymological, not just a secondary, meaning of "south," could be accidental. In Gen 36:15, Teman is the name of an Edomite ruler; and Teman is often used in poetic parallelism with Edom, once with Esau (Obadiah 9).

The ancient location of Yahweh in Teman is confirmed by the language of the Kuntillet ʿAjrud inscriptions: *yhwh tmn* and *yhwh htmn*. In light of these and analogous phrases, it is possible that *mtymn* is part of the divine name (see Emerton 1982; Hadley 1987, 1993; Renz and Röllig 1995:47–48; and the discussion of *yhwh mṣywn* in AB24A:224).

Paran. This name is not a synonym of Teman (in spite of the parallelism of Hab 3:3 and Deut 33:1). Its associations are with Ishmael (Gen 21:21), not Esau. The location of the El-Paran in Gen 14:6 is less certain. The various notices in the Hebrew Bible point to a location of "the wilderness of Paran" between Mount Sinai and Kadesh-Barnea, but the combined evidence of Num 10:12; 13:2, 26, and 1 Sam 25:1 suggests that an extensive region was covered by the term. It extends down the eastern parts of the Sinai Peninsula, west of the Gulf of Aqabah. The mention of Midian in v 7 supports this location. This is the only place in the Hebrew Bible where Paran is parallel to Teman. Parallelism associates Teman with Edom (Jer 49:20; Ezek 25:13), that is, Esau, and with Bozrah (Amos 1:12).

LXX recognized Teman as a place-name, but Paran was lost in the Old Greek (conflated in later Greek recensions). No explanation is in sight for how they arrived at "the shaded bushy mountain." Rudolph (1975:233) interprets it as "thickly-wooded." Hiebert (1986:16) has a full discussion.

Selah. The positions of this musical annotation (vv 3, 9, 13) do not correspond to the divisions we have found in the poem. No explanation has been found for their placement at these points. Thackeray (1923:50) observed that LXX read at this point "change" or "exchange," which corresponds to nothing in the Hebrew. He took it to be part of a rubric, suggesting that at one stage a lectionary reading ended at this point. If so, the break does not seem appropriate (cf. Sorg 1969).

glory. The splendor (*hōd*) of God suggests both majesty and energy, but its chief associations are with radiance. On the human level, *hōd* is ascribed mainly to kings (Jer 22:18; Ps 45:4), a gift of God (1 Chr 29:25; Ps 21:4). This connection suggests both that *hōd* is an attribute of Yahweh as king and that the human *hōd* is a sharing in the divine. It can describe the voice of God (Isa 30:30). Its commonest parallel is *hādār* (assonance); others are *kābôd*, *'addîr*, and *gĕdullâ*.

The word *hōd* is part of the vocabulary of the cult. Only here is *hōd* associated with *tĕhillâ*, *nōgah*, and *ʿōz*. Note the long list of such terms in 1 Chr 29:11. Hab 3:3 shares ideas with Pss 8:2; 104:1; 148:13 (the next verse contains *tĕhillâ*).

covered. In the MT it is not certain which noun is subject, which is object. There are several considerations here:

1. In the first colon both nouns are masculine, and either could be the subject; in the second colon both nouns are feminine, and either could be the subject.
2. The second colon has neutral syntax, SVO or OVS; the first colon, however, would be more normal (VSO) if "sky" were the subject.
3. It is true that the sequences secure chiasm, but it is more likely that the more normal syntax would be found in the first clause, the chiastic effect secured by a less normal sequence in the second clause: "sky" is the subject, and, by analogy, so is "earth."
4. The *Qal mālĕʾâ* is more likely to be stative than factitive. The transitive *Qal* of this verb seems to be a late development, characteristic of P. This factor also points to "earth" as the subject (NAB, NRSV; it is object in REB, NAB, NIV).
5. We cannot insist that the two colons should have identical syntax (apart from word order), but this is more likely; that is, parallel words have the same grammatical function in each colon. For "sky" to be the subject (which is indicated both by its position and also by the analogy with "earth"), the verb should be passive (by analogy with "is filled"; cf. NAB). There is no difficulty in pointing **kussâ*.

praise. This word is not a close parallel to "glory" because it normally denotes expressions of admiration for God, usually in song. Can the meaning of *tĕhillâ* be stretched to describe the renown that evokes such praise (cf. "fame" [v 2])? Parallelism can be made more synonymous either by changing the word or by giving *tĕhillâ* the meaning of "brilliance" (*Glänz* [Rudolph 1975 √hll I BDB]), "splendor" (REB), or "glory" (NJB). Avishur (1994:156) comes to a similar conclusion by comparing expressions in which *hôd* and *tĕhillâ* have a similar function. This loses the point that the splendor of the god in the sky evokes praise from people on earth. This is a common motif in Babylonian (and earlier Sumerian) hymns in which humans and animals alike adore the radiance of the rising sun or the beauty of Inanna (Jacobsen 1987:119–21). Egyptian parallels are also familiar.

If the earth is full of praise, it must be people on earth praising God (Pss 34:2; 71:8) for the display of glory in heaven. The corresponding praises in the sky (v 3bA) are sounded by the "myriad holy ones" (Deut 33:2 = "all his holy ones" [Deut 33:3]). Verse 5 refers to at least two members of this retinue. (But we have interpreted *qdš* as a name of God, there and here [cf. Isa 6:3]).

filled. The verbs in v 3b are in chiasmus with the same verbs in Hab 2:14, an important link between the two major parts of the book. In Exod 40:34, the cloud covered the Meeting Tent, and "Yahweh's glory" filled the Tabernacle. Habakkuk's picture is more cosmic (cf. Num 14:21; Ps 72:19).

earth. The definite article is commonly deleted (Rudolph 1975) to bring the diction in line with "heaven." This is not desirable.

4. *his.* LXX reads "his brightness." Targum adds "of his glory," as it did to *hôd* in v 3. This correct understanding of the nature of the radiance does not require the pronoun suffix to be "restored" to make *noghô*. Nor does the lack of the suffix show that the *nōgah* "is an independent entity surrounding God" (Avishur 1994:159).

radiance. The term *nōgah* describes the brightness of sun, moon, and stars; also the flash of weapons (lightning [?] [v 11]; cf. 2 Sam 22:8–13). Sunrise is clearly indicated in Isa 60:3 (the whole of that chapter is full of such images). Usage closer to Hab 3:4 is found in Ezekiel's chariot vision, where *nōgah* is repeated several times.

The noun is not necessarily masculine, making discord with the verb (Sellin 1930:36); the gender of some Hebrew nouns is indeterminate, being now masculine, now feminine; and BDB accepts Hab 3:4 as evidence that *nōgah* is feminine. Irwin's (1942:20–21) emended text is *wĕnāgah kāʾôr ḥănîtô bĕrāqîm yāśîm ḥiṣṣê ʿuzzōh*, "and flashed like the light his javelin, he made the arrows of his strength to be lightning bolts." Only two words of the original survive! Hiebert (1986:4) likewise reads *ngh* as a verb: "he shone." It is not logical to reject *nōgah* as the grammatical subject of *tihyeh* (because *nōgah* is presumably masculine) and then to emend *tihyeh* to *hawwâ*, "destruction," as Hiebert (1986:17) does.

There should be no doubt that here *ʾôr* means "sun" (NRSV). While Yahweh is sometimes revealed as a devouring fire, there is no need to gloss *ʾôr* here as "fire." Hiebert's (1986:17) quotation of Isa 31:9 as supporting this translation is inexact. That text reads *ʾûr*, not *ʾôr*. DCH agrees with HAL in recognizing that *ʾûr* sometimes may have the connotation of "light," but neither lexicon recognizes "fire" as a possible meaning for *ʾôr*. The parallelism is used again in v 11, chiastically, as well as in other places in the Bible (Isa 59:9; Amos 5:10).

The usual translations ("his brightness was like the light") are jejune and tautologous (cf. Isa 9:1). This radiance is specifically connected with the "face" of God (Pss 4:7; 44:4; 89:16). A pronoun is needed to complete the sense of this colon. It can be supplied (double-duty) from v 3b: "(his) radiance was like the sun." The same collocation occurs in Prov 4:18. The prefixed verb in parallel with the suffixed verbs in v 3b is normal. If, however, v 4a is a bicolon, then *lô*, "to him," could do double duty retroactively: "radiance like the sun was (to him)." Either result yields such good sense that emendation (such as Albright's [1950a] elaborate attempt) is quite unnecessary.

In most places where the sun is called *ʾôr*, it is at its rising. So there is something to be said for "dawn" (REB), "day" (NJB), and "sunrise" (NIV) (cf. Hos 6:3).

Once vv 3bA, 3bB, 4aA (colons C, D, and E) are recognized as a tricolon, the piecemeal approach that tries to make sense of each colon in isolation from the others can be replaced by a holistic approach that appreciates the cohesive linkages within each combination of two colons. Each colon has three words, and the verb migrates from first to second to third position. None of the three colons has the standard VSO sequence of normal Hebrew prose. Colons C and D (v 3b) have the most complete parallelism, and congruity of syntax, always salient, requires "sky" and "earth" to be the grammatical object. The SVO word order in colon D (v 3bB) is next to VSO in acceptability, and this shows up the unusual nature of the VOS sequence in colon C (v 3bA).

To come to grips with the problems in colon E (v 4aA), it is important to note and to preserve the "and" that begins it. In line with its function in this unit, the conjunction indicates that colon E is not the beginning of a new bicolon; it is part of a tricolon. When v 3b (colons B and C) is read as a self-contained unit, the parallelism of the verbs and the objects puts pressure on the subjects to bring them into line, to make *thltw* parallel *hwdw* (see the NOTE on "glory" above). But the availabilty of *ngh* in colon E to be the parallel for *thltw* (inclusion or envelope construction) relieves that pressure. Most translations tacitly recognize this match of colon C and colon E by translating "his splendor" (NAB; cf. REB, NJB) (double-duty suffix) rather than "the brightness." Taken together, colons C and E state that the arrival of Yahweh suffuses the sky with light like the radiance of the (rising) sun. It is this spectacle that arouses the praise of the whole world (colon D). The logical consequence is placed *inside* the parallel descriptions of its cause.

We are encouraged by this analysis to search for a continuation of the theme of the tricolon B–C–D in vv 4aB–4b (again "and" for the second colon of the couplet). Verse 5 turns to another feature of the event—Yahweh's retinue, a further indication that colons E and F belong with the preceding. So vv 3b–4 constitute a pentacolon in which we can recognize at least *hwdw . . . ngh . . . ʿuzzōh* as a series.

If vv 3b–4 are a pentacolon (and vv 3b–4aA have already been identified as a tricolon), vv 4aB–4b can be tested as a possible bicolon. Two details point in this direction. First, this unit presents the same shape as other bicolons in this poem—colon₁ "and" colon₂. Second, verse 5 is another bicolon with this shape, so vv 3–5 are nine colons with a symmetrical introverted structure. The series of verbs, taken all together, identify the three personages in the procession: *ʾĕlôah . . . deber . . . rešep.*

		COLON
3aA	*ʾĕlôah mittêmān **yābôʾ***	A
5a	*lĕpānānyw **yēlek** dāber*	H
5b	***wĕyēṣēʾ** rešep lĕraglāyw*	I

We have already noticed that another triad *hwdw . . . ngh . . . ʿuzzōh* unifies vv 3b–4. The verbs migrate in contrary motion and show that v 3 and v 5 constitute an inclusion. More precisely, colon G is the inclusion for colon E because of the match *hwdw . . . ʿuzzōh*, while the semantic match of *kissâ* and *ḥebyôn* leaves *šāmayim* to be the reference of *šām* (assisted by assonance).

horns. The picture painted by v 4aB is hard to recover. It is no solution to change the word *qrnym* to *brqym*, imported from v 11 (Irwin 1942:20). Because the evidence of the versions is unanimous for "horns," such a change is gratuitous. But what kind of horns? Coming so soon after so much talk about splendid radiance and shining light, and especially if vv 3–5 are one poetic unit, it is understandable that giving *qrnym* the meaning "rays" sustains congruent imagery.

A clue has been sought in the use of *qrn* in Exod 34:29–35 (Propp 1987, 1988), where the word seems to describe a radiance that Moses acquired from exposure to the divine presence; but the imagery of light is not prominent in that theophany. In any case, there is a difference between that glow, however dangerous, and the radiance of God. The interpretation receives some support here if colons E and F are a bicolon. This support is weakened, but not lost, if, as seems more likely, colons C, D, and E are a tricolon, and colons F and G are a bicolon. The imagery of light could be present in the whole pentacolon. So it is not a "forced interpretation" (Hiebert 1986:18) to find connotations of radiance in "horns." The structural position of *ʿuzzōh*, "his power," as inclusion for *hôdô* adds a connotation of splendor to its denotation of strength, and this flows to *qrnym* through the chiastic arrangement of *qrnym* and *ʿuzzōh*. The supporting parallelism of *ʿōz* and *qeren* in 1 Sam 2:10 and Ps 89:18 shows that, as a symbol of strength, *qeren* can lose its literal meaning and *tipʾeret* (Ps 89:18) gives it the attribute of splendor. This meaning comes through in Barberini: *hē dynamis tēs doksēs autou*, "the power of his glory."

Albright (1950a), followed by Hiebert (1986), preferred the literal meaning "horns," or, more exactly, "a pair of horns." The term "horn" is a common symbol of military prowess, but the presentation of Yahweh as a warrior is confined to vv 8–15. Irwin (1942:13) is dogmatic that it "must refer to lightning." Verse 11 is brought in to support this. But it is not certain that the armament in v 11 includes lightning. The construct "the light of your arrows" is dubious, and in the NOTE on v 11 we reject it. And it is not certain that the poem in vv 3–7 is congruent in imagery with the poem in v 8–15. In fact, no weapons are mentioned in vv 3–7, unless these mysterious "horns."

Progress in untangling this web of words beyond this point is handicapped by the obscurity of v 4b (colon G). If v 4b is parallel to v 4aB, *ʿōz* might support the idea that "horns" are a symbol of strength. Albright's (1950a) emendation, which requires the addition of only one letter **mĕyaddō[t]*, equips Yahweh with "tossing horns." This animal imagery does not fit in well with the remainder of the poem. Nevertheless, the identification of the horns with the regalia of deities, abundantly attested in the ancient Near East, especially in Mesopotamia, is compatible with radiance.

Hiebert's (1986) position that *qarnayim* can be only anatomical horns and not a metaphor for rays of light is not conclusive. His main argument is that there is no other clear attestation of the imagery, the logic being that nothing can occur in the Bible unless it occurs at least twice. *Hapax legomena* are abundant in Biblical Hebrew vocabulary, so why not a *hapax* trope? The trouble does not lie only in the word *qarnayim*, but in the whole colon: "a-pair-of-horns from-his-*yad* to-him." Each word is familiar and clear. If it is retained, the main difficulties are with "from his hand" and the absence of a verb. The correctness of the MT is shown by the literal translation in LXX (it does not have the third word). LXX reads *en khersin autou*, "in his hands"; Barberini (more literal), *ek kheiros auto*, "from his hand." Hiebert (1986) drops two words from colon F and accepts Albright's (1950a) rewrite of colon H; only *qarnayim* survives.

The picture of horns (coming) from God's hand has encouraged interpreters to identify the "rays" (*qarnayim*) as lightning bolts in the hand of a storm god. Roberts (1991:134–35) adduces comparative evidence. But if the sun of the first five colons supplies the picture, the "rays" could be the beams of light that come from the upper arms of the sun god in some seals—stretching the meaning of *yad* a little.

The imagery of sunrise in this part of the poem does not mean that behind it lies a hymn to the sun god, let alone an evolution of Yahweh from UTU (Shamash), to say nothing of Egyptian deities. Attributes in common can always be found to support such equations, but they prove too much. In the end, Yahweh would be traced to too many gods whom he resembles at one point or another. Poetic comparison of God with the sun is a literary resource, a commonplace, but it is going too far to find behind such language either an original hymn to the sun transferred to Yahweh or traces of an ancient identity of Yahweh and the sun god.

The same error was commonly made by scholars of the *religionsgeschichtliche* school, in interpreting the same kind of imagery in Christian hymnody. See Fauth (1984–1985) and my paper on the sun in 2 Enoch in the forthcoming Jaubert volume.

Psalm 19 presents similar problems, and Briggs (*ICC* I:166–68) interpreted it along these lines. But there, as in Hab 3:3b, the heaven and the earth, along with the sun, are creatures praising their Maker.

there. "Heaven" is the most eligible referent of "there." The evidence of the Greek versions is emphatic for *šm*, "there" (Ziegler 1943:273) or *śm*, "he placed" (LXX, Syriac). The Barberini version reads "there the power of his glory was confirmed." Margolis (1908:135, 137) thinks that the verb in the Greek is an amplification, but allows the possibility that it comes from *śm*. If so, the original Hebrew text was **wěšām šām*, with one word lost by haplography.

(un-)veiled. In LXX, the object of "put" is "the mighty love of his strength." But neither "love" (LXX) nor "power" helps to clarify *ḥebyôn* with √*ḥbb*. It is hard to surmise what this might mean in the context. Nor does the collocation of "power" help to clarify *ḥebyôn*. If *ḥebyôn* retains its traditional meaning of "concealment," we have the paradox that God is both revealed and obscured by his effulgence: "and therein his glory is enveloped" (Avishur 1994:162). The thought is similar to that in Ps 18:7–15, although there is little shared vocabulary because Psalm 18 uses the imagery of the thunderstorm, while Habakkuk 3 draws on the spectacle of sunrise. In spite of these differences, the effect on the world below, especially on the mountains, is similar in both poems.

Albright's (1950a) solution (based to some extent on previous suggestions) is very attractive. He changes only one letter, but adjusts the word boundaries:

wśmḥ byw[m] ʿzh   and he rejoiced in the day of his strength

Hiebert (1986) likewise, except that he obtains a prefixed verb by changing *wāw* to *yod.*

It might seem strange and strained to represent God as rejoicing in his day of power, but Ps 104:31 says that God enjoys (*yśmḥ*) his work. And if in Hab 3:3–4 Yahweh comes out into the world like the rising sun, that sun also comes out (*yṣʾ*) and rejoices (*yāśîś*) like a champion athlete (Ps 19:6). Albright's (1950a) emendation can be made more reasonable if the imagery of radiant light continues through v 4b, with the verb √*śmḥ* meaning "glow" as well as "rejoice." The collocation of joy with light is found in texts like Ps 19:9: Yahweh's ordinances make the heart rejoice and make the eyes sparkle. So does good news (Prov 15:30). The notion that a joyful countenance "beams" is commonplace. The parallelism of *śmḥ* with *ṣhl* in Ps 104:15 is matched by the parallelism of *śmḥ* with *ṣhl* in 2 Aqht II:9 and established the meaning "is radiant" in Ugaritic.

pnm . tśmḥ w ʾl . yṣhl pi[t]

(Daniel's) face lights up / while above his forehead shines

This passage was used by H. L. Ginsberg (*BASOR* 98 [1945], 15 n. 20) to clarify the meaning of Prov 13:9 without emendation. Further exploration is in Greenfield (1959). This meaning has now found its way into translations (REB, NAB, NJPS).

If Albright's (1950a) emendation is accepted, the phrase "in the day of his power" provides the only time reference in the unit. As such, it dates the whole episode and attaches to all the preceding verbs (see the NOTE on *taḥat ʾāwen* in v 7).

To sum up the analysis: the first nine colons could be construed as three tricolons, all discontinuous and interdigitated:

The difference between this display and that on page 283 is that colons E, F, and G are here recognized as separated from the bicolons that they go with.

There is no point in pushing the analysis to the question of which of these two displays is "correct." The moral rather is that an individual colon might have more than one thematic and structural connection. Thus colon E (the only simile in the poem) is equally eligible to complete the tricolon A–B–E or C–D–E. In other words, the coexistence of more than one structure shows that the first nine colons are a unit within the larger whole. Thus v 5 constitutes the first inclusion for v 3a, and v 7 is the final inclusion for the whole poem.

5. *In front of him.* Help in reading this verse is supplied by Deut 33:2. The more so as Deut 33:2 could almost be called a variant of Hab 3:3. In each case, there is a triumphal epiphany of Yahweh accompanied by his retinue of heavenly beings, but neither picture is complete. Deuteronomy 33 and Habakkuk 3 have important vocabulary in common:

	Deuteronomy 33	Habakkuk 3	
Right hand	*mymynw*		*'ēš*
Left hand	*bydk*	*mydw*	
In front		*lpnyw*	deber
Behind	*lrglk*	*lrglyw*	rešep

It makes no material difference to the present question what we do with *'šdt* in Deut 33:2. It is tempting to retrieve Hebrew *'ēš* from it. But the Aramaic *'ăšēdôt*, "beams of light," would do just as well. Dahood (AB 17A:472) has amply demonstrated that *yd* in parallel with *ymyn* means "left hand." One positional item is lacking from each of the texts being compared, but the locations are in the same sequence in both. The consonants *dbr* in the last word of Deut 33:3 could be the remains of an original reference to Plague.

The picture in Deut 33:2 is, then, that of the deity accompanied by the four prime attendants. Hab 3:5 has a similar arrangement. The same picture is met in Sam'al religion, where Panamuwa recognizes Hadad in association with El, Resheph, Rekib-el, and Shamash. The identity of three of the associates in Hebrew is disclosed by the combined texts (Deuteronomy 33 and Habakkuk 3). All the attendants are destructive, and are the four traditional "destroyers." In what positions do these four bodyguards surround the central figure?

In considering instances when a person of importance (king or god) is accompanied by four attendants, distinctions should be made. Their disposition in relation to the central figure is just as important as the number four. A quadriga is one thing (cf. Enuma Elish IV: 50–51); a palanquin is another; the pattern reflected in Hab 3:5 is different again.

The following ensemble would offer maximum protection, even hide the deity. There is evidently no breach of protocol here for an attendant (plague) to have his back to royalty:

		Fire	
← [Direction of march] ←	Plague	God	Pestilence
		?	

DIAGRAM 2

	Ebla		*dagan*		
	Erra Išum =		*'ēš*		
	Sam'al		*rekib-'ēl*		
	Deuteronomy 33	*deber*			
	Habakkuk 3	*deber*			
	Ezekiel	*deber*			
	Ps 97:3	*'ēš*			

Sam'al   *'ēl*

Deuteronomy 33   ?
Habakkuk 3   *ḥereb?*
Ezekiel   *ḥereb*

Ebla   *šipish*
Sam'al   *šamaš*
Deuteronomy 33   *'ēš*
Habakkuk 3   *'ēš*
Ezekiel   *rā'āb*

Ebla   *rasap*
Sam'al   *rešep*
Deuteronomy 33   *rešep*
Habakkuk 3   *rešep*

Such an arrangement resembles the disposition of guardian gods in magic amulets intended to ward off evils of all kinds. The names of deities are inscribed in diagrams consisting of a rectangle divided into four triangles by diagonal parallel lines (Reiner 1960) illustrated in Diagram 2.

The tradition of four attendants is ancient, and interpreters were not amiss to bring the living creatures of Revelation 6 into Habakkuk 3 (see the variant readings of v 2 in the Greek versions.) The background of the line "four angels round my head" in the White Pater Noster is not known. It has some affinity with the traditional Jewish prayer: "In the name of the LORD, the God of Israel: may Michael be at my right hand, Gabriel at my left hand, before me Uriel, behind me Raphael, and above me the divine presence of God" (Singer's edition of the Prayer Book, p. 297). This disposition is different from angels at the four corners of the bed in the nursery prayer.

The traditional destroyers are often met in biblical texts. As befits his leading position, when only one destruction is mentioned, it is often *dbr*. When there are two, they are *dbr* and *ḥrb* (Exod 5:3; Ezek 28:23; Amos 4:10) or *ḥrb* and *rʿb* (Jer 14:15); when there are three, they are commonly *ḥrb*, *dbr*, and *rʿb*—the sequence varies (Lev 26:25; 2 Sam 24:13; 2 Chr 20:9; many times in Jeremiah and Ezekiel). In Ezek 33:27, the three are *ḥrb*, wild animals, and *dbr* (cf. Ezek 14:15–19). The wild animals are realistic, and their inclusion represents a strong demythologizing move that brings the other destroyers down to material realities. So the original reference to the god Dabru is lost (*DCH* does not mention it). Additional destroyers are locusts (along with *rʿb* and *dbr*) (2 Chr 7:13). The "fire" of Deut 33:3 is not so common, but see Ezek 38:22 and Amos 1–2. Ps 97:3— ʾēš lĕpānāyw tēlēk, "fire marched in front of him"—is very close.

Only three attendants are named in Habakkuk 3. In view of the prominence of *ḥrb* in other ensembles, one wonders if he is the best candidate for the missing fourth attendant.

The *Epic of Erra* begins with an address to the god Išum:

10 *at-ta di-pa-ru-um-ma i-na-aṭ-ṭa-lu nu-úr-ka*
11 *at-ta a-lik ma-ri-im-ma* DINGIR^meš . . .
12 *at-ta nam-ṣa-ru-um-ma ṭa-bi-ḫ[u . . .*

10 You are the torch, and they will look at your light;
11 You are the one who marches in front of the gods;
12 You are the sword, the slayer . . .

The epithet "devouring" is common with "fire" in the Hebrew Bible (Exod 24:17; Deut 4:24; 9:3; 1 Kgs 18:24, 38; etc.). Compare "the fire of Yahweh" in Num 11:1–3. In Atra-Ḥasīs (lines 23–26) it is disease that eats the land.

23 [*ma*] EN *ut-ta-za-ma ta-ni-še-ti*
24 [*mur-ṣ*]*i-ku-nu-ma e-kal mātu*^tu
25 DINGIR^é]*-a* EN *ut-ta-za-ma ta-ni-še-ti*
26 [*mur-ṣu*]*-šá* DINGIR^meš *-ma e-kal mātu*^tu

23 Lord, mankind is groaning,
24 Your *mur-ṣu* is devouring the land;
25 Ea, Lord, mankind is groaning,
26 [The *mur-ṣu*] of the gods is devouring the land. (Lambert and Millard 1969:106–7)

Before the *Epic of Erra* had been adequately studied, its hero god had been identified as Deber, "pestilence," and the references to devouring fire were explained as clinical observations on the raging fevers that wasted those infected. Roberts (1972:48) is correct when he says that "his character as a god of pestilence may very possibly be the high fever that accompanies many epidemic diseases." Roberts (1972) has also demonstrated that Erra is more appropriately dubbed a god of war, but burning is a common act of war, and disease is a common accompaniment of war. Erra's retinue includes all the destroyers, who are as much aspects of his character as agents of his purposes (see also Bodi 1990).

Because the destroyers often appear together, they are not always distinguished from one another. See Mendenhall (1973) for the evidence that extensive plagues were a major cause, along with war, of massive depopulation of the Syria–Palestine region toward the end of the Late Bronze Age, giving a possible identification of Baal-Peor as a plague deity (not the usual Baal, the storm god) and "Yahweh's fire" as another name for the disease. In combination, war produces famine, which leads to the starvation that makes people vulnerable to infections.

In preparation for battle

The lightning he [Marduk] set before him
With a blazing flame he filled his body (*Enuma Elish* IV:39–40)

Heidel (1951:38, n. 78) compares this passage with Exod 19:16–18, but fire is the only element common to the two accounts. It is not enough to prove much, but it gives the flavor of many reports of the fiery splendor of the ancient gods.

It is not certain that Išum is (a god of) fire in its usual sense, because the normal Akkadian noun is the feminine *išātum*. Calling him a torch (*dipāru*) is not supportive evidence because Ishtar, Marduk, Shamash, Sin, and other deities can be similarly designated (CAD 3:156–57). The function of marching in front of the gods is not exclusive to Išum either.

The language in Hab 3:5 is similar, although it describes, not a ceremonial procession, but an army on the march. This conclusion is supported by several circumstances. First, there are military associations in the verbs that are used. Second, the divine associates have military roles. Ashurbanipal, describing his successes against Elam, repeatedly acknowledges the help granted by the gods Ashur and Nergal (Streck 1916:194–95). In the course of his report, he describes the latter as

DINGIR*Nergal be-lum ṣi-i-ru šà ina maḫ-ri-ia il-la-ku*

Nergal, the august lord, who marches in front of me

On the warpath (cf. Luckenbill [*ARAB* 1928: II 361])! That Nergal, god of pestilence, should be the vanguard is no surprise. The role is not reserved for any one god, and it can be filled by a pair. In the account of the flood in the eleventh tablet of the *Epic of Gilgamesh*, there is a description of the storm that causes the deluge. It is caused by Adad in his thundercloud (*ANET* 94). He is preceded by his scouts Shullat and Hanish (*Gilgamesh* XI, lines 99–100). Gelb (1950) has shown that this is one divinity, a coordinated double name of familiar type. So this might not change the picture of one god as forerunner at all. In view of the affinities of Hadad with Yahweh, it is of interest to investigate the function of Shullat-and-Hanish. But with caution, for the storm motif is not noticeably present in Habakkuk 3. In *Gilgamesh* (XI, line 100), the pair are called GU.ZA.LAL (*nāgiru*), a Sumerogram usually translated as "heralds." But the usual equivalent of Akkadian *nāgirum* is NIMGIR. There is a discussion of Išum as *nāgir ilāni* in Reiner (1960).

The term "herald" (*l'araldo* [Cagni 1969:59]) is not altogether suitable because his duty is not proclamation, but service as an advance guard. Išum could serve as rearguard as well as vanguard, as *Epic of Erra* (1:99) shows.

ù at-ta a-lik maḫ-ri-ia a-lik arkī-ia

And you are the one who marches in front of me,
    the one who marches behind me.

The role of the herald is not belligerent, and, when warfare succeeds in observing any ethical rules, heralds are noncombatants and are guaranteed safe conduct. Identification of personel in the lead as heralds does not accord with the upshot of Gelb's (1950:198) contention that Shullat and Hanish are "gods bringing death and destruction." A similar reason for seeing in Išum something more than a herald is his epithet "the killer," apparently a swordsman (literally, "the great sword" [*namṣarum*]). In the context of this discussion, it should be apparent that "the Sword of Yahweh" is an attendant angel. Gilgamesh's *namṣarum* weighed 8 talents or 240 kg [Bauer 1957:256]). In fact, Išum is "the famous slaughterer," with his terrible weapons ($^{GIŠ}kakkē^{meš}$-*šú ezzūti*). He is clearly more than a herald.

Of equal interest with Išum is the god whose *a-lik maḫ-ri-šu* he is—Erra. Roberts (1972:21–29) finds more connection between Erra and famine than pestilence, questioning the scholarly consensus. (Incidentally the earlier belief that this deity is Dibarra, "the female counterpart of Deber" and "goddess of Pestilence" [Thackeray 1923:52] and its use in the interpretation of *deber* in Hab 3:5 must be abandoned at both points. And, as we have seen, there are associations of Erra with fire and sword.)

Roles similar to those of Išum are ascribed to Erra himself in the piece of "wisdom" literature called *Advice to a Prince* (BWL 110–15). There is a threat against a king who behaves unjustly:

^{DINGIR}*Ér-ra gaš-ra*
[*a-lik pa*]-*an ummāni-šu*
immaḫḫaṣ-ma
idi [^{lú}nak]-*ri-šú illak*

Erra the mighty,
[instead of] marching with the vanguard of his army will smash
[the vanguard of his army] and will march alongside his enemy.

All this excursion into ancient Near Eastern mythology and iconography arose from an attempt to sharpen the meaning of the epithet, *a-lik maḫ-ri*, attached to several gods, including Shullat and Hanish. Before leaving this duo, we should note a liver omen text, mentioned by Gelb (1950:194), CT XXXI:9, in which Shullat and Hanish march *alongside* the army, assisting victory.

In the Babylonian story of the Flood (Lambert and Millard 1969), the first attempt to wipe out mankind was made by Namtara, god of pestilence. He sends four kinds of sickness; at least four words are used to describe the diseases, and the list, as well as the number four, seems to be conventional. The four destroyers (*Atra-Ḫasīs*, p. 108, line 28) are:

murṣu	illness
diʾu	sickness
šuruppu	plague
asakku	pestilence

All four destroyers are mentioned together (pp. 106–7, lines 11, 15 [lines 12, 16 in Akkadian], 23–26; pp. 108–109, line 28); *murṣu* alone I:371 (pp. 68–69); *šuruppu* alone (pp. 66–67, line 360; pp. 70–71, line 212 [both damaged]), where it seems to be generic; *asakku* (pp. 108–109, lines 50, 60; pp. 110–111, line 9 [damaged]), where it prevents childbirth.

To that extent the theophany in Habakkuk 3 is nearer to phase 1 of Atra-Ḫasīs in the extermination of humankind than phase 3, which concerns the Flood.

In the biblical lists, neither the number nor the sequence of the destroyers is fixed. This is due to some extent to the replacement of the gods of the old lists by natural events—human agents ("sword") and wild animals. The latter are not featured in the Mesopotamian conventions, and the Assyrians did not have a remedy for this menace (2 Kgs 17:24–28). The biblical lists remain four or three. Ezek 14:21 specifically enumerates the four punishers—sword, famine, wild animals, and plague (cf. Jer 14:12; Ezek 5:17). That there are sometimes three destroyers is suggested by the division of the people into three groups in Ezek 5:12–17, but the destroyers listed are pestilence, famine, wild animals, and sword—Ezekiel's four. There are five in 4QDibHam^a 1.3$_7$—*ḥwlyym rʿym wrʿb wṣmʾ wdbr wḥrb*, "evil diseases and famine and thirst and plague and sword" (cf. the Four Horsemen of the Apocalypse [Rev 6:1–8]).

Deut 32:24 has a similar list: "wasted by famine [*rāʿāb*] and consumed by plague [*rešep*] and bitter pestilence [*qeṭeb*] and the teeth of beasts . . . the venom of serpents . . . sword [*ḥereb*] . . . terror [*ʾêmâ*]." The three words *qeṭeb*, *ršp*, and *dbr* were current in northwest Semitic texts, as far back as the Ebla tablets. In the earlier stages they refer indistinguishably to various kinds of pestilence or to the divine beings (sometimes, but anachronistically called "demons") that were believed to cause these diseases. It is only when they are distinguished by enumeration, as in the later lists of destroyers, or given distinct locations, as in Hab 3:5, can we postulate different entities. Even then it is not possible to associate identifiable diseases with the individual gods. Avishur (1994:164–65) oscillates between regarding *ršp*, and *dbr* in Hab 3:5 as "synonymous" and "two distinct entities." The god *ršp* was prominent in early northwest Semitic religion, but hardly figures in the biblical lists. His presence in Hab 3:5 is striking evidence that the poem has ancient origins. More elaborate but unsystematic lists are found in Deut 28:21–24 and 1 Kgs 8:37–40. Second Samuel 24 is an important passage because it shows that the "avengers" are angels.

We suggest that originally Yahweh's bodyguard consisted of four "holy ones": Sword, Famine, Pestilence, and Plague (*ḥrb, rʿb, dbr,* and *ršp*). The one least attested is *ršp*, but his presence in Deut 32:24 shows that it is authentic and ancient; and Hab 3:5 shows that *ršp* is distinct from *dbr*. Perhaps *ršp* was lost early from the lists because it was more obviously a Canaanite god than the others. The other three survived in the stereotyped lists of Jeremiah and Ezekiel, by whose time the old mythology could be used without danger of polytheism. Ezekiel's fourth destroyer in now "wild animals." In Deut 32:24 the names of the old gods are already lost in words for natural dangers: famine, animals, and reptiles. In spite of such demythologizing, however, later references to such forces still suggest that they were divine agencies.

Unlike *ršp*, the words *ḥrb*, *rʿb*, and *dbr* are not attested as Canaanite deities. We can only guess at what the four may have been in the ancient poems whose fragments survive in Deuteronomy 33 and Habakkuk 3. If we are correct in finding here traces of poems that describe the descent of Yahweh into Egypt to rescue his people, then the destroyers who accompany him may be connected with the "plagues" of Egypt. But detailed identification is now out of the question. Already in the Joseph story, God sends "famine" to Egypt to achieve his purpose, and the language of 2 Kgs 8:1 shows that the Lord summons "the famine" as a king would call an officer to carry out some duty.

Returning to Hab 3:4aB, we can now suggest that God is surrounded by four quasi-divine beings. The ones in front and behind are clearly identified (v 5), while those at his side are not. The word *qarnayim*, however, suggests that they are described as "horned ones," that is, minor deities wearing, nevertheless, the customary insignia who are at his side (cf. Canaanite, *Ashtaroth-qarnayim*).

marched. The prefixed verbs are epic preterite.

Plague . . . Pestilence. The god Deber is associated with Resheph (Caquot 1956). On Resheph, see Fulco (1976) and Day (1979). Resheph (Rasap) was a prominent deity at Ebla, with one quarter of the city under his care. Three quarters in Ebla are known to have been named for the gods Dagan, Sipish, and Rasap (Mattiae 1979:566). In fact, the plan of the city of Ebla seems to correspond to the array of four deities that have been found in other sources, including Hab 3:5.

The Barberini Greek text (Thackeray 1923:52) translated *rešep* as "the largest of the birds." There is a widespread tradition among the Hellenized Jews to interpret *rešep* in terms of birds, and this tendency finds confirmation in the title *ršp ṣprm*, "Resheph of the birds (?)" in the Phoenician inscription from Karatepe (Barnett, Leveen, and Moss 1948:65). The identification is not certain, however. Some translate "he goats" (UT 475, no. 2186; Donner and Röllig 1968, II:41–42). The alternative that *rešep* is god of "fire" has enjoyed more favor in modern versions. Thackeray (1923:54) supplies also an interesting comment on the regular LXX reading—the attendant of God is "the Logos shod in the sandals of Perseus." Accordingly the matching word *deber* has been read as *dābār*. Irwin (1942:21) endorses a suggestion of Moore that this word (of might) is an armament (?) comparable with the powerful spells (*Enuma Elish* IV, lines 22–23; 61–62) used by Marduk against Ti'amat. Bévenot (1933:505) links v 5 with the curious doublet in v 2 in LXX—"in the midst of the two living beings"—so that those creatures are bird-like.

The possible mythological background of the terms "plague . . . pestilence" has been explored in the NOTES on v 4. Deut 32:24 is decisive for association of this vocabulary with disease. At Ebla, Rasap is associated with (or equivalent to) Nergal, god of death, also of disease. The same equation is found at Ugarit. In *Ugaritica* V: 45 (line 26 of R. S. 20.24 ["Panthéon d'Ugarit"]) *ršp* = Nergal (Fulco 1976). The idea of "flame" is secondary and late. This detail removes the incongruity of animals and people being burned by "the fire of god" falling from the sky (Job 1:16). In Ps 78:48, the same disaster is wrought by *brd* // *ršpym*. The parallelism of Hab 3:5 strongly supports emendation of *brd* to *dbr. The animals died of pestilence. It is more likely that *ršpy qšt* (Ps 76:4) is a reference to Resheph. By polarization, when *rešep* was adopted into Egyptian religion, he became a god of healing. Progress in establishing the role of *rešep* in Israelite thought is hampered by the fact that no *rešep* myth (story) has survived from antiquity.

The verbs *hālak* and *yāṣā'* both have military connotations. The idiom *yṣ' ršp* occurs in a personal name from Sargon times i-zi-ra-sa-ap (MDP 14, 72 ii) = *îṣi-Rasap*, "Let Rasap go out!" Otherwise, *ršp* is not an Akkadian root.

6. Earlier commentators could not accept the authenticity of all five colons in v 6. The last colon attracted the most suspicion. Wade's (1929:210) comment is typical of the older criticism: "The line is isolated, and is either the addition of a copyist, or else is part of a couplet of which one line is missing." Nowadays it is taken for granted that the pentacolon was part of the Hebrew poets' repertoire (Watson 1984a:187–88).

The first bicolon, which has four verbs, is very compact. The repetition of the consonants *md* in the first two verbs creates a striking sound effect and explains the choice of the rare root *m(w)d*. Translations tend to fill out the ellipses into a paraphrase. The apparently intransitive use of *rā'â*, "he saw," is the crux of the problem, because its absolute meaning is not "look," but "have the power of vision." To judge from other passages, the world ("mountains" [v 10], "nations," etc.) trembles when it sees God. Psalm 114 illustrates the point: "The sea saw [him] and fled" (v 3). "Earth writhed at the presence [face] of the LORD" (v 7). The behavior there of the "mountains // peaks" is exactly the same as in Habakkuk 3. The sequence "earth" // "mountains" in Ps 97:4–5 is similar:

> The earth saw him and writhed
> the mountains melted like wax before the LORD
> before the Lord of all the earth.

The title *'ādôn* used in Psalms 97 and 114 points to the Ark tradition. In Ps 97:6, "all the nations saw (him)," and this verse also contains the idea of the heavens praising God, as in Hab 3:3b. But Ps 104:32 affirms that it is God

> Who looked at the earth, and it quaked
> He touched the mountains and they smoked.

Compared with Hab 3:6, this language suggests that God is the subject of *rā'â*, with "earth" as its object:

> Earth he saw,
> and he made nations tremble.

The chiasm is good, but the two-word colons depart from the pattern of the rest of the poem. That "earth" and "nations" are parallel objects of successive verbs is suggested by comparison with "earth" and "nations" in v 12. If "earth" is the object of "saw," rather than of the preceding verb, we are spared the task of explaining he "spanned the earth."

spanned (or "he measured the earth"). Ancient evidence is split between confirming MT *ymdd*, "he measured," supported by V *mensus est* and Barberini *demetrēse*, and versions that point to "he made it shake," or the like—Tg *ʾāzîaʿ*, LXX *esaleuthē*, retrojected to *wyndd*. Duhm's (1906) suggestion of *Hipʿil wayyamʿēd*, "he made the earth wobble," makes a good parallel for *wayyattēr* (colon K). It is still recommended by BHS. Many recent translations (NRSV, REB, NJB) derive from some such emendation. The only other attested instance of *Hipʿil* of *mʿd* (unless by emendation in Ezek 29:7) is Ps 69:24, where the object is "their loins." Irwin (1942) emended to obtain *wayyabbēṭ*. This word occurs elsewhere in Habakkuk, and it is good for parallelism. But Irwin's (1942) proposal is nullified by the need to further emend *wayyattēr* into *wytwr* (cf. Thackeray 1923:54–55). This domino strategy of building reconstruction upon reconstruction is an abuse of the principle of parallelism. To change one word of a pair in order to make a closer parallel is sometimes reasonable; to change both words of a pair in order to achieve parallelism is to disdain the texts. If "earth" is the object of "measured," the nearest analogy is Ps 60:8 (= Ps 108:8), a *Piʿel*, which would eliminate the hapax *pōlēl* used in this verse. Even if a destructive act is in mind, measuring the earth does not fit into the narrative of the theophany that develops in vv 3–7.

The interpretation that takes its cue from "he saw"—"he measured the earth (with his eye)"—is too fanciful. Some creation stories include the motif of marking off the dimensions of the world with callipers (Isa 40:12). But here Yahweh is not a carpenter-builder, and his acts are destructive rather than constructive.

Our choice of "spanned" is deliberately neutral. It allows for the notion of extension, as in 1 Kgs 17:21, where Elijah measured himself upon the boy.

Other suggestions try to make *wymdd* a closer parallel to *wytr*. Albright (1950a) suggested *wayĕnōdēd*, but a *Hipʿil* would be better. Other proposals include *wayĕmōṭēṭ* or *yimmôṭ*, and *wayĕmōgēg*.

The versions supply only tenuous support for suggested emendations of *wayĕmōded*. The main arguments depend on a search for something that secures more synonymous parallelism with the next colon. Reliance on the Greek (Hiebert 1986:19) should be restrained by facts not considered by Hiebert:

1. We cannot always expect synonymous parallelism within a bicolon.
2. The scenario of other biblical passages in which God's impact on the world causes seismic convulsions has some weight; but, as we have seen many times, Habakkuk, like other prophets, does not simply recycle the clichés.
3. The closest analogy (Isa 24:20) points to reflexive *wĕhitnôdĕdâ*, which is hard to handle as the forerunner of MT.
4. Examination of the complete text of LXX (not just one word) shows extensive remodeling of the passage, including the familiar replacement of

active verbs with passives, such as *esaleuthē* "it was shaken," rather than the active "he shook" as glossed by Hiebert (1986).

The Masoretes must have had some good reason for their unique vocalization. Perhaps it was intended to be intensive or iterative.

tremble. The root *ntr* is not found often enough to permit us to determine its precise sense from attested use. It means "to jump" in some way (Lev 11:21). Metaphorically (Job 37:1), it means "to be startled with sudden fear." In this context we are inclined to find a closer parallelism with the preceding verb, identified as a biconsonantal by-form of *yrʾ*:

Earth took fright.
He startled nations.

Thackeray (1923:54–55) prefers the root *twr*, "explore," which is closer to "he looked." He gets this by emending Barberini (Zeigler 1943:273). The normal LXX confirms MT. The matter is exceedingly complicated, as Margolis's (1908:137) elaborate note shows. In some occurrences *hittîr* means "dissolve" or "release," and this definition has passed into many translations. LXX reads "the nations melted and the hills melted." But often the translations were guided by the general sense. So a feeling for parallelism can produce

He stood, and measured the earth
He scrutinized and spied out the nations.

shattered. It is more likely that the verb comes from *pṣṣ* than from *pwṣ*, "scatter." There is a similar parallelism of "mountains" and "peaks" in Psalm 114. The best historical moment to connect this with is the theophany of Mount Sinai (Exodus 19).

ruined (or "sank down"). The Greek versions point to a choice between *šḥy* ∼ *šḥḥ*, "prostrate," and *šwḥ*, "melt" (cf. V *Aspexit, et dissolvit gentes*). The distinction is hard to make because both the morphology and the semantics of these roots overlap.

highways (or "orbits"). Verse 6b is commonly deleted as a gloss or dealt with as a corruption. In his discussion of *hălîkôt*, Albright (1950a) resorted to the lexicons of Akkadian and Ugaritic for evidence that this word denotes the orbits of stars. This is only a particular application of its general meaning of "tracks" or "pathways." It could just as well be a paved road along the earth (Isa 40:3). Here the question is whether in Habakkuk 3 the LORD travels across the sky (v 3b) or in the southern desert (vv 3a, 7). And a related question is whether the ancient "roads" along the ancient mountains are to be identified with the mountains of Edom, or whether v 6b is referring to cosmic mythological mountains, not geographic ones. In our opinion, the reference to "nations" in v 6 brings the whole matter down to earth, but the mythological origins of the language are quite evident. The tradition of Yahweh marching (or driving a chariot) along the mountain ridges finds clear expression in Deut 32:13, with an echo in Hab 3:19.

Rudolph (1975) was dubious about Albright's (1950a) solution. He contended

that because vv 6a and 7 take place on earth, an intervening flight to heaven is
not likely (234). But unlikely things happen in poetry all the time, and one could
argue that the combination in vv 6–7 matches that in vv 3b–4a, where we found
a colon dealing with earth inserted into a bicolon dealing with heaven.

Avishur's (1994:205) translation—"His ways are eternal"—seems to be neutral as to the meaning of *hălīkôt*. His discussion, however, shows that he means
"God's conduct in ancient times" (170), referring originally to God's marching
forth to battle. We have resisted the tendency of scholars to bring the military
motifs of the second unit (vv 8–15) forward into vv 3–7. In any case "eternal" is
not as suitable as "ancient" as a translation of *ʿôlām*.

7. NAB is wrong to commence a new strophe with v 7. Avishur (1994) moved
v 7 to v 13. Verse 7 contains two verbs. MT assigns one verb to each half-verse
and makes the bicolon balanced (ten // nine syllables) by placing *ʾathnah* after
Kushan, even if the colons are overly long. That division makes "the tents of
Kushan" the object of "I saw" and, worse, creates a grammatical problem in v
7b with a masculine verb and a feminine subject.

The first two words of v 7 have been found to be unintelligible—"Under iniquity." To remove them as a gloss is the easy way out. The normal LXX and V ("because of trouble[s]") confirms the MT. Barberini goes its own way as usual: *autou
heneka seisthētai hē oikoumenē*, "on his account the inhabited world will quake."

The best case for retaining MT *taḥat ʾāwen* has been made by Rudolph (1975).
If this is a floating adverbial phrase that does not go with any particular verb,
but rather gives the motivation for everything that God did in vv 3–7, his interpretation ("as punishment for wickedness" [231]) is plausible. Rudolph cites
2 Sam 19:22; Jer 5:19; Zeph 2:10 in support of this meaning for the preposition.
The interpretation is ancient: Tg expands to "because the house of Israel had
worshiped idols, I gave them into the hand of the wicked Kushan" (Judg 3:7–11).
This hints at an understanding of *ʾāwen* as short for *pôʿŏlê-ʾāwen*.

In the context of two other place-names, it has been ingeniously suggested
that *ʾwn* be identified as the Egyptian city On (Heliopolis). This proposal has
been debated back and forth since Wellhausen (1892). Avishur (1994:205) accepts the reading and follows through by changing the other two words in the
colon to obtain *tēḥat ʾōn wĕtîrāʾ*, "On will fear and be frightened." (Note that
he takes the verb forms as classical, not archaic.)

A commonly adopted solution of the problem of *tḥt ʾwn* grows out of an observation of Albright (1934:132, n. 168), that Ugaritic *ttn* means "to be crushed."
The root *ḥtʾ* from Ugarit is attested also in Akkadian and Arabic. Albright (1950a)
recognized as well emphatic *l* to reconstruct a colon meaning "eternal orbits
were shattered." The argument was enormously strengthened and applied to
Hab 3:7 by Albright (1941a:49), reiterated in Albright (1950a). Irwin's (1942:23,
n. 40) out-of-hand dismissal of the result because it involves a tricolon is jejune.
The argument is unimpeachable:

1. Textually, it is elegant, for it requires no change whatsoever, only the read-
    ing of two words as one.

2. Etymologically, the root has unassailable credentials (Akkadian, CAD 6:151; Ugaritic, GUT 405, no. 1022).
3. Morphologically, the form compares with the following *yrgzwn*.
4. Poetically, the parallelism is excellent, and the tricolon is beautiful, with the repetition of *'ôlām* giving it a classical touch.

The repetition of *'ôlām* certainly invites a search for a tricolon, for otherwise v 6b is unmatched. In order to sort out the opening words of v 7, the whole of the verse has to be controlled.

I saw. The main difficulty in v 7a lies in "I saw." If an emendation such as Albright's (1950a) is not adopted, this personal note seems entirely alien to the otherwise objective description, especially if Habakkuk is reusing an ancient poem, not reporting his own experience. And the Masoretic punctuation overloads the colons. We suggest at least that the last six words make a satisfactory bicolon (eight // six syllables). This, however, seems to make things worse by leaving "under iniquity I saw" stranded.

As usual, part of the text-critical task is to account for as much of *all* the evidence as possible, particularly to explain where these three words (*taḥat 'āwen rā'îtî*) might have come from, if they are not original. The verb at least could represent the intrusion of a personal observation into the poem—an inclusion for "I heard" in v 2, or rather, a third prong along with the first-person comments in vv 2 and 16–19. Although the same diction in Hab 1:3 *tar'ēnî 'āwen* seems too far away from Hab 3:7 to have influenced a scribe to reproduce its language here, the possibility that the original author (or first editor) tied everything together by such means cannot be ruled out.

Having emended *tḥt 'wn* to *tēḥattûn*, Humbert (1944:60) permuted the subjects to secure gender concord with the verbs:

tēḥattûn yĕrî'ôt kûšān
yirgĕzûn ohŏlê midyān

It takes a lot of rearranging to achieve the familar A B C // A′ B′ C′ parallelism. Humbert claimed support for the deletion of *'ereṣ* from Barberini *tas derreis Madiam*, and accounted for *rā'îtî* as a corruption of *yĕrî'ôt*. Ingenious. But the similar shapes of the including bicolons (vv 3, 7) legitimate the MT. Once the punctuation of v 7 is revised, with possible emendation of v 7a, the rest of the verse can be left as it is. The verb *yirgĕzûn* does double duty for both subjects.

Kushan . . . Midian. The correspondence between the two place-names in this verse and the two in v 3—bicolons strategically placed at the beginning and end of the strophe—has already been pointed out. This structural fact demolishes the arguments of Irwin (1942:21–22), who found the verse totally irrelevant to the theme of the poem, but who was completely at a loss to explain it, saying that "it is the most baffling passage in the entire poem" (1942:21). When he had finished with it, Irwin read:

tēbēl kĕ'āšān tir'ad   The world writhed like smoke
tir'eh 'ereṣ middorkô   the earth trembled at his treading

Only one word of the original remains! Perhaps the most fantastic feature of this text criticism is the alteration of *yry'wt* to *yir'eh* as a better parallel to *yirgĕzûn*, followed by the alteration of *yirgĕzûn* to *yir'ad*, as a better parallel to *yir'eh*!!!

"Curtains" is such a good parallel to "tents," and always in that sequence—three times in Jeremiah (4:20; 10:20; 49:29; cf. Isa 54:2; Cant 1:5)—that emendation to *yôra'at*, "trembles" (Albright 1950a), to supply a parallel to *yrgzwn*, is quite unnecessary. The Barberini Greek version, not wishing even to personify an inanimate object, paraphrases "those who live in leather screens" (Margolis 1908:135–36).

Kushan. This is the only known occurrence of this form. This is certainly the Cush associated with Midian (and Moses), not Ethiopia or any other place. The similar forms Teman, Paran, Midian, and Kushan achieve a poetic effect, with the opening and closing bicolons of vv 3–7 constituting an inclusion. If the form ending in -*ān* is influenced by the other names, there is no difficulty in equating this locality with the Kushu that is mentioned in Egyptian texts of the Middle Bronze Age. This supports the general location of the tradition in southern Transjordan (Albright 1941b:34).

land of Midian. The longer phrase makes the usual rhythmic compensation for the incomplete parallelism of the second colon, the same as in v 3. The same kind of match is found in the writings of the eighth-century prophets: Assyria // land of Egypt or Egypt // land of Assyria (cf. Hos 11:5, 11).

VIII.2.iii. THE VICTORY OVER THE WATERS (3:8–15)

8aA	Was thine anger against the rivers, Yahweh?
8aB	Was thy rage against the rivers?
8aC	Was thy fury against the sea?
8bA	When thou didst mount thy horses,
8bB	thy chariots of deliverance?
9aA	Thou didst strip the cover from thy bow,
9aB	Seven clubs thou didst bring to view. [Selah]
9b	Thou didst split open the streams of earth.
10aA	The mountains saw thee and writhed;
10aB	the cyclone passed over;
10bA	the abyss gave forth its voice.
10bB*	The exalted sun raised his hands,
11a	the princely moon stood still;
11bA	thine arrows went streaming to the light,
11bB	thy flashing javelin to the bright one.
12a	In thine anger thou didst trample the Earth;
12b	in thy rage thou didst thresh the nations.

*The word "sun" has been attached to this colon from v 11.

13aA	Thou didst march out to deliver thy people,
13aB	to deliver thy messiah thou didst come.
13bA	Thou didst mash the head of the wicked,
13bB	Thou didst slash them from backside to neck. [Selah] ס
14aA	Thou didst smash their heads with thy two maces.
14aB	Their hair thou didst scatter to the wind.
14bA	Thou didst gloat over them . . .
14bB	like the oppressed feasting in the secret place.
15a	Thou didst trample the sea with thy horses,
15b	Thou didst churn up the many waters.

Scansion of the Victory over the Waters (3:8–15)

		BEATS	SYLLABLES	BI(TRI)COLON	
8aA	*hăbinĕhārîm ḥārâ yhwh*	3	9		
8aB	*'im bannĕhārîm 'appekā*	3	7	22	
8aC	*'im-bayyām 'ebrāteka*	3	6		
8bA	*kî tirkab 'al-sûseykā*	3	6	13	
8bB	*markĕbōteykā yĕšû 'â*	2	7		
9aA	*'eryâ tē 'ôr qašteka*	3	6	12	*selâ*
9aB	*šĕbū 'ôt maṭṭôt 'ōmer*	3	6		
9b	*nĕhārôt tĕbaqqa '-'āreṣ*	3	7	14	
10aA	*rā 'ûkā yāḥîlû hārîm*	3	7		
10aB	*zerem mayim 'ābār*	3	4		
10bA	*nātan tĕhôm qôlô*	3	6	16	
10bB	*rôm yādêhû nāśā'*	3	6		
11a	*šemeš yārēaḥ 'amad zĕbūlâ*	4	8		
11bA	*lĕ 'ôr ḥiṣṣeykā yĕhallēkû*	3	8	23	
11bB	*lĕnōgah bĕraq ḥănîteka*	3	7		
12a	*bĕza 'am tiṣ 'ad-'āreṣ*	2	5	11	
12b	*bĕ 'ap tādûš gôyīm*	3	6		
13aA	*yāṣā 'tā lĕyēša ' 'ammeka*	3	6	12	
13aB	*lĕyēša ' 'et-mĕšîheka*	2	6		
13bA	*māḥaṣtā rō 'š mibbêt rāšā '*	4	7	14	
13bB	*'ārôtā yĕsôd 'ad-ṣawwā 'r*	3	7		
14aA	*nāqabtā bĕmaṭṭāyw rō 'š pĕrāzāw*	4	9	17	
14aB	*yis 'ārû laḥăpîṣēnî*	2	8		
14bA	*'ălîṣūtām . . .*	1	4	14	
14bB	*kĕmô-le 'ĕkōl 'ănî bammistār*	3	10		
15a	*dāraktā bayyām sûseykā*	3	6	10	
15b	*ḥōmer mayim rabbîm*	3	4		

INTRODUCTION

Verses 8–15 constitute a poem (or part of a poem) quite distinct from the rest of
Habakkuk's "prayer." It has all the marks of great antiquity. If anything, it is more
archaic in its prosody than vv 3–7, although its imagery is less mythological.

This unit contrasts with vv 3–7 in addressing Yahweh throughout as "thou." The vocative "Yahweh" in the first colon marks this change in the mode of address, but it is not used again in the remainder of the unit. Verses 3–7 describe the theophany historically; vv 8–15 tell God what he has done, as though in adulation. Such a recital could be part of an act of worship in which God is praised, but there are no expressions of amazement or gratitude, as in, say, Exodus 15. Such a recapitulation of God's past achievements could be intended not to stir up admiration in a group of worshipers, but to stimulate God to new feats of the same kind.

The conjunction "and" is not used once in the entire unit. This is unheard of in Biblical Hebrew. While it is generally true that grammatical particles were used in the early poetry less frequently than in later classical prose, this is not a license for deleting them from this poem, as though particles now present must have been added by later scribes. Hiebert (1986:5) deleted six of the "ands" from vv 3–7 "for stylistic and metrical reasons" (16). But their presence there (which we have shown to be a helpful aid in exploring the poetic structure) and their absence from vv 8–15 are indicators that these two pieces were originally distinct compositions whose contrasting features have survived the leveling that one might have expected from the editor (perhaps Habakkuk himself) who joined them together into this "prayer." In any case, any attempt to reconstruct earlier stages of these poems will be so speculative that it cannot produce a text with claims to oust the canonical MT. Rather than trying to understand the poems as they might have existed in the time of David or earlier, we prefer to work on the text as it was used by the prophet in his time. While he (or any scribe at any time) may have touched up the language to make it more current, the fact that vv 8–15 lack "and" altogether shows that the conjunction was not supplied where sense required it. This requirement is met in LXX, which has "and" five times with no match in MT. Translators are not under the same constraints as a person who is just copying an old text. It should not be assumed that the generous provision of "and" in the Old Greek translation of vv 8–15 shows that these five conjunctions were already present in the Hebrew *Vorlage* used for that version. They could have been (probably were) added in the translation process. If they are authentic, why would a scribe have omitted them from vv 8–15, but not from vv 3–7?

Characteristically in vv 3–7 "and" marks the second colon of a bicolon. Its absence in vv 8–15 denies us this valuable clue, but the poetic structure can be discerned well enough in most places. There is no use of the definite article, the relative pronoun, and the *nota accusativi*. The apparent instance of the last in v 13 admits of another explanation (see the NOTE). The four occurrences of "the" with the preposition *b-* can be dismissed as a Masoretic artificiality, although the scribes correctly sensed that the nouns were definite in reference.

Another archaic feature is the use of both suffixed and prefixed verb forms as narrative past tense. Unlike vv 3–7, where the two colons of a bicolon might have a suffixed and a prefixed verb in parallel, vv 8–15 contain no mixed bicolons of this kind (unless vv 9b // 10aA). The two forms are in the same colon in v 10aA.

For the most part, the colons arrange themselves in bicolons. There is one certain tricolon (v 8a), possibly more. Verse 10 consists of three colons, each of which begins with a suffixed verb (reading **zāram* or **zārĕmû* [cf. MurXII *zrmw*]). This observation invites identification of a similar tricolon in vv 13b–14aA.

When v 8a is isolated as an introductory tricolon, the remaining twenty-four colons can be seen as a vast introverted structure. Repeated themes are arranged in a complex symmetrical pattern:

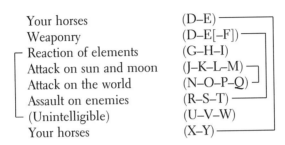

Your horses	(D–E)
Weaponry	(D–E[–F])
Reaction of elements	(G–H–I)
Attack on sun and moon	(J–K–L–M)
Attack on the world	(N–O–P–Q)
Assault on enemies	(R–S–T)
(Unintelligible)	(U–V–W)
Your horses	(X–Y)

There is a little repetitive parallelism in this unit, notably in v 8. This parallelism is not strictly classical, since it is synonymous, not climactic. Other examples are the repetition of "deliver" in v 13 and of "head" in vv 13 and 14. This is scarcely enough to warrant extensive reconstruction of tricolons by developing repetitive parallelism in the way Albright (1950a) has done.

Indeed, there is very little parallelism of the usual kind in this part of the poem. Verse 12 is a bicolon with complete synonymous parallelism: A:B:C::A':B':C'. Verse 11b has incomplete synonymous parallelism with rhythmic compensation: A:B:C::A':B'. Compare v 15. Not much else. The continual appeal to parallelism by text critics as an aid to recovering what they think might be better, that is, more "original," readings has been overdone.

The chiastic placement of related items is seen in vv 11 and 13. This device has the effect of breaking up the noun phrases. So in v 11, "exalted sun" and "princely moon" are broken up and arranged in chiasmus. In v 13, the result is a discontinuous ("broken") construct phrase: "the deliverance . . . of your anointed one." The construct phrase "the head of the wicked" is realized discontinuously in v 13b.

The themes of vv 8–15 are compatible with those of vv 3–7, but the focus is different. Both have a seismic convulsion of the mountains (vv 6, 10). The interest in the sky continues with references to the sun and moon (v 11). Both units combine two effects of the theophany—the devastation of the cosmic elements, and the terrorizing of the nations (cf. vv 6a and 12a).

The most distinctive motif in vv 8–15 is its representation of Yahweh as the chariot-driving warrior. The armament is ancient—composite bow (since it is protected by a case), mace, javelin, perhaps sword, or cleaving battle-ax. There could be a mythological vestige in the pair of special maces known from the Ugaritic texts.

The fusion of the mythological and the historical is seen in the double reference of the term *mayim*, "water," the most prominent element in the unit. (Water in some form or other is mentioned in eight colons, whereas humankind is mentioned only twice.) The rich vocabulary—"sea," "water," "rivers," "streams," "abyss"—includes technicalities that are discussed in the NOTES. The terminology comes from the old creation stories, but the historical focus is on the crossing of the Reed Sea, in keeping with the "prayer" as a whole. Yahweh dominates the scene, and only the plural "chariots" (if not to be emended) hints at an accompanying retinue. Although the warrior motif is not developed in vv 3–7, the "myriad chariots of God" were in evidence at Mount Sinai, according to Ps 68:18.

NOTES

8. The tricolon in v 8a is a perfect example of repetitive parallelism. It exploits the availability of three synonyms for "anger." We have shown the rhythm as 3:3:3 in spite of MT, which gives the first *'im* stress, but makes the second *'im* proclitic with *maqqef*. The first two colons are unified by the repeated *bnhrm*; the last two are unified by the repeated *'im* and *-kā*. Hiebert's (1986) emendation of the the the first *'im* to *h-* is gratuitous. The parallelism of "rage" (short unsuffixed form *'ap*) and "fury" (long form and feminine suffix) achieves a conventional pattern of rhythmic compensation (but see the NOTE). The parallelism suggests that "rivers" and "sea" are the same element. The days are long past when we could delete the second colon as a variant of the first (Irwin 1942:24).

anger. The complete idiom is *hārâ lĕkā 'appĕkā b-*, "it-was-angry for-you your-wrath (subject) against (someone)." The ethic referent is lacking here, except in the vocative "O Yahweh!" The standard idiom is distributed over the poetic colons: the verb in the first colon, the two synonymous nouns in the second and third colons. The syntax interdicts the versions' switch of the verb to second person (for example, *ōrgisthēs* [LXX]; "you were angry" [NIV]; "Lord, are you angry?" [REB]). The question is not whether Yahweh was angry; the unusual position of the object shows that the question is was he angry with the rivers. The delay of the subject to the second colon makes the repeated object even more prominent.

Failure to appreciate this effect, secured by the retroactive double-duty subject, along with suspicion of tricolons, led Humbert (1944:60), followed by Rudolph (1975), to delete *'im bannĕhārîm* as dittography (this was after Albright [1950a] had demonstrated [even if he somewhat exaggerated] the use of tricolons in the poem). In spite of versional support for MT, this adjustment is still recommended by BHS. Eaton (1964:151) argues for leaving the tricolon intact.

Whereas Rudolph was happy with

hăbinĕhārîm hārâ yhwh	*'appekā*
'im-bayyām	*'ebrāteka*

Humbert wanted to delete as well either *ḥārâ* or *yhwh* to obtain 3:3 rhythm:

hăbinhārîm	*ḥārâ*	*'appekā*
'im-bayyām		*'ebrāteka*

rivers. The normal plural is *něhārôt*, as in v 9, although the gender is masculine. The rare (masculine) plural occurs three times in Isaiah 18, where it refers to "the rivers of Kush" (cf. Zeph 3:10). An apocalyptic vision in Isa 33:21 describes *mqwm-nhrym y'rym rḥby ydym*, "a place of rivers, of wide streams" (cf. Job 20:17, where the emphasis is on abundance). In the present context, mythological imagery can be suspected, and since the normal plural is used in v 9, the repeated *nhrym* may not be plural at all. The parallel is *yām*, "sea." There is no geographic or historical identification, such as *yām sûp*. Nor are any human agencies included to assist historical identification. This absence and the cosmic scope of the passage point to something primeval and mythic as the source of the imagery, if not of the extract itself.

The parallelism of River and Sea is familiar in the Ugaritic *Epic of Baal and Anat*, in which there is conflict between Baal and various enemies, including "Prince Sea" // "Judge River." The identical vocabulary and parallelism is striking, but it should not be allowed to control the interpretation of the Israelite poem. The inverted poetic sequence of sea // river is a minor difference, but it is only one of many indications that the Ugaritic and Hebrew traditions, while close, are not identical. Before the Ugaritic texts were known, it was possible to find connections between the Babylonian Creation Epic and Israelite poems. In *Enuma Elish*, Marduk (storm god) overcomes Ti'amat (goddess of the water-chaos); and the cognate *Těhôm* occurs in Hab 3:10.

The story that lies behind v 8 is now lost. Only an echo remains, and the story cannot be reconstituted from the echo. The episodes or situations in the Ugaritic and Babylonian epics that offer the most promise for comparison are well down in the stream of narrative development, and the Israelite poem is not directly dependent on any of them. What little can be discerned is very simple—an immediate conflict between Yahweh and the Sea. Whether this moment is but a glimpse of the primal simplicity of an unadorned tale or the sparse effect of a story that has lost all its details cannot now be determined. The only moment recorded is the instant of angry assault on the Sea. What happened before and after is not reported—neither the cause of Yahweh's anger, nor the subsequent fate of the defeated Sea.

This same sparseness also prevents identification with any moment in Israel's history. The "river" cannot be identified with the Jordan, for instance—at least not with the certainty that would warrant input from that "crossing" story as an augment to the meager details in Habakkuk's prayer. The motif of the thunderstorm, so evident in Judg 5:4 and Psalm 18, is less prominent in this verse. The culmination of the events in "the deliverance of your people" (v 13a) brings us to history and to Israel, but it does not give us a date. Even supposing that the Exodus is the event in mind, the poetic use of imagery derived from ancient myths does not now determine the meaning of that language. The upshot is that the exact sense of "rivers" in v 8 cannot now be determined.

Guided by Ugaritic, Albright (1950a) read singular *ha-ba-nah(a)ri-mi*, "River," with enclitic *mem* (see also Hiebert 1986:23). Another possibility is to read a dual, referring to the twin rivers found in some ancient sources. There is a Mesopotamian (Babylonian, but not Sumerian [Pope 1955:63]) tradition that the primal waters distinguish a sweet and a salt sea as original elements. At Ugarit, El is domiciled at the confluence of the two streams, *mbk . nhrm* (KTU 1.2.III[129].4; 1.3[ʿnt.vi].V.6; 1.4[51].IV.21; 1.6.I.33[49.1.5]; 1.17[2.AQHT].VI.47). Either of these explanations of *nhrm* is better than the Masoretic plural. For one thing, it lessens the strain of having two different plurals (masculine and feminine) of the same stem so close to each other. But neither result supplies the narrative setting of Hab 3:8. Neither the dual streams of Babylonian cosmogony nor the twin rivers of Canaanite mythology are the objects of an assault by a chariot-riding warrior god, in any story we now have. Either the possible background of this imagery in some neighboring culture is still lost, or the motif represents a distinctively Israelite development. It is at least certain that the relationship between Yahweh and the elements is entirely hostile. If the ultimate result of successful combat is the construction of the world into its present state, then this outcome is not pursued in Habakkuk 3, as it is in Genesis 1. Nor are the preliminaries recounted. Only one moment is glimpsed—the anger of God against the elements, focused almost exclusively on the various waters. Their hostility, let alone its provocation, is not featured. The anger is Yahweh's, against them. Nor do they offer any serious resistance. The initiative and the power are all on Yahweh's side. The volcanic quality of the anger described in v 8 contrasts dramatically with the calm deliberation with which God orders all things in Genesis 1. These stories leave unanswered many questions we should like to ask about the plot: whether before all this tumult God had already made these things, but they had somehow got out of hand; whether God encounters a prevailing chaos and secures sovereignty over it by force. Some kind of primeval rebellion is implied, otherwise the LORD's fury is unaccountable.

When. This translation of *kî* is better than "that." Furthermore, this conjunction governs the whole of the following paragraph with second-person verbs—that is, the five colons of poetry in vv 8b–9.

mount. The verb *rkb* indicates riding in a chariot, not on a horse (Mowinckel 1962). This imagery explains also the plural "horses," with the singular subject, and horseback riding is excluded (see also v 15). This feature, as well as the associated armament, locates the warfare in the Middle Bronze Age or later. The equipment of the gods in the more ancient myths—the hunting net, for instance—is not in view.

In ancient armies, warriors did not ride on horses that drew a chariot. Unlike in Hab 3:3–7, where Yahweh has assistants, in vv 8–15 he fights alone. The incongruity of one person riding horses and chariots is removed once it is understood that *rkb* means "mount." This meaning is clear in Ugaritic, and the similar Hebrew usage has been sufficiently discussed (Barrick 1982; Moran 1962;

Mowinckel 1962). The two colons together paint a picture of the warrior mounting a chariot drawn by horses. The normal sequence of the phrase "horses and chariot" (Isa 2:7; Mic 5:10) is preserved, producing a superficial impression of mounting horses. This has fostered a lot of unnecessary rewriting of the passage. The poet says simply that Yahweh installed himself in his equipage.

horses. The Barberini Greek version reads "chariots," diminishing the mythological ingredient.

chariots. The plural, if it is not simply poetic, points to a whole squadron of charioteers. If v 5 is part of the same picture, Plague and Pestilence are also chariot-riding warriors. But we have concluded on many grounds that the two sections are self-contained; they reflect different stories. "Correction" to the singular, as frequently advocated, is licensed by the likelihood that the plural "horses" pulled the original singular "chariot" into congruent plural.

deliverance. The construction in which the noun "chariots" is modified by both the pronoun suffix "your" and the noun "deliverance" is strained, but not impossible. A more normal Hebraism would be "the chariots of your deliverance." The parallelism of "horses" // "chariots," however, suggests that the word "deliverance" is independent. We have already remarked on the absence of the word "and" from this poem. A phrase "your horses (and) your chariots" can be observed, with the preposition *ʿal* governing the whole. The prominence of the noun "deliverance" in v 13 (albeit in the shorter, masculine form) supplies a hint, suggesting that the preposition *l-* is to be understood in v 8—"as you came riding with your horses and chariots, for deliverance." This reading is a considerable improvement. Instead of "deliverance" being an incidental attribute of "chariots," it is the purpose of the expedition. Yahweh comes in order to rescue his people. Thus his anger is not judicial and punitive, destroying the wicked by way of penalty. It is redemptive. The defeat of the wicked is only a means to God's real intention: the deliverance of his people. And the provocation is wrong that has been done to the LORD's people (v 13). This was the problem in Habakkuk 1, where the prophet complained that the LORD was unmoved by the plight of the "righteous" surrounded by the wicked (1:4), swallowed by the wicked (1:13)—*rāšāʿ*, the same word as in Hab 3:13.

Duhm (1906) found the noun "deliverance" unacceptable because the theory of Hebrew poetry in his day looked for synonymous parallelism everywhere. A verb was needed to match *tirkab*. Duhm proposed *yiššāʾeh*, "rumbled," or *yāʿûpû*, "they flew." Humbert (1944) inserted the *yhwh* he had deleted from v 8a to obtain

kî tirkab ʿal-sûseykā
markĕbōteykā yhwh yāʿûpû

Not yet satisfied, because of the oddity of mounting horses, Humbert completed his solution by making "chariots" singular and inverting the nouns to obtain

kî tirkab ʿal-merkābĕkā
sûseykā yhwh yāʿûpû

9. *strip*. LXX *enteinōn eneteinas toxon sou*, "bending you bent your bow," while pointing back to a verb and its cognate (that is how LXX usually handled infinitive absolute + verb), does not point to any one of the several verbs that describe the readying of a bow—not necessarily *drk* (preferred by Humbert [1994]—*dârôk tidrôk qaštekâ* "Tu bandes ton arc" Thou dost string thy bow. V *suscitans suscitatis* lines up with this tradition, but agrees with 8 ḤevXIIgr (*exegereis*, "thou shalt arouse") from √ '*wr* I, "to wake." Barberini has a matching passive. Hence Eaton (1964:145) rendered "Mightily awakened is thy bow." All these translations could be no better than shots in the dark, guided by the one certain word ("bow") in a line that everyone finds unmanageable.

This action of the deity in v 9aA is a display of weapons preliminary to battle. If that is so, it reduces the probability that the next colon refers to actual combat. This warming-up exhibition is part of a convention in stories of heroic warfare. The buildup creates atmosphere and arouses expectation in the hearer. This reading fits in with the use of '*eryâ*. This rare word is simply a variant of '*erwâ*. The versions cited earlier suggest that the first word was read as the cognate infinitive absolute of the following verb. Hence BHS '*ārōh tě 'āreh*. The translation "you make bare your bow out of its cover" is due to Sellin (1922:357), who wanted to read *he'erêtā 'ôr*. (Irwin [1942:24] incorrectly says that Sellin read the first word as '*ôr*.) We believe that Sellin has hit on the meaning of the colon, but none of these changes is needed once the poetic usage is accepted.

The word '*eryâ* is always absolute (six times); '*erwâ* is absolute only twice, but it is used about fifty times as construct. This complementary distribution suggests that the difference between the two forms is purely grammatical. While commonly used to refer to nakedness as something shameful, the emphasis is not on indecency as much as on the taboo that forbids the exposure of something sacred and private. Because of its workmanship, the composite bow had to be protected from the weather. Pictures of Pharaoh as a chariot-riding archer show the bow case as part of the equipment. Yadin (1963) has many illustrations. The action described in v 9aA is, then, the extraction of the bow from its case. The identification of the verb *tě 'ôr* as √ '*wr* II, "to be bare," is therefore justified, in spite of the poor attestation of the root with this meaning *in the verb*. The cognate object demands this meaning and could have an effect similar to that of an infinitive absolute. The *Nip'al*, however, may be questioned. "Thou" (= Yahweh) is the subject of all the verbs in this section, and the preparation of the bow is an act of God. Hence Rudolph *tě 'ōrēr*. A *Hip'il* factitive ("make naked") would be better, and **tā'wîr* requires minimal emendation. Hiebert (1986:25) prefers *Pi'el*—"you laid bare."

In any case, the discontinuous (broken) "construct" phrase '*eryâ . . . qaštekā* must be recognized as the subject (if *Nip'al*) or object (if *Hip'il*) of the verb.

bow. Verse 9a apparently describes the LORD's arsenal. At least the bow can be identified in v 9aA, which describes the preparation of the weapon for action.

Seven clubs. Verse 9aB has become notorious for the range of solutions proposed. Rudolph 1975), among others, harks back to the work of Franz Delitzsch

(1843), who already knew of a hundred solutions. Others have been advanced since (Rudolph 1975:235). The frustrating thing is that each of the three words *šĕbūʿôt maṭṭôt ʾōmer* is separately recognizable. But the meaning of each is indeterminate, and the syntax is completely baffling. Even when the choice is narrowed to three prime candidates for *šĕbūʿôt* ("sworn," "seven" [revocalizing], or "sated" [√*šbʿ*]) and the two possibilities for *mṭh* ("tribe" or "staff"), the possible combinations are numerous, compounded when the meaning of *mṭh* is stretched to "arrow" to provide a parallel for "bow" and even more when, on top of that, *ʾōmer* is emended to "quiver" to complete the picture:

> according to the oaths of the tribes, even thy word (KJV)
> The oaths to the tribes were a sure word (RV)
> The rods of chastisement were sworn (NASB)
> Sworn are the rods of the word (NJPS)
> Oaths were sworn over thine arrows (NKJV)
> Sated were the arrows at your command (NRSV)
> and charge your quiver with arrows (REB)
> filled with arrows is your quiver (NAB)
> You sated the shafts of your quiver (Hiebert 1986)
> "Arrows in abundance thou didst let whiz" (Rudolph 1975)
> Tu rassesies de flèches sa corde (*sibba ʿtâ maṭṭôt yitrô*) (Humbert 1944:78, 79)
> and give the string its fill of arrows (NJB)

Humbert (1944:61) judiciously points out that, from the outset, the struggle with v 9aB depends on whether we think it completes a bicolon with v 9aA or begins a bicolon that is completed with v 9b. He explores both possibilities and settles for the first. We agree.

The difficulty of v 9aB is shown by the divergence of the ancient versions. 8 ḤevXIIgr has *rhabdous*, "rods." The two Greek translations supplied by Ziegler (1943) are quite different. LXX reads "seven ("upon the" [*epi ta*] is a corruption of *hepta*) scepters, says the Lord." Barberini does not support *Kyrios*, but reads "you fed the missiles [*bolidas*] of his [her, your] quiver." The first word obviously comes from *śibba ʿtā* and *bolidas* matches *maṭṭôt* (although it is not as defensible as *skēptra*), but the introduction of "quiver" seems to be entirely due to "bow" in the preceding colon.

The word *maṭṭeh* commonly means "rod" or "staff," or, with great frequency, "tribe." It can denote a shepherd's crook, a magician's wand, a walking stick, a ruler's scepter, an overseer's stick (for beating lazy workers), a magistrate's rod (for corporal punishment), and a threshing flail.

Because of the parallelism with v 9aA, v 9aB probably describes the readying of another weapon besides the bow. In parallel with "bow," one might have expected a reference to "arrows." Arrows are, in fact, mentioned in v 11b: *ḥiṣṣeykā*, the usual word. So why not use that word in v 9? Recognition of parallelism between *qšt* and *maṭṭôt* suggests at least that *maṭṭôt* are some kind of weapons. Given that parallelism, the suffix "thy" in "thy bow" in v 9aA continues to modify the following appropriate noun. Hence "(thy) *maṭṭôt*" can be postulated in v 9aB.

Marduk's armament in his fight with Ti'amat consists of bow (*qaštu*) and quiver with arrows, mace (*miṭṭu*), and a net (*Enuma Elish* IV:35–40). The symbolic mace of the old gods was made of stone, with fifty heads (*CAD* 10:148). Since the sources clearly describe its use—wielded in the hand—there is no basis for assuming that it might point to Hebrew *maṭṭôt* as denoting arrows. There is no story in Hebrew in which a *maṭṭeh* is used as a weapon. Jonathan has a *maṭṭeh* on the battlefield in 1 Samuel 14 (vv 27, 43), but he uses it only to convey honey to his mouth. Irwin (1942:11–12) correctly inferred from vv 13–14 that the weapon was a club, but he developed the point only in a general way. In fact, after identifying the *maṭṭôt* with Marduk's club (24), he reverted to the interpretation as arrows ("missiles") in a quiver.

It is different at Ugarit, where Anat's weapons are *mṭm* // *qšt* (KTU [3 'nt] II.15–16). Cross (1973:23, n. 59) identifies these two words as a "formulaic pair," and extends the meaning of Hebrew *maṭṭeh* from "stave" through "shaft" through "dart" to "arrow." The matter is not so straightforward. There is one episode in Ugaritic literature that describes the use of this weapon (by El, to bring down a bird [CTA 32.52]). The expression is *mṭ ydh*, "his hand-weapon." Compare Hebrew *'eben-yād* "stone hand-weapon," and *'ēṣ-yād* "wooden hand-weapon," used to commit murder (Num 35: 17, 18). This analogy leaves it open that El's weapon was not for fighting but for fowling, some kind of throwing stick, rather than interpreting *mṭ yād* as an epithet meaning "mighty," as does Cross. The shape and use of such an implement is familiar from Egyptian painting. Gordon (*UT*) did not recognize any meaning for Ugaritic *mṭ* apart from "club." Our study of *mṭyw* in v 14 agrees with this.

Whether the Hebrew weapon *mṭ-* is like the Akkadian mace or closer to the Ugaritic *mṭ*, whatever that was, those associations and the context of Habakkuk 3 indicate that it was some kind of weapon. So far, so good. Further progress in recovering the picture in v 9aB is handicapped by the difficulty in the other two words—*šĕbū'ôt* and *'ōmer*.

The task, then, is to make sense, if possible, of *šĕbū'ôt*. "The oaths of the tribes" (KJV) could refer to the covenant engagement that made the Israelites Yahweh's "people" (v 13). But, as we have already observed, the protagonists in vv 8–11 are cosmic. The human does not appear until v 12.

The reading of the first word as *śāba'tā*, "thou didst satiate," or the like, enjoys considerable vogue (cf. NEB). The idea derives general support from passages in the Hebrew Bible that speak of war weapons eating or drinking, even to the point of becoming glutted or drunk with blood (Deut 32:42). See Jer 46:10: *wĕ'ākĕlâ ḥereb wĕśābĕ'â wĕrāwĕtâ middāmām*, "and the sword will eat and it will be sated and it will be drunk from their blood."

There are three objections to this emendation.

1. The verb is usually stative in *Qal*; *śāba'tā* means "thou wast sated," and it is straining the idiom to render "you filled (the quiver) to capacity." We

need to remember, all the same, that poets say many unexpected things. This objection to the far-fetched imagery can be partly overcome by reading Pi'el. Albright (1950a) was closer to this idea when he translated "sated by the fight," but such a development would be premature at this stage of the proceedings, since v 9 describes preparation for battle, not satisfaction when it is over.

2. The verbs in this part of the poem are prefixed rather than suffixed; the time perspective is not clear.
3. The idea of satisfying (stuffing?) the quiver with arrows seems very fanciful.

The third possibility is that the numeral "seven" should be considered (LXX). If *mattôt* means "shafts" (there is a problem of gender concord between numeral and noun), then an arsenal of seven arrows would be a suitable complement to the bow of v 9aA. Such an idea ("heptads of spears") had already occurred to Ewald (BDB 990a). We need to find a tradition that a warrior had "seven shafts," but a supply of spears would be needed only in the case of javelins for throwing.

The word *'ōmer* means "saying." For the noun *'ōmer*, which is poetic, see Ps 77:9. A verb to match *t'wr* would be good for parallelism. A possibility is *t'mr*, either by dividing the *t* from *mtwt* or by reading it twice. Albright (1950a) had already reassembled *t'mr* and suggested the meaning "which thou hast decreed." As a synonym of *t'wr*, "expose to view," *t'mr* could mean "make visible" if the root *'āmar*, "see," can be admitted. Proposals to find the meaning of the Akkadian homonym attested in West Semitic (Dahood [AB 17A] was fond of this idea) have not made their way into the standard lexicons (Barr 1968:322). Accordingly, we keep that option alive (but with hesitation), mainly because it supplies a parallel to the idea of bringing out the bow from its case in v 9aA. (Elsewhere in this commentary we have been unfriendly to the stratagem of using assumed synonymous parallelism to settle the meanings of matched words; hence our hesitation.)

The common LXX *legei Kyrios*, "says the Lord," confirms the Hebrew *'mr*, but does not prove that it can mean only "say." Hiebert (1986:28) discarded this evidence because it "has all the earmarks of a gloss." What are the earmarks of a gloss? *Yhwh* might be a gloss on *'āmar*, but *'āmar yhwh* is not a gloss on the text reconstructed by Hiebert (1986)—"You sated the shafts of your quiver"—by emending all three words in v 9aB: *śb't mty 'šptk* (cf. "and charge thy quiver with shafts"[NEB]). The replacement of *'ōmer* by *'ašpâ*, "quiver," depends on back-translation from Barberini. While it is easy to explain how a Greek translator would add the quiver to complete the portrait of Yahweh as archer, it is hard to explain the replacement of an original *'šptk* by *'ōmer* to arrive at MT.

We find similar difficulties in the way of Albright's (1950a) emendation. Although his alterations to the consonants are minimal, he revocalizes every word. His resort to South Arabic *mtw* for the meaning "fight" is so adventurous that it should first be proved that *matteh* is impossible before importing an exotic replacement.

Our conclusion is that the warrior in Habakkuk 3 is armed with a bow and maces. The evidence is admittedly fragmentary and circumstantial, but cumulatively it has some weight.

1. Psalm 68, which exhibits numerous affinities with Habakkuk 3, contains the statement that "God wounded the head of his enemies" (v. 22). Furthermore, the closeness of this verse to Ugaritic poetry in diction is now commonly recognized, and the same vocabulary turns up in Hab 3:13–14. The explanation of śēʿār in Ps 68:22 as *śāʿār, meaning "split open" (AB17:144) clears up Hab 3:14 and adds detail to the picture. The injury inflicted on the head is that it is broken open. This rules out the use of an arrow, a spear, or a dagger and points to a club of sorts.

2. This reading is confirmed by Ps 2:9, where the weapon—"an iron rod" (šēbeṭ, a synonym of maṭṭeh)—smashes the enemy "like a piece of crockery." This is done not by hurling the vessel to the ground, but by hitting it. The same verb describes the destruction wrought by "the smasher" (mappēṣ) in Jer 51:20–23.

3. Another related verb is √nqb, which describes the action of the maṭṭeh in v 14. A weapon that "perforates" the skull could be the spikes on a mace.

4. All these passages (and there are more) have in common the head as the target of a blow struck with an implement. A clear instance is the smashing of the seven heads of Leviathan in Ps 74:13–17, where the pronoun ʾattā, "thou," is used seven times, once for each smashed head. The various actions (perforate, smash, and split) are more congruous with the use of a spiked mace than with any other weapon.

5. It was already pointed out by Cassuto in 1938 (1975, II:11) that the weapons used by Baal to defeat "Prince Sea" // "Judge River" were a pair of rods (ṣmdm). That the mace is the divine weapon par excellence is shown by UT (107:14), which refers to the ṣmd of El. This is the only place in the iconographic tradition where that god is presented as armed or, indeed, as a warrior in any way at all. El is pacific and benign; the weapon is obsolete; his bearing it is evidently as symbolic and ceremonial as a beadle's carrying a mace in royal and even ecclesiastical processions. Cassuto further speculated that the name of one of these clubs (áymr) might explain ʾmr in v 9. This is attractive. Adherents to the theory of a Babylonian background for Habakkuk 3 point equally to Marduk's club ina miṭišu (Enuma Elish IV:130). The general point is supported by artistic representations of gods and kings in the ancient Near East, especially Pharaohs. See Collon (1972, 1982, 1986) and the illustrations in Podella (1993:321–23).

We conclude that mṭw(t) in v 9 is similar to mṭ(y)w in v 14, and that the latter are a legendary pair of clubs similar to those in Ugaritic tradition. The words mṭwt and mṭyw (in v 14 [the only attestation of the masculine, strongly indicating that the latter is dual]) constitute a single problem. The orthographic and morphological difficulties (the strange feminine plural, the suffix "his") can be explained by an underlying dual form. The much debated and still unsettled question of duals in the Gezer Calendar illustrates the problem.

The word "sevens" may have arisen from the fact that the maces were equipped with seven spikes. Or there may be a connection with the seven heads of the chaos dragon, as shown in the Tell Asmar cylinder seal 32/738 (*Iraq* I 1934, pl. l[a]). There is a Sumerian mace head (Heidel 1951: fig. 15) on which the seven-headed serpent is engraved.

Selah (see also v 3). The insertion of a liturgical note in the middle of a verse led Thackeray (1923:51) to account for the three preceding words, which he found otherwise unintelligible, as an accompanying instruction about lessons to be read at Pentecost along with the lesson from Habbakkuk which ends at this point. In fact, he identified "a row of catchwords to the Torah lessons for each year of the triennial cycle" (51):

Oaths (= "Seven Weeks")	Deuteronomy 16
Rods	Numbers 17
Word	Genesis 12

This seems to be a case of explaining the obscure by the even more obscure. Why, for instance, should rubrics about the first lessons, as cryptic as can be imagined, be supplied in the text of the second lesson?

streams. "Earth" is a possible subject of the verb, as in LXX, which transforms to passive: "the land of rivers will be rent." Likewise Hiebert (1986): "Earth was split open with rivers," who makes "rivers" agential, a construction almost unknown in Hebrew (Andersen 1971; Müller 1985, 1995). Hiebert's category—"circumstantial accusative," also "manner" is not germane, and his "similar constructions" (1986:155, n. 66) are not similar at all. And where did the rivers come from? In v 8 (where we suggested that the forms are dual), this element is the object of Yahweh's anger.

Once more, credit must go to Cassuto (1975) for recognizing that Ps 74:15 provides the key to v 9b. That *nhrwt . . . 'rṣ* are the underground waters is proved by comparison with Ps 74:15, where the same verb *bqʿ* (albeit *Qal*) is used in a similar context to describe God's attack on "fountain and flood," in parallel with *nhrwt 'ytn.* This connection makes it clear that "rivers" is the object of the verb, the object of Yahweh's attack. This is consistent with the rest of the poem, for the watery element is the main enemy, and it would be out of keeping if the rivers are the instruments used by the LORD to cleave the earth. But Cassuto missed the connection between "rivers" and "earth"—"The rivers thou didst shatter upon the ground." This colon (v 9b) does not belong with v 9a; it continues the theme of v 8a to complete an eight-colon strophe. The object of the verb is a discontinuous construct phrase: *něhārôt . . . 'āreṣ.* This was already perceived by some ancient versions. The correction in the Washington MS (*potamous rēkseis gēs*) (Sanders and Schmidt 1927:106) resembles the reading of Alexandrinus *potamous skhiseis gēs*, and the V *fluvios scindes terrae*.

"The rivers of the earth" are the subterranean waters (cf. Gen 2:6; Andersen 1987). The arrangement permits a more precise identification of the cosmic rivers of v 8, which are associated with the abode of El.

The reference to all these watery elements are arranged in an introverted structure.

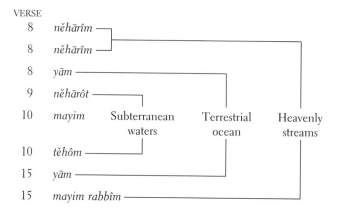

It is misleading to call these enemies "demons of chaos" (Irwin 1942:17) when the poem itself names the familiar elements of the cosmos. Nor is it adequate to describe them as "personifications of the powers of nature." That terminology and those conceptualities are so foreign to Hebrew thought that using them takes us away from the poem. The enemies are these things themselves, and, in the mythology, they are the gods.

10. Verses 8–9 describe the activity of Yahweh. Verses 10–11a describe the reaction of the elements—mountains, waters, sun, and moon. The Hebrew Bible contains several descriptions of the reactions of a human to the theophany. A conventional response of terror is recognized (Hillers 1965). The elements similarly "dissolve," but a common syndrome is to "see" and "writhe" or "flee."

rā'ûkā	mayim	'ĕlōhîm
rā'ûkā	mayim	yāḥîlû
'ap	yirgĕzû	tĕhōmôt (Ps 77:17)

This has the same verbs as Hab 3:10 and the same absence of "and." The element is water rather than mountains. Ps 77:18 continues as in Hab 3:10, and its v 20 matches Hab 3:15:

zōrĕmû	mayim	'ābôt	
qôl	nātĕnû	šĕḥāqîm	
'ap-	ḥăṣāṣeykā	yithallākû	
qôl	ra'amkā	baggalgal	
hē'îrû	bĕrāqîm	tēbēl	
rāgĕzâ	wattir'aš	hā'āreṣ	
bayyām		darkekā	
û-		šĕbîleykā	bĕmayim rabbîm
wĕ		'iqqĕbôteykā	lō' nōdā'û

Bévenot (1933:508) thought that Psalm 77 contains a quotation from Habakkuk 3. The matter is not so simple. The fact that in Hab 3:10 the subject of "writhe" is "mountains," while in Ps 77:17 it is "waters," is of no moment because in Psalm 114 the responses of these two elements are placed in parallel:

> The sea saw [you] and fled;
> > the Jordan twisted itself backward:
> The mountains jumped like rams,
> > (the) peaks like sons of the flock.

Earth, sky, waters, mountains also appear in Judges 5:4–5. In each passage, there is vocabulary in common with that in Habakkuk 3 (cf. *ḥûlî ʾāreṣ* [Ps 114:7]), and some vocabulary is distinctive of each poetic treatment. Conspicuously lacking from Habakkuk 3 is the verb that describes seismic convulsions (*rʿš*). The following display shows shared vocabulary:

ḥwl	*rʿš*	*rgz*	*ṣʿd*
	Judg 5:4		Judg 5:4
	Ps 68:9		Ps 68:8
	2 Sam 22:8	2 Sam 22:8	
	= Ps 18:8	= Ps 18:8	
Ps 77:17	Ps 77:19	Ps 77:17, 19	
Hab 3:10		Hab 3:7	Hab 3:12

Other verbs, such as *nzl*, and *nṭp*, are shared by two or more of these theophany poems. An exhaustive comparative study of the idioms would be instructive. Exodus 15 should be included. Parallelisms, such as that of *rgz // ḥwl* in Deut 2:25, are part of the tradition. In all these poems, the language of terror moves across a spectrum of referents from the primal elements of creation stories, to the Reed Sea, to Israel's historical enemies, to the hostile forces (political and cosmic) of the End Time. The focus varies from poem to poem. For an illustration, the dragon Rahab-Leviathan of the Canaanite creation myth becomes the Pharaoh of the historical Exodus. The demythologization has gone even further in the Barberini Greek translation, which paraphrases: "when you looked, the mountains were agitated."

Habakkuk 3 seems to represent the early stages of this development; the story is still told largely in terms of the primal conflict of creation. In some ways, it is nearer to Judges 5 and Psalm 68 than to Exodus 15 and Psalm 114, which have the Exodus clearly in mind, or to 2 Samuel 22 (= Psalm 18), which have updated the material to describe David's battles and present a more naturalistic description of the thunderstorm. In genre, Habakkuk 3 is very close to Psalm 77, sharing the perspective of reminiscence long after the original events, whereas in Exodus 15 and Judges 5 they are in immediate memory.

Studies of oral literature have suggested that poets manage extempore composition because of the availability of stock phrases that fit the rhythms. Habakkuk 3 is replete with such phrases. But they are not always used in exactly the same form every time; these stock phrases are not strictly "fixed." Such a phrase can be reproduced with slight variations without impairing the rhythm. Hab 3:10b and Ps 77:18 are such an instance:

nātan tĕhôm qôlô	6 syllables
qôl nātĕnû šĕḥāqîm	7

The same is true for stock pairs in parallelism. Compare, for example, the juxtaposition of "clouds" and "the wings of the wind" in Ps 18:11–12 and Ps 104:3. It follows that both Hab 3:10b and Ps 77:18 are equally acceptable, and neither should be leveled to the other; neither "abyss" nor "clouds" has a better claim to be the subject of "gave voice." The interchangeability of *tĕhôm* and *šĕḥāqîm* (both very poetic words) is facilitated by their use as poetic parallels (Prov 3:20; 8:28). In Psalm 77, *tĕhômôt* has already been used in v 17, with the conventional verb *rgz*, "quake," which again is stock-in- trade for poems of this kind. But *rgz* is not used in a fixed idiom; its subject can be heaven, earth, mountains, or lower waters. In Ps 18:8, the subject of *yirgāzû* is "the foundations of the mountains" (cf. Isa 5:25); in 2 Sam 22:8, it is "the foundations of the sky" (cf. Isa 13:13). By the way, this abundant evidence confirms our rejection of the tradition that identifies *rgz* in v 2 as God's anger. Numerous passages in Ugaritic literature that repeat formulaic language show that latitude was acceptable in the recitation within the same poem—a feature that makes it questionable whether lacunae should be filled with the precise wording found elsewhere. How much more variety, then, is to be expected when a new poem is made out of a fresh assemblage of familiar turns of expression.

Why not rewrite Ps 77:18 to conform with Hab 3:10? The reason is that throughout Ps 77:17–20 there are parallels to Habakkuk 3, but at every point the wording is slightly different:

Ps 77:17	*rā'ûkā mayim yāḥîlû*	waters saw you, they writhed
Hab 3:10aA	*rā'ûkā yāḥîlû hārîm*	they saw you, mountains writhed
Ps 77:18	*qôl nātĕnû šĕḥāqîm*	skies gave voice
Hab 3:10b	*nātan tĕhôm qôlô*	Tehom gave his voice
Ps 77:18	*'ap- ḥăṣāṣeykā yithallākû*	indeed your arrows walked
Hab 3:11	*lĕ'ôr ḥiṣṣeykā yĕhallĕkû*	to the light your arrows walked
Ps 77:19	*hē'îrû bĕrāqîm*	lightnings illuminated
Hab 3:11	*lĕnōgah bĕraq ḥănîteka*	to light the flash of your javelin
Ps 77:19	*wattir'aš hā'āreṣ*	and the earth quaked
Hab 3:12	*tiṣ'ad 'āreṣ*	you trampled earth
Ps 77:20	*bayyām darkekā*	in the sea is your way
Hab 3:15	*dāraktā bayyām*	you walked in the sea
Ps 77:20	*ûšĕbîleykā bĕmayim rabbîm*	and your paths in mighty waters
Hab 3:15	*ḥōmer mayim rabbîm*	churning mighty waters

Of particular interest is the use of a noun ("thy path") in Psalm 77 where Habakkuk 3 has a verb ("thou didst tread"). So in v 10, Habakkuk has a noun ("storm") where Psalm 77 has a verb ("stormed"), while Psalm 77 has a noun ("clouds") where Habakkuk has a verb ("passed by"). This consistent divergence argues strongly against changing Hab 3:10aB into Ps 77:18aA. Once you open the door to that, and Psalm 77 is accepted as "original," consistency demands that all of Hab 3:10 be replaced by Ps 77:17–18. This would be ridiculous. Hab 3:10 stands on its own legs; it is well wrought. In every respect, Habakkuk 3 is more archaic than Psalm 77. If Hab 3:10aB is a little more difficult than Ps 77:18aA, it should be left alone for precisely that reason.

Psalm 77 and Habakkuk 3 are personal prayers expressing the same anxieties. But Habakkuk 3 is more archaic (or more successfully archaizing), as its nonuse of "the" and "and" shows, and the mythic imagery is still largely frank, untouched by later sophisticated theology.

mountains. LXX *laoi*, "peoples," stands aside from other versions, which match the MT. Curiously, LXX does the same thing with *šimʿû hārîm* at Mic 6:2, reading *akousate laoi* as in Mic 1:2; and at Exod 19:18, reading *pas ho laos* for *kol hāhār* (v 16 has *wayyeḥĕrad hāhār*, the most likely source). If there is a tendency in LXX here, it is to make the language less mythological.

cyclone (or "storm"). The MT makes sense as it is. The three-word colon is neat; the parallelism is good; the noises of the upper and lower waters match. The noun *zerem* is unimpeachable. Compare *zerem mayim kabbîrîm*, "a tempest of mighty waters" (Isa 28:2), but this is no warrant for rewriting every word, as Irwin (1942:26) has done to obtain *zāram yam kabbîr*, "the mighty sea stormed." The noun *zerem* describes a destructive downpour of rain, a cloudburst. Six of its eight occurrences in the Hebrew Bible are in Isaiah, including this very phrase: "a downpour of water" (Isa 28:2). Nevertheless, now that MurXII attests the antiquity of the variant with the verb *zōrĕmû* rather than the noun *zerem*, it is now widely accepted to rewrite v 10aB into conformity with Ps 77:18:

zōrĕmû mayim ʿābôt	clouds poured out water
qôl nātĕnû šĕḥāqîm	skies gave voice

On first sight, this variant receives support from the use of the same idiom ("gave voice") in the following colon. But the subject is not the same in both colons. In Hab 3:10, it is "the abyss"; in Ps 77:18, it is "the clouds." It would be going too far to make v 10b the same as Ps 77:18, even though the parallelism of *ʿābôt* and *šĕḥāqîm* is excellent. Hab 3:10 already has the parallelism of *mayim* and *tĕhôm*. But if Ps 77:18 is not to dictate the reading of v 10b, why should it prescribe an emendation of v 10aB? Apart from that, there is a problem with the verb form *zōrĕmû*, which is usually construed as a rare Poʿel (Roberts's *polel* [1991:140] is inexact).

passed. The verb makes sense once it is recognized that it describes not a thunderstorm that passes overhead, but a great rainstorm that washes over the earth. The parallelism with *tĕhôm* points to the second phenomenon and makes it unnecessary to change *ʿābar* to *ʿābôt*, "clouds." In the first place, this verb can be used to describe a flood of water flowing over a land "like the Nile" (Isa

23:10), a metaphor for an invading force (Isa 8:8; cf. Job 6:15 and, especially, Job 11:16: "like waters that pass along"—a flash flood). Second, *zerem mayim* is not strictly a deluge, but an inundation caused by a cloudburst. Isa 28:2 speaks of "a flood [*zerem*] of mighty waters overflowing." A synonym of *zerem* is *šeṭep* ∼ *šeṣep*, which describes a rain flood (Job 38:25). Hence the idiom *šeṭep ʿōbēr*, "an overflowing flood" (Nahum 1:8), using the same verb as Hab 3:10, and "flood of mighty waters." Such devastations are caused not only by sudden pluviations, but also by upsurging of the great deep. In Noah's Flood, these two combined (Gen 7:11). In Hab 3:10, the question is whether the *zerem mayim* is a downpour of celestial water, in contrast with the roaring flood from the abyss, or whether *zerem mayim* and *tĕhôm* are synonyms. The association of *zerem* with the thunderstorm (as in Isa 30:30) or hailstorm (as in Isa 28:2) or windstorm (as in Isa 32:2) points to the flood consequent on sudden rain, not to the tempest as such. It is the passage of this flood that is described by the verb *ʿābar*.

voice. Irwin (1942:14) compared this outcry of Tehom with Ti'amat's outburst in *Enuma Elish* (IV:71, 89, 91). The latter is angry, defiant, scornful. The impression in Habakkuk is that the elements cry out with terror. The scrap of an ancient poem preserved in Ps 93:3 celebrates the same event. It supports the conclusion already reached in v 9, that the *nĕhārôt* are the waters of the great deep (*tĕhôm*). In Ps 93:3 and Hab 3:10bA this sound made by the deep is a storm at sea caused by the march of God, rather than the voice of a defiant enemy raised against God, provoking retaliation. Nevertheless, there is an inconsistency in the poem between water as the object of God's wrath (v 8) and water as the instrument of his judgment (v 10). This can be resolved if vv 10–11a describe the terrified response of the elements to the vision of Yahweh. So the subject of "they saw thee" is not simply "mountains," but all the elements—mountains, flood, abyss, sun, and moon:

šāmayim mē ʿal // tĕhôm rōbeṣet tāḥat (Deut 33:13)	*tĕhôm* (Hab 3:10)
šemeš // yĕrāḥîm (Deut 33:4)	*šemeš // yārēaḥ* (Hab 3:11)
harĕrê-qedem // gibʿōt-ʿôlām (Deut 33:15)	*harĕrê-ʿad // gibʿōt-ʿôlām* (Hab 3:6)

sun. The traditional punctuation should be revised, as in BH³ and BHS, to do justice to the obvious parallelism between sun and moon. The Greek translations have also done more justice to the parallelism, although apparently groping in the dark, in spite of four words for light. Here the curious Barberini recension as studied by Margolis (1908), Thackeray (1923), and (Ziegler 1943:274) shows itself to be independent of LXX. It has more poetry, but takes more liberties:

MT	LXX	BARBERINI
šemeš	*ho hēlios*	*phōs to lampron tou hēliou*
yārēaḥ	*hē selēnē*	*to pheggos tēs selēnēs*
ʾôr	*phōs*	*to pheggos*
nōgah	*pheggos*	*to pheggos*

V interprets the light as the gleam of the weapons, not the target of the assault.

There is a grammatical peculiarity in the variable gender of *šemeš*. Here it is masculine. Albright's (1950a) demonstration that *rôm* (= *rām*) is an appelative remains as impressive as ever. The title Samēmroumos, "Heaven the Exalted," clinches the point. Albright's (1950a) argument may be clarified and strengthened. In the first place, the use of such discontinuous phrases in Hebrew poetry is now more widely recognized, so there can be no grammatical objection to such a construction here. Second, Albright's (1950a) claim that *zĕbūlâ* means "his lordly dais," reading *-h* as the masculine third-person-singular suffix, not the feminine ending, although brilliantly argued, must be treated with reserve. The moon should not be given such honor. And the picture is wrong. The verb "stood" (*ʿāmad*) means "stood still" (that is, stopped moving along its orbit), not "stood up" "on" its dais. If there is a court scene here, the dais ("princely throne") is Yahweh's and moon stands as a respectful courtier before him. Third, part of Albright's (1950a) evidence is the phrase *zbl yrḥ*, "Prince Moon." Its similarity to *rwm šmš* is unmistakable, and *zbl* and *yrḥ* are correlated in Ugaritic literature. Both phrases are discontinuous, and the names and appellatives are in chiasmus:

rwm . . . *šmš*
yrḥ . . . *zblh*

For the sake of the parallelism, either *zbl(h)* is another title ("Prince") to match "exalted" or else, if *zblh* means "his princely dais," then *rôm* (a *hapax*) should be a synonym. A holistic analysis of the bicolon yields the paraphrase: "Sun and moon stood still in their elevated position (LXX *taxis*) and raised their hands." (The pronoun suffix on *ydyhw* would then be distributive.) The response of the two chief heavenly bodies must be the same—paralysis and submission to Yahweh. Or else, keeping the colons separate:

Exalted sun raised his hands;
Prince moon stood still.

Josh 10:12–13 preserves a fragment of an epic that contained just such an event (Hess 1999). The second bicolon contains the same statement "moon stood still"—and the same chiasmus of sun and moon. The prose commentary adds the detail "and the sun stood still," although the original poem says "the sun was silent." The evidence from Joshua supports the holistic analysis given earlier, which we prefer, notwithstanding Hiebert's (1986:31) reminder that the versions do not support the idea. The raising of the hands could be due to consternation, but more likely the gesture accompanies prayers—that is, incantations against the enemy.

Doubt attaches to the idea of sun and moon as enemies in this combat. There are two arguments:

1. If the imagery of combat in Habakkuk 3 comes from a creation story, sun and moon would not exist, only chaos.

2. Sun and moon are not in the retinue of Ti'amat in *Enuma Elish*; they are allies of Marduk. Both difficulties vanish if the creation motifs are secondary to a recital of Yahweh's assault on the world on a cosmic scale—his historical mighty acts of deliverance. We cannot find this motif in the accounts of the Exodus (but note the darkening of the sun as one of the plagues). The possibility exists that the attack on sun and moon is a new motif of strictly eschatological character.

raised. We have concluded from various thematic and structural features in this part of the poem, that vv 10–11a describe the terrified response of the elements—mountains, water, sun, moon—to Yahweh's ferocious assault. Just what sun expresses in the gesture of raising his hands is not evident.

his hands. The unique *yādêhû* (standard *yādāyw*) is a genuine archaism. Because of the awkwardness of the syntax, including gender agreement between noun and verb, no matter how the constituents are linked together in the grammar, and without much help from considerations of word order, many different combinations have been suggested, with varying plausibility. Roberts (1991:129), comparing v 10bB with Ps 93:3, makes v 10bB a continuation of v 10bA. It is the abyss that lifted up its hands. Avishur (1994) found the picture in v 10bB to be the same as that in Deut 32:4. It is Yahweh who raised his hands. He ingeniously recovered the divine name from the unique form *ydyhw*, emending slightly to *rôm yād(ô) YHW nāśā'*, "YHW has raised His hand to the heavens." We do not think that the significance of this gesture—taking an oath—fits the stage that the action has reached in this part of the poem. Insertion of an action of Yahweh at this point would disrupt the catalog of terrified responses of the cosmic entities to Yahweh's attack.

11. *light.* It is generally assumed that the weapons described in this verse are "the light, regarded as his arrows, and the brightness of lightning, taken to be his spear" (Irwin 1942:20). The use of the preposition *l-* makes this impossible. The interpretation offered in our commentary assumes (1) that the whole of v 11 describes an assault of Yahweh on sun and moon; (2) that *'ôr* means "sun" here, as it does in many other places; and, by extension, (3) that *nōgah* here means "moon." Clear evidence for the secondary meanings we are advocating here is supplied by Isa 60:19:

lō'-yihyeh-lāk 'ôd	it will not be again for you
haššemeš lĕ'ôr yômām	the sun as light by day
ûlĕnōgah hayyārēaḥ	and the brightness the moon
lō'-yā'îr-lāk	will not give light for you

The light of the sun is *'ôr*; *nōgah* is the light of the moon. By metonymy, the attribute becomes the denoting noun.

BDB (21) thinks that "light" in this verse means "lightning," doubtless because of the parallelism of *brq*, and does not find "sun" as one of its eleven meanings for *'ôr*. DCH has seven meanings, including "luminaries, sun, moon, stars"

(p. 161). The point is worth attention. We have already argued that *'ôr* in Hab 3:4 means "sun" (see also the COMMENT on Hos 6:5 in AB 24A:429). The term *'ôr* is often associated with sunrise, and the light that dispels darkness can only be that of the rising sun (Isa 9:1). Nevertheless, it is possible that "the light of the morning" does not describe the risen sun (2 Sam 23:4), but the first glimmerings of daylight. Since *zārah* is the usual verb for sunrise (the normal subject is *šemeš*), the idiom *zārah 'ôr* must mean "the sun rose" (Ps 112:4; cf. Ps 97:11). The word "sun" is used only once in Job (8:16); *'ôr* is common (over thirty times), and in places like Job 31:26 (where it is parallel to "moon") and Job 36:32 (where clouds cover the sun; cf. Job 37:15, 21), the equation is irresistible.

streaming. The traditional interpretation of v 11b is illustrated by KJV: "at the light of thine arrows they went." This leaves the subject unidentified. Hiebert (1986:155, n. 77) summarizes the candidates for this role. Irwin (1942:15), comparing *Enuma Elish* (IV:106–8), supposes that "they go" describes the enemy in full flight. This cannot be correct. It is insipid; indeed, what does it mean for the sun to walk in the light of Yahweh's arrows? It contradicts the preceding statement that the moon and also the sun (presumably) have been brought to a standstill, if they are the subject of "went." BDB (235) correctly sees that "arrows" is the subject, but supposes a relative clause ("thine arrows that shoot"). It is better to make the colon an independent clause, rather than attaching it to v 11a by means of referential *l-*. If *'ôr* means "sun," then *l-* marks the indirect object, and a good clause results. Hiebert (1986), however, makes the phrase adverbial: "brightly." Ps 77:18 confirms that "thine arrows" is the subject of the verb, and the *Hitpaʿel* used there suggests that the *Piʿel* in Habakkuk 3 is iterative. Hiebert (1986:31–32) provides additional analogies in support of this reading.

flashing. The proof that "the light of your arrows" (NIV) is not a discrete phrase is aided by the difficulty in its parallel: "the shining of the lightning of your javelin." This is heavy for poetry; *bĕraq hănît* is enough; the phrase occurs in Nah 3:3. The word for a flash of lightning, *bārāq*, also describes the glitter of other weapons, such as arrows and swords. There is more here than metaphor. In the iconography, the javelin brandished by the storm-god is the thunderbolt. The same parallelism of "arrows" and "lightning flash" occurs in 2 Sam 2:15 (where the singular would seem to be more primitive than the plural in Ps 18:15), and (in reverse) in Ps 144:6.

javelin. The *hănît* was a throwing spear. The plural *hoplōn* of LXX is probably due to attraction from the plural "arrows." Only here and in Ps 35:3 is it a weapon of Yahweh. The Israelite infantry of the monarchical period was armed with spear and sword. Note the wooden javelin in 2 Sam 23:7. The spear would be hurled first and the sword used in the ensuing hand-to-hand combat. The javelin was an auxiliary weapon of the chariot-riding aristocratic elite troops of the Middle Bronze Age. No Israelite war records report an archer with a javelin.

bright one. The moon, as already argued.

12. Verses 12–14 move from the mythological to the historical; rather, only

here does the human foe come on stage. The preternatural dimension of the saving theophany is described in mythological language. The parallelism of v 12 is perfect. That "trample" is a military term is shown by its use in Judg 5:4; Ps 68:8 (and possibly Isa 63:1). While "trample" can be used of the regular tramp of infantry on the march, the present context of this verse suggests rather the injuries inflicted by ferocious warhorses. This reading fits in with v 15, where tramping on the sea is an attack, not just a march. It also fits in with the parallel image of treading out the nations (v 12b) as an animal threshes grain. The same metaphor in Amos 1:3 could describe chariot warfare. Compare treading the winepress (= waging war in which the wine is blood) in Isa 63:1–3, where the phrase "and I trampled them in my anger" resembles Hab 3:12, 15.

Irwin (1942:15) compared the trampling here and in v 15 with the action of Marduk against Ti'amat (*Enuma Elish* IV:118, 129). This treatment of a prostrate foe was so universal, that it provides no firm link between the two poems.

No historical identification is possible for this verse. The general reference to "earth" and "nations" makes it universal, potentially eschatological. In keeping with the rest of the poem, the prefixed verbs should be taken as historic past—neither future nor general present.

13. *marched out.* The verb *yāṣā'* means "to set out on a military expedition" (see the NOTE on Hab 1:7). The verb describes Yahweh's egress in Judg 5:4; 2 Sam 5:24; Isa 42:13; Zech 14:3; Pss 68:8; 108:12.

deliver. The root *yš'* is found in Hebrew words traditionally translated as "save" or "salvation." The motivation for Yahweh's campaign is to rescue his people from "the wicked." This purpose was already hinted at in the use of the feminine form of "deliverance" in v 8. The masculine form, used twice in v 13, seems to have the same meaning. This is the final answer to the prophet's complaint that the LORD was doing nothing to rescue "the righteous" from "the wicked."

thy people. That the objects of Yahweh's saving acts are called his people hints at a covenant relationship. But no details are given, and covenant terminology is not evident in the rest of the book. Hiebert (1986:106) has argued cogently that, in the context of an ancient poem celebrating the military prowess of Yahweh, the term *'am* refers specifically to "the militia of the tribal confederation." In that case, the "deliverance" is not rescue of the people from an enemy, but victory of the people's army in battle.

thou didst come. Something has to be done about the *nota accusativi* in 13aB. It is completely out of character in archaic poetry of this kind. And it is grammatically impossible inserted in the phrase "the rescue of [*nota accusativi*] thy messiah," which must be parallel to "the rescue of thy people." For these reasons, the solution offered by BHS, which reads an infinitive instead of a noun, in order to have a grammatical object, moves in the wrong direction. Albright's (1950a) solution was ingenious. He replaced *'et* with *'am*, arguing that the word was lost by haplography from the letters . . . '[*m*]m. . . . He justified the reconstruction in terms of his belief that ancient poetry went in for repetitive parallelism. (The emendation is actually due to Horst). Hiebert (1986) accepts the emendation, with tortuous explanations of how the change from ʿ*am* to ʾ*et* came about. But Albright's (1950a) argument that "it was obviously inserted for the sake of the rhythm" is weak, for scanning by beats, ʾ*et* would not be counted. Counting by syllables, it makes little difference. Its insertion did not solve any grammatical problems. Even when prose grammar requires ʾ*et*, there is no indication that scribes supplied *nota accusativi* when it was "missing" from a poem. So why was it inserted here, when the preceding noun (or something) has to be emended to make ʾ*et* grammatical? If the text did have ʿ*am* originally, this might have been mistaken for ʿ*im* and changed it to ʾ*et*.

The MT ʾ*et* is confirmed by ancient versions, rendering "with"; indeed, Jerome made much of the distinction between Christ as the object of salvation and salvation achieved "with" Christ (texts in Field 1875:II:1009, n. 34).

We suggest, rather, that ʾ*et* is original and that it represents the verb ʾ*ātîtā*, in parallel with *yāṣāʾtā*. The poetry is excellent, with a discontinuous construct phrase *yēšaʿ* . . . *měšîḥekā* to match *yēšaʿ* . . . ʿ*ammekā*. The acceptability of archaic ʾ*ātîtā*, in parallel with *yāṣāʾtā*, is established by its use in Deut 33:2, a passage whose affinities with Habakkuk 3 need no further argumentation.

thy messiah. The word "messiah" led to considerable debate between Christians and Jews, so that the *Heimat* of a Greek text can sometimes be discerned in its choice of translation. The MSS are almost unanimous at this point, reading *Khristos*. Even Aquila let it through, much to Jerome's delight: *Rem incredibilem dicturus sum, sed tamen veram: isti semichristiani Judaice transtulerunt, et Iudaeus Aquila interpretatus est, ut Christianus* (Field 1875:II:1009). One Christian scribe embellished it, rendering "on account of Jesus His Christ" (attested in Field). But Barberini reads "your chosen ones," *eklektous* (plural!). Other attestatioins of the plural are documented in Field (1875:II:1009, n. 33; for Qumran parallels, see Amusin 1966). The plural is found also in some Hebrew MSS.

The word "messiah" seems anachronistic if the poem purports to describe events that took place no later than the Exodus, since the earliest historical figures to whom it properly applies are Saul and David. Here the affinities between Habakkuk 3 and Psalm 18 are noteworthy. There is a similar anachronism in 1 Sam 2:10. In neither case can this word be allowed to settle the date of the rest of the poem in general. That Habakkuk should use such a word is not surprising, although the rest of his prophecy shows no interest in the monarchy as such. The anachronism could be literary, as in Ps 105:15, where the patriarchs are called "prophets" and "messiahs," both later terms projected onto an earlier age. In similar fashion, the word "anointed" might be used to refer to Yahweh's "people" before the age of kings, in the sense of "chosen" or "favored." If so, Habakkuk did not have a king in mind at all, although the term itself does not belong with the ancient diction that he uses more correctly.

Thou didst mash (or "smash," if it took only one blow). Of fifteen occurrences of the root *mḥṣ* in the Hebrew Bible, all the verb forms are used only in poetry. Isa 30:26 contains the only attestation of the noun. The following table gives the connotations of the verb.

TABLE 5. Connotations of the Verb √ *mḫṣ*

REFERENCE	ASSAILANT	WEAPON	INJURED ORGAN
Job 26:12	God	not specified	Rahab (head? [not specified])
Job 5:18	God	not specified	human
Deut 32:39	God	not specified	human (?)
Deut 33:11	God	not specified	loins of enemies
Num 24:8	God	arrows	nations? (skull?) bones
Num 24:17	Star from Jacob	rod (?)	temples, cranium
2 Sam 22:39 = Ps 18:39	David	not specified	not specified
Ps 110:5–6	God	not specified	heads
Ps 68:22	God	not specified	heads
Judg 5:26	Jael	mallet (?)	Sisera's head
Hab 3:13	God	mace (?)	head

The verb √ *mḫṣ* is used nine or ten times to describe an action of God. Other persons who do this thing are Jael (Judg 5:26) and David (Ps 18:39 = 2 Sam 22:38). The agent in Num 24:17 is the mysterious "Star from Jacob." The occurrence of the verb in Ps 68:24 seems to be an error for *tirḫaṣ*, influenced by v 22. Thus in nine of thirteen occurrences √ *mḫṣ* is an act of Yahweh. It is described in ancient poems (Deut 32:39; 33:11; Judg 5:26; 2 Sam 22:38; Pss 18:39; 68:2), all have affinities with Habakkuk 3. Usually the head is attacked (Judg 5:26; Pss 68:22; 110:6) or the crown (Num 24:8; Ps 68:22), but Deut 33:11 specifies the loins (Gevirtz 1963:70). Hab. 3:13 is thus typical. Jael seems to have used some kind of mallet, and the Star uses a "rod"; Num 24:8 specifies "arrows" as the weapon. The prominence of the head as the target makes a club the most likely weapon, even when not identified. That this is the traditional form of divine punishment is shown by the curse in the Kilamuwa Inscription:

my mšḫt hsprz	whoever should smash this inscription,
yšḫt rˀš b ˁllet	Baal smash (his) head (lines 15, 16)

The verb is different, but the action is clear. The use of the cognate verb *maḫāṣu* in Akkadian affords numerous supportive parallels. And it also permits the event to be reconstructed with even more precision. The blow is not inflicted in combat, but to mutilate a dead foe. At least in *Enuma Elish* (IV: 130), *ina mi-ṭi-šu la pādî ulatti muḫḫa*, "with his unsparing club he split (her) skull," the victorious Marduk, standing on the buttocks of the prone Ti'amat, smashes her skull with his unsparing *miṭṭu* aiming blows at the top of her head. Some idea of what the weapon does (and therefore of what it could be) might be learned from the connotation of the verb that describes its effect on the skull. In general, the verb *letû* (*latû*) means "to split into two or more pieces." As far as the entries in *CAD* (9:148) indicate, when a weapon is used, whether sword or mace, the object is the head (*muḫḫa* or *qaqqadu*). It is cracked open, like a piece of crockery.

The most interesting victim of this kind of assault is the marine monster of Job 26:12, which is given various names, including Yam ("Sea") and Rahab. This could be the most ancient fragment of this tradition; it is replete with the diction of Canaanite mythology. This helps to work out the picture in Hab 3:13bB.

head. Since the head is the part of the victim usually struck when the verb √*mḥṣ* is used, and since "head" is well attested by the versions, there is no need to consider any other reading. Hiebert (1986:36–40), however, offers lengthy arguments for replacing *r'š* with *bmt* "back." This emendation has been accepted by Roberts (1991:142). It is fatuous to point to the repetition of "head" as evidence that v 14aA is a doublet of v 13bA, or the reverse (Roberts 1991:142). In the closely parallel Ps 74:13–14, *rā'šê* is repeated in exactly the same way. Furthermore, the plural there shows that we are dealing with the seven-headed dragon (Hydra) of the ancient myth, common to Mesopotamia and Canaan. The wound is inflicted on "the head of the wicked." A discontinuous construct phrase is evident. The inserted word "from house" is problematic. The colon is unusual for this poem in having four words, and this detail gives some support to cleaning it up, deleting "from house." A popular emendation, based on LXX, is *mwt*. It requires little change in the Hebrew text. It would identify the enemy with Mot of the Ugaritic sources. "Wicked" is then an attributive adjective: "wicked Death." Stephens (1924:291) combined the evidence of LXX, pointing to *hmwt*, and MT *mbyt* to obtain *bhmwt*, "Behemot." In this, he was influenced by his belief that *Enuma Elish* IV provides the background of the literary allusions in Habakkuk 3. The proposal is certainly ingenious, but the case is weak all the same. Yahweh in Habakkuk 3 is much like Marduk. And it is not easy to accept a textual change from *bhmwt* to *mbyt*, and the latter is the "difficult" reading. Identification of the enemy with a dragon such as Ti'amat is plausible all the same, on general grounds. The Greek plurals have taken the object as collective ("wicked ones"), but an individual enemy is probably nearer to the original. Whether "wicked" is singular or collective, a historical allusion is suspected. Rabbi Solomon saw Sennacherib as the foe (Irwin 1942:10).

Thou didst slash. The morphology of the verb is not certain. Possible roots are *'ry* and *'rr*. An infinitive construct (GKC §74n) is feasible and syntactically unobjectionable. So is a suffixed form * *'ārōtā* or * *'ārîtā*. A factitive would be better.

Some action is performed on the prostrate victim. Either he is stripped naked, "from thigh to neck." Or *mibbayit* could refer to his "insides." His brains are bashed out and his innards exposed by slicing him open "from foundation to neck." Disemboweling was a common atrocity in ancient warfare, but the case that chiefly comes to mind is that of Ti'amat in *Enuma El-ish*. She corresponds to the Canaanite sea monster. After defeating Ti'amat, Marduk splits her body in two and out of it fabricates the universe. Hab 3:13bB could be describing a similar action. Nothing comparable is known in Canaanite sources.

14. *Thou didst smash* (or "hammer" or "perforate"). This verse is largely un-intelligible, and the second part is best left untranslated. The first part seems to continue the description of the assault on the wicked given in v 13b. Once more, the target is the head, and *nāqabtā* is close in meaning to *māḥaṣtā*. In the light of our discussion of *maṭṭôt* in v 9, "his staves" in v 14 represent the twin clubs or dual maces of the god's armament. The MT presents a difficulty because of the pronoun suffix "*his* rods," which is out of place in a strophe that is other-wise second person. In this detail has been found the rather fanciful idea that the enemy "are smitten on the head with their own weapons" (Gaster 1937:26). The remedy is to read *maṭṭāyw* as dual (cf. the suffix dual -*w* in the Gezer Cal-endar). The parallelism suggests that *przw* is another reference to the enemy, but the forms *przwn* and *prznw* in Judges 5 point to some kind of peasant mili-tia, which does not fit the context of Habakkuk 3.

After this the text becomes progressively worse, and even recognizable words, such as "to eat the poor in secret," make no sense. The correctness of the He-brew text is shown by the Greek versions, or, rather, their evidence points to a text evidently the same as the MT. The vocabulary differences of the versions enhance their witness to a common Hebrew original. The key words "eat" and "poor" were rendered independently by the divergent Greek recensions:

| LXX | *hōs esthōn ptōkhos lathra* |
| Barberini | *heneken tou kataphagein tous ptōkhous lathra* |

This evidence does not mean that the text is immaculate, only that it is au-thentically ancient in its present form. Irwin's (1942:30) reconstruction, which he hails as "probably the most astonishing case of dependence on a Babylonian original in the total of Hebrew literature," is arrived at by remodeling every word, most of them drastically:

MT	*przw ys ʿrw lhpyṣny*	
Irwin	*pigro yisʿar haṣṣāpôn*	his corpse the North wind blew away;
MT	*ʾlyṣtm kmw*	
Irwin	*yaʿaleh ṣiyyatā dāmôit*	carried his blood to the desert.

One could propose almost anything by such methods.

15. The last verse of this section is a well-formed bicolon that returns to ear-lier themes. It constitutes an inclusion with v 8. Compare the similar relation-ship between v 3 and v 7. Chronologically, it comes before the successes de-scribed in vv 13–14. It also has a thematic connection with v 12. The picture is clear, although the word *ḥmr* is a problem.

Thou didst trample. Albright (1950a), following Ehrlich (1912), emended to *Hip'il*, in line with v 19. This may not be necessary in view of Ps 77:20. The difference is not material.

many waters. The root *ḥmr* has several connotations. It can describe the roar of the waters (v 10bA; cf. Ps 46:4) or the heaping up of water (the parting of the Reed Sea), or clay (the turning of the seabed into dry ground for the passage). Poetically, a verb is needed to parallel *drkt*. Perhaps an infinitive absolute should be read.

To sum up: vv 8–15 describe a foray by Yahweh in language that is largely mythological. Although the campaign is directed against the nations for the sake of his people, the main target is the cosmic order, especially the watery element, which is completely subdued. Numerous incidents in Israel's past—Creation, Flood, Exodus, the crossing of Jordan, the Battle of Beth-Horon, the Battle of Kishon—supply memories that are echoed in this poem. But the main substance is a (creation?) myth, akin to the subjugation of the primal marine dragon, in which Yahweh—armed with bow, javelin, and mace—is featured as a chariot-riding warrior. The language matches this very archaic content.

COMMENT

In a detailed study of the *Chaoskampfmythos* that includes Psalm 93 but not, surprisingly, Habakkuk 3, Podella (1993) has demonstrated the fluidity with which motifs in ancient Near Eastern sources have been subsumed under the rubric of chaos. One might object that the word is not appropriate, indeed misleading, when applied outside the Greek philosophical tradition, where it goes back to Hesiod. But since the foundational work of Gunkel, who set chaos as the antithesis of creation, the term is here to stay. Podella concluded (1993:319) that it was not possible to trace the reception and development history of the *Chaoskampfmythologem* in the Old Testament. He does show, however, that

> Aus der Discussion exemplarischer Texte zum Theme "Chaoskampf" im Alten Testament folgt, daß terminologisch explizit nur dann von einem *Kampf* gesprochen wird, wenn ein (erneutes) Eingreifen JHWHs gegen aktuelle Feinde/Gegner erwartet wird. Das Chaoskampfmythologem ist demnach fest situiert in Kontexten, wo kollektive Notzeiten sprachlich bewältigt werden. Das heißt hier, Not und Feinde werden in religiösen Symbolsystem dämonisiert und personalisiert, so daß man mit ihnen "umgehen" und die Notlage einer Lösung zuführen kann.

It follows from the discussion of representative texts that deal with the theme of the "War against Chaos" in the Old Testament that there is termino-

logically explicit discourse about a *War* only when a (fresh) intervention of
Yahweh against actual enemies/opponents is expected. The war-against-
chaos mythologem is then firmly situated in contexts in which collective
times of trouble are overcome by using language. In the present instance,
this means that trouble and enemy become demonized and personified in
a religious symbol-system so that one can engage with them and bring in
a resolution of the troubled situation.

We suggest that some such relationship exists between the pieces of ancient Israelite epic gathered in vv 3–15 and their application to the troubles and enemies that Habakkuk was struggling with.

Why are the opening statements formulated as questions? As part of a dialogue
with God, the question is presumably asked by the prophet. If the question is an
integral, original part of an ancient poem that Habakkuk has now incorporated
into his own contemporary restatement, what purpose did this form of questioning originally serve? Compare the question to the sea in Ps 114:5. A question
asked for rhetorical purposes will normally begin *hălō'*, "Was it not . . . ?"

The questions in Habakkuk 3 seem like more straightforward requests for information. As such, they resemble the inquiries addressed to the returning warrior, inviting him to give an account of his exploits (1 Sam 27:10). It is the occasion for a boasting speech (Isa 63:1–3) in reply. Such a ceremonial exchange
is part of a desacralization ritual that ends a season of war. The sanctified warrior is released when he has fulfilled all the vows he made on setting out on his
expedition. Deut 32:37–42 is a good example of such a report, formulated as an
oath of clearance that serves both to glorify the hero and to vindicate the victor.
Here the ideas of victory and justification merge. The righteousness of the returning hero consists of his successful performance of his promises. The victory
granted by the god proves the justness of his cause. Hab 3:8–15 does not develop into such a self-testimony. It remains an address to the hero, recounting
his exploits. Such a recital could be made in worship by a people grateful for
deliverance. Its purpose, in its present form, was not primarily to edify the people, by keeping alive the memories of great past events. As an address to the deity, it becomes a supplication. Habakkuk 3 is similar to Isaiah 63 in this regard.
The ancient feat is to be repeated. Israel's hope for the future was the expectation of a new Exodus.

What provoked Yahweh's anger against the sea? In a pioneering study, Cassuto (1943:69–109) tried to retrieve an ancient Israelite epic from scraps such
as Hab 3:8–15, which are scattered through the Hebrew Bible and survive mostly
as literary allusions. The vocabulary he recovered is particularly abundant in
Hab 3:8–15. The occasion is the revolt of the sea against Yahweh. Its naturalistic counterpart is the threat of the ocean against the land. The outcome is the
restraint of the sea and the safety of the land. In some respects, this is regarded
as a creation story, in the sense of an etiology, an explanation of how the present world order came about.

Very little of this scenario is germane to Hab 3:8–15. The time, the setting, the motivation, and the outcome are all different. The object of God's wrath is "the wicked"; his motive is to rescue his people (v 13). This content puts the poem into history, involving humans. Yet the wicked enemy is not explicitly identified as human. While the sea is the most prominent target of the assault, other cosmic elements (sun, moon, mountains, underworld) are also involved. It is not certain whether this warfare against the elements provides images and parallels for the LORD's campaign against Egypt or some other oppressor; whether Egypt is the only antagonist, described metaphorically as "sea," "earth," and so on; whether references to the sun and the other elements describe events collateral with the campaign against Pharaoh and his army—the various "plagues," including thunderstorm (Yahweh's typical weapon), and the darkening of the sun (the chief deity of Egypt). All this is suggestive, but it remains elusive. The sea is not entirely recognized as an independent, alien power, a threat to Yahweh. A moral cause for his indignation (political oppression of his people, one of the motives for the Exodus) is barely hinted at in the word "wicked" (v 13).

The recurrence of the theme of anger in v 12 could supply the answer to the questions in v 8a. Verse 12 marks the transition to the second part of the recital within vv 8–15. At this point, the human enemies come clearly into view, and suffixed verbs are more prominent. The implied answer could then be "No." Yahweh's anger, this time, was not against the sea and other cosmic elements, as in the original victory of creation. It was against the nations.

VIII.2.iv. HABAKKUK'S RESPONSE (3:16–19)

16aAα	I heard, and my stomach churned,
16aAβ	at the sound my lips trembled;
16aBα	Rottenness entered my bones,
16aBβ	and my feet shook beneath me.
16bA	I waited for the day of disaster
16bB	to come up against the people who had invaded us.
17aAα	Although the fig-tree has not sprouted,
17aAβ	and there is no yield from the vines;
17aBα	although the olive crop has failed,
17aBβ	and the fields have made no food;
17bA	although the flocks are cut off from the fold,
17bB	and there are no cattle in the yards—
18a	Nevertheless I, I will rejoice in Yahweh,
18b	I will exult in the God of my deliverance;
19a	in Yahweh the Lord of my success.
19bA	And he made my legs like does,
19bB	and he made me trample on my high places.

Scansion of Habakkuk's Response (3:16–19)

		BEATS	SYLLABLES	BI(TRI)COLON
16aAα	*šāma'tî	wattirgaz biṭnî*	3	8	16
16aAβ	*lĕqôl ṣālălû śĕpātay*	3	8	
16aBα	*yābô' rāqāb ba'aṣāmay*	3	8	15
16aBβ	*wĕtaḥtay 'ergāz ['šr]*	3	7	
16bA	*'ānûaḥ lĕyôm ṣārâ*	3	6	15
16bB	*la'ălôt lĕ'am yĕgûdennû*	3	9	
17aAα	*kî tĕ'ēnâ lō'-tiprāḥ*	4	7	15
17aAβ	*wĕ'ên yĕbûl baggĕpānîm*	3	8	
17aBα	*kiḥēs ma'ăśēh-zayit*	3	5	13
17aBβ	*ûśĕdēmôt lō'-'āśâ 'ōkel*	3	8	
17bA	*gāzar mimmiklâ ṣō'n*	3	6	14
17bB	*wĕ'ên bāqār bārĕpātîm*	3	8	
18a	*wa'ănî b-yhwh 'e'lôzâ*	3	9	
18b	*'āgîlâ bē'lōhê yiš'î*	3	9	25
19a	*yhwh 'ădōnāy ḥêlî*	3	7	
19bA	*wayyāśem raglay kā'ayyālôt*	3	8	17
19bB	*wĕ'al bāmôtay yadrīkēnî*	3	9	

INTRODUCTION

The last four verses (seventeen colons of poetry) represent the prophet's personal response to the theophany or, rather, to the recital of the poem in vv 3–15, which has been composed from "report(s)" (3:2) of the epic deeds of Yahweh. The first part of his response has already been given in v 2. The repetition of the verb "I heard" at the beginning of v 16 provides a connecting link between these two more personal parts of the "prayer." The root *rgz* (v 2) is used twice in v 16. The mood of terror continues, and 16a describes the syndrome of fright at the theophany in conventional terms. This mood changes to relaxation and expectation (v 16b) and then to an ecstasy of joy (v 18). The loss of all things (v 17) is accepted. The final bicolon (v 19b) is a kind of coda in which the triumph of Yahweh is shared with the poet. Verse 19c is simply a concluding musical annotation.

The four sections (corresponding to the verses) of this unit that register the prophet's changes of mood are of diminishing length (six colons, six, three, two).

The contrasts within the unit are extreme and dramatic. The terror of v 16 gives place to the confidence of v 19b—legs like jelly become like magnificent athletic animals. And the conquered becomes the conqueror. The total deprivation of v 17 gives place to the complete satisfaction with God expressed in v 18. These related passages are chiastically arranged.

Terror (v 16)
    Deprivation (v 17)
    Satisfaction (v 18)
Confidence v (19)

The poetry is well formed, with colons of consistent length and good parallelism. Sixteen of the colons have three beats; the only variant, four beats in v 17aAα, is of no consequence: the Masoretes did not make *kî* proclitic. There is similar regularity in the colons and bicolons when length is measured by the number of syllables. The mean length is 7.7 syllables per colon. The mean for the whole poem is exactly seven syllables per colon.

The two six-colon stanzas are internally integrated by various connecting devices. The first four colons of v 16 are unified by the list of four organs weakened by the sound of the story—stomach, lips, bones, feet. The verbs are not so straightforward. The prefixed verb forms in v 16aB must be taken as past tense, and this extends to the verbs in v 16b as well. The repetition of the root *rgz* in the first and fourth colons creates a chiasmus and also constitutes a link with earlier parts of the poem (vv 2 and 7). But the form *'ergāz,* "I shook," makes the fourth colon difficult.

The six colons of v 17 are unified by the list of basic commodities that represent the staples of the mixed subsistence farming characteristic of the Israelite economy—figs, grapes, olives, cereals, sheep, and cattle. All six clauses are governed by the introductory conjunction "although," and the whole of the verse constitutes the protasis whose apodosis comes in v 18. Verse 17 adds up to total disaster, as far as the food supply is concerned.

The syntax of these six clauses is interesting. Three of them have suffixed verbs, past tense. The one prefixed form (v 17aA) joins them in pointing to a realized, rather than a hypothetical, condition. The six privations are expressed by two negations (*lō'*), two negative existentials (*'ên*), and two privative verbs ("deceived," "cut off"). No one bicolon contains two clauses with the same kind of negation.

The change to future tense in v 18 is clearly marked by the long (cohortative) forms. The tricolon is tightly integrated. The first two colons are linked by the parallel verbs and by chiasmus. The second and third colons are linked by the similar phrases "the God of my deliverance" and "the Lord of my success." The first and third colons have the word "Yahweh" as an inclusion. Or, to put it another way, the phrase "Yahweh, the God of my deliverance," which is distributed over the first two colons, corresponds to "Yahweh, the Lord of my success," which constitutes the third colon. This parallelism shows that *b-* governs all these names and is to be understood in v 19a as well. This good tricolon makes it quite unnecessary to suppose that a colon might have been lost (BHS) or to make v 19aA a new clause (KJV, Albright 1950a, and others).

The concluding bicolon (v 19b) reverts to the past tense. The colons are rather long for this poem, but the parallelism is good. The chiasmus brings the last verb to the end, finishing on a strong note.

NOTES

16. *I heard.* What is heard is not the voice of God in the revelatory vision (2:2). Nor is it the noises made in the theophany, by either the voice of Yahweh (Psalm 19) or the sound of the convulsing elements (3:6). The connections of v 16 with

Hab 3:2 show that what disturbs the prophet is hearing the report (*šēmaʻ*) of Yahweh's deed—that is, the recitation of the traditional poem(s) found in vv 3–15. This audition might well have taken place in some cult setting, when the LORD is in his holy Temple, and everyone is silent in his presence (2:20). Habakkuk's experience is thus like that of the Psalmist who went into the sanctuary of God, and then understood the end of the wicked (Ps 73:17). The conventional language of v 16 shows that the effect of this experience was the same as that of the original theophany. For a similar response to hearing a report, see Deut 2:25; Isa 21:3–4.

churned. The same verb is translated "shook" in the fourth colon. The √*rgz* describes the agitation that goes with violent emotions—surprise, anger, grief, terror. It describes also the convulsions of nature, such as earthquake. This is the only place where the verb is given a psychological connection with organs of the body. The examples gathered by Waldman (1976) do not include many in which the viscera are the organs prominently affected in the syndrome of fear, however caused. As far as comparison with other creation stories goes, the poet's response here is more like that of Ti'amat (*Enuma Elish* IV:90) or ʻAnat (*ANET* 136).

trembled. This verb usually describes the effect on the ears of horrifying news of Yahweh's judgment (1 Sam 3:11; 2 Kgs 21:12; Jer 19:3). Only here does it refer to lips, but the connotations are the same. Habakkuk is rendered speechless.

bones. The bones, as vital organs, are very significant in Israelite psychology. Rottenness of the bones describes the devastating effects of a complete loss of self-esteem, due to resentment (Prov 12:4) or envy (Prov 14:30). The effect is paralyzing; all capacity to act is lost. A similar combination of symptoms is described in Ps 22:15 (cf. Lam 1:13). Belly and bones are associated in a contrasting description of well-being in Prov 3:8 (cf. Prov 16:24), and according to Prov 15:30, "Good news makes the bones fat."

my feet. Once more, the psychology is realistic. A person in a state of shock has difficulty in locomotion. Tottering footsteps and general lack of coordination due to a drop in blood pressure can lead to a complete faint. The physiology of fear is very complex and varies from person to person. The sympathetic and parasympathetic nervous systems might work in opposite ways. The Bible describes discouragement as a slippage of the feet (Ps 73:2). There is a progression through the four symptoms, the collapse of the feet being the last and worst state. And it is to the feet that the cure is applied in v 19.

The text that we have translated "and my feet shook beneath me" is difficult, and various attempts have been made to solve its problems. Modern editions (BHS) are correct in putting ʼšr with the words "and underneath me I shook." The relative pronoun is out of the question. The accusation, made by Goodwin (1969), that scholars wish to eliminate this word in order to make the poem more archaic does not dignify debate. The authenticity of the relative pronoun in any occurrence is not sacrosanct. The critical scholar must be free to question it.

There is wide agreement that instead of *ʾšr* should be read *ʾăšūray*, as in Pss 17:5; 40:3; 73:2, etc., or *ʾaššūrî*, as in Job 31:7. The first-person verb might remain, with "[my] steps" as referential. Albright (1950a) wanted to emend this word to a dual verb, making the subject concrete ("my two feet"). No emendation of consonants is needed. Only the vowels have to be adjusted, since the possessive pronoun is available by double duty from the three preceding colons.

I waited. The verb √*nwh* is so restful that the abrupt change of mood has perplexed commentators. Various solutions have been proposed. If v 16b begins the resolutions that continue in v 18, we would expect a long form * *ʾānûḥâ*. In v 16, the prefixed verb forms are past tense: "I waited in repose." BH³ lists three possible emendations, and BHS offers a fourth (*ʾăhakkeh*), which would represent obedience to the command in Hab 2:3. Albright (1950a) suggested *ʾānûs*, "I was sick," which continues the theme of the preceding colons. Jer 17:16 does not give much support to Albright's proposal. The difficulty with the verb "I was at ease" lies as much in bringing sense out of the remaining words of v 16. Albright has to make three more changes to carry his point.

disaster. The phrase "day of distress" is often used in the Hebrew Bible. It never describes the trouble experienced by the wicked when justice is done to them in retribution. It always describes the distress of the LORD's people, caused by an oppressor, a distress from which he should deliver them. The Israelites, and especially their prophets, often refer movingly to their "day of distress" when praying to God for help. It would fit in with the book of Habakkuk as a whole if this is Habakkuk's last prayer of this kind. But it does not fit with the rest of v 16. In v 16a, the prophet's anguish is entirely caused by the terror of the LORD. All this would be wasted if he reverts to the frame of mind of his first prayers. Hence, for once, "the day of distress" can be taken as retribution by *jus talionis* "for the people who raided us."

Whether *ʾānûaḥ* is left as it is or is changed to *ʾăhakkeh*, fear at the majesty of God can be mingled with a patient waiting for him to bring his justice in his own time and in his own way. In fact, such opposites can coexist in their extreme forms, as the juxtaposition of v 17 and v 18 shows. Even if the devastation is total, even if there is no retribution and no restoration, Yahweh, my God, my Lord, my Strength, my Salvation, has become the sole and sufficient object of Habakkuk's ecstatic hope and joy.

It is only a bloodless rationalistic analysis that finds contradiction between the reverence of v 16a, the delight of v 18, the devastation of v 17 and the tranquillity of v 16b. The ancient pieces that are closest to Habakkuk 3 in genre — Exodus 15, Judges 5, Psalms 18 and 68 — contain a lyrical synthesis of the fear of Yahweh with admiration and confidence, a synthesis of faith and love that is the height of adoration — Yahweh, terrible and compassionate.

17. The textual difficulties in v 17 are minor and make no material difference to the final result. It is interesting that all the problems listed in v 17 are due to a failure of nature (or of Yahweh as the God of farm and flock), not to the depredations of a conqueror. Even when these most familiar and reliable tokens of God's goodness are withdrawn, God himself will be more than enough for fullness of joy.

Attempts have been made to link this verse with a harvest festival. This interpretive move detaches this verse from the rest of the poem. It is too small to constitute an independent composition and could hardly have been "penned . . . for a harvest festival" (Thackeray 1923:48). Its negative assertions hardly fit such a thing, and the range of products, from the reaping of wheat to the gathering of olives, spans too long a part of the agricultural year to suit any one festival. The same range is recognized in the curses of Leviticus 26, which are very numerous and assorted. There the yield of grain is eaten by enemies (v 16), and neither field nor orchard will yield (v 20) "increase" (yĕbûl).

Stephens (1924) and Bévenot (1933) identified this verse as an account of famine—a third phase of destruction in some serial stories, such as Atra-Ḫasīs. The treatment decreed by Enlil to teach the misbehaving humans a lesson is described as follows:

> Cut off food supplies from the peoples,
> Let plant life be in short supply in their stomachs,
> Let Adad above make his rain scarce,
> Below, let (the river) be blocked up
>   and let it not raise the flood from the Abyss.
> Let the fields diminish their yields,
> Let Nisaba turn aside her breast,
> Let the black fields become white,
> Let the broad plain produce salt,
> Let the earth's womb rebel,
> Let no vegetables shoot up, no cereals grow,
> Let pestilence be laid on the peoples,
> That the womb may be constricted
>   and give birth to no child. (Atra-Ḫasīs iv:41–51)

Gaster (1937:26) saw in v 17 a trace of an ancient fertility myth in which the earth suffers "from drought and blight." His suggestion follows that "the victory over sea and river" described in the preceding text is the means to fertility. It is the victory of the god of rain. But in Habakkuk, the waters are wholly hostile, and if the iconography of Yahweh is that of a storm god, it is the destructive zerem, not the gentle rain from heaven.

sprouted. It makes little difference to read the MT *tprḥ* or *tprh*, "fruited," as LXX evidently did.

vines. As with *tĕ'ēnâ*, the singular collective *gepen* is the standard term (fifty-two times). The plural occurs only here and in Cant 2:13. The explanation is found in the artistry of the six colons:

fig	vines
olive	fields
fold	yards

Singular and plural alternate throughout.

yield. This term is used mainly in a general way for the produce of "the earth." This is the only place in the Hebrew Bible where it is connected with vines.

failed. On the use of this verb in such a context, see the COMMENT at Hos 9:2 (AB 24A:524). To make "olive" the subject of the verb, in line with the grammar of the other statements, the object can be read as "its work" with little or no change of the text. Although the word order (verb, object, subject) is abnormal, it could be due to the chiasm, which achieves another pretty word pattern in the six colons:

FIG	sprout	:	produce	VINES
work	OLIVE	:	FIELDS	work
FOLD	flock	:	herd	YARDS

fields. This poetic word for cultivated lands is always plural. It is found in Ugaritic. We are reluctant to change the verb ʿāśâ to plural, in agreement with the subject, because the same thing happens in Isa 16:8. The noun could be collective. The clash of gender can be eased by reading an infinitive absolute (suggested by David Noel Freedman).

food. This word generally refers to cereals.

cut off. The active voice of the verb is a problem if "flock" is the subject. For the passive, meaning "was destroyed" (or eaten), the Nipʿal is available (BHS). Otherwise, a passive participle (Albright 1950a) or an internal Qal passive might be read. The problems of "made" and "cut off" might be solved together if God is the understood subject. Otherwise, the cause of all this catastrophe is not identified.

fold. The singular must be intentional (see NOTE on *vines*), for the other two occurrences of the word are plural (spelled with *alef*).

yards. This is the sole occurrence of this word, whose derivation is unknown. The combination of plant and animal cultivation is noteworthy. The contrast between agriculturalist and pastoralist is not present. Yahweh is God of all natural forces. To designate him as, even originally, a shepherd's God in contrast to a God of crops, such as Baal, is a fiction of scholars. From earliest times in the civilized Near East, the fertility gods combine jurisdiction over both aspects of mixed farming, which were economically integrated from the earliest beginnings we can trace (for the evidence from seals, see Frankfort 1934:13–14).

18. *Nevertheless I.* The use of the personal pronoun is very emphatic and indicates a tremendous assertion of faith. The response is intensely individual. There is no prophetic outreach to the people. It supports our argument that the whole of this prophecy is a testament of Habakkuk in his private crisis of faith. If this is so, it is an exception to the rule that God's dealings with the prophets were always for public purposes.

exult. The prophet's jubilation is the answer to the illicit joy of the heathen, which he had deplored in Hab 2:15. They worshiped their instruments of war because they gave them rich food (*maʾăkāl*); Habakkuk worships Yahweh even when he withholds food (*ʾōkel*).

deliverance. This is the fourth time this root (*yšʿ*) has been used in Habakkuk 3. Habakkuk began his passion with a complaint that Yahweh had not delivered him (Hab 1:2); at the end, he acclaims Yahweh as "the God of my deliverance," even though it would seem to be still a matter for hope, not a fact of experience. Habbakuk has learned to live by faith.

19a. For arguments that v 19a forms part of a tricolon with v 18, see the INTRODUCTION.

Yahweh the lord. The usual title is "My Lord Yahweh." The phrase "the Lord of my strength" is indicated by the parallelism with v 18b. It requires repointing. The majestic plural of *ʾādôn* is rarely used for God, except in suffixation, where it is ubiquitous.

does. The affinities of v 19a with 2 Sam 22:34 and Ps 18:34 have long been appreciated, but the details are hard to work out. The Psalms are identical, except for minor orthographic variations. The main differences lie in the verbs: Hab 3:19 is secondary. "And he set" is a prosaic synonym for the original *mšwh*. The original "he made me stand" is a closer parallel. The emphasis is on firm footing as an enablement from God. Habakkuk has changed this to "he made me trample." This is more energetic, and matches the action of Yahweh's horses in v 15.

The most important thing is that David's triumphal ode confirms the authenticity of the simile and of the reading "on my high places," which is found also in Deuteronomy.

Deut 32:13	*yarkîbēhû*	*ʿal-bam(w)tê*	*ʾāreṣ*
Deut 33:29	*wě ʾattä*	*ʿal-bamôtêmô*	*tidrōk*
Ps 18:34	*wě-*	*ʿal bamôtay*	*yaʿămîdēnî*
2 Sam 22:34	*wě-*	*ʿal bamôtay*	*yaʿămîdēnî*
Hab 3:19	*wě-*	*ʿal bamôtay*	*yadrīkēnî*

Ps 18:34 and 2 Sam 22:34 are identical in everything but orthography, using *L* as the standard. Some editions show a trend to more *plene* spellings. Thus Hahn's (1867) edition has

Ps 18:34	*wě-*	*ʿal bamôtay*	*ya ʾămîdēnî*
2 Sam 22:34	*wě-*	*ʿal bamôtay*	*ya ʾămîdēnî*

For our purposes, the only point in the spelling variants is their possible use as clues for the relative antiquity of the tradition. With such sparse evidence, any inference cannot be very robust. Even so, the variants in Habakkuk are on the conservative side. By a paradox, both the *plene* spelling in *bamôtay* and the *defective* spelling in *yadrīkēnî* point in this direction (Freedman, Forbes, and Andersen 1992:70). Apart from such considerations, Psalm 18 and 2 Samuel 22 may be treated as one composition. All four compositions contain the same word *bāmôt*, with the same preposition. Except for Ps 18:34, *bāmôt* is spelled *plene*, even in Deut 32:13, in spite of its deviant vocalization. Hab 3:19 agrees with

TABLE 6. Comparison of Hab 3:19 with Three Parallel Passages

	Deut 32:13	Deut 33:29	Ps 18:34	Hab 3:19
Last colon of a poem		×		×
Second colon of a bicolon	×	×	×	
Similar preceding colon			×	×
Same noun	×	×	×	×
Same preposition	×	×	×	×
Same verb (root)		×		×
Same verb form (*Hipʿil*)	×		×	×
Suffixed verb	×		×	×
Verb last in the clause		×	×	×
Vocalization of *bāmôt*		×	×	×
First-person pronoun object			×	×
Verb is third person	×		×	×

the word order of Ps 18:34, and both have first-person pronouns. Deut 33:29 resembles this word order partly (verb last), but it is second person. Deut 32:13 has a different word order (verb first), but it resembles Ps 18:34 and Hab 3:19 in having a *Hipʿil* verb with pronoun object. By contrast, Deut 33:29 is simply "you tread on their high places." Three different verbs are used in the four "recensions," if we may use that term, and they are not synonyms. Hab 3:19 agrees with Deut 33:29 in using *drk*. With *rkb* in Deut 32:13 compare Ps 66:12—*hirkabtā ʾĕnôs lĕrōʾšēnû*, "You made men ride over our heads"—where the *Hipʿil* shows that God gives men a military success like his own. The similarities among these texts may be shown in a table above.

These features cannot be given equal weight as a measure of affinity, so merely adding up the scores does not prove much. For what it is worth, this metric shows Ps 18:34 to be the closest to Hab 3:19, differing in only the verb root. Deut 32:13 is the least close, and its different word order (verb first) sets it apart from the others. Yet Deut 33:29 has two features shared with Hab 3:10 and not found in Ps 18:34, and they deserve considerable weight as an index of affinity. They are the use of the same verb root (albeit the stem form is different) and the same structural placement (at the end of the poem). The latter fact, coupled with the similar feature that both poems begin in the same way, is very telling. Yet against this has to be set the unique feature of Deut 33:29—address to God in second person—with the associated thematic difference that in Deut 33:29 tramping on the heights is what God does, whereas in the others that is what God enables the poet to do.

The simile is usually paraphrased as "like the feet of does." This misses the point. It makes David (Habakkuk) himself like a hind. But to judge from the Song of Songs, the various parts of the body are compared to plants and animals, not with the corresponding parts of animals. By changing the verb, Habakkuk has changed the picture. Neither poet is emphasizing the fleetness of the deer. David is sure-footed; Habakkuk tramples his enemies.

he made me trample. One of the most impressive features of this persistent tradition, in spite of the diversity of its expression in four distinct compositions, is the use of the prefixed verb forms in their archaic preterite sense. From clause-initial position in Deut 32:13, the verb has moved to clause-final position in the other three poems. In Hab 3:19bB, the question is whether the verb usage has departed from the ancient meaning and has its classical future-tense reference. LXX has already adopted a neutral present tense. The parallelism (with chiasmus) of this verb with a *wāw*-consecutive construction ("and he set") suggested that Habakkuk is recording an experienced fact, not expressing an unrealized hope, and certainly not stating a general truth.

The tradition of Deut 32:13 and of the last colon in Deut 33:29 might have contributed to Habakkuk's result. The similar use of *Hip ʿil* forms is certainly striking. The fuller phrase of Deut 32:13 ("the back of the earth") makes us hesitate to follow Albright (1950) in restoring "the back of [Sea]." True it is the sea that God treads on in v 15. The connection might remain if "earth" in Deut 32:13 is the underworld, not the land; for "the back[s] of Sea" probably refers to the humps or coils of the primal sea dragon, still represented by the waters of the underworld (v 9). But Deut 32:13 has probably historicized this myth to describe the occupation of the promised land. Habakkuk ends his prophecy on the same note of triumph.

VIII.3. DEDICATION (3:19c)

19c   For the conductor in my string ensemble.

INTRODUCTION

Because no break was shown in the original text, the Greek translators supposed that this half-verse was part of the poem and continued the sentence to the end—"Upon the heights he sets me in order to conquer by means of his ode." The Barberini translation similarly incorporated the last words, but with different results—"and upon the necks of my enemies he sets me; having hastened, he came to rest." It is possible to explain the first of these readings, since the title of the musical director (*měnaṣṣēaḥ*) has a root that means "conquer." The variant is harder to account for. Thackeray (1923:50) reconstructed an underlying Hebrew meaning: "the day after the sabbath"—a lectionary rubric.

COMMENT ON HABAKKUK 3

That Habakkuk 3 contains echoes of ancient myths is generally recognized. There is no agreement about where these echoes come from. Detailed comparisons with the Babylonian creation story *Enuma Elish* have been made, notably by Irwin (1942), consolidating the work of Stephens (1924). Cassuto (1975) rejected Stephens's hypothesis. Irwin (1942:12) said that Cassuto was "certainly wrong" to do so. Irwin's study was thorough, pushing the Babylonian connection to the limit. It was dismissed out of hand by Albright (1950a) as completely misguided. But Albright's own search for Canaanite connections was also one-sided, with Ugaritic evidence prompting many solutions to problems.

The search for the original voices of these echoes is limited by the meager evidence available. It has been done piecemeal, selecting any motifs and allusions that are turned up by comparative study. Recognition of a genuine parallel is often influenced by the general preference of the scholar, and behind this preference are usually theories about the cultural relations of the nation of Israel with its neighbors. Sometimes one or two impressive parallels are enough to convince investigators that they have found that background. Once a sighting has been made, more equations are discovered or recovered with the aid of the hypothesis.

There are two chief candidates: Canaan and Mesopotamia. A third, Egypt, now receives very little backing. Scholars have lined up against one another on these two sides. Proponents of the Babylonian connection are Gunkel (and dependent German commentators), Thackeray (1911), Stephens (1924), Bévenot (1933), and Irwin (1942, 1956). Proponents of the Canaanite connection are Gaster (1937), Cassuto (1938), Albright (1939, 1950), Béguerie (1954), and Mowinckel (1939, 1953).

The debate among these and other scholars up to the time of his work was studied by Jöcken (1977:290–310). Of the literature available, the chief candidates are the Creation Epic (*Enuma Elish*), the Flood Legend (*Atra-Ḥasīs*), and the *Epic of Erra* (all from Babylon), and the Baal cycle from Ugarit. Mowinckel (1955) tried to take a mediating position, recognizing Mesopotamian background, but suggesting that earlier Canaanite borrowing from that source brought the material within range of Israelite poets. After the standoff between the polarized positions, most subsequent scholars have been content to point out the affinities piecemeal, without attempting to explain them in terms of borrowing. May (1955) highlighted the combat with the dragon (a marine monster), while Wakeman (1969, 1973) spoke about a primeval earth monster that was split open to release underground waters. Most recently, Avishur (1994), while distancing himself from the one-sided assertions of Albright (1950a), and even more of Dahood, for direct *literary* borrowing from Canaanite (mainly Ugaritic), recognized nevertheless, and illustrated by many parallels, that there was a *cultural* dependence, natural enough considering the geographic proximity and linguistic kinship between Canaan and Israel. For a balanced review of the debate see Lambert (1965, 1988).

That each candidate has a case arises from the fact that Habakkuk 3 does not correspond closely to any other text that we now have. Its nearest congeners are within the Hebrew Bible itself. Yet even when they are taken all together, a myth or cycle of myths cannot be recovered that corresponds to any other corpus. One of the methodological difficulties that is encountered in all this work is the small

scope of the biblical poem, which is only a few colons compared with the
Ugaritic and Babylonian epics. The alleged parallels are only motifs and allusions. The textual and literary difficulties within Habakkuk 3 compound the
problem, and some of them are so desperate that any glimmer of light, from
whatever quarter, is welcomed with gratitude. Extraordinary ingenuity has been
shown in these procedures, but there is one tactic that should be considered il-
legal. Comparative materials should never be used to resolve a textual problem
that defies all other solutions. At the very least, such proposals should always be
marginal, provisional. They should be brought in only in the later stages of the
investigation. Thus the main thrust of Stephens's (1924) paper is to emend *mbyt*
in v 13 to **bhmwt*. But having done that, encouraged by the expectation of finding allusions to *Enuma Elish* in Habakkuk 3, he is obliged to infer, from the
fact that Behemoth is not the name of the dragon of the Babylonian myth, that
Habakkuk was using a variant of the legend. At this point the argument is seen
to be very frail.

   First of all, a firm foothold must be secured in places where the text is clear
and where comparisons can be made with confidence. Second, that solution is
to be preferred that explains the most places in the text and does not seriously
collide with others. It would be helpful if we could use another criterion and
say that a myth that explains the dramatic structure of Habakkuk 3 as a whole
has a claim to be a close relative. But we cannot do that until we know with
more assurance what Habakkuk 3 is. More precisely: Is Habakkuk 3 an Israelite
version of a myth that might, perhaps, be found somewhere else? Is it a historical recital from Israel's own past, told in poetic form using imagery drawn from
myths? Not from complete myths, but only as literary motifs that come through
as fragments, so that other parts of the myth cannot be taken as riding in on
them. Is it so distinctively Israelite that the search for comparable material is
likely to be futile or, if taken too seriously, positively harmful?

   There is a concession that is commonly made in the debate between proponents of Canaanite background and proponents of Babylonian background. Material that cannot be traced to any known source, material that supports the opponent's case most strongly, is attributed to a common Semitic background.
Thus Irwin (1942) admits that the parallels adduced by Gaster (1937) and Cassuto (1975) are valid. But, he says, "they indicate no more than a common store
of cosmic mythology of the ancient Near East" (12). Stephens's (1924) position
is more nuanced. He says of Habakkuk 3 that "the background for it was fur-
nished by an ancient Semitic legend, one version of which is found in the Babylonian Creation Epic" (290).

   Cassuto's (1975) nuanced position, stated with great caution, seems to be that
the comparable material from Ugarit suggests that the Israelites had *similar*
myths, of which only fragments survive in biblical literature. Certainly, there is
no place in the Hebrew Bible where the myth can be found, or even an episode
from it, in any sustained narrative form. And even the numerous scraps that Cassuto was able to gather cannot be reassembled into a coherent story.

   Speiser's (AB1) sustained explanation of the numerous similarities he found

between patriarchal traditions and cuneiform literature was that it fitted the Israelites' belief that their ancestors had migrated from Mesopotamia in the Middle Bronze Age. When there are differences, however, Speiser recognized two
possible lines of adjustment. One scenario is the modification of Babylonian materials to fit the new ideology of Israel. At various places in Genesis, this revision is so polemical as to amount to a complete reversal on vital issues, notably
monotheism. The second suggestion is that the Hebrews did not derive their
parallel materials from sources similar to the cuneiform texts we now happen to
have, but by way of some intermediary channel, in which adjustments had already been made: "[B]efore they reached the Hebrews these entries had gone
through a secondary center of dissemination, where they were transformed in
accordance with local needs and conditions" (AB1:36). Speiser refers to Albright
(1939:91–93), reiterating the point in connection with the genealogies of Genesis 5: "It is thus apparent that the underlying traditions had been subjected to
considerable modification in some intermediate center." In a more nuanced
statement, Speiser suggests that "the Hurrians could have served as intermediaries in the transmission of the antediluvian lists to biblical chroniclers" (42);
and, in connection with the Flood traditions, that the intermediate source was
"evidently northwesterly" (55)—the Ark grounded in the Ararat mountains.

Lambert, in postscripts to his 1965 paper, takes a position that is method-
ologically similar to Speiser's, except that Lambert suggests the Amorites as intermediaries and the Late Bronze Age as a more likely period for the migration
of these influences. At least it can be seen that the possibilities are more numerous than those recognized in the either / or debate between the Canaanites
and the Babylonians. Yet all admit that Habakkuk 3 is not directly related to either tradition. Direct quotations are not claimed. The relationship should then
be stated in terms of affinity—a purely relative matter.

The tenuous connections, then, may be explained in one of the following
ways:

1. The Israelite tradition is dependent on an earlier tradition, which is best
represented by Canaanite, Babylonian, or other (lost) sources. But it differs substantially because Israel has gone its own way. In particular, the demythologizing that came with Israelite monotheism emptied the myths of dramatic content, so their motifs survived as only literary ornament. If the Israelite poems
have undergone a radical theological change in content and a radical literary
change in form, the recovery of ancestral prototypes is mainly an antiquarian
pursuit doomed to yield only a few fragments. Of course, the history of literature is a valid subject for research. But it does mischief to interpretation if knowledge of the prototypes is considered a requirement for understanding the later
developments. It could be quite wrong to label Habakkuk 3 as "the Israelite version of the myth." At best, such discoveries can help to recover the ancient imagery as it is used in the Israelite poem, and even then the original mythology
has been bleached out. To understand that image, (for example, Yahweh smashing the head of a dragon) we should not import into an Israelite poem the meaning that that image had in a similar Canaanite or Babylonian work. We need to

ask, rather, what the image meant to the Israelite author and the Israelite reader (or listener).

2. The limited match between Israelite versions and original Canaanite and Babylonian myths is due to modulation of the source material as it passed to Israel through intermediaries—Hurrians (Speiser) or Amorites (Lambert) in the case of Babylon, Phoenicians in the case of Canaan or rather Ugarit. The difficulty with these theories is that practically no literature has survived from these intermediate stages.

3. If the similarities between Israelite motifs and the nearest exotic parallels are too few and too tenuous to sustain a theory of "borrowing," they may nonetheless be the outcome of independent derivation from common sources in Semitic mythology, too ancient to have left traces other than these divergent traditions.

No matter which of these theories is considered to be the more likely, Habakkuk 3 has its own identity and integrity as a monument of Israelite culture. And, as its reuse in the book of Habakkuk shows, the understanding of the poem, and of its several constituent images is never captured and frozen, for Habakkuk the prophet is well down the stream, almost at the end of the classical period of Israelite prophecy and literature. Earlier than him, we have primeval Hebrew poets who composed one or more poems that acquired a strong hold on the tradition. Habakkuk (or a scribe) was able to incorporate some of this verse into his own collection, with few or many changes. Probably the material changes to the poem itself were very few, as the archaisms show. Even so, the setting is different—historically and in the accumulated associations of long use. And since then, the process of copying and reinterpreting has continued. We have only to think of the Qumran *pešer* on Habakkuk, which, alas, does not include the third chapter. It would be fascinating to discover what the Qumran sectaries made of the final "prayer." The processes of interpretation and modernization are more obvious when it comes to the versions. The theological and literary changes in the family of Greek manuscripts represented by Barberini, for instance, are so substantial that we should recognize two distinct works, each to be interpreted in its own right. When Thackeray (1923) found Perseus in the Greek and used the legend to clarify the mythology of the Hebrew (working back into time) his procedure was just as dubious as that which finds Baal or Marduk and uses Canaanite or Akkadian mythology to clarify the Hebrew (working forward).

At the very least we have three moments to discover and to keep apart:

1. The composition of the source myths in their definitive form, and their meaning in their own cultural and historical setting.
2. The composition of the classical Israelite poems, and their meaning in their period and community.
3. The composition of Habakkuk 3 in its present form, and its meaning in its present literary setting against the historical background of its period.

The obligation to be rigorous places great restrictions on the investigator, who might feel totally discouraged by this reminder that the task is much more difficult than a mere search for similarities. The cumulative effect of the many weak (or missing) links in the chain of argument—the treachery that lurks in inference by analogy and the warnings given by the discredited movements, such as pan-Babylonianism, and now, it would seem, a similar reaction against the alleged pan-Canaanism of some members of the Albright school, which have taken such things to excess—might well breed a caution, even a skepticism that paralyzes all research.

If this Anchor Bible volume seems overly cautious, it should be pointed out that there is a big difference between evidence and inference. The evidence for creation myths in which a god triumphs over an opponent is abundant and very interesting. To gather it together is worthwhile. To explain it by means of hypotheses on cultural connections and literary developments within the ancient Near East is legitimate, although admittedly speculative, and always provisional. So long as too much is not claimed, no harm is done.

INDEXES

◆

INDEX OF AUTHORS

◆

INDEX OF SUBJECTS

◆

INDEX OF BIBLICAL AND OTHER ANCIENT SOURCES

◆

INDEX OF LANGUAGES

◆